Alaskan John G. Brady

ALASKAN
JOHN G. BRADY

Missionary, Businessman,
Judge, and Governor,
1878-1918

Ted C. Hinckley

Published for Miami University by the
Ohio State University Press

Miami University, through an arrangement with the Ohio State University Press initiated in 1975, publishes works of original scholarship, fiction, and poetry. The responsibility for receiving and reviewing manuscripts is invested in an Editorial Board comprised of Miami University faculty.

Library of Congress Cataloging in Publication Data

Hinckley, Ted C.
Alaskan John G. Brady, missionary, businessman,
judge, and governor, 1878-1918.

Bibliography: p.
Includes index.
1. Brady, John Green, 1848-1918. 2. Alaska—
Politics and government—1867-1959. 3. Alaska—
Governors—Biography. 4. Businessmen—Alaska—
Biography. 5. Missionaries—Alaska—Biography.
6. Judges—Alaska—Biography. I. Title.
F908.B8H56   979.8'03'0924 [B]   81-19030
        ISBN 0-8142-0336-1   AACR2

For

CARYL FAY CHESMORE

who said, "We can do it"

Contents

Illustrations ix

Acknowledgments xi

Introduction xv

1 The Formative Years 3

2 The Sitka Mission 25

3 An Alaska Advocate 44

4 A Mercantile Ministry 54

5 Sitka Society and the Pattons 74

6 Judge Brady 87

7 Politics, Profits, and Progeny 111

8 Legal Limbos and Land Hunger 133

9 The Pace of Change Quickens 150

10 Klondike Governor 169

11 Civilizing the Civilizers 188

12 Sovereignty, Domestic and National 210

13 Education and Native Conundrums 236

14 Safeguarding and Settling Alaska 263

15 Administrator and Politician 287

16 The Go-Getter Virus 316

17 Resignation 348

18 Home Again 370

Bibliographic Sources 377

Index 381

Illustrations

Detail of Sitka from
  Baranov Castle (p. 127, below)   Frontispiece

Judge John Green   7

John G. Brady, 1874   17

Sitka from the Harbor   32

The Reverend John G. Brady   39

Amos T. Whitford   55

Interior of the Sitka Trading Company Store   62

The Sitka Trading Company Store at Juneau   69

Women of Sitka   77

Sitka Harbor from Baranov Hill   102

Governor Alfred P. Swineford   113

A Log Raft   125

Sitka from Baranov Castle   127

The Brady Children   143

The Brady Lumber Mill   151

Sitka Commons   177

The Last Potlatch   252

Native Alaskans with Governor Brady   257

Interior of Satchahnee   275

The Brady Garden   281

ILLUSTRATIONS

Governor John Brady   291

Sitka Commons on the Fourth of July   318

Collecting Totem Poles   337

Alaska Day at the Saint Louis Exposition   341

Incoming Governor Wilford B. Hoggatt with Brady   355

x

Acknowledgments

How warmly satisfying it is to recognize those who assisted in the production of this book. Unfortunately omitted are hundreds of students and academic associates whose questions and suggestions also helped hammer this biography together. Perhaps these individuals can enjoy the solitary satisfaction that comforts the anonymous donor.

At the outset the author wishes to thank the preeminent expert on Alaska, Robert N. DeArmond, for his unceasing guidance. Three other Great Land scholars whose knowledge proved particularly valuable are Isabel Miller of the Sitka Historical Society and professors Robert A. Frederick and Claus-M. Naske. Quite as beneficial was the tonic of forthrightness provided by native Alaskans Ellen Lang Hays and Walter Sobeloff. Sitka's Sheldon Jackson College has repeatedly enabled this researcher to savor John Brady's beloved hometown, and staff members Frank Roth and Charles Bovee seem never to tire of playing host. Even more astonishing has been the enduring patience of Governor Brady's family, and especially the unflagging enthusiasm of his son Hugh.

For over twenty years this historian has been pestering his coworkers at San Jose State University. Despite his vexatious requests, these good people continue to walk the extra mile. Among the most footsore are librarians Nancy Emmick, King Wah Moberg, Jerome B. Munday, and Christine G. Simpson. No less weary must be instructional technologists Romaldo Lopez, Richard W. Mills, Richard F. Szumski, and Tom Tutt. However, for sacrifices above and beyond the call of duty, the palm goes to history department secretaries Marlene S. Bosanko and Leslie Brand. Somehow they sustain serenity midst an encroaching jungle of paperwork and not a few snarling professors. A partial list of industrious student assistants who did their best to ferret out the author's errors must include Patricia L. Donohue, Joan Garrett, Ellen Goldberg, Roderick C. Johnson, Benjamin Kline, Ann B. Lewis, Scott MacArthur, Jon Carl Moses, and Clay Trost.

Librarians and archivists are for historians what the genie was for Aladdin. Lacking their necromantic powers, we are helpless. Among that legion of magicians to whom this scholar bows in deep appreciation are: Archibald Hanna, Beinecke Library; Dorothy Kurtz, Presbyterian Historical Society; Phyllis De Muth, Selma Doig, Susan Johnston, and Paula D. Scavera, Alaska State Historical Library; Phillip E. Lothyan, Federal Records Center, Seattle; Robert Monroe, University of Washington; Paul McCarthy, University of Alaska; Robert Becker, Bancroft Library; and Renate Hayum, Seattle Public Library. Summer research assistance from Alaska Methodist University, the American Philosophical Society, the Henry E. Huntington Library, and the Washington State Historical Society advanced this project.

Writing history is a lonely occupation. Certainly each writer stands accountable for his words and his interpretation of events. Nevertheless, without the steady encouragement of professional friends, this author's pen would have stalled years ago. For their criticism and counsel, both kind and harsh, I am indebted to the following colleagues: Eugene Asher, Ray Allen Billington, Robin Brooks, Charles Burdick, Donald C. Cutter, Clifford M. Drury, Richard N. Ellis, Theodore Grivas, Howard R. Lamar, Jack Miller, Virgil Mitchell, Rodman W. Paul, Lawrence Rakestraw, Morgan B. Sherwood, Victor Small, Dwight L. Smith, Lynn Turner, Norman E. Tutorow, Gerald E. Wheeler, John E. Wickman, William H. Wilson, and Charles Winkler.

Anchorage sourdoughs whose historical preservation labors have enriched the lives of literally hundreds of thousands of cheechakos, including this author, are George Hall, William S. Hanable, Alfred Mongin, and Michael S. Kennedy. Six editors whose demanding standards have consistently challenged me and to whom I am grateful are Robert E. Burke, S. George Ellsworth, Robin Higham, Doyce B. Nunis, Charles S. Peterson, and Richard A. Pierce.

Professors Ronald Shaw and Frank Jordan of Miami University, Ohio, undertook the burdensome task of reducing my refractory, overweight manuscript. That we remained on amiable terms throughout this ordeal confirms that scholars and gentlemen still do exist. Last, and surely not least, cheers for book editor Carol S. Sykes of Ohio State University Press, under whose management a box of tired bond became a book.

Finally, a profound thank-you to those who administer the California State University and Colleges for their generous support.

Grateful acknowledgment is made to the following individuals and institutions for permission to use materials from archives and personal files: The Bancroft Library, University of California, for the R. B. Crittenden Manuscript; The Beinecke Rare Book and Manuscript Library, Yale University, for the John G. Brady Papers and the Mottrom D. Ball Papers; The Huntington Library, San Marino, California, for the Charles Watts Correspondence; the Indiana Historical Bureau for quotation from the *Tipton Tribune*; the Presbyterian Historical Society for the Sheldon Jackson Correspondence and the Sheldon Jackson Scrapbooks; Princeton Theological Seminary for the Sheldon Jackson Collection; San Francisco Theological Seminary for the Edward Marsden Correspondence; Sheldon Jackson College for the C. L. Andrews Collection; the University of Alaska, Fairbanks, for the Andrew T. Lewis Papers; Hugh P. Brady, the Alaska State Historical Library, the Beinecke Rare Book and Manuscript Library, Yale University, The Huntington Library, San Marino, California, and the Sitka Historical Society for the illustrations; Robert N. DeArmond, Lawrence Rakestraw, the Seattle Public Library, and Teachers College, Columbia University, for information in personal correspondence with the author; and Hugh, John, Mary, and Elizabeth Brady for invaluable assistance through letters and interviews.

Introduction

Biographies reveal different things to different people. Within John Green Brady's life at least four major historic themes are interwoven. First, he superficially personified the Horatio Alger figure. Second, as a corollary to his personal success, the Irish immigrant's son was swept up in his enthusiastic endorsement of America's business triumphs at home and abroad. Only belatedly did he awaken to Mammon's threat. Nevertheless, like so many Victorian-age Protestants, he held firmly to the belief that man was an instrument of God; God had saved him from Manhattan's wretched slums, now he must in turn "do likewise for his fellow man." Finally, there is Brady's paradoxical relationship with his Northwest Coast Indian neighbors. Just as he ultimately tarnished his Alaskan political reputation by his speculative aspirations for that magnificent region, so did his quite normal ethnocentrism flaw his labors among the Great Land's natives.

It has now become fashionable to ridicule the Horatio Alger aspect of American history. In fact, a few historians, conveniently overlooking such Americans as Abraham Lincoln and Andrew Carnegie, would have us believe that the Alger symbol was never anything but a myth. The "roots" mania, family history, and widespread use of computer quantification have intensified our concentration on America's Mr. Average Man. Surely the roots of the runaway New York City ragamuffin Johnny Brady were common enough. Yet how well he confirmed the unpredictable power, the grinding, and the intermixing of diverse elements within American society. In truth, the unique reality of Brady's life embodies the framework for a rags-to-riches fable.

Imagine an 1850s eight-year-old street gamin rescued by the Children's Aid Society, his mind, body, and character refurbished by rural

Indiana, working his way through Yale and Union Theological Seminary, and then after but two years as a Presbyterian missionary in Alaska, embracing a secular ministry that culminated in the territory's governorship during the gold-crazy Klondike-Nome epoch. Like Horatio Alger's Ragged Dick and Tattered Tom, Brady was rewarded for his pluck and luck with profits and public esteem. However, unlike the victories of Alger's heroes, Brady's triumphs proved short-lived. In 1904, at the very moment that Alaska's governor warmed to the crowd's cheers at Saint Louis's memorable Louisiana Purchase Exposition, forces were at work that terminated his financial security and public acclaim. Despite these reverses and a humiliating self-imposed exile from Alaska, Governor Brady eventually returned to the northland he loved so much. Regrettably, his 1878–1918 role in Alaska has never been adequately detailed.

John Brady's solid contributions to the territory's schools, law enforcement, business development, government, and a wide variety of public services for all Alaskans mark him as one of its foremost leaders. Although a close friend and humanitarian ally of that remarkably durable Alaska publicist-lobbyist Sheldon Jackson, Brady fought and defeated his political partner on the embattled liquor control question. This policy debate, like other Far North controversies over land disposition, native rights, and conservation, spilled into the national political arena. Indeed, angry echoes from these emotionally charged disputes reverberate right down to present-day Alaska.

Today's forty-ninth state remains every bit as dazzling and perplexing as was the District of Alaska to Brady's contemporaries. Thrust far out atop the Pacific Basin, Alaska, with its vast resources and vital strategic significance, serves as an American-Asian bridge. Yet despite its trans-Pacific position and the facility of space-age communications, the population still suffers from provincialism. Not a few citizens revel in this isolation from urbanized America and urge a life-style closer to nature. Of course, burgeoning metropolitan Anchorage mocks such notions. Ambiguities abound. Natives blame the white man for ruining their traditional existence but match him in their insatiable consumption of necessary unnecessaries. Common wisdom claims that giant corporations run the state, but denied its thousands of little entrepreneurs, the country could not function. With one hand Alaskans shake their fist at federal intervention and with the other extend a tin cup to Washington, and although its communities can exude an exploitive materialism reminiscent of a nineteenth-century mining town, almost everywhere there breathe a sociability and a grassroots interest in the arts that invite emulation.

As missionary, trader, judge, and governor, Brady wrestled with each of these contradictions. In his annual reports and as the territory's unofficial representative to the nation's capital, he struggled to represent his commonwealth's diversity and to speak for all Alaskans. He was condemned because he too frequently protested impositions on the aboriginal population. Today the appelation "Indian Governor" would be an accolade. We may laugh at farmer Brady sweating in his Sitka garden seeking to demonstrate Alaska's potential agricultural self-sufficiency, but who cannot respect his vision of the Far North's future role in world affairs.

Americans hear much about Alaska yet comprehend little. Thanks to the interaction between the Alaskan settler John Brady and his adopted Great Land, we may enjoy a clearer view of the awesome dynamics of American values and institutions within Alaska.

Alaskan John G. Brady

CHAPTER ONE

The Formative Years

Not until retirement did John Green Brady summon the courage to track down the correct date of his birth and retrace his Manhattan childhood. He had been born on 25 May 1848 in an ill-lighted, shabby flat located on the East Side between the lower end of Roosevelt Street and Park Row. One wonders if his desperately impoverished parents, James and Catharine Brady, genuinely welcomed the arrival of their only son. Among John's few faint memories of his mother, before she died, was that of an exhausted, frail young woman soothing him from the discomforts of smallpox, vainly trying to keep her son's hands from tearing open his inflamed blisters.[1]

For all of New York City's astonishing growth and bustling commerce, it, too, was infected. Among the city's working classes, the 1840s and 1850s were a "hungry" time. The continued infusion of European immigrants only worsened the city's overcrowding, social degeneration, and misery. Brady's father and mother were bit players in this act of the vast trans-Atlantic drama, the Irish exodus to America. Manhattan's common laborers seldom earned more than five dollars a week, and unskilled dock workers like his father never knew when even this pittance might be cut off.[2] The frequent whippings that John suffered were probably the frustrated reaction of an impoverished "foreign laborer," a fugitive from Ireland's potato famine, now trapped in a hostile city.

Not long after John's mother's death, Brady's father remarried. One result of this union was another burden, a baby girl. When employment could be found, both parents worked, forcing John to spend hour upon hour babysitting in the dingy flat. He rebelled against the confinement and fled. When brought home, he was flogged. This sequence of

3

events was repeated with dreary regularity, for the exciting activities of New York's streets proved irresistible. By the time he was seven years old, the child vagrant was tied to a bed post before being beaten. Had times been good, his father's large stevedore's belt and steel hook might have been a source of pride. As it was, that strap became a tool of terror for the errant son. James Brady had joined the mass of unemployed workingmen, victims of New York City's mid-fifties business oscillations. Unable to find work, he sought escape through liquor; now the beatings that he administered to his son became savage. Outraged by such treatment, the street-wise eight-year-old hid out until his father tired of searching for him. John never saw his father or half sister again. About all he carried from his home were the pockmarks on his face and the scars on his back where his father's belt had torn the flesh.[3]

It was the spring of 1855 when John Brady became a "street arab." Long before fleeing his miserable home, he had learned how to survive in the Bowery and along New York's East Side. Judging from his unpublished reminiscences, the "Zigzags," Brady's hand-to-mouth existence was not devoid of fun and adventure. To be sure, he was often hungry. And there were distinct limits to what a boy could earn shining shoes and running errands. One night his shelter might be under a saloon table, and the next might find him in a refuse-filled alley kicking away rats to obtain sleeping space in a packing crate.

Like one of Fagin's band, Johnny became a skilled thief. Either on his own or working with other gamins, he pilfered food stands at Fulton Market. On dark nights he and his chums raided the docks. Shortly before the steamboats docked at the Ferry Building in the early morning hours, the vessels dumped their refuse overboard. Fishing for breakfast midst this garbage ofttimes provided an edible catch. But money assured a more satisfying meal, and for a lad with Johnny's quick mind, there were numerous ways in which small change could be earned.

With all its callousness, his enormous hometown offered its citizens, rich and poor, a variety of recreations. Street musicians, clowns, dancers, and singers were common. They could be paid or ignored as one's taste or treasure dictated. For endless entertainment, nothing could match the saloon. Boys quickly discovered that in these taverns the usually inhospitable adult male world could become friendly and often generous of purse. Running messages or carrying food and drink invariably merited a few pennies.[4] Occasionally when he sang an Irish ballad, John received a tip so munificent that he was able to afford the twelve-cent charge required by the Chatham Street theater. What a glorious escape the antics of the theater's comedians provided!

One evening in late December 1857, unable to pay for either the theater or the delicious steaming corn sold there, he lingered at the theater entrance. Experience had shown him that some people tossed aside half-eaten cobs. Waiting to scavenge, John fell asleep against an iron grating where the sidewalk met a place of business. Half-starved and in a fitful slumber, he heard a man describing food. "His voice was so wonderful that he soon won me." Many years later Brady identified his benefactor as Theodore Roosevelt, Sr., father of the future president. Very likely representing the Children's Aid Society, Roosevelt quietly urged the waif to go with him to the police and hence to the orphanage at Randall's Island. Here he could taste good food and find comfortable lodging with other boys. The street urchin had already spent one night in jail; the thought of actually cooperating with the police instead of running from them seemed positively dangerous. Another crowded imprisonment with drunks and vagrants was repugnant. However, the society's agent "was so kind . . . I consented to take his advice."[5]

The Children's Aid Society was an enlightened response to the social agony produced by America's nineteenth-century mushrooming cities. Founded in 1853 by the Reverend Charles Loring Brace, it sought to salvage pathetic tatterdemalions such as Brady. The society aimed to remove youngsters from the streets and send them west to a small town or farm. Here, it was hoped, a more ordered environment, a Christian home, and hard work would erase the vices imprinted by urban pauperism.[6] Furthermore, the program assured the foster parents of an additional farmhand, and Manhattan's more stable citizens could sleep with a little more comfort: a potential ruffian had been "drained from New York."

On Randall's Island these children first obtained nourishing food, clean uniforms and quarters, and an elementary education. The orphanage was a crudely managed program, but in it Brady's enthusiasm for learning germinated. Part of John's peer initiation had been the painful self-application of a *JB* on his right elbow and a cross on his left wrist. These ash needle tracings he carried to the grave.[7]

Not long after his arrival on Randall's Island, Brady was informed that as soon as it could be arranged he would be transferred to a foster home in the West (which might mean any place from western New York to Kansas or Iowa).[8] Brady was permitted to read letters from boys earlier dispatched from the orphanage under the "placing out system" to states in the Ohio Valley. Especially alluring were the youths' descriptions of rural America's gastronomic delights. After a daily diet of "mush, milk and bread, I wanted to go to a country where all they had to eat was 'apples, chicken, and watermellons.'"

5

In his second year, Brady's turn came. Along with a group of other boys, he was lined up and asked, first, if he desired assignment to a farm in Indiana and, second, if his parents were alive. To the first question he gave a lusty affirmative; to the second he replied with a cool lie. John was one of twenty-seven selected. A few days later, after being presented with a new suit of clothes, the now apprehensive youngsters were taken to a city minstrel show and to the headquarters of the Children's Aid Society. Here the Reverend Mr. Brace, among others, wished them God's blessing and presented each with a personally inscribed Bible. An agent of the society then escorted them to the railroad station and they were on their way to Indiana.[9]

For a boy who had never gone beyond the boundaries of New York's Lower East Side, the August 1859 railroad ride west might as well have been a trip to Latin America. Where were all the people? The houses seemed so far apart. And the profusion of trees, some of which appeared to be on fire, so upset him that a deluge of tears ensued. Only later would John become familiar with the land-clearing technique called girdling.

Good food and a night's slumber aboard their passenger car restored the exuberance of Brady and the other twenty-six worried youngsters. Seated beside Brady was another orphan designated for an Indiana adoption. Although John recognized him, he had never made the boy's acquaintance. The ice was quickly broken; Andy Burke proved to be a lively traveling companion.[10] It was a curious twist of fate: at the journey's end they would separate, not to meet again until 1897, at Carlisle Indian School, after Andrew Burke had served as governor of North Dakota and John Brady was being considered for the governorship of Alaska.

After a brief stop in Peru, Indiana, to await the arrival of the Peru and Indianapolis train, the youngsters resumed their journey, headed for Noblesville. Each child was still ignorant of his destination. Noblesville was merely the point for the orphans to disembark. As they passed by Tipton, had Brady possessed the power of foresight, he would have carefully scrutinized the community that lay thirty-one miles north of Indianapolis. Until almost the end of the decade, Tipton would be young Brady's hometown. And on this particular morning one of its most distinguished personages also boarded the train for the ride to Noblesville. Whether Judge John Green was primarily interested in resolving a legal question at Noblesville or really had planned to select an orphan from among the Children's Aid Society band is now impossible to tell.

6

Judge John Green, Brady's Hoosier foster father and small-town patriarch, about 1870. (Property of the author.)

John Green had first cast his future with Tipton in 1848, when it was hardly more than a name on a surveyor's plat, a mere clearing dotted with twenty-five log cabins isolated in dense woods broken only by patches of swamp. Before long it became a thriving town and boasted a good public school, an attractive central square, gravel access roads, and, above all, a railroad. At the time of Brady's arrival, it had a population of 513; a decade later its citizens would number 890.[11]

In 1856 Judge Green had been elected to the state senate for a four-year term. Some time during the late fifties, the veteran Whig joined the Republican party and remained a GOP stalwart thereafter. Years before, during the war with Mexico, he had raised a company of troops and only at the last moment decided against going south. His oldest boy, Milton, however, had marched off to Mexico. Now, in 1859, with the nation moving toward war, his second son about to leave the nest, and his legal and political responsibilities mounting, the judge felt the need of a fresh farmhand.

After boarding the train at Tipton, Judge Green stepped into the Children's Aid Society passenger coach. For some time he stood in the doorway studying the travel-weary juveniles. Brady recalled that the magistrate was attired in a dark suit with a soft black hat and a cane. When the train ground to a halt at Noblesville, the judge hurried off. His client could not wait.[12]

From the station the children were taken to Aunt Jenny Ferguson's hotel. If Judge Green had realized how many citizens were genuinely desirous of accepting a placed-out child, he might have delayed his business. The hotel was alive with people. The youngsters sat in the dining room devouring large quantities of food while dozens of officious adults buzzed about them. When the judge arrived at Ferguson's Hotel, he was surprised to find out how rapidly the children's ranks had thinned. Green later commented that Brady appeared to be the home-liest and least promising of the boys; John described himself as "rather jug nosed, marked by smallpox and no doubt the mickiest one of the lot." He was the best, however, that could be had. The judge chose him and returned to Tipton.[13]

If the New York orphan expected this new world to be anything like that from which he had departed, he must have been sadly disappointed. Tipton possessed little to excite the eye. A recently completed brick courthouse had cost the hardly impressive sum of ten thousand dollars. Beside it a log cabin lodged the U.S. Post Office. The judge's law office, a small square structure, stood nearby. The editor of the *Tipton County News* boasted that the town was "thoroughly ditched and drained," supported three organized denominations—an Old School

8

Presbyterian church, a Christian church, and a Methodist Episcopal church—and two "good schools."[14]

In 1859 Judge Green's home was still the rather unpretentious white frame dwelling that he had earlier constructed at one corner of his two-hundred-acre farm. This property was located on the west side of Tipton, about a half mile from the square. The immediate reaction of the judge's family upon the arrival of the eastern waif is best told in Brady's own words: "When I stepped across the threshold of that home the sensation of all the inmates was profound. There were—Mrs. Green a motherly woman in cap and side puffs, Mary her youngest child, a lovely looking girl of sixteen, John the youngest son about twenty, Will Dougherty a boarder . . . and Sarah Piles the servant girl who regarded me doubt-fully."[15] With his acceptance by his foster family, John Brady became John Green Brady.

The Tipton region, for all its still undrained swampland and extensive timber cover, possessed an acknowledged resource in its rich, deep soil. From this fertile earth Green had produced many a crop. Now he proceeded to change John into a farmer. Some of the tyro's initial blunders were laughable, if not hazardous. Aware that August Belmont, the Judge's prized white Durham bull, had a large baglike appendage between his hind legs, Brady inquired why he was never milked along with the rest of the cows. This nearly convulsed Will Dougherty, the hired hand, but it incensed the distaff side of the household. A few days after the milking episode, John was ordered to "bring the cows into the back lot." Knowing that the bull Belmont belonged to the cow family, Brady ushered him into the yard along with the cows. August Belmont of Wall Street fame might have called the ensuing pande-monium a "bull market"; then again, he might have said it was a "panic."[16]

The judge's oldest son, Milton Green, working an eighty-acre farm not far from his father's, was told to "take the greenhorn and turn him into a farmer." Milton proved a kind and patient teacher for John. First, to satisfy himself that the boy was robust enough to be a tiller of the soil, he employed him as a partner in removing the many patches of brush still growing on the Green homestead. Tearing out the blackberry, raspberry, and hazelnut shrubs was hard, painful work, but the city boy stuck with the experienced Milton. From these clearing chores Johnny graduated to the building of "worm [rail] fences." Every cultivated patch had to have its fence to keep out stock. When split, the fine white oak and walnut trees made excellent fence rails. The actual sheaving of the oak and walnut trunks was labor for a powerful and adept woods-man and far too demanding for the eleven-year-old. Brady was kept busy leading the horses as they dragged the logs to the axeman, laying the fences, and feeding the numerous fires burning around the girdled trees. Those moments when the men relaxed from their labors were quite special to John for Milton possessed an immense repertoire of stories.[17]

Planting, plowing, and picking—it was an endless cycle, and, although broken by moments of laughing companionship, increasingly vexing to Brady. He particularly disliked separating the wheat from the straw. His job was to ride one horse and lead another around and around the barn floor where Milton had spread the sheaves in a large circle. The monotony of it was stultifying. "I became like a patient in a sick room who notices every crack and defect in the ceiling and combines them into all kinds of pictures."[18]

And John, like nearly all inhabitants of that region, had his bout with the dangerous "ager," or "swamp fever." His fingernails turned blue and he shook till he thought his teeth would rattle right out of his head. He survived despite the heavy doses of calomel, quinine, and other home remedies. "It was a sort of badge by which one was identified as a citizen."[19]

The barn's loft and his corner bedroom provided the lad with places for quiet reflection. What had become of his father? Would he, John, ever again get an opportunity to go to school, or must rural drudgery forever be his lot? Of one thing he was certain: in Tipton Judge John Green was somebody. His foster father's standing was not due to the extent of his fields nor to his bright black boots, which Johnny regularly shined—other men in Tipton held land and wore handsome boots. What the judge had was a title.

It would be some years before Brady understood what lay behind that title, the power implied in being a "professional man." But the wonderment of a printed page required no explanation. When it came to the books in the judge's library, the lad's thirst was unquenchable. Judge Green's sons had done poorly in school. In light of this, he surely must have been delighted at the many penetrating questions posed by his foster son during their Sunday morning rides.

In the fall of 1860 John Brady entered Tipton's public school. The schoolmaster, William Phillips, labored in an unadorned building situated at the northeast corner of town. John's first week was a triumph: when the class cock of the walk tried to "measure" him, the orphan laid him flat. His academic labors quickly proved no less successful. The schoolroom in which Brady scribbled on a slate, competed in spelling bees, recited, and batted at flies was essentially the same as that made so famous by Edward Eggleston.[20]

John's proper upbringing required that the boy also attend Sunday school. In the morning Brady went to the Presbyterian church; during the afternoon he frequently attended the Methodist program. After the drudgery of farm work, the extended religious exercises were not onerous; indeed, the Old and New Testament stories afforded him real pleasure. It was the Methodist Sunday school that most stimulated Brady's mind. His teacher, Dr. Joseph Blount, was the local physician. Well-educated, urbane, and a man of means, Blount had spent many years studying the Scriptures and biblical history. Brady was struck by the doctor's excellence as a Sunday school teacher, as well as by his bearing. "There was a graciousness in his face and manner which won me at once."[21]

School or no school, Johnny had multiple daily chores. It was his responsibility "to pour water on the ash hopper to get the lye for making soft soap for all the ashes were saved as well as all the trimmings from the slaughtered animals and all the waste grease from the kitchen." Milking, gathering eggs, racing to get in a harvest before it was cut down by a storm—be the task routine or exceptional, farm work came first. In all truth, he later affirmed, "While such matters broke in upon my school course I long since have realized that there was no loss to me in learning these homely industries."[22]

In the summer of 1861 John Green Brady was thirteen years old and, although not yet a man, had grown to realize that the world beyond Tipton possessed neither its simplicity nor its tranquility. In mid-April South Carolinians fired on Fort Sumter and America's Civil War began. Even before Lincoln's call for troops, the Hoosier farm lad may have sensed that black people played a critical role in this national tragedy. How the ex-slave Jim became a hand on the judge's farm can only be surmised. Apparently in either 1860 or 1861 he arrived via the underground railroad. Although the judge was no Quaker conductor, he, along with many another Hoosier, had welcomed these fugitives. The outbreak of the Civil War assured the virtual freedom of men like Jim. Certainly his strong back and good humor proved a blessing for the Green family during the war years.[23]

News of the outbreak of war reached Tipton on the thirteenth of April. Two days later President Lincoln issued a call for seventy-five thousand volunteers. Strongly Union in sentiment, the town responded immediately. Edward T. Wallace, Tipton's local harness maker and brother of General Lew Wallace (later renowned for his novel *Ben Hur*), set about recruiting a company of volunteers. In less than five days his roster was complete. It included Judge Green's youngest son, John. Brady never forgot the surge of emotion that swept over the Hoosiers as they saw their neighbors and loved ones march off to war. "Old men who were hard hearted and infidels cried like children."[24] Even without a war, Judge Green's responsibilities as magistrate of the common pleas court would have complicated managing his farm. His son's departure was a blow. Soon his foster son Brady also heard the fife and drum. The lad's pleas to join up as a drummer boy fell on deaf ears. Periodic protests that he was needed at the front remained unsuccessful. Parental rebuttals that it was a man's war were countered by his reply that for some years he had been doing a man's work. Whenever his foster mother decried war's violence and horror and reminded him of its human waste, so evident in the crippled backwash of war in Indiana towns, his mind pictured only the youthful veterans who returned as soldier heroes from Antietam and Shiloh. The judge was adamant; two of his sons had risked their lives for the nation, and he refused to surrender a third. John was indispensable on the farm.

To formalize his fifteen-year-old's role as a minor partner in the business of farming, the judge gave him a stunning "ornamental saddle of a kind of patent leather with a low horn." His foster father, who had taken to calling him Jack, in a half-humorous, half-grave manner, chided him: "Now Jack, if you won't make any more efforts to go into the army, I will give you this saddle."[25] Brady accepted the saddle. Before long Judge Green also sold him some unfattened stock. Doubtless the price was well below that of the market, and Jack not only made money but became more closely tied to the total farm operation.

The last two years of the Civil War brought major changes in the life of Judge John Green. At last freed from his circuit court duties, he was able to devote more attention to his farm and private practice. Furthermore, loved ones were reaching maturity and slipping away. On 9 April 1865 General Robert E. Lee surrendered the army of Northern Virginia. About this same time Judge Green lost his wife. Jack did what he could to keep the household and farm operating. Nonetheless, the war was over and he felt that his agreement with the judge had ended. "I was worked so hard and saw things going so much to waste that I got discouraged."[26]

In fact, his manhood was asserting itself. No longer could a saddle, a young calf, or promises of a farm or even a share in a local law practice keep him bridled on the Green property. Other country boys had proved their virility in deadly combat. Fortunately the judge had insisted that his foster son attend to matters of the mind and spirit. Now in 1865 these elements demanded fresh stimulation and expanded horizons, challenges that the Green household could no longer meet.

Periodic visits from the Children's Aid Society representative reminded John Green Brady of his orphan childhood. Three times in 1864 and at least once a year during 1865, 1866, and 1867, Mr. H. Friedgen visited him at Tipton.[27] This was a difficult period for young Brady; he was no longer a boy and not yet a man. John knew that he did not want to be a farmer, but until 1867 he was perplexed by what should be his chosen vocation. Judge Green was proud of John's steady growth. With considerable satisfaction he reported to the society that their human investment was now capitalized at two hundred dollars cash, a horse, seven acres of land, and "was respected by everyone." Earlier his foster father had written: "He is a very attentive boy to his books, is a good arithmetician and is learning grammar and algebra. He is posted in national affairs and seems to be disposed to make a man of himself."[28]

One day in mid-1866 John observed a group of young people approximately his own age standing quietly outside Tipton's courthouse. On inquiry he was told that they were waiting to enroll for a teacher training institute preparatory to being certified by examination. Although some of them ranked him in age, the stripling felt confident that when it came to education he would equal, if not exceed, most of the group. John's competitive instincts were aroused. Once he weighed his pleasure for study against his impatience with the dull routine of farming, he resolved to put himself to the certification test. After a few weeks of tutoring by an elderly Tipton teacher, Brady took the examination and passed.

This triumph was succeeded by another. Popular for his Celtic wit and admired as a worker, John was promptly recommended for a teaching position in a rural school east of Sharpsville at a salary of forty dollars a month. The seventeen-year-old Hoosier schoolmaster described his Mud Creek school as "about 24 feet square covered with clapboards. The desks were driven into the logs and the flat side of the slab was used." Seats were equally primitive, but there was "a cast iron stove on rather high legs." He was forewarned that his assignment was a difficult one. From the Tipton Bible Agency he secured some Testaments. At the first meeting of his class, John found himself victim of stage fright; even a familiar prayer proved beyond recall. Luckily John's oral Bible reading saved the day. His first day behind him, the apprentice began a successful term of schoolmastering.[29]

During the 1866–67 teaching year, Brady roomed with the hospitable Brookbank family, owners of a large Sharpsville farm. In fact, the Mud Creek school was located on a corner of their land, and three of the farmer's children were in attendance. His auspicious Mud Creek experience was abruptly overshadowed by an outbreak of the dreaded cholera. All of the Brookbank family caught the disease; both the kindly farmer and his elderly mother died. It was a sad end to an otherwise productive year.

For a time during the cholera epidemic, Brady had nursed the entire Brookbank household. Afterward he was glad for a sojourn at the Tipton home and was especially warmed to find out how well the second Mrs. Green fitted into the household. Before the judge brought her to Tipton, Catherine Hummerrikhouse had resided with her farmer father not far from Peru. To Brady she would become a generous friend.[30]

Judge Green still wanted John to return to his hearth. Brady's scholarly ability pleased the small town patrician. The lad's successful teaching stint had confirmed John's fiscal independence; his assiduous book work and back work were publicly acknowledged. The judge came flat out with it: "By continued application you can become a lawyer in my office, or you can take full charge of the farm. I will pay taxes, make the improvements and give you half of what the farm produces." It was a most generous offer, particularly when one realizes that Brady was not his legal heir. John had long sought to prepare himself for this confrontation with his future. The grave moment demanded forthrightness, and he told his well-intentioned foster father that he desired to pursue neither farming nor law. Judge Green "was disappointed and changed, and when we parted for the night I was so overcome with emotion that when I went out on the road I fairly fell on my face and rolled in the dust with agony of tears. I felt that I had lost my best friend in making my decision." As it transpired, his ties to Judge Green remained unbroken.[31]

Following John's residence at Mud Creek, he lived for a period with Edgar Rumsey. Rumsey not only taught a common school but also acted as superintendent of a Presbyterian Sunday school. Possibly through his association with Rumsey, Brady came into intimate contact with a Presbyterian minister, the Reverend Isaac Montfort, and was thus drawn to that church. It was Montfort who first proposed to Brady that he enter the ministry. John had already publicly affirmed Jesus Christ as his savior, yet he had never seriously contemplated the ministry as a vocation, "but I gave it consideration, and [the] more I thought of it the more it seemed along the line that was most impressing to me."[32]

In the fall of 1867 John Green Brady was formally taken under the care of the presbytery at Muncie, Indiana. He first studied at Waveland Collegiate Institute, a Presbyterian-sponsored school isolated in the southwest corner of Montgomery County, some fourteen miles from the county seat of Crawfordsville. Waveland Academy, as it was first identified, had been founded to fulfill a college preparatory role in the

14

absence of any local free public high schools. Specifically its object was "to be the intellectual and religious training of pious youth for the gospel ministry."[33] The Presbyterian Board of Education voiced its confidence in him as a candidate for the ministry and appropriated one hundred dollars for his first year's expenses at Waveland. His church expected him to be "thorough in all your studies; to be watchful to improve well your time; to be careful to take abundant corporeal exercise, and use whatever means are necessary to maintain vigorous health; to avoid bad and luxurious habits; . . . to 'give thyself wholly' to preparation for the great work to which you have consecrated yourself, and to which we trust the Lord Jesus has truly called you."[34]

Novice Brady spent three academic years at Waveland—1867 to the summer of 1870. He had selected Waveland because his friend Edgar Rumsey had a brother-in-law on the faculty who offered him a very reasonable board and room in return for his labor. John ended the first year at Waveland with his savings exhausted. Janitorial tasks paid for his second-year expenses; and fiscal needs for the last year were met by selling his husbandry skills.[35] Brady remembered Waveland as a "Godly community." "I think," he later recalled, "during my first year there I did not hear a person swear." Levity, however, was not entirely absent. Decades afterward John laughingly regretted that he had not joined the reprobates who had organized a square dance—then an "unpardonable sin."

By 1869 Brady had fastened upon the next rung on his educational ladder. His decision to pursue schooling in the East was arrived at easily enough, yet it posed further financial worries. During the summer of 1868, in order to supplement his agricultural wages, he accepted a colporteur's commission. The Presbyterian Board of Publication expected its salesman "to circulate as extensively as possible the religious Books, Tracts and Periodicals . . . but none others without permission from the Board." When John first expressed a wish to go to Yale, he doubtless surprised many a Hoosier friend. Apparently the Connecticut institution had been first brought to his attention many years earlier by guest speakers at Randall's Island, visitors who had been introduced as Yale graduates. Now in 1869 his orphan status favored him. Some eastern philanthropists heard that a Children's Aid Society urchin had become a sedulous student, a model farm boy whose pluck was blocked by lack of money. Once again aid was promised him.[36]

Brady proudly forwarded to his foster father a copy of the letter assuring him of some eastern support, "not, however, asking him plainly to assist me, leaving that to his own judgment and good will." A reply was soon forthcoming, "in substance saying that if a Western

15

man was going to spend his time in the West, he thought a Western college was good enough, but as for himself he had come to the conclusion to let every fellow hoe his own row." That meant no assistance from the judge.[37] Happily the affectionate respect that the two men held for each other never ended. But after 1870 only random visits to Tipton renewed Brady's Hoosier boyhood ties.

In September of 1870, his savings sewed in his coat lining, a stuffed carpetbag in hand, he headed east. Seated aboard a car on the New York Central Railroad, the same line that had carried him west eleven years before, John Green Brady returned to New York City. Although curious to learn whether his real father still lived, he could not bring himself to renew the relationship. However, he did promptly visit the staff at the Children's Aid Society.[38]

In the fall of 1870 Yale was still esteemed as the "mother of colleges and outstanding citizens."[39] In truth, Old Eli of pre-Civil War America was fading away; the institution was being transformed from a college into a university. Yale was composed of four professional "schools" or departments. John enrolled in Theology, the oldest school, begun before the American Revolution but not formally organized until 1822. In 1869 the Theology School acquired a totally new building designed by the Gilded Age's illustrious architect, Richard Morris Hunt. For Brady's fifty-five divinity classmates, this structure became a residence and study center.[40]

The Yale that Brady experienced was still essentially an orthodox institution. Despite the fact that it had granted the first Ph.D. awarded in the United States (1861), supported the Sheffield Scientific School, a school of fine arts, and a graduate school, Yale's president, Noah Porter, found the word *university* offensive. It was a pretentious word. The college's paramount task, he insisted, was not training specialists but building character, molding students into citizens.[41] Porter also continued the ministerial tradition. He officiated as pastor of the Yale chapel, and many of his beliefs would later be reflected in John's philosophy of life. "Strength and perfection of character are the supreme aim of all right-judging men." "A personal God is needed by man to give his conscience energy and life." Evolution is God acting in history. "So soon as we know that God rules over man for man's moral discipline, and that Christ is setting up a kingdom of righteousness and peace and joy in the Holy Ghost, then we lift up our hearts, and gather courage for man's future history."[42]

In 1870 theology professor Timothy Dwight wrote: "Yale College is the largest and highest educational institution, under real and pronounced Christian influence in the country."[43] Few would have disa-

John G. Brady's Yale College graduation photograph, 1874. (Courtesy of Hugh P. Brady.)

greed, considering the time Yale then allocated for religious obser-
vances. Besides required daily morning chapel, there were two services
of an hour or so on Sundays. Twice a week, at the close of the Sunday
morning service and again on Tuesday evening, each class usually held
a voluntary prayer meeting, which lasted about a half an hour. Brady's
diary confirms how seriously he considered these prayer sessions. Then
on Friday a special voluntary college prayer meeting was held in the
president's lecture room. Attendance was sparse at the evening gatherings unless a revival enthusiasm swept the campus; then large crowds
were often present and additional prayer meetings were scheduled.[44]

Housed in a temporary garret room, John soon took his entrance
exams. The Hoosier passed everything but "conditioned" in Latin and
Greek. Being "conditioned" necessitated a private tutor, "studying up,"
and a belated admission to his classical language classes.[45] "Full-time
studies" during Brady's freshman and sophomore years were Greek,
Latin, and mathematics; "part-time" included some work in hygiene,
Roman history, and rhetoric. Most of the rhetoric was devoted to dec-
lamation and composition.[46] He also studied Cicero, Demosthenes,
Herodotus, Livy, Horace, Tacitus, Aeschylus, and Plato, reading about
them in Latin or Greek. In his last two years, his assignments included
works by Shakespeare, Dickens, and Tocqueville.[47]

Among the most impressive teachers of the early seventies were
Thomas A. Thacher in Latin, Timothy Dwight, III, in sacred literature,
Cyrus Northrop in rhetoric, and the brilliant young social scientist
William Graham Sumner. An ordained clergyman, Sumner taught that
it was "the duty of the Pulpit" to prepare for the dawning scientific
age. "Sumner," Brady noted, "makes . . . lessons interesting and profitable."[48] In April of his senior year, Brady was a house guest of the
distinguished sociologist.

At times John's impecuniousness forced almost a hand-to-mouth existence. In summer he labored in a sawmill near Williamsport, Pennsylvania. A sawyer's duties were arduous and not without hazard, but
the smell of cut wood and its utilitarian qualities appealed to him.
Fortunately the subsidies earlier promised by eastern Presbyterians and
the Children's Aid Society reduced his tuition costs. President Porter
took a personal interest in the young man and gave him a job tending
the furnace at his home. During his senior year he rang the bell in the
Old Lyceum, and Professor Sumner hired him for yard tasks at his
home on Whitneyville Road.

John's work kept him from participating in organized sports. However, his 1873 diary reveals precious stolen hours when he iceskated,

played baseball or football in the empty lots along Elm Street, or merely hiked in the countryside. John bemoaned the wasteful attraction of "Elm St. football." Usually minutes not consumed in earning money were exhausted in getting through his books. Once when terriby weary, a letter from his foster father bolstered him. The judge counseled: "Rise and fight again. . . . Self reliance is the only safe protection to an independent mind."[49]

It is perhaps unfortunate that Brady's monetary resources did not permit him to enjoy Yale's fraternal festivities. Participation in Skull and Bones ribaldry could have mellowed him. Laughter and sociability would forever flow from his warm personality, but idle jollification— being one of the gang merely for the sake of being one—was not part of his personality. Later when John became a politician, his inability to relish cavalier good fellowship proved costly.

One hundred twenty-two bachelor of arts degrees were awarded to the class of 1874. John joined nine who went on for ministerial study.[50] Gone were the days when almost half the class became clergymen. From first to last, from frosh capers to the smug smoking of the long clay pipes specially issued at commencement, Brady's years at Yale remained forever a treasure store of vibrant memories and profound inspiration. In large measure, John's lasting affection for Yale lay in his attachment to the men of 1874.[51]

The members of the class of 1874 entered upon their respective careers when President Grant was still in the White House and Congress sought to hurry along the closing years of Reconstruction. In a unique way this difficult chapter of American history touched Brady's class. Edward Alexander Bouchet, Connecticut-born and of Negro parents, was part of that class, whose members referred to themselves as the "Black and Tans."[52] Two years after graduating sixth in the class, Bouchet became Yale's first Negro Ph.D. Bouchet's singularity can hardly have been lost on Brady; he, too, was born an outsider.[53]

Why did John Brady choose to take his three years of ministerial training at New York's Union Theological Seminary? Both sentiment and economics probably affected his decision. The founders of Union believed that "a large city presented advantages for the training of young men for the Gospel ministry and the pastoral office, no less numerous and important than those which invite such large numbers to prepare for the professions of Law and Medicine." Presbyterian in affiliation, it was "open to students from every denomination." Its theological position was recognized as significantly more liberal than that church's historic and conservative-minded Princeton. To matriculate

Brady was obliged not only to show membership "in good standing in some Evangelical Church" but once again to "be examined by the faculty."[54]

At Union his financial burdens, although still weighty, appear to have lightened. New York City merchant William E. Dodge had heard of Brady's bootstrap progress from his son Arthur, one of John's classmates at Yale. For over a quarter century William Dodge, a Union trustee, had underwritten foreign and domestic missions, education for the ministry, Indian and Negro philanthropy, and the extension of temperance. He now extended to Brady $250 a year for spending money. Furthermore, he arranged a room-and-board scholarship for him. In later life John repeatedly praised Dodge's generosity.[55] Brady supplemented his sparse income by custodial labor in city churches and welfare services throughout Manhattan's slums.

Brady's understanding of the wretchedness he saw in New York took on a more reflective cast than had been possible when he was there as a boy. His own experience on Randall's Island and his subsequent treatment by Brace's welfare organization confirmed that social cancers of poverty and unemployment could be treated. Brady and his seminary classmates confidently believed that the march of science, reinforced by popular education and the Christian message, heralded cures for civic sicknesses of every sort.[56]

John arrived at Union at a time when reform-conscious "liberal Protestantism" was becoming influential. The Congregational minister Washington Gladden, often referred to as the "father of the Social Gospel," editorialized in the New York *Independent* on the ugly social consequences of the new industrial age. Gladden and other contemporary Christian mavericks insisted that the laboring classes were not getting their fair share. Writing in the *Presbyterian Quarterly and Princeton Review*, Lyman Atwater chided the employer who sinned against his employee by paying him inadequately and who thus sinned against God.[57] John had sweated for too many days as field hand, millhand, and now social worker not to agree with such sentiments.

Union's library of thirty-six thousand volumes included many rare and valuable European works. Perhaps John mused over the strange objects that foreign missionaries in Asia and the Pacific had sent back to the seminary, and his later fascination with aboriginal crafts may have been first aroused here.[58] He seems to have been too preoccupied with books and budget balancing to have cultivated many friends. At Yale he had been the rustic. Now seminarians from western colleges such as Knox, Oberlin, Wabash, and Ripon may have envied Brady his Yale-bred assurance. This urbanity earned him a reprimand when he communicated his familiarity with cards and the Bowery to some less worldly classmates. Frivolous raillery was not condoned at University Place. Happily there were off-campus occasions for socializing. One dinner date he recorded in his 1875 diary recalled his Hoosier gusto for the dance floor. "We went through the Lancers and Virginia Reel and some round dances. . . . Got to bed by 12."[59]

Union's course of study demanded a full three years of two terms each. In line with longstanding tradition, Union, like other Presbyterian seminaries, "continued to favor systematic theology and its foundations in Biblical studies over against the newer disciplines." The catalogue listed a most intimidating array of courses: in the first year, propaedeutics (theological methodology and bibliography), philology, exegesis, apologetics, Hebrew, and mission work; followed in the second year by exegesis, history, dogmatics, ethics, church polity, catechetics, homiletics; and in the third year much more of this, plus pastoral theology. In addition to the foregoing, the seminarian was expected to find time for training in sacred music, Syriac and Arabic languages, and vocal culture, and for study of "the relation of Civil law to ecclesiastical polity, discipline and property." No student could enroll in Union before he signed a pledge swearing "to complete a full course, either here or elsewhere."[60]

John's intellectual growth continued to be seasoned by his outside employment. In the summer of 1875 he signed on as a deckhand aboard a trans-Atlantic Black Ball steamer and was thus able to visit the land of his forebears. On his return to New York City, he began a search for his immigrant father and also attempted to discover what had happened to his half sister. This led him in turn to the Bellevue Hospital. Here confirmation of his father's death greeted him. Of his half sister no record could be found; she had vanished as completely as had the pockmarked Irish street gamin by the name of John Brady.[61]

1. Certificate of baptism from the baptismal register of Saint Andrew's Church, New York City, 9 August 1972. John G. Brady Papers, Beinecke Library, Yale University, John G. Brady Microfilm No. 2, "The Zigzags of a New York Street Boy," which Brady wrote some time after 1907. There are also handwritten and typed versions of "Zigzags." Hereafter items from the Brady Papers, Yale University, will be cited by microfilm roll number and specifically identified—i.e., JGB, mf. 2, "Zigzags," or, if not microfilmed, JGB, unfiled (for example). Park Row was then called Chatham.

2. David M. Ellis et al., *A Short History of New York State* (New York, 1957); Allan Nevins and M. H. Thomas, eds., *The Diary of George Templeton Strong*, vol. 3 of *The Turbulent Fifties, 1850–59*, 4 vols. (New York, 1952).

3. JGB, mf. 2, "Zigzags." Another version of the boy's transition to street vagrancy may be found in a letter he apparently wrote to Charles Loring Brace (*The Dangerous Classes of New York and Twenty Years Among Them* [New York, 1872], p. 261). According to this document, he was for awhile sheltered by an aunt by the name of Julia. "She had me in charge for some time, and made known some things to me of which I have faint remembrance. She married a gentleman in Boston and left me to myself. . . . I could not have been more than seven or eight years of age at this time. She is greatly to be excused for this act, since I was a very bad boy, having an abundance of self-will." This letter was also reprinted in Helen Campbell, *Darkness and Daylight; or, Lights and Shadows of New York Life* (Hartford, Conn., 1892), p. 130.

4. *New York Times*, 19 December 1918.

5. JGB, mf. 2, "Zigzags." Corinne Roosevelt Robinson, "My Brother Theodore Roosevelt: The Nursery and Its Deities," *Scribner's Magazine*, February 1921, p. 132; statement from Children's Aid Society to Hugh P. Brady, 7 August 1968.

6. Pertinent studies of American poverty are Robert Bremner, *American Philanthropy* (Chicago, 1965); idem, *From the Depths: The Discovery of Poverty in the United States* (New York, 1966); and idem, *Children and Youth in America: A Documentary History*, 3 vols. (Cambridge, Mass., 1970), vol. 1, *1600–1865*. On the Children's Aid Society see Bremner, *Children and Youth in America*, pp. 401 ff.; Miriam Z. Langsam, *Children West* (Madison, 1964); and Annette Riley Fry, "The Children's Migration," *American Heritage* 26 (December 1974): 4–10, 79–81.

7. JGB, mf. 2, "Zigzags."

8. Ibid.

9. Ibid.

10. Ibid. On Governor Andrew H. Burke see C. A. Lounsberry, *The Record*, May 1895; and Lewis F. Crawford, *History of North Dakota* (New York, 1931), pp. 376–78.

11. JGB, mf. 2, "Zigzags"; George Pence and Nellie C. Armstrong, *Indiana Boundaries* (Indiapolis, 1933), p. 772; Louis Wood, Indiana State Library, to author, 21 May 1968.

12. JGB, mf. 2, "Zigzags."

13. Ibid.

14. G. W. Hawes, *Indiana State Gazeteer and Business Directory for 1858 and 1859* (Indianapolis, 1858), pp. 376–77.

15. JGB, mf. 2, "Zigzags."

16. Ibid.

17. Ibid.

18. Ibid.

19. Whether "ager" actually was malaria, or at least what John suffered from was malaria, is impossible to tell. If it was, he later evidenced no traces of it.

20. Edward Eggleston, *The Hoosier Schoolmaster* (1871) in many editions.

21. JGB, mf. 2, "Zigzags."

22. Ibid.

23. M. W. Pershing, *History of Tipton County, Indiana* (Indianapolis, 1914), p. 142.

24. JGB, mf. 2, "Zigzags."

25. Ibid.

26. Ibid.

27. Ibid; statement from Children's Aid Society. Children's Aid Society to author, 30 September 1968.

28. Children's Aid Society to author 30 September 1968.

29. JGB, mf. 1, "Zigzags."

30. Ibid. *A Biographical History of Eminent and Self-Made Men of the State of Indiana* (Cincinnati, 1880), p. 16 (hereafter cited as *Men of Indiana*). The judge's second wife died in 1875, after which he took a third and last wife, Mrs. Caroline Paswalter of Noblesville, a judge's daughter.

31. JGB, mf. 2, "Zigzags."

32. Ibid.

33. *History of Montgomery County*, 2 vols. (Montgomery, Ind., 1913), I:205–7.

34. JGB, unfiled, William Speer to Brady, 9 December 1867.

35. Ibid., mf. 2, "Zigzags."

36. Ibid.; ibid., colporteur's commission filed in "Letters from Friends, 1867–1880."

37. JGB, mf. 2, "Zigzags." Undated Tipton *Tribune* clippings, Indiana State Historical Society. *Men of Indiana*, p. 16.

38. Statement from Children's Aid Society.

39. George Wilson Pierson, *Yale College: Educational History, 1871–1921*, vol. 1 of *Yale: College and University, 1871–1937*, 2 vols. (New Haven, 1952), p. 4.

40. Graduate of '69, *Four Years at Yale* (New Haven, 1871), p. 33.

41. Pierson, *Yale College*, 1:53.

42. Interview with Hugh Brady, 6 June 1962, Seattle; Ralph Henry Gabriel, *Religion and Learning at Yale: The Church of Christ in the College and University, 1757–1957* (New Haven, 1958), pp. 180–82.

43. Pierson, *Yale College*, 1:10.

44. Graduate of '69, *Four Years*, pp. 524–26; JGB, diary for 1873, 23 August entry.

45. Interview with Hugh Brady, 6 June 1962; and Graduate of '69, *Four Years*, p. 546.

46. Pierson, *Yale College*, 1:706.

47. Graduate of '69, *Four Years*, pp. 558–66; JGB, diary for 1873.

48. Pierson, *Yale College*, 1:54; Gabriel, *Religion and Learning*, p. 160; JGB, diary for 1874, 7 January entry.

49. Foster Rhea Dulles, *A History of Recreation: America Learns to Play* (New York, 1965), p. 197; JGB, mf. 3, John Green to Brady, 7 October 1873.

50. *Catalogue of the Officers and Graduates of Yale University in New Haven, Connecticut: 1701–1895* (New Haven, 1895), pp. 122–23.

51. Pierson, *Yale College*, 1:5.

52. Interview with Hugh Brady, 24 November 1967, Seattle.

53. Yale College, *Biographical Record of the Class of 1874 in Yale College, Part Fifth, 1909–1919* (New Haven, 1919), pp. 81–84; and Yale University, *Obituary Record of Graduates of Yale University, 1918–1919* (New Haven, 1920), pp. 919–20.

54. *Catalogue of the Officers and Students of the Union Theological Seminary, in the City of New York, 1880–1881* (New York, 1880), p. 14. George Lewis Prentiss, *The Union Theological Seminary in the City of New York: Historical and Biographical Sketches of Its First Fifty Years* (New York, 1889), pp. 207–8. Elwyn Allen Smith, *The Presbyterian Ministry in American Culture: A Study in Changing Concepts, 1700–1900* (Philadelphia, 1962), p. 171.

55. Interview with Hugh Brady, 24 November 1967. JGB, mf. 3, Dodge to Brady, 14 July 1874; JGB, diary for 1874, 17 February entry. Dodge was his paramount benefactor but not his sole one (JGB, mf. 2, Collins & Fen, commission merchants, to Brady, 1 May 1876).

56. Kenneth Scott Latourette, *The Great Century: In Europe and the United States of America, A.D. 1800–A.D. 1914*, vol. 4, *A History of Christianity* (New York, 1941), p. 1.

57. Charles Howard Hopkins, *The Rise of the Social Gospel in American Protestantism, 1865–1915* (New Haven, 1940), pp. 27–34; John Dillenberger and Claude Welch, *Protestant Christianity Interpreted through Its Development* (New York, 1954), p. 245.

58. *Students of the Union Theological Seminary*, pp. 15 ff.

59. Interview with John G. Brady, Jr., 14 August 1968, Seattle. JGB, mf. 2, "Zigzags"; JGB, diary for 1875, 21 January entry.

60. Lefferts A. Loetscher, *The Broadening Church: A Study of Theological Issues in the Presbyterian Church since 1869* (Philadelphia, 1957), p. 75. Ibid., pp. 13, 16–17; Prentiss, *Union Theological Seminary*, pp. 88–93.

61. Interview with Hugh Brady, 6 June 1962; JGB, penciled record of 1875 trip. The date of his father's death is unknown.

CHAPTER TWO

The Sitka Mission

In May 1877 John Green Brady and forty-five other seminarians graduated from Union Seminary. Shortly afterward the nation experienced an industrial upheaval, a frightening series of urban explosions caused by widespread unemployment exacerbated by wage cuts among railroad employees. Pittsburgh and Baltimore burst into flaming battles between mobs of infuriated workers and volley-firing militia. Before it burned itself out, the Great Railroad Strike seared the humanitarian conscience of Brady's generation, some of whom, no doubt, wondered whether revolution lay ahead. The violence certainly magnified the immediate social challenge confronting Brady.

But precisely how was he to apply a Christian's healing touch to such urban agonies? Very likely Brady had pondered the activist evangelical approach when Dwight L. Moody and Ira D. Sankey returned triumphant in 1875 from their ministry in England. Like other seminarians, he varied his place of worship. In the city's affluent churches he listened to such nationally recognized sermonizers as Thomas DeWitt Talmage, Henry Ward Beecher, and Henry Van Dyke.[1] Too often these churches preferred to channel their funds into foreign missions instead of fighting pervasive urban poverty.

Unquestionably Brady possessed an acute understanding of Manhattan's cruelty. He had personally tasted New York's dregs. Revulsion at its appalling degeneracy never left him; thanks be to God, the Reverend Mr. Brace, and Judge Green, the Irish street arab had escaped the slum's horrors. Inner city welfare work during his years at Union had regularly renewed harsh memories of his orphan days. Occasionally Brace asked him to give an inspirational talk before an audience of urchins corraled at the Children's Aid Society. How John must have

25

empathized with those amoral, unhealthy, and virtually abandoned children! "I could see they looked upon me with confidence, that touched me very much, and I did not forget it." He knew that his words to them about each having a chance to make good were but half-truths. Some of these "God-forsaken creatures" would end up behind bars, or worse.[2] Brady determined that his ministry should be to such youngsters.

In January 1876 a friend in Denver recommended that Brady contact Colorado's synodical secretary, Dr. Sheldon Jackson.[3] Jackson, the self-styled Presbyterian "Rocky Mountain Superintendent," had made quite a name for himself as a western home missionary organizer. The remarkable five-foot-tall Jackson, traveling over his gigantic eleven-state charge by stage, mule, and on foot, was fast becoming legendary.[4] Always on the qui vive for hard-driving young ministers whose vivacity might match his own, Jackson was impressed with Brady's credentials. He suggested that the New Yorker assume a pastorate in Colorado's Silverton mining district.

But how could John reconcile his attraction to the West with the demands of conscience to assist juveniles trapped within America's urban-industrial centers? Brady's solution may have been Brace's suggestion. The plan does seem to have jelled one evening at the Children's Aid Society. Texas had plenty of cheap land. Why not create there an industrial school to rescue eastern street lads? Here Brady could unite the best features of the Randall Island manual arts training with certain of his skills mastered on an Indiana farm.

Arthur Dodge soon heard of his friend's aspirations. His father urged Brady to go west and investigate the practicality of such a school. Theodore Roosevelt, Sr., whose family had endowed Union's chair of systematic theology and who had himself been a founder of the city's Newsboys' Lodging House and the Young Men's Christian Association, was approached for aid. Possibly Brady chose not to remind the patrician of their first encounter on the sidewalks of New York. Roosevelt extended only a qualified promise of support.[5] Especially encouraging was a "lady friend," apparently one of considerable means and quite active in the Children's Aid Society. She assured him that once he located a site for an industrial school, nine thousand dollars would be forthcoming.[6]

Thus armed with assurances of financial support and letters of introduction, Brady headed west. To a Yale alumnus he wrote: "I am going to Texas to see if I can in any way organize a farm for boys between fourteen and nineteen. This class of boys in New York is as helpless and worse off than foundlings."[7] Brady made sure his contact with Dr. Sheldon Jackson remained cordial. If the Texas dream did not

26

materialize, he might like to have that job in Silverton. A letter to Jackson described his Texas scheme. "The idea is to have a well organized farm upon which a boy can receive a good training in a year. When so trained, a home with a good farmer is to be procured for him, or he is to be placed in a position where he can industriously hoe his own row."[8]

On his way west Brady relaxed briefly with "nice little visits" at Tipton and Waveland. He arrived in Dallas in June of 1877. After a week discussing his proposition with local businessmen and church leaders, he hired a horse and commenced a personal tour of northwestern Texas. His route took him to Denton, thence to Weatherford, from there to Thorpe's Springs in Hood County, back to Weatherford, and then straight back to Dallas. William Dodge's letters secured passes for him on all of the Texas railroads. Brady visited San Antonio, Houston, Austin, Waco, and Palestine. He found his promised land not far from Weatherford. Located on the Brazos River, "the tract was 1700 acres and could be purchased for approximately $7000." As he later informed Dr. Jackson, "I selected a farm twelve miles south of Weatherford for it combines nearly every good thing—rich bottom soil, with black upland prairie, water, timber. . . . I have strong faith in its success but the only way is to try it."[9]

While Brady roamed over the windswept land that banked on the Brazos and dreamed of erecting an industrial reform school, America's great railroad strike swept his hopes into oblivion. When he returned east in 1877, his "lady friend had lost her money." And after a pleasant evening welcome at Dodge's home, Arthur broke the bad news. "Now Brady, you know my store down on Cliff Street. It is not bringing me 2%. I am not only spending my income but part of my capital to keep things going. . . . I can take on nothing new." Although John appreciated his friend's frankness, "it was then out of the question for me to start this proposition of a training farm in Texas."[10] Brady was familiar with defeat. He rationalized his intense disappointment with sour observations on Texas's weather and renewed his search for a fresh "calling."

While the restless Brady had been hunting for a school site in Texas, Jackson had opened the door for a Presbyterian mission in Alaska. As if that zealous organizer's multistate synod were not a sufficient field of labor, Jackson's intense ambition had compelled him to plow fresh ground. Before the summer of 1877 had ended, and before his eastern superiors in the church realized exactly what he was about, Jackson had inaugurated a mission outside the contiguous United States. The Presbyterian Board of Home Missions was painfully familiar with his impetuous obsession to sow religious seeds. Now, unless the board acted to throw Jackson out of the church—and to have initiated such a process against the well-publicized "Rocky Mountain Superintendent" would have been calamitous—they must accept his fait accompli, while praying that he could make good on his promise to raise the necessary money to nourish his embryo Alaska mission. Certainly Brady's Texas reversal signified how mercurial philanthropy had become.[11]

Jackson's action not only irritated the board's secretaries but nettled Dr. Aaron L. Lindsley, influential pastor of the First Presbyterian Church of Portland, Oregon. Lindsley had likewise dreamed of becoming the "first Christian to plant a Protestant Church" in America's recently acquired Far North frontier. Both men could have relaxed, at least when it came to historical precedent. Well before America's annexation of Russian America in 1867, the Lutherans had operated a chapel at Sitka.[12] Vanity notwithstanding, there was no denying the need for aroused Christian action on the Alaskan frontier.

Jackson's 1877 tour touched only a tiny portion of the vast District of Alaska: the village of Wrangell, a ramshackle embarkation and supply point for miners boarding steamers to British Columbia's gold country up the nearby Stikine River. Here he witnessed Indians suffering the familiar problems of acculturation.[13] Only in its particulars did this native tableau differ from that which Jackson had too often seen across America's Far West. The vigorous Northwest Coast Indians of the Alexander Archipelago, marine warriors who had once held their own against Caucasian invaders, appeared to be succumbing to a self-destructive trinity of lasciviousness, liquor, and lassitude. Before the invaders' power and tacit contempt, their self-esteem eroded. Many a proud Tlingit or Haida family had slipped into a dangerous cultural staleness. Some sold their daughters to miners in exchange for whiskey. Intoxication at least provided one sure means of escaping the social disarray into which they had fallen.[14] Jackson was appalled. Before he left Wrangell he arranged with local American officials to help maintain a Presbyterian missionary, Mrs. Amanda McFarland, an old friend and the widow of an Arizona churchman. Using the lever of his privately owned newspaper, the *Rocky Mountain Presbyterian*, Jackson assured Amanda McFarland that he would pry out donations to underwrite her courageous commitment.[15]

Brady soon heard of what Jackson had initiated. Drawing upon an arsenal of promotional devices, the Rocky Mountain superintendent made certain that an increasing number of Americans were informed about what had to be done for Alaska. The Great Land, according to him, had no government, no law, no morality, and no protection for the native people. Protestant churches, and first of all the Presbyterians, had a sacred obligation to remedy this tragic state of affairs. Jackson exaggerated, of course, but his polemical theme hit home. Certainly the indomitable Mrs. McFarland bravely sheltering teenage girls from lecherous prospectors epitomized the aroused Victorian belatedly and angrily protecting mistreated Alaska. This symbol, in a variety of shapes, was paraded before ladies' auxiliaries, propounded from pulpits, and set in type throughout the country. The impact of his publicity proved irresistible—the Wrangell mission succeeded. Ultimately Jackson would dot the district with Christian teachers.[16]

Jackson's exciting description of the Great Land captivated Brady. Before 1877 ended, the Board of Home Missions appointed the tyro a "missionary to preach the Gospel" at an annual salary of twelve hundred dollars in the "Sitka Vicinity." At the February 1878 meeting of the Presbytery of New York, Brady was ordained. Even before the gathering had concluded, he boarded the train for Portland, Oregon; only once a month did an Alaska-bound steamer depart Portland. The young missionary possessed but a hazy idea of what was awaiting him at Sitka. Few accurate sources were then available.

Settlers at Sitka and Wrangell, the only two towns of consequence in Alaska's Panhandle, felt shamefully neglected by the American government. Alaskans' grumbles exceeded the normal Far West self-pity. Easily available scapegoats for their slow development were the federal government and the Alaska Commercial Company. However, whereas the fur company had conscientiously and pragmatically exerted itself to assist Alaska, Washington, D.C., had done all too little. Gilded Age congresses had more than they could handle: embittered Reconstruction politics, the burgeoning Far West, and, above all, the nation's amazingly rapid industrialization with all of the harsh imponderable adjustments that this entailed. To a Congress so burdened, Alaskan affairs appeared exceedingly inconsequential.[17]

Brady could hardly have envisioned these overriding historic facts as he steamed north during late February 1978. Enroute across the United States, he had been briefed first by Jackson and then by Lindsley at Portland. Conversations abroad the S.S. *California* and voracious reading improved his knowledge of Alaska before the steamer docked at Sitka in mid-March. Nothing, however, fully prepared him for the district's polyglot population.

Alaska claimed no more than a couple of hundred white Yankee inhabitants, but it could boast of tens of thousands of other diverse Americans. Russian blood ran in the veins of approximately two thousand natives. Such mixed bloods, raised in Russian settlements or oth-

29

erwise heavily immersed in Russian culture, were called Creoles.[18] For simplicity, Alaska's aboriginal population usually was divided into four major classifications. In the far northwest, bordering on the Arctic Slope and the Bering Sea, were the Eskimos. Brady would not become personally familiar with them until some years later, when official duties carried him into their isolated country. Second were the Aleuts, whose habitation on the Aleutian Islands had proved disastrous for them. Their north Pacific islands had provided convenient steppingstones for Russia's ruthless fur-hunting *promyshlenniki* as they swept eastward in the eighteenth century. Alaska's third major aboriginal group were the Northwest Coast Indians of southeastern Alaska, Panhandle natives among whom Brady would be preaching and teaching. An admirer of wood and woodworking, he soon commenced a collection of their remarkable wood artistry. A fourth group, also categorized as Indians, were the Athapascan natives of the Yukon Valley. The Athapascans, like Alaska's great river, extended deep into Canada's Yukon Territory. Together this indigenous population reached a total of about thirty thousand people.[19]

Brady quickly discerned that these general classifications were hazardous—about as foolish as trying to lump Manhattan's citizens by three or four commonalities. For the remainder of his life he continued to learn about and from Alaska's Northwest Coast Indians, that is, his regional Alexander Archipelago neighbors, the Tlingit, Haida, and Tsimshian. Although many would eventually call him a friend, John conceded that his understanding of their utterly unique and sophisticated cultures must forever remain superficial.

In 1878 the callow young minister was blissfully unconscious of the challenge that awaited him. The "Terms of This Commission" delineated three fundamental duties: "First. You are required, at the end of every quarter . . . to forward to the Secretaries a full and accurate report of your Ministerial labors; noticing in detail the various departments of your work, and the various encouragements, and trials therewith connected, together with any facts or suggestions that may be of service to the board. . . . "[20] Second, it was his obligation to complete an annual statistical report. The form made provision for such things as "stations where you have preached," "the number of Sunday schools and scholars," "whole number of communicants," "baptisms of adults," and "number of church edifices." And finally, he had to inform his New York Home Board superior of the amount of any contributions he received—this so it might be deducted from his salary.

The "Rules of the Board of Home Missions" were longer but more broadly drawn. Among the most important:

The grand object of the Missionary should be to build up the kingdom of Christ, by constant and prayerful labor for the conversion of the unregenerate, the edification of the Christians, and the training of the children of the Church.

As soon as may be, the Missionary is to organize, in every suitable locality in his field, where one does not exist a church . . . he will be careful not to interfere improperly with existing church organizations . . . not to be governed by mere sectarian considerations.

He will organize a Sabbath School in each suitable locality.

Congregations should steadily aim at self-support as soon as possible.[21]

Brady would do what he could to organize a traditional Presbyterian church at the capital; however, he soon discovered that his ministry was primarily to the natives.

Sheldon Jackson, Amanda McFarland, John Brady, and other missionaries to follow were distant participants in America's ruinous red-white encounter—the three-century tragedy enacted across western America. In 1819 Congress had begun a regular annual appropriation of ten thousand dollars (the "Civilization Fund") to be used by churches and benevolent groups for Indian education. During President Grant's administration these Christian bodies had involved themselves in what was referred to as the Quaker or Indian peace policy.[22] Throughout Brady's lifetime America's newspapers had lamented the sanguinary "Indian Wars." Brutal and wasteful of people, they were the consequence of two radically different societies grinding together. Christian leaders had labored long and hard to ease the red man's adversity, but by 1878 the Bureau of Indian Affairs and the military, both charged with protecting the red man, were in low public esteem.[23] If the army had been too prone to apply force, philanthropic agencies had been reluctant to admit the appalling complexity of the social disaster and too unrealistic in their efforts to save the Indians with the white man's tools.

Repeatedly the U.S. commissioner of education, John Eaton, had urged some kind of native education program in Alaska. The Bureau of Education, like the Indian bureau, was in the Department of the Interior. Congress ignored him. Commissioner Eaton, an active Presbyterian, had welcomed Jackson's impetuous move into the Far North. Eaton not only endorsed the incipient Wrangell and Sitka missions but maneuvered to bring both the military and civilian branches of government to assist his church's Far North educational efforts. Indeed, by 1878 the Presbyterian Home Board obligated itself to provide Christian schools for Chinese, Indians, Mormons, and Mexicans, and also to uplift the "natives of Alaska."[24]

When Brady arrived at Sitka on 17 March, one of his first questions

View of Sitka from the harbor looking southeast, in the mid-80s. Baranov Castle is on the right rise, the Customs House between the masts of the *Leo*, part of the Sitka Trading Company building to the rear of the main, and the Governor's House at the far left. (Reproduced by permission of the Beinecke Rare Book and Manuscript Library, Yale University.)

was, "What is the danger of an Indian outbreak?" With relief he reported that the "people of Sitka have no anticipation of any thing of this kind. Everything is quiet, and there is no rumor of any disturbance." He was likewise comforted by the cordial welcome that both Sitka's few merchants and the priest of the Russian Orthodox Church extended him.

Although his stay at Sitka had to be brief, for he was soon to leave on the steamer for a month's duty at Wrangell, Brady promptly contacted leaders in the contiguous Indian Ranche, as the native village was called. His translator was the official U.S. interpreter, the convivial Sitka-born George J. Kostrometinoff. After introducing himself to the natives, John described his God. "The God who made the mountains the sea and made also the Indian, Chinese, white man and all men. We were all sinners before that God but Jesus Christ his son came to save us all from sin by believing upon him." With the aid of native carpenters Brady proposed to build them a school. He concluded by singing a couple of hymns, "Knocking" and "Hold the Fort," which "seemed to please them." Sitka's Indians, who for some time had been asking for a school, assured him that "if they could not learn at school, they would make their children learn."[25]

Decades afterward, Brady sadly recalled the avidity with which Sitka's natives had embraced "whiteman vices." Furthermore, their segregation from central Sitka made him "sick at heart." Yet in 1878, in letters to both Lindsley and Jackson, John declared that the only certain way to save the Indians was to separate them from the whites. This contradiction reveals the insoluble dilemma that has challenged men of good will since time immemorial. How can people whose culture is incompatible be brought into a more aggressive, technically superior society without the latter wrecking the former's way of life, that is, without inducing a devastating culture shock? Even if the weaker mingle freely with the invader, they cannot for many years master the stronger culture's sophisticated talents. Indeed, too often the weaker people imitate the coarser habits of those thrust among them. Invariably the hedonism of frontier toughs hastened the decay of the aboriginal's social structure.[26]

On the other hand, to isolate native peoples, though perhaps sensible in theory, was impractical. America's Indian reservations had failed to protect them from socially undesirable whites. Hundreds of mounted soldiers had repeatedly proved incapable of halting gold seekers and nesters infiltrating Indian country.[27] In Alaska the military played a similar frustrating game of hide and seek with those who illegally imported liquor for Indian customers.

After purchasing Alaska the U.S. government assigned the primary police role in the district to the army. Some capital residents told Brady that before the troops were withdrawn in 1877 they had only accelerated the demoralization of the Indians. For the moment U.S. Treasury Department customs officers were responsible for governing the district. It was generally agreed that policing of the natives should be done either by a U.S. Revenue Marine cutter or a naval vessel; an armed steamer promised far more mobility throughout the Alexander Archipelago than the soldiers ever possessed.[28]

Upon his arrival at Wrangell, Brady was reassured to hear from the deputy collector that "the Indians here are not a band of cut-throats and pirates that require bayonets and brass cannon to keep them in subjection." Throughout the mid-seventies Wrangell had benefited from transient gold seekers enroute to British Columbia gold fields. But by 1878, as the easy pickings declined, so had the port's population.[29] It was the harmful effects on Wrangell's natives produced by this oscillating wave of miners that had so alarmed Jackson and given birth to Widow McFarland's Indian school. "I was astonished and gratified by all that I saw," Brady reported. "Some big boys I may say men, were learning their A B C some little chicks as cute as could be were learning to spell. A few boys were in short division as well as one or two of the girls. The lessons in primary geography were well recited. . . . Some of the scholars were married women."[30]

Doubly encouraging to Brady was the sizable number of Wrangell's adult Indians who had not lost their sense of self-worth. Indeed, some had already been evangelized. These pre-Presbyterian converts had been proselytized by visiting Tsimshians from British Columbia.[31] One such Indian teacher, Sara Dickenson, a full-blooded Tongass and wife of a white trader, had become Mrs. McFarland's right-hand woman. More than likely Mrs. Dickenson's commitment and multilingual capacities were what sustained the evangelized Indians' interest in Christian education.

At Brady's first prayer meeting, he could not understand a word of what one elderly Indian was saying. So moved was John by the man's intense and dignified supplication, however, "I could not help crying."[32] After one month's work at the Wrangell mission, much of it hard physical labor clearing ground for permanent buildings, he returned to Sitka as he had been instructed. His Wrangell internship had introduced him to native life: the matrilineal family structure and the delightful raven legends, as well as the Indians' barbaric exploitation of slaves. The youthful clergyman probably did not realize how he had vexed Mrs. McFarland when he encouraged the natives to continue their dancing.

She had been trying hard to discontinue the practice. John did discover, however, that Portland's Aaron Lindsley had become quite envious of Jackson's Alaska achievements.[33] For the moment Brady sensibly avoided the Jackson-Lindsley spat. He needed to remain on good terms with the Portland minister.

Upon his return to Alaska's capital in April of 1878, Brady probably saw the community through less romantic lenses. In contrast to its picturesque harbor dotted with rocky islands against a backdrop of cloud-shrouded volcanic peaks, Sitka was itself dolorous. Its mild, misty temperature was pleasant enough, and the surrounding forest cover ribboned with mountain streams was forever lovely, but Sitka's large number of empty, decaying buildings, particularly the chaotic Ranche waterfront, revived Brady's memories of eastern slums. So, too, the stench from the Indians' open sewer, and the wild yells from their frequent drunken rampages discouraged him.[34]

Brady understood the humanitarian necessity of keeping the Indian from firewater. The federal government had designated Alaska as Indian country precisely for this reason. Ostensibly the entire 586,000 square miles was off limits to spirituous liquors.[35] Merely to control this clandestine traffic into Wrangell and Sitka was, however, difficult. The West Coast supply seemed inexhaustible. Especially disturbing, the Indians had now become adept at distilling their own special brew. Indeed, when the S.S. *California* had first delivered Brady to his mission field, it had also disembarked some twenty barrels of molasses, which, as everyone knew, would end up as fiery hoochinoo.[36]

A Northwest Coast missionary leader, Father William Duncan of British Columbia, had developed one means of practicing controlled acculturation. At his rigidly supervised, Indian-run community of Metlakatla, anyone caught trafficking in liquor was thrown into jail by uniformed Tsimshian police. Attesting to the success of his enterprise were its impressive buildings—church, schoolhouse, shops, and neat cottages—and Metlakatla's almost complete economic independence.[37] Duncan's amazing enclave argued for the concept of a strict separation of Indian and white, excepting only those occasions where tightly regulated cultural exchanges might take place. But it was too late to apply a Duncan blueprint to Alaska. Furthermore, his was too radical a variance from the historic American pattern.

By 1878 Americans had tried a variety of educational techniques to introduce Indian youth to white ways: boarding schools both on and off the reservation; Indian day schools; special scholarships to offer Indian youth the finest possible eastern educational experience; work apprenticeships; "the outing system" (placing the Indian child in a Christian

35

home).[38] None of them ever seemed to produce the results that its advocates had predicted. Too much was always made of the failures. A special target of the critics was the "fallen Indian girl" who, rejected by her own people for her adoption of a white life-style, became a squaw man's partner when her dark skin denied her acceptance in Caucasian society. The record was disappointing. Only reluctantly did Victorian reformers recognize that "civilizing the Indian" could not progress rapidly.

In 1877 the American anthropologist Lewis Henry Morgan published his *Ancient Society*, in which he portrayed mankind as evolving from savagery to barbarism to civilization. The lesson seemed clear enough: as quickly as possible the red man should be reshaped into a white man. A contemporary of Morgan, the well-known ethnologist Major John Wesley Powell, who had also lived among the aboriginals and carefully probed the "Indian problem," proposed that their nomadic existence be phased out for a farming way of life. To further accelerate acculturation, diverse Indian languages and habits should be homogenized.[39] These goals guided Brady and his coworkers. Failure, they believed, could happen only if public giving and missionary sacrifice failed.

In 1878 Fannie Kellogg, Aaron Lindsley's niece, joined Brady at Sitka. From all descriptions, Kellogg was an attractive, strong-willed female. Assisted by Sitka trader Amos Whitford, who had "bought up every old trap when the soldiers left," Brady furnished living quarters for his missionary partner—with what grace we can only imagine. No doubt he was chagrined when Fannie's sudden illness after her arrival forced him to begin the Presbyterian mission school without her. Aided by three Indians, John prepared a classroom in the abandoned soldiers' barracks, "determined to fulfill every promise" that he had made to the natives.

School opened on 17 April "with about fifty of all ages and sexes present."[40] After asking God's blessing on the undertaking, Brady began "to teach A B C." His students' "mental vigor" surprised him, just as their teacher's rapidly increasing use of the Tlingit tongue fascinated the Indians. Brady's linguistic talent, which he later attributed to his polyglot New York boyhood, was remarkable. Greek, Latin, and Hebrew were educational gifts. Tlingit and Russian came from independent study, and in later years, as leisure time permitted, he found pleasure in acquiring a familiarity with the Romance languages.[41]

Writing to Jackson in the spring of 1878, Brady exuded confidence. "The progress which [the Indians] have made in the past month is a matter of amazement to me." Native pupils who met on Sitka's streets or in stores reviewed their alphabet; sometimes they chorused songs such as "Come to Jesus" and "I Need Thee Every Hour." When Fannie Kellogg jestingly told them that they could not become good Americans until they learned how to whistle "Yankee Doodle," townspeople soon had their full share of that tune. In a few weeks Brady and Miss Kellogg had "thirteen now reading in the primer, and twenty-five have learned all the large letters." Improvisation was imperative, but educational enthusiasm was abundant: "We have but six primers. This want of apparatus retards the work very much. Miss Kellogg has been careful to see that they do not learn in the parrot manner. They are taught the meaning of what they learn. . . . money spent in teaching and Christianizing these people will not be thrown away. 'Blessed are they which do hunger and thirst after righteousness for they shall be filled.' This promise will surely be willed to these people for they are hungering and thirsting for more light."[42]

On Sundays Brady held divine services attended by both Indians and whites. Among the latter he was surprised to see Amos Whitford. The veteran trader's skill as an illicit liquor dealer was commonly acknowledged. Fannie Kellogg reported that Brady obtained "the signatures of all the merchants to an agreement that they would send for no more molasses for rum." The next steamer brought a large cargo of brown sugar.[43]

Indian curiosity satisfied, attendance declined in the summer: some students succumbed to the seasonal urge to fish; others found temporary employment in a recently begun salmon cannery. Itching to see more of the Great Land, Brady seized the opportunity to escape the confines of the classroom. Twice he secured a canoe and, aided by some strong hands, visited archipelago tribes, among them the Hoonahs on Chichagof Island and the Kootsnoos on Admiralty Island. Frequently he came ashore soaked from an open voyage. Indian welcomers quickly dragged his canoe up on the beach fronting their log homes. "I preached boldly against witchcraft [he still used an interpreter] and the medicine men, against gambling, drunkenness and licentiousness. I took with me to the Hoonas a magic lantern and some fine views of the Holy Land. You may imagine the astonishment of these people." A maritime people, the natives of one village asked him to repeat the slides of Jesus walking on the water. It may well have been a shaman who requested that he explain how Lazarus had been raised.[44]

At another community he was relieved to find that "the women are comparatively unpolluted, and the children numerous. They have constant communication by canoe with Sitka and Fort Wrangell. We should make this one of our chain of mission stations among the Thlinket speaking people." A visit with the Chilkat Indians marked the northern limit of his 1878 tours. They "filled the house of the chief, where we spoke, to suffocation," Brady wrote, "and some who could not get in climbed upon the roof and listened through the aperture . . . enduring the cold for two hours at a time rather than miss any of the message." The missionary was amazed. "Your words are food to our hearts," they declared. The Chilkats insisted he should "preach again and again."[45]

After he returned to Sitka Brady counseled Jackson that, despite the lack of a stable congregation, the formation of an Alaska presbytery would soon be justified. But by the autumn of 1878, the leaves of his Sitka mission had begun to fall; indeed, they had begun to turn as early as July.

Several factors caused Brady to leave his field at year's end. Some can only be surmised. Quite possibly Fannie Kellogg was one. Brady groused to Jackson that he "absolutely refused to notice her bids for courtship and thus gained her ill will." Fortunately Fannie found another Alaska missionary, the Reverend S. Hall Young, a Jackson appointee.[46] A recent graduate of Western Theological Seminary, Young arrived at Wrangell in July of 1878 as a coworker for Mrs. McFarland. He wooed and won Fannie. John married them, and another illustrious Alaska missionary career was launched.[47]

Brady fortuitously avoided the egregious political blunder made by S. Hall Young, who allied himself with Fannie's uncle, Aaron Lindsley. By underestimating the spreading, churchwide power base that Jackson was building for himself and linking up with the disgruntled Portland pastor, Young probably ruined his chances to win the territorial political eminence he later sought.

By September Brady's relations with Lindsley had deteriorated. More serious, the youthful missionary had begun to grumble about his station's inadequacies to his New York superiors, Presbyterian Home Board secretaries Henry Kendall and Cyrus Dickson. Kendall was esteemed for his patience, but Dickson expected Home Board missionaries to adopt an obedient, if not a mendicant, role.[48] Possibly Brady's irritability was caused by despair with his Sitka Indians. Culture shock sends current both ways, and frequently the more eager the missionary, the greater the odds that he will suffer a malaise when he finally comprehends that the natives with whom he is laboring not only are exotic and bright-eyed, but also can be lazy and cruel to one another, and sincerely prefer living a life that is repugnant to an outsider.

The foregoing was never acknowledged by Brady. Unquestionably Alaska's prospects for Christian labor had aroused his exuberant humanitarianism. How could America's church or lay leaders expect peo-

Photograph of the Reverend John G. Brady, probably taken in 1881 in San Francisco. (Courtesy of Hugh P. Brady.)

ple like himself to "save the heathen" when frontier settlements at Sitka and Wrangell possessed neither pioneers nor rudimentary government? After ten years of waiting, America's homestead laws still did not apply to Alaska. "The manner in which the government has neglected this country, for the past year," he snapped, "is nothing short of criminal neglect." "To leave the people another year without any means of settling difficulties," he warned, "would be extremely culpable."[49] To a degree this was hyperbole. However, the capital's collector and his deputies at Wrangell and Sitka were virtually the district's entire civil government. And these bedeviled public servants could only enforce regulations issued by the far-off Treasury Department. More alarming, distressful instances of red-white friction recurred about Sitka during the late summer and early fall of 1878. "A raid on the town" was imminent, the Indians warned. For Brady, Alaska's administrative deficiencies could no longer be endured; he must personally inform the Home Board as well as officialdom in Washington of Alaska's deplorable conditions.

1. Allan Johnson and Dumas Malone, eds., *Dictionary of American Biography*, 2d ed. rev., 11 vols. (New York, 1957), 9:287; Henry F. May, *Protestant Churches and Industrial America* (New York, 1967), pp. 42, 67 ff.; Sydney E. Ahlstrom, *Theology in America: The Major Protestant Voices from Puritanism to Neo-Orthodoxy* (Indianapolis, 1967), p. 74; G. L. Prentiss, *The Union Theological Seminary in the City of New York: Its Design and Another Decade of Its History . . .* (Asbury Park, N.J., 1899), pp. 414–17.

2. May, *Protestant Churches*, p. 62; JGB, mf. 2, "Zigzags."

3. JGB, mf. 2, "Zigzags"; ibid., mf. 3, Isaac W. Monfort to Brady, 8 January 1876.

4. The standard, if eulogistic, biography of this remarkable man is that penned by his admirer, Robert Laird Stewart, *Sheldon Jackson: Pathfinder and Prospector of the Missionary Vanguard in the Rocky Mountains and Alaska* (New York, 1915). For comparison refer to Colin B. Goodykoontz, *Home Missions on the American Frontier* (Caldwell, Idaho, 1939). Useful for tracing Jackson's pre-Alaska Far West labors are the articles by Alvin K. Bailey entitled "Sheldon Jackson, Planter of Churches," *Journal of the Presbyterian Historical Society* 26 (September and December 1948): 129–48, 193–214; 27 (March 1949): 21–40.

5. JGB, mf. 2, "Zigzags." Henry F. Pringle, *Theodore Roosevelt: A Biography* (New York, 1956), p. 8; JGB, mf. 4, Brady to Jackson, 20 February 1902. This latter document is also found in the Sheldon Jackson Correspondence Collection of twenty-six bound typescript volumes, Presbyterian Historical Society, Philadelphia, Pa. (hereafter cited as JCorr.).

6. JGB, mf. 2, "Zigzags."

7. Yale College, *Biographical Record with Report of the Triennial Meeting of the Class of 1874 in Yale College* (New Haven, 1879), p. 55.

8. JCorr., 7:116, Brady to Jackson, 28 August 1877.

9. Ibid.

10. JGB, mf. 2, "Zigzags."

11. Ted C. Hinckley, "The Alaska Labors of Sheldon Jackson, 1877–1890" (Ph.D. dissertation, Indiana University, 1961), pp. 10–32. "Soldier Brown and Sheldon Jackson," *Alaska Journal* 1 (Autumn 1971): 60–62.

12. Toiva Harjunpa, "The Lutherans in Russian America," *Pacific Historical Review* (May 1968): 123–46.

13. At this time Wrangell was still often called Fort Wrangell. Opinions differ on the condition of the natives as they came under the influence of American institutions. See Hubert Howe Bancroft, *History of Alaska, 1730–1885* (New York, 1960), pp. 607–9; Vincent Colyer, "Report on Indian Tribes and Their Surroundings in Alaska Territory, from Personal Observation and Inspection, 1869," in *Report of the Board of Indian Commissioners* (Washington, D.C., 1870); and the annual reports of the Bureau of Indian Affairs for the seventies and eighties. Helpful for the comparative picture are A. L. Kroeber, "American Culture and the Northwest Coast," *American Anthropologist* 25 (January–March 1923): 1–20, and A. Grenfell Price, *The Western Invasions of the Pacific and Its Continents: A Study of Moving Frontiers and Changing Landscapes* (Oxford, 1963).

14. A reliable introduction to these remarkable people is Philip Drucker, *Indians of the Northwest Coast* (Garden City, N.Y., 1963). Aspects of this social deterioration may be traced in F. W. Howay, "The Introduction of Intoxicating Liquors amongst the Indians of the Northwest Coast," *British Columbia Historical Quarterly* 6 (July 1942): 159–69; Edwin M. Lemert, *Alcohol and the Northwest Coast Indians* (Berkeley, 1954); and Frederica de Laguna, *The Story of a Tlingit Community . . .* (Washington, D.C., 1960).

15. Sheldon Jackson, *Alaska, and Missions on the North Pacific Coast* (New York, 1880), pp. 140–65. *Rocky Mountain Presbyterian*, October 1877.

16. Ted C. Hinckley, "Publicist of the Forgotten Frontier," *Journal of the West* 4 (January 1965): 27–40.

17. Ted C. Hinckley, "Reflections and Refractions: Alaska and Gilded Age America," in *Frontier Alaska: A Study in Historical Interpretation and Opportunity*, ed. Robert A. Frederick (Anchorage, 1968), pp. 91–105; William H. Wilson, "Alaska's Past, Alaska's Future: The Uses of Historical Interpretation," *Alaska Review* 13 (Spring and Summer 1970): 1–3. To appreciate America's domestic implosion, see Edward C. Kirkland, *Industry Comes of Age: Business, Labor, and Public Policy, 1868–1897* (New York, 1962).

18. Ivan Petroff, *Population and Resources of Alaska* (Washington, D.C., 1881), p. 85.

19. Ibid.

20. JGB, mf. 3, "Terms of This Commission."

21. Ibid., "Rules of the Board of Home Missions."

22. S. Lyman Tyler, *A History of Indian Policy* (Washington, D.C., 1973), pp. 45–47. Scholarly accounts of this post–Civil War program may be found in Henry E. Fritz, *The Movement for Indian Assimilation, 1860–1890* (Philadelphia, 1963); Loring Benson Priest, *Uncle Sam's Step-Children: The Reformation of United States Indian Policy, 1865–1887* (New Brunswick, N.J., 1942); and Frances Paul Prucha, *American Indian Policy in Crisis: Christian Reformers and the Indian, 1865–1900* (Norman, Okla., 1976); and for a precise summary, see Robert M. Utley, "The Celebrated Peace Policy of General Grant," *North Dakota History* 20 (July 1953): 121–42.

23. Excellent general introductions to the Indian are William T. Hagan, *American Indians* (Chicago, 1961); Alvin M. Josephy, *The Indian Heritage of America* (New York, 1973); and Wilcomb E. Washburn, *The Indian in America* (New York, 1975). Robert Winston Murdock, *The Reformers and the American Indian* (Columbus, 1971), pp. 163–67.

24. John Eaton, *Report of the Commissioner of Education for the Year 1870 with Accompanying Papers* (Washington, D.C., 1870), p. 24. Private agencies had also long

advocated Indian education in Alaska, and for different reasons. For example, the busi-
ness-oriented *Alaska Herald* (San Francisco) urged it so that commerce would be safe
(15 May 1865). Presbyterian Church, *Minutes of the General Assembly of the Presbyterian Church . . . 1878* (New York, 1878), p. 167.

25. JGB, mf. 4, Brady as sworn to U.S. Commissioner, 26 March 1903; JCorr,
7:287–89, Brady to Aaron Lindsley, 17 March 1878; JGB, unfiled, "Sunday, March 17th,
1878" summary by Brady.

26. John G. Brady, "The Present Status of the Alaskan Natives," *Lake Mohonk Conference, Report of the 29th Annual Meeting, 1911*, p. 78. JCorr, 7:287–89, Brady to
Lindsley, 17 March 1878; Jackson, *Alaska and Missions*, p. 214.

27. Ray Allen Billington, *Westward Expansion: A History of the American Frontier*
(New York, 1960), p. 633.

28. Bobby Dave Lain, "North of Fifty-three: Army, Treasury Department, and Navy
Administration of Alaska, 1867–1884" (Ph.D. dissertation, University of Texas, 1974),
is a worthy and recent contribution to this phase of America's history. R. W. Meade,
"Alaska," *Appleton's Journal* 6 (22 July 1871): 91; *Alaska Herald*, 1 March 1875; *New
York Times*, 13 April 1877.

29. William Gouverneur Morris, *Report upon the Customs District, Public Service,
and Resources of Alaska Territory* (Washington, D.C., 1879), p. 154. Clarence L. Andrews, *Wrangell and the Gold of Cassier* (Seattle, 1937), pp. 36–55.

30. JGB, unfiled, "Tuesday, March 19, 1878" summary by Brady.

31. Charles A. Anderson, ed., "Letters of Amanda R. McFarland, II," *Journal of the
Presbyterian Historical Society* 34 (December 1956): 226–44.

32. Jackson, *Alaska and Missions*, p. 144.

33. Anderson, "Letters of Amanda McFarland, II," pp. 238–39. Jackson, *Alaska and
Missions*, p. 176; JCorr, 8:117, Brady to Jackson, 9 July 1878.

34. Morris, *Report upon the Customs*, pp. 79–81.

35. To trace the confusing territory-wide prohibition, see U.S., Congress, House, *Jurisdiction of the War Department over Alaska*, 44th Cong., 1st sess., Exec. Doc. 135,
26 February 1876; U.S., Congress, Senate, *Report of a Special Agent on the Territory
of Alaska and the Collection of the Customs-revenue Therein*, 44th Cong., 1st sess.,
Exec. Doc. 37, 20 March 1876.

36. Morris, *Report upon the Customs*, p. 80. Hoochinoo ("hooch") was the alcoholic
drink distilled by archipelago natives.

37. John W. Arctander, *The Apostle of Alaska: The Story of William Duncan of
Metlakahtla* (New York, 1909), and Henry S. Wellcome, *The Story of Metlakahtla*
(New York, 1887), give reasonable, if laudatory, summaries of this man's fascinating
saga.

38. Robert F. Berkhofer, Jr., *Salvation and the Indian Response, 1787–1862* (Lex-
ington, Ky., 1965); Arthur H. DeRosier, "Cyrus Kingsbury—Missionary to the Choc-
taws," *Journal of Presbyterian History* 50 (Winter 1972): 267–87; Priest, *Uncle Sam's
Step-Children*; and Fritz, *Indian Assimilation*.

39. John A. Garraty, *The New Commonwealth, 1877–1890* (New York, 1968), p. 18.

40. These Indians were essentially the same group that Brady had spoken with in mid-
March when he first, and momentarily, visited Sitka. Therefore the embryo for what is
today Sheldon Jackson College is sometimes dated from 17 March instead of 17 April
1878. Brady first crossed into Alaskan waters on 13 March 1878 and came ashore at
Wrangell on the fifteenth and at Sitka on the seventeenth (JGB, unfiled, "Sunday, March
17, 1878"). C. L. Andrews Collection, Sheldon Jackson College, Sitka, Alaska, Brady
to Andrews, 9 November 1915 (hereafter cited as CLASJC); Ted C. Hinckley, "Sheldon
Jackson College: Historic Nucleus of the Presbyterian Enterprise in Alaska," *Journal
of Presbyterian History* 49 (Spring 1971): 64; Morris, *Report upon the Customs*, p. 79.

41. JGB, notes by him utilizing workbook written by J. W. Powell, *Introduction to the Study of Indian Languages, with Words, Phrases, and Sentences to be Collected* (Washington, D.C., 1877); Morris, *Report upon the Customs*, p. 79; interview with Hugh Brady, 6 August 1968, Seattle.

42. Jackson, *Alaska and Missions*, pp. 207–8.

43. Ibid., pp. 212–13; *Rocky Mountain Presbyterian*, February 1879.

44. JCorr, 9:6, Brady to Jackson, 11 November 1878.

45. Jackson, *Alaska and Missions*, p. 245.

46. Ted C. and Caryl C. Hinckley, "Ivan Petroff's Journal of a Trip to Alaska in 1878," *Journal of the West* 5 (January 1966), entry for 26 July; JCorr, 9:151, Brady to Jackson, 21 March 1879. S. Hall Young, *Hall Young of Alaska, the Mushing Parson* (New York, 1927). Ted C. Hinckley, "The Early Alaskan Ministry of S. Hall Young, 1878–1888," *Journal of Presbyterian History* 46 (September 1968): 175–96.

47. Sheldon Jackson, *The Presbyterian Church in Alaska: An Official Sketch of Its Rise and Progress, 1877–1884, with the Minutes of the First Meeting of the Presbytery of Alaska* (Washington, D.C., 1886), p. 4; Young, *Hall Young*, pp. 78–79. CLASJC, Brady to Andrews, 9 November 1915.

48. JGB, mf. 3, Brady to Lindsley, 10 September 1878; JCorr, 9:150, Brady to Jackson, 21 March 1879. Thomas Stratton Goslin, "Henry Kendall and the Evangelization of a Continent" (Ph.D. dissertation, University of Pennsylvania, 1948).

49. JCorr, 8:118, Brady to Jackson, 9 July 1878. *Presbyterian Monthly Record*, August 1878, p. 234.

CHAPTER THREE

An Alaska Advocate

Sheldon Jackson must assume some of the responsibility for Brady's abrupt departure from his Sitka field. Jackson was anxious to talk with Brady about Alaska affairs, above all to assure himself of the young minister's loyalty. The District of Alaska fell under the Synod of the Columbia, and although Jackson was not without friends in the Pacific Northwest, he feared that in this particular Presbyterian governing body Lindsley's supporters could probably outvote his interests. It was imperative for Jackson to have a vigorous Alaska ally at any Portland meeting. Just how strenuous a spokesman he had in Brady was soon manifest.[1]

The two men met in Denver. Brady delivered a box full of native artifacts to Jackson—his mentor was similarly captivated by Northwest Coast Indian art—and brought him up to date on the Sitka and Wrangell missions. John proposed nothing less than transplanting his Texas industrial school to Alaska. He had evangelized the red man, sweated like a common laborer, preached to miners and traders, stood up to smuggler and shaman alike, and done his best to teach the rudiments of a "Christian education" to his Tlingit students. Admittedly much had proved futile. A discouraging number of natives continued to be distracted by the vile habits of white and red riffraff.[2] And how could he inculcate habits of "civilized living" when his pupils daily returned to their "demoralizing Indian village"?

Missionary answers to Brady's questions existed across the Mississippi Valley to the Kingdom of Hawaii to distant China: establish a boarding school that would isolate the native youth from the "barbarism of their parents' world" and transform them into progressive models of nineteenth-century Caucasian society. Amanda McFarland was already initiating a home for girls at Wrangell. Brady envisioned a much larger, more diversified Sitka school. He may well have read of the educational breakthroughs performed for nonwhites by General Samuel Chapman Armstrong at Hampton Institute, Virginia. Surely Brady must have had some knowledge of the trade schools (or manual arts or industrial schools—the terms often described similar endeavors) spawned during Reconstruction to educate the freed slaves and of the concomitant and expanding institutions for American Indians.[3]

Brady correctly guessed that the district's economic growth was about to improve; ahead lay fresh opportunities for skilled labor. He admired the manual dexterity of his Tlingit students, and he knew how prosperous and law-abiding Father Duncan's Tsimshians had become at Metlakatla. A well-equipped Sitka industrial school would be a crucible for testing the worth of America's institutions. Surely the Home Board secretaries in New York would grasp the merit of this vital experiment.

Brady knew all about the challenge of big city juvenile vagrants, but New York maintained schools and private agencies to succor disadvantaged youth. Too many Sitka youngsters had little or nothing. Brady's idealism collided with the gloomy financial realities bedeviling his Home Board employers. The New York churchmen doubtless reminded him that Sitka was merely one of dozens of Presbyterian mission stations that cried for increased aid. Like that of others before and since, Brady's isolation and preoccupation with his special mission led him to overstate Sitka's very real needs. Vexed by the more detached perspective of his superiors, he determined to secure funds for his industrial school elsewhere. His seminary patron William Dodge appears to have offered some tentative backing, and possibly it was his son Arthur who suggested that Brady journey to Yale to see if contacts there might lead to a major bequest.[4]

Before he left for New Haven, a reporter from the *New York Herald* interviewed him concerning a reported increase in red-white tension at Sitka. A settler had recently been murdered by some Indians. Judging by what appeared in print, Brady was already parroting Jackson. He mingled praise of Alaska's resources with condemnation of his government's apathy. Ivan Petroff, one of the few Americans personally familiar with the Great Land, reprinted and edited Brady's New York City interview in his San Francisco–published newspaper, the *Alaska Appeal*:

"In the western part of Alaska," Mr. Brady says, "the natives are held like slaves by a monopoly"; But Mr. B. has never been to the west and speaks from hearsay. . . . The missionary claims that the natives of Eastern Alaska are a much better people than is generally supposed.

45

. . . He stated that Alaska was emphatically "a poor man's county," forgetting that a poor man would find it rather difficult to get there. He expressed the opinion that the Territory should have at once a civil government of its own, having evidently no conception of its vast dimensions, appalling distances and thinly scattered native populations of the north and west of Alaska.[5]

Petroff was right. The Alaska Commercial Company held no Aleuts as slaves, and boomer myopia had infected Brady. Although Brady was guilty of misinformation, "If we had many such warm advocates of the neglected Territory," Petroff concluded, "there would be some hope of having its wants attended to at last."

At Yale both students and professors were impressed with Brady's Frank Merriwell spirit. After the newspapers reported an Indian uprising that placed Sitka in grave and imminent peril, John's Yale associates urged him to take the train to Washington and apprise the solons as to what must be done. "You go down to Washington," Professor Benjamin Silliman told him, "and tell what you know. I'll give you a letter to Secretary Evarts who is a classmate of mine." Flattery was backed by action. Other Yale men came forward with letters of introduction to Washington politicians. "Rutherford Hayes Platt, the President's nephew, was then a student in Columbia Law School," Brady later wrote. "I explained matters somewhat in detail to Platt who listened with great interest. . . . He accordingly gave me a straight forward letter to his Uncle."[6]

Just how serious was the 1879 Indian threat to Sitka? Certainly there was much native bombast, and the timorous response of certain Sitka whites abetted Indian demagoguery. Part of the problem was a status conflict among Sitka's aboriginal leadership as to who could protest the loudest. But the grandiloquent chiefs did not precipitate a conflict. Shipboard Gatling guns and howitzers had effectively demonstrated what havoc they could wreak upon native seaside villages. To the frightened whites it seemed an eternity before a war vessel finally arrived. Doubly humiliating, it was the H.M.S. *Osprey* that "saved Sitka from massacre." The situation was not clarified when the captain of the American naval vessel that relieved the *Osprey* implied that the whole business was a hoax and ridiculed the Indians' warlike gestures.[7]

Certainly the rather sensational columns about America's forgotten frontier facilitated Brady's mission to Washington. "I determined to call upon the President first," he recalled later, "and work down the line." Armed with "my letter from R. H. Platt," Brady went directly to the White House. Moments after the clerk took the introductory letter from him, he was ushered into the president's office. "I want to have a talk with you," President Hayes said, "But I am busy right now and this evening I must attend a reception. . . . You come here at 10 o'clock [P.M.] for I expect to return at that hour and if I do not, wait for me. I shall instruct the doorkeeper." "It was 11 o'clock before the President returned and we went to his office room where there was a cheery fire in the grate. After seating me in a large comfortable chair he excused himself for a few minutes. When he returned he seated himself near his desk and I then began to tell my story of Alaska. . . . This interview lasted until after 1 o'clock. When near the close he said: ' . . . I was in favor of that purchase (and with a gesture of his arm) it is like a huge sickle gathering in the whole North Pacific Ocean.'" Brady returned to his hotel room confident, he wrote, "that I had done poor Alaska a service at the right moment."[8]

The next day, as requested by President Hayes, Brady spoke with Secretary of the Interior Carl Schurz. "He received me kindly enough and listened while I briefly ran over the matters which I thought he should know." Brady stressed the uniqueness of the Northwest Coast Indians. "Many sensible miners with whom I have conversed, and who have had great experience with the Indians of the plains, have no hesitancy in pronouncing the Alaska Indians much superior. . . . They are self-supporting, and are always ready to do the hardest kind of labor." Furthermore, he emphasized, "There is no need for soldiers to keep the natives subdued" and "no reason why these natives should not be made citizens of the United States, when they become as enlightened as they are at Tongas, Wrangel, and Sitka."[9]

Brady went next to the State Department. Professor Silliman's letter opened the door and "I was conducted right to Mr. [W. M.] Evarts in his office." When he had finished, the secretary "shook my hand cordially and remarked—'We had better make you Governor of Alaska.' I answered by saying there was no law for that . . . " Not wasting a moment, Brady went at once to the Navy Department, "where I met Secretary [R. W.] Thompson." He promised that Sitka would henceforth have better naval protection. The cabinet member actually charged with Alaskan administrative duties was Secretary of the Treasury John Sherman. Brady refused to call on him. "I was prejudiced against him," he afterward recalled. Sherman had urged the withdrawal of troops in 1877, and Brady was probably correct when he averred, "Mr. Sherman often wished that he had never heard of Alaska."[10]

Brady returned to Sitka in May 1879 without church support for either his long-cherished dream of an industrial school or himself. At least the blessings of Home Board secretary Kendall went with him. Thankfully the end of his Presbyterian employment left little rancor.[11]

Brady could still play a vital role in the creation of the new Presbytery of Alaska. Furthermore, his recent idea of going into business at Sitka and training Indian boys in his Sitka firm might well be, as Brady thought, "God directing him."

Other forces abetted Brady's shift from a pastoral ministry to one of commerce and, ultimately, politics. Brady, like Jackson, was too much the man of action to find professional contentment as a humble Christian apostle. His temperament rejected a self-effacing Franciscan role. Imprisonment in a traditional classroom with restless natives no longer appealed to him. Brady's church could have offered him other positions, less confining tasks more suited to his personality. Why, therefore, especially after three years at seminary, numerous avowals of Christian commitment, and untold hours of prayer, was John's separation from a ministerial career so final?

There was no question about his commitment to Christ, but, as he growled in one letter, he could not accept Lindsley as a Presbyterian pope, nor did he believe any human institution provided the final repository of worldly or religious wisdom.[12] John Brady's character had been forged by a far more syncretic value system than that which had shaped the character of most of his eastern peers. The Ten Commandments, the sanctity of the home, and a robust Fourth of July—on matters like these he was typically conservative. Yet, because of his varied experiences, not the least of which were his years at Union midst the depression of the seventies, he was distinctly not an orthodox Presbyterian.

Consciously or subconsciously, he sought philosophical rationalization to justify his vocational apostasy. Social historians now point to the late nineteenth century as one of conflicting moribundity and rebirth among churchmen. The new theology that was vitiating the critical redemptive role of Christ was in considerable measure a product of not merely America's material wealth but also the growing worship of science and the concomitant belief in the perfectability of man. For all its naivete, this view did not mean that Christians could relax. The coming of the 1880s "marked an era in the development of social Christianity."[13] Over the next few decades the social gospel would be defined by religious leaders such as Washington Gladden and Walter Rauschenbusch. Brady's Sitka mission was his recognition of a living gospel.

John's random visits to Tipton immersed him in an old-time religion whose emotional fervor hardly squared with the questions considered at Union. In truth, the doctrinal rungs on his earlier religious ladder had been weakened, if not cracked, by the higher criticism, Darwinism, and the wonder-working accomplishments of modern technology. And

Brady was not alone in eschewing the verities of yesterday because of an enlarged philosophical outlook. Among others of his classmates at New Haven and seminary, he was a modernist long before the conflicting terms *modernist* and *fundamentalist* were coined. In later years Brady may have envied the comforting theological absolutes of his Hoosier boyhood; by 1879, however, age, education, and a world in flux denied him this intellectual pillow.

On 29 May John Brady celebrated his thirty-first birthday. Quite possibly the clergyman, who soon was to become a businessman, had suffered through what psychologist Erik H. Erikson so well described in *Young Man Luther*. Young man Brady had urgently searched for a "combination of freedom and discipline, of adventure and tradition." He had subjected himself to "hardship and discipline," sought "sanctioned opportunities for spatial dispersion," followed "wandering apprenticeships," heeded the "call of frontiers," and manned the outposts of a new nation. "The crisis in such a young man's life," Erikson hypothesized, "may be reached exactly when he half-realizes that he is fatally overcommitted to what he is not."[14]

The attention paid Brady at New Haven and in the capital had removed the sting from Secretary Dickson's censure at the Board of Home Missions. Likewise, John's vanity was flattered when his opinions on Alaska were solicited by William Gouverneur Morris, special Alaska agent of the Treasury Department. Certainly Brady returned to the north country better informed on how the United States administered her boreal territory. "The whole machinery at Washington impressed me as fearfully cumbersome."[15] Tangible evidence that he was eager to speed up that machinery was a press that he shipped north. Brady intended to issue "a monthly publication in the interest of Alaska."

Accompanying Brady to Sitka was an old New York City friend and fellow welfare worker, Alonzo E. Austin. Austin had operated a Manhattan produce business until the depression of the 1870s. He and his family then became street missionaries to New York's impoverished children. As a volunteer tutor, John had assisted him while at seminary. Intrigued by Brady's enthusiasm, Austin headed north and Alaska acquired another pioneer.[16]

The previous year, when Brady had initiated a native mission day school at Sitka, Pauline Cohen, daughter of Sitka's brewer, also commenced a day school for the white (Yankee as well as Creole) youngsters. After Brady and Fannie Kellogg departed, both schools closed. It was this dual program that Austin revitalized. Like Brady, Austin quickly saw that Alaska's youth would benefit from skilled manual arts teachers. He soon returned to New York City for his wife and daughters. The oldest daughter, Olinda ("Linnie"), was commissioned by the Board of Home Missions to instruct native girls in sewing. His youngest, Ettie, replaced her father as teacher for the white children.[17] For the moment Austin devoted his energies to working with the native boys.

Although 1879 is memorable in Sitka's history for the "dire Indian threat" during January and February, it is equally noteworthy for the midyear arrival of the U.S.S. *Jamestown* and its outspoken commander, Lester A. Beardslee, who found himself virtual governor of Alaska, or at least of its Panhandle. The navy "ruled Alaska" until relieved by civilian administrators in 1884. Beardslee described Sitka, as composed of "Indians, creoles, and white men of various nationalities, including English, Irish, German, Austrian, Italian, Turks, and Jews, among whom were numbers of idle, dissolute characters, and a sprinkling of men, who though experienced with law, had learned to have no good opinion of it, and had sought Sitka as a home because there the law could not reach them." Drunken debauchery emanating from the nearby Ranche likewise offended Beardslee. "The first and only step by which Alaska can ever be saved or developed," emphasized the *Jamestown*'s commander, "will be the enactment by Congress of a law which shall place the importation of molasses and coarse sugar under such restrictions that the manufacture of 'hootchenoo' can be stopped." Wasting little time, Beardslee organized a raid upon the illicit distilleries. "I had but awaited sufficient provocation. A murder in the white settlement and a continued drunken row, ending in a big fight, which I had to send an armed party to suppress, in the Indian village, furnished me with a cause." Thirty-eight stills and "150 gallons of liquor, and as much mash" were destroyed.[19]

On 9 July, "ably assisted" by John Brady and the assistant collector, Beardslee initiated action to provide Sitka with a local civil government. This was the second such undertaking. Shortly after Alaska's purchase Sitkans had pieced together a civil administration, but by 1873, as the *Alaska Herald* then satirized, "Sitka no longer maintains a city government. The people have become so virtuous that it is unnecessary."[20] It was just as unnecessary at the end of the decade, for the people were hardly less virtuous then. The district collector, Mottrom D. Ball, was chosen as "Chief Magistrate," and Sitka's new "selectmen" represented merchant, mining, cannery, and Russian constituencies.[21] It would be the last time in the politics of pioneer Alaska that the Presbyterian missionary element was totally unrepresented.

With Sitka's white population fluctuating around four hundred (many were miner transients), Beardslee came to admit that the capital did not then possess a sufficient number of responsible citizens to support a local government. Or, to put it another way, Sitka was as yet too heterogeneous (many of the Creoles were not enumerated) to fit itself together. "The problem presented me," Beardslee reported, "was how to govern a mixed community of whites and Indians with no code of laws but the Revised Statutes of the United States, the United States Naval Regulations, and the treaty with Russia."[22] Sitkans "manifested a disposition to rely upon the government forces for everything," Beardslee groused, "and to look upon me, the commanding officer, . . . to supply all of the deficiencies incident to the entire absence of any other governing power or code of laws." The officer's town council soon folded. He then asked Brady, George Pilz, an educated miner, and M. P. Berry, one-time Sitka customs collector, to join three of his officers in a "mixed commission" to inquire into some of Sitka's shooting affrays. Its ad hoc nature made the mixed commission slightly more productive than Beardslee's ephemeral council.[23]

Certainly Sitka merchants and San Francisco investors insisted upon a modicum of law and order in the capital. Without it their respective interests could not be advanced, be they social or economic, or, as in Brady's case, both. Along with a growing number of Pacific Coast businessmen, John watched the rising volume of Alaska salmon being shipped south to San Francisco markets. Indeed, Brady's arrival in 1878 had coincided with the conception of this salmon-canning industry; before long these fish became her most valued replenishable resource. The following year Cutting and Company of San Francisco shipped out some five thousand cases of salmon on the *California*. "The Western Fur and Trading Company, the Alaska Commercial and American Russian Companies," Petroff's *Alaska Appeal* exclaimed, "have also put up large quantities of salmon on Kodiak Island and at Cook's Inlet."[24] Most of this was in barrels and thus destined for a more restricted market. But those who cared to inform themselves appreciated that, just as the salmon industry had ballooned earlier in the Pacific Northwest, it must soon prosper in Alaska.

Brady also had faith in the Great Land's mineral wealth. Given Alaska's immense size and the current mining booms all over America's Far West, it appeared but a matter of time before the Far North's riches were likewise exposed. Brady was equally sanguine about the Great Land's agricultural potential. In December of 1879, when he accompanied Austin on his trip east to bring his ladies to Alaska, John carried samples of the vegetables he had recently raised at Sitka.[25] By this time he no longer saw himself as merely a struggling missionary but also as a builder determined to attract settlers and investment to Alaska. But John remained as eager as ever to create an industrial school for natives; he was pleased to be listed as an "independent missionary without charge" by the board.[26]

Brief visits with eastern friends further stimulated John's predilection to become an outspoken Alaska advocate. They were so ignorant of his Great Land! In January he delivered a series of Alaska lectures in various Washington, D.C., churches.[27] Once again he strongly urged a civil government for the Far North territory. Responding to eastern investors who voiced anxiety about Alaska's Indian threat, Brady cited the accomplishments of the officers and men of the U.S.S. *Jamestown*. Beardslee confirmed the wholesome changes:

> During the autumn and winter of 1879 the white population of Sitka was greatly increased, and, as many of the new arrivals were of a far higher class than the average of the residents at the date of our arrival, the tone of the community was greatly improved. Missionaries had been sent by the Presbyterian Board of Home Missions, and their work soon began to be apparent upon the Indians. Businessmen, and miners who had been deterred from bringing their families to Sitka on account of the absence of law, became satisfied that it was safe to send for them, and a church for whites, another for Indians, and Sunday schools sprang into existence.[28]

Alaska's capital had definitely turned a corner. Among a small handful of bona fide resident Alaskans who stood to benefit from the district's steadily growing commercial and extractive activities would be the archipelago trader and Sitka merchant John G. Brady.

1. JCorr, 9:6, Brady to Jackson, 11 November 1878. JGB, mf. 3, Brady to Lindsley, 10 September 1878. Clifford M. Drury, "Beginnings of the Synod of Oregon," *Journal of the Presbyterian Historical Society* 37 (December 1959): 255.

2. Interview with Hugh Brady, 23 June 1962, Seattle.

3. Harold Winfield Kent, *Charles Reed Bishop: Man of Hawaii* (Palo Alto, 1965), p. 146. Jackson, *Alaska and Missions*, pp. 166 ff. John Hope Franklin, *Reconstruction after the Civil War* (Chicago, 1961), p. 38.

4. Presbyterian Church, *Annual Report, Board of Home Missions, 1879* (New York, 1879), p. 103. Morris, *Report upon the Customs*, p. 75.

5. *Alaska Appeal*, 6 March 1879.

6. JGB, mf. 2, "My Visit to Washington in the Spring of 1879."

7. *Alaska Appeal*, 22 March 1879; *Daily Evening Bulletin* (San Francisco), 18 March 1879; *Portland Oregonian*, 19 March 1879; *New York Times*, 10 April 1879. JGB, mf. 2, "Katleean's Attempt on Sitka in 1879." *San Francisco Call*, 26 June 1879; U.S., Congress, Senate, *Reports of Commander L. A. Beardslee, Commanding U.S.S. Jamestown, from June 15, 1879 to January 22, 1880*. 46th Cong., 2d sess., Exec. Doc. 105, 5 March 1880, pp. 4–6.

8. JGB, mf. 2, "My Visit to Washington."

9. Morris, *Report upon the Customs*, p. 83.

52

10. JGB, mf. 2, "My Visit to Washington."

11. Presbyterian Church, *Minutes of the General Assembly, 1881* (New York, 1881), p. 761; JCorr, 9:150–52, Brady to Jackson, 25 March 1879.

12. JCorr, 9:150–52, Brady to Jackson, 25 March 1879.

13. Dillenberger and Welch, *Protestant Christianity*, pp. 213–24. Smith, *Presbyterian Ministry*, pp. 229–30, 237–48. Hopkins, *Rise of the Social Gospel*, p. 67.

14. Erik H. Erikson, *Young Man Luther: A Study in Psycho-analysis and History* (New York, 1962), pp. 42–43.

15. *Presbyterian Monthly Record*, August 1878, p. 234. Morris, *Report upon the Customs*, pp. 78–83. JGB, mf. 3, 7 March 1879. JCorr, 9:152–53, Brady to Jackson, 21 March 1879. Ibid., pp. 170–71, 31 March 1879.

16. JCorr, 9:153, Brady to Jackson, 21 March 1879. Ibid., p. 219, 9 March 1879. JGB, mf. 2, "Zigzags."

17. John G. Brady, *Annual Report of the Governor of Alaska, 1899* (Washington, D.C., 1899), pp. 35–36. Jackson, *Presbyterian Church in Alaska*, p. 5. On 15 August 1881 Ettie married another Presbyterian missionary, Walter B. Styles, and moved to Cross Sound among the Hoonah Tlingits (Mrs. Eugene S. Willard, *Life in Alaska*, ed. Mrs. Eva McClintock [Philadelphia, 1884], pp. 28 ff.).

18. U.S., Congress, Senate, *Report of Captain L. A. Beardslee, U.S. Navy, Relative to Affairs in Alaska, and the Operations of the U.S.S. Jamestown, under His Command, while in the Waters of the Territory, 1882*, 47th Cong., 1st sess., Exec. Doc. 71, 24 January 1882. Helpful for grasping the larger picture are Mel Crain, "When the Navy Ruled Alaska," *United States Naval Institute Proceedings* 81 (February 1955): 198–203; and Robert Erwin Johnson, *Thence Round Cape Horn: The Story of United States Naval Forces on Pacific Station, 1818–1923* (Annapolis, 1963), chap. 9.

19. *New York Times*, 7 August 1879.

20. Beardslee, *Affairs in Alaska*, p. 22; *Alaska Herald*, 24 June 1873.

21. *New York Times*, 18 August 1879. Beardslee, *Affairs in Alaska*, p. 22.

22. Beardslee, *Affairs in Alaska*, pp. 13, 34–37, 17. Population reports for Alaska varied. See George W. Bailey, *Report upon Alaska and Its People 1879* (Washington, D.C., 1880), p. 5; and Ivan Petroff, *Population, Industries, and Resources of Alaska* (Washington, D.C., 1884).

23. Beardslee, *Affairs in Alaska*, pp. 17–25.

24. *Alaska Appeal*, 30 September 1879.

25. Ibid., 1 December 1879.

26. *Minutes of the General Assembly, Presbyterian Church, U.S.A.* (New York, 1886), p. 285; Albert N. Marqus, ed., *Who's Who in America, 1910–1911* (Chicago, 1910), p. 211. JCorr, 10:4, Brady to Jackson, 2 January 1880; ibid., p. 315, 11 October 1880. Secretary Henry Kendall continued to hope that Brady would assume another Home Board assignment (JGB, unfiled, Kendall to Brady, 6 April 1881).

27. *National Republican*, 27 January 1880.

28. Beardslee, *Affairs in Alaska*, p. 34.

CHAPTER FOUR

A Mercantile Ministry

One can only surmise why the frontier-hardened Amos T. Whitford consented to a commercial union with the more cultivated Brady. The salty, Brooklyn-born trader had attended John's sermons, facilitated his acquisition of native artifacts, and helped furnish the mission school. After Alaska's annexation Whitford had oscillated between Sitka junk dealer and archipelago gold seeker. His steam launch *Rose* became notorious for its cargoes of smuggled liquor; no less a trade facilitator was the frontiersman's "droll way" and easy familiarity with both white men and natives. By 1879, probably sensing a shift in Sitka's tide, Whitford cooperated with Beardslee and those seeking socioeconomic stability. In fact, Brady's interisland evangelizing had been assisted by the *Rose*.[1]

Brady insisted on three things before binding himself in 1880 to their oral partnership: the seaborn salesman must marry the mother of his current brood, never open their store on Lord's Day, and utterly divest himself of any connection with the liquor traffic.[2] Another trader, John Picken, was brought in as a minor stockholder, and although he afterward removed himself, Picken continued to remain John's friend and business ally on Puget Sound.

They named their new firm the Sitka Trading Company.[3] Their business occupied a rectangular, log-framed building originally constructed by the Russian-American Company. Over one hundred twenty feet long, the structure faced the town's parade ground. This Lincoln Street site could not have been more central to the community's life—the Brady-Whitford store lay approximately halfway between Saint Michael's Cathedral and Sitka's primary wharf. Just below the rear wall of their establishment the bay slapped against sand and rocks. Next door was

Amos T. Whitford, veteran archipelago trader and partner with Brady in the Sitka Trading Company. Photograph probably taken aboard their schooner, the *Leo*, in the mid-80s. (Reproduced by permission of the Sitka Historical Society.)

the capital's tiny post office, and at an angle behind it rose the height capped by "Baranov's Castle." By 1880 these half-century-old structures smelled of decaying wood and presented a dilapidated appearance.[4] Yet for all of the Sitka Trading Company's sagging roofline, none could mistake the vivacity of its new occupants. As John had once sublimated his humanitarian and religious fervor by zealously adopting the cause of neglected Alaska, he now switched his Protestant work ethic from building a Presbyterian outpost to erecting a profitable business.

The subtle connection between countinghouse and God's house in American sociointellectual history is common knowledge. Henceforth Brady would be coupled with Alaska's commercial and civic affairs. He remained, however, a vigorous Presbyterian. This side of his career was in large part sustained and channeled by his alliance with Sheldon Jackson. In time their relationship would border on that of son to father. Dr. Jackson had early sensed the futility of keeping John behind the pulpit; indeed, by 1883 Jackson moved his own residence to Washington, D.C. Here he could apply pressure on those legislators who did not wish to be reminded of America's northland problems. Concurrently, Brady's skills as a carpenter and archipelago trader would advance the Home Board lobbyist's plans for Indian education in Alaska.

Critics later asserted that the Christian workers wanted to exploit the natives, to brainwash them and eradicate their culture. The charge contains a measure of truth. If "exploit" meant to inveigle aboriginal youths, both male and female, into manual arts classes at a mission school, frequently working as actual laborers, learning skills of value to an American commercial community, they were guilty as charged. Likewise, the missionary preferred that adult natives attracted to white settlements be employed in a mill or a cannery. Neither Wrangell nor Sitka offered a social matrix that could adequately supplant the Tlingits' seasonal fishing-trading domestic cycle. Given their tragic susceptibility to the white man's diseases and his liquor, idle town life courted disaster. To prevent this, as the missionaries saw it, required keeping the Indian constructively employed and making him a homeowner—in short, a socially functional, Victorian-age Christian.

Certainly these humanitarians stand indicted for indoctrinating the natives in the four Rs (reading, 'riting, 'rithmetic, and religion) and encouraging them to abandon their inherited habits. However, well before the arrival of Jackson and Brady, the confines of Sitka's Ranche had provided only diminishing evidence of the aboriginals' once vigorously creative culture. Regrettably, squalor, drunken violence, and native social disorganization also occurred at other commercial communities after 1880.[5]

Proof that Brady and Jackson genuinely appreciated the sophisticated native art and crafts was evident by the way they squirreled away the finest examples of these fast-disappearing artifacts. With his own limited resources, Jackson erected first a temporary wooden unit and then the district's first concrete building to protect these remarkable expressions of Northwest Coast culture. And both museums were constructed *in* Alaska so that the indigenes as well as visitors could honor this heritage.[6]

At the beginning of the 1880s, natives found employment as mine and cannery laborers as well as merchant seamen. The Great Land boasted its first sustained boom town when a gold discovery gave birth to Juneau; soon, across Gastineau Channel on Douglas Island, the Treadwell works began to take shape. Time would confirm that forest- and shore-loving Indians could not readily adjust to the regimented confines of either mining mill or fish cannery. However, in the early eighties Sitka Indians insisted that this means of earning money be theirs, and the missionaries were gratified.[7] Brady conjectured that the nearby Ranche might be transformed into a commercial colony like Metlakatla and wrote Jackson about a possible native-operated cannery: "The natives can be taken in hand and brought under strict control. Sitka is doubtless the best place as the fish can be had here as abundantly as anywhere else; it can be reached by sail easily from San Francisco. . . . for such an enterprise they have decided good qualities. I have held out and prayed for such a work to be given to these people and may God grant that they have it by another season."[8]

The Presbyterians never had even a remote chance of reshaping the capital's Ranche into a regimented village like Duncan's Metlakatla. Nevertheless, reinforced first by Commander Beardslee and then by his successor, Captain Henry Glass, Sitka's missionaries accomplished much. First, naval personnel attacked the Indian Ranche's mucky streets with shovels and left them properly drained. Then, after whitewashing some natives' houses, navy men assisted in the organization of Sitka's Indian boarding school.[9]

In the spring of 1881 Jackson and Henry Kendall had shepherded a plan for a boys' boarding school through the church's Board of Home Missions. Shortly afterward Jackson received a letter from Brady that must have delighted him: "Capt. Glass and his wife and Lt. Symonds, Mr. Austin and myself had a talk about organizing a Boys Home. The Capt. said that he had only a few months to be here and wanted to begin work at once. He would furnish carpenters and men from the ship to refit, repair and clean up. The Collector gave his full consent that the building [an abandoned hospital] should be devoted to such a purpose as he had authority from Washington allowing it. I agreed to furnish material from the store and wait for the pay till the Board could act."[10] Now, as he had done three years earlier, Jackson energetically broadcast his fund-raising formula: sacrificial Christian field workers have enabled citizens of America to save the bodies, minds, and souls of Alaskan children—we cannot let them down. Fate smiled when a half-dozen Ranche lads impetuously approached Brady and Austin and begged to live at Sitka's Presbyterian school. Often thereafter Jackson recounted the plight of these boys before East Coast audiences. "At home there was so much drinking, talking, and carousing that they could not study. . . . They were so much in earnest that they said they would provide for themselves. Upon receiving permission, 7 Indian boys, 13 and 14 years of age, bringing a blanket each, left their homes. . . . Thus commenced the boarding department of the Sitka school." And thus did John Brady at last have his boys' school.[11]

Henceforth he gave unstintingly of his own time, treasure, and talent. His vital contributions ranged from trustee-patron to business manager, pastor, woodshop teacher, plumber, and, finally, employer of its graduates. In 1881 the school was casually labeled the "Boys Boarding School," and in a few years it resembled a properly equipped manual arts school. Dr. Jackson's strenuous lobbying and private fund raising caused Austin to call the burgeoning institution the "Sheldon Jackson Institute"; others labeled it the "Sitka Training School" or merely the "Industrial School."[12]

Protecting the native Alaskans, in the opinion of white humanitarians, required a number of actions, but few had greater priority among Presbyterians than guarding female dignity and instilling a Protestant work ethic among the boys. One way to accomplish these ends was to remove the aboriginal youth from his crowded, multifamily dwelling and convince him of the superiority of a one-house, one-family home. Brady reported to Jackson on what was needed: "While both the church and the state hold to individual rights and responsibilities yet the family is regarded as the unit in each community. . . . Now they live in large houses and have but one fire. . . . a chief told them it was not possible to keep their girls pure on account of being overcrowded. If they are to be separated into families of one man and wife and children they must be assisted by the missionary society."[13] To recast youthful indigenes in such a radically different social mold while permitting them to return to the Ranche each evening appeared self-defeating.

58

Skeptics who questioned Jackson about the wisdom of separating parents from their children were reminded of the boarding schools operated by army captain Richard Pratt at Carlisle, Pennsylvania, and Booker T. Washington at Tuskegee, Alabama. Jackson was familiar with these innovations and was gratified that some Alaskan youth were already enrolled in Lt. M. C. Wilkinson's newly instituted government boarding school at Forest Grove, Oregon. However, Jackson thought Forest Grove's location, like Pratt's Carlisle, less attractive for native Alaskans than Sitka. Commander Glass agreed. "Here in Sitka the improvement of the boys from day to day will be seen and appreciated by those older than themselves, and will more immediately affect the habits and customs of the Indians." Brady concurred; "I do not think it would be wise to send boys and girls away from here."[14]

In 1881 Sitka's training school possessed a large beachfront campus—the handsome site occupied today by its academic heir, Sheldon Jackson College. Assisted by Lt. F. M. Symonds, Brady first surveyed the one-hundred-sixty-acre property. John seems to have acquired the site by using Civil War veterans' land script that he had carefully accumulated during the previous few years. He then transferred his title to the Board of Home Missions. Although Brady's patent was hardly official, it later enabled his church to claim the site legally. Jackson promptly found donors to erect a one-hundred-by-fifty-foot, two-story building, the nucleus for the boarding-training school. Brady took care of book and equipment needs. After he outfitted the entire student body in overalls, navy men saw that each pupil was uniformed with a sailor's cap.[15]

In 1884 the Wrangell Girls' School burned to the ground and Mrs. McFarland's boarders were transferred to Sitka. Within but a few years Sitka's training school boasted an impressive program, one that the growing number of tourists were invited to inspect. The ecstatic praise of one prominent eastern lady was exaggerated but not atypical: "I am not a Christian woman; my faith is that of the chosen people who were led out of Egyptian tyranny . . . but my whole nature is in accord with these Christian men and women. . . . I and those ladies and gentlemen who accompanied me through the rancherie and schools at Sitka can vouch for the fact that it is only a half mile from savage, uncivilized ignorance . . . to education, deportment, thrift . . . "[16]

By the mid-eighties links in the Presbyterian mission chain stretched beyond Wrangell and Sitka to include stations at Hoonah, Chilkat, Juneau, and Howkan. But competent manual arts instruction at these localities, and at the other missions that would follow, could not be afforded. The church was taxed enough merely sustaining a missionary

couple in each of these remote points. Sitka's boarding school necessarily became the educational center to which the most promising of
the Northwest Coast mission children would be sent.

During the spring of 1884, after persistently pressuring his fellow
Presbyterian, Senator Benjamin Harrison of Indiana, Jackson lobbied
Alaska's Organic Act through the United States Congress. Thereafter,
the Far North region had a governor, judge, district attorney, and skel-
eton civil administration. Within less than a year the territory would
also have a General Agent for Education in Alaska with an office in
Washington, D.C. To no one's surprise the position went to Dr. Jackson.[17]

Eighteen eighty-four marked a milestone to Jackson and Brady for
other reasons. Fifteen thousand dollars were pried loose from Congress
for their training school. Of notable symbolic import was the formation
of the First Presbyterian Church of Sitka and the initial meeting of the
Presbytery of Alaska. Since the Lindsley-Jackson feud had first begun
to simmer, Brady had done his best to block any possible ecclesiastical
control of Alaska by the Portland minister. In November 1883, while
en route back to Sitka from a marketing venture in San Francisco, John
attended the annual meeting of the Oregon presbytery. "I was ready,"
he wrote Jackson, "for a square fight if Dr. L. . . . would enter the
first round." Brady was "treated very kindly by many of the members."
However, "Dr. Lindsley did not offer to speak to me but brushed by
me as if I were not there." To Brady's disappointment, at the conclusion
of the Portland gathering Alaska remained "under the care of Oregon
Presbytery. This I am afraid will checkmate your plans, but as you are
rich in resources you will doubtless work out of it."[18]

Jackson was indeed "rich in resources," for already he had maneuvered the Presbyterian general assembly, convening at Saratoga
Springs, New York, "to perfect the organization" of the Presbytery of
Alaska the following September. Accordingly, on 14 September 1884
the newly constituted body held its inaugural meeting at Sitka. Jackson
had arranged to have John serve as the convener and preach the "opening sermon of Presbytery," but coastal winds determined otherwise and
trader Brady missed the meeting. S. Hall Young was thus "elected
Moderator and constituted Presbytery with a prayer." Sheldon Jackson
was elected temporary clerk, and "after recess Presbytery met in the
school room of the Mission, and listened to a popular sermon by Mr.
Alonzo E. Austin."[19] Brady no doubt would have appreciated the historical honor his mentor had sought to extend him.

In 1881 Brady reported to Jackson that "the service on Sabbath is
of course optional [but] nearly the whole ranch attends and they have
to be stowed away like sardines in a box. For the past three Sabbaths

the number has amounted to at least 300." When Sitka's Presbyterian church was organized three years later, those qualified for membership included forty-four natives and five white communicants.[20] Throughout the 1880s Brady frequently occupied the pulpit and delivered an evangelical message.[21]

In his sermons Brady often alluded to the progress of the archipelago's native population. This recital of aboriginal achievements annoyed some of his white audience, just as it pleased the local Indians and gratified the Board of Home Missions.[22] In 1889 Secretary William Irvin praised John for the vital part he was playing among the Northwest Coast peoples. "It is a real refreshment and encouragement to know that the heart of men like you is so entirely with us." Increasingly optimistic about the church's Far North enterprise, Dr. Irvin cheerily reminded Brady that the nation now had a Presbyterian president. "Under President Harrison and other friends in the new administration we are sure of considerate treatment and all the help we deserve."[23]

For the owners of the Sitka Trading Company, commercial success must have seemed a long way off in 1880. But what they lacked in capital they made up for in experience. Amos T. Whitford was as familiar with Alaska's southeastern littoral as were his Tlingit customers with their innumerable fishing sites. Years before, the veteran trader had learned how to remain solvent by what the *Alaska Herald* described as "strategy." His "Grand Emporium," as he had advertised his Sitka store in 1877, sold "Clothing, Dry goods, Notions, Boots, Shoes, Tobacco, Segars, Rifles, Ammunition, etc." to natives and whites alike. Whitford listed himself as "General Dealer in Dry Goods, Groceries and Hardware"—he and John were prepared to sell just about anything they could stow aboard their steam launch *Rose*.[24]

At sea as well as ashore the partners met with energetic competition, particularly from J. M. Vanderbilt, who had succeeded the notorious W. K. "King" Lear at Wrangell and who had joined with others to form the Northwest Trading Company. After Vanderbilt moved to Sitka, and despite the competition of his steamer *Favorite*, he and Brady became friends.[25] Larger corporations like the Portland-based Oregon Steam Navigation Company lacked the flexibility of these smaller shippers and do not appear to have cut deeply into the limited archipelago traffic.

More aggressive in hustling customers were the capital's ephemeral "general merchandisers." Their inventories were as eclectic as that of the Sitka Trading Company; however, unlike Brady, too few of these proprietors had any qualms about selling liquor to the natives. In 1880, when Brady and Beardslee sought to form a local government to regulate the liquor trade, storekeeper Lazar Caplin growled, "De captain may

The interior of the Sitka Trading Company store, 1887. To the rear center is H. A. Bauer, and directly to the right is B. M. Behrends. (Reproduced by permission of the Beinecke Rare Book and Manuscript Library, Yale University.)

go to hell wid his tam gov'ment; I'll bay no daxes."[26] Beardslee recalled that among Sitka's whites were "shop-keepers, Indian traders, saloon keepers, and loafers, who . . . supported themselves by distilling hoo-che-noo, which they traded with the Indians for food."[27]

Much of the miner flotsam that washed north through Sitka no doubt dallied at these amoral places of business. Certainly the Sitka Trading Company was glad to supply and transport gold-hungry argonauts. But its management aimed at more reliable customers, individuals and businesses promising a larger yield than a miner's seasonal purchases. Brady's sanguine commercial projections were based on the rising number of public servants, both in and out of uniform, who, with their families, were establishing their residences at the capital. Profitable expectations were reinforced by Juneau's expanding market, the proliferation of Panhandle canneries, and, by the mid-eighties, the swelling number of Inside Passage summer excursionists.[28] Although Brady functioned primarily as a retailer of consumer necessities, the vocation of village merchant ultimately induced him to wear many hats: moneylender, town booster, journalist, lawyer, community peacemaker, civic planner, and, finally, territorial politician.[29] Certainly there was no better way to become an indispensable figure than by operating a general store.

Within the Sitka Trading Company's poorly lighted, overstuffed quarters, John's fellow townsmen purchased such staples as sugar, flour, "Japan tea," coffee (usually green), onions, cabbage, apples, and oranges. Steady sellers included traps, kerosene lanterns, hip gum boots, hand tools, blankets, and clothes. Contemporary photos taken of the interior of the Sitka Trading Company store reveal that it was usually well stocked with "Indian curios." Tlingits with pelts or fresh food to barter took forever poring over the company's wares; equally exasperating were tightfisted tourist browsers.[30]

In August of 1882 the steamer *Dakota*, equipped with a "fine band of music," introduced a load of vacationers to southeastern Alaska, a region in which "the scenery is a magnificent panorama of wondrous grandeur." Further facilitating a "grand Pacific Northwest land and sea tour" was the completion a year later of America's second transcontinental railroad, the Northern Pacific. Inside Passage summer tours quickly won the attention of businessmen and churchmen alike. Particularly gratifying to Jackson and Brady were the influential politicians who junketed north—thereby getting a firsthand glimpse of the educational deficiences that cried for remedial legislation. Throughout the eighties and nineties the volume of East Coast pleasure seekers rose steadily.[31] Many of the summer sightseers swarmed into Sitka. By July

63

of 1887 Brady reported that his clerks, James H. Shields and Bernard M. Behrends, were "wrestling with tourists in the curiosity room."[32]

Brady and Whitford appear to have garnered their fair share of profits from sales to the capital's public agencies. One time none other than the secretary of the treasury, William Windom, ribbed Sitka's collector for his heavy reliance on "corn brooms, whisk brooms, buckets, and feather dusters" from the Sitka Trading Company. Repeatedly the company won the contract for repairing Sitka's jail, its Custom House, and public structures. John found pounding nails and sawing planks a welcome release from the confines of his log-walled emporium.[33]

The agricultural potential of the northland had attracted John almost from the moment he arrived there. He had been quite impressed by the colorful vegetable garden of deputy collector R. B. Crittenden at Wrangell.[34] Thereafter, despite a variety of authoritative reports detailing serious limitations to Great Land husbandry, Brady's farming energies never waned. His Alaska horticultural hobby was turned to good account: vegetables sold by the Sitka Trading Company usually came from his garden. "Brady's garden" was not only a standard topic of capital conversation; his oversized vegetables served also as yet another sight on the tourist itinerary. To all who would listen he insisted, "one can raise something in Alaska besides quartz mills and icebergs."[35]

Akin to this enterprise was Brady's importation of some cows. Their manure could fertilize his garden, their milk would afford dairy products for the capital's children, and, if all went well, they eventually promised the capital's populace fresh beef. Indian children were fascinated by the beasts. But after John's cattle had chomped their way through neighboring gardens, it was clear that he had imported a headache. For awhile he consigned the animals to mission hands, but, weaned as the lads were on a coastal diet, they showed little avidity for cheese and milk. Somehow the lumbering beasts got loose, and there was more chomping, followed by more outcries. A harbor island supplied at least a temporary solution.

Tourist inquiries about Sitka's nearby mineral hot springs spurred Brady into another business venture. Located about sixteen miles south of Sitka, a pleasant two- to three-hour voyage by sea, these warm waters had comforted Slavic flesh long before the annexation of Russian America. A few years after the purchase, General Jefferson C. Davis, army commander in Alaska, urged Whitford to thin out the ground cover there and erect bath houses for the benefit of Sitka residents. Tubs and sheds were installed, but the business slump of the 1870s that had so retarded the district's growth cast its shadow over Whitford's spa. The prosperity of the eighties led Whitford and Brady to refurbish

"Sitka's Hot Springs" accommodations. Sitka's environs have "suddenly become a popular summer resort for invalids, artists, and sportsmen, the counterpart of which does not exist on the continent," extolled sportsman Charles Hallock. "With her towering mountains, pretty islands, her extinct crater, her river, Indian picnic grounds, her hot springs . . . she offers attractions hard to duplicate."[36] Zealous to promote their resort, the partners unblushingly employed the inflated claims so much a hallmark of their age. A two-week "course of baths at the Hot Sulphur Springs" promised much: "For all diseases of the skin and rheumatic ailments, the effect is almost magic." Notwithstanding their improvements on the grounds, the proprietors never realized their anticipated returns. John later moaned, "It was always much money out and less money in."[37]

A facet of their partnership that produced greater commercial rewards and infinitely greater pleasure to Brady was the business afforded by their steam launch *Rose* and later by the handsome schooner *Leo*. When it became obvious that the stubby *Rose* could not handle all the cargo demands required by mission stations, canneries, and mining ventures, the partners acquired the *Leo*. Laid down at Baltimore just after the Civil War, the oak, 102-foot-long *Leo* had first appeared on the Pacific coast as the U.S. revenue cutter *Reliance*. Originally a topsail schooner, she was condemned by the government; later, after being rerigged as a topmast schooner, lumber shippers operated her between Humboldt Bay and San Francisco.[38] Eventually she became a liquor smuggler along Alaska's Bering coast and, on an unlucky day, was captured by her one-time owners, the U.S. Revenue Marine. Confiscated, she was purchased by the Sitka Trading Company. Brady and Whitford first planned to employ the *Leo* in salmon and halibut fishing, but her commodious hold into which a payload of "250 tons of general merchandise" could be stowed dictated otherwise. Like the launch *Rose*, the *Leo* eventually performed a wide variety of maritime tasks.[39]

Although Brady and Whitford offered imaginative trade routes and thus won an expanding clientele, they thereby threatened the profits of the Pacific Coast Steamship Company and its tough-minded agents, Goodall, Perkins and Co. An irreconcilable squabble compelled court action. Years afterward Brady recalled that the litigation with Captain James Carroll of the Pacific Coast Steamship Company "did me great financial injury. But in time we became good friends and remained so." Before the matter was finally resolved, the Sitka Trading Company found itself in court, encumbered with legal fees, and required to secure formal incorporation papers at San Francisco. After a steam engine was installed in the *Leo*, Brady and Whitford had the last laugh.

Throughout the eighties the auxiliary schooner, with its enormous main-sail, low silhouette, and aft cabin, became a familiar sight from San Francisco to Kodiak.[40]

Manifestly John Brady delighted in the bracing smell of the cold northern salt air and the always dangerous puzzle of operating a vessel throughout an archipelago notorious for submerged reefs, wild currents, and ill-charted channels. A sixteen-day sail, beating his way home from San Francisco, awakened a better appreciation of his garden, his neighbors, and even of himself. Later, after marriage and civic charges entrapped him, the duration of such voyages began to diminish. In June of 1884 he wrote Jackson: "We shall now load the Leo and start westward to sell goods and buy furs. I shall be on her and do not expect to return here before Sept. 1st—of course I shall pick up all curios that come in my way. Hoping that you may have secured the $25,000 appropriation, I shall feel like spying out the land for future missions."[41]

A steady increase in lumber shipments from Seattle required a purchasing agent at that lusty Puget Sound city. Fortunately they obtained the services of Herman A. Bauer, who, like the partners' Sitka clerks, Frederick T. Fischer and B. M. Behrends, would in time direct his own business and enjoy financial success. Behrends was already fast becoming his "own man," for by 1887 he was managing a Juneau branch of the Sitka Trading Company.[42]

Occasional jocular moments helped keep afloat a trading business that was rarely serene. Acting abruptly and without anthorization to assist some seamen in distress, the Rose's owners were once fined "one thousand dollars for wilfull violation of the steamboat laws." Jackson promptly communicated the facts to the acting secretary of the treasury. Soon afterward Sitka's officious collector received a scorching rebuke. "It is evident to the dullest comprehension that there was an emergency existing which appealed strongly to the sympathetic feelings of the owners of that vessel . . . the voyage was plainly a voyage of charity and not of profit or private venture."[43] Once Brady carelessly shipped blasting powder in company with some hardrock miners, and the capital collector again heard from Secretary Daniel Manning. "You are informed that section 4472 Revised Statutes, absolutely prohibits the carriage on passenger steamers, of Nitro-Glycerine and other dangerous explosive substances."[44]

With each passing year Brady grew more adept at avoiding human explosions, and his blend of industry and Irish good humor attracted a widening circle of district and southside friends. Less energetic, envious neighbors, and an occasional sensation-seeking member of the press, muttered about the merchant-missionary. Sitka's "leading missionary," carped the *St. Louis Globe Democrat*, "has joined partnership with a trader. He has prospered beyond all measure in his commercial venture . . . others have taken his place in the soul saving work." A reporter for the *San Francisco Chronicle* took aim not merely at Brady but at all missionaries. "I do not say that all the men who have come to Alaska as missionaries are all schemers, but still they do have that reputation. They are adept at antagonizing. Every settler distrusts them. . . . They locate missions and women live and labor in them. There is war between the settlers and the missionaries. . . . these men do not begin to accomplish the good their sisters do, they should go away."[46] The California critic was guilty of gross distortion, yet within his shotgun indictment there was a hard pellet of truth. Devil-may-care frontiersmen *were* angered when churchmen condemned their exploitive liaisons with native women and freehanded distribution of both disease and liquor. Tirelessly, Brady argued the missionary's side of the case. Addressing a group of church women, he declared: "A Christian Indian, properly, . . . feels that their own safety is in having a separate house, where they can have the privacy of family life. . . . To meet this increased expense the Indians . . . must be put in the way of earning more money. To Christianize the Indians without helping them to new industries and new methods of earning money is to impoverish and make them more wretched. The work of the church is only half done in giving them the gospel; she must also assist them in their efforts to live a Christian life."[47]

By the mid-eighties a hard fact of Alaskan reality was dawning on John Brady: Alaska's pioneer occupation was not duplicating the farming model typified across mid-America. In happier contrast, it appeared that Alaska's natives would not have to endure the socioeconomic ordeal forced upon their brothers to the south. Quite often Brady and Jackson drew invidious distinctions between the Plains Indians and the "superior" marine societies of the Northwest Coast. Indeed, they abjured the application of the word *Indian* to Great Land indigenes, preferring *Alaskan* in the belief that for too many whites *Indian* was synonymous with *nigger*.

On the matter of uplifting Alaskan peoples through education, Brady and Jackson saw eye to eye. In 1885, when Jackson became general agent for education in Alaska, he forthwith commenced a day school program to supplement his church's Panhandle missions. To initiate Alaska's schools, Congress, in 1884, provided a miserly grant of twenty-five thousand dollars. Clearly reinforcements were critical. Commissioner John Eaton accordingly reported to his superior, Secretary of the Interior L. Q. C. Lamar: "Through the visit of Dr. Jackson to the

Secretaries of the several educational bodies . . . there have been assurances of a desire to cooperate in this work of establishing schools in Alaska on the part of the representatives of the Presbyterian, the Baptist, Methodist, Moravian, Episcopal and Congregational Churches. I also saw personally the representatives of the Catholic Church. All acknowledge the courtesy of the Government and expressed a desire to cooperate."[48]

As the public schools spread, it was not always easy for the casual observer to differentiate between the secular and the church-related contract schools. Wives of missionaries often became public school teachers, and mission facilities assisted the tax-supported institutions. By 1891 Jackson had scattered schools as far as Point Barrow among the Eskimos on the Arctic coast.

Without the efforts of the Sitka Trading Company, the remarkable school system would have spread less rapidly. Indeed, the general agent considered Brady his "Chief Assistant" in the undertaking.[49] Champing to advance native educational opportunities of the Panhandle and "to the westward" along the Gulf of Alaska, Jackson leased the *Leo* to carry a group of teachers and school equipment as far as Unalaska in the Aleutians. The *Leo*'s voyage from Seattle in 1886 lasted 104 days, and when it ended, children of Afognak and Unga enjoyed the mixed blessing of compulsory school.[50]

For that memorable adventure Jackson encouraged Brady to "take merchandise and trade at the several stations . . . while we are locating the teachers."[51] Wisely the general agent parceled out his office's educational purchases to a variety of firms both inside and out of the territory. Although the Brady-Whitford business consistently did well, their schooner paid them only a slight profit. Brady complained that even with a gross return of $4,535 (passage, board, and room), the Sitka Trading Company did not clear much from the *Leo*'s lease for three and a half months in 1886 to the U.S. Bureau of Education. The following year Brady collected $1,796 for transporting lumber and school supplies; the next year, building materials used for public school construction at Juneau and Sitka cost Jackson's office $1,832. Eighteen-eighty-nine marked the apex of the Sitka Trading Company's business. During the nineties Brady continued to collect smaller sums for services rendered the government, but by then the money went directly into his own pocket.[52] The Whitford-Brady partnership had drawn to a close.

A variety of factors accounted for Brady's decision to ease out of his business association with Amos Whitford after 1889. Primary was the pull of his recent marriage: a warm Sitka hearthside was much more inviting than a cold, sloppy night watch aboard the *Leo*. Furthermore,

The Sitka Trading Company store at Juneau, 1887. (Reproduced by permission of the Beinecke Rare Book and Manuscript Library, Yale University.)

the schooner's near-fatal wreck in 1888 had cost John too much money and an infuriating amount of time. Finally, he wanted to remove himself from operating a general store, if selling to tourists dictated the admission of Jim Crow. Whitford desired both a separate section and a separate entrance for natives so that tourists would no longer be obliged to rub elbows with smelly, lamp black–smeared Tlingits. John's protests to no avail, their partnership terminated in August of 1891; fortunately the dissolution was amicable.[53] On 17 October the *Alaskan* reported that the Sitka Trading Company had "considerably enlarged the floor-room. . . . the goods have been divided in a general way into two departments; one for . . . the white residents the other . . . for natives. The company intends within a few days to furnish two entrances in the front of the building, which will give admittance to the departments above mentioned."[54]

In December 1893 a destructive fire swept the firm. This disaster, plus the rigors of old age, forced Amos Whitford to retire to Mount Vernon, Washington, where he died on 13 October 1899. By 1893 the *Leo* also lay in retirement—sinking into the mud near the capital. Useful to the end, the vessel built as a revenue marine cutter closed her career as a part-time quarantine station and "supplementary jail."[55] Doubtless there were poignant moments when John's eyes happened on this rotting hulk. But busy with family obligations, political affairs, and a rewarding lumber business, Brady had little time to reflect on the past—his present was too consuming.

1. Brady to J. W. Witten, 2 September 1903, National Archives, Microfilm Record Group 430, U.S. Department of the Interior, Territorial Papers Alaska, 1869–1911, roll no. 9 (hereafter cited as TAP). JGB, mf. 2, untitled reminiscenses. Beardslee, *Affairs in Alaska*, 24 January 1882, pp. 38–39. Interview with Hugh Brady, 30 June 1962, Seattle.

2. Interview with Hugh Brady, 30 June 1962.

3. TAP, mf. 9, Brady to Witten, 2 September 1903; JCorr, 10:315–16, Brady to Jackson, 11 October 1880.

4. An 1867 map of Sitka may be found in C. L. Andrews, *Sitka: The Chief Factory of the Russian American Company*, 3d ed. (Caldwell, Idaho, 1945), endpaper. Richard A. Pierce, "The Ghost of Baranov Castle, Folklore or Fakelore," *Alaska* 36 (May 1970): 25 ff.

5. JCorr, 11:238–39, Brady to Jackson, 11 August 1881. Ibid., 10:315–16, Brady to Jackson, 11 October 1880. Jackson, *Alaska and Missions*, pp. 202–15.

6. Ted C. Hinckley, "Sheldon Jackson as a Preserver of Alaska's Native Culture," *Pacific Historical Review* 33 (November 1964): 411–24.

7. A careful reconstruction of Juneau's earliest years is given in R. N. DeArmond, *The Founding of Juneau* (Juneau, 1967). Morris, *Report upon the Customs*, pp. 129–30;

"Letter of Rev. Sheldon Jackson," *Report of the Secretary of the Interior . . . Forty-Seventh Congress* (Washington, D.C., 1884), 4:278–80.

8. JCorr, 10:315–16, Brady to Jackson, 11 October 1880.

9. Hinckley, "Sheldon Jackson College," pp. 59–79. Henry Glass, "Naval Administration in Alaska," *Proceedings of the United States Naval Institute* 16 (January 1890): 1–19. JCorr, 11:106, Brady to Jackson, 24 March 1881. Jackson, *Alaska and Missions*, pp. 388–91.

10. JGB, unfiled, Brady to Jackson, 12 June 1881.

11. U.S., Congress, House, *School for Indian Children in Alaska*, 47th Cong., 1st sess., Report No. 236, 4 February 1881, pp. 1–2. This first boarding school building, a one-time hospital, burned down on 26 January 1882, and until the permanent campus was acquired, the students temporarily were housed in a stable (*Alaskan*, 23 April 1898). "Letter of Rev. Sheldon Jackson," p. 280. JGB, unfiled, Kendall to Brady, 6 April 1881. Brady had speculated about "starting a boys' farm," but events so identified him with the training school that he eventually abandoned the idea (JCorr, 11:107, Brady to Jackson, 24 March 1881).

12. JGB, unfiled, Kendall to Brady, 6 April 1891. JCorr, 11:197, Austin to Jackson, 12 June 1881; ibid., 13:152–53, Austin to Jackson, 13 June 1883. *Alaskan*, 23 April 1898. In his own book published in 1880–81, the rarely modest Jackson referred (in quotes) to the educational nucleus as the "Sheldon Jackson Industrial School" (*Alaska, and Missions*, p. 389). A few years later, in his *Presbyterian Church in Alaska*, Jackson wrote, "The school was afterward named the 'Sheldon Jackson Institute' by the missionaries" (p. 5.).

13. JCorr, 10:290, Brady to Jackson, 6 September 1880.

14. "Letter of Sheldon Jackson," p. 280. U.S., Congress, House, *Report of the United States Naval Officers Cruising in Alaska Waters*, 47th Cong., 1st sess., Exec. Doc. 81, 24 February 1882, p. 31. JCorr, 11:106, Brady to Jackson, 24 March 1881.

15. JCorr, 12:149, Austin to Jackson, 12 April 1882. On Jackson's astonishing promotional skills see Hinckley, "Publicist of the Forgotten Frontier," pp. 27–40. Sheldon Jackson, *Facts about Alaska: Its People, Villages, Mission Schools* (New York, 1903), pp. 25–28. *Alaskan*, 23 April 1898. Interview with Hugh Brady, 12 July 1973, Sitka.

16. A girls' program had been set up at the training school as early as December of 1882 (Jackson, *The Presbyterian Church in Alaska*, p. 5). Septima M. Collis, *A Woman's Trip to Alaska: Being an Account of a Voyage through the Inland Seas of the Sitkan Archipelago in 1890* (New York, 1890), pp. 119, 124.

17. Ted C. Hinckley, "Sheldon Jackson, Presbyterian Lobbyist for the Great Land of Alaska," *Journal of Presbyterian History* 40 (March 1962): 3–23; idem, "Sheldon Jackson and Benjamin Harrison," *Pacific Northwest Quarterly* 54 (April 1963): 66–74. JCorr, 14:34, appointment; Sheldon Jackson Scrapbook Collection, 65 vols., Presbyterian Historical Society, Philadelphia, Pa., vol. 64, p. 139, appointment (hereafter cited as JScrap).

18. JCorr, 10:31, Brady to Jackson, 30 January 1880; JGB, mf. 3, Jackson to Brady, 19 March 1880; ibid., unfiled, Jackson to Brady, 7 July 1883; JCorr, 13:234, Brady to Jackson, 12 November 1883.

19. *Minutes of the General Assembly of 1883*, p. 631; Jackson, *The Presbyterian Church in Alaska*, p. 809.

20. JCorr, 11:107, Brady to Jackson, 24 March 1881. Jackson, *The Presbyterian Church in Alaska*, p. 5.

21. JCorr, 13:308, Brady to Jackson, 24 February 1884.

22. JCorr, 12:36, Alonzo Austin to Jackson, 5 January 1882.

23. JGB, unfiled, Irvin to Brady, 14 March 1889.

24. *Alaska Herald*, 24 July 1873; *Sitka Post*, 5 June 1877; *Alaska Appeal*, 6 March 1879.

25. *Alaska Appeal*, 15 September 1879 and 15 April 1880; Piseco [L. A. Beardslee], "Alaska Ichthyology," *Forest and Stream* 15 (9 September 1880).

26. Beardslee, *Report . . . Affairs in Alaska.*

27. *Alaska Appeal*, 15 February 1880; Beardslee, *Report . . . Affairs in Alaska*, pp. 17–18.

28. Ted C. Hinckley, *The Americanization of Alaska, 1867–1897* (Palo Alto, 1972), chaps. 3 and 4.

29. Lewis E. Atherton, *The Frontier Merchant in Mid-America* (Columbia, Mo., 1971), chap. 1.

30. JCorr, 10:288, Brady to Jackson, 6 September 1880; JGB, unfiled, James Jones to Whitford, 2 January 1882; ibid., mf. 2, Dan to Brady, 4 October 1881; JCorr, 11:198, Brady to Jackson, 12 June 1881; ibid., 13:236, Brady to Jackson, 23 November 1883.

31. Ted C. Hinckley, "The Inside Passage: A Popular Gilded Age Tour," *Pacific Northwest Quarterly* 56 (April 1965): 67–74.

32. To sample the travel literature that blossomed forth, see Abby Johnson Woodman, *Picturesque Alaska* (Boston, 1889), and Eliza Ruhamah Scidmore, *The Guide-Book to Alaska and the Northwest Coast* (London, 1893). *New York Evening Post*, 24 January 1887; JGB, mf. 1, Brady to his wife, 3 July 1887.

33. U.S. Treasury, Alaska Custom House Records, Federal Records Center, NARS, Seattle, Wash. (hereafter cited as CHR), vol. 35, Windom to custodian, 16 September 1889; ibid., scattered vouchers.

34. R. B. Crittenden Manuscript, Bancroft Library, University of California, Berkeley. *Alaska Appeal*, 15 July 1879.

35. *Alaska Appeal*, 22 March 1879; *New York Times*, 25 November 1880. Brady's unrestrained enthusiasm for the Panhandle's horticultural prospects can be found in his numerous newspaper interviews and his annual reports as territorial governor (*Alaskan*, 12 November 1887).

36. JScrap, 18:10.

37. *Alaskan*, 8 May 1886 and 5 December 1891. CHR, vol. f74–s89, S. M. Hockslayer to A. Swineford, 18 June 1887. TAP, mf. 9, Brady to Witten, 2 September 1903.

38. JGB, mf. 3, "The Cruise of the Rose in 1878"; JCorr, 10:316, Brady to Jackson, 11 October 1880. Willard, *Life in Alaska*, pp. 232–33; JCorr, 13:108, Brady to Jackson, 20 April 1883. *Alaskan*, 17 August 1889. E. W. Wright, ed., *Lewis and Dryden, Marine History of the Pacific Northwest* (Portland, 1895), p. 338.

39. C. L. Hooper, *Report of the Cruise of the U.S. Revenue Steamer Corwin . . . 1880* (Washington, D.C., 1881), pp. 21–22; JCorr, 10:291, Brady to Jackson, 6 September 1880. *Alaskan*, 17 April 1886; W. R. Abercrombie, "Report of a Supplementary Expedition into the Copper River Valley in Alaska, 1884," in *Compilation of Narratives of Explorations in Alaska* (Washington, D.C., 1900), p. 418. *Alaskan*, 6 March 1886; JCorr, 14:200, Brady to Jackson, 24 April 1886; ibid., 13:308, Brady to Jackson, 24 February 1884. *Alaskan*, 21 April and 17 November 1888. JGB, mf. 1, Brady to his wife, 28 June 1889. Ted C. Hinckley, "Cutter, Smuggler, Colporteur, and Trader—the *Leo* . . . ," in *The Sea in Alaska's Past* (Anchorage, 1979), pp. 182–205.

40. JCorr, 13:244, Austin to Jackson, 16 October 1883; ibid., p. 236, Brady to Jackson, 27 November 1883; ibid., 12:234, Brady to Jackson, 12 November 1883; ibid., 14:98, Jackson to his wife, 27 August 1885; ibid., 13:251, Austin to Jackson, 15 December 1883; ibid., 14:200, Brady to Jackson, 24 April 1886. CLASJC, Brady to Andrews, 28 May 1912. *Juneau City Mining Record*, 16 January 1890. JGB, mf. 1, articles of incorporation; *Seattle Post-Intelligencer*, 17 December 1886. Ship history file, Robert N. DeArmond, Juneau.

41. JGB, Elizabeth Brady diary for 1887, 13 February entry. Ibid., unfiled, Brady to Jackson, 18 June 1884.

42. *Seattle Post-Intelligencer*, 17 December 1886. Robert N. DeArmond, *Some Names around Juneau* (Sitka, 1957), pp. 7–8; JGB, unfiled, Frederick T. Fischer to Elizabeth Brady, 24 December 1918. Alan Jergens, Seattle Public Library, to author, 23 July 1973.

43. JScrap, 8:135, clipping. CHR, vol. 2, February 1881–December 1883, John C. New to collector, Sitka, 23 September 1882.

44. CHR, vol. 30, Daniel Manning to collector, Sitka, 11 March 1886. Details of the altercation may be traced; see CHR vol. 2, correspondence of August and September; ibid., vol. 23, Whitford and others to W. G. Morris, 14 August 1882.

45. Quoted in the *Independent*, 13 September 1883.

46. *San Francisco Chronicle*, 23 November 1884. As Alaska grew, and acquired more newspapers, some territorial editors echoed the familiar accusations about the "do-gooder missionary." See, for example, *Alaska Journal*, 16 September 1893.

47. JScrap, 7:12, clipping, ca. 1881.

48. *North Star*, February 1888. JCorr, 24:27, Eaton to Lamar, 24 August 1885.

49. For the details of Jackson's achievements, see his annual reports to the commissioner of education for the period 1885–1907 and the summary in Ted C. Hinckley, "The Presbyterian Leadership in Pioneer Alaska," *Journal of American History* 52 (March 1966): 742–56. JGB, unfiled, Jackson to Brady, 7 July 1883.

50. Sheldon Jackson, "Schools in Alaska," *Report of the Commissioner of Education* (Washington, D.C., 1893), p. 750. Idem, "Report on Educational Affairs in Alaska," *Report of the Commissioner of Education for the Year 1892–93* (Washington, D.C., 1893), p. 1738.

51. Jackson to Brady, 16 April 1886, "Alaska Schools," 5 vols., 3:120, Sheldon Jackson Collection, Princeton Theological Seminary, Princeton, N.J. (hereafter cited as PTS).

52. Expenditures by the Bureau of Education paid to Brady may be found in "General Agent's Letterbooks," 63 vols., National Archives, Washington, D.C., vols. 1 and 2; and TAP, mf. 5.

53. *Juneau City Mining Record*, 27 September and 6 December 1888. JGB, mf. 1, Brady to his wife, 7 June, 3 July, and 12 July 1889.

54. *Alaskan*, 29 August and 17 October 1891.

55. Ibid., 23 December 1893 and 18 November 1899; JCorr, 16:254, Brady to Jackson, 30 December 1892. JGB, unfiled, caption on photo of *Leo* hulk.

CHAPTER FIVE

Sitka Society and the Pattons

Sitka in 1885 presented a healthier, happier scene than it had a decade earlier. By no means had it become a boom town; flourishing Juneau and neighboring Douglas, lying across the Gastineau Channel, boasted that sobriquet. Although Juneau's white population quickly exceeded Sitka's, Alaska's capital imparted an air of progressive orderliness. As one returning visitor observed, Sitka "has waked up from her long lethargy. New dwellings have been added and old ones restored and fresh painted. . . . new fences, new sidewalks, and in fact everything new."[1] Capital sightseers snorted, however, at the "half-starved dogs which infest the neighborhood as they do the slums of Constantinople and Amsterdam." Even Sitka's local newspaper had to confess that the untethered cattle, hogs, goats, and mules that roamed about were "a growing nuisance."[2]

No agricultural hamlet surrounded by waving croplands, Sitka lay in a munificence of ocean, islands, and mountains. In some ways the Yankee-Creole-Indian enclave could be compared to an eighteenth-century New England town. A "house of God" thrust up its steeple from Sitka's center. Here and there about the village green stood white-painted, clapboard structures. Nearby nestled a cluster of boats.[3] Much as the Atlantic Ocean had given birth to Plymouth, so the Pacific favored the location of Alaska's inconspicuous commercial and administrative capital. In 1885 its Yankee residents aspired to make it the vestibule for northbound pioneers. But most Americans still envisioned life at Sitka as difficult. The West still seemed far from "won." Seattle had yet to shed its pioneer vestments, and Washington, as was true of most of the Pacific Northwest's budding commonwealths, remained a territory. In the public mind the Great Land was a distant realm of icebergs and discomfort.

Invariably those women whom Dr. Jackson recruited as schoolteachers, like their missionary counterparts, possessed a goodly portion of "missionary spirit." They were also among the most independent-minded of their sex. Three women who ultimately cast their lot with Alaska and who would play integral roles in John Brady's life were Cassia, Elizabeth, and Gertrude Patton, daughters of Hugh Patton. In June of 1885 a friend of this Cochranton, Pennsylvania, family, Miss Margaret Powell, opened the public school at Sitka. Elizabeth Jane Patton later recalled how impressed the Patton family was by Miss Powell's tales of Alaska. Twenty-one-year-old Elizabeth was pleasantly surprised to hear that, because of her Pennsylvania teaching, only a few months of additional normal school training were required for a similar Far North position, either in a common school or at a mission station. Cassia was less enthusiastic. She was "not fool enough to be a missionary." "I am conceited enough," Elizabeth snapped back, "to think that I am good enough!"[4]

A year later, equipped with the supplementary courses from Normal Park in Chicago, Elizabeth departed for Alaska. At Portland she was invited to stay with Dr. Aaron Lindsley. He properly counseled her on northland dos and don'ts, perhaps even warning her about a certain apostate missionary who had embarked upon a mercantile career.

On 13 March 1886 residents of Alaska's capital had their first sight of Powell's coworker. Elizabeth Patton had been in Sitka for less than a week when Margaret introduced her to one of the owners of the Sitka Trading Company. Dressed in a heavy sheepskin-lined coat, in need of a bath, and preoccupied with repairing his *Leo*, Brady hardly made much of an impression on Elizabeth. To her family she wrote, "I have met the homliest man I have ever seen." However, a few weeks later when "the homliest man" delivered some food to the Powell cottage, Elizabeth met him at the door and inquired, "Why don't you ever call on Margaret and me, the other gentlemen in the town have called?" "Thank you," John replied, "I will now that I have been invited."[5]

On matters of the mind, Elizabeth and John shared much. Each had a similar theological outlook, an abiding concern for Alaska's natives, and a love of literature. John's calls at the Powell-Patton residence became habitual. Sitkans watched and wondered how long it would be before Whitford's partner proposed to one or the other of the schoolmarms. Margaret and Elizabeth laughed at the gossip. Particularly hilarious were the repeated efforts by capital residents to maneuver

John and Margaret into being alone—the neighbors bet on Miss Powell.[6] Erelong John had to admit that he could not deny his emotions. Elizabeth Patton's charm and remarkable abilities, even her penchant to bristle, captivated him. However, at a long-anticipated party at Sitka Hot Springs, he tried to show off a bit—and she left him feeling foolish and frustrated. Edward De Groff, the boyish young merchant from New York, appeared seriously attracted to her. That worried him. But what really alarmed John was the sight of her having so much fun dancing with the naval officers from the U.S.S. *Pinta*.[7]

Discerning John's unhappiness, Margaret Powell conveniently left her home the afternoon of 3 July 1886, when he asked to "come over to see Elizabeth." Afterward Elizabeth recalled: "Brady came sure enough, he proposed. He wanted to know if I had any interest in him. I said, 'No, I had not any more interest in you than anyone else.' He said he would like to stir some interest in me. You were a very different person from any man I had ever thought I would get interested in. . . . So we talked awhile and he said. 'Well would you be willing to consider me for awhile, for a month say?'" It was Elizabeth's turn to get snared. "I shall," she replied, "but I do not promise anything." She promised more than she knew, for persistence was among her suitor's strongest qualities. In less than a month she accepted his proposal and announced her engagement.[8]

To her parents Elizabeth wrote, "I suppose you will think me dreadfully silly and spoony when you see us together, but I do love him so, he is everything that will call forth a woman's profoundest love. Everything but handsome, you know I have told you before that he lays no claim to fine looks, but he does lay claim to an honest upright life. I do want you all to see him and know him and like him not for my sake, but just because you can't help admiring and liking him."[9] Neither of the betrothed could have anticipated the anxiety they would suffer before they said their vows. The *Leo* kept Brady at sea and Elizabeth was sure he was marooned, or worse. By early summer 1887, after she had returned to Cochranton to prepare for the wedding, she realized just how powerful were her feelings. "Indeed if you could know what I have gone through this summer," she wrote him, "you would pity me. At times I have been almost distracted." Elizabeth became so distracted that she forgot to mail her final report to Dr. Jackson, but he forgave her and along with her paycheck sent his congratulations.[10] Doubtless the impatience Brady suffered was as painful, if not worse. In a July letter he opened his heart: "I think of you often and love you more than I ever told you."

The women of Sitka, about 1889. Elizabeth Brady appears at front left in the polka-dot dress; in the center, to her left, in button-up black, is Mrs. Behrends; at front right is Pauline Cohen; and teacher Margaret Powell is in the white dress with ribbon belt and bow. (Reproduced by permission of the Beinecke Rare Book and Manuscript Library, Yale University.)

Somehow that glorious day finally came, and the *Cochranton Times* gushed: "The marriage of John G. Brady and Miss Elizabeth Patton was solemnized at the residence of the bride's father, Mr. Hugh Patton, on Thursday, Oct. 20. . . . The rooms were beautifully decorated and the air was heavy with the perfume of flowers. As the hour for the ceremony approached the library was filled with guests. . . . the rooms were filled with gay repartee and light laughter until the first tones of Mendelsohn's wedding march was sounded, when a hush fell upon those assembled."[11]

By February of 1888 the Bradys were back in Sitka. On the first morning after their return, Elizabeth evidenced her shrewdness. While John lay abed, she arose and busied herself about their new home but fixed no breakfast. First the kitchen fire had to be prepared, and that her husband could attend to. Finally, at about eleven o'clock, hunger propelled John to the woodpile, a chore he continued thereafter. By March they had "entertained a number of invited guests in admirable manner," as the *North Star* described the Bradys' housewarming.[12]

Equally indispensable for both of them were solitary avocations such as reading, writing, home crafts like sewing and carpentry, and merely walking silently through the woods at nearby Indian River. But for a vigorous man in his late thirties with a vivacious wife not yet twenty-five, such a private existence was unthinkable. Work, both vocational and civic labors, was mandatory. To some degree it was Calvinist compulsion: "Work now for the time cometh when no man can work." For the present the Sitka Trading Company could support them. But what about children and a future Sitka home? Furthermore, John was impatient to operate his own business.

As in other ports across the Pacific Basin where American values and life-styles predominated, such as San Francisco and Honolulu, life tended to be directed by a WASP elite. The *Alaskan* referred to the Bradys and their social milieu as the "exclusive set" and numbered it less than fifty members, "gay and gallant officers and officials from the service of his Honor Uncle Samuel."[13] The local newspaper summarized the capital's pacesetters: "There are the Governor of the Territory and his family, the Marshall and his dark-eyed daughter, and other Government officials, too, with wives and daughters. A few wealthy Russians, old residents in Sitka, with unpronouncable names. . . . But the last and the best are the officers of the United States ships which cruise about the Alaska waters with the brave hearted young wives who follow their liege lords and young masters for the sake of being with them when their ships are in port."[12] Among these vessels was the U.S.S. *Pinta*. Its ship's company and capital-stationed complement of marines formed the district's resident police force. America was at peace, and Sitka's press found it pleasant to romanticize about the uniform and all that it symbolized. "The white toy war-ship Pinta, as pretty and dainty as a maid at her first communion, the coast survey steamer Hassler and her jolly crew, the Mohican all are in the harbor at times."[15]

Although the *Alaskan* rarely, if ever, listed natives among Sitka's sociopolitical leadership, the newspaper frequently noted certain Russian "old residents" who had been assimilated, such as the Kashevarovs, the Bolshanins, and the Shutnovs. Among these George J. Kostrometinoff, longtime United States interpreter at the capital, was unquestionably the most respected. Kostrometinoff had assisted Brady when he first set foot in Sitka. Thereafter, despite occasional differences, John and the "Colonel" were good friends.[16]

Yet Kostrometinoff was the exception. Most of those who had Russian blood in their veins fell outside of the capital's ruling elite. A free press had early provided the Creoles a chance to reply to the disparaging charge that they personified sloth. "They are poor, but poverty is no crime," one of them had protested in 1879. "The Creoles may be lazy, but it is not fair to judge of that at a time when there is nothing for them to do."[17] Brady continued to fret over the slowness of their assimilation until after the turn of the century. Elizabeth periodically employed Creoles to assist her about the house and praised them generously.[18] She and John were already in the vanguard of those advocating preservation of Russian-American historic sites, especially the Governor's Castle and the Cathedral of Saint Michael.

The Abraham Cohen family, although non-WASP, like the "old resident Russians," remained an important part of Sitka's establishment. From the outset of the American frontier in Alaska, Jewish businessmen had played significant roles. Born in Prussia, Abraham Cohen had come to Alaska during its earliest years under army rule and had built up a successful brewery. After Juneau ballooned he joined other Sitkans who gambled that the noisy mining town would flourish; his son Marcus was sent north to establish another brewery.

Sitka's residents honored the Cohen family for its three stunning and talented daughters as well, all of whom added immeasurably to the charm of capital society. In 1890 daughter Augusta married Lt. Robert E. Coontz of the *Pinta*, later a four-star admiral. Pauline Cohen had assisted Brady and Fanny Kellogg in their abortive efforts to educate Sitka's children. And Henrietta married the Treadwell Mine physician. Beauty, brains, and beer easily swept aside any latent anti-Semitism that might have come their way. When their brother Marcus died, his friends were legion, and he was buried by the Knights of Pythias, of whom he had been a prominent member.[19]

Journalists who visited the Panhandle, where most of its Caucasian inhabitants lived, too often undervalued Alaska's prodigious economic prospects. Many of them took delight in spoofing the territory. "It is a dreary, lonesome spot," one wrote in 1885; "of the four hundred Americans there, I think three hundred would leave if they had the money to get away."[20] Yet a highly mobile population was hallmark of America, and most assuredly of its western regions. Those able, middle-class whites who had the good sense, or luck, to settle down in a town that was growing would quite likely gain a degree of upward mobility.[21] Pioneers like Brady, who found Alaska agreeable and adopted it as their home, were in a distinct minority, for the majority of Americans who came to the Great Land during the nineteenth century were as seasonal as Yukon Valley geese. Maritime personnel, argonauts, government workers, and, after 1879, an expanding number of cannery workers knew that their residency had a termination date. Too frequently this fact, plus their geographic isolation, bred a careless and sometimes ruthless attitude toward Alaska. In 1890 Ivan Petroff summed up the social threat posed by these seasonal workers. "I refer chiefly to mining camps and fisheries; all of which are now without any [legal] authority of this kind whatever. Such places during the summer attract a numerous assemblage of ignorant Italians, Greeks, Portuguese, and Chinese, who are easily led to excesses of various kinds. In four or five such locations, shooting and stabbing affrays and murders have occurred during the past summer, and in every case there was a total failure of justice."[21]

In the eyes of its residents, Sitka was an oasis of civility. Some Juneau businessmen even maintained a home in the capital so that their familes would be immersed in "refinement" instead of being exposed to frontier rowdiness. During the eighties and nineties Sitkans engaged in a losing battle to convince themselves of the capital's ascendant, more civilized milieu.[23] These towns really had much in common: both were maritime communities; both rejoiced in 1888 at news that mail would be delivered twice a month instead of once; neither boasted a resident dentist; and both experienced occasional importations of "la grippe." Invariably the flu deaths of native residents outnumbered those of whites. "As far as the white population are concerned the malady is not malignant," declared Sitka's *Alaskan* in 1892, "but it has stricken terror into the hearts of the natives."[24]

John and Elizabeth were keenly conscious that not only aboriginal Americans lay outside Alaska's Yankee mainstream. To have one's shirts laundered by Sitkan Lung Sing assured quality cleaning. Yet the capital's Chinese were outsiders. Brady was gratified that his friends Lt. Robert Coontz and Alonzo Austin gave a drowned Chinese a "decent Christian burial" despite the objections of some whites.[25] Intercultural ignorance existed and racial slurs crept out even when the opposite was intended. Once the Douglas *Miner* failed a press run due to an abrupt lack of water power. Its competitor sniped: "The *Alaskan* uses 'man power' to run its presses, and does not have to depend on such an uncertain thing as water. We can remmend [*sic*] it to the *Miner* man. If he had had a good buck 'nigger' and a crank the Douglas subscribers would not have experienced such a calamity."[26] Unhappily the classifications "John Chinaman," "Buck Nigger," and "Siwash" exposed America's prevalent ethnocentricism. However, Alaska's natives also disliked the Chinese. In fact, the curse of xenophobia was multicultural.

As with most humanely inclined people, John and Elizabeth may have only rarely admitted to themselves how thin was the tissue of decency that shielded human dignity from crudity and even depravity. Patriotic celebrations, card parties, balls, dances and concerts, a weekly newspaper, charity bazaars, a lyceum and debating society—each in its own fashion stimulated neighborliness and community consciousness.[27] They were creatures of an age in which Americans still viewed themselves as a people apart, a "chosen people." The Bradys' Calvinist legacy, an abiding distrust of man's sinful predilections, had been diluted by their age's extraordinary achievements. For John and Elizabeth the turn-of-the-century epoch was so swollen with excitement at the realization of rising expectations that it was almost impossible to accept man as inherently evil. Confidence in mankind's creative powers was renewed at every hand. Within Alaska there was the slow but steady absorption of natives into a "Christian society." On their trips to the East Coast it became almost a game to spot the changes in city skylines. Seattle was knocking down its hills; Denver was spilling out over the countryside; Chicago's and Philadelphia's swelling polyglot populations and enormous physical transformations verged on the unbelievable.

Absolutely critical in reinforcing the Bradys' confident humanism was their commitment to a well-read public. For too long Sitka had lacked a newspaper. Indeed, the district had been without a domestically printed weekly since the withdrawal of the army in 1877. San Francisco papers, such as the *Chronicle* and the *Bulletin*, did supply an occasional column or two on Alaska affairs, as did those of Portland and Seattle. A partial solution to the problem of inadequate local news coverage had been Ivan Petroff's San Francisco–printed *Alaska Appeal*, but in 1880 it had folded.[28] On 7 November 1885 the weekly *Alaskan* broke the silence of the district's fourth estate. Fortunately this four-page, twelve-by-nineteen-inch sheet, with a five-column spread, survived until well into the next century.

Sheldon Jackson, Mottrom D. Ball, Brady, and Alaska's second governor, Alfred P. Swineford, cooperated in the *Alaskan*'s birth. Governor Swineford, who had earlier been editor of the *Marquette Mining Journal*, became president of the Alaskan Printing Company. Exactly what its corporate structure was and who first set policy is not clear.[29] What is verifiable was the *Alaskan*'s restrained, decorous quality. Unlike so many frontier weeklies aflame with vitriolic charges and political bombast, Sitka's sheet assumed a reasonably calm, reportorial tone. From the outset it was promissionary, pronative, and pro-Brady. A few years later John helped launch the Sitka Industrial School newspaper, the *North Star*.[30]

Another form of communication, one in which Elizabeth delighted, was the art crafted by Northwest Coast natives. Their masks, argilite carvings, decorated wooden containers, and much else were exhibited for sale at her husband's store. By the end of the tourist season, excursionists had snapped up the trading company's best pieces—sometimes to her regret. Jackson's successful efforts to build a museum in which to preserve these fast-vanishing creations has already been noted. A vital antecedent to that museum was Sitka's Society of Alaskan Natural History and Ethnology. John and especially Elizabeth were vital in its formation.

Usually one or two resident generations, or approximately half a century, are required before a frontier community awakens to its historical legacy and takes vigorous steps to preserve it. In the hiatus, much that was irreplaceable has been destroyed, discarded, or carried off. Indeed, just two years after the purchase of Russian America a captain, Edward S. Fast, announced his plans for the establishment of an "Alaskan Museum" at San Francisco. Paradoxically, as the aboriginal antiquities flowed southward, the Northwest Coast peoples' regard for their handicrafts waned. By 1880 C. T. Tate, of Bella Coola, British Columbia, informed Jackson that the natives not only did not like to talk about their "curiosities" but had even burned some.[31]

To protect remnants of Alaska's past meant alerting and educating Creole and Yankee alike. Always eager to embark upon yet another excuse for socialization, Elizabeth grabbed at the idea of forming a local enthnological association. Sitka's Society of Alaskan Natural History and Ethnology was organized on 24 October 1887. Thereafter its members met approximately once a month, at which time papers were usually read on facets of Alaskan anthropology, natural history, and even linguistics. Perusal of the original "Secretary's Book" and "Minutes" confirms that it was the Bradys, joined by Cassia Patton, who formed the society's mainspring. Elizabeth broadened her neighbors' reading resources and occasionally lectured on topics of public interest. For example, in 1890 the society listened to her deliver a paper on the Bering Sea Eskimos. It was the Bradys who inaugurated the pleasant custom of cake and coffee after the society's evening proceedings had closed, and after they built their new home, John and Elizabeth took pleasure in hosting numerous meetings.[32]

The society also encouraged Sitkans to initiate numerous acts of restoration and preservation. Local marines cleaned up some old cannon and remounted them on the capital green. Other residents salvaged the fast-decaying blockhouses that once had warned away threatening Tlingits. And, after considerable delay, federal money was secured to pay for a major overhaul of Baranov's Castle. Sitka's Russian Orthodox priests took a renewed concern for their jewelbox sanctuary; and the Reverend V. P. Danskoy set about writing a record of Saint Michael's under the Russian flag.[33]

While the Bradys applauded these enhancements of the capital's past, the more immediate concerns of the present pressed in upon them. The Sitka Industrial School hospital had never been equipped with facilities for adult natives. In conjunction with their friends and fellow Sitkans, such as Lt. and Mrs. George T. Emmons, the Coontzes, and the missionary physician Dr. Clarence Thwing and his wife, the Bradys began a maternity hospital for native women. A "Maternity Society" raised funds by featuring "a sewing bee to make up some sheets for the native Maternity Hospital."[34]

While the distaff side of society busied itself with female matters, menfolk confronted the endemic scourge of fire. Hardly a year passed without some overheated wooden building going up in smoke. As a businessman, Brady was understandably an active member of the Sitka Fire Brigade. In 1891 he joined with Peter Callsen, the brigade's president, in advocating better fire-fighting equipment. Three years later, not long after carpenter Callsen, contractor C. W. Young, and John and other townspeople had rejoiced at their handsome restoration of Baranov's Castle, Sitka's fire brigade fought and lost an agonizing battle to save this "Pride of Sitka."[35]

A municipal responsibility that John assumed, doubtless at the urging of the general agent for education, was service on Sitka's local school board. By 1890 the Panhandle's growing number of schools exhibited considerable self-direction. Accordingly, Jackson created a number of local unpaid school committees. With his strong opinions on what was right and wrong in pedagogical matters, Brady could hardly have rejected this community chore.[36] And he had another, personal reason in his concern for his sisters-in-law, Gertrude and Cassia Patton. John's and Elizabeth's letters extolling the unique surprises awaiting visitors to the Great Land continued to arouse the curiosity of the Hugh Patton family. First it was Elizabeth's sisters who came north for a short stay and remained. One event after another drew Hugh Patton's attention northward. Both Cassia and Gertrude had secured Panhandle teaching positions. The youngest daughter, Gertrude, fell in love with the district governor's son and insisted on a prompt marriage. After the elder Patton heard that he was to become a grandfather all constraints vanished. With three daughters lost to Alaska, Hugh and his wife tore loose their Pennsylvania stakes and headed for Sitka.[37]

At first Cassia taught the students in Juneau's public school, while Gertrude operated public school No. 2 at Sitka. After Gertrude married George E. Knapp, eldest son of Governor Lyman E. Knapp, in August of 1890, her husband dropped his teaching position at the capital for a job in the collector's office, thus enabling Cassia to join her sister at Sitka as teacher of public school No. 1.[38] Hugh found employment with John. Within a few years "Father Patton" would become the much-loved "grandfather" of the five Brady children. All would have been well for the Pennsylvanian-turned-Alaskan had not Gertrude's marriage soured. George Knapp drank too much, made a fool of himself over some ladies, and forced John to have him arrested for violating public decency. Before the matter terminated, Gertrude had a baby, the couple was divorced, and George left the district.[39] For John the family rupture became doubly painful when Governor Knapp injected himself into the matter. After the dust had settled, Elizabeth was grateful that her mother's death had spared her "all the sorrow and suffering we have passed through." Fortunately Gertrude was able to rejoin Cassia in the classroom, occasionally assisted by Elizabeth, and the Patton-Brady family remained intact.[40]

It may well have been one of the Patton girls who, in 1892, urged Alaskans to celebrate their first quarter century as part of the United States. The proposal was greeted with apathy and scorn. The territory had suffered "utter neglect at the hands of congress," some growled. Why should Sitka exert itself when her treatment by the government was "worse than Gaul . . . at the hands of Roman Empire"?[41] Paradoxically, in just six years, the United States, like ancient Rome, was herself rapidly expanding an overseas empire. Concurrently "Klondike" had become a household word, and within Alaska the name John G. Brady was everywhere recognized.

1. Kirk H. Stone, "Populating Alaska: The United States Phase," *Geographical Review* 42 (July 1952): 390. JScrap, 18:10, clipping, ca. 1885.

2. Collis, *A Woman's Trip*, p. 109; *Alaskan*, 14 March 1893.

3. Maturin M. Ballou, *The New Eldorado: A Summer Journey to Alaska* (Boston, 1890), chap. 22. To contrast this frontier hamlet with other pioneer towns, see the excellent compendium by John W. Reps, *Town Planning in Frontier America* (New Jersey, 1969).

4. Typescript in possession of author, typed from statement by Elizabeth Brady owned by her daughter Mary, ca. 1948. (hereafter cited as MsEB).

5. Ibid.

6. JGB, Elizabeth Brady diary for 1887, 6 February entry; MsEB.

7. MsEB; *Alaskan*, 24 April 1886.

8. MsEB.

9. JGB, Elizabeth Brady diary for 1887, 13 February entry.

10. MsEB; JGB, mf. 1, Elizabeth Patton to Brady, 7 October 1887. "General Agent's Letterbooks," 1:118, Jackson to Elizabeth Patton, n.d.

11. JGB, mf. 1, Brady to his wife, 3 July 1887; *Alaskan*, 12 November and 3 December 1887.

12. Interview with John and Hugh Brady, 23 June 1962, Seattle. *North Star* (Sitka), March 1883.

13. Gavan Daws, *Shoal of Time: A History of the Hawaiian Islands* (New York, 1968); Ralph S. Kuykendahl, *The Hawaiian Kingdom, 1834–1874: Twenty Critical Years* (Honolulu, 1966); Merze Tate, *The United States and the Kingdom of Hawaii: A Political History* (New Haven, 1965). *Alaskan*, 14 October 1893. An entertaining picture of this aspect of Sitka life may be found in Robert E. Coontz, *From the Mississippi to the Sea* (Philadelphia, 1953), pp. 120 ff. Coontz estimated "real society" to be about one hundred (p. 120).

14. *Alaskan*, 14 October 1893; Collis, *A Woman's Trip*, p. 115.

15. *Alaskan*, 14 October 1893 and 11 April 1890.

16. Andrews, *Sitka*, p. 91. Article on Colonel Kostrometinoff, *Alaska Yukon Magazine*, October 1907, p. 147; Jackson, *Alaska and Missions*, p. 205.

17. *Alaska Appeal*, 1 December 1879.

18. JGB, mf. 4, Brady to Emily L. Gage, 27 May 1901; MsEB.

19. Helpful for appreciating the very real part these pioneers played is Rudolf Glanz, *The Jews in American Alaska, 1869–1880* (New York, 1953). On the Alaska Commercial Company's Jewish leaders see Gerstle Mack, *Lewis and Hannah Gerstle* (New York, 1953). Within a year after Alaska's annexation, Jews were holding religious services at Sitka (Emil Teichmann, *A Journey to Alaska in the Year 1868*, ed. Oskar Teichmann [New York, 1963], p. 199). DeArmond, *Founding of Juneau*, pp. 144, 152; and idem, *Some Names around Juneau*, pp. 7–8. *Alaskan*, 12 August 1899. DeArmond to author, 25 May 1973.

20. JCorr, 25:24, plain statement about Alaska, 21 April 1885.

21. Robert V. Hine, *The American West: An Interpretive History* (Boston, 1973), pp. 326–27.

22. Alaska Governors' Papers, Federal Records Center, NARS, Seattle, Wash. Knapp Box 2, Ivan Petroff to R. P. Porter, 21 October 1890 (hereafter cited as AGP).

23. Charles Hallock, *Our New Alaska; or, The Seward Purchase Vindicated* (New York, 1886), p. 32. A more detailed sketch of this town rivalry is found in Hinckley, *Americanization of Alaska*, pp. 227–41.

24. *Alaskan*, 12 May 1888. Ibid., 30 January 1892.

25. Coontz, *From the Mississippi*, pp. 126–30.

26. *Alaskan*, 30 September 1890. Douglas's *Miner* was absorbed by the *Alaska Miner* in 1897 (James Wickersham, *A Bibliography of Alaskan Literature, 1724–1924* [Cordova, Alaska, 1924], p. 264).

27. JScrap, 18:10, clipping; *Alaskan*, 22 May 1886; ibid., 10 July 1886.

28. Interview with Hugh Brady, 30 June 1962. Wickersham, *Bibliography*, p, 250.

29. Collection of Agnes Shattuck (daughter of Governor Swineford), Juneau, Brady to Swineford, 31 October 1885; JCorr, 14:180, Ball to Jackson, 3 March 1886. JCorr, 14:392, Henry E. Hayden to Jackson, 16 December 1887. *Chicago Tribune*, 23 November 1885.

30. In 1879 Brady, then a missionary, had the satisfaction of seeing his written opinions included in William Gouverneur Morris's *Report upon the Customs*, pp. 78–81. Wickersham, *Bibliography*, p. 265. JScrap, 5:47b, clipping.

31. JCorr, 26:199, Jackson to Edwin Hale Abbott, 19 October 1887; *San Francisco Evening Bulletin*, 7 July 1869; JCorr, 10:181, Tate to Jackson, 9 June 1880.

32. PTS, small booklet, *Constitution and By-Laws of the Society of Alaskan Natural History and Ethnology, Sitka, Alaska*. Ted C. Hinckley, "Sheldon Jackson as a Preserver of Alaska's Native Culture," *Pacific Historical Review* 33 (November 1964): 416–17. Jackson originally conceived of two societies, the second to be primarily concerned with overseeing the museum (JCorr, 26:199, Jackson to Abbott, 19 October 1887). *Alaskan*, 8 October 1887. *Thlinget* (monthly newsletter published at Sitka), January 1909; *North Star*, November 1890. The society's official records are housed in the Sheldon Jackson Museum, Sitka. JGB, mf. 1, A. A. Meyer to Elizabeth, 6 April 1887. *North Star*, January 1890. *Juneau City Mining Record*, 27 January 1894. Minutes of the society of 17 December 1901.

33. CHR, vol. 34, T. C. Jewett to William Windom, 8 June 1889; *Alaska Journal*, 13 May 1893 and 27 January 1894; JGB, mf. 2, report of historical society chairman.

34. *Alaskan*, 16 May and 19 September 1891.

35. Ibid., 21 January 1891 and 27 January 1894; *Alaska Herald*, 19 March 1894.

36. TAP, mf. 2, report of Bureau of Education for 1890, Brady's three-year assignment to Sitka school committee. JCorr, 24:307, Jackson to William T. Harris, 5 April 1890.

37. TAP, mf. 5, "Education in Alaska," exhibit A, teachers' salaries. JCorr, 15:272, William Kelly to Jackson, 17 April 1890.

38. *Alaskan*, 16 August 1890; *North Star*, October 1889.

39. *Alaskan*, 18 February and 16 December 1893. Interview with John and Hugh Brady, 23 June 1962. U.S. Commissioner's docket book, Sitka, 11 July 1889–6 June 1892, United States v. George E. Knapp, 29 July–3 August 1891.

40. JCorr, 16:49, Elizabeth Brady to Mr. and Mrs. Sheldon Jackson, 24 November 1891; ibid., 193–94, Elizabeth Brady to Jackson, 1 August 1892; ibid., p. 293, Brady to Jackson, 11 February 1893. Cassia and Gertrude continued for varying periods as Alaska public school teachers. Sheldon Jackson, *Annual Report of Commissioner of Education* (Washington, D.C., 1891–97). *Alaskan*, 18 November 1899. Fortunately there was a happy ending to the story. Gertrude Patton Knapp was married to J. Sydenham McNair in 1901 (ibid., 30 November 1901).

41. *Alaskan*, 10 September 1892 and 2 April 1898.

CHAPTER SIX

Judge Brady

Alaskan pioneers sought what America's westward-moving citizenry had almost invariably insisted upon. First of all, their territory must be blanketed with its own organic act. Civil officers chosen solely in Washington, D.C., should be dispensed with as quickly as practicable. To block Great Land settlers from enjoying the hallowed right of electing their own representatives, passing their own laws, judging what taxes they should pay—in essence, governing themselves—was intolerable. Alaska required a delegate in Congress to explain the district's unique problems. Finally, statehood must be achieved—again, the sooner the better.[1] Although the stridency of these demands faded after the collapse of the late-sixties Sitka boom, they were still quite audible when John Brady arrived in 1878.

Brady soon understood that, though these recurrent appeals to Congress were reinforced by both constitutional and historic precedent, it was unrealistic to envision all these "political rights" suddenly being granted by legislative legerdemain. Those of his fellow Alaskans who pointed to the precedents of Texas and California needed to consider the meaning of the word *organic*. The Great Land, for all its enormous size, possessed but a fraction of the white population of either Texas or California when they bypassed the traditional territorial stepping-stones to statehood. Could a few thousand American pioneers concentrated in the Alexander Archipelago form the necessary warp and woof from which to weave a state government, much less a commonwealth capable of covering its financial obligations? And what about the fate of the district's native peoples in a premature transition? Were they prepared for citizenship?

Within weeks after his introduction to the Great Land, John had sought some means to check the Ranche's periodic pandemonium. A visit to Wrangell had familiarized him with Deputy Collector I. C. Dennis's employment of Indian police for maintaining public order. On 12 November 1878 John circulated a letter among the people of Sitka: "The bearer, Tom, has frequently asked me to appoint Indian policemen to arrest those who steal, get drunk and fight. . . . I think that it would be well to try the plan for one month. There is no fund to pay such policemen for their services. All those who feel like aiding such a project will please subscribe their names to this paper and the amount opposite which they feel inclined to pay *per week*. The wages will not be over $5.00 per month for each man."[2] Eleven of the capital's whites responded, including Abraham Cohen, George Kostrometinoff, A. T. Whitford, and Mottrom D. Ball.

The ill-starred town government contrived during mid-seventy-nine by Commander Beardslee had not been without its lessons. Some months after its collapse, Mottrom D. Ball, the district's collector of customs and former Confederate cavalry officer, was chosen by a public meeting to "go to Washington in order to urge upon the attention of Congress the necessity of legislation for Alaska."[3] When he arrived in Washington in 1880, Ball joined other such unofficial delegates as Jackson, Dall, Morris, and Brady, all promoting an organic act.[4]

These entreaties were not merely balloons floated by men with inflated egos. As Brady pointed out in 1879, "There are no officers to arrest criminals, though crimes are from time to time committed. Men die in Alaska as well as elsewhere, and some leave property behind them but there is no legal way to take possession of it. . . . there is no way of collecting debts."[5] The following year the *New York Times* declared, "There is no reason why Alaska should not have a local civil government of some kind, even though the sparseness of its population will not warrant the expense of a territorial organization."[6] By 1884 a medley of lobbyists, reinforced by developments in mining, canneries, and tourism, finally spurred a reluctant Congress to grant an organic act.

Among the spurs was the crude, bustling, and always volatile Juneau. Its shooting affrays, lynching parties, and friction with the still testy Chilkats, as well as with occasional British Columbians, caused the district's naval officers repeatedly to urge congressional resolution of Alaska's law-and-order dilemmas. Portland, Seattle, and San Francisco suppliers were equally insistent. So were the nearby missionaries. Juneau's impetuous boosters held a territorial convention to "rightfully appeal for the sanction of their action and the relief of their extremity."[7]

Clearly the August 1881 convention had been some time in planning.

The Pacific Coast Steamship Company seems to have given reduced passage to the delegates, and Governor W. A. Newell of Washington Territory was invited to give an address. It was strictly a Panhandle affair; there were no representatives "from the westward." Wrangell, Sitka, and Juneau sent delegates, but Brady, busy establishing the Sitka Trading Company, was not among them. The Reverend S. Hall Young, representing Wrangell, was chosen secretary of the convention.[8] Certainly Governor Newell's peroration was what the Juneau convention wanted to hear: "I will say in conclusion that if the Government of the United States cannot afford you the usual appliances for the protection of life and liberty, . . . [to] allow you as a free people, to establish a Government of your own . . . it would have been far better for Alaska to have remained under the Russian despotism than be held in its present ungoverned, unprotected helpless and most unfortunate condition."[9] It was frontier bombast, but the delegates loved it.

A year and a half later, a *San Francisco Chronicle* reporter encountered the good-natured, persevering Ball in Washington, D.C., and inquired how far he had advanced Alaska legislation. "Slowly enough," was the colonel's reply. "The Election Committee keeps postponing and postponing waiting for the Committee on Territories to act on the message before them in regard to the bill making Alaska a Territory. . . . I won't be surprised if both are left unacted upon." And then to hearten his Far North friends and supporters, he commented, "I propose, however, to keep knocking at the doors and kicking up a noise until I am admitted or fired out altogether."[10] Ball's cloakroom machinations helped, but it was the massive ground swell of public opinion created by Dr. Jackson that finally won Alaska her 17 May 1884 organic act.

Evidently the tenacity of the Alaskans had angered some of the legislators, for Congress inserted in section 9 of the Organic Act, "nor shall any Delegate be sent to Congress therefrom." Jackson circumvented this restriction by becoming Alaska's general agent for education with his office *at* the nation's capital.[11] Furthermore, on his annual cruises about the district aboard cutters of the U.S. Revenue Marine, he succeeded in visiting the Aleutians and Bering Coast, something the pioneer governors longed to do but were rarely able to accomplish.

"I have put in your name as Commissioner at Sitka," Jackson wrote Brady on 13 June 1884"; if you are appointed do not decline at least until we have had an opportunity of talking it over together." Hall Young wanted Jackson to block "a Catholic or one of these traders or miners" from such preferment. Other citizens advised the general agent on who and who not to recommend to President Chester Arthur for the district's first governor, judge, attorney, marshal, clerk, and four commissioners.[12] Their importunings were wasted; senatorial patronage had to be served. Senators from Nevada probably named the new governor, the veteran Far West politician John H. Kinkead. In 1868 he had served as Sitka's first postmaster. Afterward he had advanced himself from a Nevada businessman to its governor. Ward McAllister of San Francisco became the district judge and Munson C. Hillyer its first marshal. E. W. Haskett of Iowa received the district attorney slot, and Andrew T. Lewis of Illinois became clerk of the court. The only resident of Alaska included in the embryo administration was John G. Brady, commissioner.[13]

Commissioner Brady joined a motley company. In the pages of history, territorial appointees give off a musty aroma. "Spavined old war horses and disgruntled political hacks" is what one scholar calls them.[14] Certainly as far as Alaska was concerned, the negative image has been overdrawn. As a rule her district governors and judges were not seedy opportunists. Burdened by a vast geographical responsibility, a region with sparse settlements dependent on marine transportation, theirs was not an enviable job. Compounding their Sisyphean labors was a dismal lack of communication to the "outside" and a discouraging lack of precedents for administering what the *New York Times* referred to as an "anomaly." According to its organic act, Alaska was henceforth under "The general laws of the State of Oregon now in force . . . so far as the same may be applicable and not in conflict with the provisions of this act or the laws of the United States." In time the inconsistencies, indeed, the impossibilities of trying to apply Oregon's code to the Great Land would become embarrassingly obvious.[15]

News that he had been appointed one of the district's four commissioners doubtless pleased John. The three other commissioners, also appointed on 25 July 1884, were located at Wrangell, Juneau, and Unalaska in the Aleutians. The position of U.S. commissioner was a familiar one across the Far West. Brady quickly discovered that he was expected to be Sitka's probate judge, justice of the peace, land office registrar, notary public, and considerably more.[16] If he expected any thorough elucidation of his duties in the Federal Blue Book, he must surely have been disappointed. This 1884 publication, *Compilation of the Laws of the United States Applicable to the Duties of the Governor, Attorney, Judge, Clerk, Marshall, and Commissioners of the District of Alaska*, contained but eight pages on "laws applicable to duties of commissioners." According to its twenty specific instructions, Judge Brady could administer oaths, take bail and affidavits, imprison or bail offenders of the law, issue warrants for search and arrest, and discharge

90

poor convicts. His location at Alaska's capital enabled him to gain advice and experience by observing the operation of the district court under district judge Ward McAllister. Brady burned midnight oil "reading at the law" and on 6 May 1885 became the fourth person admitted to the bar in Alaska.[17]

Erasing debts in a bankruptcy case, incarcerating a dangerously drunken squaw, and witnessing a thick-skinned hard-rock miner dissolve into tears were among the wretched scenes that quickly matured Sitka's municipal judge. As he passed sentence Brady looked directly into the faces of the condemned, the broken in spirit, the social pariahs. From every indication he found his magisterial robe, if not sackcloth, a wearisome cloak. But this judgeship strengthened his self-confidence and resignation to personal abuse. Elizabeth was astonished at how, despite the "very unkind things" said about him, John could forgive and forget. "I don't see how you can do it," she once commented. "What need to remember those things," he replied, "they did one no harm."[18]

It is easy to make either too much or too little of the violent human behavior manifested throughout the Alexander Archipelago during the years 1867–87. Mercifully Alaska was spared any Indian wars. Yet the military had felt compelled to destroy some Tlingit villages.[19] Recalling his eight and a half years at Wrangell, 1878–86, Colonel R. B. Crittenden declared, "There has been but one murder, and the man who committed the deed was taken by the people and hanged."[20] And in this instance the condemned miner, "Boyd" (he refused to reveal his true identity), had received a jury trial of sorts. What about Juneau's pattern of violence? Here again, for all the bombings and shooting affrays, the actual mortality rate among whites was not high, certainly nothing like the legendary rate of Dodge City or Tombstone. Murderous lynch law fell most heavily on the two Indian villages that straddled Juneau.[21]

What appears to have been a relatively small number of homicides by whites against whites may in part be accounted for by the territory's tiny, fluid settlements scattered over a huge land area, much of it dissected by sea and mountain. The sobering impact of the district's brutal northern climate cannot be overlooked. Many a hostile tough must have headed south after a few years in Alaska's vast continental interior with his overheated masculinity cooled and thankful to be alive.[22] And until Alaska boasted reasonably large, prosperous centers, the professional criminal found little in the northland to attract his talents. Sacramento or Tucson offered numerous ways one could exit after a holdup. The only way out from a Panhandle community was by

boat. Once Alaska's settlement-space-mobility balance got out of kil-
ter—as it later would at Klondike-born Skagway—violent, organized
crime appeared.[23]
   Although Governor Kinkead and his fellow public servants never had
to cope with the likes of Skagway's Soapy Smith gang, they did inherit
an abundance of administrative headaches. For years Congress had
agreed that "it was just and proper" that the citizens of southeastern
Alaska "should have a judiciary."[24] But a judiciary required more than
the handful of civil officials created by the organic act. Sitka's jail was
branded "unfit," and a recent fire in the Custom House had eliminated
an adequate courtroom. No funds existed to pay for the subsistence or
transportation of prisoners; in fact, "The district has no revenue from
taxation, licenses, or any other domestic commerce," moaned Governor
Kinkead.[25]
   In office but a few months, Judge McAllister requested of the *Pinta*'s
commander the use of his brig "as you have so kindly done in other
urgent cases." Otherwise, explained the judge, he would have to release
the prisoners for lack of funds. Captain H. E. Nichols's snippy reply
was correct: "While I consider myself under every obligation to assist
the civil authorities of Alaska in the execution of the laws for the district
government, yet I cannot under any circumstances place myself in the
position assumed by you." And then, in case any doubt lingered as to
what he meant, Nichols stated, "I decline in every particular to be the
pivot on which the success of this new civil government of Alaska shall
swing."[26]
   Kinkead must have wondered if indeed it could swing. Given the
small resident population of naturalized Americans, it was not going
to be easy to impanel many juries. Sitka's lawyers questioned whether
a jury was even legal in Alaska. The Oregon code, now ostensibly in
force, required that, to be a member of a grand or petit jury in a civil
or criminal case, one had to be a taxpayer. Yet neither Congress nor
Alaska's residents had been able to levy an operable tax.[27] Queries to
U.S. attorney general B. H. Brewster seemed to take forever, and his
interpretations were necessarily just that. Although Unalaska was made
a judicial point, an Aleutian litigant carrying his case to the district
court at Sitka traveled far more than the twelve hundred miles separating the two points. No direct transportation existed. Thus a litigant
would have to go and come via San Francisco, a distance of nearly four
thousand miles.[28]
   Judge McAllister must surely have been jolted when he learned that,
within legally dry Alaska, breweries bubbled at both Sitka and Juneau.
Governor Kinkead forthrightly recommended that Congress terminate

the Alaska prohibition fiasco. In its place he urged a system of licensed liquor distributors in order to provide a badly needed source of income for the district while excluding those irresponsible traders who so recklessly bartered the fiery brew among the indigenes. To Brady "high license," as this policy came to be identified, seemed worth considering. Somehow, some way, there must be a system that would inject sanity into the current prohibition folly. To Jackson advocates of "high license" were dangerous men.[29] Actually Kinkead seems to have been a "good, church going Christian"; indeed, his wife had helped initiate a temperance society at Sitka.

It seems evident that Kinkead, McAllister, and Haskett misjudged Jackson. He was physically small, a crusty Puritan, and a leading missionary. If these qualities did not cast him in a dim light before the civil administrators, his exaggerated pronative position was sure to do so. Very few of the Panhandle's "floating population" could comfortably identify themselves with a minister who insisted that the Indian too had rights. On the other hand, the miners easily empathized with the earthy Kinkead. As President Arthur's appointees underrated Jackson's strength, they also overestimated their own.

Governor Kinkead certainly did not itch to have a fight with Jackson. The governor was aware that "some of the Indians at Sitka had become converted and desired to get out of their dirty village and to build houses near the Indian land." Unfortunately, he noted, "the citizens there objected. They sent me a protest signed by themselves. . . . I see no real reason why these Indians should not go there except that the white men do not want them. The whites [primarily Creoles] have absolutely no title to the land."[30]

Since the American occupation the Creoles had sensed that their property and status were slipping away to the Americans. They felt incapable of resisting these encroachments. Envious of the attractive Presbyterian-subsidized, Indian-built cottages adjacent to the training school, the Creoles voiced their resentment to District Attorney Haskett. In January of 1885 Haskett checked the boundary claims of the Sitka Training School and found them to be extensive. Brady had laid out this tract and, with native help, cleared it. "This territory," Haskett wrote the attorney general, is "the only territory adjoining the City of Sitka suitable for residents or other buildings." By that he meant land developed for construction. "The missionaries have taken this entire territory," he fumed, "fenced up the road to the grave yard and are assuming control of all the improvements thereon."[31]

During February and March Haskett appears to have played upon the Creoles' loss of self-esteem by drawing invidious comparisons between them and the local Indians. No doubt he overstated their jux-taposed class standing with the heretofore inferior natives, some of whom were now domiciled in attractive new cottages. Jackson asserted that "two or three public meetings were held and harrangued by the District Attorney until an intense race prejudice was created between the Russians and natives, which made a riot liable at any time."[32] At one of Haskett's meetings Jackson attempted to be heard and was shouted down. At another, Brady attempted to speak and ended up in a fist fight, while Jackson "took to the woods for safety." After a group invaded his office, Jackson took the steamer south.[33]

By himself Haskett probably could not have produced the crisis that overtook the Kinkead government. Judge McAllister, a competent and well-connected San Francisco attorney, no doubt looked upon his Alaska service as more of a sacrifice than a public duty. Political preferment was flattering, but Sitka had neither Palace Hotel nor Cliff House. During March of 1885, with court not in session at either Sitka or Wrangell, McAllister left the district for a brief period. Upon his return aboard the same vessel that took Jackson south, he discovered that Haskett had kicked over a beehive.[34]

Whether or not the judge had originally abetted Haskett's verbal and legal assault on the Sitka Training School is not easy to discern. "The people despise the missionaries," was the attorney's caustic comment. One can imagine Brady's reaction. Clearly there was no love lost between Haskett and Jackson. In a letter to President Grover Cleveland, Jackson described Alaska's first district attorney as "an uneducated man, rowdyish in his manner, vulgar and obscene in his conversation, low in his tastes; spending much of his time in saloons, a gambler and confirmed drunkard with but little knowledge of the law."[35]

During Judge McAllister's absence the district attorney had been required to appear before Commissioner Brady on charges of assault and battery. Although "the case was compromised," there seemed no way to quiet Haskett's anger at the missionaries. McAllister agreed with the district attorney that the Sitka Training School's boarding pupil contract verged on indentured servitude. "Slavery," Haskett called it. He adamantly refused to accept Brady's explanation for the contract: unless the native children were removed from their parents for five years there could be no real implanting of American values. Haskett now convinced two Sitka Indians to withdraw their child. But when he asked Brady to institute legal action and "free" the Indian girl, John "utterly refused to issue the writ, or act in the matter in any way whatsoever."[36] A. J. Davis, the current director of the training school, then wrote Jackson what happened: "You will be surprised and grieved to learn that we have lost more than half of our children. A spirit of persecution seems to have seized some of the people, including several officials of the civil government. . . . The District Attorney has been violent and will continue to cause us further trouble. . . . our efforts are nobly seconded by Mr. Lewis [Clerk of the Court] and Mr. Brady."[37] Judge McAllister dissolved the injunction when it came before him. Why is not clear. Very likely some Sitkans reminded him that it was one thing to stir up a group of passive Creoles but quite another to incite Indians who six years earlier had threatened to burn the capital. Taking no chances, Sitka's teachers posted an extra night watch over their campus.[38]

Brady watched all of this with mounting fury. It was just as well that he was in and out of town on business matters, for as his behavior at the school meeting reminded him, the fuse to his temper was shorter than he cared to admit. His opinion of McAllister was just a few notches above that of Haskett. On Alaska's judge the *Chicago Tribune* quoted Brady: "His legal experience was . . . a brief term as Assistant United States District Attorney at San Francisco. His father, a New York caterer, was an intimate friend of Attorney-General Brewster, and Brewster insisted on the appointment. He was less than 30 years old, was an eastern dude and Anglomaniac, and has been a short time on the Pacific, and was destitute on almost every attribute which would entitle him to the supreme control of the judicial . . . affairs of a great, half-civilized Territory." Brady's animus for McAllister was personal as well as professional. "With his little velvet jacket, high collar, gloves and dandy cane," John jested, "I tell you he was a rare curiosity in Sitka."[39]

After watching the Haskett-McAllister assault on the school, Lt. T. Dix Bolles, executive officer of the *Pinta*, made a sworn statement: "The District Attorney, an intemperate man, even openly by words incited the Russians and Indians to overt acts of violence and arson. The course of Judge McAllister in permitting a woman—not the mother of the child—to take the child away from the school where its parents had placed it . . . led to a loss of almost one-half of the scholars, many of them young girls, who represented to their parents just so much coin by the sale of their virtue."[40] Consequences of the furor were not restricted to Sitka. A missionary among the Chilkat, two hundred miles distant, reported: "When the word reached our people that 'the new white men' (Government officials) said the teachers were 'no good,' that they maltreated the children under their care, 'starved, beat and witched them to death,' it was believed. Our people became insolent and unteachable, suspicious and contemptuous toward us. . . . Hooch-

ALASKAN JOHN G. BRADY

inoo making became for the first time in the history of our mission open
and fashionable. Men women and children were drunk. . . . it became
necessary to suspend the mission work at Haines."⁴¹

The climax was reached in May when a grand jury composed of
numerous Creoles brought a list of indictments against Jackson. For
a few hours even Alaska's general agent for education found himself
behind bars. By hindsight the political ramifications of the struggle do
credit to Gilbert and Sullivan. Incoming president Grover Cleveland
swept out all of the officials except Jackson, Brady, and Lewis.⁴² The
Great Land had a new set of leaders, but with a Democratic party
pedigree. To erase animosities and bid a fond farewell to the deposed
Republicans, Sitka held a costume ball. Brady came clad in torn sheets,
his beard whitened, a bent cane in one hand and a lantern in the other.
When the revelers inquired who he represented, Brady walked up to
the late district judge, looked him in the face, and cracked, "Diogenes
looking for an honest man."⁴³

Evidently the 1885 educational rupture left no permanent scars on
native schooling throughout the archipelago. In fact, the triumph definitely increased the general agent's prestige. The victory may be said
to have launched what later came to be called "the Presbyterian hierarchy." For Brady it was an education in the rough-and-tumble of
Western politics.

The appointment of Alaska's second governor, Democrat Alfred P.
Swineford of Michigan, renewed the district gripe that their territory
was run by "carpetbaggers." This indictment conveniently overlooked
the fact that virtually every non-Creole white was an opportunistic
latecomer to Alaska. Many years later, after his own governorship had
ended, Brady wrote that the 1884 appointees were "followed by a lot
of hangers-on from all quarters, anxious for pickings. Alaska was then
made a dumping ground for politicians, and has continued to be such
to the present day, as the history of federal appointments will prove."⁴⁴
His sweeping generalization, with its negative imputations, was as unfair
as another common accusation that would also take root: that the Presbyterian hierarchy ran Alaska and was to blame for the territory's lack
of progress. Although palpable exaggerations, both of these oft-made
charges gained public credence in the district. By the mid-nineties they
had become a part of Alaska's political mythology, the sententious
carpetbagger shibboleth even gaining currency among scholars.⁴⁵

Not long after Brady arrived in the district, a group of Portland
businessmen erected a ten-stamp mill at Silver Bay, twelve miles south
of Sitka. In the early seventies some soldiers stationed at Sitka had
struck pay dirt there. "At first water power was tried and then steam,"

Brady later recalled. "Wherever there was a wrong way to do a thing in the management that way was followed." In 1880, poorer of purse but wiser in the ways of Western mining, the Oregonians shut down the Stewart mine. Three years later their claim was jumped, and there matters stood for some years.[46] Sitkans watched these vacillations intently. If the Silver Bay diggings would boom, so must Sitka.

Nicholas Haley was one of the soldiers who labored so hard to scratch riches from the mountains surrounding Silver Bay. Brady concluded that he was a "fanatic," but confessed, "Fortune may yet smile upon him for his strength of purpose."[47] Fortune was not so kind. "Nicholas toiled on year after year, keeping up his assessments and living on hopes until at last he passed over the Great Divide to a Better Digging." The equally persistent miner Edmund Bean talked Brady into gambling some of his scarce capital in a development they labeled "The Great Eastern." As an archipelago merchant, Brady had found it good business to become a competent assayer, and the Great Eastern glittered with promise. Later Brady's father-in-law, as well as Cassia and Gertrude, filed claims at Silver Bay. But, as one correspondent observed, "The fortunes of Silver Bay mines have waxed and waned. . . . Abandoned mills, wharves, and buildings are going to ruin, trails and wagon roads are overgrown, and actual mining is not being carried on anywhere in the Sitkan district."[48] After the turn of the century, a geologist had to admit that "none of the properties at Silver Bay have been put on a productive basis. . . . some remarkable mining failures have taken place on Baranof Island."[49]

Little wonder, then, that in 1885 Sitkans, too many of whom had vainly sought gold on Silver Bay's nearby ledges, took heart. To the north on Douglas Island, a large corporation, armed not with shovel and pick but with enormous extraction and refining machines, resolved to secure a profit from the site's low-grade ore. Heretofore gold in this Paris Lode had proved too thinly scattered to fill a single miner's poke. Beginning in 1885, and continuing until well into the next century, bullion bricks became a regular export from the Juneau-Douglas region. By 1900 the complex of mines facing Gastineau Channel, collectively identified as the Treadwell Mines, was the largest operation of its kind in the world, yielding an annual return running to hundreds of thousands of dollars.[50]

Andrew T. Lewis, clerk of the district court and close friend of John's, recalled that the patent for the Treadwell mining property "was the first to be issued in the territory by the new civil government." Lewis received the fee properly enough; "however there was some question raised by Government officials as to his right to receive money in such transactions." Two and a half years passed before he got his money. Obtaining payment from Washington bureaucrats could be as difficult as extracting Douglas Island gold.[51]

Cases paraded before Judge Brady's bench usually received more immediate resolution. He had been granted the powers, both civil and criminal, permitted a justice of the peace under the general laws of Oregon. The organic act limited his jurisdiction "in civil cases to two hundred dollars or more, and in any criminal case" to "a fine of more than one hundred dollars."[52] John's compensation depended on the fees he collected. They must have been minimal, for Judge Brady's magisterial obligations were usually light; the greater portion of his working hours continued to be taken up with the Sitka Trading Company. Because most of his cases dealt with Creoles and Indians, Brady wisely gave over his Monday evenings to instruction in both Russian and Tlingit. Tillie Paul, a native mission worker, found him an eager student, for though his Chinook jargon, the lingua franca along the Northwest Coast, might suffice when out on the *Leo*, it hardly fitted courtroom precision. Besides, it annoyed John to have to depend on his interpreter, George Kostrometinoff.[53]

Commissioner Brady's first case was typical of so many that would follow: a local white was charged with "selling malt liquors to Indians." In this instance the Caucasian was Michael Travers, a Sitka personality who had arrived with the army and then remained behind as a "squaw man" and town nonconformist. If Travers had confined his liquor exchanges to his current Indian companions, he probably would have remained out of jail. But under the influence, he could not tell a red friend from Sitka's Indian policeman. The first time he stood before Brady, he was given a few months to dry out in Sitka's jail.[54] Regrettably, the alcoholic remained a familiar figure in Sitka's court.

Creoles who came before Brady were generally charged with assault, petty larceny, or trafficking in liquor.[55] "Some eleven Indians living in the same house as Anna Shoomahoff" accused her of "keeping a dreadful house." "After examining this case," John reported, "I discharged Anna after warning her that if again [she came] before me I would send her to jail. She appears to have 3 little children to support."[56] A month later Anna was accused of "throwing stones at a little Indian boy and cutting his head." Because the boy was a nephew of the town's Indian policeman, the venerated Chief Annahootz, Brady felt required to fine her ten dollars. Anna must have had a temper. Another woman came before him and charged Anna with assault. After he investigated the circumstances, Brady informed the plaintiff, "The charges against said defendant Anna Shumakoff, in said complaint are . . . prompted

by jealousy. It is therefore ordered that said defendant be discharged."
Anna may have appreciated Brady's Solomonic wisdom and also, it
seems, the excitement of the court proceedings. Before long *she* was
bringing charges against Yankees for selling liquor to the Indians.[57]

Alaska's judicial processes invariably favored the "American element." Both their cultural affinity with employees of the court and
their familiarity with its procedures assured the frontiersmen of such
an edge. Nevertheless, the latter's roughneck habits too frequently discredited their law-abiding pretensions. Barton Atkins, Cleveland's appointee as U.S. marshal, nearly had his head blown off by an infuriated
Byron Cowles toting a double-barreled shotgun. Brady passed the as-
sault-with-a-deadly-weapon case on to the district court—such maniacal
behavior required plenty of cooling-off time.[58] When author Frank
Myers refused to retract a story printed in the *Alaskan*, a fistfight
exploded in the newspaper's front office. Brady gave up on the case
after district attorney Mottrom D. Ball alleged that the fight did "not
come within his jurisdiction." At least that was how it was recorded in
the commissioner's docket book. Possibly Judge Brady concluded that
Myers's sharp-tongued journalism was needed in Sitka, for like most
small towns, Sitka tended to be parochial, if not obtusely protective.[59]

Eliza R. Scidmore, a widely traveled and discerning author, wrote
that in Alaska "no cloud of witnesses can convince a jury that any one
has stolen timber from the public domain; nor would a grand jury
convict any one of selling or smuggling intoxicating liquors. Justice can
be deaf and dumb as well as blind when there is no other resource
against laws which nineteenth-twentieths of the citizens oppose."[60] No
nonwhites and only a relatively few Creoles seem to have sat on Panhandle juries. During August of 1886 the *Alaskan* evidenced Sitka's
prevailing ethnocentrism.

> John Chinaman . . . has become a figure in our judicial proceedings,
> and the striking ceremony (no pun intended) of shivering the saucer has
> been exhibited for the purpose of binding the Celestial conscience to the
> utterance of the truth, the whole truth, and nothing but the truth. . . .
> One Chinaman has been convicted before Justice Brady of an assault,
> and compelled to fork over . . . the sum of twenty-five dollars to help
> support the government they are menacing with overthrow and another
> has been sent to court . . . [for] selling whisky to a blarsted heathen
> siwash.[61]

That same month anti-Chinese violence eminently more alarming
than such journalistic sinophobia erupted. In an attempt to cut his costs
and increase production, mine superintendent John Treadwell imported
Chinese labor.[62] His supposition proved correct: the Orientals outpro-

duced both their white and red counterparts. What Treadwell failed to consider was that many of the territory's itinerant prospectors had also imported their "Chinese must go" bigotry. In February a bomb blast shook the Chinese quarters at Juneau. Governor Swineford hurried north to investigate. "The explosion," he informed his chief, secretary of the interior L. Q. C. Lamar, "was undoubtedly the work of placer miners and prospectors, who being unable to pursue their calling during the months of December, January, and February, flock into town, and being unused to restraint are prone to indulge in all manner of excesses." He reminded Lamar that the Juneau-Douglas locale was a "thousand miles beyond the reach of telegraph or railway, and when the emergency arises, we will be perfectly helpless during the two months that would necessarily elapse before a response could be had to call for military aid." The governor urged that some soldiers be stationed at Juneau by fall at the latest.[63]

Swineford certainly knew the miner temperament. On 6 August a large crowd of miners concentrated at the Douglas Island works and shouted for the immediate expulsion of Treadwell's "damn coolies." Although the Asians were willing to fight, their superintendent refused to arm them. Treadwell wisely, if seethingly, bent to mob rule. Eighty-six Chinese were crammed into two schooners and dispatched southward. By the time Swineford and Commissioner Brady arrived at Juneau, the Chinese had been evicted.[64] Governor Swineford angrily condemned the rioters and swore that the Chinese would return to their Douglas Island works. To protect them he requested the support of navy commander Nichols, his *Pinta*, and especially a portion of his marine guard. Once again Nichols stubbornly refused to assist the civil authorites in a moment of great need, claiming that Juneau's housing was inadequate for the marines. Not until Swineford contacted Washington and the secretary of the navy did the *Pinta* steam north. By that time the Chinese were scattered. "Nichols is a pompous, brainless coxcomb," Swineford fumed to the secretary of the interior, "infatuated with the gaieties of Sitkan society and cannot be depended upon."[65] Douglas and Juneau had joined a shameful list of western communities: Seattle, Tacoma, Rock Springs, Denver, and too many others during the eighties had gained notoriety eradicating the "Chinese threat." Brady's immediate reaction to the wretched affair seems to have been a stunned silence.

For almost five years John Brady served as Sitka's commissioner. His judicial chores consisted of a miscellany of virtually everything related to Alaska's inhabitants. Estate litigation expanded to such a degree that he decided to sit as probate judge on the first Monday of each month.[66] Duty as Alaska's ex officio land registrar alerted him to the steady increase of East Coast investors in the territory's mineral prospects. During October 1888 Brady gave formal notice, as obliged to do by law, of Thomas S. Nowell's file for a land patent. Nowell, president of the Juneau Placer mining Company, proved to be a rarity: an eastern speculator who, after a business disaster in Boston, came to Alaska (once or twice each year) and by shrewd mining transactions pyramided a small fortune. Before he finished, the one-time wholesale shoe dealer speculated with such mining and milling companies as the Ophir Gold Mining Company, the Berners Bay Mining and Milling Company, and the Alaska Nowell Gold Mining Company.[67]

Two matters passed before Brady's bench that served to remind him that Alaska was immensely larger than its southeastern littoral. Both cases dealt with violence against living creatures. In September of 1887 Frank Fuller, the accused murderer of Roman Catholic bishop Charles John Seghers, appeared for preliminary examination. It was a dual tragedy. Bishop Seghers, approaching the peak of his career and eager to lay the groundwork for Catholic missions in Alaska's vast interior, had been shot to death at a remote campsite on the Yukon River.[68] Fuller was the killer, but the environment was an accessory. Marooned in a cruel white hell, Fuller had lost his mind. Bishop Seghers became the victim of Fuller's dementia. After the accused provided Commissioner Brady with some vague details of the crime, his case moved up to the district court.[69] "Fuller is a good-looking young man with mild blue eyes and light hair," Brady commented not long afterward, "the last person you would suspect of being a murderer."[70] Brady had yet to tour the Great Land's gigantic Yukon Valley. Later he would be awed by how easily it could break even the toughest of men.

Killing of quite a different type riveted American attention on its northern province during 1886. Prohibited from slaughtering seals on the Pribilof Islands and determined to lay their hands on the fur seal profits being garnered by the Alaska Commercial Company, a number of pelagic hunters irresponsibly killed the animals at sea. Fearful that this would lead to the destruction of the Pribilof seals, federal authorities precipitously seized four of the poaching vessels, one of which was American, the other three Canadian. These craft had been operating well outside U.S. territorial waters when they were boarded by men from the U.S.R.M.C. *Corwin*. All four of the sealers were forced to go to Unalaska. Forthwith the affair was catapulted into world headlines.[71]

Commissioner Brady can hardly have grasped the enormousness of the conservation challenge that historical hindsight now affords. After the *Corwin*'s captain swore out complaints, Judge Brady issued the

View from Baranov Hill looking northwest. Anchored in Sitka's harbor are two historic vessels—in the foreground the schooner *Leo*, and with the smokestack the U.S.S. *Pinta*; ca. 1889. (Reproduced by permission of The Huntington Library, San Marino, California.)

necessary warrants "for taking into custody the masters and mates of the seized vessels." Being a small businessman, a considerable portion of whose income came from maritime labors, Brady doubtless sympathized with the half-angry, half-dispirited captains who were paraded into his courtroom. The label "fur seal pirates" was obviously a newspaperman's concoction. One of the skippers, terribly morose over his capture, slit his throat with a razor while awaiting trial.[72] Ultimately the proceedings begun in Brady's court would call forth a large U.S. naval police force and would only finally be resolved by an international tribunal in which were represented Britain, America, Japan, and Russia as well.[73]

Sitkans watched these events, but merely as distant spectators. Judge Brady was far more aroused over another indigenous creature in danger of extinction: Alaska's natives. Repeatedly Brady did what he could as local migistrate to shore up native dignity and hope. But he did not discount their transgressions. Whenever the northwest Coast Indian indulged in lawless behavior, Judge Brady, however reluctantly, tried to make the punishment fit the crime. Attempting to communicate in Tlingit was exasperating, but it did emphasize his respect for their culture.

In 1880, while formulating Alaska's organic act, Congressman Henry L. Muldrow revealed America's common ignorance of Alaskans and America's prevailing ethnocentrism. In a report from the Committee on the Territories, Muldrow wrote, "Any one at all acquainted with Indians and their life will at once admit the futility of . . . courts of justice or trials by jury. . . . It is the 250 white citizens of Alaska only who are deprived of those legal rights and privileges and protection that the committee must keep in mind."[74] But what about Alaska's Indians who already lived in clapboard homes, sent their youngsters to mission schools, worked for the canneries and shipping companies, had replaced Treadwell's Chinese, and cheered Old Glory on Independence Day? Did they not deserve due process? Brady believed that they did.

Among Panhandle natives none had a more belligerent reputation than the Chilkat Indians who resided northeast of Juneau. In 1886 a group of them pugnaciously compelled Bishop Seghers, then about to enter the interior on his fatal mission, to pay an excessive sum for their packing service. Miners had repeatedly complained that the Chilkats' fees were exorbitant. Swineford, after collecting a Sitka posse, steamed up to the Chilkat country to end such monopolistic extractions. Once there, he lured Chief Klanat aboard the *Idaho* and promptly returned to the capital with the protesting native as his prisoner. Hauled before Commissioner Brady, Klanat was immediately released. The governor,

Brady snapped, had broken the law. He should have first secured a warrant for the chief's arrest.[75]

Quite as damaging as the habit of classifying all Indians alike was the tradition of distrust between red and white Alaskans. One missionary to the Tlingits remembered that "Among white people of Alaska the natives have the reputation of having little regard for the truth. Their testimony in court, unless corroborated by the testimony of a white person will not be considered by the average juryman." Too many were prone to believe the worst of the Indian, but "it is safe to say that as many natives have been killed by white men as white people killed by them."[76] Judge Brady quickly recognized that Sitka's natives, like New York City's poor, perpetrated far more crimes on each other than they ever did on the town's established citizens.

Witchcraft among Alaskan natives was no joking matter. One of John's earliest cases concerned a woman who insisted that her brother had been bewitched. After a shaman at Killisnoo confirmed her worst fears, Brady had the three principals brought before him. He required the "woman who caused the trouble . . . to give a deed to her house as security to keep the peace for a year." Another time an old Indian woman commonly denounced as a witch was viewed as the party whose incantations had killed a man's daughter. Alone in the world, depressed at being a social outcast, "She tried to cut her throat. Very old and has no one to protect her," Brady noted. He admonished the bereaved father to be careful whom he accused. To prevent any further misuse of his tongue, the embittered parent was forced to deposit with the court two camphorwood trunks, ten blankets, and one button blanket.[77]

As with the Creole poor, a majority of the Indian cases dealt with minor thefts, assaults, or some form of breaking the public peace. Indian policeman Chief Annahootz had few compunctions about arresting Ranche inhabitants who stubbornly refused to stop screaming whenever they became inebriated. Indians, like convicted whites, had the option of paying a fine or going to jail. Unlike the whites, most chose imprisonment. Their average sentence seems to have been between two and eight weeks. Prisoners were exercised by patching streets and repairing sidewalks. Whenever good behavior or the dictates of humanity justified the reduction of incarceration, Swineford and Brady seem to have been glad to do so.[78]

Certainly the Indian was acutely conscious that it was white man's law and white man's justice. Nevertheless, thievery was a crime with no color line, and after Chee-tee-teek stole food from the training school, she got a month in jail. "Charley" admitted that he had robbed one of his peers and was given a sentence of three months behind bars. When Yas-touch encouraged a student to escape the confines of the classroom for the freedom of the forest, Brady imposed a week's imprisonment on Yas-touch; the seductive charms of Mother Nature could not be taken lightly among Tlingit students.[79] There were moments when the judge appreciated the superiority of native cultural rubrics. Given Alaska's climate, it was difficult to defend the traditional "decent Christian burial." Northwest Coast cremation was eminently more practical. Unfortunately, the commissioner's docket does not clarify what his final decision was in an angry dispute between different Indian groups over the disposal of a deceased Ranche inhabitant.[80]

One thing is glaringly clear. Many of those hailed before Sitka's commissioner could have avoided the unpleasant experience had they denied themselves the bottle. Brady, unlike the Patton girls, was no teetotaler: whenever a doctor recommended a spirituous drink as tonic for a cold or fever, Brady had no difficulty subscribing to the remedy. Some of his neighbors chuckled at the effect of alcoholic beverages on the natives, but Brady saw little that was humorous. The *Alaskan* reported that the "charge against Charles Schaeffer first sergeant of the Marine Corps, of supplying intoxicating liquors to 'Lucy' an Indian woman, whereby she came to her death, was held before Commissioner Brady. . . . A post mortem examination of the remains . . . showed that death ensued from failure of heart's action, brought on by excessive drinking of alcohol."[81] Brady placed Schaeffer in jail, awaiting trial in the district court. Katz-Kay-ish also became wildly drunk in the company of another Indian woman. In this instance a knife became the murder weapon. There was a pathetic truth in the Tlingit's appeal to Judge Brady: "It was not me that killed this woman, it was whiskey. I did not know what I was doing. Next morning all the Indians were sorry and told me what I had done I paid ten and twenty blankets, two guns and shirts. Woman was related to my wife. White men do same thing. I am willing to be punished—have been bad man but will never be bad any more."[82] Katz-Kay-ish's case was also too serious to be resolved by the commissioner's court.

Fortunately the bulk of the cases involving liquor did not result in homicide. For "drunkenness and disturbing the peace," Kahkeitch was "sentenced to jail in Sitka at hard labor for 20 days." For "gross drunkenness" Kla-sha was "to be confined in the jail at Sitka at hard labor for the period of 30 days." Elias Rankin received "two months hard labor in the jail at Sitka" for selling liquor to Indians. In addition to Brady's lectures on the evils of hoochinoo, jail sentences, fines, and penal labor, he even resorted to a temperance weapon. One educated native was required to swear in writing that he would not use any intoxicating liquor for a period of six months.[83] On 15 April 1889 Judge Brady adjudicated his last case: W. Bolshanin had been apprehended outside Alga Shmakoff's home "calling her by name at the hour of 2 am."[84] Of the approximately two hundred cases he had heard, at least the last one was relieved by a touch of levity.

1. The paramount study detailing the drive for full territorial government is Jeannette Paddock Nichols, *Alaska: A History of Its Administration, Exploitation, and Industrial Development during Its First Half-Century under the Rule of the United States* (Cleveland, 1924). Nichols's meticulous scholarship has been of immense assistance to the author. Also useful are Ernest Gruening, *The State of Alaska* (New York, 1954); and George Washington Spicer, *The Constitutional Status and Government of Alaska*, Johns Hopkins University Studies in History and Political Science, vol. 45 (Baltimore, 1927).

2. JGB, Brady diary for 1878, 18 March entry; JGB, unfiled, Brady to the people of Sitka, 12 November 1878.

3. Morris, *Report upon the Customs*, p. 83; *Alaska Appeal*, 15 February 1880. Beardslee, *Affairs in Alaska*, p. 25.

4. *Congressional Record*, 46th Cong., 2d sess., 12 January 1880, p. 275; *National Republican*, 16 April 1880.

5. *Alaska Appeal*, 6 March 1879.

6. *New York Times*, 9 February 1880.

7. DeArmond, *Some Names around Juneau*, pp. 26–27. House, *Report of United States Naval Officers*, 47th Cong., 1st sess., Exec. Doc. 81, 24 February 1881, pp. 27 ff. *San Francisco Chronicle*, 25 and 26 May 1881; *Portland Oregonian*, 16 January and 16 March 1882.

8. *San Francisco Evening Bulletin*, 26 August 1881; Young, *Hall Young*, pp. 258–59.

9. *San Francisco Evening Bulletin*, 26 August 1881.

10. *Alta California*, 23 September 1881. JGB, unfiled, "Brief of Argument for Admission of M. D. Ball as Delegate from Alaska in the 47th Congress." *San Francisco Chronicle*, 4 January 1883. The Forty-seventh Congress was not kind to Ball. After proposing to pay him $4,665.00 for "furthering legislation for said Territory," it ultimately reimbursed him nothing (Mottrom D. Ball Papers, Beinecke Library, Yale University; see his note scribbled on bottom of House Resolution No. 366, 47th Cong., 2d sess., Report No. 1988, 28 February 1883).

11. For the Senate's debate on S.153 (Organic Act), see *Congressional Record*, 48th Cong., 1st sess., 21–25 January 1884, pp. 527–31, 564–69, 593–602; Nichols, *Alaska*, pp. 71–82; Hinckley, "Sheldon Jackson, Presbyterian Lobbyist," pp. 3–23. Nichols, *Alaska*, pp. 411–17, contains a copy of the Organic Act, as does Fred F. Barker, comp., *Compilation of the Acts of Congress and Treaties Related to Alaska from March 30, 1867 to March 3, 1905* (Washington, D.C., 1906), pp. 25–30.

12. JGB, unfiled, Jackson to Brady, 13 June 1884. *Congressional Record*, 48th Cong., 1st sess., index to vol. 15, pp. 7–8. JCorr, 12:115; Young to Jackson, 16 March 1882; ibid., 11:284, John Foster to Jackson, 31 October 1881; ibid., 13:341, Brady to Jackson, 7 April 1884.

13. James W. Hulse, *The Nevada Adventure: A History* (Reno, 1965), pp. 120–22. *San Francisco Evening Bulletin*, 30 July 1884; Joseph G. Cannon to Andrew T. Lewis,

7 July 1884, Andrew T. Lewis Papers, University of Alaska, College, Alaska (hereafter cited as ATLewis).

14. Clark C. Spence, "The Territorial Officers of Montana, 1864–1889," *Pacific Historical Review* 30 (May 1961): 123–24. Vital for an understanding of territorial government is Earl S. Pomeroy, *The Territories and the United States, 1861–1890: Studies in Colonial Administration* (Philadelphia, 1947). Also insightful are the more recent studies: Jack E. Eblen, *The First and Second United States Empires: Governors and Territorial Government, 1784–1912* (Pittsburgh, 1968); idem, "Status, Mobility, and Empire: The Territorial Governors, 1869–90," *Pacific Northwest Quarterly* 60 (July 1969): 145–53; and Kenneth N. Owens, "Pattern and Structure in Western Territorial Politics," in John Porter Bloom, ed., *The American Territorial System* (Athens, Ohio, 1973), pp. 161–79.

15. Gruening, *State of Alaska*, chaps. 8 and 9. *New York Times*, 9 February 1880; Barker, *Compilation*, p. 9; Spicer, *Constitutional Status*, pp. 57–58.

16. *Rules of Practice of the District Court of the United States for the District of Alaska* [adopted 27 September 1890, revised 2 March 1896] (Sitka, 1896); JScrap, 17:27, clipping.

17. Arthur K. Delaney, *Alaska Bar Association and Sketch of Judiciary* (San Francisco, 1901), p. 21, lists the date of Brady's admission to the bar as October 1885. Probably the date used here is correct (it is listed in *Rules of Practice*, p. 2).

18. JGB, Elizabeth Brady diary for 1887, 15 April entry.

19. In 1869 the army burned three Tlingit villages and shelled the native village at Wrangell. A combined force of the navy, revenue marines, and marines burned Angoon in 1882. In each instance, it can be argued, the destruction may have checked future native violence. It is significant that the military carefully avoided taking human life. At least the violence against property was disciplined violence. *New York Times*, 25 April 1869; U.S., Congress, Senate, *Bombardment of Indian Village at Wrangel, Alaska*, 41st Cong., 2d sess., Exec. Doc. 6, 21 March 1870. U.S., Congress, House, *Shelling of an Indian Village in Alaska*, 47th Cong., 2d sess., Exec. Doc. 9, 21 December 1882; and Beardslee, *Affairs in Alaska*, part 2. Ted C. Hinckley, "Punitive Action at Angoon," *Alaska Sportsman*, January 1963, pp. 8 ff., and February 1963, pp. 14 ff.

20. R. B. Crittenden MS, Bancroft Library, University of California, Berkeley, California.

21. *San Francisco Chronicle*, 4 January 1879. Robert R. Dykstra, *The Cattle Towns* (New York, 1968), p. 146. Dykstra's chapter 3, in fact, discredits the popular image of exuberant homicide in the cattle towns.

22. For a contemporary's candid recounting of how harsh that interior was, see W. H. Pierce, *Thirteen Years of Travel and Exploration in Alaska*, ed. Prof. and Mrs. J. H. Garruth (Lawrence, Kans., 1890).

23. A stimulating essay on Western violence is Joe B. Frantz, "The Frontier Tradition: An Invitation to Violence," in *Violence in America, Historical and Comparative Perspectives: A Report to the National Commission on the Causes and Prevention of Violence, June 1969*, ed. Hugh Davis Graham and Ted Robert Gurr (New York, 1969), pp. 119–43. Also useful are John W. Caughey's *Their Majesties, the Mob* (Chicago, 1969) and W. Eugene Hollon's *Frontier Violence: Another Look* (New York, 1974).

24. U.S., Congress, House, *Courts of Justice in Alaska*, 46th Cong., 2d sess., Exec. Report No. 754, 6 April 1880, p. 3.

25. U.S., Congress, House, *Civil Government of Alaska*, 48th Cong., 2d sess., Exec. Doc. 227, 16 February 1885, pp. 2–3; U.S., Congrerss, House, *Court-Houses and Jails in Alaska*, 48th Cong., 2d sess., Exec. Doc. 249, 23 February 1885, pp. 1–2.

26. House, *Civil Government of Alaska*, pp. 3–4.

27. Gruening, *State of Alaska*, p. 58.

28. ATLewis, Haskett to Brewster, 10 January 1885. Spice, *Constitutional Status*, pp. 51–52. John H. Kinkead, *Annual Report of the Governor of Alaska, 1884* (Washington, D.C., 1884), p. 5.

29. John G. Brady, *Annual Report of the Governor of Alaska, 1898* (Washington, D.C., 1898), pp. 181–98, contains a well-documented summary of this protracted and costly problem. In 1869–70 Kinkead had fallen afoul of the territory's liquor prohibition. *Alaska Herald*, 9 February 1870. Kinkead, *Annual Report, 1884*, p. 643.

30. JCorr, 24:15, notes on Alaska (furnished by Governor Kinkead), 1885.

31. ATLewis, Haskett to Brewster, 10 January 1885.

32. JCorr, 14:50c, Jackson to Grover Cleveland, 3 April 1885; PTS, Alaska schools, 1:327, Jackson to H. Goode, 13 August 1885.

33. *Victoria Standard*, 26 June 1885.

34. One side of this quarrel is detailed in Sheldon Jackson, *A Statement of Facts Concerning the Difficulties at Sitka, Alaska, in 1885* (Washington, D.C., 1886).

35. JCorr, 14:50c, Jackson to Cleveland, 3 April 1885.

36. Ibid., p. 176, Jackson to L. Q. C. Lamar, 8 March 1886; ATLewis, Haskett to Brewster, 25 March 1885.

37. JCorr, 14:35, A. J. Davis to Jackson, 10 April 1885.

38. Ibid., 26:4, Jackson to Cleveland, 17 June 1885.

39. *Chicago Tribune*, 23 November 1885.

40. Jackson, *Statement*, p. 16.

41. Ibid., p. 18.

42. National Archives, Washington, D.C., unfiled correspondence, Department of the Interior, Alaska education, grand jury May term 1885; and ibid., petition to the superintendent of the Bureau of Education, 16 June 1885. *Portland Standard*, 11 September 1885. JCorr, 14:99, A. L. Palmer to E. B. Cobb, 27 August 1885.

43. Interview with John and Hugh Brady 23 June 1962. In 1886 Sitka missionary teachers had their five-year pupil contract upheld. (*Alaskan*, 3 April 1886).

44. John G. Brady, "The Mal-Administration of Affairs in Alaska," *Commerce and Industries*, September 1911, p. 113.

45. David Starr Jordan, "Colonial Lessons of Alaska," *Atlantic Monthly*, November 1898, p. 579; Nichols, *Alaska*, pp. 149–50.

46. John G. Brady, *Annual Report of the Governor of Alaska, 1900* (Washington, D.C., 1900), pp. 25–26. *West Shore*, May 1879, p. 166.

47. JGB, mf. 2, diary for 1878, 18 March entry.

48. Andrews, *Sitka*, p. 113. *Alaska Appeal*, 30 October 1879. Ibid., 1 December 1879; Hugh Brady to author, 15 December 1969; and *Alaskan*, 27 August 1887. E. Ruhamah Scidmore, "Alaska's Mining Regions," *Harper's Weekly*, 14 May 1892, p. 466.

49. Adolph Knopf, *The Sitka Mining District*, U.S. Geological Survey Bulletin 504 (Washington, D.C., 1912), p. 8. Horatio C. Burchard, *Annual Report of the Director of the Mint to the Secretary of the Treasury, June 30, 1884* (Washington, D.C., 1884), p. 36.

50. John G. Brady, *Annual Report of the Governor of Alaska, 1897* (Washington, D.C., 1897), p. 192.

51. ATLewis, clipping; JCorr, 14:91, A. J. Davis to Jackson, 23 July 1885; interview with John and Hugh Brady, 23 June 1962.

52. Spicer, *Constitutional Status*, p. 49; Barker, *Compilation*, p. 9. The commissioner's docket (3 November 1884–26 June 1889) kept by Brady may be found in the State Superior Court House, Sitka, Alaska. The actual limits of his power were anything but clear. Judge James Wickersham later wrote, "In the annals of American Legislation, this

act stands glaringly and conspicuously forth as a stupendous piece of stupidity" (James Wickersham, *Alaska Reports Containing All the Unpublished Decisions of the District Courts of the Territory of Alaska from May 17, 1884 to January 1, 1903*, 6 vols. (St. Paul, Minn., 1903), 1:15.

53. JCorr, 14:270, Paul to Jackson, 8 February 1887. T. N. Hibben, *Dictionary of the Chinook Jargon* (Victoria, B.C., 1887); and Horatio Hale, *An International Idiom: A Manual of the Oregon Trade Language or Chinook Jargon* (London, 1890).

54. House, *Civil Government*, p. 13. CHR, vol. 23, Travers to W. G. Morris, 14 December 1882; commissioner's docket, case no. 75.

55. Commissioner's docket, 17 December 1884 and 20 January 1887; ibid., case no. 73.

56. Ibid., 3 and 4 November 1884; ibid., 17 December 1884, 17 July 1885; ibid., case no. 33.

57. Ibid., case no. 21.

58. Ibid., 23 March 1887.

59. Ibid., case no. 111.

60. Scidmore, "Alaska's Mining Region," p. 471.

61. *Alaskan*, 28 August 1886. Apparently a saucer was quite literally broken before the Chinese to symbolize what would be his fate if he gave false testimony (commissioner's docket, 18 August 1886).

62. The details of this unhappy experiment may be traced in Ted C. Hinckley, "Prospectors, Profits, and Prejudice," *American West* 2 (Spring 1965): 58–65.

63. *Alaskan*, 23 January 1886. TAP, mf. 1, Swineford to Lamar, 19 February 1886.

64. Francis C. Sessions, *From Yellowstone Park to Alaska* (New York, 1890), pp. 77–79; and idem, "Alaska," *Magazine of Western History*, December 1886, pp. 274–75. *Alaskan*, 14 and 18 August, 1886; *New York Times*, 15 August 1886.

65. TAP mf. 1, Swineford to Lamar, 17 August 1886 (including enclosures).

66. Commissioner's docket, note on p. 28. *Alaskan*, 10 April 1886.

67. *Juneau City Mining Record*, 4 October 1888; Donald Deschner, "Frank H. Nowell," *Alaska Review* 3 (Fall–Winter 1968–69): 193. *Alaska Journal*, 27 May 1893.

68. Gerard G. Steckler, "The Case of Frank Fuller: The Killer of Alaska Missionary Charles Seghers," *Pacific Northwest Quarterly* 59 (October 1968): 190–202.

69. Commissioner's docket, 5 September 1887. *Alaskan*, 10 September 1887.

70. *Daily Colonist*, 24 September 1887.

71. JScrap, 17:51, clipping. A good summary of the fur seal problem is found in Thomas A. Bailey, *A Diplomatic History of the American People*, 7th ed. (New York, 1964), pp. 410–14, 536–37. Overall Anglo–U.S. relations during these years is summarized in H. C. Allen, *Great Britain and the United States: A History of Anglo-American Relations (1783–1952)* (New York, 1955), chap. 14. On the Pribilofs, a first source remains: H. W. Elliott, *Our Arctic Province: Alaska and the Seal Islands* (New York, 1887).

72. *Alaskan*, 28 August 1886. Commissioner's docket, 25 August and 7 October 1886.

73. H. W. Elliott, "The Salvation of the Alaskan Fur Seal Herd," *American Forestry*, November 1912, pp. 702–8.

74. House, *Courts of Justice*, p. 2.

75. *Seattle Times*, 18 August 1886. *Alta California*, 28 August 1886. *Alaskan*, 14 August 1886.

76. Livingston F. Jones, *A Study of the Thlingets of Alaska* (New York, 1914), pp. 218–19.

77. Commissioner's docket, 27 October 1884 and case no. 70.

78. Ibid., 2 June 1887. *Alaskan*, 26 June 1886 and 19 January 1889. JGB, mf. 2, Swineford to Brady, n.d.

79. Commissioner's docket, case no. 57; ibid., 24 January and 2 February 1889 and 5 October 1888.

80. JGB, mf. 2, hearing in commissioner's court, 10 March 1887.

81. *Alaskan*, 17 December 1887.

82. Commissioner's docket, case no. 48.

83. Ibid., case nos. 28, 32, and 15. JGB, mf. 3, "As sworn to . . . ," 25 October 1888.

84. Commissioner's docket, 15 April 1889.

CHAPTER SEVEN

Politics, Profits, and Progeny

Alaska's second governor, Democrat Alfred P. Swineford, surely looked the role. A muscular frame, his lean face punctuated by sharp eyes and a trim gambler's Vandyke, Swineford's appearance bespoke the Western politician. The longtime Michigan resident had gained renown as businessman-journalist, state legislator, and Marquette mayor. Swineford's political currency remained reasonably high in his party despite his Civil War record as a copperhead and negrophobe.[1] Like his predecessor, John Kinkead, he well understood what Westerners desired to hear. To win and hold their popularity, a politico must espouse home rule and slavishly back every activity that stimulated territorial economic development. Anyone who questioned either of these frontier verities or who might have qualms over blindly rushing Americanization was suspect. Boomers who acclaimed home rule were, unquestionably, the sturdy pioneers.

Swineford's 1887 *Annual Report of the Governor of Alaska* rang the familiar tocsin. The Great Land deserved "representation in the popular branch of Congress—rights never before withheld from any fraction of the American people, however small, since the adoption of the Articles of Confederation." He damned as "enemies, those who desire to retain the country in its wild state as a great fur preserve for their own exclusive benefit," especially that "giant corporation, which thus far has succeeded in defeating nearly every proposed act of legislation calculated to ensure the settlement and development of Alaska."[2] Every Alaskan knew that his Goliath was the Alaska Commercial Company.

District oldtimers can hardly have been surprised, if disappointed, when a congressional investigation exonerated Swineford's "dreadful monopoly."[3] Nevertheless, it was impossible not to respect his executive energy and be impressed by his facility with words. Indeed, early hopes of capitalizing on Swineford's acknowledged communicative skills had induced Brady and Jackson to unite with him in the creation of Sitka's weekly *Alaskan*. But the general agent found it impossible to hide his distaste for Swineford's exuberant advocacy of a pell-mell transformation of the territory. And before long Swineford found Jackson to be "dictatorial, arbitrary, untruthful and a persistent mischief maker" and withdrew from the newspaper.[4] What probably disturbed the outspoken governor almost as much as Jackson's unbending nature was the stubby Presbyterian's pervasive influence among powerful eastern philanthropists and important solons.

Nevada's mineral wealth had colored Kinkead's Alaskan design. Similarly, Michigan's mineral riches imbued Swineford with heady dreams of Great Land mining prospects. Restless, able, and determined to become Alaska's first official congressional delegate, he correctly estimated that a swelling Far North commerce would propel his political ambitions. Swineford quickly realized that he could not easily manipulate the power levers within the district capital. Thereafter he sought to build the base of his popular support in neighboring Panhandle communities, particularly in Juneau. Regrettably, Jackson's ingrained skepticism of on-the-make territorial appointees, as well as his supersensitivity to any criticism of his management of Alaska's spreading aboriginal schools, resulted in a second quarrelsome governor-general agent relationship. No different than the politically seasoned governor, Jackson identified those who endorsed his goals as friends: "Christian citizens," he called them. Only self-seeking opportunists, purblind fools, or scoundrels would oppose his humanitarian objectives. By early 1886 Jackson had already classified Alaska's second governor with the first group.

Unlike his mentor, Brady was a twelve-month resident of Alaska. Despite Swineford's rhetoric and imprudent generalizations, John had to accommodate himself to reality. As an archipelago merchant, John could ill afford the territorial enmities that a Washington-based Jackson too readily accumulated. After all, Swineford had promptly pushed for expanded educational funds from Congress; his complaint that Sitka's "Government wharf . . . is so dilapidated and insecure that it cannot be used" might stretch the facts, but not very far. And what Sitkan could not favor the variety of pork barrel recommendations repeatedly advocated by Swineford in his eloquently worded annual reports?[5] Jackson's woeful litany, one that had emphasized American negligence in the northland, took on a more mellifluous interpretation from Swineford's pen:

Governor Alfred P. Swineford sometime during his administration, 1885–89. (Reproduced by permission of the Alaska State Historical Library.)

. . . as soon as Congress shall conclude that there are indeed here in Alaska all the natural elements essential to the growth of a rich and prosperous State, and acting upon that theory shall conclude to enact such legislation as will encourage and promote their development, then, and not till then, may we look for the dawn on that era of prosperity which should have followed close after the transfer of the Territory from the Russian to the American Government, which will populate Alaska with a hardy, industrious, enterprising people, dot her main and island coasts with thriving villages, towns, and cities . . . [6]

Jackson placed top priority on native uplift; Swineford favored an entirely different group: he felt that Alaska possessed the "right and urgent need of representation in the popular branch of Congress and of some kind of legislature to provide laws to meet our recurring local necessities. . . . The people of this great and truly magnificent Territory should no longer be left to the 'abomination of desolation' but as speedily as possible provided with a form of government . . . and the enjoyment of 'all the rights, advantages, and immunities of citizens of the United States.'"[7]

Here was familiar frontier rhetoric, and when Swineford delivered it before an audience of Juneau miners, they responded with roars of approval. Alaskan natives, on the other hand, could hardly have concurred with Swineford's "abomination of desolation" remark. Predictably, the governor began to zero in on Jackson's pronative allies as "enemies" who handicapped Americanization. The isolation of the Far North, the historical rightness of his governmental demands, and the applause of an antimissionary vox populi so in contrast with their contemp for mugwump-minded Jackson deceived Swineford into overestimating his political strength.

The leverage of public economic policy—and in an emerging Far West territory that certainly included federal monies—could make or break any business, large or small. Brady, like his fellow merchants, was acutely conscious of this, as well of it its corollary: the necessity for maintaining cordial relationships with Alaska's collector, the governor, the district judge, the general agent, the chief naval office, and their subordinates. Those who did so received consideration when it came to public works contracts. Being politic also guaranteed less legal harrassment over petty regulations randomly enforced, usually against itinerants or Indians. Brady endorsed a number of the governor's recommendations: improved district-wide transportation, a more sensible control of hoochinoo, and a reorganization of the court system.[8] Furthermore, Swineford's prompt, if futile, action to block Juneau's anti-Chinese mob had exhibited real courage. When Swineford punished a

114

lawbreaking Killisnoo shaman by shaving the Tlingit's head and painting it with red lead, however, John was aghast.

The ex–Marquette mayor was impatient to be an activist administrator: to quicken corporate investment, to accelerate pioneer settlement, in essence, to create in Alaska the kind of capitalistic expansion
that had benefited Northern Michigan when Americans exploited the
wealth of Great Lakes ore and timber resources.[9] But Michigan had
dynamic neighboring cities like Chicago and Milwaukee, as well as
Detroit's ballooning population. Above all, Michigan enjoyed easy water
and railroad accessibility. David Starr Jordan discerned why the development of America's noncontiguous territory would not soon parallel
the growth of other commonwealths: "Alaska is not a region of homes
and householders. The widely separated villages and posts have few
interests in common. The settlements are scattered along a wild coast,
inaccessible one to another; . . . the white men knowing 'no law of God
or man.' With these elements, a civic feeling akin to the civic life in
the United States can in no way be built up."[10] Everyone agreed that
vital for Great Land growth was a continuing intermingling of private
and public enterprise.[11]

Throughout the eighties frequent contact with Alaska's government
provided Judge Brady lessons in public administration. Some days he
could only commiserate with the district officials vainly seeking sensible
answers to impossible riddles. Dr. Jackson kept him abreast of the
capital scene and reminded him of the thankless toil of combatting
congressional apathy. The Swineford governorship opened Brady's eyes
to the unique quandaries facing Far North administrators.

Deeply grateful that Jackson had safeguarded his reappointment as
Sitka's commissioner, John would have been chagrined had he known
that Swineford had written to the attorney general requesting that "a
change be made in his case."[12] By mid-1886 Alaska's governor found
it difficult to hide his antipathy toward Sitka's pro-Jackson element.
John was not worried about the general agent's ability to protect himself, but he could not be indifferent to local quarrels boiling up between
Swineford's friends and detractors. In half jest, half annoyance, John
wrote Jackson: "The spirit of antagonism appears to be an epidemic
over the whole land. It must come here on a Southeast wind which is
now blowing. . . . I am sick of all this contention and often wish that
I were in some other part of the land but sin is everywhere."[13]

Swineford's unrelenting determination to expand territorial government in order to advance his own career was common gossip among
capital residents. In December of 1887 Sitkan Henry E. Hayden en-

capsulated this distrust of political boosterism: "Any legislation other than putting into effect the General Lands laws, would be absurd at this time. None of us wish to be handicapped by the broils of political factions, with the certainty that the scum will surely come to the top. Without a dollar of taxable property—with only a mere handful of intelligent people in the territory, with three fourths of our population made up of disreputable adventurers, why do we wish for release from the protection of the present forms, unless we too be political adventurers?"[14] But Swineford represented the frontier tradition, for as Senator Thomas A. Hendricks of Indiana once commented, every territorial governor expected that appointment "to be a stepping stone either to the House of Representatives or to the Senate."[15]

For the moment, at least, Judge Brady had less interest in political adventures than in Alaskan land ownership. Once he had deeded over to the Presbyterian church the plat that formed the campus for the Sheldon Jackson Training School, John set about examining other untouched pieces of Sitka real estate on which he might stake out a future homestead. He surely knew that he was on "questionable ground." The 1884 organic act had provided for mining, municipal, missionary, and Indian claims but had done nothing for the homesteader. Nevertheless, preemptive rights, legal as well as muscular, were another hallowed Western tradition; Brady had no compunctions about importing them northward.[16]

By 1887 Judge Brady quite understandably viewed himself as a community pillar. The gracious hospitality extended capital visitors by Judge and Mrs. Brady was widely acknowledged, even if their living quarters within the musty-smelling Sitka Trading Company store provided only a crude setting for such amenities. But John and Elizabeth wanted to have a family, and that meant a comfortable home. Furthermore, John was eager to enlarge his lumber trade, to become a well-equipped millwright. He envisioned a piece of property sufficient to accommodate a lumber mill, a subsistence farm, and, above all, a home.

Having parted with his initial land claim at the east end of town, John searched for fresh, undeveloped business-domestic acreage on the other side of the native village. The land upon which he set his heart lay just northwest of the line of Tlingit houses fronting on Sitka's beachfront opposite Channel Rock. The tract included much of Swan Lake, actually a befouled pond. On its seaward side was a rising knoll perfectly situated for an ocean-view home. Like the soil that he had earlier claimed, this area's crop-raising prospects were superior to almost any other thereabouts. Its close proximity to the Indian Ranche offered mixed blessings.

Exactly why in mid-1887 Governor Swineford chose to dispute Brady's title to the Sitka Trading Company's centrally located log structure, the Hot Springs claim, and then seek to stop John's preemption of a home site is impossible to determine. An explanation depends on whose opinions are accepted. Swineford informed secretary of the interior L. Q. C. Lamar that Sitka's commissioner "should at once be authoritatively informed that the erection of . . . buildings, and actual occupation of the lands, will not invest in him any preferred claim . . . [after] the general land laws shall have been extended to this territory."[17] The one-time Michigan legislator was painfully familiar with settler land rapacity, and wherever sloppily drawn claims were carelessly endorsed, judicial thickets invariably took root. At this time Arthur K. Delaney, Alaska's newly appointed collector and veteran Wisconsin Democrat, warned John that "the log building in which you are now doing business . . . appears to be the property of the United States." Brady promptly refuted this.[18] Not so easily refuted was the governor's accusation that his envisioned home-farm-mill tract encroached on an Indian cemetery. In a smoldering letter to Secretary Lamar, Brady hotly denied Swineford's indictment. "The natives have no ancient cemetery or burying ground. They have always burned their dead on piles of dry cedar logs. . . . it is only recently since the establishment of the missions among them that they have consented to bury their friends."[19] Swineford "wants me removed and he has seized this opportunity to pose as the defender of the poor natives, upon whose rights I am committing 'an unjust and unnecessary infringement and sacrilegious outrage.'" Brady went further. He reviewed Swineford's use of physical violence in humiliating native leaders, mentioning that as judge he had released one of them from jail after the governor had acted without a warrant. "If you could properly understand the motives of this bad man," Brady sputtered, "the villany of his letter would be apparent. He is possessed of an itching almost a feverish desire to magnify his office; and whoever objects to his arbitrary acts encounters his enmity." Not unlikely the politically experienced governor wanted to weaken Brady's gubernatorial chances in the upcoming quadrennial appointments. Swineford went so far as to imply that Sitka's judge was dealing in stolen goods. "A willful liar," John labeled him to Elizabeth.[20]

In the Indian land controversy Swineford seems not to have acted as arbitrarily as Brady. Supporting the governor was a group of Ranche Indians who argued against the judge's occupation of their cemetery.

Brady had recently put one of them under bond: Tlantich had been judged guilty of condemning an old Indian woman of witchcraft, an act that could have brought on her death. Was this Indian's accusation of cemetery sacrilege fully justified? There was no question that John had unilaterally occupied the area. To justify his aggressive conduct, Brady reminded Lamar: "I have been living in Alaska nearly ten years and have waited patiently for the extension of the land laws in this Territory. I am in business here and all of my interests are identified with Alaska. . . . it is my desire to make as respectable a home as I can afford. The place which I have selected is public domain, is not nor never has been in the possession of a native or other person. . . . Many of the reputable people here have assured me that they will make affidavit to this fact if necessary."[21] While insisting that the land was not an Indian burial ground, he admitted that two native sheds housing cremated bodies did remain on the "ground which it is my intention to fence, but not on the piece I have already cleared of brush and humps and upon which I have built a road from the beach to the top of the hill, where I have excavated the earth for a cellar."

John's dream home was no longer merely a dream. To abandon it now was unthinkable. "In April last the natives delivered to me on this ground, one thousand fence posts and since that time I have hired them to do most of the work which has been performed." "Not one native," he insisted, "ever came to me, and objected to my building there."[22] Brady could hardly expect Sitka Tlingits to voice any objections to the white man who paid for their services, who was among the most esteemed of the capital's population, and who, when they got drunk, decided on their punishment. For the present they remained silent. Weather permitting, Brady continued the excavation of his cellar, ground clearing, and fence extension.

Like the 1884 presidential contest, the 1888 campaign remained, until election eve, a toss-up. President Cleveland found himself opposed by the Republican standard bearer, Benjamin Harrison. Both Brady and Jackson rejoiced at the triumph of the Grand Old Party and the election of fellow Presbyterian Benjamin Harrison. Although the general agent had few illusions that he could dictate Alaska appointees to the president-elect, Jackson believed that his recommendations would be seriously reviewed at the White House. Twice, in Jackson's opinion, Alaska's management had been retarded by governors who rejected his philosophy for Far North development, incompetents who dared to criticize his educational leadership. America's new chief executive had authored Alaska's organic act. Surely it was not being unduly optimistic to hope for more cooperative Far North civil appointees.

Predictably, outgoing governor Swineford did not depart silently. "Aside from the partial administration of justice by the United States district court and the four United States commissioners acting principally as justices of the peace, the civil government of Alaska is little, if any, better than a burlesque both in form and substance."[23] Alaska's governmental deficiencies had not been due to Swineford's lack of persuasive skill or persistent advertising; he appreciated that he had administered the least consequential of America's trans-Missouri political properties. Long years in politics had taught him to be a good loser. At the 1888 Christmas Eve party hosted by Sitka's mission staff, Governor Swineford was among the overflow of guests. As Brady recapitulated the scene to Jackson, the governor "was called upon and eulogized the Mission and its work and Mr. Austin in particular. . . . he tried to be pleasant by referring to his own determination to resign and to me as the prospective governor."[24]

To reward Judge Brady with Alaska's governorship would quiet at least the Far North's threadbare shibboleth about "damn carpetbagger appointees." None other than the outgoing governor's brother, C. A. Swineford, urged Harrison to appoint Brady. "Having resided in Alaska the past two seasons, where I have mining interests, and feeling that residents of the Territory necessarily better understand and appreciate the existing conditions of affairs . . . I take the courage to pen these lines." John G. Brady "is an educated, Christian gentleman with a thorough knowledge of the Territory. . . . There exist grave abuses in the Territory, notably that of the sale of intoxicants. Arrests are made. . . . Yet owing to the . . . apathy and indifference of the officials it is impossible to convict. . . . Though a brother of the present governor of Alaska, I am not numbered with his party, and he being an advocate of the maxim, 'To the victor belong the spoils,' I believe at an early day you will receive his resignation of the office."[25] And pro forma Alaska's second governor did step down as Benjamin Harrison took charge of the country. Republican party lieutenants and district special pleaders, such as Sheldon Jackson, showered the new president with names of possible gubernatorial successors.

The motives that caused John to let himself be actively championed by mentor Jackson can only be guessed at. Prestige, civic duty, commercial connections—the reasons ranged from self-sacrificing to self-serving. Jackson's lobbying connections in the nation's capital, the wide-reaching public pressure that he could bring to bear, and his past links with Benjamin Harrison were impressive. On 22 January 1889 Jackson addressed himself to a "Dear Brother," soon to be sworn in as America's chief executive. "It gives me great pleasure to transmit to you the action of the Presbytery of Alaska, and also of the Missionaries and teachers of Southeastern Alaska recommending to your favorable attention Mr. John G. Brady of Sitka, as Governor of Alaska." It was not a long letter, but it reminded Harrison, "Alaska has suffered so much from Godless, drinking officials that we are looking to you for a different kind." The Presbytery of Alaska wanted him to remember that "eight tenths of our population are Indians or natives just emerging from barbarism." When it came to caring for their interests, the letter insisted, no better man could be obtained than John Brady.[26]

Support for Brady's candidacy piled upon Harrison's desk, almost all of it marshaled by Jackson. Members of Congress, ex-Alaskan officials, and a wide spectrum of American Protestants ranging from ecclesiastical leaders to numerous women's auxiliaries wrote letters urging his appointment.[27] By mid-March the president announced that John W. Noble would serve as his secretary of the interior. Forthwith Noble heard from pro-Brady advocates, among whom were the WCTU and, of course, Sheldon Jackson.[28] Evidently, and correctly as it turned out, the general agent suffered no fear over his own reappointment.

Predictably Juneauites were divided on Brady's value as a territorial spokesman. The *Juneau City Mining Record* editorialized:

> He is the unanimous choice of the better element in Alaska. . . . He is a Christian gentleman of high intellectual abilities, and has used every effort to aid the missionaries in reclaiming Indians from barbarism. As a businessman he has been successful, and has gained an almost unlimited knowledge, through long residence, of the habits and customs of the Indians. . . . Mr. Brady is a staunch Republican. . . . the only opposing faction in either party consists of those who ridicule missionary efforts and are engaged in the sale of intoxicating liquors, illegally in Alaska.[29]

This was hardly the kind of copy to win support among the town's citizens, men generally apathetic to Indian welfare. Editor Frank Myers surmised as much. His column had appeared in an extra edition. "I did not print it in my regular issue," he wrote Jackson, "for the reason that it would have the effect to incite those of Juneau who are opposed to Mr. Brady to action against his appointment." Copies of the paper were forwarded to "places where I thought they would do the most good." Myers was confident that "the better portion of Juneau's citizens are favorably disposed toward Mr. Brady's appointment." The editor regretted the "severe things about you and also about Mr. Brady" that appeared in Juneau's *Free Press*. He was also annoyed by Thomas S. Nowell, of Boston, who "now wants me to 'buy' his influence by using my paper to 'boom' certain mining schemes in Alaska in which he is interested, and which are of doubtful nature."[30] Juneauite John G. Heid informed Jackson that local Democrat W. F. Reed, "who at all times prides himself as being a 'reb,'" was one of the several "malicious persons" trying to stir up opposition to Brady. Like Myers, Heid believed that John Brady was "held in esteem by the solid element of the District."[31]

Other than circulating some petitions, Judge Brady seems to have done little to forward his candidacy. Experience had taught him that all vital Alaska management decisions were resolved in Washington, D.C. Far North political rallies were healthy vents for public exuberance, but their political impact was nil. In a lengthy letter to Henry Kendall and William Irwin at the Board of Home Missions, written in early 1889, Brady revealed his view of the opposition. At a Juneau Democratic meeting, "the Chairman was intoxicated and when missionaries were mentioned he would cry out 'Damn 'em.' There is a class of men in the Territory who are opposed to religion. They constantly revile missionaries." Brady expressed genuine apprehension over a "groundless and false" document prepared by Swineford whose release would soon "create a sensation."[32] Swineford's "bitter attack" did erupt, but its primary target turned out to be the general agent. Jackson not only dodged Swineford's charges but also skillfully combined them in a pronative document he was preparing.

Years later Jackson stated that President Harrison did not select Brady as governor in 1889 "on the ground that both he and Mr. Brady were Presbyterians and he did not want to appear before the country as giving special favor to his own church."[33] In part, this was true. Still, the defeat chastened John. It seemed such an inevitable prize. "Personally," he snapped, "I am heartily sick of Mr. Harrison and his administration as far as Alaska is governed."[34] For all his sour grapes, John could not long dwell on the gloomy side of things. Indeed, for Alaska businessmen the nineties appeared to herald gratifying growth. And for Mr. and Mrs. Brady, progeny proved to be a pleasant accompaniment to profits.

Since the early 1880s Brady and a handful of other Far North lumbermen had been turning Alexander Archipelago's forests to good account. During these years the finite nature of "America's limitless timber reserves" became painfully apparent. New England's supremacy had passed. The nation's lumber-producing regions had shifted to the south and west about the Great Lakes. A booming Pacific Slope economy extracted larger and larger quantities of wood from Puget Sound stands as well as from abundant forests stretching over much of northern California.[35]

America's voracious appetite for wood products required a doubling of the country's sawmills. Of the manufacturing industries, only flour milling and a few other giants loomed larger than the nation's lumber industry.[36] Inevitably as the demand skyrocketed, so did the looting of the national domain. One suit instituted by the federal government required a California firm to account for sixty million feet of lumber. Not even the more isolated regions were spared. Several hundred square miles of countryside around Eureka, Nevada, were laid waste, and the trespass by timber cutters in New Mexico was notorious. Rapacious men were the villains, but steam-driven tools and vehicles were their weapons.[37]

Primarily due to its isolation, which increased transportation costs, but also because its wood was less marketable, late-nineteenth-century Alaska was spared such rapine. The green-carpeted mountains of the Alexander Archipelago offered a timber resource neither as generous in its yield nor as easy to shape as what lay around Puget Sound. It was "too gummy and resinous for the ordinary use of house-building and furniture making."[38] Yet, if the Panhandle's hemlock and spruce were not attractive to lumbermen, the region's hundred-foot giant cedars possessed a Pacific-wide fame.

American settlers helped themselves to the Panhandle's surrounding forests, as had their Slavic predecessors. Simultaneously lumber from California and Oregon mills was unloaded at ports from Wrangell to Unalaska in the Aleutians. Some of the materials came ashore in a prefabricated state to facilitate assembly.[39] To ship the lumber all the way from Portland, and later from Puget Sound, was expensive. Yet the superior building qualities of Pacific Northwest timber, plus the efficient operation of that region's mills, some of which were decades old, invited competition. In fact, America's Pacific Slope cargo mills had been shipping their wood products all over the Pacific Basin, from Australia to North China to Chile, since mid-century. Zealously independent, their fierce rivalry had often benefited the consumer.[40]

Brady and a handful of other part-time millmen who lumbered Panhandle trees exemplified the half-century-old West Coast merchant-millwright. In 1822 a Yankee had constructed the first mechanical sawmill on the Pacific Coast not far from Mission San Gabriel, and by the mid-1840s the quiet near Bodega Bay, California, was broken by the West Coast's first steam-powered mill. After 1867 Sitka's venerable Russian-built, water-driven lumber mill, with its large waterwheel falling into decay, was periodically activated by mechanically minded settlers.[41] Sometime during the early eighties, Theo Haltern acquired this centrally situated mill. Sitka's old-timers claimed that Macao and Canton, China, possessed structures erected from Alaska spruce processed at their pioneer Russian mill. Brady may have occasionally leased this historic facility, but it was his primary competitor, W. P. Mills, who, in the nineties, put the mill to regular use, and, in 1903, purchased it from Haltern.[42] Fortunately the increase of mining, canning, and multiple archipelago wood requirements throughout the eighties and nineties afforded generous opportunities for both Brady and Mills.

In 1880, even before John had shed his missionary's sackcloth for a lay ministry, he had informed Jackson of a Tlingit chief who had told him that his people desired lumber "to build houses." "They did not want it given to them, but they would pay for it, another said that so many living in one house threw the boys and girls together too much." To the ears of money-short mission organizers, the suggestion that the Indians help pay for their Christianization was welcome. Before his eastern audiences Jackson proclaimed the virtues of a single-family home, which a sawmill could provide, and erelong the machinery was on its way north.[43]

The crude "missionary saw-mill" that the Presbyterians imported in 1882 possessed two advantages: it was steam operated and small—so portable, in fact, that it provided saw logs for the mission facilities at Hoonah before it was permanently situated at Sitka. Initially Brady appears to have operated this mill. Soon training school students were being instructed in its use, and some of the school's lumber needs were met by their apprenticeship. At the same time, John and Whitford, aided by millwright Douglas Reynolds, marketed a portion of the sawmill's output about the capital and at scattered archipelago mines, salteries, and canneries. Quite early John hired Indian graduates of Sitka's training school as millhands. Subsequently native employees, such as George Bartlett and Peter Simpson, became "excellent mechanics and engineers."[44] Jackson and Brady took special pride whenever these aboriginals with anglicized names and a "christian education" constructed "suitable cottages" adjoining the mission's campus.[45]

Historians have noted how quickly San Francisco grew to dominate the Pacific Slope lumber industry during the latter half of the nineteenth century.[46] After Brady's cargo aboard the *Leo* had become embroiled there, he realized that he was but an Alaska fingerling among California sharks. Fortunately he could concentrate his energies on the district's own growing domestic lumber market. Because his own funds were distinctly limited, John might never have prospered had he not benefited from a unique labor supply and the archipelago's abundant stands of timber—his twelve-hour days and mercantile perspicacity notwithstanding.

During the eighties and nineties, aboriginal employment in Panhandle mining and canning enterprises increased. Indians were vital as packers and longshoremen, but they could also be seen setting type for local newspapers, teaching school, and swabbing decks on the U.S. men-of-war. At Sitka a significant proportion of them were earning respectable livings as loggers, sawyers, boat builders, coopers, and carpenters.[47] Mission youths stood in the forefront of these activities. After fashioning boxes and barrels "for the Alaska fish trade," they turned their energies to becoming "fishers of men" and built a Presbyterian church. The *Alaskan* lauded their craftsmanship. The edifice "can be creditably compared with any church in any western town with population ten times as large as that of Sitka." Brady could no longer apportion much time to supervising these diverse training school endeavors; as his "ministry" became more secular each year, so did his identity with younger, "Christianized Alaskans" assume a more practical form. Nowhere was this better evidenced than at his own sawmill.

Financial assistance from Thomas C. Doran and Herman Bauer enabled John to erect a completely new sawmill in the spring of 1889. Approximately eighty feet long and forty feet wide, the initial building stood without walls; heavy vertical posts carried the roof. Within hummed and screeched a steam-driven saw; a forty-two inch planer provided buyers with dressed cedar, spruce, or hemlock. On 20 January 1891 the Sitka Sawmill Company's total daily mill capacity of six thousand feet was suddenly terminated when a furious gale leveled the mill. John was lucky. Although the storm flattened the eighty-foot structure, its boiler and machinery survived undamaged.[48] After surveying the wreckage, inventorying his own capital, and weighing his future prospects, John offered to buy out Doran and Bauer. By selling his remaining shares of the Sitka Trading Company to Amos Whitford, he managed to meet their price. Thus by 9 August 1891 the *Alaskan* could report that John had "closed out all his interest in the Sitka Trading Company" and had become "the sole owner of the Sitka Sawmill." Shortly thereafter he signed a contract for the cutting of one hundred thousand feet of rough and dressed lumber for two government buildings, one of them the new marine barracks. The contract may have been the reason why he hired as his engineer Andrew Usher, a Tlingit from the training school.[49] Usher's diligence had earned him a millhand's charge; other Indians would become quite as indispensable.

Panhandle loggers had to contend with dense undergrowth, swampy muskeg, and rocky terrain. Equally burdensome was the lack of machinery, which dictated hand logging. Usually spruce and hemlock were felled near the shore, so close their tops crashed into the water. Logging areas in the proximity of the capital included Silver Bay, Fish Bay, and

A log raft manned by native workers approaches the Brady lumber mill, sometime in the 1890s. (Reproduced by permission of the Beinecke Rare Book and Manuscript Library, Yale University.)

Chicagoff Island. Once trimmed, the logs were formed into a raft and then kedged to Sitka or hauled there by a tug. Congressman James Tawney of Minnesota "paid a flattering tribute to the character and disposition of the Indians, who . . . did much of the work. . . . All of their work is done by hand; that is, the timber near the stream is selected, felled and put in without any mechanical device of any kind."[50]

During January 1893 Sitkans heard about the establishment of the first Alaskan business enterprise built and managed entirely by natives. Among the Tsimshians who constituted the leadership of the new, all-Indian mill on the eastern shore of Gravina Island (about midway down the Tongass Narrows) were Peter Simpson and Mark Hamilton. Jackson, Brady, and William Duncan had all played educational roles in preparing them for this exciting business venture. Within a few years Hamilton, Simpson and Company employed fifteen millhands, all Indians, and its steam-powered saw sliced out a daily capacity of fifteen thousand feet of sawed and planed lumber. From these materials the Gravina community erected both a church and a schoolhouse. What better confirmation of the missionaries' faith in Alaskans.[51]

Just as John Brady had confidence in the abilities of his native neighbors, he had a strong faith in his own future. Ten years earlier, in 1880, self-doubt and guilt had plagued him after he rejected a missionary's abnegation. Now, public life, and family life as well, cheered him with bright prospects. Writing to Dr. Jackson, Elizabeth confided: "We have made some changes in our business, have made some exchanges with Whitford and Bauer. Have now half of the building where we live, and building between it and Custom House, the garden lot and stable, the store property at Juneau, the sawmill and all belongings. We are not connected with Mr. Whitford in any way. . . . the sawmill has been running steadily for three months. There is now more of a demand for lumber than can be supplied."[52]

On the face of it, Elizabeth's optimism may seem excessive, if that vital statistic, population increase, is considered. According to the 1890 census, Sitka had only 1190 inhabitants. Even Juneau topped this by no more than one hundred citizens. The *Alaskan* grumbled that "the larger part of the business transacted by the merchants here, is with the natives, and we could not advise a newcomer to enter the field." Furthermore, "the homestead law is not in force in Alaska." Worse, "not a stick of timber can be exported from Alaska and working of sawmills is only permitted to supply the local consumption of lumber." However, only two sawmills operated at Sitka. And although Wrangell and a few other archipelago communities also operated sawmills, various ephemeral mills came and went, and the century ended with Sitka's

Photograph of Sitka taken from the site of Baranov Castle, about 1889. The large structure in the left foreground is the Sitka Trading Company store. By this date Brady's lumber business was growing, as was the volume of tourists visiting historic Saint Michael's (center). (Reproduced by permission of the Beinecke Rare Book and Manuscript Library, Yale University.)

same two mills supplying a sizable portion of the "marketable lumber" cut in southeastern Alaska. After 1897 the Klondike boom added greatly to the rising demand for timber. With that in mind, it is not difficult to grasp why as late as 1900 "the largest part of the [Panhandle] lumber consumed [was] shipped from points farther south, including Seattle and Tacoma."[53] Clearly Sitka's two medium-sized mills enjoyed a sellers' market.

Alaska's population figures were just as deceptive as the lumber statistics. Salteries, mines, canneries, even much of Alaska's shipping operated on a seasonal basis. San Francisco–owned corporations employed a sojourner work force in Alaska; their payrolls were spent outside the district. Equally as serious, the profits of these parasite corporations were largely spent elsewhere. But these firms did consume quantities of archipelago forest products, and for Brady that spelled money.

Republican Governor Lyman E. Knapp, Swineford's successor at Sitka, stated a painful truth:

> The white population of [Alaska's] towns consists, for the most part, of traders, miners, artisans, and laborers, comparatively few of whom have accumulated any considerable amount of wealth. Besides, these accumulations . . . are largely invested in doubtful mining claims, improvements upon land to which they have no title and can have none . . . that every resident who erects a shanty to protect himself and his family . . . is a trespasser and liable to be ejected by legal process; that the cutting of a walking stick, or the gathering of wood to boil his coffee, is a breach of the law.[54]

Judge Brady knew the law. Both the projected homesite to which he proposed to lay down a road and the timber he logged and rafted to his millsite bruised if not broke the law. The U.S. statutes "did not fit Alaska," congressional obfuscation aggravated the mess, and "if persisted in, must be equally potent to bar future progress."[55] Surely the lawmakers would soon pass adequate legislation. Until then Brady would persistently demonstrate that Alaska could provide both a comfortable livelihood and comfortable living.

But the carousel of commerce required business dexterity. If one was to catch Alaska's financial rings, he could not long relax. Any need for wood found Brady attentive to the need: yellow cedar paneling for a handsome Tacoma home, timbers to repair a hull tunneled by teredo worms, quantities of hemlock sawlogs for mine supports, and strips of sawn spruce for barrels and salmon cases.[56] And in December 1894 the *Alaskan* reported: "There may now be seen in the vicinity of Mr. J. G. Brady's saw mill the rearing of a schooner thirty eight feet long on deck, nine foot beam and of about eight tons when measured." John usually had plenty of lumber available for the restoration of Sitka structures: boardwalks and bridges, waterfront buildings, mission and public school repairs, and never-ending home improvements. By the mid-nineties his ambitions had been handsomely realized.[57]

To an age wedded to expanding production in all its forms, Elizabeth's creation of five healthy babies in the space of approximately six years was almost routine. For the parents it was never routine. John Green Brady, Jr., arrived on 1 August 1889. Certainly if Elizabeth wished to dissuade her husband from further commercial voyages aboard the *Leo*, the sight and sound of an animated son proved to be a stout domestic anchor. On 19 February 1891 a second son, Hugh Picken, joined the Brady household. The following year, "On September 22nd our third son was born," John informed his mentor. "We have named him Sheldon Jackson," Elizabeth then delivered two daughters, Mary Beattie on 29 April 1894 and their youngest child, Elizabeth Patton, on 1 September 1896.[58]

Once his namesake appeared, John Green Brady's aspiration to build a family nest became imperative. Elizabeth's third pregnancy (one had miscarried) by the summer of 1890 spurred John's determination to push rapidly ahead with his residential development west of the Ranche. What arose might be described as a modified Queen Anne style dwelling. By Sitka standards the two-story hemlock framed structure was imposing, if not elegant. John named his home "Satchahnee," his interpretation of Tlingit for "top of the hill." Although atop merely a low ridge, the culmination of his domestic dreams enjoyed a view of the channel. The surrounding meadows rolled down toward Sitka's bay front and enlarged the house's proportions. Throughout 1891, motivated by the multiplication of his family, John shoveled earth, pounded nails, and did everything time allowed to expedite Satchahnee's completion.

During November of 1891 John and Elizabeth commenced that exciting, if tedious, task of moving. Satchahnee was not finished, nor like any beloved home would it ever be, but its master was impatient to command his castle. Writing to Dr. Jackson, Elizabeth cheered, "Our new house is almost ready for us to move into, we hope to move in by Christmas." "We are all quite well. Our little ones are growing nicely. John tries to repeat all the words he hears. Hugh is a great rollicking boy of nine months without teeth."

For all his elation at Elizabeth's motherhood and her profound contentment, John was neither serene nor secure. Brady knew that he lacked a confirmed title to his property. Elizabeth could rejoice that "the sawmill has been running steadily for three months. There is now more of a demand than can be supplied,"[59] but until millsite and home-site were officially his, he could ill afford to relax. Elizabeth seems not to have been disquieted by the possible loss of their home or business. Indeed, her confidence in "Mr. Brady" was manifest among Sitka society.

John Brady, however, was gritting his teeth. Years afterward he re-called "that the most severe struggle" he ever had in the northland "was in trying to get the government to give [me] a patent to [my] home and it seemed to be the determination of the department not to grant it."[60] This prolonged contest to possess a clear title to his property and the ancillary struggle, clarification of the legal limitations on cutting Alaska timber, obliged him to become familiar with both district and national law. Indeed, his tenacious campaign to obtain adequate laws covering district land use and ownership became a decade-long contest. It sharpened John's political acumen and, in doing so, forced him once again to consider appointment as district governor.

1. *Alaska Searchlight*, 1 June 1895. Interview with Agnes Shattuck, 4 August 1962, Juneau.

2. Alfred P. Swineford, *Annual Report of the Governor of Alaska, 1887* (Washington, D.C., 1887), p. 728.

3. Bancroft, *History of Alaska*, pp. 636–59, well summarized the Alaska Commercial Company's scapegoat role on the Far North frontier, and the company's privately printed *Reply of the Alaska Commercial Company to the Charges of Governor Alfred P. Swineford, of Alaska, against the Company in His Annual Report for the Year 1887* (San Francisco, 1888) defends its constructive role in the northland.

4. AGP, vol. 1, Swineford to Lamar, 13 October 1885.

5. Ibid., 14 October 1885. The late senator Ernest Gruening characterized Swineford's official reports as "classics in the literature of protest" (*State of Alaska*, p. 54). Swineford, *Annual Report, 1887*, p. 737.

6. Swineford, *Annual Report, 1887*, p. 698.

7. Ibid., p. 728.

8. JGB, mf. 1, Brady to Lamar, n.d. (ca. July 1887).

9. *Alaska Searchlight*, 1 June 1895; *Oregonian*, 21 August 1885.

10. Jordan, "Colonial Lessons of Alaska," p. 579.

11. Stuart Bruchey, "Economic Growth and Change to 1860," in John Garraty, *Interpreting American History: Conversations with Historians*, 2 vols. (London, 1970), 1:180.

12. AGP, vol. 1, Swineford to Lamar, 12 October 1885; ibid., Swineford to A. N. Garland, 17 November 1885.

13. JCorr, 14:200, Brady to Jackson, 24 April 1886.

14. Ibid., 15:392, Hayden to Jackson, 16 December 1887.

15. *Congressional Globe*, 40th Cong., 2d sess., 3 June 1868, p. 2800.

16. No comprehensive, scholarly study has yet been written on the utilization of the

public domain in Alaska. For an introduction to the settlers' frustrations, see Hinckley, *Americanization of Alaska.* Suggestive of various approaches to the complex subject are Hugh A. Johnson and Harold T. Jorgenson, *The Land Resources of Alaska* (New York, 1963); and Richard A. Cooley, *A Challenge in Conservation* (Madison, 1967).

17. JGB, correspondence 1881–89, Swineford to Lamar, 18 May 1887.

18. JGB, mf. 3, Delaney to Brady, 12 May 1887; CHR, vol. 32A, Herbert F. Beecher to Delaney, 11 May 1887; and ibid., Brady to Delaney, 13 May 1887.

19. JGB, mf. 1, Brady to Lamar, n.d. (ca. July 1887).

20. National Archives, unfiled Alaska education correspondence, Swineford to N. H. R. Dawson, 26 May 1888. Ibid.; and JGB, mf. 1, Brady to his wife, 28 July 1887.

21. JGB, mf. 1, Brady to Lamar, n.d. (ca. July 1887).

22. Ibid.

23. Alfred P. Swineford, *Annual Report of the Governor of Alaska, 1888–1889* (Washington, D.C., 1889), p. 1001.

24. JCorr, 15:119, Brady to Jackson, 27 December 1888.

25. JGB, Brady correspondence 1881–89, C. A. Swineford to Benjamin Harrison, 1 February 1889.

26. Ibid., Jackson to Harrison, 22 January 1889.

27. Ibid., recommendations and petitions for governor; JGB, mf. 1, Jackson to Harrison, 21 March 1889; *North Star*, February 1889; JCorr; 15:175, Jackson to Robert de Schweinitz, 28 February 1889; ibid., p. 149, list of endorsements; and ibid., 24:293, Oscar L. Jackson to J. P. White, 7 March 1889.

28. JGB, Brady correspondence 1881–89, Elliott Shepard to Noble, 14 March 1889; and ibid., Jackson to Noble, 22 March 1889.

29. *Juneau City Mining Record*, 3 January 1889.

30. JCorr, 15:149, Meyers to Jackson, 9 February 1889.

31. Ibid., p. 189, Heid to Jackson, 7 April 1889.

32. Ibid., p. 163, Brady to Kendall and Irwin, 6 February 1889.

33. PTS, SJ letters, 13:425, Jackson to Lewis S. Welch, 14 December 1903.

34. JGB, unfiled, Brady to Jackson, 19 April 1890.

35. A good summary of the movement is David C. Smith's "The Logging Frontier," *Journal of Forest History* 18 (October 1974); 196–206; and a superlative study of the cargo trade is Thomas R. Cox, *Mills and Markets: A History of the Pacific Coast Lumber Industry to 1900* (Seattle, 1974). Bernhard D. Fernow, "American Lumber," in Chauncey Depew, ed., *One Hundred Years of American Commerce,* 2 vols. (New York, 1895), 1:200.

36. Fred A. Shannon, *The Centennial Years: A Political and Economic History of America from the Late 1870s to the Early 1890s* (Garden City, N.Y., 1967), pp. 253–54; and John Ise, *The United States Forest Policy* (New Haven, 1920), pp. 26ff.

37. Ise, *Forest Policy*, pp. 81–82.

38. Kate Field, "Our Ignorance of Alaska," *North American Review*, July 1889, p. 86.

39. Petroff, *Population and Resources of Alaska*, p. 15.

40. Cox, *Mills and Markets*, pp. 71–100. To taste just how competitive they could be, see John R. Finger, "Seattle's First Sawmill, 1853–1869: A Study of Frontier Enterprise," *Journal of Forest History* 15 (January 1972): 25–31; and Alan Hynding, *The Public Life of Eugene Semple: Promoter and Politician of the Pacific Northwest* (Seattle, 1973), pp. 42–49.

41. *Alaska Appeal*, 1 September 1879; JCorr, 13:107, Brady to Jackson, 20 April 1883. Eliza Ruhamah Scidmore, *Alaska, Its Southern Coast, and the Sitkan Archipelago* (Boston, 1885), p. 172.

42. *Verstovian* (Sitka), November 1914. "The Sawmill at Sitka," *Alaska-Yukon Magazine*, October 1907, pp. 148–50.

43. JCorr, unfiled, "Notes on Trip to Alaska 1881," 5 August 1881 entry; *Occident*, 8 November 1882; JCorr, 12:159, Brady to Jackson, 15 April 1882. Ibid., 10:17, Brady to Jackson, 7 June 1880.

44. Hugh Brady to author, 15 December 1969.

45. *Alaskan*, 3 August 1895. The elementary frames of these cottages exist within a few Sitka homes to this day, testimony not only to their teachers' instructional talents but to the Indians' inherited woodworking skills.

46. Richard C. Berner, "The Port Blakely Mill Company, 1876–1889," *Pacific Northwest Quarterly* 57 (October 1966); 158–71; Cox, *Mills and Markets*, p. 125; and Earl Pomeroy, *The Pacific Slope: A History of California, Oregon, Washington, Idaho, Utah, and Nevada* (New York, 1965), pp. 124–25.

47. Jackson, *Alaska and Missions*, pp. 209–10. JScrap, 18:18, clipping. Lyman E. Knapp, *Annual Report of the Governor of Alaska, 1891* (Washington, D.C., 1892), p. 492.

48. *Alaskan*, 18 May 1889. JCorr, 15:19, Brady to Jackson, 18 April 1889. JGB, unfiled, Elizabeth Brady to commissioner of education, 12 October 1925. *Alaskan*, 24 January 1891.

49. *Alaskan*, 29 August and 18 July 1891. *North Star*, February 1891. *Alaskan*, 9 July 1891.

50. *Thlinget*, August 1908. *Alaskan*, 11 June 1891 and 17 December 1895. Interview with Lawrence Rakestraw, 14 July 1974, Saratoga, Calif. J. E. Defenbaugh, ed., "Alaska and Its Timber," *American Lumberman*, 5 September 1903, p. 18.

51. Patricia Roppel, "Gravina," *Alaska Journal* 2 (Summer 1972): 13–15.

52. JCorr, 16:50, Elizabeth Brady to Jackson, 24 November 1891.

53. *Alaskan*, 24 March 1894. Report by Inspector George H. Miller in Brady, *Annual Report, 1900*, p. 57. Miller, the census agent, must have taken a narrow definition of what constituted marketable lumber, for it seems unlikely that the other ten sawmills then operating in the Panhandle sold none of their mill products, despite the fact that they had been established by missions or corporations primarily to satisfy their own immediate requirements. Brady noted twelve mills in his article "Alaska: Its Resources and Its Needs," *Independent*, 18 January 1900, p. 167.

54. Lyman E. Knapp, *Annual Report of the Governor of Alaska, 1889* (Washington, D.C., 1890), pp. 222–23.

55. Ibid., p. 223.

56. *Alaskan*, 2 July 1893, 16 May 1894, and 17 October 1891. Lawrence Rakestraw to author, 12 December 1970.

57. *Alaskan*, 1 December and 4 April 1894, 21 October 1893, and 19 January 1889; ibid., 19 March 1892; TAP, mf. 5, U.S. Bureau of Education, account with Sheldon Jackson, Brady items, 1888–94.

58. *Alaskan*, 21 February 1891. JCorr, 16:221, Brady to Jackson, 19 November 1892. Henry W. Farnum, ed., *Biographical Record of the Class of 1874 in Yale College* (New Haven, 1912), p. 22.

59. Interview with John and Hugh Brady, 23 June 1962. JCorr, 16:50, Elizabeth Brady to Jackson, 24 November 1891; and ibid., p. 51, Miner W. Bruce to Jackson, 24 November 1891.

60. JCorr, 16:35, Mrs. Haydon to Jackson, 8 November 1891. Defenbaugh, "Alaska and Its Timber," p. 18.

CHAPTER EIGHT

Legal Limbos and Land Hunger

Visions of rapid real estate winnings had excited Sitka's earliest Yankee pioneers. "Speculative minds," reported the *Sitka Times* in 1868, "were soon busy staking off City and water lots, and with such a degree of spirit as to endanger the whole of the Indian village that had been held sacred for years against land grabbers."[1] Nor did the white man's land hunger abate after the collapse of the postpurchase boomlet. A decade later Captain Beardslee felt compelled to fall back on his superiors to force a Sitkan to relinquish his claim to the capital commons.[2]

One does not have to embrace the Turner hypothesis to appreciate how the frontier's "free land" stimulated western settlement. Fee simple ownership promised subsistance, status, and singular freedoms without peer. And because land usually appreciated in value, it provided an attractive means of growth capital; some pioneers made not a single improvement and still reaped a lucrative windfall. Alaska settlers who hacked away at Panhandle forest knew that they "trespassed." Yet it was a rare pioneer whose conscience pricked him for raiding the public domain. To be a ground-breaker was among the most noble of encomiums.

Predictably, Alaska was subjected to this land hunger and its baneful accompaniment of land disputation. A Great Land census taker, Ivan Petroff, warned that "Creoles, being both indolent and shrewd, have settled upon the most desirable ground yielding the most to the least labor, just such lands as speculators and grabbers would seize upon." In 1872 the scientist William H. Dall lambasted Congress for its failure to create "inducements for immigration" such as "extending the land laws of the United States over the Territory."[3] Two decades later, Brady

133

and his fellow Alaskans still remained without America's oft-liberalized homestead legislation.

Although no comprehensive history of Alaskan land policy has yet been written, it seems safe to assert that the territory was in part penalized for illegalities practiced outside Alaska. Throughout the sixties and seventies fraudulent violations of the Homestead Act, the Timber Culture Act, and the Desert Land Act occurred across the western United States. Understandably, Congress was reluctant to open another Pandora's box in the north. The possibility of a fresh shower of contended titles must have produced cold shudders within the General Land Office, an agency already submerged under a deluge of western land litigation.

On the other hand, Great Land citizens never tired of citing these inducements to settlement, just as they never stopped complaining how a "neglectful Congress" unfairly injured their development by denying them this "historic right." Wisely they soft-pedaled the uniqueness of America's Far North frontier—the remoteness of so much of their prodigious territory and its sparse, transient population. These harsh realities remained, even after the Klondike and Nome rushes, and the scattered search for gold throughout the vast Yukon Valley at the beginning of the next century. Finally, and despite John Brady's ceaseless rationalizations to the contrary, Alaska was agriculturally atypical. Occasionally Brady conceded, "Alaska is no agricultural country." More frequently he insisted, "there is plenty of land for growing vegetables for a vast population which can be easily cleared and cultivated."[4]

By the mid-eighties the lamentable abuses of America's beneficent homestead legislation lay revealed. It was Brady's misfortune, as well as Alaska's, that his determination to possess his own quarter section, the hallowed 160 acres, coincided with these unsavory revelations. Pioneer cupidity and corporate fraud were a national disgrace. U.S. Land Commissioner William Andrew Jackson Sparks's solution in 1885 was to suspend from final land entry a considerable portion of the public domain. Westerners roared in rage. For a time President Cleveland defended his courageous subordinate, but in November of 1887 Sparks was dismissed.[5] Fortunately Sparks and a number of public-spirited citizens were alerting politicians that the runaway dispersal of the nation's material heritage must be braked. The wild 1889 Oklahoma land rush dramatically portrayed how imminent was the end of free farmland. The sobering 1890 census declared an end to the continuous frontier line. Few, if any, Alaskans were alarmed by these historic warning signs. Many Americans who were conscious of these events preferred

134

to ignore them. John Brady, and he was not alone, was astonishingly ebullient in his estimates of what modern man's technical wizardry could accomplish. Like those Arizonians who would make the desert bloom, he would create farmland from muskeg.

From the outset, however, the overwhelming preponderance of Alaska settlers sought land not to farm but for resident-commercial purposes. Governor John Kinkead was doubtless correct when he predicted, "Without such legal right to property, progress in the direction of advancement will be slow and very uncertain."[6] President Harrison's 1889 gubernatorial appointee, Vermont Republican Lyman E. Knapp, echoed his two predecessors. However, unlike Governor Swineford, Governor Knapp persistently championed native as well as white land ownership. Indisputably his was a more equitable policy, if one that further complicated the disposition of Alaska's lands.

A churchgoing Christian, Governor Knapp quickly established a reasonably healthy working relationship with both his neighbor Brady and Alaska's man in Washington, Sheldon Jackson. Although in neither instance did the association become a friendship, Knapp's genuine sensitivity to the problems of Alaska's aboriginal peoples encouraged the Presbyterians' initial confidence in him. Alaska's third governor espoused a native policy that reflected America's General Allotment Act of 1887. The General Allotment, or Severalty Act, had been shepherded through Congress by Senator Henry L. Dawes and aimed to transform America's tribal nomadic Indians into self-supporting farmers. Dawes and Jackson were allies in the highly vocal friends-of-the-Indian movement. Indeed, Jackson had recently importuned the Massachusetts senator to come north and inspect the advances of Panhandle natives.

In his 1889 *Annual Report* Knapp observed that the life-style of the Alaska natives had "never led them in the direction of cultivation of the soil. But they . . . have even stronger desires than the whites to acquire property." He recommended a "law giving some method of acquiring homesteads and fields for cultivation . . . where the land is suitable, either by preemption or otherwise, and especially giving them to the natives without purchase, upon certain conditions of cultivation."[7] It was Dawes's severalty philosophy applied as a panacea for Tlingit, Haida, or Tsimshian acculturation dilemmas. Four years later, when he was replaced by a Democratic governor, Knapp still urged fee simple land allotment for the natives.

What is significant here is not the governor's dubious notion that the southeastern littoral could support "fields for cultivation" but that he advocated an Alaskan Indian homestead policy more generous than that proposed for white men. Like the pronative "pesky missionaries,"

Knapp had been converted. Writing to Senator Orville H. Platt, he warned, "There seems to be insufficient provision for the protection of the Indians, or *native*, as I prefer to call him." He needs "protection against the rapacity of unscrupulous whites who are better educated than he is in the art of *grabbing* for the best places. . . . protection to the natives is my especial object."[8]

It seems inescapable that concern for Alaska's natives was also a factor in the reluctance of Congress to extend the nation's liberal land laws northward. Sheldon Jackson said little on the matter. When he addressed himself to the problem, he urged the application within Alaska of the Agricultural and Mechanical College benefits.[9] Brady and others might view every additional white arrival as additional dollars, but not Jackson. In his eyes too large a number of white migrants were just additional crosses to be borne by unassimilated natives.

In 1890, thoroughly disgusted by Washington's unattentiveness, Alaskans held another nonpartisan convention. As at the 1881 gathering in Juneau, the participants formally communicated to Congress a brief list of grievances. To represent them they dispatched an official delegate, the popular steamer captain James Carroll. The *Alaskan* kept its readers informed on their "indefatigable" agent who was buttonholing legislators and busy at "conferences with the Secretary of the Interior on the . . . regulations governing the taking of timber from the public domain, and the extension of the land laws over the Territory."[10]

Carroll reminded the House Committee on Territories that "the fact of scarcity of population does not justify neglect of it by the National Government, nor can it ever be peopled unless the land laws of the United States are put in force therein and government surveys made so as to insure a title to settlers." His remarks were concluded in terms his listeners understood. Alaska "was purchased from Russia at the cost of $7,200,000, and up to the present time has returned to the Treasury of the United States from industry alone $8,694,965.67." Alaska "shipped last year out of the Territory fish, oil, bone, furs, gold, etc. amounting to about $11,000,000."[11] Did Captain Carroll have unlimited confidence in the persuasive pull of hard cash, or was he merely twitting Washington? Before returning home he grandly offered to purchase the boreal territory if the federal government no longer desired it!

Any politically ambitious Alaskan laboring to form a political constituency faced a herculean task. In 1890 the Great Land could not even claim five thousand prospective voters. Even when turn-of-the-century gold rushes substantially increased its inhabitants, the miners' sojourner outlook and the geographic disunity of Alaska's gold fields badly handicapped the formation of articulate, territory-wide pressure groups. Alaska, like other Far West territories, had to suffer through that ignominious early stage of political organization described by Kenneth N. Owens as "chaotic factionalism," years "characterized by disruptive, confused, intensely combative, and highly personal politics."[12]

For diversion in 1884 Brady had polled Sitka's electorate when Republican presidential candidate James G. Blaine ran against Grover Cleveland. Blaine won handily at Sitka, though he lost nationally. Brady's poll confirmed nothing more than Sitkans' durable ties with the Grand Old Party.[13] Not until 1888 when two Alaskans participated in the national Democratic convention would a national party directly address itself to Alaska's appeals. It would require the stampede to Dawson City ten years hence and its mining aftershocks to induce a majority of stateside legislators to be attentive to Far North spokesmen. Nevertheless, the presence of Alaskans at a national political convention set a significant precedent. Thereafter Sitka, and especially Juneau, hosted a variety of political gatherings. If the organizers took them seriously, the participants frequently did not. Robert E. Coontz remembered how quickly a presidential election victory banquet could bring about an exchange of party buttons among the losers.[14] Nor could Alaskans become very aroused over such national controversies as the tariff, silver certificates, or "the plight of the farmer at the hands of the railroad monopolies." Merely the vaguest promise of a railroad monopoly linking Alaska with the United States would have produced jubilation. Boreal settlers and their stateside allies fractured into varying splinters of opinion on the degree of home rule. On the matter of legislation for facilitating bona fide land ownership, however, there was general agreement: homesteading rights had been too long withheld.

While Brady and his coworkers pressed for the importation of the homestead law, an even older federal law, the 1841 Preemption Act, supplied a faint silver lining to their dreams of possessing real property. Preemption had legalized a historic reality. Westerners, Thomas Jefferson had prophesied, "will settle the lands in spite of everybody." Yet for Alaska's land-hungry Yankees, even preemptive occupancy was no safeguard. Elsewhere it had "democratized the American land system and placed the actual settler on an equal basis with the speculator." However, that had been true only for publicly surveyed land, which did not exist in the district.[15]

The Land Act of 1891, also called the General Revision Act of 1891 or the Forest Reserve Act, may well have been the "most important agrarian measure ever passed by Congress."[16] Sections of that omnibus enactment seemed to portend a new day for Alaskans. Eliza Scidmore predicted, "The pioneers have partially triumphed, . . . [and can] secure public lands for town-site purposes at the rate of one dollar a quarter of an acre, with the costs of survey added; and land for trading and manufacturing purposes at two dollars and half an acre. Settlers and miners may cut timber, for use on their own claims or lands, from any public lands not reserved or appropriated. Under these conditions the pioneer may now have a home."[17] Sitkans talked excitedly about lots being "sold to occupants for $10. each" and "160 acres for trading or manufacturing purposes at $2.50 an acre." It was not long before fourteen pages of instructions arrived from Washington, detailing how "parties desiring to make entries" might do so. "The law," observed the *Alaskan*, places the native Alaskans upon the same footing as the white people of the Territory," and rejoiced that "it will enable present residents of Alaska to make improvements of a substantial character and to feel that such improvements . . . can be held permanently and securely during their chosen or enforced absence from the Territory."[18] Furthermore, the law "will . . . tend to create some movement in real estate because parties having real property to sell will be enabled to transfer it in a tangible form."[19] To expedite the 1891 act a number of meetings were held. Brady exuded optimism. "I think that an application for the United States patent of the Sitka town-site will not meet with any obstacles and that the people . . . have the matter in their own hands." He reminded his neighbors that there were only "20 de facto property holders in this town." "Let us have a townsite under a U.S. patent so every man who owns a house in this town will stand on an equal footing," John urged.[20] Some of his neighbors were dubious. Where would Sitka's Russian-American citizens find the money to pay for their survey and title? Also, the legislation did too little for any future corporations. In his typically querulous manner, Henry Hayden complained, "Alaska itself stands as an Ishmael among the sisterhood of States and Territories."[21]

By August of 1893 Alaska's ex officio surveyor general specified that under the 1891 act "there have been received 77 applications for which orders and instructions have been issued." Sixty-eight official surveys were executed in the field, with 252 plats of all descriptions being drawn up.[22] The plats were no more than a house of cards. At the turn of the century, the Alaska Bar Association reported: "Owing to the strict and somewhat forced construction placed upon the section providing for the entry of trading and manufacturing sites made by the General Land Office, only two patents have been issued . . . for Southeastern Alaska."[23]

Federal indifference, smothering even this belated land legislation, confounded Brady. His resentment can only have increased when he discovered that the highly touted 1891 omnibus law had also teminated America's historic preemption. With preemption dead, his frustration about securing a confirmed land title was magnified by fear that he might lose his home and mill. It was just as well that he did not then know that this struggle to obtain a title would drag on for another ten years!

Judge John S. Bugbee editorialized on how badly the 1891 legislation discriminated against Alaskan business.[24] Other Sitkans angrily protested that southside investors "exploited the northern colony." For all of Alaska's "rich possibilities," lamented Governor Knapp, "unless there is an accumulation of wealth, . . . power to carry financial burdens may be small indeed." Although annual exports exceeded imports by nearly seven million dollars, Alaska's business was "carried on with foreign capital, and with imported laborers who leave the country as soon as the work is done. Its carrying trade is done with foreign ships. . . . no money is spent in the Territory except to carry on business with a view to the greatest immediate profit." In summary, "Nothing is left in the country which can be carried away."[25] The governor not only exaggerated but erred when he stated that "none of its products are retained within its borders." Brady was amassing a swelling bank account by doing exactly that. Yet the thrust of Knapp's admonition was correct: too often the northern territory was treated like a colony.

Although apprehensive at the prospect of losing his sawmill site, John forged ahead. Experience had taught him to persist in his property claims, expect a joust with officialdom, defend himself with righteous indignation, call on Jackson for aid when necessary, and then, if he must, be satisfied with half a loaf. Like Amos Whitford he had few compunctions about benefiting from that which lay at hand and possessed latent value—witness his quasi-expropriation of the Sitka Hot Springs, idle mooring buoys in the harbor, the initial Sitka Trading Company store, and his unblushing trespass on archipelago timber.[26] An acutely discomforting result of this acquisitiveness was his land dispute with Ranche Indians.

The Sitka Tlingits, aggrieved at Judge Brady's encroachment upon their burial grounds, understood only dimly the historic and tragic encounter between red and white Americans. Certainly Brady would have been stunned had a contemporary called him a hypocrite. His defense of Alaska Indians and his unflagging efforts to prepare them for entry into his society were manifest. Perhaps John's driving compulsion to be his own man made him incapable of penetrating the Indian mind. He sweated to dominate nature, to affix his imprimatur on it, to capitalize on it, and to make it return a profit. In contrast the aboriginal possessed an environmental empathy that was essentially static. This is not to say that Northwest Coast Indians did not energetically utilize the resources of sea and shore. As one 1890 visitor discerned, "The Indians here store up everything they get their hands on: old sea chests, uniforms, carpenter's and blacksmith's tools all find their way to their storehouses."[27] Paradoxically, this aggrandizement of personal property was epitomized at every potlatch, their popular gift-giving celebration. However, privately owned land with precisely defined boundaries was another matter. Trees rotted; showers and ocean storms altered a beach, a forest, even a mountainside. Winter villages and summer fishing sites changed as necessity and whim dictated. Life's vagaries were personified in those spirits who inhabited sky, sea, and slope. Such unfathomable enigmas humbled these preindustrial peoples and ineluctably checked their conceit.

John had been ruffled and then angered when Governor Swineford had thrust himself into the Indians' burial site quarrel. Three years later, in December of 1893, when Brady's lumbermill had long since become a "Sitka business establishment" and his growing family was about to move into their handsome new house, the natives again acted. Some thirty Ranche Indians, among them a few chiefs, denounced his occupancy before Alaska's ex officio surveyor general and registrar of the U.S. Land Office. George Kostrometinoff joined them as interpreter. "They said that when Mr. Brady swore that the Indian population made no claim to the land applied for—in common English he told an untruth. The fact is they . . . lay claim to all the property [he] has applied for as their own in fee simple." In his defense Brady presented papers demonstrating that he had "applied in due form for 160 acres." To this the Tlingits reported that the ground had been granted them by the Russians over half a century ago; "the land is as much their own as the other portions of Sitka are the property of the white race." Furthermore, they insisted that the United States had confirmed their claim and that they should be protected in the enjoyment of it. Governor Swineford had sought to have the federal authorities block Brady from continuing his building projects, but Alaska's white chief had failed. Now these structures stood on their land. White man and red profited from Brady's mill, but the land remained theirs. They insisted "that the Great father at Washington should be informed of these proposed wrongs to his Indian children in Alaska."[28]

For John the friction was embarrassing, to say the least. Not for a moment did their resentment or his distress dissuade him from the rightness of his occupancy. During January of 1894 Alaska's district attorney, Charles S. Johnson, officially filed the natives' protest. April was set as the time for resolving the matter.[29] The white man's law stated that in support of final title proof the applicant must swear "That no portion of the land applied for is occupied . . . or claimed by any native of Alaska." John Brady's Satchahnee home and his Sitka sawmill buildings visibly reminded the Ranche elders how costly their procrastination had been. Justice was due them, they insisted, "for their village by increasing in population from year to year, the houses are more numerous and closer together, . . . they cannot extend their village on account of Mr. Brady's land." It was a shrewd argument, and it carried a double edge. Among the capital's white residents, not a few wanted the Indians to push their enclave to the northwest, away from Sitka proper. Tlingits recalled that their "trail back of the Indian village extending to Harbor Mountain" had been used for many years to collect wood. At the base of the mountain they constructed their canoes. Furthermore, they claimed "that cranberries and other berries grow on the land, which they use for domestic purposes and derive quite a revenue from the same in the market."[30]

In May the *Alaskan* reported that "John G. Brady and the Indians met in arbitration and the matter was amicably settled by . . . compromise." In truth it would seem that prosecutor Johnson and defendant Brady once again confirmed the meaning of blood brothers. A document now resting in the National Archives gives a glimpse of what happened:

> Brady agrees that said Indians may gather berries for their own use on said land, and that the Indians may cross the land by any trail that they have to reach the land beyond Brady's land. Brady is to put gates not over two on the outside boundary line of the land he wants, where the Indians may suggest, but will not be required to move them when once fixed, and as many gates elsewhere as are necessary for the Indians to follow the trails they have to reach the Ranche. . . . whenever the Indians cease to use it all rights are to belong to Brady. . . . Brady agrees not to throw away any bones of dead Indians into the Sea, or to expose them to public view, but whenever he sees or finds any to bury the same out of sight.[31]

Finally, "For the consideration of all these things Brady acknowledges the payment of a dollar to him from the Indians, and the Indians a dollar from him. Brady agrees never to throw filth in or pollute the water of Swan Lake." Seven natives then scratched their *X*'s below Brady's signature.

It was a sorry business and was all the more unpardonable because it seems that neither Brady nor his white neighbors sensed the unfairness of the arrangement. Paradoxically, the only white to go on record opposing Brady's action had been Alfred P. Swineford, a man who, according to his daughter, was an outspoken white supremacist. Proof that the Indians knew that they had been scalped occurred the following year when a Ranche inhabitant, Tlingit Charles Morse, offered his house for sale at five hundred dollars. His neighbors drew up a document that "unanimously resolved that Mr. Morse had no right to sell his house to any white man, . . . that the land belonged to the Indians as a whole and not to individual members of the tribe." In self-defense they notified "all people that the Indian village real estate is owned by Indians collectively and no one Indian can sell any portion of it."[32]

Various interpretations can be drawn from John Brady's implacable and protracted struggle to obtain title to "his" quarter section. One view sees him as just a typical land-hungry frontiersman. Another explanation, and surely an element in his own rationalization, was John's awareness that his campaign was also Alaska's, that his eventual victory would be in the best interests of Americanization. To him continued denial to Far North pioneers of America's historic fee simple title of 160 acres was intolerable.

Once John had resolved the burial ground dispute, he had every reason to assume that his survey would be approved. Sitka's registrar and surveyor, their investigation completed, accepted Brady's final proof. He paid his fee, and "all the papers [were] forwarded to the General Land Office for a patent." The commissioner's reply surely must have shaken him. Instead of granting John 160 acres, Washington officialdom had approved twenty. Of course he immediately appealed to the secretary of the interior. And of course months of delay and anxiety ensued. Finally it was conceded that John's improvements spread over fifty acres and he was justified to own that much Sitka real estate. John then discovered that if he accepted this he must have it surveyed again at his own expense and pay $2.50 per acre besides— that there was no provision of law to reimburse him for the money that he had already laid out. Needless to say, he paid. In 1898 Alaska's governor could report, "The Land Office has issued one patent only under the law of March 3, 1891 for trade and manufacture."[33]

John's citizen-versus-state contest to secure a bona fide land patent paralleled a similar tug-of-war to win legal authorization for timber cutting. The campaign, although less arduous, proved almost as prolonged. Somehow the rules of the timber trespass contest were every bit as murky as those pertaining to Alaska land claims. The fact that John waged both struggles concurrently, and in both instances the U.S. government was his adversary, unquestionably toughened his political combativeness. A self-righteous attitude born of these abrasive land-

The Brady children pose before the governor's home, Satchahnee, in 1904. (Reproduced by permission of the Beinecke Rare Book and Manuscript Library, Yale University.)

lumber squabbles may in part explain John's aggressive insensitivity to the Tlingits' property rights.

In 1885 and again the following year, land commissioner William Sparks had counseled resident Alaskans that they might cut timber "for their own use in the vicinity where obtained, for building, agricultural, mining and other domestic purposes." On no account, he had warned, must Alaska timber be exported.[34] Although the General Land Office chose for the moment to overlook Alaskans who logged on the public domain, that is, trespassed, Commissioner Sparks, with his customary diligence, energetically pursued those who exported archipelago lumber. In 1887 San Francisco's U.S. district attorney availed himself of Commissioner Brady's services for a suit against "two vessels, with cargoes aggregating somewhere between half and three-quarters of a million of valuable lumber, cut at the mills on Prince of Wales Island."[35] Captain William Thonegal of the *Gem* was eventually found guilty of having cut five hundred thousand feet of lumber from government land. For his blunder Thonegal paid a fine of $8,145. The defendant had broken the law by selling Alaskan wood outside the district, yet Governor Swineford bemoaned "the embarrassment caused by the timber law which allows no white person to lawfully use wood and timber from the public lands, even for domestic or other local purposes."[36]

Fortunately for Brady, the U.S. Land Office had chosen to avoid the "severe consequences of strict compliance" of the timber trespass laws. "Nearly, if not quite all, of the timber consumed by these mills in Alaska," one inspector reported, "is cut from public lands. . . . This has time out of mind been the custom, the people of Alaska having felt that their isolated condition and the demands made upon them . . . justified them in doing so."[37] No prosecution had been brought "against parties using timber and wood for local purposes." Logging for "local purposes" had generally been tolerated by the government all over the West.

During 1889 Sitkans received word that a U.S. timber agent would soon visit them to attempt to resolve "the very important question as regards the rights of local residents to remove trees from the government land in this Territory and convert them into lumber for domestic use." Charles Gee had been ordered north to halt "depredations occurring on the national domain." Upon his arrival in September Gee found plenty of evidence of timber trespass scattered around Alaska's capital. It lay afloat within rafts, piled on beaches, and in various stages of manufacture about the local mills. Somehow Gee consumed almost a year "collecting a resume of his observations."[38] Instead of being stigmatized as a prying government snooper, he soon wore the label of "our popular U.S. Timber Agent," who "has no wish to inflict hardship or injustice on anyone, nor to interfere with the growth and development of the Territory's resources." But the delights of Sitkan hospitality notwithstanding, he had a job to do. In August of 1890 Gee requested U.S. District Attorney Johnson to commence "actions for damages for timber trespass against: The Lake Mountain Mining Co. for $225. John G. Brady et al., for $450. The Alaska Mill and Mining Co. $12,750. The Eastern Alaska Mill and Mining Co., for $900." Brady was ordered to close his mill.[39]

It almost seems to have been a charade. Although Agent Gee fully expected Alaska's lumbermen to heed him, he probably presumed that the local courts would act to compromise if not nullify his suits. Furthermore, these pioneer entrepreneurs, like their counterparts to the south, could be counted on to plead for special dispensation from Washington. Then, after an appropriate pause, the sawmills would renew their ripping whine and the march of progress could continue unimpeded.

After shutting down his mill, John promptly called for help from Alaska's general agent for education. Jackson, it may be recalled, also happened to be an employee of the Department of the Interior. Meanwhile, Brady's neighbor, district attorney Charles Johnson, pressed the government's suit against the Panhandle lumbermen. The latter first stalled and then practically admitted "that the [U.S. government] is entitled to stumpage." One defendant "actually made an offer to pay at the rate of 20 cents for each tree cut down." Even during the period when his mill lay mute, John did not lose much production. He temporarily shifted his operations to the training school. Gee obliged by promising not to "interfere with the mission sawmill unless he found them selling lumber."[40]

By mid-1891 Panhandle mills were again humming. Facilitating their reopening was the passage of the Land Act of 1891. Just as it confused the issue of fee simple Alaska land claims, the land legislation failed to clarify archipelago cutting practices. Brady, Haltern, and other sawyers preferred to believe that the law and the subsequent 5 May 1891 "Rules and Regulations Governing the Use of Timber on Public Lands" did not totally prohibit trespass. Apparently loggers henceforth had to file an application for cutting timber with the U.S. Land Office at Sitka, afterward admitting the scale of their "innocent trespass," and, when requested, pay the federal government according to a predetermined rate. Trespass would be quasi-legal, what the *Alaskan* labeled a "compromise." Of course, "innocent trespass" presumed that Far North lumbermen would submit reasonably accurate reports. The De-

145

partment of the Interior had little alternative. To assign a timber agent to shadow each woodsman and check his annual harvest of spruce, hemlock, and cedar was impossible. Gee had not even been able to afford a launch to chase British Columbians felling Panhandle trees.[41]

The *Alaskan*, unhappy with the ambiguous timber law, fervently wished for a remedy to "the absence of any legislation [specifically] authorizing the cutting down of trees in Alaska." In the meantime, the newspaper suggested that signs be placed about Alaska's forests reading, "Who touches it will prick himself," and the beautiful but nettle-covered devil's club flower "should occupy a conspicuous place in the design of the territorial seal."[42] For Alaskans like Brady, businessmen striving to import and implant Americanization, it was gallows humor. For all the Great Land's magnificent vistas and munificent resources, those who labored to transform the territory into an Illinois or an Oregon struggled against ominous geo-economic odds. Whenever action, or lack of action, by the federal government worsened those odds, the probability of bankruptcy became harrowingly real. Journalists and tourists might applaud this Great Land; its authentic pioneers knew better. Alaska was a hard land.

To Brady's generation man's rational powers had accomplished miracles in raising the standard of living. The ability to dominate his environment had not been matched, however, by a recognition of how finite were the earth's resources. Well before the twentieth century began, American's conservation movement was launched.[43] Alaska might be remote, unappreciated, with a puny voice in national councils, but her riches would not be slighted by a "people of plenty" with gargantuan appetites. Thankfully, embryo conservation awareness had slowed the destruction of Alaska's Pribiloff seals and the far-flung assault on her "unlimited salmon."[44]

During 1892 Alaska loggers were reminded that a permit to cut trees on public lands granted no "more than 50 per cent of the timber of each class growing on any acre." Henceforth monthly statements, under oath, would be required, giving the description of the tracts from which the timber was cut, "the amount cut and how disposed of." Furthermore, no one would be permitted "to fell or remove any kinds whatsoever, less than eight inches in diameter." And loggers would be responsible for the "tops and brush of the trees . . . to prevent forest fires, and be held liable in damages for the spread of any fire attributable to his neglect." A fine of five hundred dollars and an added six months' imprisonment awaited those found guilty of such neglect.[45] Congress had replied with its own "neglect thesis."

LEGAL LIMBOS AND LAND HUNGER

"There need be no fear of Alaska being denuded of its timber," asserted Brady in 1898, "as long as rain falls as it does, and that will surely be as long as the Japan current flows and the mountains stand."[46] Sixty-five years later gigantic Japanese-owned mills would be processing Alaska's spruce and hemlock forests while environmentalists complained that whole mountainsides of denuded archipelago islands were slipping into the sea. In fact, even before the nineteenth century ended, technology's capacity to speed up time, shrink space, and swell waste spectacularly evidenced itself in the northland. The catalyst was a gold discovery. Ironically, Klondike Creek sparkled in Canada's Yukon Territory, yet despite its location, the mad rush to get there marked the end of one Alaskan epoch and the genesis of another.

1. *Sitka Times*, 24 October 1868. See also *Alaskan Times*, 30 July 1869.

2. *Alaska Appeal*, 15 February 1880.

3. Ibid., 15 January 1880. William H. Dall, "Is Alaska a Paying Investment," *Harper's Monthly*, January 1872, p. 257.

4. Ballou, *New Eldorado*, p. 302. Essential in understanding the evolution of Alaska's land policies are the annual reports of the commissioner(s) of the General Land Office during these years. For the overall national picture see Vernon Carstensen, ed., *The Public Lands: Studies in the History of the Public Domain* (Madison, 1963), and Paul W. Gates, *History of Public Land Law Development* (Washington, D.C., 1969). An excellent appraisal of Alaska's agricultural prospects is James R. Shortridge, "The Evaluation of the Agricultural Potential of Alaska, 1867–1897," *Pacific Northwest Quarterly* 68 (April 1977); 88–98.

5. Roy M. Robbins, *Our Landed Heritage: The Public Domain, 1776–1936* (Lincoln, Nebr., 1962), pp. 291–95. Kent L. Steckmesser, *The Westward Movement: A Short History* (New York, 1969), pp. 387–90.

6. Kinkead, *Annual Report, 1884*, p. 640.

7. *Alaskan*, 31 August 1889. Knapp, *Annual Report, 1889*, p. 224.

8. Lyman E. Knapp, *Annual Report of the Governor of Alaska, 1892* (Washington, D.C., 1893), p. 540. AGP, box 1, Knapp to Platt, 31 March 1890.

9. *Juneau City Mining Record*, 29 January 1891.

10. *Alaskan*, 7 February 1891.

11. U.S., Congress, Senate, *Proceedings of a Convention in Alaska*, 51st Cong., 2d sess., Exec. Doc. 39, 13 January 1891. *Alaskan*, 2 March 1891.

12. Owens, "Pattern and Structure in Western Territorial Politics," pp. 163–64.

13. JScrap, 11:128, "Blaine and Cleveland."

14. *San Francisco Chronicle*, 23 June 1887; *Alaskan*, 9 November 1888 and 20 September 1890. Coontz, *From the Mississippi*, pp. 163–64.

15. Roy Robbins, "Preemption—A Frontier Triumph," *Mississippi Valley Historical Review* 17 (December 1931): 349.

16. Ibid. For the 1891 law's application to Alaska, see Fred F. Barker, comp., *Compilation of the Acts of Congress and Treaties Relating to Alaska from March 30, 1867 to March 3, 1905* (Washington, D.C.), pp. 31–39.

147

17. Scidmore, "Alaska's Mining Regions," p. 465.

18. *Alaskan*, 4 April 1891.

19. Ibid., 18 July 1891.

20. Ibid., 26 December, 1891.

21. Ibid., 19 December, 1891.

22. *Alaska Journal*, 19 August 1893.

23. Arthur K. Delaney, *Alaska Bar Association and Sketch of Judiciary* (San Francisco, 1901), p. 13.

24. Bugbee's editorials ran in the *Alaskan* from 25 October to 30 November 1895.

25. Knapp, *Annual Report, 1891*, p. 487.

26. CHR, vol. 2, February 1881–December 1883, Brady to Teller, 12 June 1881; ibid., vol. 25, J. C. Coghlan to Brady, 15 March 1884; ibid., vol. 1, December 1889–September 1890, Brady to Max Pracht, 31 July 1890; ibid., vol. 32A, Herbert F. Beecher to Delaney, 11 May 1887; ibid., Brady to Delaney, 13 May 1887; ibid., vol. 3, April 1887–January 1888, I. H. Maynard to Delaney, 5 December 1887.

27. E. J. Glave, "The Village of Klukwan," ed. Jo Sherman, *Alaska Journal* 4 (Spring 1974): 86.

28. *Alaska Herald*, 11 December 1893.

29. *Alaskan*, 27 January 1894.

30. *Alaskan Herald*, 5 May 1894.

31. Ibid.; TAP, mf. 3, agreement between Brady and Indians, Sitka, 2 May 1894.

32. *Alaskan*, 9 February 1895.

33. Brady, *Annual Report, 1898*, p. 199; and *Alaskan*, 27 August 1898.

34. CHR, February 1874–September 1889, Sparks to ex officio receiver of public money, 27 October 1885; *Alaskan*, 13 February 1886.

35. JGB, mf. 1, Brady to his wife, 3 July 1887. Sessions, "Alaska," p. 276. Alfred P. Swineford, *Annual Report of the Governor of Alaska, 1886* (Washington, D.C., 1886), p. 246; *Alaskan*, 29 May and 5 June 1886 and 30 March 1889.

36. Knapp, *Annual Report, 1889*, p. 225.

37. James W. Witten, *Report on the Agricultural Prospects, Natives, Salmon, Fisheries, Gold Prospects, etc. of Alaska, 1903* (Washington, D.C., 1904), p. 91.

38. *Alaskan*, 8 June, 31 August, 14 and 28 September 1889.

39. Ibid., 21 December 1889; and 16 August, 20 September and 25 October 1890.

40. Ibid., 30 August and 20 December 1890. JGB, unfiled, Brady to Jackson, 19 April 1890. AGP, box 11, Brady to Charles Valentine, 9 March 1898; National Archives, unfiled Alaska education letters, O. D. Eaton to Jackson, 17 December 1890.

41. Lawrence Rakestraw to author, 12 December 1980. *Alaskan*, 20 December 1890, 28 November and 12 December 1891, and 2 January 1892; *Juneau City Mining Record*, 29 January 1891. A few years earlier encroachment and abuse of the public domain had become so serious at Yellowstone National Park that the U.S. Army had been called in (H. Duane Hampton, *How the U.S. Cavalry Saved Our National Parks* [Bloomington, Ind., 1971], pp. 80–112).

42. *Alaskan*, 7 March 1891.

43. Douglas H. Strong, *The Conservationists* (Menlo Park, Calif., 1971), pp. 10–11. Paul W. Gates, "Public Land Issues in the United States," *Western Historical Quarterly* 2 (October 1971): 373.

44. Although a thorough study of conservation in Alaska is yet to be written, an introduction is the author's "Alaska and the Emergence of America's Conservation Consciousness," *The Prairie Scout* 2 (Abilene, Kans., 1974): 79–111; and for the larger

national picture, see Lawrence Rakestraw, "Conservation Historiography: An Assessment," *Pacific Historical Review* 41 (August 1972): 271–88, and Roderick Nash, *Wilderness and the American Mind* (New Haven, 1967).

45. *Alaskan*, 2 January 1892 and 13 April 1895.

46. Brady, *Annual Report, 1897*, p. 180.

CHAPTER NINE

The Pace of Change Quickens

The nineties in America have been described as "gay," "mauve," and even "black." Obviously a contemporary's opinion depended on the individual's specific circumstances. The master of Satchahnee subscribed to a sanguine view, for while John Brady's lumber mill buzzed profitably his toddlers chattered happily at home. In harsh contrast was America's mid-nineties business collapse. Beginning in 1893 it shoved men into bread lines from Philadelphia to San Francisco, a depression so bitter as to compel an Ohio businessman to lead a protest march on the nation's capital. The impact on John's affairs appears to have been slight. Although West Coast lumber mills wallowed in "a desperate struggle for survival," his financial position steadily brightened.[1]

Predictably, the *Alaskan* saw sunny times ahead for the capital community: the Union Pacific Company planned to build a new hotel at Sitka, and recent homestead legislation practically invited a "cooperative colony" to settle nearby. Luckily an attempt to move the capital to Juneau "by a clique of unscrupulous speculators" had been defeated. "The outlook for Sitka," purred the *Alaskan*, "is undoubtedly of a roseate hue and those pioneer residents whose ardor has been so frequently deferred by hope long deferred should take courage."[2] Brady did not need courage, simply more hours in each day to keep pace with orders for lathes, tunnel beams, packing boxes, and lumber of considerable diversity. Swelling construction demands from Juneau-Douglas, archipelago native hamlets, and the scattered salmon canneries provided fluctuating markets that his low overhead, flexible firm met handily.

The district's salmon pack had multiplied from some six thousand cases in the early eighties to over 966,000 by 1896. Fifty-three steamers,

The Brady lumber mill at Sitka, obviously busy (date unknown). (Reproduced by permission of the Beinecke Rare Book and Manuscript Library, Yale University.)

over seven hundred lighters and boats, and thousands of employees canned salmon for the 1897 season approaching a market value of nearly three million dollars.[3] Californians had virtually destroyed their once enormous salmon catch. Columbia River fishermen seemed equally intent on eliminating their waterborne wealth. Witnessing the spreading assault on Pacific salmon, one-time U.S. fish commissioner Eugene G. Blackford groaned, "There can be no question as to the speedy extermination of the salmon in some Alaskan rivers."[4] Special agent Howard M. Kutchin described the devastating decline at Karluk River on Kodiak Island. "By the existing [fishing] methods the approaches to the river on both sides are completely cleared of fish, and it is no exaggeration to say that now where a single salmon makes its way to the lake there were formerly 10,000."[5]

In 1889, alarmed at the Pacific Coast mayhem, Congress belatedly prohibited the use of barricades. Two years transpired before feeble enforcement began. Money was then found for one inspector and an assistant, this for a territory with a longer coastline than the contiguous United States. Little wonder that one cynical observer of Congress's Alaska enactments observed, "there is no law north of fifty-four forty." "While in a degree that caustic remark was doubtless meant as hyperbole," replied Agent Kutchin, "it is a very grave fact that the enforcement of the law in the District of Alaska is surrounded by so many obstructions, and there are so many persons not averse to taking advantage of the fact, that . . . the laws . . . are by no means scrupulously observed."[6] A few years later Charles P. Elliott, a retired U.S. Army officer, put it more bluntly: "There is no inclination on the part of the canneries in Alaska to obey the laws or orders of the Fish Commission. As far as I could see there was no pretense to do anything except to catch fish in whatever way they could."[7]

Certainly the cannery corporations had no desire to preside at their own financial burials, and they most certainly understood the danger of overfishing. "Paradoxically though it may appear," reported one Treasury Department special agent, "it is nevertheless true, that none are more anxious to save and perpetuate the salmon than the salmon canners themselves, and yet their methods are such as if continued, will very soon destroy them."[8]

In the greedy pursuit of dollars, it was once again the aborigines whose life-style altered the most markedly. Wherever a cannery arose, native acculturation sped up. By the mid-nineties over a thousand natives found summer employment in and about the processing centers. Others accepted the white man's money economy after bringing in their catch to be canned. As with Indian women who journeyed south to find seasonal employment at Victoria and Vancouver, the assimilation was not particularly edifying, nor was what they spent their earnings on always wise. Yet many natives were not beguiled by a cannery payroll. A large percentage of those who did join the imported Chinese workers invariably left, bored by the tedium of long hours spent racing a clock and feeding tireless machines. Indigenes who preferred their own less hurried summer fishing could not remain oblivious to the widening intrusion of the salmon canneries. Was it not enough that the invader pockmarked the earth looking for the gold and removed their towering cedars? Must he now carry off their elementary food supply?

A rising number of Indian cannery employees dissipated their earnings on liquor. The merchant John J. Healy informed Governor Knapp that the situation up the Lynn Canal "demands your immediate presence." Healy predicted, "*There will be serious trouble here before long if something is not done to restore confidence to these natives.*" Not only were the Chilkat Canning Company and the Pyramid Harbor Packing Company encroaching on the Chilkats' ancient fishing grounds, but, according to Healy, men from the Chilkat Canning Company were selling lemon extract to the natives.[9] Twice the *Pinta* with its marine policemen had steamed into this region to pacify hostile Chilkats. This time before it arrived the Indians killed one white man and wounded another. "Killers Tom and Qualth" quietly gave themselves over to the *Pinta* for white man's justice. The *Alaskan* pointed the finger of guilt at "a free indulgence of firewater" and "sheer neglect of Alaska's interest by the General Government."[10] Seeking to head off just such sanguinary frictions, Governor Knapp had earlier issued to the Indians "'papers' with big seals attached and recommendations and certificates of good character . . . to warn white men against fishing for trout or salmon in the creeks and bays." The *Juneau City Mining Record* scored Knapp's temerity for taking it upon himself "to create a small sized siwash land office as well as a sort of court for the adjudication of siwash difficulties."[11]

Brady watched these abrasive episodes with reactions that are not hard to imagine. For years representatives of Pacific Slope corporations had come north and elbowed aside the Northwest Coast peoples. Although grateful for the lumber purchases of these well-financed San Francisco and Portland corporations, John protested illegal acts perpetrated by their employees. Finally, his patience exhausted, he concluded that a show of force was required to check such arrogant deployment of nets and traps—offenses certain to enflame red-white relations. Not long after the Chilkat killings, Skookum Bob, a Klawock Indian, hurried to Sitka and lodged a formal complaint against the cannery superintendent, A. S. Wadleigh. Wadleigh and his men had installed traps across the Klawock River, thereby "hindering the run of salmon, depriving the Indians of their years stock of fish for support of themselves and families." When Skookum Bob first protested, Superintendent Wadleigh had countered by unabashedly demanding rental money, asserting that the Tlingit's home occupied ground on the corporation's fishing site.[12]

Satisfied that the Indian told the truth and Wadleigh's men cared little for the law, John had himself appointed assistant district attorney. Accompanied by Sitkans William Kelly, currently a U.S. commissioner, special deputy marshall George Kostrometinoff, and his old friend Navy lieutenant R. E. Coontz, and reinforced by the *Pinta*, Brady acted with what for Panhandle justice was astonishing dispatch. Coontz double-checked the *Pinta*'s auxiliary launch; chasing lawbreakers and making arrests would require a shallow-draft, swift-moving craft. Like Brady, he was impressed by Skookum Bob's earnestness; now was the moment to bear down hard on the pugnacious whites. Before the cruise ended, Superintendent Wadleigh and a number of others were placed under arrest, slapped with a heavy bond, and ordered to appear at the next sitting of the U.S. district court.[13] Violations of the 1889 law continued, but respect for Indian fishing rights had taken a turn for the better.

Brady's efforts to protect Panhandle natives by enforcing fishnet and trap restrictions formed a minor ripple in the expanding conservationist ground swell. Ironically, the much-maligned Land Revision Act of 1891 advanced Alaska's piscatorial future. Section 14 had invited the U.S. Commission of Fish and Fisheries to establish fish culture stations on Kodiak and Afognak islands. Accordingly, in December of the following year President Benjamin Harrison proclaimed that parts of the public domain "known as Afognak Island, are in part covered with timber, and are required for public purposes, in order that salmon fisheries in the waters of the island, and salmon and other fish and sea animals, and other animals and birds, and timber, undergrowth, . . . about said island may be protected and preserved unimpaired . . . [Afognak Island] is hereby reserved from occupation and sale, and set apart as a public reservation, including use for fish culture stations."[14] Alaska had its first forest reserve. Paradoxically, salmon propagation had in part brought it to pass.

Whereas the tourist business and salmon canning injected dollars into the economy only at mid-year, at least in the Panhandle mining could be a year-round business. And as visitors to Juneau could testify from the deafening roar, the Douglas Island stamping mills continued to pound out profits, jobs, and civic growth. Gazing at Douglas Island's mile-long shorefront of gold refineries, California governor George Stoneman reflected that "the entire island is nothing less than a mountain of ore . . . sufficient to pay off the whole national debt." "It is surely coming," predicted the city's *Alaska Journal*, "the period of development, the union of money and labor, and in that union will be found the strength which will prove the salvation of the territory . . . when that old cry of discontent . . . is changed from 'Alaska for Alaskans' to 'Alaskans for Alaska.' "[15] "Alaska To Be The Greatest Mining Center In the World," headlined Juneau's *Mining Record* of 29 April 1895.

From the first, Alaskans had pinned their fondest hopes on an eventual Forty-niner-type boom—a gigantic lucky strike, a super bonanza that would incite a stampede duplicating California's mid-century madness. As Governor Knapp observed, "Our mineral resources are the subject of more discussion and still create a greater fever of excitement than any other." At Alaska's capital the dream refused to fade. "This dingy little hamlet," wrote the *Alaskan's* editor in 1891, "will doubtless be the center of great mining operations."[16] During the eighties Brady's prospecting had earned him little but aching muscles. Throughout the period 1886–91 John dallied with some coal sites near Kootznahoo Inlet. He reckoned that they might be as lucrative as the deposits on Vancouver Island. Pro forma, the *Alaskan* gave the venture its blessings, trusting "that the expectations of the prospectors may be realized this time and that the discoveries may prove to be paying investments."[17] For John, at least, it was not to be.

By the nineties the Great Land was no longer unexplored. Scientific parties had crisscrossed Alaska's great continental Yukon interior and probed the forbidding Bering Sea and Arctic coasts. Brady read about her explorers Frederick Schwatka, H. Seton-Karr, Frederick Funston, E. J. Glave, and numerous others with as much avidity as his countrymen traced the adventures of Henry M. Stanley in Africa. Journalists, missionaries, and even a growing number of sportsmen also helped eliminate geographic ignorance.[18] As on other frontiers, miners frequently familiarized their countrymen with what to expect across Alaska's terra incognita. None of them, however, ever produced a historic drama to equal Canada's Klondike. Yet even before George Carmack's celebrated 1896 Yukon Valley strike, hardy trappers, traders, and miners—and in the north country a gold seeker was often all three—had opened Alaska's section of the sprawling Yukon Valley.

Commercial voyages aboard his *Leo* had afforded Brady opportunities to journey across the immense Gulf of Alaska and touch the coast of Alaska's vast mainland. But the hinterland north of the towering coastal Alaska Range remained quite as remote from him as it appeared to people living in Oregon and California. Over two decades would pass before Brady actually traveled up Alaska's Yukon aorta into its continental heartland. To gauge the impact on John's imagination of this northwest mass is impossible, as impossible as estimating Kentuckians' response to the gigantic Louisiana Purchase or Missourians' to the Mexican Cession. While events in southeastern Alaska preoccupied Judge Brady, other Americans pried open Alaska's vast hinterland.

The 1880s had witnessed an increasing trickle of Pacific Slope prospectors, Indian packers, and river steamboats breaking down Alaska's mid-continent isolation. Americans were entering the Yukon Valley from the river's mouth on the Bering Sea or from the east over Panhandle mountains via Canada's Yukon Territory. This latter route was by far the more arduous. After ascending the mountain gateways lying at the end of Lynn Canal, they followed hazardous trails northward. Miners, recently warmed by Juneau's "drugstores" and dance halls, had to endure a stretch of foot-wearying, muscle-aching labor before reaching the Yukon's headwaters. Thereafter, river transportation sped them across the 141st meridian boundary line into Alaska's Yukon Valley.[19] Despite the awful loneliness of this wilderness and its sixty-below-zero winters, the number of gold seekers slowly increased throughout the eighties. But as one observer noted, "The long severe winters of the interior, left a mining season of four months too short to be profitable."[20] Understandably, each winter most of the valley's miners retreated southward with the emigrating geese.

Nevertheless, pressures outside as well as inside the Great Land assured the occupation of its enormous interior. An attractive and well-circulated Pacific Coast Steamship Company book publicized "The Route to the Yukon . . . How to Go and What the Trip Costs." Eastern newspapers regularly reported that Alaska's "gold fever is setting in early." Rumors grew wings: oil had been tapped near Juneau; and "work will soon commence on the first railroad in Alaska, to run from Juneau to Chilkat."[21] By the mid-nineties Indian packers carried so large a miner traffic over the Chilkoot Pass from Dyea to Lake Lindemann that some natives demanded fourteen dollars per one hundred pounds carried. One local inventor sought to promote a sled tramway to short-circuit these Chilkat capitalists. The *Alaskan* conjectured that it was a matter of time before Icelandic immigrants and a long-overdue railroad connecting North America and Asia opened the forbiding interior to settlement.[22] Surely it was significant that the Treadwell Gold Mining Company now listed Rothschild and Company along with San Francisco's Bank of California in its *Annual Report* and that the West

Coast's famed mining engineer, Adolph Sutro, had come north to spy out the land. In 1895 the U.S. Geological Survey granted its first federal funds "to investigate the mineral wealth of Alaska." Brady must have mused over these reports, factual and fictional, and, like his counterparts everywhere, pondered on who would lay hands on the "lion's share of the Alaskan trade."[23]

In 1893 the veteran northland trader John J. Healy formed the North American Trading and Transportation Company. Aided by Chicago capital, Healy's group aimed to tap the vast northern valley at its western entrance. John Brady took note, and so did a *Seattle Post-Intelligencer* reporter. The usually laconic Healy explained: "I have lived in Alaska for seven years, having kept [a] store with[in] a few miles of the headwaters of the Yukon river the past six years. It has been costing 15 cents a pound to pack freight across the mountains, but by carrying it around by boat up the Yukon [from the Bering Sea] it can be gotten there for half that amount." That country is "hidden from the world," and we are "going in there, opening it up and letting the world know something about it." "I have always been a pioneer," Healy reminded the newspaperman, "I lived twenty-five years in Montana. . . . Our steamer will be named the P. B. Weare. We expect to run her up the Yukon at least 1,600 miles."[24]

The unmistakably bearish outlook of Knapp's successor, Governor James Sheakley, disappointed Brady. A resident of Wrangell, Sheakley escaped the carpetbagger brand. However, because his words and actions marked him promissionary, he quickly found himself identified as a tool of Sheldon Jackson. Certainly the general agent rejoiced when Grover Cleveland returned to the presidency in 1893 and appointed the one-time Pennsylvania congressman as Alaska's fourth governor. Sheakley, like his predecessors, proved to be his own man, an honest public servant who took his job seriously enough. But unlike Swineford's, his public relations were bland. Sheakley lacked both Swineford's journalistic flair and his combativeness. Despite Sheakley's experience in Alaska as a businessman, commissioner, and educator, his was a lackluster governorship. In essence his policy was not to rock the territorial boat.[25] When others decried lawbreaking in Alaska, Knapp's successor wore blinders: the law "has been observed and complied with so far as I have been able to learn." However, Sheakley did recommend establishing a military base "in the Yukon Valley, to remain until the country is further developed and its needs become known."[26]

Alaska promoters no doubt winced when they read the governor's sober warnings to Seattle citizens contemplating Far North prospecting. With regret Sheakley had learned that so many citizens from the Pacific

Northwest and East were "flocking into the territory . . . the result will be that many of the men will perish from hunger and cold . . . no one who is not inured to hardships should go into Alaska . . . men should all have at least $1000 cash." He cautioned that the man unused to the [Yukon] climate and country is indeed lucky if he can get over [the Chilkoot Pass] with anything on his back at all."²⁷

Sheakley's neighbor, Brady, viewed matters quite differently. John warmed with optimism in an article that he wrote for the September 1896 *Chautauquan*. "The mines of Alaska are drawing hundreds of prospectors. The placers on the Yukon and its tributaries and upon the head waters of Cook's Inlet promise richer rewards than the fleece of which Jason dreamed. The Argonauts are coming from all parts . . . they are a fine lot of fellows and have made up their minds to endure hardship. The Yukon appears to draw the largest number. It is probable that one million dollars was cleaned up in the Yukon district during the season of 1895."²⁸ Brady went on to inform readers about southeast Alaska's "spruce, hemlock, and cedar. It is abundant but will not have great commercial value for years." And in truth, except for the cedar, Alaska's timber did lack the quality of the Puget Sound stock, which, John noted, continued to be shipped northward in large quantities.²⁹ Innovative, industrious, and alert to the vicissitudes of the Panhandle's seasonal economy, Brady, like a handful of other small-scale, resident entrepreneurs, was at last banking substantial savings.

Although Sheldon Jackson possessed an even broader overview of the territory's astonishing diversity than most, an appreciation enriched by his annual farflung school inspections, he remained considerably less sanguine about Alaska's future than Brady. "The civilization of Alaska is progressing slowly on account of the inaccessability of the country. . . . After all these years Sitka has less than 200 white inhabitants," Jackson blurted out. "The entire town, Indians and all live off the federal salary list." Governor Sheakley, equally candid, gloomily estimated that the native population was "slowly decreasing."³⁰

And then, abruptly, "Klondike!" The gold strike of 16 August 1896 formed an epochal watershed. Thereafter a man who claimed to have been a Far North frontiersman before the rush was an old Alaskan, a "sourdough." Greenhorn Klondikers had to bear the good humored slur "cheechako" before they, too, earned the encomium "sourdough." As with California's mother lode discovery a half century earlier, news of the gold strike slipped out. Readers of Juneau's *Alaska Searchlight* of 24 October 1896 would have missed the following tidbit unless they first waded through two and a half columns of copy on the more newsworthy diggings near Circle City and Fortymile: "Forty Mile has once more been thrown into a fever of excitement over the recent gold dis- coveries in the Clondike district. The discovery was made . . . upon Bonanza Creek, a tributary of the Clondike."

Appropriately it was a Canadian prospector, Robert Henderson, who first guessed what glittering prospects awaited development in that part of the Yukon; but it was an American, George W. Carmack, assisted by some Indians, who unearthed and publicized the rich deposits on Bonanza Creek. Until then a majority of the Yukon Territory miners had been concentrated at Fortymile, sixty miles down river. When Car- mack arrived there to stake his Bonanza Creek claim, Fortymile's pop- ulace stampeded. By mid-1897 that virulent virus, the Klondike fever, had spread across North America.[31]

The surge of humanity that swept down upon Klondike Creek and within less than two years created Dawson, a city approaching twenty thousand people, flooded northward in three waves. Initially only a few arrived from "the outside, mostly miners from the Treadwell, old trap- pers and prospectors." Overnight Circle City and Fortymile became virtual ghost towns. These men staked out the original claims and cleaned off the paydirt. Next among the would-be Klondikers were Americans and some western Canadians, North Americans free of strong domestic ties. During the spring and early summer of 1897, as news of Far North gold was telegraphed about the outside world, these blithe spirits headed north. But by far the mightiest wave of gold seekers was the group that built up at Dyea and Skagway throughout the winter of 1897 and then in the spring of '98 surged down the Yukon River into Dawson City (or simply Dawson, as it came to be called in quieter, less frantic times).[32]

Although Juneau was never forested with a fleet of abandoned vessels like that which had collected along the San Francisco waterfront in 1848–49, shipboard desertion became common enough. Brady reported that thirty crewmen from the U.S.S. *Concord* jumped ship at Juneau, and when her captain approached Sitka, he "stood off in the western passage" to safeguard his men from the gold fever. Employees at the Pyramid Harbor Cannery abruptly quit their jobs, as did thousands of other workers up and down the Pacific Coast and to a lesser degree, across the country at large.[33] One might suspect that miner G. H. Cole was intoxicated when he penned the following from Dawson City: "Some of the old miners . . . say it beats anything they ever saw. Around some of the camps they have [gold] piled up like farmers have their wheat, and in other camps they have all their cooking utensils full of gold, and standing in corners as if it were dirt. Some are taking out $100,000."[34]

To extract Yukon Valley treasure demanded the cruelest kind of labor, but that was not what many a footloose fortune hunter wanted to hear. Florence Marvin, Seattle "prophetess," understood what the argonauts desired: "I now predict that the strike on the Klondyke is but a drop in the bucket compared to what will be found in Alaska."[35] The sorrowful warnings of Klondike busters appeared only after Seattle boosters—"the gateway to Alaska," Seattle's masterful publicist Erastus Brainerd labeled their strategically located city—and hundreds of newspapermen had showered the country with Klondike hoopla.[36]

Half amused, half amazed, Brady watched the swelling Klondike torrent. An exhuberant Yale classmate, Oliver Sumner Teal, informed him that the class of '74 had organized "Grub Stakes for Klondike— The Cooperative Grub Staking Co." Brady's aid was vital. "We will appoint you as our representative in Alaska and give you control of as many of our men as you think you can profitably direct from Sitka."[37] Wisely John demurred. His sons recalled that their father did grubstake two miners, supplying each of them with a white mule. Somewhere between Skagway and Lake Bennett, Bob and Fanny joined other quadrupeds on Dead Horse Trail.[38]

The lag between George Carmack's August 1896 gold discovery and the flash flood of humanity during spring-summer of 1898 assisted Alaskans in preparing themselves for the inundation of gold seekers. Sitkans grudgingly recognized that their obstreperous neighbor Juneau, not Alaska's capital, would win the lion's share of Panhandle commerce. Juneau lay at the entrance to Lynn Canal, a natural waterway that pointed straight toward the Yukon. Distribution boom towns Dyea and Skagway sprouted grotesquely in Yankee soil at the canal's termini. Second only to Dawson itself, Skagway became the gaudiest, indeed, the most parasitical of mushrooming spores fertilized by Yukon riches.

Perhaps it was the roaring prospector pandemonium of 1897 that once again attracted Brady to the noisy game of politics. President Cleveland's departure in 1897 obligated William McKinley to bestow the usual political patronage. In far-off Alaska Governor James Sheakley packed his personal papers and prepared to welcome his Republican successor. The territorial colossus still lacked a stable population, West Coast corporations continued to drain off much of its wealth, and congressmen, as ever, had little time for, and less interest in, its affairs. Now it had to endure the frenzy of being "rushed"—run over by men and women obsessed by the thought of gold. Yet the Great Land did not lack gubernatorial aspirants.

Designating Alaska's territorial appointees was hardly a matter of real importance to McKinley; helping the nation recover from its worst depression was. Like his predecessors he expected his secretaries of the treasury and the interior and their subordinates to manage Alaska. Certainly the incoming president was not ignorant of America's trans-Missouri provinces. A few years earlier Congressman McKinley had cheered as six western territories triumphantly marched under the statehood arch: Montana, Washington, the Dakotas, Idaho, and Wyoming.[39] And now in 1896 even "polygamous Utah" entered the statehood parade. Merely a matter of time and lobbying perseverance seemed to detain Oklahoma, Arizona, and New Mexico from winning the same political parity. But as for Alaska, ex-judge John Keatley snapped, there was not even "any necessity for maintaining the office of governor, and the consequent annual expense of about five thousand dollars per year, including salary, contingent fund and fuel at public expense."[40]

Alaska's newspaper editors and budding politicos, observing the gestation of new Far West commonwealths, adamantly insisted that they too deserved broadened home rule. Congressional leaders were skeptical. Consider the paradoxes of this sprawling geographic giant: in size it was one-fifth that of the United States, and it possessed incalculable natural wealth, yet residents of Alaska's capital appeared unable to afford a fire engine. This immense dependency cried for expanded policing, but because of its sparse population Sitkan Charles Isham formed "the entire militia of Alaska from its brigadier general to sole private." Ohio senator John Sherman conjectured that the territorial stepchild might be adopted as a county by the state of Washington.[41]

In 1896 the House Committee on the Territories voted in favor of providing Alaska with an official delegate to Congress. To no one's surprise the legislation went no further.[42] But the matter's very discussion seemed to suggest that Alaskans walked America's historic territory-to-statehood trail. In a bittersweet fashion the defeat of the delegate bill also reminded Far North pioneers that they had few friends on Capitol Hill.

President McKinley probably knew that among the 1896 GOP platform planks lay a recommendation that the "Territory of Alaska be granted a delegate in Congress." Very likely Jackson reminded him that four years earlier the Democratic platform had urged "that the officials appointed to administer . . . Alaska should be *bona fide* residents of the Territory or district."[43] President Cleveland had obediently responded to this in 1893 and named James Sheakley as governor. Now Alaskans asked themselves whether McKinley would select another Far North resident or flout their wishes by appointing one more carpetbagger.

Indicative of Alaska's growing political maturity were the district's 1896 Democratic and Republican conventions. The Republicans met at Juneau during May; their primary chore was to elect delegates for the national convention to be held in Saint Louis. Apportionment of Republican delegates to their territorial convention reflected Alaska's lopsided population. Juneau was allocated eleven delegates, Douglas City three, and Sitka four, but Unalaska obtained only two, and Saint Michael on the Bering Sea one.[44] Most outspoken of the Republicans was John S. Bugbee of Juneau, who from 1889 to 1892 had been Alaska's district judge. Brady thoroughly disliked him. Indeed, so strongly did he feel about the judge's penchant for Juneau's brothels and his inability to handle liquor that six years earlier he had written directly to president Benjamin Harrison bitterly decrying an official who "for moral turpitude surpasses them all."[45] Bugbee's leading role at the Juneau convention made it easier for John not to attend. The convention's attempts to concern itself with an improved legal code for Alaska and better representation were sidetracked by a heated parliamentary squabble. Before it ended two different factions, the "Squawmen" and the "Aristocrats," almost came to blows. So uncontrolled became chairman Bugbee's anger that he suddenly pitched forward, dead from an apoplectic stroke.[46] After the body was removed, Alaska Republicans elected regular and contested delegates for the Saint Louis meeting. A month after the Republican gathering, the Democratic territorial convention met at Juneau, chaired by Brady's one-time clerk, B. M. Behrends, now a prominent Panhandle man of commerce.[47]

On 24 November John Brady reacted to William McKinley's presidential victory by writing to Jackson: "News of the election has just reached us and of course we are pleased." Confident that Jackson preferred him in the governor's office, John tactfully speculated, "I hardly know what to do about making an effort to secure the Governorship. Mr. [Charles S.] Johnson will be a candidate if Alaska is not allowed a delegate during the coming session of Congress. If a delegate is allowed he will make a fight for that office. I feel disposed to strike out and make an effort. What would you advise?"[48] Four years earlier Brady had written Jackson, "I have no political aspirations and I have not the slightest idea that anything will be offered to me."[49] But that was before a Republican and staunch Methodist had won the presidency.

Aspiring to win Alaska's governorship quickly took hold of John. "Mr. C. S. Johnson told me he will be a candidate for governor, and of course I should like to get that place myself," he informed Jackson. "Support from yourself, Gen. Eaton and others might secure me the appointment. Will you not talk the matter over with Gen. Eaton and give me the result of your deliberation." As for the general agent's controversial program for feeding starving Eskimos by the importation of Siberian reindeer, Brady promised, "If I should be Gov. I shall do all that I can to sustain the reindeer project."[50]

Both Presbyterians had come to realize that Alaska's uniqueness assured political controversy. By having his office a continent apart from the territory, Jackson had enjoyed considerable insulation. For the moment, at least, Brady was free of newspaper vilification or political feuds. John even patched up his quarrel with Swineford. "He and I are on good terms now," Brady informed Jackson. "I think he has changed for the better."[51] Brady and Jackson had nurtured a healthier relationship with outgoing Governor Sheakley than with any of his predecessors. At Sitka the Sheakleys and the Bradys had become quite close socially, so much so that Jackson humorously rebuked Alaska's governor: "I think you are getting very dissipated in Sitka. First, I hear about the Governor making a dinner party of so many courses and inviting all the Ministers and their wives; and then I hear about Judge Brady doing the same; then I read about a 'Progressive euchre party' in which the Governor got the booby prize. Now you have to be careful or you will get a bad reputation up in that country."[52]

Despite Sheakley's cautious leadership, he had not escaped scurrilous accusations of "malfeasance in office." Nor had the usually mild-mannered Sheakley been able to control his own temper when his predecessor stepped down. He had slammed Knapp as a "blackmailer," and after he left Alaska he rejoiced that "I would never in all my life have to do business with or come in contact with such a contemptible character as Lyman E. Knapp."[53] Clearly the humdrum monotony of Far North village society magnified personal slights and political differences to an inordinate degree.

By February of 1897 Brady decided to join the throng of office-seekers traveling to Washington to honor America's new president and, he hoped, receive his patronage favor. Before departing from Sitka John signed a petition addressed to the incoming Congress. The document urged four "rights and privileges of American citizenship": an Alaskan delegate in the House of Representatives; homestead rights "as have been heretofore granted . . . in other territories"; "authority to incorporate our towns and villages"; and "repeal of the Prohibitory liquor law and the substitution in lieu thereof of a stringent and well guarded license law." The *Alaska Searchlight*, which seems to have sparked the petition, placed Brady among the top of those listed in its three-column spread of signatories. Noteworthy was the attention given "Residents of Kitchikan," an emerging Panhandle community, a number of whose citizens listed their occupation as fisherman.[54]

Keenly aware that territorial appointments were confirmed in the

U.S. Senate and that backing by some key Western politicians was imperative, Brady stayed a few days at Seattle, Portland, and San Francisco promoting his availability. In his correspondence with Elizabeth, John expressed confidence that Juneau, Sitka, and New Metlakatla stood under his banner. Pacific Slope friends supplied him with letters of introduction to power dispensers such as Republican senators George C. Perkins of California and John L. Wilson of Washington.[55] At first Brady seems to have been surprised that his old missionary associate the Reverend S. Hall Young had raised his own banner and sought to substitute an Alaska governorship for his Wooster College professorship. Young would return to Alaska, but as a "mushing parson," not as a politician.[56]

Inauguration Day, 4 March 1897, cast its traditional rays of patriotism over the assembled multitude. Exactly a month later John met America's still unseasoned chief executive. That evening John penned a letter to Elizabeth recalling how he had brought the president up to date on Alaska's gold frenzy and how McKinley had replied with consideration but without commitment. In turn, Elizabeth kept him well informed on Sitka happenings and wrote to the Jacksons to thank them for assisting her husband. "I do hope Mr. Brady will be successful in securing the appointment he wishes, it would be very discouraging to have some bad or even indifferent people in our important places."[57]

John devoted March and April to contacting and conversing with as many East Coast Alaska-minded people as possible. E. K. Martin, a New York realtor, Republican party worker, and old friend, proved of great aid. But as Martin warned John, "your danger is not in having plenty of strong backing but in having the right kind. . . . there is a certain prejudice in public life especially in Washington life against what are known as Missionary Candidates. . . . Why this is so I don't know."[58] Brady, of course, knew and was equipped to handle it. Support from amiable Louis Sloss, senior figure of the Alaska Commercial Company, as well as from his venerable friend General Eaton, assured John that crucial capital doors would swing open. Charles Loring Brace assisted him with an introduction to the new secretary of the interior, C. N. Bliss, who would be his boss if he attained the governorship. Endorsements of Brady ranged from that of steel magnate Mark Hanna to that of Tsimshian Indian Edward Marsden.[59] Fellow Presbyterians Eaton and Jackson carefully circularized over a thousand reprints of various statements that John had made on Alaskan affairs. By mid-May the president still had not made up his mind. And although John was having a grand time renewing old friendships along the northeast seaboard, he became impatient. "The Cuban question gives McKinley an excuse to delay office seekers," he wrote his wife.[60] For Brady the Sheldon Jacksons and their two daughters, Leslie and Delia, were gracious hosts. The general agent departed in May for the annual meeting of the Presbyterian church's general assembly, which began at Winona Lake, Minnesota, on the twentieth. When the Presbyterians adjourned a few days later, Jackson had been chosen moderator, the church's highest honor.[61]

When he arrived at Seattle on 8 June, preparatory to boarding the *Queen* for home, John, though as cordial as ever, according to a *Daily Times* reporter, was noncommital on his gubernatorial chances. The newspaper chose to emphasize his connection with Jackson, citing him "as the leader of the missionary element . . . opposing the liquor traffic . . . and bettering the educational facilities in Alaska." And then in a series of sweeping generalizations, the *Daily Times* sketched a stereotype that already was a folk truth on the Pacific Slope. Although believed by many, the statement was in fact an exaggeration: "For a generation the missionaries have gone North—families of them—and generally have remained there. The young members of the families have grown up and scattered through Alaska in different callings, but always in sympathy with the missionaries' cause. Then the mission teachers themselves practically have charge of many settlements and hamlets. . . . The natives are almost entirely under their influence and protection."[62] In the kingdom of Hawaii some second-generation Yankees of missionary parentage had become quite influential, but this was certainly not so in the Alaska of 1897. And when measured against the total influence of miners, traders, and trappers, the missionaries' impact on Alaska's native peoples was relatively limited. Both Brady and Jackson understood how preposterously overblown was the supposed power of Alaska's "missionary element." They not only had become inured to the canard but also had learned how to employ it to serve their purposes.

On 25 June Secretary of the Interior Bliss informed Brady: "There is transmitted herewith, under separate cover, a commission from the President for your appointment to the office of Governor of Alaska . . . you having been so nominated to and confirmed by the Senate." The actual date of his appointment was 23 June 1897, but John did not take his oath of office at Sitka until mid-July.[63]

For the present John's days as a free-wheeling, independent businessman were finished. Although his lumber mill would continue to operate, he was now a public servant, territorial governor of the District of Alaska, with all the pleasure and pain this position promised. His preparation for the task was superior to that of any Great Land governor to date. Whether he could successfully adjust his talents to meet the rumbling requirements of Alaska's 1897 watershed remained to be tested.

1. Robert H. Walker, *Life in the Age of Enterprise: 1865–1900* (New York, 1971), p. 13; Thomas Beer, *The Mauve Decade: American Life at the End of the Nineteenth Century* (New York, 1926); Harold U. Faulkner, *Politics, Reform, and Expansion: 1890–1900* (New York, 1959), p. 278; Cox, *Mills and Markets*, p. 226.

2. *Alaskan*, 26 September 1891.

3. Jefferson F. Moser, *The Salmon and Salmon Fisheries of Alaska* (Washington, D.C., 1899), p. 49; Howard M. Kutchin, *Report on the Salmon Fisheries of Alaska* (Washington, D.C., 1898), p. 20. Useful summaries of salmon's role in Alaskan development are C. L. Andrews, "The Salmon of Alaska," *Washington Historical Quarterly* 9 (October 1918): 243, 244; and Alfred H. Brooks, *Blazing Alaska's Trails* (Fairbanks, 1973), chap. 24.

4. Eugene G. Blackford, "American Fish Foods," in Depew, *One Hundred Years of American Commerce*, 2:394.

5. Alexander Badlam, *The Wonders of Alaska* (San Francisco, 1890), p. 121; Kutchin, *Report on the Salmon*, p. 21.

6. Kutchin, *Report on the Salmon*, p. 11.

7. Charles P. Elliott, "Salmon Fishing Grounds and Canneries," in Edward F. Glenn, comp., *Compilation of Narratives of Explorations in Alaska* (Washington, D.C., 1900), p. 738.

8. Joseph Murray, *Seal and Salmon Fisheries and General Resources of Alaska*, 4 vols. (Washington, D.C., 1898), 2:406.

9. Kutchin, *Report on the Salmon*, p. 20; AGP, vol. 2, Healy to Knapp, 9 July 1891.

10. *Alaskan*, 23 July 1892.

11. *Juneau City Mining Record*, 26 March 1891 and 28 January 1892.

12. *Alaska Journal*, 19 August 1893.

13. Ibid. Coontz, *From the Mississippi*, pp. 153–55, 165.

14. Thomas H. Carter, *Report of the Commissioner of the General Land Office, 1891* (Washington, D.C., 1891), p. 183; Frank T. Wolcott et al. comps., *The Compiled Laws of the Territory of Alaska* (Washington, D.C., 1913), pp. 174–75.

15. Northern Pacific Railroad Company, *The Official Northern Pacific Railroad Guide* (St. Paul, Minn., 1897), p. 429. John Burroughs, *Far and Near* (Boston, 1904), p. 34; and Charles W. Stoddard, *Over the Rocky Mountains to Alaska* (St. Louis, 1899), p. 71. *Alaska Journal*, 1 April 1893.

16. Knapp, *Annual Report, 1891*, p. 489. *Alaskan*, 7 November 1891.

17. *Alaskan*, 15 December 1888; 18 May 1889 and 28 March 1891.

18. Morgan B. Sherwood, *Exploration of Alaska, 1865–1900* (New Haven, 1965), ably reviews these various expeditions. *Alaskan*, 24 May, 6 June, 16 August, and 20 September 1890; James Sheakley, *Annual Report of the Governor of Alaska, 1896* (Washington, D.C., 1896), p. 193.

19. A. P. Swineford, *Alaska: Its History, Climate, and Natural Resources* (Chicago, 1898), p. 175. *Alaskan*, 1 May 1886. Robert Stein, "The Gold Fields of Alaska," *Review of Reviews*, June 1896, pp. 697–99. Richard Mathews, *The Yukon* (New York, 1968), pp. 75 ff.

20. Sessions, "Alaska," p. 275.

21. Pacific Coast Steamship Company, *All about Alaska* (San Francisco, 1888), pp. 20–21. *Washington Evening Star*, 31 March 1887; and *West Shore*, 3 May 1890.

22. *Alaskan*, 17 February 1894; ibid., 18 July 1891 and 3 February 1894. Ibid., 13 December 1890 and 21 March and 3 October 1891.

23. *Alaska Treadwell Gold Mining Company First Annual Statement—Year Ending May 31st 1891* (document located at the Henry E. Huntington Library, San Marino, California). Pacific Coast Steamship Company, *All about Alaska*, p. 36. Brooks, *Blazing*, p. 514. *Alaska Journal*, 27 May 1893.

24. *Alaskan*, 16 July 1892.

25. Ibid., 22 July 1893; *Juneau City Mining Record*, 13 July 1893. Clifford P. Reynolds, comp., *Biographical Directory of the American Congress, 1774–1961* (Washington, D.C., 1961), p. 1589.

26. James Sheakley, *Annual Report of the Governor of Alaska, 1895* (Washington, D.C., 1895), pp. 320, 323.

27. *Alaskan*, 30 March 1895.

28. Brady, "Alaska," p. 735.

29. Ibid., p. 734, and *Alaska Herald*, 19 May 1894. *Alaskan*, 13 July 1895.

30. *Tacoma Ledger*, 20 May 1895; and James Sheakley, *Annual Report of the Governor of Alaska, 1894* (Washington, D.C., 1894), p. 328.

31. Fortymile (it is still often spelled "Forty Mile"), Yukon Territory, is now abandoned. The site is located where the Yukon has its confluence with Forty-Mile River, so named because it lay forty miles downstream from old Fort Reliance (James W. Phillips, *Alaska-Yukon Place Names* [Seattle, 1973], p. 52). Alaska-Yukon Directory Company, *Alaska-Yukon Directory and Gazetteer, 1902* (Seattle, 1902), p. 474. The Klondike story's supreme chronicler is Pierre Berton, *The Klondike Fever: The Life and Death of the Last Great Gold Rush* (New York, 1958). His film *City of Gold* is recognized as a masterpiece of cinema art.

32. Morris Zaslow, "The Yukon: National Development in a Canadian-American Context," in Mason Wade, ed., *Regionalism in the Canadian Community, 1867–1967* (Toronto, 1969), pp. 187–88; Addison Mizner, *The Many Mizners* (New York, 1932), p. 97; F. W. Howay et al., *British Columbia and the United States: The North Pacific Slope from Fur Trade to Aviation* (Toronto, 1942), chap. 14; and David B. Wharton, *The Alaska Gold Rush* (Bloomington, Ind., 1972), chap. 6.

33. *Alaskan*, 4 September and 28 August 1897.

34. A. C. Harris, *Alaska and the Klondike Gold Fields* (Washington, D.C., 1897), p. 61.

35. William R. Hunt, *North of 53°: The Wild Days of the Alaska-Yukon Mining Frontier, 1870–1914* (New York, 1974), pp. 14–51; and Berton, *Klondike Fever*, pp. 146–70. JScrap, 28:73, clipping.

36. *New York Sun*, 25 December 1897; *San Francisco Examiner*, 29 July 1897; *Seattle Post-Intelligencer*, 19 July 1897. Jeannette Paddock Nichols, "Advertising the Klondike," *Washington Historical Quarterly* 13 (January 1922): 20–26. Murray Morgan, *Skid Road: An Informal Portrait of Alaska* (New York, 1951), pp. 159–64; Pomeroy, *Pacific Slope*, p. 257; and Dorothy O. Johansen and Charles M. Gates, *Empire of the Columbia: A History of the Pacific Northwest* (New York, 1967), pp. 369–71.

37. JGB, mf. 2, Teal to Brady, 22 April 1898.

38. Hugh Brady to author, 1969.

39. David Starr Jordan, *Imperial Democracy: A Study of the Relations of . . . Democracy to the Demands of a Vigorous Foreign Policy and Other Demands of Imperial Dominion* (New York, 1899), pp. 192–93. H. Wayne Morgan, *From Hayes to McKinley, 1877–1896* (Syracuse, 1969), p. 343.

40. Sheldon Jackson Collection, Philadelphia, Pa., Testimony before Committee of Territories, U.S. Senate, 23 February–12 April 1892, p. 39.

41. *Alaskan*, 3 February 1894; 11 September 1897, 24 March 1894.

42. U.S., Congress, House, *Report from Committee on Territories*, 54th Cong., 1st sess, Report No. 751, 12 March 1896. *Alaska Searchlight*, 21 March 1896. *Alaskan*, 2 December 1896.

43. Kirk H. Porter and Donald Bruce Johnson, *National Party Platforms, 1840–1968* (Urbana, Ill., 1970), p. 89.

44. *Alaska Searchlight*, 14 March 1896.

45. JGB, unfiled, Brady to Harrison, 29 November 1890.

46. JScrap, 24:24, clipping from *Salt Lake Tribune*, 26 May 1896. *San Francisco Examiner*, 25 May 1896; *Seattle Post-Intelligencer*, 2 June 1896.

47. *Alaska Searchlight*, 6 June 1896.

48. JCorr, 17:375, Brady to Jackson, 24 November 1896.

49. Ibid., 16:220, Brady to Jackson, 19 November 1892.

50. Ibid., 17:384–85, Brady to Jackson, 14 December 1896. On Jackson's introduction of reindeer into Alaska, see Dorothy Jean Ray, *The Eskimos of Bering Strait, 1650–1898* (Seattle, 1975), pp. 226–40.

51. Ibid., p. 141, Brady to Jackson, 2 May 1895.

52. *Alaskan*, 21 November 1896. AGP, box 7, Jackson to Sheakley, 19 January 1897.

53. *Port Townsend Weekly Leader*, 27 July and 10 August 1893. PUTS, 3:96, Sheakley to Jackson, 10 December 1892.

54. *Alaska Searchlight*, 27 February 1897.

55. JGB, mf. 1, Brady to his wife, 11 and 12 February and 21 April 1897; JCorr, 18:34, Brady to Jackson, 15 February 1897; JGB, mf. 1, Louis Sloss and Co. to Perkins, 17 February 1897.

56. *Alaskan*, 20 March 1897. *Boston Herald*, 11 March 1897. Young, *Hall Young*, p. 315.

57. JGB, mf. 1, Brady to his wife, 4 April 1897; JCorr, 18:39, Elizabeth Brady to Jackson, 19 February 1897.

58. Edward Marsden Correspondence, San Francisco Theological Seminary, San Anselmo, California, 3:67, Marsden to John H. Devore, 1 May 1897 (hereafter cited as EMC). JGB, mf. 1, Brady to Martin, 22 April 1897. JCorr, 18:35, Brady to Jackson, 17 February 1897; and ibid., p. 87, Brady to Jackson, 1 May 1897.

59. EMC, 3:190, Marsden to Elizabeth Brady, 26 June 1897; and ibid., p. 171, Marsden to McKinley, 15 June 1897. William Gilbert Beattie, *Marsden of Alaska: A Modern Indian* (New York, 1955), pp. 82–83. JGB, mf. 1, Brady to his wife, 2 May 1897.

60. JGB, mf. 1, 4 May 1897. JCorr, 18:88, Brady to Jackson, 1 May 1897; and ibid., p. 87, Brady to Jackson, 29 April 1897. JGB, mf. 1, Brady to his wife, 17 May 1897.

61. Robert Laird Stewart, *Sheldon Jackson: Pathfinder and Prospector of the Missionary Vanguard in the Rocky Mountains and Alaska* (New York, 1908), pp. 424–37.

62. *Seattle Daily Times*, 8 June 1897.

63. AGP, box 5, Bliss to Brady, 25 June 1897. JCorr, 18:110, Brady to Jackson, 15 July 1897.

CHAPTER TEN

Klondike Governor

John Brady began his official duties as Alaska's fifth governor after taking the oath of office at Sitka on 15 July 1897. In a brief address John "stated he would try like his esteemed predecessor to live up to the eleventh commandment, i.e., mind his own business."[1] The fact that he entered an office bereft of aides, patronage, or statutory muscle assured Alaskans that they needed fear neither executive bureaucracy nor an autocrat at their capital.

In mid-1897 the full impact of "klondicitis," as John phrased it, had not yet been felt. Alaskans forwarded routine congratulations to what they presumed would be still another benign district governor. Juneau's *Searchlight* and the *Mining Record* sent their good wishes. Understandably his loyal hometown newspaper, the *Alaskan*, gave him plenty of space. One of his well-wishers, Nicholas R. Peckinpaugh, recently a Sitkan and now a successful Louisville, Kentucky, lawyer, was especially effusive. Peckinpaugh recalled their earlier campaign fight for "sobriety, honesty and decency."[2] It cheered John, of course. His Washington superior, secretary of the interior Cornelius Newton Bliss, quickly eliminated any self-congratulatory reverie. Bliss reminded him that "great interest is manifested by the public as to the District of Alaska, in view of recent discoveries of gold therein." Forthwith the government wanted data on "means of transportation thereto, the cost thereof, transportation facilities within the District," principal business enterprises, and much else.[3] Within a few weeks John visited the Panhandle entrepôts to the Klondike at Dyea and Skagway, and before the year ended he began planning for a trip westward. Thereafter not a year passed when he did not complete an extensive inspection tour of some section of his huge geographic charge.[4]

Historic circumstances benefited John Brady's' governorship, although at first glance conditions would appear to have created quite the opposite result. The United States still felt the lingering effects of the depression, while within Alaska klondicitis ignited a series of mining booms that ultimately scattered death and dishonesty from Skagway in the Panhandle to Nome on the Bering Sea. And then, as if national economic maladies and territorial social boils were not sufficiently ominous, there was the political rupture with Spain. Jingoists cheered America's "splendid little war," but some Alaskans worried that an expanded Pacific Basin empire might sidetrack congressional concern for the Great Land.

Two Interior Department employees working in tandem labored to prevent such an omission. Alaska's general agent for education, Sheldon Jackson, had long since become a Far North gadfly in Washington. Now, thanks to President McKinley, Dr. Jackson had been reinforced by his well-armed ally Brady, who would prove equally persistent in advancing Great Land legislation. Jackson had exuded an Old Testament moralistic approach, and although lawmakers respected him, they found his badgering irksome. In sharp contrast was his coworker's bonhomie.

John Brady's governorship paralleled the Progressive period of American history.[5] Swept along near the close of the nineteenth century by fiery winds of protest from the agrarian Midwest and South, as well as from the metropolitan centers, the Progressive movement blew up a political storm. Demands were made at "both state and national levels that legislative bodies must consider the common good before partisanship."[6] Somehow America's "vested interests" had to be checked. Unquestionably the winds of change that swept across the United States affected territorial politics. Within the nation's capital the liberalizing process enabled western spokesmen to win a better hearing from Congress. By 1912 every contiguous territory had become a state; even Alaska had gained its own legislature and full territorial status. Governor Brady's Far North accomplishments were only indirectly influenced by this trans-America reform surge; however, its force doubtless strengthened his leverage among Potomac solons.

Foreboding, indeed, turbulent, developments arising from the stampede into Yukon Territory consumed an excessively large proportion of Brady's time during his first three years of office. Wisely he refused to let this abrupt increase in social discord long detour him from a well-marked pathway of district priorities, needs that his gubernatorial predecessors had faithfully, if futilely, advocated. John's first annual report (1897) to Secretary of the Interior Bliss provides a laundry

170

list of those well-worn requests. Predictably, John gave top priority to settler land ownership, the historic right of homestead.[7] Legal protection and improved living conditions came next. He threw an impressive bouquet to the man whose role had been central in his own life. "The education of the children of school age in the Territory of Alaska without reference to race . . . has been done under the care of the Bureau of Education, with Dr. Sheldon Jackson as general agent. It is safe to say that no work under the care of any department of the Government has been more fruitful of good results than the labor of this Bureau here in Alaska." Among the other matters his report reviewed were agriculture, fisheries, treatment of natives, mining, pressing administrative reform, and protection for the vanishing sea otter. Free of a carpetbagger's misdirected officiousness, he could be philosophical about a rich land so poorly handled. "If variety is the spice of life," he joked, "Alaska has not lacked for seasoning during these years." Quite frankly, he conceded, the present state of affairs was "far preferable to that which existed" when he first had arrived in the northland.[9]

Confident that he understood this gigantic territorial enigma as well as anyone, Brady held no lofty notions that he could transform Alaska. Like it or not, his district duties had to be more educational than executive, more promotional than political. Reinforced by neither a meaningful territory-wide Republican party phalanx nor a territorial assembly, John Brady somehow had to strive to be a fair-minded spokesman for his complex and prodigious district. Concurrently Congress and the executive branch expected him, as the most important civilian official in the territory, to represent the federal government's will in Alaska. That authority might be an expression of the War Department or the secretary of state, the Treasury Department or the attorney general, but usually it expressed the wishes of the secretary of the interior.

John's Washington head had been a highly successful New York businessman and longtime GOP treasurer before assuming the interior secretaryship. An unenergetic administrator, Secretary Bliss did not lean very heavily on his Far North subordinate.[10] Bliss stepped down in 1898 and was replaced by the punctilious Ethan Allen Hitchcock, who remained John's superior for the next eight years. Regrettably, Hitchcock's unbending, excessively formal personality was incompatible with Brady's relaxed manner. But if this communication handicap was troublesome, and at times it could be more than that, John's bond with the veteran lobbyist in the Bureau of Education easily compensated for it. Jackson had made enemies in the capital. He could be insufferably self-righteous, and on matters such as Alaskan liquor prohibition, he and Brady disagreed. Yet the doctor had mastered the intricacies of Washington politics, and Alaska's new governor quickly became an apt apprentice.

Governor Brady's immediate challenge was to minimize the social disorganization that had been intensified by the 1897–98 gold rush. From distant Saint Michael on the Bering Sea coast he received word, exaggerated, in fact, of an alarming accumulation of "gamblers, saloon men and some desperados." Delayed from ascending the Yukon to Dawson by a passenger steamer bottleneck, frustrated miners threatened to turn nasty. Fortunately the arrival of the revenue cutter *Bear* helped curb any serious violence.[11] Brady urged the government to maintain a careful check on the exodus from British Columbia and Puget Sound ports. This "moving multitude," he warned, might require navy or army units to preserve order. For the moment Sitka's absence of cable communications with Washington did not worry him unduly. Certainly he was gratified at the quality of his coworkers, especially Charles S. Johnson, who had been promoted to the difficult job of district judge.[12]

What did cause John increased anxiety were the rising incidents of crime in the vicinity of Juneau, Dyea, and Skagway. The burgeoning influx of cheechakos and the limited provisions caused prices to soar. Avarice then bred dishonesty and callousness. Shrewd Chilkat Indian packers, emulating mercenary whites, tripled their freight rates. They in turn were snared by whiskey smugglers. "If he can tempt the native to take a drink," John commented, "he is sure to make a sale for when Mr. Thlingit drinks he wants to get drunk."[13] A prospector, C. W. Watts, informed his wife that "you will see more money in Juneau in one hour than you will see in Albany in a year." At Skagway, Watts noted, "at least every other house is a saloon or dance house." "A spirit of lawlessness" flared up at Douglas, across from Juneau, and the jail was broken into. Before the escaped prisoners were back behind bars, one marshal was killed and another nearly so.[14] But whereas Juneau, Alaska's largest community, benefited from almost two decades of sociocivic maturation, Dyea and Skagway suffered the usual boom town excesses. Of the two, Skagway quickly became the more notorious: it was "conceived in lawlessness and nurtured in anarchy." A Frenchman, apprehended raiding a cache, was accorded miners' justice despite his screams for mercy. For three days the thief's bullet-riddled body hung suspended from his tent pole to remind others so tempted. In June 1897 four additional commissionerships were created: Saint Michael, Circle City, Unga, and Dyea.[15] For the moment, however, what judicial muscle existed lay in the miners' hands.

John's inspection of Skagway and the subsequent reports that reached his Sitka office left him ambivalent. Writing to Secretary Bliss he mused, "I can hardly bring myself to realize all this commotion so suddenly brought about. Can it be simply a thirst for gold or are there factors at work in our society of today that we are not rightly weighing and considering?"[16] The *New York Times* quoted him: "Recently the steamers have been carrying great lists of passengers. Many of these are gamblers, thugs and lewd women from the worst quarters of the cities of the coast. They have taken in the situation at Skagway and Dyea, and . . . the United States Marshal is powerless, because he can appoint only a few deputies, and when they undertake to act they are singled out as targets by this ruffianly element."[17] Fortunately Skagway attracted more than ruffians lusting after gold. "These people reflect the goodness of our institutions," Brady insisted. "They set about putting themselves in order without any pressure from outside authority. They united and built a church . . . a school was begun in this building." Fifty children had been enrolled. But of particular import, *"A meeting was called and a town council was elected."* "Here is a true American town," he boasted. "Only a little over a year old, with a railway, water- works, electric lights, four wharfs, lumber yards, hotels and shops of all kinds, with one daily and one weekly newspaper . . . well laid out . . . it wears an air of permanency."[18]

By mid-winter 1897–98 seven ships regularly steamed back and forth from America's Pacific Northwest ports to the Panhandle. The volume of humanity debouching at the Lynn Canal termini compelled even relatively restrained Alaskans such as Brady to wonder if this were not 1849 California all over again. "If the coming multitudes can compare with what we beheld at Skagway and Dyea," Brady conjectured, "Alaska will have a wealth of material out of which can be constructed one of the most notable states in the Union."[19]

During the summer of 1897 John completed his first annual report. He also did his best to stay abreast of the mounting stream of corre- spondence from southside citizens curious about Far North mining pros- pects. Most inquiries dealt with the Yukon region, but "hundreds are anxious to know about the Copper River country" north of Prince William Sound. John tailored his replies to the interrogator. A pastor from Kalama, Washington, aspired to bring his flock northward and commence a colony. John advised the dreamer to first spend at least one month in residence. Gold-struck Hoosiers were reminded that dur- ing an Alaska winter "everything becomes solid, and prospecting must be done with fire." "It is not worthwhile to try this venture," John counseled, "unless you can give it 3–5 years." However, he informed the mayor of Gas City, Indiana, "There are very few persons at present who are dissatisfied."[20] San Francisco businessmen were likewise encouraged to place their bets on Alaska's future. In answer to an inquiry from William Adams of Levi and Company, the governor wrote, "I am simply amazed at the growth of Skagway and Dyea and the great quantity of goods being sent there." Rough lumber "has been in such a demand there that it sold at thirty-five dollars per thousand." Americans also wrote President McKinley asking about Klondike opportunities. Alaska's governor dutifully handled these replies. One such gentleman anxious to work for "God and humanity" requested his brother Methodist's patronage in order that he might set up a facility at Dawson in which hot chocolate would be substituted for hard liquor.[21]

Joining John in the amusement afforded by answering such letters was Alaska's ex officio secretary and first surveyor general, W. L. Distin. Not so laughable were Sitka's land office records. Distin found them to be "in a most lamentable chaotic condition." Brady gave him his full support, insisting, "This is the most important office in the territory, and too much care cannot be taken to preserve the records."[22] By Thanksgiving Day the governor reminded his fellow Alaskans that, for all of the current confusion, "The people of Alaska have much for which to be thankful to Almighty God. . . . many who have decried Alaska as good for nothing are now admitting that it has wonderful possibilities."[23]

John's ebullience was in part dissimulation. The widening circle of criminal behavior at Dyea and, especially, Skagway alarmed him. Furthermore, he was apprehensive lest the Yukon Valley settlements be hit by starvation as well as lawlessness. Incapable of communicating directly with Secretary Bliss, John abruptly decided to journey to Seattle. Seattle provided prompt contact with the capital; it also afforded him a chance to talk with West Coast leaders whose backing could be critical in blocking any gold-seeker anarchy. Without authority to leave his district, John used the excuse of private business and paid for his own transportation.[24]

In Seattle and Tacoma John spoke with "a number of prominent men," all of whom "promised to use their influence with their Senators and Representatives urging them to vote for a Commission to draw up a code of laws for Alaska." Already on record favoring this code was California's senator George Perkins. During an interview with newsmen, Alaska's governor insisted that what his district desperately needed was an "amplification of the laws." John's proposed commission would be composed of a senator, a representative, and three bona fide Alaskans

174

"to consider the needs of Alaska on the ground." His first annual report carried a similar message.[25]

In the same 27 November 1897 interview in Seattle, Brady admitted that "many think Alaska should have a territorial form of government." Territorial status was popular among embryo politicos, for it promised a profusion of elected and appointive offices. Prior to klondicitis, northlanders had blown hot and cold in their demands for full territorial government, unsure if they were prepared for an elected assembly, an appointed governor, and a delegate to Congress. Now, however, they agitated for such a step. John found himself in the uncomfortable position of having to remind his fellow Alaskans, "The objections to this are manifold. Chief among them is the sparse population of the country. A territory means taxation, and the people are not there to be taxed."[26] Brady understood only too well how unstable an electorate he administered. A territorial structure appeared inevitable. But to advance that form of government in 1897–98, given the current transient nature of Alaska's population, was clearly to build a house on sand.

While John's Seattle trip garnered some reassurances from his Washington superiors, news of lawless behavior, sometimes with murderous results, continued to reach him at Sitka. Marshals and commissioners had been intimidated by a mindless mob of gold seekers, and now some lawmen were reported to be colluding with criminal elements. Another was killed in the line of duty.[27] Wherever legitimate law enforcement broke down, men could be counted on to take the law into their own hands. At Sheep Camp, not far from Dyea, vigilante justice sentenced two thieves to death. One shot himself; the other luckily got off with fifty lashes well laid on by an ex-muleskinner.[28] David Starr Jordan condemned the federal government, whose negligence had invited such excesses. It was typical Progressive rhetoric. Jordan conceded that the gold seekers were a naive throng: "A very large percentage of the Klondike adventurers know nothing of mining, nothing of Alaska, little of the sea, and little of hardship." Nevertheless, he insisted that "good government would have checked this whole experience of fraud." Had he lived for a few months at Skagway during 1898 and studied the fraud practiced by "Soapy" Smith, Jordan might have been more reserved in his sanguine confidence in "good government." More realistic was John Brady's reaction to the summary justice dealt out at Sheep Camp. "This may not be legal but it will be salutary for thieves for sometime on the trail and will be better than a whole lot of moral suasion."[29]

Ernest Gruening described Soapy Smith as "the lone dramatic example of classic border banditry in Alaska." Certainly Jefferson Randolph Smith fit the physical requirements for such a role. Erect of bearing on foot or horseback, he made his handsome face even more imposing with a thick black beard. Not satisfied with mere cardsharking in western mining camps, Soapy and his gang had seized virtual control of Creede, Colorado, in 1892. Ultimately the wheels of justice forced him to move elsewhere, and in 1897 the Klondike beckoned.[30] Dawson sparkled with nuggets and dust, but the steady hand of the Royal Canadian Mounted Police warned him off. The way Soapy and his confederates fastened their predatory grip on Skagway and waylaid miners by "fair means and foul" surely confirmed Professor Jordan's observation on the naivete of many of those infected with klondicitis.

Because they avoided Skagway's resident establishment and euchred only transients, Soapy's bunch were at first tolerated. Brady informed Hitchcock that Soapy Smith "seems to have the gambling element completely under his control."[31] By spring of 1898 the greed of Soapy's thieving rogues led them to armed robbery. That July a crowd of angry citizens rallied, determined to topple the "King of Skagway." His majesty boldly joined them—with two revolvers at his waist and a Winchester rifle in his arms. Frank H. Reid, a former school teacher, barred his way. In the resulting shoot-out, Soapy received a bullet in the heart and Reid one in his groin. Smith died instantly; Reid was not so lucky.[32] Brady recounted the aftermath for Smith's comrades. "Some whose company was no longer agreeable were given free transportation out of the country, and eleven were turned over to the United States marshal. . . . This was self-purification. Skagway and Dyea were now models of good order."[33]

Throughout this frenzied gold hunting, Alaska's capital remained an oasis of tranquility. On 2 January 1898 the Bradys, assisted by the Charles Johnsons, greeted the new year with a gala public reception, hosting their neighbors to what surely was the biggest party yet to enliven Sitka. Handsomely decorated rooms in the venerable Custom House sheltered the "sumptuous repast." Russian and Anglo members of Sitka society shook hands with the Bradys and Johnsons "under a tastefully made canopy consisting of flags and evergreens."[34] Brady's governorship was marked by receptions, large and small, for all kinds of domestic and foreign groups by those who had a soft spot in their hearts for "charming old Sitka" and the convivial governor and his lady.

After John renovated Sitka's historic Governor's House, the white washed, picket-fenced bungalow facing the commons, he transferred his office from its cramped second-floor quarters in the Custom House to this refurbished "executive mansion." Gertrude Knapp, his recently

The Governor's House, used by Brady as an office, at left; the Indian School, or School No. 2, behind the flagpole; and, at right, the Presbyterian church, where the Brady family worshipped; about 1899. (Reproduced by permission of the Beinecke Rare Book and Manuscript Library, Yale University.)

appointed "private secretary," assisted him here with the flow of paper and people.[35]

On 2 April 1898 John and Elizabeth, accompanied by two of their youngsters, left for Washington aboard the steamer *Cottage City*.[36] John's primary purpose in journeying east was what it would remain for the next eight years: to get congressional action on pending Alaska legislation. To a *Post-Intelligencer* reporter in Seattle he admitted, "a very small percentage of those flocking over the gold fields intend to make their homes in Alaska." But then, "as they perceive its limitless possibilities, as they learn that it has other resources than gold mining that are filled with promise of comfort and plenty to thousands, they will settle where they have come to find a fortune . . . build up their homes and send for their families." This could only happen, however, if Congress enacted laws "to govern the rights and actions of these men." Just because an Ohioan or Missourian had left his southside constituency, Brady insisted, did not free his congressman from an obligation to that American.[37] Unconsciously, Alaska's governor bespoke the isolated frontiersman's dependency on a strong federal government. News that robust America had declared war on "decadent Spain" greeted the Bradys on their arrival in Washington.

Alaskans welcomed the conflict with all the patriotic fervor of their fellow citizens to the south. Sitka's Indian band soon was blaring "There'll Be a Hot Time in the Old Town Tonight," which, along with "Hail! Hail! The Gang's All Here," became universal wartime favorites. The *Alaskan* bubbled with patriotism, although expressing disappointment that no Alaskans had been called to the colors. It was just as well; Alaska's militia was a joke. In December Secretary Bliss had informed John that he should organize "the militia of the District in such manner as in your judgment may be deemed best." Secretary of War R. A. Alger then deemed best an allotment of $7,105.60 "for Quartermaster's and Ordnance stores." Only a few months from his own death, Soapy Smith volunteered to lead a group of Skagway's best against the Spanish foe.[38] And when Dewey destroyed the Spanish Asian squadron on 1 May, one would have thought that Alaska's capital had been saved from Admiral Montojo's rusting fleet. Just a year earlier John had warned that Alaska "is entirely defenseless. . . . Japanese and other eastern nations are showing so much activity . . . and the English have forts and a depot for supplies at Esquimalt [British Columbia]."[39]

Few leaders in either the United States or Canada could have estimated America's chauvinistic reaction to McKinley's decision to fight. America's passion for war proved so powerful that it diverted men from

178

Klondike gold to martial glory. As John summed it up, "The declaration of war against Spain checked the tide."[40] Dawson had already become an American city on Canadian soil, that is, American citizens dominated its streets if not its courts. Word that America and Spain were at war caused the town "to go wild." One resident remembered the day as "the most exciting time Dawson ever saw" except for the big parade on July Fourth. "The band played the National Anthems and excitement ran high. I asked if I could get 1000 volunteers in 1000 minutes, and Yes, Yes, came from that many yelling men."[41]

Even without the Spanish-American War, the Klondike flood would have ebbed in 1898. By summer the region's rich claims had been staked and the easy pickings had vanished. Canada's leaders breathed sighs of relief once the war diverted American pugnacity to the Caribbean and far Pacific. Too many Yankees still viewed Great Britain as America's "century-old enemy"; the "great rapprochement" had yet to be confirmed by World War I.[42] Furthermore, contention over the Alaska-Canada boundary, although not explosive, remained a slow-burning fuse.[43]

Fresh anxiety troubled Governor Brady and his fellow Far North pioneers once the Spanish-American War ended. Alaska now found itself but one of a number of overseas possessions. "Colonies" some were already calling them.[44] Northlanders' apprehensions were unduly magnified; the Great Land really was never bereft of friends on Capitol Hill. Their remote homeland simply never had enough such friends, nor were a sufficient body of lawmakers ever aroused over district "neglect" to ram bills out of the territorial committees and through the gauntlet of both Houses. As Professor Jeannette P. Nichols summed it up, "beginning soon after the Organic Act was passed, bills to partially organize Alaska were presented with fair regularity in the House and spasmodically in the Senate."[45] Perhaps the Klondike stampede, which not only threatened law and order in Alaska but exacerbated the Canadian boundary friction, might compel Congress to act.

Quite early Governor Brady assumed a petulant stance on the boundary matter, insisting that Canada's cabinet was "trying to drive the Americans from their territory." He charged the Canadians with "exacting tribute in all manner of ways that will add to [their] government's revenue" and with vascillating in their management of the miner throng.[46] In March 1898 John hiked to the top of Chilkoot Pass. He "found the British flag flying there and some officers of the Canadian Mounted Police . . . collecting customs from the miners who were so laboriously getting up their outfits." Brady asked the officer in charge when and by what authority they had stationed themselves on the Chil-koot ridge. "The previous month and by command of his superiors," the Mountie replied.[47] It may well be that the half-anarchistic, half-civilized tradition so concomitant with America's frontier West reached its apogee atop that famous pass. From Chilkoot Pass down the Yukon River to Dawson, "Victorian respectability" prevailed.[48] When a mob of Yanks tried to lynch some Yukon Indians who had attempted robbery, the Mounties restrained their frolic. When American braggadocio ran up the Stars and Stripes on Yukon river craft, the Mounties tolerated it just so long as the Union Jack floated above it. And when libertarian Far West gold seekers angrily denounced the Mounties for insisting that they must obey the queen's law, their scorn quickly abated once they arrived at Dawson. For while Skagway endured lawlessness, Dawson, the City of Gold, had no murders, not even a major theft, during the wild year of 1898.[49] Superintendent Samuel B. Steele meant it when he warned the Americans: "There are many of your countrymen who have said that the Mounted Police make the laws as they go along, and I am going to do so now for your own good, therefore the directions I give shall be carried out strictly." It may have been irksome, but the thin red line saved lives. Everywhere the cool-headed police work of the Mounties, reinforced by the Yukon Field Force, won a respect for law that helped stay national passions.[50]

Washington had not been oblivious to the gravity of law enforcement so shredded by klondicitis. Indeed, for decades the Revenue Marine had been doing admirable work aiding natives and whites along the Gulf, out across the Aleutians, and northward along the Bering and Arctic Sea coasts.[51] But like the navy, these federal maritime arms could do little to ferret out criminals and intimidate lawbreakers over Alaska's vast interior. Without anything to correspond to the Mounties, even an effective district militia to match Canada's diminutive Yukon Field Force, the situation seemed to call for the U.S. Army.

Hardly had John returned from the capital in July 1898 when he departed for Unalaska and the Seal Islands. His purpose was to gather firsthand information on conditions to the west. Although rough seas left him seasick for much of the voyage aboard the U.S.S. *Wheeling*, John interviewed a sampling of Americans recently returned from lo-calities along continental Alaska's southern and western flanks. Back at Sitka by September, John exuded his usual optimism. "The West-ward," he predicted, "will in the near future become one of the richest and most populous districts of our great territory."[52] Rumors had begun to circulate that the cheechakos scattered over this isolated hinterland faced starvation during the coming winter. John inquired carefully of the masters of the vessels plying between Cook Inlet and Prince William Sound. With relief he reported, "there are no prospectors left on the beach, who wish to return."⁵³

Doubly reassuring to Alaska's governor was the knowledge that a year earlier army officers had entered the great interior valley on a similar fact-finding humanitarian mission. Captain P. H. Ray, along with Lieutenant W. P. Richardson, had been instructed to report "as fully and frequently as you can, the condition of affairs, and make recommendations as you may deem best."⁵⁴ They were told to make Circle City their headquarters. Ray and Richardson arrived at Saint Michael during August. Winter's advent and low water stopped them from proceeding up river any further than Fort Yukon. Like Brady, Ray somehow had to evaluate rapidly changing conditions over an enormous area—the Yukon River country all the way to Dawson. "Few, if any" of the settlements, he wrote, "can be called permanent." The North American Transportation and Trading Company operated stores at Saint Michael and Circle City, and for the rest of the interior. "The missions at Kudlik, Anvik, Nulato, Tananah, and Fort Yukon are simply native settlements, aside from the priests and sisters engaged in the work. The Alaska Commercial Company has stores at Andreasfky, Nulato, Nukeukahyet (Tananah), Rampart City (Manook), and Circle City. The white settlements are Circle City and Rampart City, the first 1,200 and the second 977 miles from St. Michaels. Circle City is practically abandoned."⁵⁵ To the present time, Captain Ray reported, "the laws in this country have not been enforced nor does there exist any means of enforcing them." Despite this state of nature, memorials were circulated "petitioning Congress to divide the Territory and erect a full Territorial government in North Alaska." Ray recommended that "so long as the present chaotic conditions exist some semimilitary form of government would most readily meet the emergency." One company of infantry "will be an ample force."⁵⁶

Faced with what seemed to be the spectre of starvation in the interior, business groups at Tacoma and Portland telegraphed Secretary of War Alger and President McKinley urging government purchase and distribution of food for "the relief of the destitute gold seekers." At first satisfied that the threat of hunger was quite real, Captain Ray proclaimed martial law at Fort Yukon, took charge of the NAT&T Company food stores, and put the community's citizens on rations.⁵⁷ Fortunately, during neither the 1897–98 nor the 1898–99 winters did the much-deplored starvation occur. Yukon steamboats, plus Superintendent Steele's unbending insistence that incoming Klondikers carry with them a year's supply of food, alleviated hunger. As always there were isolated prospectors whose stomachs shrunk during the winter. Drink apparently was abundant. Ray was disgusted that the "transportation companies in forwarding large quantities of liquor . . . had greatly aggravated the present conditions."[58]

It is not hard to understand why the U.S. Army only reluctantly renewed permanent stations in the Far North. Historic precedent had established "the general principle . . . that territorial authorities should be left to work out practical details and to make all possible use of local resources."[59] Nor could the army forget its thankless 1867–77 Alaskan duty that had produced no glory, only disparagement. In 1890 the Senate Military Affairs Committee expressed its aversion to the creation of a military post in Alaska's interior: district whites were too few, and the natives, if left alone, rarely bothered anyone. After his 1897 experiences Lieutenant Richardson believed that to hold soldiers in Alaska's harsh interior would require extra pay.[60] And though the Plains Indian wars had faded into history, urban, ethnic, and labor riots thrust new and onerous demands on the American army.

Obviously Alaska's scale, her transmarine location, and various post-1897 peculiarities dictated that America's century-old frontier administrative patterns be twisted, and possibly broken. During the winter of 1897–98 reverberations of klondicitis reached President McKinley, his cabinet, and various congressmen.[61] Spurred on by the reports from Captain Ray, the War Department in September of 1897 ordered Lieutenant Colonel George M. Randall of the 8th Infantry, with two officers and twenty-five enlisted men, to establish a military station at Saint Michael on Norton Sound. By 20 October all land within a one-hundred-mile radius of the garrison flagstaff was declared a military reservation. Before long, detachments of the 8th Infantry were showing the flag in the interior at Rampart City and Circle City. Units of the 14th Infantry, sent to maintain law and order at Dyea and Skagway, were recalled after the outbreak of war with Spain.[62] Previously Captain R. T. Yeatman, commander of Lynn Canal Military District, had not been reluctant to act against Skagway's Soapy Smith. On 9 July he had written his superiors, "I deem it proper to report that last night a notorious character passing under the name of Smith was killed in Skagway. . . . I have carefully avoided any interference with matters here as civil authorities have been able to attend to them but stand ready at any time to accept any responsibility necessary to carry out my instructions here."[63] Over the next few years Yeatman's philosophy bespoke that of America's thin brown line in its widely dispersed Yukon Valley police duties. With real pride Major General A. W. Greely later declared,

"Assuming control in all emergencies, the army extended assistance, afforded relief, discouraged violence, and when absolutely necessary made arrests and administered condign justice."[64]

Certainly Alaska's governor was grateful for the army's support during the widespread mining rushes. Yet John, like others of his generation, wished to see the troops supplanted by civilians as expediently as possible. However, for this to occur within a year or two was impossible. Alaska's prospector enclaves were too scattered, too inchoate. Thus, as the new century began, Alaska's governor requested "a military police system" at points about western and northern Alaska. Eminently preferable to John would have been permanent settlements capable of maintaining their own law and order.[65] Conscious of the quasi-military administrations fastened upon America's new Pacific Basin dependencies, Brady argued: "If, instead of setting up a military or naval government, with a military or naval commander whose word was law, and practically driving the people out, they would have given it a regular form of civil government, I have no doubt that Alaska would have had by this time a large population. But nobody wants to go to a country where they can not acquire titles to lands or homes."[66] Here was barbed irony. This statement, Brady informed his readers, had been made by Governor Swineford twelve years earlier!

From the day he entered office, John had done his best to win Alaska the long-sought-for right of homestead. For a moment in 1898 he thought Alaska had triumphed. Entitled "An Act Extending the Homestead Laws and providing for Right of Way for Railroads in the District of Alaska," the law at last provided homesteads for Alaska, or so it seemed. Present at the act's tortured congressional birth, Brady was not surprised at the resulting deformation. He labeled the land law "valueless," or at best "a feeble attempt to extend homestead rights to Alaska."[67] It cut back the 1891 provision of 160 acres to 80 acres. "Why there should be a departure from the long-established practice of granting 160 acres to settlers," he protested, "is beyond comprehension." With an eye on the Spanish-American War veteran, the act allowed acquisition of title through soldiers' scrip. Brady condemned this feature as "the work of some shrewd land lawyers at the capital." Twelve months later the scrip had appreciated, but not a single actual homestead entry had been made.[68] "It still remains a fact," Brady groaned, that "a poor man can not take up a piece of land for his home and go to the land office and obtain title to the same." The 1898 law was "inoperative, from the fact that homesteads can be located only upon surveyed land," and Alaska remained without base or meridian lines or monuments.[69]

Too many congressmen held an *idée fixe* when it came to homesteads.

Unless it sprouted corn or wheat or cattle grazed on it, the land could not be homesteaded. In a sense their shortsightedness was justified: Alaska's rural family sites would have to be radically different. Because neither Jackson nor Brady possessed reliable data to describe such alternate Far North living modes, and because they were themselves simplistic in their defense of Alaska's agricultural prospects, they sometimes injured their case. Missouri's senator George C. Vest, who had visited Alaska in 1889, insisted, "It is impossible to make a farming country out of what God has never intended to be such. You cannot carry the cattle of the United States there and graze them." "I was told at Juneau," he informed his Senate colleagues, of an old army mule that "became so lonesome that he deliberately walked down into the ocean, waited for the tide, and committed suicide. (Laughter). I sympathize with that mule. (Laughter)." Vest blasted the profligacy of expenditures required in surveying Alaska.[70] In his 1898 *Annual Report*, Brady angrily recalled how lingering—indeed, how entertaining— the Seward's Folly image remained in Washington. "Under the heat of the debate on this measure," one congressman "waxed warm and exclaimed: 'Gentlemen, men are not going to flock to Alaska for the purpose of taking homes. Men would not want to take homes where they would in many instances have to take dynamite in order to blow off the ice to reach the ground. (Laughter).' "[71]

Despite John's remonstrances, he was charged with being "the only man in the Territory who will reap a direct benefit from this law."[72] The 1898 legislation no doubt expedited John's final fee simple patent to Satchahnee. But even Alaska's governor would have to wait a few more years before he obtained clear title. John had his own *idée fixe*: Satchahnee should be a living symbol of what incoming Alaska settlers might realistically aspire to achieve. Lacking such striving homeowners and beset by footloose men addled by mineral opiates, Alaska seemed to have a bleak future. Fortunately, across America's Far West the cycle of amoral, shiftless predators appeared to be in steady retreat before more stable citizenry. The Great Land, John preferred to believe, no less than its vigorous sister commonwealths to the south, would eventually see the homebuilder win out.

By late fall of 1898 it was manifest that Dawson's boom had peaked. Disgruntled with Canadian regulations and disappointed at not striking it rich, Americans rapidly retreated, most back to the states. Others, more persistent, journeyed downriver, entering America's Yukon Valley in search of "fresh pickings." That November Alaska's governor informed Washington, "matters in the District at this time are all quiet."[73] As in the past, John's focus rested on southeastern Alaska. Across the

Yukon River Valley and along the Great Land's seemingly infinite western coastline, everything was definitely not "all quiet."

1. *Alaskan*, 17 July 1897. Alaska's public officials have now been carefully compiled in Evangeline Atwood and Robert N. DeArmond, comps., *Who's Who in Alaskan Politics: A Biographical Dictionary of Alaskan Political Personalities, 1884–1974* (Portland, Ore., 1977).

2. Brady, *Annual Report, 1897*, p. 176. *Alaskan*, 10 July 1897. JGB, mf. 1, 19 July 1897.

3. AGP, box 5, Bliss to Brady, 1 July 1897.

4. *Alaskan*, 4 September 1897.

5. Introductions to the dynamics of Progressivism are Benjamin Parke De Witt, *The Progressive Movement* (Seattle, 1968), and George E. Mowry, *The Era of Theodore Roosevelt, 1900–1912* (New York, 1958).

6. A. Bower Sageser, *Joseph L. Bristow: Kansas Progressive* (Lawrence, Kans., 1968), p. 65.

7. Brady, *Annual Report, 1897*, p. 173.

8. Ibid., p. 178.

9. Ibid., p. 175.

10. Johnson and Malone, *DAB*, 1:369.

11. JGB, mf. 1, Jackson to Brady, 1 April 1897. TAP, mf. 4, Brady to Bliss, 5 October 1897. U.S., Congress, Senate, *Alaska Gold Fields*, 55th Cong., 2d sess., Doc. No. 14, 13 December 1897, p. 5.

12. TAP, mf. 4, Brady to Bliss, 21 August 1897.

13. Ibid., 16 September 1897.

14. Charles Watts Correspondence, Henry E. Huntington Library, San Marino, California, Watts to his wife, ca. December 1897 (hereafter cited as WattsCorr). John G. Brady, *Annual Report of the Governor of Alaska, 1905* (Washington, D.C., 1905), p. 11.

15. Berton, *Klondike Fever*, p. 149; Brady, *Annual Report, 1897*, p. 176.

16. TAP, mf. 5, Brady to Bliss, 21 December 1897.

17. *New York Times*, 19 February 1898.

18. TAP, mf. 5, Brady to Bliss, 21 December 1897. Brady, *Annual Report, 1898*, p. 222.

19. *Portland Oregonian*, 5 February 1898. TAP, mf. 5, Brady to Bliss, 21 December 1897.

20. JCorr, 18:129, Brady to Jackson, 5 November 1897; AGP, box 11, Brady to A. R. Johnson, 22 December 1897; *Alaskan*, 11 December 1897; AGP, box 11, Brady to F. A. Brasier, 22 December 1897.

21. JGB, unfiled, Brady to William Adams, 21 December 1897; TAP, mf. 5, John Woodruff to McKinley, 18 January 1898.

22. *Alaskan*, 20 and 13 November 1897.

23. JGB, unfiled, 25 November 1897, Thanksgiving proclamation.

24. JCorr, 18:182, Brady to Jackson, 5 December 1897.

25. Ibid., and p. 148, Perkins to Brady, 11 November 1897. *Alaskan*, 11 December and 6 November 1897.

26. *Alaskan*, 11 December 1897.

27. TAP, mf. 5, Brady to Bliss, 3 February 1898.

28. Amelie Kneass, "The Flogging at Sheep Camp," *Alaska Sportsman*, October 1964, pp. 18 ff.

29. Jordan, *Imperial Democracy*, pp. 203–4. Carl L. Lokke, *Klondike Saga: The Chronicle of a Minnesota Gold Mining Company* (Minneapolis, 1965), pp. 45–46.

30. Gruening, *State of Alaska*, p. 336. Hunt, *North of 53°*, pp. 35–43.

31. TAP, mf. 4, Brady to Bliss, 16 September 1897; ibid., 7 July 1898.

32. Berton, *Klondike Fever*, chap. 10. James Wickersham, *Old Yukon: Tales—Trails—and Trials* (Washington, D.C., 1938), pp. 19–23. *Stickeen River Journal*, 16 July 1898.

33. *Alaskan*, 11 March 1899.

34. Ibid., 8 January and 12 March 1898.

35. TAP, mf. 5, Brady to Bliss, 3 February 1898. *Alaskan*, 8 April and 27 May 1899.

36. *Alaskan*, 2 April 1898.

37. Ibid., 16 April 1898.

38. Ibid., 30 April, 7 May, and 23 July 1898. AGP, box 5, Alger to Brady, 30 November 1897. C. L. Andrews, *The Story of Alaska* (Caldwell, Idaho, 1938), p. 195.

39. *Alaskan*, 21 and 28 May 1898. Ibid., 3 April 1897.

40. Brady, *Annual Report, 1898*, p. 213.

41. WattsCorr, Watts to his wife, 14 August 1898.

42. For an illumination of the larger Anglo–U.S. diplomatic background to the boundary dispute, see Allen, *Great Britain and the United States*, chap. 15, and Bradford Perkins, *The Great Rapprochement: England and the United States, 1895–1914* (New York, 1968), chap. 7.

43. Ottawa also knew that the loyalty of her own Dawson citizens was rather tepid. To appreciate the Canadian dilemma see David R. Morrison, *The Politics of the Yukon Territory, 1898–1909* (Toronto, 1968).

44. America's war with Spain has been well recounted in Frank Freidel, *The Splendid Little War* (Boston, 1958), and Walter Millis, *The Martial Spirit* (New York, 1931). Exactly how Alaska fitted into the new overseas jigsaw has yet to be examined.

45. Nichols, *Alaska*, p. 121.

46. *Alaskan*, 11 December 1897; and AGP, box 11, Brady to William P. Harley, 24 February 1898.

47. JGB, mf. 4, Brady as sworn to U.S. commissioner, 26 March 1903.

48. Zaslow, "The Yukon," chap. 11.

49. Lokke, *Klondike Saga*, p. 83. Berton, *Klondike Fever*, pp. 318–65.

50. Zaslow, "The Yukon," pp. 190–91.

51. Stephen H. Evans, *The United States Coast Guard, 1790–1915: A Definitive History* (Annapolis, Md., 1949), provides an overview of this service's activities.

52. *Alaskan*, 9 July, 6 August and 24 September 1898.

53. TAP, mf. 5, Brady to Bliss, 5 October 1898.

54. Senate, *Alaska Gold Fields*, p. 5, Useful, if uncritical, in reviewing the military impact is U.S. Army, *The Army's Role in the Building of Alaska* (Anchorage, 1969).

55. Senate, *Alaska Gold Fields*, p. 9.

56. Ibid., pp. 10, 5, 7.

57. A. W. Greely, *Handbook of Alaska: Its Resources, Products, and Attractions in 1924* (New York, 1925), p. 28.

58. Ibid., pp. 12–14. Zaslow, "The Yukon," p. 190. Senate, *Alaska Gold Fields*, p. 5.

59. Pomeroy, *Territories and the United States*, p. 25.

60. U.S., Congress, Senate, *Military Post in Interior*, 51st Cong., 1st sess., Report No. 557, 28 March 1890. U.S. Army, *Army's Role*, p. 29.

61. TAP, mf. 5, F. W. Dunham to McKinley, 16 December 1897.

62. U.S. Army, *Army's Role*, pp. 30–34.

63. TAP, mf. 5, Yeatman to adjutant general, Department of the Columbia, 9 July 1898.

64. Greely, *Handbook*, p. 28.

65. *Alaskan*, 21 April 1900.

66. Brady, *Annual Report, 1900*, p. 48.

67. Brady, *Annual Report, 1898*, pp. 198–99.

68. John G. Brady, *Annual Report of the Governor of Alaska, 1901* (Washington, D.C., 1901), pp. 10–11.

69. Brady, *Annual Report, 1899*, p. 38.

70. *Congressional Record*, 55th Cong., 2d sess., 3 March 1898, p. 2418.

71. Brady, *Annual Report, 1898*, p. 199.

72. *Alaskan*, 13 August 1898.

73. TAP, mf. 5, Brady to Bliss, 8 November 1898.

CHAPTER ELEVEN

Civilizing the Civilizers

Since coming to Alaska John had dreamed of an opportunity to visit the district's distant interior. Certainly the Yukon Valley's proportions were in scale with the Great Land. Its river stretched almost 2,000 miles. By itself that serpentine waterway drained an area of almost 330,000 square miles. With the ebb of defeated Klondikers during 1898–99, Alaska's Yukon villages swelled with fresh life. Only reluctantly would these stubborn "sons of failure" accept the harsh reality that a boreal miner "must work in very much richer ground than would be necessary in the States in order to make mining pay."[1] Hitherto, maps had enabled John to trace gold seekers pursuing routes other than those leading from the Lynn Canal entrepôts. To the west along the gulf coast, argonauts penetrated the Yukon interior via Prince William Sound and Cook Inlet. Others pressed their hurried search for the yellow mineral to the northwest along Alaska's myriad bays and inlets. An increasing importation of expensive hydraulic mining equipment foretold the replacement of the solitary miner by the corporation.[2]

In the summer of 1899, after winter months of lobbying in Washington, Alaska's governor headed far north. John's inspection trip to the sprawling hinterland lying north of the towering Alaska Range commenced in Canada. Unlike his predecessors who had sweated their way over Skagway's White Pass and watched in dismay as horses toppled to their death along Dead Horse Trail, John rated a preview ride on the unfinished White Pass and Yukon Railway. "The scenery along this short road" he found "grand." "It can be enjoyed so easily from the cars, it is now added to the tourist route."[3] Times were indeed changing. Skagway's Americans already had begun to institutionalize their historic quest. John joined their Arctic Brotherhood fraternal or-

188

ganization. Not yet a year old, the brotherhood put "its members to the test in climbing the trail and crossing the range in much the same manner as all good Shriners have to cross the hot sands of the desert."[4]

By the first of August Brady had passed the headwaters of the Yukon, run the dangerous Whitehorse Rapids, and reached Dawson. Accompanying him on his voyage, or for parts thereof, were members of President McKinley's Joint High Commission. For months "in speeches at Seattle, Tacoma and other places," John had urged "upon the Chambers of Commerce, Boards of Trade and all corporate bodies and private individuals the absolute necessity of the Commission visiting the Territory." Among these notables was the powerful Indianan Senator Charles Warren Fairbanks. A man of humble "log cabin birth," Fairbanks had become a highly successful lawyer before entering the Senate as a Republican. In 1898 McKinley had appointed Fairbanks chairman of this commission trying to resolve all of the U.S.–Canadian differences.[5]

At Eagle, six miles downriver from the Canadian boundary, Brady was a guest of the Reverend and Mrs. James W. Kirk. The governor praised the Kirks' domesticity among such rugged surroundings, particularly their home garden. "People are learning that vegetables can be raised here," Brady observed. "The native wild fruits are delicious, as this blueberry pie proves." He recommended that the missionaries try planting cranberries, which he and Elizabeth so much relished.[6] Brady also bestowed reassuring accolades on Colonel P. H. Ray, now in command of nearby Fort Egbert. The colonel, Brady wrote Elizabeth, "has an abundance of stores, cattle, mules, horses, sawmill, etc." One-third of Ray's command were "mechanics," that is, civilian communications workers. Fort Egbert's soldiers and their counterparts elsewhere found linking up the Great Land with copper wire and wagon roads eminently more appealing than policing miners. John thought "the region between Prince William Sound and Eagle City" to be the "most alluring" for gold hunters. "It is across here," he predicted, "that we confidently expect to see the Alaska Central Railroad built in a few years."[7]

Brady's Yukon Valley tour left him with mixed feelings. To the press and to Congress he was all effusiveness. "Within a very few years there will be hosts of busy people here, intelligent and aspiring bone of our bone, and flesh of our flesh. When they send their petitions and knock at the doors of Congress, what are the Eastern statesmen going to say?"[8] The "bone of our bone" that John described were "as fine specimens of manhood as the country affords. . . . Preachers, lawyers, doctors, gamblers, machinists, railroad men, lumbermen, farmers, etc."[9] How pleasant if his Alaska tours revealed only this civilizing edge among its pioneers. But the frontiers of continental Alaska could no more escape the tension between home builder and restless nomad than had colonial Virginia or the Missouri Territory. Within each new Alaskan lay the symbiotic seeds of reckless individual and selfless communitarian, romantic and realist, wrecker and conservator. Fortunately, combating political centrifugalism was not the nightmare for Alaska's governor that it had been for America's territorial governors a century earlier.

Invariably, however, the exploitation of additional mineral wealth within Alaska's Yukon Valley, as along its southern and western reaches, attracted additional criminals. Unlike Soapy Smith, with his immaculate dress and pretentions of fine Southern stock, outlaw H. Homer Bird lacked class. When he and his coterie departed from New Orleans for Yukon country, they had fully intended to use Bird's attractive girl friend as bait for luring homesick miners to their riverboat. Once they had a victim on board, the dupe would be robbed and murdered and his body conveniently disposed of in the river. But before these cutthroats could begin their murderous mining of the miners, Bird killed two of his gang. It was months before the whole story broke.[10] John was aghast. Poignant letters from parents and wives pleading for information on a silent son or husband infected with klondicitis were among his most frequent inquiries. When the conditions that bred loathsome parasites like Bird showed few signs of abating, John warned the secretary of the interior: "Numbers of murders are being committed in this District and no murderer has yet been hanged for his crime. We must do everything in our power to protect lonely prospectors. . . . The honor of the nation is involved."[11]

Eventually Bird dangled from a quite legal hangman's noose at Alaska's capital. Across the district's vast subarctic vacuum, violent crimes inevitably took their toll. Not all of them demanded the governor's attention. But all reinforced John's belief that man must wrestle evil, particularly when he or she was freed from the restraints of hearth and home. Each year Revenue Marine officers and their army counterparts compiled a sorry list of human depravity. Brutal robberies, premeditated and random killings, gruesome "accidental" gunshot wounds, some of which proved fatal, rapes of native women, and mutilating gang fights formed a record that John never publicized.[12]

Brady's Yukon Valley and Bering seacoast tours of 1899 and 1900 revealed that Jackson had not exaggerated the sad decimation of its indigenous population. Eskimos and Athapascans had been succumbing to Russian-borne diseases since the eighteenth century. During the following century Yankee whalers and traders hastened native destruction by recklessly bartering guns and liquor along Alaska's northwest littoral.[13] But it was the white invader's diseases—syphilis, smallpox, measles, tuberculosis, diphtheria, and so on—whose impact proved so fatal. By 1896 scientist William Dall reported that one group north of the Arctic Circle, attacked by an "epidemic of scarlet fever, introduced some years before through contact with other tribes trading to the coast, had [been] swept absolutely out of existence. Not an individual was left."[14] Dogsled missionary Hudson Stuck believed that the "valley of the upper Kuskokwim was almost depopulated" by diphtheria, and a "disease resembling measles took half the population of the lower Yukon villages in 1900."

Governor Brady was dismayed by the degree of native helplessness. At Greyling, on the Yukon, some five hundred miles from Saint Michael, "so many of them were sick that there was no one to wait on them and many of them were actually starving to death for want of attention."[15] With prophetic resignation the *Alaska Searchlight* echoed the "vanishing American" theme: "The Eskimo on the Arctic Coast and Saint Lawrence Island, utterly demoralized by the unchecked importation of spirituous liquors by whalers and traders, are rapidly decreasing under the alternate effects of wild intoxication and of starvation, the latter being the consequence of utter recklessness engendered by the former. Their extermination will probably follow that of the walrus—their staff of life—now being wantonly destroyed by thousands for ivory alone."[16]

Brady and Jackson, like almost every contemporary acquainted with the Eskimos, held them in high esteem. To a group of senators Brady said, "the Eskimos are the most intelligent race we have on the continent. I admire the Eskimo. Everything he uses is stamped with intelligence—his boat, his dress, his house; in fact all his implements."[17] Since the early nineties Jackson had poured his energies into the importation of Siberian reindeer.[18] Breeding reindeer in northern Alaska was for Jackson a means to a number of ends: reindeer milk and meat would in time reverse native starvation; reindeer would provide better mobility for both Eskimo and Athapascan, currently compelled to adjust to encroaching mining camps, canneries, and logistical hubs; reindeer herds required careful attention, certain to preoccupy the indigene and thus prevent his loitering about the ubiquitous saloon; and under native ownership reindeer could constitute a valuable trade item with whites.

Jackson's annual arctic school inspection cruises convinced him that the reindeer scheme was succeeding. Brady was no less convinced. "The reindeer is as valuable in its way to an Eskimo as the bamboo is to a

Chinaman. It affords him food, shelter, clothing, utensils, and trans-portation."[19] At century's end Alaska's governor noted that the animals' prolific numbers would soon top three thousand. On the actual total of Alaska's entire native population John could not be so optimistic. Observing their increase in certain areas and their decline elsewhere, he repeated his estimate of 1898: "natives and Russian creoles, 31,064." Despite the exodus of disappointed Klondikers, the increase in the num-ber of Alaskan white inhabitants was impressive. "A great many" of those who had left Canada's Yukon, he believed, had "scattered out in all directions through Alaska. Twenty-four thousand whites may be taken as a conservative estimate."[20]

It was not solely this Klondike residue that had caused Alaska's nonnative population almost to double between 1890 and 1900. His-torians have quite justifiably identified the Cape Nome gold rush as "America's Klondike." Like Dawson, boom town Nome lay between the 64th and 65th parallels, but whereas Dawson was imbedded in North America's interior, Nome gazed across Norton Sound and the north Pacific. With astonishing suddenness, gold-fed Nome mush-roomed on Alaska's remote Seward Peninsula.[21] In certain ways Nome's bizarre 1898–99 birth and subsequent growth was a replay of the cre-ation of Juneau and Skagway. But for the most part the Nome story was unprecedented. Without modern technology the unbelievable town could never have existed. Assaulted by wind and waves from violent ocean storms, this scramble first of tents and then of quickly assembled balloon-frame structures shouted modern man's impertinent contempt of weather and geography. Nome lacked any shelter whatsoever for anchored ships. Fronted by a shore so shallow that vessels could only unload at sea, and provided with a water supply polluted by its own inhabitants' filth, this madcap spectacle situated on a treeless strip of tundra somehow succeeded. Obviously anything so isolated, so super-ficial, and so feverishly dedicated to avarice must invite vice and vio-lence.

Panhandle residents had watched far-off Nome's evolution with a mixture of bewilderment and pride. At the town's inception in Septem-ber of 1898, Anvil Creek's gold traces had seemed little more than just another paying strike. However, before winter forced the "three lucky Swedes" to return to their base at Golovin, they had panned and rocked almost two thousand dollars of the "yellow stuff" from Anvil's gravel. Having staked their claims, they swore each other to secrecy. Of course, word leaked out, and even before weather permitted, north country miners quickly staked out Anvil's banks from its source to its mouth. By April of 1899 the entire area extending twenty-five miles both north and west from Cape Nome had been staked. "A village," Brady reported, "sprang up in a short time as if by magic."[22]

Once paying quantities of fine gold glimmered along the cape's wave-lashed beaches, Anvil City (shortly renamed Nome) erupted with adventurers. "The greatest shallow placers ever discovered," one journalist wrote. "It offered an opportunity for a large number of men to make a small stake quickly." Thereafter, except for the brothels and bars, nothing about Nome seemed quite the same. Thirty-five hundred miles to the southeast, at San Francisco, Tacoma, Portland, and Seattle, the response was typical. By June, the Seward Peninsula's frozen tundra melted, West Coast steamship companies obligingly lightered ashore thousands of men and thousands of tons of heavy equipment, lumber, food, and every conceivable object remotely desired by Nome's inhabitants. Alaska pioneer Carl Lomen stepped ashore and could hardly believe his eyes. "The confusion was appalling. Machinery, hay and grain, hardware, provisions, liquor, tents, pianos, mirrors, bar fixtures, household furniture were all stored in the open." And not only eyes were offended. "Stovepipe chimneys were everywhere, all breathing out a slow black smoke that settled in a dark fog over everything, biting at a man's throat and making his nose run."[23]

With a working season of scarcely three months—before the indispensable water froze—mining equipment was at a premium. One who succumbed to Nome's golden promise never forgot the exotic mass of machinery littering its shoreline. "Among the many strange sights on the beach was an enormous machine, built upon huge barrels. . . . It represented a great deal of money." After it was "launched, and tons of sand had been taken by it from beneath the sea, not five cents' worth of gold" appeared. Alaska historian Clarence L. Andrews, a contemporary of this bedlam, recalled:

> The rains pelted down, drenching everything and turning the flat, level-lying stretch of land that lay back towards the hills into a slippery, muddy quagmire. . . . Streets began to be laid out parallel with the water front. As traffic passed over them the mud became bottomless. Horses mired and lay helpless until they were pulled out with block and tackle. . . . Claims to town lots were jumped. The cabins that had been erected were hauled away at night by horses brought by gangs of men, some of the owners still in the cabins, and before they could get back to their location another structure would be occupying the ground.[24]

Afterward some men claimed that it was only the arrival of Lieutenant Oliver Spaulding with soldiers from Fort Saint Michael that kept one particularly xenophobic gang from "cleaning out" the "lucky Swedes" much as Californians had "cleaned out" their Chinese miners.

Governor Brady visited this carnival of frivolity and force—of both man and machine—and departed shaken. As at Skagway he soon found it necessary to initiate legal action against the local commissioner. Worse, there was a repeat of the murderous Soapy Smith–Frank Reid encounter after a Nome townsite trespass argument terminated in a double murder. And again John breathed a sigh of relief when the army filled the vacuum; nearby Fort Davis helped prevent the gold-propelled merry-go-round from spinning apart. Nome's lurid qualities, captivating as they did the imaginations of so many fortune seekers, invoked a touch of Shakespeare from Alaska's governor:

> Such wind as scatters young men through the world,
> To seek their fortunes farther than at home,
> Where small experience grows.[25]

With his abundant experience Sheldon Jackson could well imagine the undesirable elements now besetting northwest Alaska's Eskimos. Later he would encounter white opposition to the admission of native youngsters into Nome's local public schools, a painful repetition of what he had confronted at Juneau and Ketchikan. But for the moment Alaska's general agent set in motion his teacher-missionary reinforcements. "Hurry on to Nome!" was his encouraging hello and goodbye to the Reverend S. Hall Young. "You will find the greatest task of your life in that new Camp."[26]

Isolated Nome cried for its own judge and civil administrators. District judge Charles Johnson and his neighbor Governor Brady were acutely conscious of how weak—indeed, how nebulous—was their authority in distant Nome. Alaska required more than a single judicial district. The intervention of the army had kept men from each others' throats, but soldiers could not adjudicate disputed claims and miscellaneous legal embroilments. On-the-site inspection by Brady and Johnson convinced them that Nome's inhabitants should immediately establish their own municipal government.[27] They did so, but events promptly demonstrated how frail the town's stopgap authority was. Lawbreakers quickly grasped this fact. Too many congressmen did not.

On the one hand, the Spanish-American War, with its ensuing "colonial problems," and the related and swiftly shifting events in East Asia overshadowed the Far North gold rushes of 1898–1901. Had there been no war, no "New Empire," the Klondike and Nome stampedes might possibly have attracted more constructive attention from Washington lawmakers. On the other hand, the acquisition of Hawaii in 1898 and the Philippines the next year compelled representatives and senators to concern themselves with the management of not merely one huge noncontiguous territory but scattered islands halfway around the earth.[28]

For a brief period Americans admired these spoils of their "wonderfully successful war." "The taste of Empire," as a *Washington Post* editor commented, was "in the mouth of the people." Exactly *what* people seemed manifest to Albert Jeremiah Beveridge, a thirty-seven-year-old senator from Indiana. "God has not been preparing the English-speaking and Teutonic peoples for a thousand years for nothing but vain and idle self-contemplation and self-admiration." According to Senator Beveridge, God had been preparing the English-speaking peoples "to administer government among savage and senile peoples. . . . He has marked the American people as His chosen nation to finally lead in the regeneration of the world. This is the divine mission of America."[29]

John Brady would come to depend on his fellow Hoosier in the Senate, but of Beveridge's impassioned faith in America's skill at administering "savage and senile peoples," John was increasingly dubious: he long since had abandoned his youthful notion that the keys to the kingdom of righteousness were largely American. In his official *Annual Report* of 1902, where all might read it, Alaska's governor gave his skepticism full vent. After lauding the Eskimo as "kind and hospitable to a fault," John groaned, "To the ways of most of what we call civilization he is a child. We have invaded his country and have killed and driven off the whales, walrus, seals, and caribous, and in places have made fish scarce. We have gone along the shores of Bering Sea and have burned up the driftwood on the beach, set fire to the tundra, have driven off the birds, and in our mad hunt for gold we have burrowed under his rude barrabbara and allowed it to tumble, even when the inmates were sick and dying."[30] In fact, there had always existed thoughtful people on both sides of the Atlantic who questioned whether Great Britain and the United States were specially equipped or selected by God "to civilize the world."[31] In 1899 an American magazine, *McClure's*, published the poem "White Man's Burden," in which the Englishman Rudyard Kipling cautioned that managing an empire extracted a terrible price.

Americans could only dimly perceive how critically fresh administrative mechanisms and attitudes were needed in managing their Pacific empire. Typically shortsighted was Senator William M. Stewart's opposition to expanded federal jurisdiction in Alaska's mushrooming mining centers. "The system of allowing the miners to make their own rules," the Nevadan asserted, "allowing the local courts to decide upon them has worked so admirably in the United States that our laws and regulations have become proverbially the best that ever existed in any mining country." Stewart's simple faith in his fellow westerners rings with a romanticism more befitting 1800 than 1900. "There is no complaint that miners have ever trampled upon vested rights when there was a deliberate meeting." And what of the mining camp's razor thin edge between fellowship and hostility? "The more excitement there is the more care is always taken to adjust matters to the satisfaction of everybody. I believe we had better not inaugurate the policy of having any other rules for mining." Senator Joseph V. Quarles of Wisconsin objected. "Toward this great, wonderful district are [moving] constituents of mine, who are investing large sums of money this winter in machinery which they propose to take to this district during the coming season." Stewart, Quarles insisted, was "seeking to turn over to that primitive and erratic tribunal, a miners' meeting, an entirely new jurisdiction. It is not within their experience. They have handled the spade and the pick and the rocker. They can control that kind of mining, but the mining that is under consideration now is to be carried on by expensive and intricate machinery."[32] The onrush of industrialization commanded Americans to march to a different drummer. Similarly, the disharmonies certain to emerge in remote and unfamiliar peoples commanded fresh policies.

Governor Brady and his coworkers, men and women who had assumed responsibility for Alaska's future, were not deaf to foreign and domestic bells ringing "change, change, change." Yet precisely what responses were required neither presidents nor governors nor congressmen—not even discerning if imperious intellectuals like Henry and Brooks Adams—could agree. Furthermore, what might function best in Hawaii might be ludicrous in Alaska. As for John Q. Public, he was increasingly preoccupied with what Mark Twain called "the limitless multiplication of necessary unnecessaries." The electorate preferred to believe that their leaders knew best, and their 1898 ballot returns reflected this faith. By off-year election standards, McKinley's party did well. Republicans held their own in the House, gained a few Senate seats, and even captured the governorship of New York.[33] Interior secretary Bliss viewed it as a good time to step down.

For Bliss's successor McKinley selected Ethan Allen Hitchcock, and old China trader who had built his first fortune in Hong Kong, his second in Saint Louis. A Calvinist in his work habits and personal integrity, Hitchcock required as much dedication from his subordinates as he did from himself. "A man of iron will," the wealthy public servant remained secretary of the interior longer than any who had preceded him. For his unbending guardianship of the public domain, land-hungry westerners would come to hate him. Before Hitchcock finally left office, he had dismissed a commissioner of the General Land Office for mis-administration and indicted over a thousand of his fellow citizens in twenty states for land fraud.[34]

Eighteen ninety-eight marked John Brady's first full year as a territorial governor. His annual reports delineated a chart of priorities. Of Brady's stated imperatives, congressional action on land, liquor, and improved territorial law were uppermost. "Valueless" was Brady's opinion of Congress's 1898 homestead legislation.[35] He would return to that issue, but for the moment Alaska's governor turned to his second and third priorities: liquor and law. He astutely linked the two, while concentrating his time and energy on the extremely controversial district-wide prohibition. Alaska's governor had embarked upon a thankless political struggle, one in which even he and his mentor Jackson held quite differing opinions.

A humane hope of safeguarding the territory's aboriginals from alcoholic drink had early recommended a policy of prohibition for Alaska. Although sound in theory, in execution the policy became a cynical joke. Everywhere traders had gone in Alaska, and by 1898 that included its entire coast and subarctic, firewater had blazed its destructive path. Not long after he arrived at Sitka as a missionary, Brady had written an article on its pernicious impact on the peoples of southeastern Alaska.[36] Henry Wood Elliott, William H. Dall, William Gouverneur Morris—virtually every public official who served in Alaska shook his head at what devastation it wrought among the natives. Ivan Petroff resigned himself to the Eskimos' alcoholic suicide, declaring in 1880, "they have acquired a craving for [liquor] that can no longer be subdued."[37] Futile exertions to enforce prohibition by U.S. customs officers on land and the Revenue Marine at sea, as well as at varying times by the three military branches, demonstrated its folly. Generally nonnative Alaskans cooperated in keeping the aboriginal from alcoholic drink, but nowhere did whites deny themselves their accustomed spirituous liquor. The result was endemic violation of the law.[38] After leaving his post as Alaska's district judge, John Keatley wrote: "It is practically impossible to arrest the illegal introduction of intoxicating liquors into our Alaska territory. If public sentiment were practically unanimous in favor of enforcing the law, which it is not by any means, there is no remedy, under existing conditions, in a prohibitionary laws. . . . a coastguard of 5,000 men loyally attempting to do their whole duty could make it little better than it is now."[39]

For decades West Coast collectors had permitted vessels engaged in commerce with Alaska to carry aboard ten gallons or more of whiskey as ship's stores, usually justified in the manifest for "medical use." But this legal-illegal importation was not all that was transported northward. Disguised in an infinite variety of ways, large quantities of cheap smuggled whiskey came ashore. Whenever bootlegging skippers sighted an approaching Revenue Marine vessel, they routinely jettisoned their illicit cargoes. Those caught importing unlawful liquor—not approved for "medical, mechanical, or scientific" purposes—lost their shipment. Drilling a hole through the floor of either a dock or warehouse where customs officers had stored seized barrels of booze and then draining off the confiscated merchandise became a popular Panhandle prank.[40] Punishment for bootlegging, although usually only a wrist-slapping, could be far more serious, particularly if one had been engaged in distributing the liquor directly to natives. Even in those instances, antiprohibition juries generally handed down light sentences, if any. "Grand juries refuse to indict, and petit juries refuse to convict," snapped Governor Knapp. His successor, Sheakley, apologized, "That all of these defendants [forty-five saloon keepers] have sold liquor in violation of the existing prohibitionary law is a matter of common notoriety. That one of them will be convicted by a trial by jury is, I am sorry to say, not believed for a moment by any resident of Alaska."[41]

In their concern for Alaska's natives, the missionaries, almost without exception, adhered to the rigid prohibitionist policy so adamantly espoused by Alaska's general agent. Their outspoken strictures against spirituous liquor and all who engaged in its traffic won them few white friends in the northland. When some of these teachers and ministers tried to enforce the law, they were beaten up, and two were murdered.[42] First as a missionary and then as a trader, John had supported prohibition. Exactly when he admitted the absurdity of trying to hold water in a sieve can only be guessed; probably the awakening occurred during his commissionership.

By the 1890s America's evangelical churches were casting aside the temperance banner in favor of total abstinence; indeed, the Anti-Saloon League, founded in 1893, called itself "the Protestant Church in action." In the nineties, with its war chest and membership swelling, "America's cold water army" was winning local option battle after battle.[43] To dry up a county in South Carolina or Kansas was one thing, but to squeeze dry anything so immense as the Great Land was preposterous. Whereas Sheldon Jackson and thousands of auxiliaries in America's beverage crusade stubbornly refused to admit this, Governors Swineford, Knapp, and Sheakley had vainly sought "high license." Quite simply, high license aimed for a regulated sale of liquor in the territory by authorized, dependable retailers, men certain not to traffic with natives.

By September 1896 the *Chautauquan* featured an article on Alaska by John Brady in which he summarized the bizarre, Alice-in-Wonderland ambiguity of his homeland's restrictions on "spirituous drink":

> One law prohibits the manufacture, importation, and sale of intoxicating liquors. Nine tenths of the criminal cases tried in the courts are directly or indirectly a violation of this law. The officers' hands are tied by the action of one of the departments, for when they try a brewer for manufacturing beer he comes before the jury and shows the license which the United States internal revenue collector has issued to him and the stamps which he has bought to put on the bung holes of his kegs. The saloon keeper when he is brought up shows his receipts for which he has paid as internal revenue. The jury invariably brings in a verdict, "not guilty."[44]

John noted that southeastern Alaska sustained six breweries and Juneau operated over thirty saloons. He asked his *Chautauquan* readers: "What can more forcibly illustrate what Macaulay calls 'unwise neglect' than this conflict of action in regard to the liquor laws?"

Mindful of the howls his advocacy of high license would evoke, John set out to convince Alaska's lawmakers, the U.S. Congress, that statutory reform could no longer be shelved. The first eighteen pages of his 1898 *Annual Report* were devoted exclusively to Alaska's liquor anomaly. Nothing quite like Brady's official statement had ever appeared before. Systematically, document by document, fact by fact, Alaska's governor detailed how his gubernatorial predecessors had repeatedly tried to convince Congress that prohibition was not merely farcical but wasteful. To buttress his case John's brief for high license included testimony from men of the cloth.[45]

Prohibition, John estimated, "is repugnant to nineteen-twentieths of [Alaska's] population. . . . Saloons are open in all of the towns and in all of the mining camps. . . . This was the status before the rush to the Klondike and no doubt the number has doubled up to the present writing."[46] John injected chauvinism for the ears of congressional jingoists angry over Canadian restrictions on Dawson-bound Americans: "The more that the collector and his force stop the importation of liquors on the steamers, the better it is for those who are engaged in smuggling. The chief smugglers send their orders and checks to Victoria, British Columbia. The liquors are put up according to order and shipped at Port Simpson which is just across the American line. . . . For the past year much foreign liquor has gone up to the summits on the Dyea and Skagway trails. A portion of this has found its way back to be sold in the numerous saloons in each of these towns."[47] He compared the District of Columbia, with its licensed flow of liquor within

a tiny area easy to police, to the Great Land and its prodigious proportions, in which prohibition was somehow to be maintained. His
clinching argument was directed at economy-minded lawmakers. By
establishing a high license fee Congress could not only reduce those
scummy, fly-by-night saloons but also assist the taxpayer by generating
a healthy tax income within Alaska. To verify the nonpartisan nature
of his position, John quoted ex-governor Swineford's opinion that an
annual license fee of one thousand dollars for each dealer would "reduce
the number of retail dealers 75 per cent and the consumption of intoxicating liquors correspondingly, while, at the same time the business
of the smuggler being destroyed, the quality of the liquor sold would
be much improved."[48] Earlier he had written to Juneau attorney A. K.
Delaney, among others, soliciting opinions on high license. Delaney's
answer was precisely what John desired. He included the lengthy letter
in his 1898 brief for high license. "I have no faith in its passage," replied
Delaney. "Experience has taught us to believe that Congress cares but
little for us or our destiny." Pessimistically he concluded, "I do not
believe [Congress] has the moral courage to enact such a law in lieu
of the present one against the opposition of an undoubtedly sincere, but
none the less misguided prohibitionary sentiment throughout the
States."[49]

Surely Sheldon Jackson had warned Alaska's governor what a storm
would follow. Even Jackson had been bruised by intemperate temperance zealots.[50] During 1899 as John lobbied to crystalize his 1898 words
into legislative action, the prohibitionists marshaled their legions. The
Alaskan correctly guessed that there would be a phalanx of Methodist
and Presbyterian preachers lining up against Brady's proposal. His journalistic voice half facetiously hoped that the ministers would be con-
sistent and see that "America's other colonies" were also dried up.[51]

Among those spearheading opposition to Brady's high license was
the Reverend Wilbur F. Crafts, superintendent of the capital-based
Reform Bureau. Crafts was a formidable adversary. A vibrant speaker
and prolific writer, he had at different times held pastorates in the
Episcopal, Congregational, and Presbyterian churches. The Reform
Bureau he headed sought to advance "Christian reforms on which the
churches sociologically united while theologically differing." Its stated
aims were: "defense of the Sabbath and purity; the suppression of
intemperance, gambling and political corruption; and the substitution
of arbitration and conciliation for both industrial and international war."
Among its advisory board members it listed notables Booker T. Washington, former senator Henry W. Blair, and that peerless purifier Anthony Comstock.[52] To defeat Brady's heterodoxy Superintendent Crafts

wasted no time. On 5 January 1899 Crafts scrawled a terse letter to none other than President McKinley decrying the possible termination of prohibition in Alaska. Aware that John's measure formed only part of a new Alaska civil code working its way through Congress, Crafts had Representative Nelson Dingley attempt to stall repeal by pushing for a congressional inquiry into enforcement of the district's current prohibition law. Congressman William H. Moody, another Crafts ally, tried to sidetrack the high license provision into a separate bill. Jackson rallied the Presbytery of Alaska. Obligingly, the churchmen notified Congress that what was required was "further trial and enforcement of the existing law."[53] Doubtless the well-known David-and-Jonathan relationship between Brady and Jackson weakened the general agent's persuasiveness.

When the Presbytery of Washington declared that it could no longer support an unenforceable law, Crafts was stunned. "It is the heaviest blow I have had in this desperate fight," he advised Jackson.[54] In a ringing speech to the Anti-Saloon League meeting in Cleveland, Crafts coupled the fate of America's new empire with liquor in Alaska. "The supreme question before Congress is whether Alaska and our new islands and our soldiers shall be protected against the saloon? If we deliver these islands over to that horrible triumverate, the spoilsman the monopolist and the saloon, they may well pray for a return to Spain." Crafts's speech interwove a fascinating array of reform strands, ranging from concern with an "enlarged army" and the need to protect it from the "regimental saloon or canteen," to WASP guilt over liquor's place in the annihilation of aboriginal Americans.

How, Crafts rhetorically asked, "could such good men as Governor Brady and John Sherman and President Jordan and Secretary Bliss call on the nation that has just sunk the whole navy of Spain to haul down its flag to the whiskey pirates of Alaska?" Crafts shouted the answer, "Repeal of prohibition in Alaska is the hideous Judas cry for 'revenue.' Columbia is asked once again to sell her virtue for gold. How can men who have read even school histories overlook the fact that nations have not died of free trade, or free silver, but of free love?" Doctor Crafts even called on the blood and iron of Manifest Destiny: "To surrender Alaska to the saloons at this juncture would not only invite our saloonists everywhere to violate laws in order to secure their repeal, but would also assure them that our new possessions are to become their spoil. Alaska is the key to the situation. As goes Alaska so goes Manila."[55] Crafts matched his strident eloquence with a well-orchestrated series of antirepeal maneuvers. Prohibitionists were urged either to write their congressmen or to buttonhole them, or both: "I believe we can do more in the next thirty days to increase the temperance host by concentrating our energies on carrying the anti-canteen bill [restrict alcoholic beverages from army bases] and maintaining Alaska prohibition than in any other way." Crafts claimed that almost two dozen groups had been thrown into the breach in the campaign to stop intoxicating liquor from reaching "Alaska and our islands, and our soldier boys."[56]

By 1899 the whole matter of inadequate law enforcement in Alaska had become a wearisome headache for the nation's legislators. Since the 1870s official reports and investigations had decried alcoholic havoc in the Far North. Was there no solution to Alaska's chief cause of lawlessness? During late January, with debate on the Alaskan legislation soon to enter its second year, the Senate Committee on Territories held hearings on the district's pending legal code; high license remained the major hurdle.[57] The Reverend James B. Dunn of Brooklyn, New York, asked the senators why "we are talking of sending fleets to Manila to subjugate the inhabitants, why can we not send a few of these small vessels to go up and down the coast of Alaska and enforce the law?"[58] Crafts told how he had "heard from lady missionaries, descriptions of the horrible physical condition of hundreds of Indian women, victims of frontiersmen crazed by whiskey illegally sold." Senator William J. Sewell, apparently an admirer of good whiskey, found this too much to bear. "You gentlemen who live comfortably in New York and Washington," he growled at Dunn and Crafts, "expect people in Alaska to carry out a prohibitionary law they do not believe in . . . to shiver in a temperature of 40 degrees below zero and not drink whiskey. . . . In my opinion you make a mistake."[59]

The distaff side was predictably proprohibition and took less than a couple of minutes of the "gentlemen's time." Mrs. M. D. Ellis, superintendent of legislation for the Northern Women's Christian Temperance Union, pleaded: "I am here representing the homes. I had the great privilege and pleasure last year of meeting Mrs. Brady, the governor's wife, and her little children. . . . I think Mrs. Brady would have a heavy heart . . . if her boy was made drunk on liquor obtained under the thousand dollar license law as if he was made drunk on smuggled liquor . . . I ask you to remember the mothers and to remember the homes in Alaska. There is a higher law than the high-license law and that is the law of moral righteousness. And may God direct you!"[60] Wisely Alaska's governor did not reply to Mrs. Ellis. After all, who could disagree with motherhood and moral righteousness? However, when Crafts commented that in Alaska, "The marriage law is broken almost as commonly as the liquor law," John angrily interrupted him with, "I deny that statement."

It appears that the senators took the prorepeal spokesmen more seriously. Brady did not hesitate to lace his logic with enough color to add piquancy to his argument. "If all Dewey's fleet were up there you could not keep [the smugglers] in order."[61] But it was the testimony of three relatively neutral special agents from the Treasury Department whose facts thrust aside emotion. In essence their well-prepared statements underlined Brady's 1898 brief. Howard M. Kutchin "did not find a single man who argued in favor of the existing conditions; although it is understood that a minority of the missionary element, on purely moral grounds, are unalterably opposed to recognition of the traffic on any terms." Impatient at such an ostrich stance and the folly of continuing a prohibition that actually abetted public corruption, and impressed by the one-time missionary's temerity, Congress adopted high license. Of greater import, congressmen also produced an improved legal code for Alaska.[62]

Brady had recognized that Alaska's code could only survive the congressional obstacle course piecemeal. For the moment he would be content with a criminal code and repeal of prohibition. Not until 6 June 1900 did Senator Thomas H. Carter see the bill he sponsored in 1898, "An Act making further provision for a civil government for Alaska, and other purposes," finally passed.[63] However, on 3 March 1899 a bill entitled "An act to punish crimes in the District of Alaska and to provide a code of criminal procedure for said district" did see the light of day. It was a lengthy document of 127 pages; the fine points of high licenses were spelled out in an appendix.[64]

The penal code and the code of criminal procedure were primarily the achievement of an ad hoc code commission, which covered everything from "offenses against the public health" to the intricacies of due process. Brady may have expected Alaskans to greet the document and prohibition's repeal with praise, if not with jubilation. If he did, he was disappointed. Paying a regular tax soured the taste of victory. Liquor retailers who henceforth had to remit five hundred dollars or more for a license (the fee depended on the size of the community served) and wholesalers two thousand dollars objected to the "unfair tax." Within days the complaint took on a more historic ring: "taxation without representation." The *Alaskan* regretted that "the new license feature of our new criminal [code] has not met with the hearty approval of the people of Alaska and has been condemned by many newspapers and citizens."[65] The negative response should have been expected. Heretofore Alaskans had existed virtually tax free. Representative Thomas H. Tongue had been surprised to find that "the largest stamping mill in the world, the Treadwell mine," did "not contribute one cent of taxation."

Liquor dealers formed a small minority of the businessmen taxed.

As of July 1899 forty-two categories, beginning with abstract offices, banks, boarding houses, brokers, billiard halls, bowling alleys, breweries, bottling works, and cigar manufacturers and ending with "waterworks furnishing water for sale," were required to secure a business license. Alaska's two leading sources of income, mining and fishing, were not overlooked. Quartz mills were charged three dollars per stamp per year. Salmon canneries paid four cents per case, exactly what Brady had recommended.[66] "Compared with the licenses paid in the states they are extremely low," the *Alaskan* explained. "Capital and business should not be frittered away by the hue and cry of a high and unjust tax when it is neither." The newspaper voiced disgust at "the men who are to pay the smallest amount of taxes [for] making the loudest noise about it." One "party raving about paying an unjust and burdensome tax" moaned that he "would have to go back to the old country." What was his burdensome tax? "Eighty-five cents per month if he continues his business, Awful! Terrible!"

Another source of resentment puzzled the *Alaskan*. "The residents of Alaska, for years have been demanding the enactment of such laws as would concede something to the expression of the will of the people. In the new liquor license law this demand has been exactly met." And indeed the law's local option provision thrust the responsibility directly on the people. Before a license could be granted by the district court, the consent of a majority of the residents, "other than Indians," within a radius of two miles had to be obtained. Forbidden was the disposal of liquor to an "Indian or intoxicated person."[67]

Rather quickly the tax revenue accumulated. By the end of September ninety-nine licenses had been issued to various businesses, and the total amount collected was $112,370, of which $88,000 was connected with the liquor trade. During Governor Brady's 1899 summer trip through the Yukon Valley, he collected another $33,544.88 in license fees. To the secretary of the interior John wrote, "The new liquor law is operating most satisfactorily, at least in so far as it restricts the number of saloons. I learn that the number is reduced enormously. The city of Skagway has now 10 as against 65 formerly . . . other places proportionately."[68] John was so pleased at the disappearance of Sitka's saloons that he pointed out the recently emptied structures to his sons. He was premature. "There has been more drunkenness, fights and rows in Sitka during the six weeks of high license law and the two legalized saloons," reported the *Alaskan* in mid-August, "than there was during the previous six months of prohibition and nine saloons."

To the surprise of no one, every Alaskan town opted for a licensed saloon. When the general agent needled John that drunken Indians had

not vanished from the Panhandle, Brady conceded, "Mr. Wadleigh
. . . brought up Italian and Chinamen to do the work which he had
trained the natives to at Klawock. This he was obliged to do because
of drunkenness of the workers."[69] Another discouraging event was the
resignation of his close friend, Alaska's district judge, Charles Johnson.
To some degree it may have been a case of "if you can't beat them,
join them." Having survived a humiliating series of corruption charges,
and confronted by the alarming growth of lawlessness at Skagway and
then at distant Nome, the Great Land's district judge decided, at least
for the present, "to practice law at Nome."[70]

Each Alaska businessman, no different than his peers the world over,
felt that the territory's tax pinched him inequitably. As John noted in
his 1899 *Annual Report*: "The men who are in the fish business say
that the tax laid upon them amounts to 1 per cent of the value of their
products while . . . the sawmill man, who is paying 10 cents per thousand, thinks that he is paying more in proportion than the miner."[71]
Curiously, asperity toward the levy echoed historical antecedents leading back to America's colonists and their anger at distant Parliament.
It was bad enough to suffer taxation without representation, but
Alaska's outflow of always scarce money to far-off Washington worked
an unconscionable hardship. Congressmen rebuked Alaskans for their
forgetfulness. Far North pioneers should realize that the labors of the
U.S. policemen at sea as well as on land, not to mention a wide variety
of other federal services operating in the northland, were costly. Such
a budgetary caveat had not satisfied the distant colonists in 1775, nor
did it pacify their Alaskan counterparts in 1899. What was obvious to
Panhandle businessmen by mid-1899 was that the Klondike-induced
prosperity had passed its zenith.

With an adroit sense of political tit for tat, Governor Brady moved
to short-circuit his fellow Alaskans' resentment at the tax money outflow. The following year, when legislation finally permitted Alaskan
communities to incorporate, fifty percent of the business license tax
money remained in the district's towns for educational purposes. This
anodyne surely eased Jackson's pain at prohibition's demise. No sooner
had Governor Brady produced this trump than politician Brady called
for another. Did the U.S. Treasury genuinely need that remaining fifty
per cent tax slice as badly as Alaska's natives? Had not the 1884 Organic
Act stated that "the Secretary of the Interior shall make needful and
proper provisions for the education of the children of school age in the
Territory of Alaska without reference to race"? Alaska's governor wanted to see that commitment fulfilled: "If 50 per cent of the license money
which is collected [and sent to Washington], excluding the amount from

the incorporated towns, could be used by the Secretary of the Interior, he could nearly comply with the law in furnishing the proper educational facilities." Once again Brady succeeded. But though pioneer town dwellers willingly accepted the necessity for public schools, too few Alaskans, red and white, living in the scattered unincorporated villages did so. Equally serious, the indigenes' portion of the tax dollar had a way of slipping away from them.[72]

More so than most of Alaska's governors, John Brady was poignantly conscious that native grievances frequently went unheard—drowned out by vociferous cheechako boosters sojourning in Alaska's gold-inflated boom towns. Nor were these lusty whites satisfied with disemboweling the earth. A December 1898 conference in Juneau with some Tlingit chiefs doubtless sobered Alaska's governor. Chief Yashnoosh of Juneau now understood that possession of land meant life or death:

> Things that I am saying now did not used to happen in olden days. The government now sells land. Our people we have simple patches of ground raising vegetables and place where our people go hunting; creeks where they fish, we want you to give them back to us. We never had any trouble with the white people of America. . . . The Indians in the States made great deal of trouble for you about the land. We never make any trouble. We love you. . . . We ask you to give to the Thlingit the places that brought us food. If you refuse to do that, then our people will starve.

Chief Kah-du-shan from Wrangell understood that his people were putty in white hands:

> We know that the same God made us. And the God placed us here. White people are smart; our people are not as smart as white people. They have a very fine name; they call themselves white people. Just like the sun shining on this earth. They are powerful. . . . They have men of wars. It is not right for such powerful people as you are to take away from poor people like we are, our creeks and hunting grounds. . . . We do not want all these things we ask for by force. We have eyes, and we have sense. We see you are powerful. We do not want to be angry with you. We want to be friends with you.[73]

Afterward John may have asked himself just who were the civilized inhabitants of this Great Land.

---

1. Mathews, *Yukon*, p. 302. Morgan Sherwood, ed., *The Cook Inlet Collection: Two Hundred Years of Selected Alaskan History* (Anchorage, 1974), p. 125.

2. Hunt, *North of 53°*, pp. 84–91.

3. *Alaskan*, 22 July 1899. AGP, box 11, private secretary [Gertrude Knapp?] to Marsden, 5 January 1899. Brady, *Annual Report, 1899*, p. 47

4. *Alaskan*, 19 August 1899. JScrap, 13:49, untitled clipping, 30 July 1900.

5. *Alaskan*, 15 April 1899. Johnson and Malone, *DAB*, 3:248–49; and Brady, *Annual Report, 1899*, p. 41.

6. James W. Kirk, *Pioneer Life in the Yukon Valley Alaska* (Buffalo, 1935), pp. 20–21.

7. JGB, mf. 1, Brady to his wife, 9 August 1899. Brady, *Annual Report, 1899*, p. 39. The historian Morgan Sherwood is rather critical of the army's Alaska exploratory activities throughout these years (Morgan Sherwood, *Exploration of Alaska, 1865–1900* [New Haven, 1965], chap. 10).

8. Brady, *Annual Report, 1899*, p. 51.

9. *Alaskan*, 25 February 1899.

10. Ibid., 28 October 1899, 25 January 1902, and 7 March 1903.

11. TAP, mf. 8, Brady to Hitchcock, 1 August 1901.

12. Ibid., mf. 5; and *Alaskan*, 1898–1901, numerous references.

13. Wendell H. Oswalt, *Alaskan Eskimos* (San Francisco, 1967), pp. 75–76. Herbert L. Aldrich, *Arctic Alaska and Siberia, or Eight Months with the Arctic Whalemen* (Chicago, 1899), pp. 143–46; and George Wardman, *A Trip to Alaska: A Narrative of What Was Seen and Heard during a Summer's Cruise to Alaskan Waters* (Boston, 1885), pp. 149–50. C. Harley Grattan, *The United States and the Southwest Pacific* (Cambridge, Mass., 1961), pp. 84–88.

14. *Alaska Searchlight*, 15 February 1896.

15. Hudson Stuck, *Ten Thousand Miles with a Dogsled: A Narrative of Winter Travel in Interior Alaska* (New York, 1915), pp. 359–60. TAP, mf. 7, Brady to Hitchcock, 3 August 1900; *New York Times*, 2 September 1900; *Alaskan*, 1 September 1900.

16. *Alaska Searchlight*, 1 August 1896.

17. CLASJC, unfiled offprint, *Statement of Hon. John G. Brady, Governor of the Territory of Alaska, Before the Senate Committee on Agraiculture, February 7, 1900*, p. 9.

18. Jackson's introduction of reindeer remains a source of controversy within the Great Land. For a recent historical evaluation see James and Catherine Brickey, "Reindeer, Cattle of the Arctic," *Alaska Journal* 5 (Winter 1975): 16–24. Standard pro-Jackson summaries are Andrews, *Story of Alaska*, pp. 178–79; and Vilhjalmur Stefansson, *The Northward Course of Empire* (New York, 1922), pp. 54–69.

19. Brady, *Annual Report, 1897*, p. 5; CLASJC, *Statement of Hon. John G. Brady*, p. 10.

20. Brady, *Annual Report, 1899*, pp. 27–29.

21. Cape Nome's gold was not the first bullion to be extracted from Seward Peninsula; almost twenty years earlier silver had been mined at Omilak (Dorothy Jean Ray, "The Omilak Silver Mine," *Alaska Journal* 4 [Summer 1974]: 142–48). Nome's history is engagingly recounted in Hunt, *North of 53°*, pp. 95–135, and David Wharton, *The Alaska Gold Rush* (Bloomington, 1972), chap. 10.

22. Brady, "Alaska," p. 167. Leland H. Carlson, "The First Mining Season at Nome Alaska—1899," *Pacific Historical Review* 16 (May 1947): 163–64.

23. E. H. Harrison, *Nome and Seward Peninsula: A Book of Information about Northwestern Alaska* (Seattle, 1905), p. 37. Carl J. Lomen, *Fifty Years in Alaska* (New York, 1954), p. 12.

24. Lanier McKee, *The Land of Nome: A Narrative Sketch of the Rush to Our Bering Sea Gold Fields, Its Mines and Its People, and the History of a Great Conspiracy, 1900–1901* (New York, 1902), pp. 45–46. Andrews, *Story of Alaska*, p. 202.

25. Leland H. Carlson, "The Discovery of Gold at Nome Alaska," *Pacific Historical Review* 15 (September 1946): 274; Lomen, *Fifty Years*, p. 12. Brady, *Annual Report, 1900*, p. 17.

26. Sheldon Jackson, *Annual Report on Education in Alaska, 1902* (Washington, D.C., 1903), p. 11. Young, *Hall Young*, p. 388. Leland H. Carlson, *An Alaskan Gold Mine: The Story of No. 9 Above* (Evanston, Ill., 1951), p. 45.

27. Andrews, *Story of Alaska*, p. 203. Brady, "Alaska," p. 167.

28. Contrasting views of the Philippine-American conflict are John Morgan Gates, *Schoolbooks and Krags: The United States Army in the Philippines, 1898–1902* (Westport, Conn., 1973); and Henry F. Graff, ed., *American Imperialism and the Philippine Insurrection* (Boston, 1969).

29. *Congressional Record*, 56th Cong., 1st sess., 9 January 1900, p. 708.

30. John G. Brady, *Annual Report of the Governor of Alaska, 1902* (Washington, D.C., 1902), p. 26.

31. Ernest R. May, *American Imperialism: A Speculative Essay* (New York, 1968), pp. 95–128.

32. *Congressional Record*, 56th Cong., 1st sess., 28 March 1900, pp. 3420–21.

33. George H. Mayer, *The Republican Party, 1854–1964* (New York, 1967), p. 265.

34. Johnson and Malone, *DAB*, 5:74–75.

35. *Congressional Record*, 55th Cong., 2d sess., 4 March 1899, p. 2470; and ibid., 3 March 1899, p. 2412. Brady, *Annual Report, 1898*, p. 19.

36. John G. Brady, "Hoocheenoo," *Presbyterian Monthly Record*, August 1878, pp. 233–34.

37. William T. Harris, *Annual Report of the Commissioner of Education, 1904*, 2 vols. (Washington, D.C., 1906), 1:1099.

38. Spicer, *Constitutional Status*, pp. 52–54.

39. *Congressional Record*, 52d Cong., 1st sess., 3 February 1892, p. 790.

40. *Alaska Herald*, 15 June 1869. *Alaskan*, 27 August 1892, 18 September 1897. Senator Vest reminded his colleagues that "opium boats" also flaunted "their nefarious trade" along the Panhandle's coast (*Congressional Record*, 55th Cong., 3d sess., 2 March 1899, p. 2704). Customs seizures periodically listed in the *Alaskan* confirm this (testimony of Sheldon Jackson, *Annual Report of the Board of Indian Commissioners, 1893* [Washington, D.C., 1894], p. 144).

41. *Alaska Searchlight*, 27 May and 14 September 1895. Lyman Knapp, *Annual Report of the Governor of Alaska, 1890* (Washington, D.C., 1890), p. 4. Sheakley, *Annual Report 1896*, p. 204.

42. *Seattle Post-Intelligencer*, 12 and 13 May 1892. JCorr, 25:510–24, report to attorney general on murder of Charles H. Edwards, 29 September 1892. JScrap, 22:26 ff., clippings on Edwards's murder. Maurice Montgomery, "The Murder of Missionary Thornton," *Pacific Northwest Quarterly* 56 (October 1963): 167–73.

43. Andrew Sinclair, *Era of Excess: A Social History of the Prohibition Movement* (New York, 1964), pp. 65–68; and James H. Timberlake, *Prohibition and the Progressive Movement, 1900–1920* (Cambridge, Mass., 1966), pp. 10–18.

44. *Congressional Record*, 55th Cong., 3d sess., 4 January 1899, p. 394. Brady, "Alaska," pp. 730–31.

45. Brady, *Annual Report, 1898*, pp. 190–91.

46. Ibid., pp. 185–86.

47. Ibid., p. 185.

48. Ibid., pp. 197–98. Senator Perkins reinforced Brady's opinions on the ironic contradictions between the two districts (*Congressional Record*, 55th Cong., 3d sess., 2 March 1899, p. 2701). *Alaskan*, 28 January 1899.

49. AGP, box 11, Brady's private secretary to John G. Heid and others, 22 August 1898. Brady, *Annual Report, 1898*, pp. 188–89.

50. JCorr, 15:247, Sara D. L. Detra to Jackson, 7 February 1890; ibid., p. 248, representatives of WCTU to President Harrison, 30 January 1890. PTS, SJ letters, 2:205, M. L. Washburn to Jackson, 30 December 1891; and JCorr, 24:467, J. E. Connett to Jackson, 20 March 1892. *Washington Post*, 1 December 1891.

51. *Alaskan*, 14 January 1899.

52. Sinclair, *Era of Excess*, p. 31. TAP, mf. 6, Crafts to President McKinley, 5 January 1899.

53. TAP, mf. 6, "Alaska Liquor Laws."

54. JCorr, 19:6–7, Crafts to Jackson, 9 January 1899.

55. TAP, mf. 6, clipping, "Drink Problems in Congress"; extracts from Crafts's address.

56. Ibid., Moody memorandum.

57. *Congressional Record*, 55th Cong., 2d sess., 26 February 1898, pp. 2119 ff. U.S., Congress, Senate, *Criminal Code for Alaska*, 55th Cong., 3d sess., Doc. No. 122, 15 February 1899.

58. Senate, *Criminal Code*, pp. 20–21.

59. Ibid., pp. 12–19, 21.

60. Ibid., p. 22.

61. Ibid., pp. 15, 5.

62. Ibid., p. 11. *Congressional Record*, 55th Cong., 3d sess., 2 March 1899, p. 2702. Roland L. DeLorme, "Liquor Smuggling in Alaska, 1867–1899," *Pacific Northwest Quarterly* 66 (October 1975): 151, notes how events within the territory strengthened Brady's argument. *Alaskan*, 11 and 18 June and 9 July 1898. Two years later Crafts gained some consolation when Congress forbade the sale of alcoholic beverages from army canteens (Sinclair, *Era of Excess*, p. 117).

63. *Alaskan*, 14 January 1899. Thomas H. Carter, comp., *The Laws of Alaska, Embracing the Penal Code, the Code of Criminal Procedure, the Political Code, the Code of Civil Procedure, and the Civil Code* (Chicago, 1900), p. xviii.

64. Carter, *Laws of Alaska*, p. xviii; Barker, *Compilation*, pp. 208–14. The House's final vote on this criminal code left no doubt that dry constituents had communicated their "moral righteousness"; over half of the representatives voted neither "yea" nor "nay" (*Congressional Record*, 55th Cong., 3d sess., 11 January 1899, pp. 580–87).

65. *Alaskan*, 15 April 1899. U.S., Congress, Senate, *Petition from the Alaska Chamber of Commerce*, 57th Cong., 1st sess., Doc. No. 238, 6 March 1902, pp. 4–5. Predictably, it was not long before the prohibitionists began their counterattack (U.S. Congress, Senate, *Proposed Restoration of Prohibition to Alaska*, 57th Cong., 2d sess., 14 January 1903).

66. *Congressional Record*, 55th Cong., 3d sess., 4 January 1899, p. 395. Alaskans, like other settlers, had not hesitated to tax themselves voluntarily as circumstances required (*Congressional Record*, 56th Cong., 1st sess., 17 May 1900, p. 5668). Barker, *Compilation*, pp. 209–10; Senate, *Criminal Code*, p. 2.

67. *Alaskan*, 15 April and 20 May 1899. Barker, *Compilation*, p. 211.

68. Brady, *Annual Report, 1899*, p. 46. TAP, mf. 6, Brady to Hitchcock, 7 July 1899.

69. Interview with John and Hugh Brady, 23 June 1962. *Alaskan*, 12 and 5 August 1899. JCorr, 19:113–14, Brady to Jackson, 27 November 1899.

70. *Alaskan*, 9 July 1898 and 23 December 1899.

71. Brady, *Annual Report, 1899*, p. 38.

72. *Alaskan*, 9 December 1899. Brady, *Annual Report, 1900*, p. 44; idem, *Annual Report, 1902*, p. 54.

73. Ted C. Hinckley, ed., "The Canoe Rocks—We Do Not Know What Will Become of Us," *Western Historical Quarterly* 1 (July 1970): 265–90, is a complete transcript of this meeting between Governor Brady and the distressed Tlingit chieftans; TAP, mf. 5, contains the original.

CHAPTER TWELVE

Sovereignty, Domestic and National

For John Brady the twentieth century began triumphantly. After lobbying for three winters in Washington, largely at his own expense, John rejoiced when his district obtained an admirably revised and expanded civil code—Senator Carter's Bill, as some chose to identify it. Henceforth Alaska benefited from not one but three judicial divisions. Courts were to convene in Juneau and Skagway, Eagle in the Interior, and Saint Michael, which also embraced Nome. Each judge would be assisted by a district attorney, a marshal, and the necessary staff.[1] Lawlessness would continue to cast ugly shadows across the Yukon interior and distant Nome, but threats of anarchy had passed. And although the homestead enactment had proved a hollow victory, Congress at last promised to extend America's public land surveys northward. For better or for worse, the recent gold rushes had raised the Great Land's white population to over thirty thousand, or more than that of the natives.[2]

A few weeks before the nineteenth century slipped into history, Alaska's governor enjoyed the privilege of personally reviewing district affairs with President McKinley. Earlier that year Senate leaders had assured John of reappointment.[3] Attesting to his successful leadership was a banquet celebrating him and the Great Land at New York City's Waldorf-Astoria Hotel on 8 May 1900. "John G. Brady, once a waif in the streets of New York and now Governor of Alaska," reported the *Mail and Express*, "was the guest of honor at a dinner last night. . . . Fifty well-known New Yorkers were present and letters of regret were received from a dozen more, among them former Secretary Bliss, Senator [Thomas] Platt, Senator [Chauncey] Depew. . . ."[4] Writing to Elizabeth, John admitted that he "felt much pleased with the whole proceeding. . . . Mr. E. H. Harriman did me the honor to come

210

to the feast and greeted me most cordially." John insisted, "the occasion was not used for advertising at all."[5] Actually, the boosterism wafting about the Waldorf-Astoria's Myrtle Room that evening was palpable, the presence of railroad titan Harriman left no doubt of that.

The cover of the handsome menu card featured a photograph of Alaska's governor. Printed within, just before the entrees, was a tribute to Alaska's commercial potentialities. The district was "in no way a failure. . . . *bought at a valuation of about two cents per acre, is now yielding dollars per pan.*"[6] The toastmaster for the evening, former state senator C. P. Vedder of New York, began the speechmaking: "The statesmen of 1867, seemed to believe that the United States Government was great enough and grand enough and good enough to own everything from the southern cross to the north pole. Then it was supposed that Alaska had nothing but northern lights, cinnamon bears, and totem poles. But of late it has been discovered that Alaska has gold 'beyond the dreams of avarice.'" His introduction completed, Vedder presented Governor Brady with a bust of William H. Seward, a gift for the people of Alaska. "Alaska's Governor," declaimed the toastmaster, "illustrates the possibilities open to any American boy. Grander victories than those of Napoleon are won on the common fields of life. It is the farmer in his field, the laborer in his shop, the student in his closet, who has fought out this matchless fabric of the American's Government."[7]

John's response mingled the hortatory beliefs of missionary, merchant, and northland advocate: "It will be my pleasure to bear this gift to the people of the coming State of Alaska. We have studied Mr. Seward. His name has always been before us. He had about him something of an Isaiah—something of a political prophet. . . . We know that at that time a great cry went up against 'Seward's folly'. . . . We in Alaska want to be bound to you. We want your institutions, your thought. . . . Our prospects are very promising, but there is a darker side. Congress has been very slow in doing anything for us."[8] John went on to bemoan the legal disabilities under which Alaska was suffering. Wisely, he closed on a high note. "In carrying our institutions to other lands we are simply following the beckoning hand of a divine Providence." An oversize twenty-by-thirty-two-inch handout with John's effusive comments and his photo memorialized the evening.

Earlier John had been regaled by a few New York friends at the fashionable Union League Club with a banquet featuring handpainted menu cards. Other dinners and receptions that winter and spring included a Washington Board of Trade gathering that enabled John to rub elbows with some twenty governors and a dozen senators.[9] Not long before, he had met Governor Frank Steunenberg of Idaho, who also labored to resolve the demands of impatient western miners.

Klondike followed by Nome, the vast New Empire, McKinley's "full dinner pail prosperity," the flattery of prominent Americans—Brady would have been an odd American indeed had he not glowed with expectations on his return home in June of 1900. A *Wall Street Journal* reporter caught up with him at Satchahnee. "The Governor's life is all wrapped up in the country," enthused the New Yorker. "The story of his own life is so remarkable, and his rise to distinction so unique, that he naturally is in great love with American institutions, and naturally is using his present power to extend them fully over Alaska."[10] The governor's ebullience was unmistakable. A few months before, he had informed his Waldorf-Astoria audience about the "coming state of Alaska." With the passage of the "new Alaska Code bill . . . [the governor] now expects to see Alaska take a long stride forward," noted the reporter. "Property here is now more secure and there is remedy at law for cruelty and injustice. . . . the new law means also a larger occupation of the land." What Alaska now needed, Brady insisted, was "simply to have the great undeveloped wealth of Alaska made known [to] the enterprising, struggling and suffering people of the crowded centers of the civilized world."[11]

That same month an article penned by John permitted the American public to share his buoyant belief in Alaska's tomorrow: "The vast majority of the men who are going to Cape Nome to seek their fortune . . . will be for the most part a picked and select class of men. . . . Within a few years there will be a large population scattered over that vast expanse of that part of the continent. The people will organize and soon appeal for statehood, for they know a territorial government is only a makeshift."[12] Brady's imagination had over-reached itself. Alaska would not have a large population within a few years, nor even in as many as seventy.

"Wise statesmanship," Brady believed, "will approve Alaska's be-coming a state as soon as possible. It is only thus that the people can enjoy to the full the blessings of our institutions."[13] A year earlier he had concluded his annual report with an admonishment to Congress that "Statehood appears to be the only remedy. . . . A people can attain under our form of government to their greatest degree of political happiness under a State and not as a Territory." If Brady now antici-pated statehood, subsequent developments dimmed his hopes. By 1901 the Nome skyrocket was already losing its most dazzling allure, and despite Felix Pedro's 1902 gold discoveries and the subsequent founding of Fairbanks, Alaska's frenzied gold stampedes had peaked.

Alaskans could not then discern that, like California, Colorado, and

Arizona, the district had already written the most dramatic chapter of its gold mining history.[14] Too many adventurers dreaming of ever larger and more lucrative gold deposits had staked their entire savings, invested years of harsh, physical sacrifice, even risked life itself. Incapable of admitting that their luck had played out, they required a scapegoat. Across America's concurrent Great Plains frontier, disillusioned farmers had damned the lack of water; Alaska miners cursed its volume. Kansans and Nebraskans were convinced that railroads had profited outrageously; Alaskans quite as heatedly condemned the "extortionate shipping companies." But there is no better scapegoat upon which to pin one's disappointments than the government, and most especially a political figure in that government. By 1898, not yet a year in office, Brady felt the pricks of such malcontents.[15]

District judge Charles Johnson's decision to step down doubtless had been encouraged by the carping of discontented Alaskans in Skagway and Juneau. Prior to the passage of the new civil code and its provision for three judicial divisions, he had endeavored to do the work of three judges by holding court in various places in northern and western Alaska. Johnson's innovation had permitted cases at law, license payments, applications for American citizenship, and the appointment of constables and notaries to be completed without journeying to distant Juneau or Sitka. Brady had accompanied and assisted his friend and coworker on an exhausting four-thousand-mile tour. One such trip had been enough for the district judge. Brady, however, continued to make arduous official tours about Alaska. The resentful voices and personal sniping at him during 1898–99 had not weakened his resolve to ram through the civil code.

When some senatorial friends moved to increase John's annual salary, apparently without urging from him, representative John W. Gaines bewailed the costs of "colonial administration": "I feel sorry for the man who has to go to Alaska to make a living. . . . he goes to a political refrigerator, a place where there are savages, a place that is cold, a place where they have to slide around on sleds, a place where we had to go to Norway and get reindeer at a cost of millions to haul the people about to hunt gold. . . . I ask how now in all seriousness for some one to tell me why you raised the salaries of the governor of Alaska from $2,700 to $5000?"[16] After representative John F. Lacey reminded his House colleagues that Alaska's overworked and underpaid district judge had recently resigned and that within Alaska "roast beef and potatoes cost $2.50 a meal," John's raise won approval. He probably viewed his pay increase as a by-product of the too long "pending Civil Code" that was finally crystallized in 1900.[17]

That same memorable year Hawaii, only two years a U.S. possession,

213

adopted a territorial form of government. As in Arizona and New Mexico, Hawaiians operated their own legislature and enjoyed the privilege of sending a delegate to Congress. Of course Alaskans envied the mid-Pacific territory. Brady bit his tongue and tried to avoid any invidious comparisons.[18] Next to his colossal homeland, these Polynesian islands were geographic midgets.

Klondicitis and its aftershocks had accomplished what Sheldon Jackson's quarter century of public relations and Governor Brady's promotional labors could never have done. Now Nevada senator William M. Stewart urged removing all restraints: "Let foreigners or anybody else go into that region; the more the better. We want gold. . . . Do not throw any obstructions in the way, and you will have plenty of gold. The gold standard may be all right if we have plenty of gold." Senator Henry M. Teller of Colorado speculated that Alaska, "if properly developed, will produce probably anywhere from fifty to seventy-five million dollars a year in gold." Congressman Vespasian Warner reminded his peers: "In the Yukon country the mining is placer mining, which . . . 'peters out,' but at Juneau it is quartz mining, and the hills are full of the mineral which will last for centuries." Montana's senator Thomas Carter saw Alaska as "destined in the future to be the great, strong, unfailing source of gold supply for this country."[19] Certainly the general agent's anxiety for native rights and the governor's dream of an Alaska occupied by resident home builders had little in common with such bullion bombast.

Within the territory this golden rhetoric fell on cynical ears. Marooned in dreary ramshackle communities, Alaska's miners endured disagreeable living conditions and outrageous prices. Denied the amenities of Sioux City or Chicago, they relieved their aggravations with shallow sloganeering, mutual duplicity, and politically naive demands. The *Alaskan* suggested that northlanders stop "to think of the extra large amount of business that came before the last congress, and its committees, incident upon the war, and many other important matters." Seen in that light, it was "a wonder that Alaska received any attention at all. . . . Governor Brady deserves the congratulations of every one for his indefatigable efforts for the advancement of our Territory."[20] Alaska, bragged Senator Carter, "has been provided by Congress with a system of statutory law more elaborate than has heretofore been enacted for any partially organized territory of the United States." The U.S. attorney, Robert A. Friedrich, praised the civil code and asked that it be given a fair and impartial trial. Friedrich rebuked those "people of Alaska [who] have been wanting laws for the Territory for years past, and now that we have them, many of the same people and several of the newspapers are condemning the very thing they have been wanting." One Great Land visitor thought it most strange that Alaskans were "in favor of a code of new laws and representation on the floor of Congress, but [were] decidedly against taxation. In other words, the anomaly is presented of a desire for representation without taxation in any form."[21]

Alaska's fourth estate provided one of the traditional escape valves for pent-up territorial frustrations. Certainly the district press never let Governor Brady suffer from a magic-mirror complex. The *Douglas Island News* blasted his amendment to the Carter Bill, which provided for a resident judge at Sitka.[22] John's enthusiasm for Alaskan agricultural potential was greeted with sarcasm from Juneau's *Alaska Miner*; later the newspaper decried his failure to secure homesteads for Alaska. Skagway and Ketchikan usually parroted the standard dissatisfactions heard about the streets of Juneau: Sitka should give up its claim as the district capital; a popularly elected delegate to Congress would put an end to taxation without representation; Alaskans, not carpetbaggers or the "Alaska Lobby"—which generally meant corporations with considerable business in Alaska—should direct the Great Land's future.[23] No less threadworn was the sniping both within the district and without at those "pesky missionaries." Brady had not worn the collar since the early eighties, but this fact did not protect him. "It is impossible for him to get away from the missionary idea," insisted the *Tacoma Daily News*; "he looks at everything from the missionary standpoint." In 1902 John wrote an old friend: "I am performing the duties of my office to the best of my abilities [yet] I have many bitter enemies." Some of this recrimination mystified him: "There must be something in my temperament that produces this. Something of which I am not conscious. All men in Alaska do not speak well of me. For one thing I belong to the 'damn missionary set', and those who voice this sentiment are numerous."[24]

Sitkan William Kelly believed that much of the antimissionary vituperation originated with Alfred P. Swineford, who had returned to the Panhandle as journalist, business promoter, and, of course, political aspirant. "Swineford," Kelly informed William T. Harris, the commissioner of education, is a "personal enemy of Dr. Jackson and always antagonistic to missionaries": "He has a coterie of henchmen who, like him, daily assuage their thirst with whiskey until their tongues are limber and their language often vile in their denunciation of missionaries. They are just as unreasonable in their denunciation of Congress, the Alaska Boundary Commission, and the members of the Committee that drafted the laws for Alaska."[25] Although nothing came of it, Swineford, as foreman of the 1899 grand jury, succeeded in bringing charges against Jackson. Shocked, General Eaton wrote John: "What about this miserable assault on Dr. Jackson, said to be made by the Grand Jury of Juneau? Is there no end to this kind of persecution of a faithful and devoted public officer?" Alaska's governor decried Swineford's "animus of long standing" and called the accusation of educational misman-agement "altogether unworthy of the ex-governor." Five years into his administration, Brady could be philosophical about Swineford's relish at making a whipping boy of the general agent. Swineford "now runs the *Ketchikan Mining Journal*. . . . He is especially hostile toward Dr. Jackson and anything he undertakes. He has his influence and of course we must battle against it. But from my way of thinking he is of Satan's own."[26]

A sizable portion of southeastern Alaska's anti-Brady ferment doubt-less emanated from Swineford's unrelenting criticism. Nevertheless, Alaska's fifth governor and its second remained on speaking terms. Certainly Swineford itched to become the miners' paladin and Alaska's first official delegate to Washington. Two conditions, however, favored Brady. The remoteness and transience of Alaska's prospector-settler enclaves severely weakened their potential political muscle. Second, John's office was appointive, and therefore he never had to campaign among such an inchoate electorate. To glue together party solidarity between distant Nome and nearby Ketchikan was virtually impossible. Consider the dilemma of any prospective office-seeker trying to speak for "all Alaskans" when each year one-third of his northern "supporters" were hibernating in Seattle and points south. No, Brady was in one sense quite fortunate—the territory's immensity seriously handicapped the emergence of a powerful district-wide opposition.

This lack of anything but a narrow Panhandle base dissuaded neither Swineford nor younger politically ambitious Alaska champions from repeatedly throwing down the gauntlet at Brady's feet. Wisely, John met these challenges with neither outrage nor contempt. Often he agreed with their demands: a territorial delegate to Congress, home-stead legislation, federal aid for improved transportation, better schools, and much else. It behooved him to channel their discontent, not con-demn it. Alaska could ill afford to dissipate its weak political energy.

On 9 October 1899 Juneau hosted Alaska's third "nonpartisan" con-vention. Of course, it was partisan, focusing upon particular grievances and prescribing specific remedies. As might have been expected, few Nome or interior Alaskans were present, but lawyers and businessmen from the territory's southeastern communities were well represented. Swineford served as chairman of the convention. Apparently he was kept busy mollifying maverick remonstrances.[27] Sitkans judged the entire gathering to be an attempt by Juneau to steal the capital and sent no delegate. The *Alaskan* facetiously claimed that the meeting violated law and insisted that "the most charming town in Alaska for a resident is Sitka. It also has the best climate, the prettiest residences and churches, and the smallest number of saloons and less vice and crime than any other place in the whole country." To this the *Juneau Mining Record* replied, "And we might add less population." Sitka's *Alaskan* made sure that it got the last word: "Yes, and we should have included in our former statement . . . less typhoid fever, and other contagious diseases . . . prevalent in some of our larger neighboring cities . . . caused from foul sewers, poor drinking water and dirty streets and back yards."[28]

After meeting in various committees for ten days, the Juneau convention framed a number of urgent requests to be made to Congress. As at Juneau's earlier nonpartisan conventions, a memorial was drafted. Chosen as a delegate to carry it east was John Garland Price, only a few years earlier an Oklahoma and Colorado boomer, now a Skagway attorney. The *New York Times* noted that the convention hoped that Price would actually be Alaska's representative to Congress.[29]

Another lengthy appeal was forwarded eastward the following February after a Skagway mass meeting accused Brady of "not properly attending to the needs of the people he represented." One part of the Skagwayans' message insisted "that John G. Price is the only person who has been clothed with even a shadow of authority by the people of Alaska to speak for or represent them in Washington." And to keep the capital at Sitka any longer "would be nothing short of a crime against our people." Price was asked what the current governor had done that was "hostile to Alaska" to which Price supplied the standard response: "He belongs to the damn missionary set."[30]

By the time the district's Republican party convention convened in Juneau in May of 1900, a few of the Panhandle's restless young turks had become unduly aggrieved about Brady. The governor's skepticism of a popularly elected delegate particularly infuriated them.[31] After the Republican convention terminated, Congressman Warner pointed out the inaccuracy and self-serving argument of the Panhandle politicos: "It would cost more to hold a general election in the district of Alaska than it would to hold a similar election in the State of New York. . . . The people generally do not remain in any one place longer than they find it profitable to do so. . . . Not one tenth of the population of Alaska would be represented by any vote that could be taken there." As to who would compose the less than one-tenth, Representative

217

Warner was embarrassingly specific: "A convention was held at Juneau which denounced Governor Brady and other officials of that district who reside in Sitka. There is a fight between the two towns, and I venture the opinion that there were not fifteen people in that convention who live out-side of Douglas Island and Juneau. So it would be of any election held in that district. The attendance would only come from a few towns along the coast. . . . we would never hear from the great interior, Circle City, Eagle City, Nome, Unalaska, and other places similarly located."[32]

Brady welcomed Price's support at the nation's capital. As with hundreds of other Far West would-be Jack-the-giant-killers who had preceded him, Price's pugnacity fled after he entered the halls of Congress. Skagway's shortcomings had aroused his knight errantry; the Washington stadium sobered him. Henceforth Price had to recognize that there were other territories—New Mexico, Arizona, Oklahoma—that also vied for congressional favors. When at mid-year the Carter Bill became law, Price agreed that most of what the previous October nonpartisan meeting had thumped for was now achieved. Indeed, he called it "a very satisfactory bill."[33] Now, however, Swineford and Price conjectured whether southeastern Alaska might not become a distinct political entity preparatory to statehood.[34] Nor had the new Alaska code swept away all the political tinder: Brady had failed to obtain a delegate for Alaska, and Sitka remained the de facto capital.

Although the passage of the 1900 code significantly strengthened Brady's standing both in Washington, D.C., and in Alaska, neither Sitkans nor Juneauites were happy with the compromise that he and Senator Perkins negotiated for delaying the transfer of the district's capital. Congress agreed that stripling Juneau had now become Alaska's dominant center and thus was entitled to supplant Sitka. Indeed, almost a decade earlier the House Committee on Public Lands had reported that Sitka "never will be a town of any commercial importance." Except for a special 1898 term of court held by Judge Johnson in Sitka, the district court's regular meetings had been in Juneau since 1892.[35] From the outset of the Sitka-Juneau tug-of-war, Brady had loyally pulled for his hometown, and as governor he continued to favor sedate Sitka over sensual Juneau. In 1900 his old friend Charles Johnson chided him for his stubbornness: "I think no one blamed you . . . even though they may feel from a personal standpoint that the capital ought to be in Juneau." But Senator Perkins, no doubt armed by John, made a convincing case that before moving it "the Government may first procure suitable sites . . . for the location of the capitol and other buildings."[36] It was a stall, but it worked, and despite what the law specified, Sitka

218

continued at least for a few more years to assert a slender claim on the capital. In 1902, when John tried to get money for rebuilding Sitka's deteriorating public structures, the Alaska Chamber of Commerce (located in Juneau) slapped his wrist: "If the government is going to erect any new buildings they should be erected at Juneau, which has been designated as the capital." That same year, John hedged when answering a question about why he continued to oppose the transfer: "It is best to let the matter rest for a few years for the people will settle the question when they get control of affairs."[37]

On the capital's relocation John probably sensed that he fought a losing battle. For all the economic benefits accompanying a capital, the campaign to obtain this distinction also had its sociopsychological overtones. These historic intrastate municipal contests could be traced as far back as the seventeenth-century colonial frontier. Be the locale Virginia or Alaska, such zealous provincial partisanship reflected the rootless, hard-driving parvenu's struggle for identity and status. Certainly when the Carter Bill enabled Alaska's burgeoning younger communities to organize their own municipal governments, the action helped alleviate many a recent immigrant's feeling of anomie. It was not happenstance that among the first to incorporate were youthful Skagway and Ketchikan.[38]

Far more universal sources of dissatisfaction than the site of the capital were Alaska's ineffective homestead legislation and the absence of an official territorial delegate to Congress. In 1900 Governor Brady listed these two priorities along with an improved status for Alaska's natives as the three matters he "most earnestly desired" to see remedied by Congress.[39]

Two grave executive concerns that required Governor Brady's attention were the concurrent land controversies at Cape Nome and along Alaska's eastern boundary with Canada. In each situation his adjudicatory influence proved negligible. Yet, paradoxically, each was injected with such an urgency that both could be credited with assisting him in the final passage of the civil code.

After their personal tour extending from Skagway to Nome, Governor Brady and Judge Johnson understood what mere stopgaps the scattered army units were. Fortunately, the creation of the second judicial division forged a weak administrative link between the physically marooned boom town facing the Bering Sea and Alaska's capital thousands of miles to the southeast. Unfortunately, history provided Governor Brady only faint precedent for his proper role in handling the criminal conspiracy that fastened itself upon Nome.

With the possible exception of friction over business license provisions, nothing had stirred so much congressional concern as the costly litigation certain to arise among Alaska's mining claimants. Senator Newlands not only summed up the problem but exhibited prophetic skill: "The source of title is in the United States Government, but the litigation over mines reaches stupendous proportions, not only in the amount involved, but in the number of cases which arise. That is inevitable in a new country. . . . I have not the slightest doubt that in Alaska, within the next one or two years, a single case will arise that will absorb the entire time and attention of a court from three to six months."[40] The staking of claims by attorneys around Nome was "detrimental and wrong," Brady warned. Claims would "be held for nearly two years without doing a dollar's worth of work upon them. Mines have thus been staked and held simply for speculation." So extensive was the greed that "hundreds of good miners who went to Nome this season and who went many miles into the interior to prospect found stream after stream staked, and very seldom could they find where the smallest prospect hole had been sunk." He predicted continued trouble.[41]

Although Brady had rejoiced that "the District is now blessed with a good body of laws," Alaska's governor reminded everyone who would listen to him that the legislation did not "give adequate protection to life and property in all parts of the district." Communications in 1900 between the Panhandle "and the Bering Sea and Upper Yukon regions were so limited," believes one Alaska historian, "that any centralized territorial government would have been faced with almost insuperable difficulties." "Without the presence of troops in northwestern Alaska," wrote Lieutenant W. P. Richardson, "riot and disorder would prevail in many places." Richardson urged that a "form of government . . . similar in general outline to that of the Northwest Mounted Police of Canada" be instituted.[42] Brady did not concur. Instead, he hoped that Alaska's expanded judicial network, plus new municipal administrations, might fill any governmental vacuums.

In an exaggerated form, Nome embodied the worst qualities of unchecked, exploitive American capitalism. A long letter to Brady from one of its citizens acclaimed Nome "the greatest place on earth." Because of the relatively low cost of transportation, its environs had become crowded, "forcing people beyond the explored limit and as a result the entire country for a distance of four hundred miles has been more or less prospected." Yet it was "no Poorman's country; She has too many of that class already," John's correspondent grumbled. Alaska is "so very expensive in which to operate that combined capital alone will be able to cope with conditions." The letter bitterly indicted the trans-

SOVEREIGNTY, DOMESTIC AND NATIONAL

portation companies that had made such rapid profits. In fact, their ships had provided just what the gold-famished multitude wanted: "Never in the history of the mining world was any country so shamefully treated as Nome. She has enriched and benefitted thousands but very few have done anything for Nome. . . . all the broke men in the United States, who, inflamed by the stories of sudden wealth in the Klondike came here entirely without any permanent intentions, buoyed up with the hope that in some way they could get hold of a [site?] and leave the country before the close of navigation."[43] Letters such as this help explain the governor's hesitancy to turn the Great Land over to what the anti-Brady men described as the "sovereign will of the people." Captain P. H. Ray stated, "An election by the floating population for the local civil officers would be a farce," and Senator Carter commented, "to hold an election in Alaska during the gold excitement would be something like holding a general election at a circus."[44]

When the civil code created two additional judicial divisions for the Yukon Valley and northwestern Alaska, everyone understood that the judges of these remote federal courts would be "not only the judicial but in large measure the executive officers of the district." The three appointed judges were expected to "issue licenses for all purposes, issue franchises to business corporations, grant charters to incorporated towns, appoint United States commissioners who are the local justices of the peace, coroners and recorders and the officers of the courts, and collect the occupation tax."[45] Clearly the federal judge had to be trustworthy; if he proved to be a rascal, who could tell what thievery he might not welcome.

Little different than other territorial governors, Brady had virtually nothing to say about those whom Washington appointed to administer district affairs. By far the greater number were carpetbaggers, but then so were a majority of the white Alaskans. Judge for the new second judicial division was Arthur H. Noyes of Minneapolis. Noyes arrived at his Nome post in July of 1900, accompanied by his staff and an ex–frontier sheriff, Alexander McKenzie. One-time Republican national committeeman from North Dakota, McKenzie had served as a lobbyist for the Northern Pacific and Great Northern railroads. Aided by some unsavory Nome attorneys, McKenzie had recently sought to amend the Carter Bill so as to cheat the "lucky Swedes" out of their rich Cape Nome claims. Blocked on Capitol Hill, the "Spoilers," as Rex Beach later dubbed them, conjured up an even more brazen scheme.[46] Noyes would see that McKenzie was designated receiver of disputed claims at Nome. Thereafter the Alaska Gold Mining Company would mine the jumped claims. Due process requires time; thus, even if the jumpers lost, they would win. For by the time the courts decided against them, the Spoilers would have skimmed the contested mines clean. Their design was so blatantly crooked as to defy probability— that is, until one recalls how tumultuous the Nome setting was in 1900–01. In the opinion of a recent chronicler, "Nome was as lawless a community as ever existed in the West. It was crowded with gamblers, con men, whores, pimps, trigger-happy ne'er-do-wells, and honest adventurers."[47]

One month after the Spoilers came ashore, Governor Brady visited Nome. He was gratified by the recently appointed judges for divisions two and three. Holding court on the upper Yukon at Rampart, Circle, and Eagle was James Wickersham. Brady had previously met Wickersham at Tacoma and was glad to renew their association at Eagle. Later, Brady wrote president Theodore Roosevelt: "My impressions were favorable of the man." In his diary Wickersham recorded his opinion of Alaska's governor. He "is stout, short, straight and vigorous: he has a clear eye and is a fearless man. I judge that there is never but one side of any case, to him, and that he sometimes makes mistakes." In time the energetic judge would play a paramount role in northland history.[48]

At Nome Brady encountered Judge Noyes. "Never was a man sent to fill a more trying position," John wrote in his annual report for 1900. "Everybody and everything is pellmell. There are several claimants for each town lot, beach claim and creek claim—25,000 people waiting for the court to open its door." While at Nome John decried the town's endemic claim jumping; he evidently did not discern what the Spoilers were about. One feature of the new civil code that did disturb him, however, was the fee system by which the enlarged force of district lawmen, commissioners, and deputy marshals were compensated. The "weakest part," he labeled it, "so uncertain [that] men will not, in many places, accept an appointment."[49] In other words, precisely where law enforcement needed the most qualified individuals, a niggardly Congress had practically invited shoddy law enforcement.

Nineteen hundred had not ended before Noyes and company found their illegal actions challenged by a Nome attorney who had resorted to the Ninth Circuit Court of Appeals at San Francisco. On the advice of Judge Noyes, McKenzie refused to comply with an order of the circuit court. They must have believed that Nome's isolation gave them immunity from the long arm of the law. President McKinley consulted Governor Brady about the rumors of this nefarious plunder. Lacking all the facts, Brady suggested that Judge Noyes be transferred to Juneau until an investigation could be completed. Thereupon the president said,

"I command you so far as the President can command you to go to the Attorney General and discuss the matter with him." For some reason the question of Noyes's transfer did not seem to strike the attorney general as pressing. Brady's contention that "it was of great importance" got nowhere.[50] When John requested Secretary of the Interior Hitchcock to give him "three-quarters of an hour to go over Alaska matters with him," his customarily brusque chief snapped, "Boil it down." To Elizabeth John expressed fear that "there will be bloodshed if there is persistence in appointing receivers."[51]

By October of 1900 a San Francisco judge had issued a bench warrant charging McKenzie with contempt of court. The last steamer departing Nome before winter's onset carried McKenzie south, under arrest and soon to stand trial in California. On 31 January 1901 Governor Brady informed Secretary Hitchcock that Noyes's "actions during the past season were very much condemned and have created a feeling [of] insecurity. Some men are openly asserting that if the same course is pursued during the coming season, namely the appointment of receivers to work the rich claims, the action of the court will be resisted and the receivers will be shot. . . . In the meantime Mr. Alexander McKenzie is in the hands of the Appellate Court of San Francisco for contempt."[52] One group at Nome confidently expected Alaska's governor to resolve matters: "He is the one man that all the people have absolute confidence in."[53]

In February McKenzie received two consecutive six-month sentences, as the California judge William W. Morrow commented, for "intentional and deliberate and in furtherance of the high-handed and grossly illegal proceedings initiated almost as soon as Judge Noyes and McKenzie had set foot on Alaska territory at Nome, and which may be safely and fortunately said to have no parallel in the jurisprudence of this country."[54] McKenzie had been too stalwart a Republican warhorse. Despite the furor, President McKinley pardoned his old GOP ally. The summer of 1901 found Noyes still in the saddle at Nome. John groaned, "This sham is now holding court." Before long a San Francisco court order, backed up by Nome vigilantes, speeded Noyes's departure southward. The Department of Justice temporarily transferred Judge Wickersham to the vacated judgeship; he quickly restored public confidence in the court's integrity. Noyes was lucky and received only a one thousand dollar fine.[55]

But for President McKinley, whose trust McKenzie and Noyes had abused, all luck had run out. On 6 September 1901 McKinely was assassinated by a deranged anarchist. News of the president's death stunned Alaskans. For Brady the loss was particularly painful. Mc-

223

Kinley had shown a sincere concern for "that vast and remote and yet promising portion of our country."[56] Furthermore, despite the president's busy schedule, he had found time to listen patiently to John's appeals on Alaska's behalf. McKinley had been so pleased with Brady's administrative skill that he had urged Congress to strengthen John's executive power. And despite the anti-Brady agitation, Alaska's governor had won quick reappointment on 6 June.[57] Now, suddenly, less than a year after McKinley's easy reelection, the president was dead. Brady wrote a formal letter to Secretary Hitchcock on behalf of the citizens of Alaska expressing "their heart felt sympathy and condolences to Mrs. McKinley and other stricken relatives." It offers a glimpse of Brady's philosophy at middle age: "I believe in the depravity of the human heart and the killing of WILLIAM MCKINLEY is one of the most awful exhibitions of it. Satan seems to be let loose for a season and his ministering spirits are doing his bidding. Science will never save humanity. All anarchists are apostles of science. They are all filled with and preach scientific theories. Unless human society can be guided by the principles of Jesus Christ which he has left us in the sermon on the mount, there is no hope for humanity."[58] Unlike a growing number of his twentieth-century countrymen, Brady had not discarded his Calvinism for the newer narcissistic worship of a man-machine centered world.

Catapulted into the White House by Leon Czolgosz's mad act, Theodore Roosevelt became a dynamic American president. Strangely—particularly so in light of his love of the outdoors—he never visited Alaska. Brady first met Roosevelt during the 1900 presidential campaign when the New York Republican, McKinley's running mate, visited Portland. A number of western governors had convened there to honor the Empire State leader. When Roosevelt entered the banquet room, each of them introduced himself; the last to do so was Governor Brady.

> Brady: Governor Roosevelt, the other governors have greeted you with interest simply as a fellow governor and a great American, but I greet you with infinitely more interest, as the son of your father, the first Theodore Roosevelt.
> Roosevelt (while shaking John's hand warmly): In what special way have you been interested in my father?
> Brady: Your father picked me up from the streets in New York, a waif and an orphan, and sent me to a western family, paying for my transportation and early care. Years passed and I was able to repay the money which had given me my start in life, but I can never repay what he did for me, but it is through that early care and by giving me such a foster mother and father that I gradually rose in the world, until today I can greet his son as a fellow governor of a part of our great country.[59]

It was a nice personal touch. Perhaps it later served to strengthen John's frail ties with the new president.

Despite what those who lashed out at the "Jackson-Brady cabal" may have at times thought, John Brady did not enjoy a close working relationship with Theodore Roosevelt. Like his gubernatorial predecessors, Brady never had other than a respectful association with the current occupant of the White House. As a post–Spanish-American War president, Roosevelt had to deal not only with huge contiguous western territories but also with new and difficult overseas territories extending from Puerto Rico to the Philippines. Although Governor Brady recognized that "the results of the war are momentous," he worried how the New Empire might diminish Alaska's relative position. He pleaded, "Congress may remember that Alaska is thirteen times larger than Cuba, that it has been in our possession for thirty-one years, and that its value has been unknown and unappreciated. . . . Above all we beseech Congress to regard us as American citizens and not undertake to classify us with Kanakas, Filippinos and Cubans."[60] From Alaska's governor President Roosevelt heard that "both parties have made pledges in their platforms and both have made Alaska a dump[ing] ground [of appointees]." And Roosevelt's annual messages do reveal the influence of his Far North deputy. At times his utterances were pure Brady. In Roosevelt's *Second Annual Message* one finds: "No country has a more valuable possession in mineral wealth, in fisheries, furs, forests, and also in land available for certain kinds of farming and stock growing. It is . . . well fitted to support a large permanent population. Alaska needs a good land law and such provisions for homesteads and preemptions as will encourage permanent settlement . . . to the building up of homes therein."[61] Nor was the president deaf to both Brady's and Jackson's preachments on aboriginal needs. In his 1903 *Annual Message* Roosevelt reminded his countrymen: "Attention should be paid to the Alaska Indians . . . to study their needs, relieve their immediate wants, and help them adapt themselves to the new conditions." The next year Roosevelt joined Brady in urging regular salaries for Alaska's commissioners so as to end "the discredited fee system" as well as a delegate to Congress. Once again the president accorded Alaska's natives attention not customarily granted their brethren to the south: "Alaska's natives have come under the influence of civilization . . . have proved their capability of becoming self-supporting, self-respecting citizens, and ask only for the just enforcement of the law and intelligent instruction and supervision." Who can doubt that Jackson cheered such assertions? Like McKinley, Roosevelt exhibited his confidence in John by requesting Congress to enlarge the administrative power of Alaska's governor.[62]

Roosevelt's most notable historical link to Alaska concerned the district's contentious eastern boundary with Canada. By the time Roosevelt became president, Governor Brady had long since embroiled himself in the complex issue.[63] Traceable to the ambiguous language in the Anglo-Russian treaty of 1825 and unresolved when the United States purchased Russian America in 1867, the problem demanded resolution. The stampede to Dawson, succeeded by America's astonishingly successful imperialistic war, had heightened the gravity of the disputed Alaska-Canada boundary. According to the 1825 treaty the Panhandle border with Canada followed a mountain range parallel to the sea, or, if this fell too far inland, a serpentine line ten marine leagues (thirty miles) from the ocean. But from the Portland Canal in the south to the 141st meridian in the north, no clearly distinguishable mountain range existed, only a jumble of unconnected peaks. The two powers therefore differed on what constituted the actual line. Understandably Canada favored the maritime line, because at points this would afford her egress to the sea. Preliminary boundary surveys left many questions unanswered; and by the late eighties Canada began to favor an expanded interpretation of what was her zone. With the 1896 Klondike discovery the sovereignty fat really was in the diplomatic fire.

In fact, once the gold rush gave prominence to Dyea and Skagway, Canadians insisted that the ten leagues should be measured from the outer limits of the irregular coast. By this theory Alaska's Lynn Canal boom towns would fall within Canada's embrace. The assertion was excessive, and premier Wilfrid Laurier and his minister of the interior admitted as much. Ottawa fully expected to reduce its expanded claim at the negotiating table, just as the Canadians depended on London's support to maximize the final settlement. Numerous Americans believed London, not Ottawa, to be their real adversary in the controversy.[64]

An obvious means of reminding forgetful legislators that Alaska was also worth fighting for was to assume a strong, if not truculent, stance opposing Ottawa's boundary claims. At first Governor Brady did not act impetuously. John's 1898 tour of Skagway, Dawson, and the disputed region satisfied him that Canada's claims were exaggerated. Furthermore, though he respected Ottawa's effective regulation of the chaotic throng of American miners, his eyes and heart told him whose sovereignty must win out. Before long John pumped his own advanced, if illogical, claims: "British diplomats are craftily clamoring for everything in sight." It was "foolishness our act of making England a present of the south half of Vancouver's island . . . [which] from a military standpoint commands the entrance to Puget Sound, and thus places all of the leading cities of Washington at England's mercy."[65] Although not unreluctant to engage in testy rhetoric, Alaska's governor did not want to foment a war. John frowned on the suggestion of Skagway's commissioner that a body of men be formed to remove the Canadian flag forcefully from the summit of Chilkoot Pass and carry it back down to Lake Bennett. As he later reassured Secretary Hitchcock, "I do not wish to have our people in a contest with the Canadians and my every effort shall be to prevent it."[66]

Among those who held the levers of power in Ottawa, London, and Washington, war talk was virtually nil. After all, Great Britain had just refused to join other European powers in condemning America for her war with Spain. President Roosevelt promised that he would "not forget . . . England's attitude during the war" and expressed pleasure in seeing "a gradual coming together of the two peoples." From England's standpoint it unquestionably served her interests to have Uncle Sam a clearly recognized "defender and policeman of the New World."[67] Even while Yankees and Spaniards were killing one another in Cuba, a Joint High Commission began gearing up to adjudicate the troublesome boundary line and its related questions. President McKinley, entrapped by postwar dilemmas and apprehensive about the anglophobic Irish vote, had permitted the negotiations to drag on through the summer and winter of 1899. Fortunately a modus vivendi was reached, somewhat easing the situation. Further complicating a settlement were the outbreak of the Boer War and Washington's desire to revoke the 1850 Anglo–United States treaty restricting construction of a transisthmian canal.[68]

Brady was privy to none of these high-level diplomatic maneuvers, albeit by 1899 he was caught up in the troubles with Canada. To both Senator Perkins and Secretary Hitchcock he denounced "encroachments of British jurisdiction upon territory in the Stickine Valley" and "unfair and unreasonable" actions by British Columbia officials.[69] Angry reports to him from Panhandle citizens were capped by a telegram forwarded from two hundred Alaskans "in convention assembled" in Seattle, urging that the Joint High Commission meet not only in Quebec and Washington but also in Victoria and Seattle. They also insisted that British Columbia's impositions, or what they felt to be unfair extractions, be terminated.

Mid-February of 1899 found Brady in the nation's capital. An interview with Secretary of State John Hay produced little. He advised John to put his concerns in writing and give them to Secretary Hitchcock; that way the governor's worries might be taken up at the next cabinet meeting.[70] John, no doubt considerably cooled down, compressed his fulminations into three typed pages. "The Canadians, from our way of looking at matters," he wrote, "have constantly shown a spirit of aggressiveness so far as the boundary line is concerned." They

227

were currently collecting duties on American goods moving along the Stikine River at a point "which for years has been regarded upon [our side] of the boundary line." Quite as grave, American packers had been imprisoned by the Mounties in the Chilkoot Pass region after Canadians had peremptorily advanced the Dominion flag to the summit. And last, John argued, British Columbia authorities had suddenly changed their customs regulations to the great injury of Americans at the recently opened Porcupine Creek diggings (a tributary of the Chilkat River). Alaska's governor wondered how long it might be before the Canadians would "move down and claim this [disputed] country as belonging to them." No responsible cabinet member could take lightly John's closing paragraph: "I think I know the temper of our people and feel sure in saying that if such a step [further Canadian aggression] is attempted . . . conflict will ensue. This danger is so imminent that I deem it wise that our troops in Alaska be ordered to take possession of these lines and maintain our sovereignty over the soil which we claim. I see no other step for us to take if we want to avoid a conflict with Great Britain."⁷¹

With the best of intentions he had blundered. It was one thing for a territorial administrator to submit an exaggerated report to the secretaries of state and the interior on a disintegrating situation, but to balloon a border friction into a potential war was dangerously intemperate. Even less excusable, John communicated similar apprehensions to the press. A conflict with Great Britain, in light of the current harmony between the two nations, was improbable. As Senator Frye mused, "Our relations with Great Britain would be pleasant enough, but Canada is continually undertaking to do something which is unsatisfactory to us. . . . We are a great, good-natured mastiff, and we allow this little fellow to bark around."⁷²

John's officiousness coupled him with Alaska's jingoistic hotheads, probably some of the same restless breed who currently sought his political scalp. If his pugnacity momentarily sidetracked the censure of testy Alaskans in Juneau and Skagway, it produced a quite different effect outside the district. His regrettable intrusion into foreign affairs may have helped destroy a tentative arrangement between the United States and Canada. The plan called for Pyramid Harbor to become a free port under Canadian administration. Angry pressure from West Coast citizens quickly crushed this proposal, which was heatedly denounced as a "surrender of sovereignty" because it permitted "Canadian vessels to frequent Lynn Canal harbors reciprocally with American vessels."⁷³

Brady's role in all of this is not entirely clear. Both Hay and Hitchcock agreed that his participation was "entirely out of place and calculated to do great harm." On 25 March Secretary Hitchcock admonished Alaska's governor to beware of "incendiary talk or action upon a question of the utmost delicacy."[74] John's reply to his chief of 6 April was also routed to Secretary Hay. Brady warned of other resentments. Juneau's merchants were only beginning to bridle at "the license features of the criminal code just passed by Congress." "As we have never paid a cent of tax of any kind, any imposition at this time would be criticized," John explained. Once again Brady cautioned Washington that American miners in the Porcupine Mining district, if pushed by Canadian authorities, would "bring on a conflict." He reassured Hitchcock that the newspaper reports, although "substantially correct," were wrong if they painted him as warlike. John closed his letter with, "We all wish that this vexed question may be amicably settled but I do not want this administration or the Republican party committed to a policy which will give Canada either by cession or compromise a sea port on Lynn Canal and a right of way across S.E. Alaska."[75] A letter from Senator Perkins seconded John's outlook. "The administration," the Californian wrote him, "is unduly sensitive about the matter and they will find that the people of the Northwest and of the Pacific Coast will be a unit in resisting any treaty that yields to Canada any of our rightful possessions in Alaska."[76]

What the senator and the district governor conveniently failed to mention were the harassments occasionally inflicted on Canadian miners in Alaska. Doubly distressing, and something Pacific Slope politicians also preferred to ignore, was how rapidly the Lynn Canal emporiums had slumped. The fourth estate was not so myopic. By mid-July 1899 the press reported, "Skagway is a live town and American to the backbone. Dyea is a dead town and willing to become a Canadian port. Pyramid Harbor is no town at all, but is the one possible site for a city that Skagway fears."[77]

Concurrently, the Chilkat Indians became restive at the vague extension of Canadian control around the Pyramid Harbor area. Governor Brady informed Hitchcock: "The natives of Klukwan are greatly exercised ... about the possibility of becoming 'King George's Men.' They would desert their old homes and settle farther down the coast rather than come under the British flag. These Chilkats are eminently a trading people and it hurts them very badly to be met by a Canadian Customs officer and be made to pay duty for taking in goods where they and their ancestors for generations have traded without molestation."[78] Fortunately for white and red men alike, the Chilkats' sharp fighting edge had been dulled; words were about all they could employ to restrain Anglo-Yankee territorial encroachments.

On 10 October what some Juneauites hailed as "Alaska's first Territorial Convention, attended by delegates from every section of the Territory," met in Juneau to condemn the surrender of any land to Great Britain. Ex-governor Swineford acted as chairman.[79] Their powder was abruptly dampened when a modus vivendi between the contending powers fixed a provisional boundary line at the head of Lynn Canal. The agreement set three short stretches of boundary on the most convenient routes to the gold fields. At two of the points Hay had his way, and even at the third the Canadians were shoved back a few miles from navigable water. Native assertiveness may well have strengthened America's hand. The Indians not only obtained "virtual free trade privileges in the Chilkat" area but enabled Uncle Sam to extend his sovereignty another twenty miles "beyond the temporary boundary in the Chilkat area."[80] To no one's surprise, jingoists in all three countries damned the modus vivendi as a sellout.

Governor Brady's introduction to the diplomatic game left him with no critical bruises. Thereafter, however, Washington kept him on a short leash on all district issues touching upon U.S. foreign relations. In 1901, when the inebriated brother of the prominent author Joaquin Miller tore down the Canadian customs flag at Skagway, John refused to let either that peccadillo or the equally drunken condemnation of the Stars and Stripes by Sergeant Primrose, RCMP, win undeserved headlines. Momentarily Brady fretted that the Canadian government might act precipitously over a "possible insurrection by Americans in the Klondike." One and all, these incidents proved tempests in a rapidly cooling klondicitis teapot; Dawson and Skagway had seen their great days. "Newspaper sensation untrue," Brady later telegraphed Washington, "all quiet here."[81]

Boundary disagreements bounced about Brady's office for the next two years. Finally, on 31 October 1903 the lead column of the *Alaskan* jubilantly proclaimed, "United States Wins Boundary Award." Muscular bargaining by president Theodore Roosevelt, reinforced by harmonious U.S.–British relations, had indeed given America just about everything it desired along the Alaska-Canada border.[82] From the first John had considered Canada's claims "baseless." Wisely, he had no stomach for war among what he called the "Anglo-Saxon race."[83]

To the end of his administration and afterward, Governor Brady never stopped reminding his countrymen how Far North geography ineluctably intertwined the Great Land's future with international developments across the Pacific Basin. He continued condemning ruthless overkilling by foreign seal hunters, as well as the "wanton depredations" within Panhandle forests by British Columbians.[84] John foresaw the economics of the great circle route across the North Pacific, although he badly overestimated the attraction of Alaskan markets. "Alaska is bound to be a very great factor in swelling the volume of [American] commerce," he predicted. "The great ships that go to Siberia, Japan, China and India will find it profitable to call at Alaskan ports. They will not travel over thousands of miles of ocean waste, when they make the distance in quicker time by circling around a coast that can furnish valuable cargoes." Like so many Americans before and since, Governor Brady was beguiled by the dream of vast commercial possibilities in the Far East. "The United States needs and must have larger markets," he insisted, "and our surest outlet is to reach the millions of consumers in the Orient."[85]

Brady definitely understood the Mahan corollary: naval might to match a commercial empire. "Extensive plans for the fortification of the Hawaiian Islands" gained his endorsement, just as he urged that Unalaska in the Aleutians be armed. He believed that Dutch Harbor was "probably the key to the situation" in that quarter of the North Pacific. A few years after John left the governorship, he penned an ominous prediction: "I believe in the full and complete fortification and defense of the Philippines and a strong stand for our share of all the trade and advancement in Manchuria in fact in all China and all the Orient and I am convinced that our efforts to secure and maintain our rights must be fought for at no distant day. Therefore, why this continued neglect of Alaska?"[86] A pioneer's hyperbole carried him even further. In the same manuscript he wrote that Alaska's "ice-free harbors nearer to the Orient than Pearl Harbor are many and inviting. Adjacent to them are deposits of coal that is of the finest quality. . . . There is fine iron ore. Alaska could build and launch her own navies if she chose. If she had a sufficient population to employ her natural resources she could maintain herself very nicely. . . . Will there come a day far in the future when Alaska will be a powerful independent nation or the most powerful and resourceful part of the United States?" Alaska as an independent nation may have been wild hypothesizing, but John was a creature of his age and he astutely comprehended what his nationalistic countrymen wished to hear.[87] And manifestly, for John Brady, Alaska *was* the Great Land.

1. JCorr, 18:182, Brady to Jackson, 5 December 1897; *Alaskan*, 23 July and 13 August 1898; 25 March, 8 April, and 1 July 1899; 16 June 1900; Brady, *Annual Report, 1900*, pp. 5–6.

2. Wolcott, *Compiled Laws*, p. 167. O. P. Austin, comp., *Commercial Alaska in 1901* (Washington, D.C., 1902), pp. 4027–29.

3. JGB, mf. 1, Brady to his wife, 21 December 1899. AGP, box 10, Thomas Ryan to Brady, 22 December 1899. PTS, SJ letters, 1:425, Jackson to Lewis S. Welch, 14 December 1903.

4. JGB, mf. 2, clipping from *Mail and Express*, 9 May 1900.

5. JGB, mf. 1, Brady to his wife, 9 May 1900.

6. Dinner program and menu, unfiled, in the archives of the University of Alaska, College, Alaska.

7. JGB, mf. 2, *Mail and Express*, 9 May 1900.

8. Ibid.

9. Ibid.; JGB, unfiled, includes handbill, hand-painted menu, and list of those who attended Board of Trade reception.

10. JGB, mf. 2, Dow, Jones & Co., news bulletins, *Wall Street Journal*, 5 July 1900.

11. Ibid.

12. John G. Brady, "Peculiar Problems in Alaska," *Assembly Herald*, June 1900, p. 619.

13. AGP, box 11, Brady to Lucy G. Hargrave, 24 October 1900. William T. Perkins, "Alaska, an Empire in Itself," *World's Work*, August 1905, p. 6535, and Herbert L. Heller, ed., *Sourdough Sagas: The Journals, Memoirs, Tales, and Recollections of the Earliest Alaskan Gold Miners, 1883–1923* (Cleveland, 1967), p. 229. Brady, "Peculiar Problems," p. 619.

14. Brady, *Annual Report, 1899*, p. 47.

15. *Alaskan*, 10 June 1899, 18 August and 1 and 8 September 1900.

16. *Congressional Record*, 56th Cong., 1st sess., 22 May 1900, p. 5869.

17. Ibid.; other district officials got salary increases as well: governor and judges, $5,000; the surveyor general, $4,000; and attorneys, $3,000 (Gruening, *State of Alaska*, p. 112).

18. Ralph S. Kuykendall and A. Grove Day, *Hawaii: A History from Polynesian Kingdom to American State*, rev. ed. (Englewood Cliffs, N.J., 1961), chap. 19. Ellis Paxon Oberholtzer, *A History of the United States since the Civil War*, 5 vols. (New York, 1937), 5:612. Gerrit P. Judd, *Hawaii: An Informal History* (New York, 1961), p. 123.

19. *Congressional Record*, 56th Cong., 1st sess., 14 April 1900, p. 4173; ibid., 58th Cong., 2d sess., 18 April 1904; ibid., 56th Cong., 1st sess., 17 May 1900, p. 5666; ibid., 24 March 1900, p. 3273.

20. *Alaskan*, 8 and 22 April 1899.

21. Carter, *Laws of Alaska*, p. xviii. *Alaskan*, 12 February 1898.

22. *Douglas Island News*, 22 December 1899.

23. Cited in *Alaskan*, 20 May 1899, 18 August 1898. The Seattle Chamber of Commerce actually affirmed that the "Alaska Lobby . . . would be done away with were the people officially represented as the people of other parts of the Union are." *Congressional Record*, 56th Cong., 1st sess., 2 March 1900, p. 2460. *Daily Alaskan* (Skagway), 15, 22, 23, and 29 May and 1, 4, and 28 June 1902.

24. *Alaskan*, 19 August 1899; JGB, mf. 4, Brady to R. E. Prime, 22 January 1902.

25. JCorr, 19:90, Kelly to Harris, 21 July 1899.

26. JGB, mf. 2, Eaton to Brady, 21 June 1899. Brady, *Annual Report, 1899*, p. 36. JGB, mf. 4, Brady to Prime, 22 January 1902.

27. Nichols, *Alaska*, p. 173.

28. *Alaskan*, 25 November and 2 December 1899.

29. *New York Times*, 27 October 1899. Edmond S. Meany, "Alaska's Provisional Delegate to Congress," *Alaskan Magazine*, May 1900, pp. 73–74.

30. *Seattle Post-Intelligencer*, 14 February 1900. JCorr, 19:215, Brady to Jackson, 13 June 1900.

31. JCorr, 19:215, Brady to Jackson, 13 June 1900.

32. *Congressional Record*, 56th Cong., 1st sess. 24 May 1900, p. 5973.

33. *Seattle Post-Intelligencer*, 15 February 1900.

34. Hinckley, in *Americanization of Alaska*, examines some of the earliest ferment for dividing the district into a number of states.

35. Scidmore, "Alaska's Mining Regions," p. 466; U.S., Congress, House, *Town Sites in Alaska*, 51st Cong., 1st sess., Report No. 2450, 14 June 1890, p. 4; *Alaskan*, 12 February 1898.

36. *Alaskan*, 13 August 1898. JGB, mf. 2, Johnson to Brady, 7 May 1900. *Congressional Record*, 56th Cong., 1st sess., 17 May 1900, p. 5666. Ibid., 21 March 1900, p. 3122. *Alaskan*, 28 April 1900.

37. Senate, Petition, 57th Cong., 1st sess., Doc. No. 238, 6 March 1902, p. 4. JGB, mf. 4, Brady to J. W. Sutherland, 22 March 1902.

38. AGP, box 13, Robert A. Friedrich to Brady, 2 October 1902.

39. Brady, *Annual Report, 1900*, p. 45.

40. *Congressional Record*, 56th Cong., 1st sess., 22 May 1900, p. 5866.

41. *Alaskan*, 8 December 1900.

42. Brady, *Annual Report, 1900*, p. 5. Clarence C. Hulley, *Alaska Past and Present* (Portland, Ore., 1958), p. 289. W. P. Richardson, "The Yukon as Seen and Explored," in Austin, *Commercial Alaska*, p. 4013.

43. AGP, box 13, E. B. McCowan to Brady, 15 February 1901.

44. *Congressional Record*, 56th Cong., 1st sess., 14 April 1900, p. 4156. Ibid., 55th Cong., 2d sess., 22 March 1899, p. 3083.

45. John Scudder McLain, *Alaska and the Klondike* (New York, 1905), p. 260.

46. Howard Roberts Lamar, *Dakota Territory, 1861–1889: A Study of Frontier Politics* (New Haven, 1956), pp. 215–16. Rex Beach's novel *The Spoilers* does not purport to be an accurate recounting of the Noyes-McKenzie conspiracy. A good summary of the notorious cause célèbre is William W. Morrow, "The Spoilers," *California Law Review* 4 (January 1916): 89–113.

47. Hunt, *North of 53°*, p. 113. Nichols, *Alaska*, p. 193, agrees with this assessment.

48. JGB, mf. 3, Brady to Roosevelt, n.d. (ca. spring 1902). AGP, box 6, Gertrude P. Knapp to E. H. Flynn, 15 August 1900. James Wickersham Papers, University of Alaska, Fairbanks, diary entry for 23 May 1900 (hereafter cited as JWD). Important for measuring Wickersham is Evangeline Atwood, *Frontier Politics: Alaska's James Wickersham* (Portland, Ore., 1979).

49. *Alaskan*, 8 September 1900. Brady, *Annual Report*, 1900, pp. 7–9.

50. JGB, mf. 4, Brady to E. B. McCowan, 30 September 1901.

51. Ibid., mf. 1, Brady to his wife, 23 December 1900.

52. Lamar, *Dakota Territory*, p. 216. TAP, mf. 8, Brady to Hitchcock, 31 January 1901.

53. JGB, mf. 2, unidentified clipping, "Fear of Cape Nome Reign of Terror."

54. Wickersham, *Old Yukon*, pp. 356–57, cited in Tom Murton, "The Administration of Criminal Justice in Alaska, 1867–1902" (Master's thesis, University of California, Berkeley, 1956), p. 32.

55. JGB, mf. 4, Brady to J. L. Osgood, 9 October 1901; Wickersham, *Old Yukon*, pp. 361–78.

56. AGP, box 11, Brady to J. R. Richards, 30 September 1901. JGB, mf. 4, Brady to McCowan, 30 September 1901. James D. Richardson, comp., *A Compilation of the Messages and the Papers of the Presidents*, 20 vols. (New York, 1917), 14:6269.

57. Richardson, *Messages and Papers*, 14:6401–2. The governor's term did not officially expire until 5 June 1904 (*Alaskan*, 8 June 1901).

58. TAP, mf. 8, Brady to Hitchcock, 21 September 1901.

59. Corinne Roosevelt Robinson, "My Brother Theodore Roosevelt," *Scribner's*, February 1921, p. 132.

60. Brady, *Annual Report, 1898*, p. 225.

61. *Alaskan*, 15 November 1902. Richardson, *Messages and Papers*, 15:6725.

62. Richardson, *Messages and Papers*, 15:6799. *Alaskan*, 19 December 1903. Richardson, *Messages and Papers*, 15:6918–21.

63. Among the various scholarly studies that deal with the disputed boundary are Charles S. Campbell, *Anglo-American Understanding, 1898–1903* (Baltimore, 1957); Norman Penlington, *The Alaska Boundary Dispute: A Critical Reappraisal* (Toronto, 1972); and Charles C. Tansill, *Canadian-American Relations, 1874–1911* (Toronto, 1943). To grasp the problem as it arose in American minds, see U.S., Congress, Senate, *Report on the Boundary Line between Alaska and British Columbia*, 50th Cong., 2d sess., Exec. Doc. No. 146, 2 March 1889; and Eliza R. Scidmore, "The Alaska Boundary Question," *Century*, May 1896, pp. 143–46. For an overview summary see Professor Peter Buzanski's "Alaska and Nineteenth Century American Diplomacy," *Journal of the West* 6 (July 1967): 451–67.

64. *New York Times*, 23 August 1895. Geographer George Davidson stated that Canadian cartographers had "washed out" whole mountains. Ivan Petroff foolishly did the same thing for the United States until he was caught and fired. George Davidson, *The Alaska Boundary* (San Francisco, 1903), p. 5; Hinckley and Hinckley, "Ivan Petroff's Journal," p. 15. Perkins, *Rapprochement*, pp. 162–63.

65. *New Voice* (New York), 25 February 1899.

66. TAP, mf. 6, Brady to Hitchcock, 6 April 1899.

67. Luella Day, *The Tragedy of the Klondike* (New York, 1906), pp. 115 ff; C. R. Tuttle, *The Golden North* (Chicago, 1897), p. 97. *Nation*, 29 July 1897, pp. 83–84. Howard K. Beale, *Theodore Roosevelt and the Rise of America to World Power* (New York, 1962), p. 94; and Perkins, *Rapprochement*, p. 161.

68. H. Wayne Morgan, *William McKinley and His America* (Syracuse, N.Y., 1963), pp. 451 ff. Margaret Leech, *In the Days of McKinley* (New York, 1959), pp. 353 ff.

69. TAP, mf. 6, Brady to George C. Perkins, 21 January 1899; ibid., Brady to Hitchcock, 24 January 1899.

70. TAP, mf. 6, Western Union telegram, John Stanley (for Seattle Committee) to Brady, 20 January 1899. AGP, box 10, Hay to Hitchcock, 23 February 1899. TAP, mf. 6, Brady to Hitchcock, 23 February 1899.

71. TAP, mf. 6, Brady to Hitchcock, 23 February 1899.

72. *New York Times*, 21 March 1899. *Congressional Record*, 55th Cong., 2d sess., 4 March 1898, p. 2471.

73. Penlington, *Alaska Boundary Dispute*, pp. 39–40.

74. National Archives, Record Group No. 48, Secretary E. A. Hitchcock's private correspondence, vol. 1, Hitchcock to Hay, 25 March 1899; ibid., Hitchcock to Brady, 25 March 1899 (hereafter cited as EAH).

75. EAH, vol. 1, Brady to Hitchcock, 6 April 1899.

76. AGP, box 10, Perkins to Brady, 1 June 1899. Penlington, *Alaska Boundary Dispute*, p. 55.

77. JScrap, 31:49, clipping from the *Seattle Post-Intelligencer*, 30 July 1899.

78. EAH, vol. 1, Brady to Hitchcock, 6 July 1899.

79. *New York Times*, 15 October 1899.

80. Fifty-Sixth Congress, *Papers Relating to the Foreign Relations of the United States* (Washington, D.C., 1901), pp. 328–32. Penlington, *Alaska Boundary Dispute*, p. 55. AGP, box 10, Hitchcock to Brady, 27 October 1899; and TAP, mf. 6, Brady to Hitchcock, 15 November 1899.

81. TAP, mf. 8, Brady to Hitchcock, 29 June 1901; ibid., Acting Secretary of the Interior to the Secretary of the Treasury, 27 July 1901; ibid., Acting Secretary of State to Hitchcock, 30 July 1901; ibid., Hay to Hitchcock, 23 November 1901; ibid., Brady to Hitchcock, 12 December 1901; ibid., Hitchcock to Brady, 24 June 1901; ibid., Brady to Hitchcock, telegram, 16 December 1901; "The Conspiracy," *Alaska-Yukon Mining Journal*, December 1901, pp. 2–4.

82. AGP, box 13, Thomas R. Lyons to Brady, 21 March 1903; *Commercial Appeal*, 13 April 1902, cited in Edwin S. Balch, ed., *Letters and Papers Relating to the Alaskan Frontier* (Philadelphia, 1904). Thomas A. Bailey, "Theodore Roosevelt and the Alaska Boundary Settlement," *Canadian Historical Review* 18 (June 1937): 123–30. Allen, *Great Britain and the United States*, pp. 610–13; Beale, *Theodore Roosevelt*, pp. 116–25.

83. For the U.S. view of the settlement and the actual treaty, see John W. Foster, "The Alaskan Boundary Tribunal," *National Geographic Magazine*, January 1904, pp. 1–14; Canada's reaction can be seen in Charles Thonger, *Canada's Alaskan Dismemberment: A Tribunal Award* (Niagara, Ontario, 1904). JGB, mf. 4, Brady to Thomas W. Balch, 21 January 1903. Brady, *Annual Report, 1899*, p. 47.

84. Brady, *Annual Report, 1901*, pp. 18, 30.

85. Ibid., p. 39. How limited to Yankees that potentially prodigious emporium was is summarized in Paul A. Varg, "The Myth of the China Market, 1890–1914," *American Historical Review* 73 (February 1968): 742–58.

86. JFB, mf. 3. This manuscript, written in 1910, may well have been the draft for an address he delivered that year in either Boston or New York City.

87. Arthur A. Ekirch, *Progressivism in America: A Study of the Era from Theodore Roosevelt to Woodrow Wilson* (New York, 1974), chap. 12.

CHAPTER THIRTEEN

Education and Native Conundrums

John Brady's abiding faith in the benefits of native education won him little praise from generally apathetic white Alaskans. At the very least, he urged, the most talented among the aboriginal youngsters must obtain training in the four Rs. To deny them these tools blighted the development of future native leaders. Arm in arm with Sheldon Jackson and John Eaton, Brady voiced the conviction that schooling was vital if native Alaskans were successfully to withstand the onrush of American culture. Indeed, their belief that the indigenes could be best protected by being assimilated into America's "Christian educated" middle class embodied the general consensus of those caught up in the late-nineteenth-century campaign for Indian rights. Education would hasten an end to the Indians' demeaning status as wards. Concurrently, the General Allotment Law of 1887 (Dawes Severalty Act) would replace tribalism with American citizenship and individual land holdings. As President Theodore Roosevelt succinctly stated in his *First Annual Message*, "the time has arrived when we should definitely make up our minds to recognize the Indian as an individual and not as a member of a tribe."[1]

America's turbulent 1890s, plus misplaced overconfidence in the efficacy of the Dawes Act, muffled the public outcry at the fate of the "vanishing American." A number of Indian schools suffered cutbacks. Nevertheless, both public and private support remained committed to the Americanization of the country's aboriginals. Of the institutions dedicated to this end, none attracted wider public attention than Captain Richard Henry Pratt's Carlisle Indian Industrial School. In 1896, accompanied by Dr. Jackson, the soldier-turned-educator toured the

Sitka Training School.[2] The following year Pratt invited Brady to address his Carlisle, Pennsylvania, Indian student body. To his pleasure John found himself seated on the speakers' platform with Jackson, Eaton, and Andrew Burke. Burke was also a Children's Aid Society foundling who had risen to become a western governor; forty years before they had been fellow passengers on the same train that first brought John to Indiana.

With some notable dissenters, those seeking justice for the red man accepted the premise that Indian absorption into the dominant white society was inevitable. The quicker total assimilation could be effected, the better. To perpetuate native values and lifestyles only accelerated the aboriginal's "vanishing." And because tribalism insulated—indeed, fostered—these "archaic and self-destructive attitudes," Yankee individualism and full citizenship must supplant it. With minor qualifications, Alaska's missionary element continued to espouse this prevailing humanitarian position at the beginning of the twentieth century.[3]

An important exception was the missionary William Duncan. In his eyes such policy among Northwest Coast people was anathema. As he wrote the commissioner of education, William T. Harris: "What the Indians need in their new environment is what we all need while we are children, namely *protection* and *education*." So strongly did the patriarch feel about protecting his Tsimshian flock that in 1887 he left British Columbia with his followers and recreated New Metlakatla on American soil on Annette Island. On the Scotsman's tight little island, his Tsimshian police maintained an autocratic, if benign, theocracy. Indeed, Duncan's policy of rigidly shielding his wards while concurrently arming them with marketable skills to adjust to the Caucasian dominated world neatly fit what anthropologists would later describe as "controlled acculturation." Sadly Duncan proved himself all too human. By the time of Brady's governorship, the renowned and respected leader had become badly self-centered and stubbornly shortsighted. So intractable had he become that when his one-time protege Edward Marsden returned with degrees from Marietta College and Lane Theological Seminary, prepared to be his successor, he rejected him. But then Duncan may have thought that he had no alternative. His one-time pupil unabashedly advocated accelerated Indian assimilation, absorption into what Marsden aptly characterized as a "push and pull" America. In 1895 Marsden chided Duncan: "Are [Metlakatlans] by a constant and progressive Christian education . . . being prepared for that day" when Annette Island would not be held in common but in severalty? "I would rather, by all means," Marsden blurted out, "own a piece of property by deed, pay my taxes and vote, as a citizen of the United States, than to hold it in common with others and be isolated on an Indian reservation."[4] To turn the clock back and transform the Great Land into one gigantic Annette Island, to emulate New Metlakatla's tightly regulated acculturation, was patently impossible. One alternative was to scatter native reservations about the Great Land. However, the dismal record of southside reservations discredited them in the northland. Although water-isolated, New Metlakatla was, in an administrative sense, a reservation; its populace's economic viability and high self-esteem were the antithesis of the typical Far West Indian reservation lying under the pall of cultural stagnation. Duncan's Tsimshians were proud and independent carpenters, shopkeepers, and fishermen—not shattered Plains Indians subsisting on annuity goods and slipping into beggary.

Since 1886 Jackson had helped Alaskan native youth journey east to attend Pratt's Carlisle Indian School. This practice angered Duncan, who insisted that the unsatisfactory condition of missions and education in Alaska was primarily due to "taking the children away to distant schools." To which Brady countered, "If he refers to children brought East to such schools as Northfield, Massachusetts; Carlisle, Pennsylvania; Chemwa, Oregon; Puyallup, Washington; etc. I would reply that the Records of the Indian Office show that only 70 Alaskans are now in the Indian schools of the country. Certainly 70 Alaskans in the very best of schools outside of Alaska cannot demoralize the 1500 Alaskans attending school in Alaska."[5] It seems clear that Duncan had, as John informed Secretary Hitchcock, "lost his hold upon the young men of his community." Understandably the benevolent despot was mortified at the loss of parental control suffered by some Tsimshians. "I feel sorry for him," John wrote Elizabeth. "He cannot confine these young men to their present state. . . . He has had his own way so long that there is not a particle of the spirit of conciliation in him. They must bend to his will or he refuses to sanction or to cooperate."[6]

In 1901 Alaska's governor gently rebuked the honored patriarch, reminding him how contradictory his testimony on Indian reservations was, and suggested that the good father's excessive paternalism had become "a step backwards." Four years later, after a cordial visit with Duncan, John again reported to Elizabeth on Annette Island's inhabitants:

[Mr. Duncan] berated Col. Pratt and work at Carlisle and said that the Col. was teaching children to disobey their parents and was therefore breaking God's commandment. . . . Mr. D. has taken a dead set against any higher education than they are now receiving. They [the Metlaka-

238

tlans] told him that they wanted some to be doctors and lawyers and other professional men but at the mention of lawyers he grew robustly emphatic in his denunciation of the ilk. . . . I told [the Metlakatlans] they had my sympathy in their aspirations for a higher education for some of their children.[7]

For a few days in 1900, both the governor and his lady had the pleasure of being guests at the renowned Carlisle Indian School. Pratt's aim to destroy tribalism was reflected by the diverse student body of some nine hundred Indians representing over sixty different tribes. One and all, the Carlisle boys wore a similar uniform, and well-tailored, graceful dresses clothed its girl pupils. Every student was soaped, scrubbed, and shined. To the south at Booker T. Washington's Tuskegee Institute, black-skinned Americans under a similar spit-and-polish regimen laughingly referred to it as the "gospel of the toothbrush." When queried about the Carlisle School and its director, John endorsed both wholeheartedly: "He is a mighty man and has done a wonderful work. They have a full corps of able teachers—fine grounds and good buildings and in fact lack for very little to carry on that kind of work." The governor was glad that "quite a number of Alaskan children have been sent there and are there now. They have uniformly done well. The fine Eskimos are the brightest in the school."[8]

In 1905 Brady and Jackson lobbied through Congress a provision specifying that "Eskimo and Indian children of Alaska shall have the same right to be admitted to any Indian Boarding School as the Indian children in the States or Territories of the United States." Initially this seemed to offer natives a considerably expanded educational opportunity in the south. Congress chose not to provide the requisite support money, and their ploy failed.[9]

Forever astonished at Jackson's capacity to sustain a work load that would fell a younger man, John made a point of lifting the old man's spirits with heartwarming reports: "Returned from Prince of Wales Island. I was much gratified to see what progress has been made by the natives upon that side of the Island for as you know less has been done for these people than for any other portion of S.E. Alaska. The mission boys who were at Shakan, George Demmert, George Field, and Billy Benson, are surely letting their lights shine and [have] been doing so for the past two years. They even frown upon smoking. The white people who are there all acknowledge the good work that has been done."[10] Distinguished young Tlingits validated Brady's hopes. William L. Paul was already respected in Seattle's Presbyterian church. In the years ahead Paul would win prominence as a lawyer, an author, and a powerful spokesman for native rights. Not one but two of his sons also became attorneys.[11] In 1904 Frances A. Willard coauthored with William A. Kelly, one-time Sitka Training School principal, a *Grammar and Vocabulary of the Thlingit Language of Southeastern Alaska*. The commissioner of education, Harris, was proud to have his bureau publish their praiseworthy achievement.[12]

Governor Brady was delighted when the captain of Sitka's Marine Corps unit organized a cadet drill unit from among Indians in the public school. After one of the training school alumni marched with Captain Pratt's Carlisle Indian band at William Mckinley's inaugural parade, Sitka's native band expanded its repertory of patriotic airs. John frankly admitted a preference for the boys' catchy "There'll Be a Hot Time in the Old Town Tonight," and the native musicians indulged him by blasting it forth whenever an appropriate occasion arose. Indians at Kake decided to emulate their brothers at Sitka. "I am pleased to learn that you have organized a brass band," John congratulated the villagers. "I am glad the Kake people are waking up and are determined to push ahead."[13]

If it seemed easy for youth to "push ahead," the reverse too often proved to be the case for adults. Nevertheless, John applauded that "their old style of house is giving way to the more comfortable frame dwelling. Some of their new buildings are large and are communal, but very many now accommodate but a single family."[14] Like the *Alaskan*, his annual reports lauded their accomplishments: "They are a hardy, hardworking, industrious people, and have always been self-supporting." John wrote of the Panhandle Indians in 1905, "They take quickly to mechanic arts, and are desirable workers in the canneries, salteries, and mines. They are really in a transition state, abandoning their old customs and accumulating property. They make use of the post-office, travel by the local steamers, get married according to our laws, and pay licenses like other people when they establish little stores."[15]

John stood well in advance of his peers when it came to accepting Alaska's natives as potential equals. Among the Tlingits his unflinching, fumbling exertions to speak to them in their tongue must have been appreciated. Like few other territorial governors in Great Land history, he strove to make the noun *Alaskan* ethnologically indistinguishable. "It is in this spirit and hope (of E Pluribus Unum) that we have come to build up our homes, schools, churches, and political institutions," John declared in 1904. "Children of the native men who were regarded as uncivilized forty years ago are joining us in patriotism. . . . They rejoice to unfurl the Stars and Stripes in front of their houses and from their canoes, and celebrate the Fourth of July in a truly American fashion."[16]

Since the mid-eighties Alaska's general agent for education had insisted that Far North educational appropriations be made "without reference to race." Within the emerging white settlements the provision created a degree of restiveness. After 1890 Jackson rapidly relinquished control over the white-dominated town schools in order to concentrate his attention on native education. He had no other course. Gold seekers who became Alaskans insisted that they control local school affairs, just as they had done back in Scranton or Cedar Rapids.[17] Jackson correctly estimated that these whites would take care of their own youngsters while paying only slight attention to the schooling of native children. Until an Alaskan community incorporated and possessed a town council and school board, he controlled the educational purse strings.

After 1899, when the incorporated towns began to receive money from business taxes and school districts were formed, white Alaskans quickly took charge. Predictably some natives lost ground. "It seems a pity that such of the native children who desire to learn," members of Juneau's Board of Education wrote Brady, "should be unable to do so, and we lay the matter before you in the hope that you may be able to suggest some way in which it may be done."[18] Alaska's governor spoke to Alaska's general agent for education, and Juneau obtained further aid. Whites at Nome and Ketchikan acted just as irresponsibly in fulfilling their obligations to nonwhite Alaskans.[19]

In all fairness to the white boards of education, native youngsters not only posed a puzzling educational challenge but often proved uneducatable because they never came to school. Wherever an Indian policeman resided, Alaska's governor directed him to enforce attendance. To a white Alaskan disturbed about delinquent natives John wrote, "I have no authority in this matter. I only instruct the native policemen to visit the homes and urge and scold and try to get the children out. I have done so and will continue to do so; but the parents know that no punishment can be prescribed." And then, to encourage the dispirited humanitarian, John counseled: "It is a pity to see them so neglectful of the best interest of their children. However, if you are doing missionary work you first learn to take a steady pull and be patient. These people have been very low and long time in darkness. They are making progress but it is in a slow way. It is line upon line, precept upon precept, here a little, and there a little. Do not lose heart in your work."[20] John promised "to nudge the Washington authorities" about compelling native attendance. Indeed, he had been doing so for years. Sometime before when reviewing the problem with Secretary Hitchcock, John admitted: "It will be difficult" to require attendance "in all parts of

Alaska, but in towns like Sitka, Ft. Wrangell, such a regulation should be enforced as well as in any New England town."[21]

Since Brady had become governor he and Jackson had vainly lobbied for an increase in Alaska's annual educational appropriation of $30,000. Finally, in 1905, the niggardly sum was tripled, and then during the last year of his governorship it reached $145,153. Sheldon Jackson's achievement—and the victory was primarily his—benefited natives and whites alike.[22] Probably a combination of Jackson's persuasiveness and his own commitment to public education induced John to agree to become "ex-officio superintendent of public instruction" for Alaska. Congress confirmed this post in January of 1905. For John the responsibility for advancing the education of "white children and children of mixed blood who lead civilized lives" became another unrelenting burden. Henceforth his office struggled to assist schools at Afognak, Chignik, Ellamar, Haines, Hope, Kenai, Kodiak, Seldovia, Seward, Sitka, Teller City, Unalaska, Unga, and Wood Island.[23]

From numerous points about his remote and heterogeneous academic charge, Alaska's ex officio superintendent was deluged with questions, appeals, and threats. In most instances he could do little. John even found himself temporarily at odds with Harris over Sitka school properties. After an irate Alaskan, William J. Hunter of Cook Inlet, obtained no response from the district's general agent for education, Hunter voiced his frustrations directly to president Theodore Roosevelt. If President Roosevelt did not read the four-page letter, his secretary of the interior did. Because the 1905 legislation had transferred the management of nonnative schools (especially those outside of settled communities) to Alaska's governor, Hunter's angry letter ended up on Brady's desk. In Hunter's opinion, inadequate money could not justify closing the Cook Inlet public school, forcing the children to attend a Russian Orthodox–operated school. "Go into any of their houses," he protested, "and you will see the picture of the Czar of Russia on the walls of their houses, but no President of the United States." He also lambasted the nearby agricultural experimental farm, claiming that "its Officials generally are Grafters."[24] John totally disagreed with this latter indictment. However, he conceded that some priests did equate the czar with the president and promised to do what he could to disabuse them of their error.

Sheldon Jackson probably saddled this extra burden on his close friend to ease his own administrative load. Although the general agent now had a full-time Washington assistant, his health was failing. For some years the scope of his duties had exceeded even Jackson's fourteen-hour day. To add to Alaska's educational difficulties, in 1905 Secretary

Hitchcock felt "compelled to close many of the old schools that had been in operation many years, and to refrain from opening new schools though the latter were urgently needed."[25] At first glance these economies seem inexplicable, particularly in light of the increased congressional appropriations since 1903. They resulted in part from confusion in Washington and throughout Alaska on how to handle the business tax revenue, portions of which had earlier been misappropriated by a few of the incorporated towns. Brady took the blame for some of the cuts. "The probabilities are that we will be unable to open some of the native schools next fall for the want of funds," Jackson commiserated. "I feel somewhat blue over the situation."[26]

In his annual reports John preferred to review the positive aspects of district affairs. Accordingly, he praised the vitality of school management in the incorporated towns of Ketchikan, Wrangell, Juneau, Douglas, Treadwell, Skagway, Eagle, Nome, and Valdez. They show, he declared, "that the people are alive to the advantages of an education for their children." To relieve himself from some of the cross fire incurred as ex officio superintendent, John encouraged those Alaska settlements that did not have school districts and boards to emulate those that did.[27]

The pedagogical chores of the governor of America's largest territory ranged from the routine to the bizarre. In 1906 John found it necessary to appeal to Congress for a special act for two unpaid teachers to receive what was owed them. Complaints of inadequate fuel and lighting by two very miserable Seward school teachers so aroused his concern that during the winter of 1905 he inspected not only their meager teaching facilities but also buildings at Yakutat, Valdez, Ellamar, and Kyak.[28] When the Department of State notified him that "under the will of the late Right Honorable Cecil John Rhodes" there had been bequeathed "scholarships at Oxford for students from the British colonies and the United States." he made certain that an Alaskan be considered. John repeatedly urged that a Far North youth be awarded an appointment to Annapolis or West Point: "We have some boys here who are setting their aims correctly. They want to become admirals and generals—we want them to have a chance."[29]

Well before his appointment as Alaska's ex officio superintendent of public instruction, John had cooperated with the Bureau of Education and the General Land Office to reserve parcels of district land for future school sites.[30] The formation of new school districts at Seward with sixty-two children and at Sitka with over a hundred was heartening. However, when John sought to establish school districts at Kodiak and at Catella, he found himself blocked by division three's court clerk,

who insisted that there were "less than 20 resident *white* children between the ages of 6 and 20 years" in the proposed district.[31] "White,"
of course, meant WASP white, not Russian-Aleut white. In his ignorance or bigotry—probably both—the clerk overlooked the fact that
the complexion of many a Creole was fairer than that of first or second
generation Yankee Alaskans. Secretary Hitchcock, like Brady, repeatedly noted that the federal legislation provided "for the maintenance
of schools for white children and those of mixed blood, both in incorporated towns and in districts outside of incorporated towns." In their
annual reports each chose to reflect the bright side of territorial affairs.
The interior secretary reported in 1905: "Many schools have been established in such places by the Governor . . . and 14 schools have been
transferred from the Bureau of Education to his supervision."[32]

The 1905 legislation that strengthened local control over public education often encouraged the evolution of two distinctly different
schools, white and native. Blatant racists could justify the move as
necessary to protect Caucasian children. Humanitarians could ration-
alize a dual program on pedagogical grounds. Neither Brady nor Jackson desired inadequate schools in any corner of the Great Land; however, budgetary consideration and the territory's sheer immensity, not
to mention the complexity of its diverse population, hamstrung their
best efforts. Seventy years later Alaskan educators would confront the
same obstacles. What forever troubled John were the ethnocentric
blinders so stubbornly worn by his fellow pioneers. As district visitors
quickly discovered, he believed "firmly that the Indian should be made
to feel that he is a citizen of the United States."[33] After members of
the Juneau school board took a turn to the racist right, the governor
warned them that they were "really responsible for the education of
native children within [their] corporate limits." He advised congressmen to amend the law "to compel the school boards" to expend the
educational money "without distinction of race," knowing, of course,
that strict enforcement could only be haphazard.[34]

Governor Brady had to resign himself to discrimination against civilized "mixed bloods" at far off Kodiak or Unalaska, but when the same
injustice seared Sitka, he reacted immediately. On 26 January 1906
Sitka's school board notified Rudolph Walton that "your children cannot attend the White school while living in the Indian Ranche." The
following day Alaska's governor inquired why the Tlingit's two little
girls had been rejected. John could not accept the board's reply. To the
U.S. district attorney, John J. Boyce of Juneau, he vainly protested:

> Notwithstanding, that the school board say in their letter that their opin-
> ion has been sustained by you I desire to place these communications
> before you and have you give me your opinion of the law. Mr. Rudolph

Walton feels that his children by right of Section 7 of the school law are entitled to school privileges in the Sitka School District. They are of mixed blood. . . . I may say that there is hardly a citizen in the town who has more reason to be treated with courtesy and respect than he has. He was educated at the mission here, reads and writes, owns his own property, conducts a store . . .

Walton was "an ivory carver and silver engraver and also repairs watches and clocks with suitable tools for the same. The children who are denied the privileges of the school are his stepchildren by his wife, a half blood, whom he recently married." As to Mrs. Walton, Brady continued, "She is a woman well respected. The children have always been kept tidy and clean."[35]

Earlier Walton had joined Daniel S. Benson and James Jackson, among other natives, in a petition to Brady denouncing customhouse employees for insisting that Sitka's Indians carry a pass to use the wharf. The officials' apparent justification was that the natives carried disease. Years afterward Mrs. Brady recalled how repeatedly she and John had remonstrated against the native children being "driven from the parade ground through race prejudice." One must wonder if John ever cursed himself for agreeing in 1889 to the formation of a second Sitka Presbyterian church "necessitated by the fact that the native church could not understand a sermon in English, and the white church could not understand one in the Tlinkit language." For those among Alaska's aboriginal population struggling to assimilate into the dominant culture, the contradictions and humiliations must at times have been almost unbearable.[36]

John and Elizabeth suffered no illusions that either their goals or the Lord's could be reached in a lifetime. In his speeches, his lobbying, and his written reports, Alaska's governor unceasingly extolled the native's remarkable "upward tendency." "They aspire to citizenship," Brady declared. "One law in Alaska for everybody and everybody amenable to that law should be the motto. Equal rights and opportunity for all. The native is willing to take equal chances with the white man in the race. Today he is handicapped."[37] Indeed, those spurred by an "upward tendency" received no praise from those not so motivated. As the *Alaskan* observed, "the Indians who divorced themselves from their own society have done so against difficult odds. Their people sneer at them, yet are secretly envious." A graduate of the Sitka Training School wrote from Juneau: "My little son is well. I hope God will spare him life so he can help his people. I want to educate him so he can be a doctor."[38]

The death rate of children both within the Ranche and among the cottage Indians exceeded that of Sitka's pioneer families. Physical deformities were the most visible of the crosses borne by Sitka's nonwhites.

Having miscarried a baby herself, Elizabeth felt a special empathy for pregnant native women. Their prenatal care was primitive, at times barbarous. The native maternity facility she had earlier established evolved into a mission hospital with a resident physician, and although it occupied merely a couple of rooms at the training school and was concerned primarily with sick pupils, it welcomed Ranche Indians as well as Tlingits from archipelago villages. Some Indian patients remained, studied health care, and then returned to solace their fellows. By 1905, confident that there resided at the capital a cadre of native Christian health workers, Elizabeth, assisted by native women Esther Gibson and Olga Hilton, instituted the Cottage Missionary Society. A large part of their energies sought to awaken the Indian to rudimentary hygiene.[39]

In April of 1901 the spectre of a smallpox epidemic darkened Sitka. The governor immediately appealed to Washington for aid. Smallpox, he warned, had in previous years caused "the extinction of whole communities." John tried to quarantine the sick on Japonski Island, and missionaries to the west acted to immunize their respective communities. Transported by the Revenue Marine cutter *Rush*, a medical team toured Alexander Archipelago canneries and villages; Brady personally assisted them in inoculating the natives against smallpox. Everywhere he lectured on cleanliness. To allay Indian qualms, he took along his son Hugh, who could exhibit his quite visible vaccination scar. At Hoonah the smallpox epidemic was particularly virulent. "All the people of this village that could be reached, were vaccinated," John reported, "but when they all left their homes in the spring, when so many of them died, they shut up their houses and went away." After the steamer *Senator* docked at Sitka with smallpox victims aboard, John insisted that all of the vessel's crew and passengers be inoculated.[40] During July of 1904 Yukon Valley Indians in the vicinity of Fort Yukon felt the ravages of still another epidemic—diphtheria. The Episcopalians' Alaska leader, Bishop P. T. Rowe, asked his friend and neighbor Brady to request federal aid in combating the scourge. The bishop was not disappointed.[41]

Brady, like his gubernatorial predecessors, never gave up the campaign for a large, well-equipped territorial hospital to minister to sick and broken natives. He believed that consumption was "the disease which is most terrible in its ravages upon the Indian" and that "recent awakening on the subject of tuberculosis has taught whites a great deal as to how the disease may be prevented. This the natives know nothing of." A "hospital rightly conducted" would be "the greatest blessing to these people." Equally understandable was John's advocacy of an orphan asylum for aboriginal children: "We have in various towns children who are the offspring of sailors, soldiers, United States marines, miners, and all kinds of people who have come here simply as sojourners and adventurers. . . . it is a problem to take care of them legally. Some of them are entering upon the first steps of criminal lives."[42]

Criminality of a different sort appeared in the Copper River country. The region's inhabitants had been reduced to destitution in part because of the prospectors' wanton destruction of game. After alerting his superiors to the Indians' starving condition, Captain W. R. Abercrombie wrote directly to Herbert Welsh of the Indian Rights Association. The War Department was soon distributing rations among the hungry. During 1900 the cutter *Bear* performed similar acts of mercy for the Bering coast Eskimos. Brady apparently did not fret unduly about the curse of Indian annuity goods fastening itself on Alaska, for when he received reports of destitution among the Copper River Indians he requested that discounted food be dispatched from military stores.[43]

Before Brady became governor in 1897, the historic check against Alaskan natives being sold "breech loading rifles and suitable ammunition" had been removed everywhere except in the Pribilofs. Although troubled by the aboriginals' tendency to shoot at everything that crossed their gun sights, he insisted that they have an equal chance at killing game. In 1902 secretary of agriculture James Wilson agreed with him that "no limit should be placed on the number of sea lions captured by natives for food or to furnish skins for their bidarkas."[44]

As teacher, judge, employer, and civil administrator, John's personal affiliations with Sitka's Tlingits never approached those of patriarch William Duncan with his Tsimshians. Like Metlakatla's autocrat, however, John had been seasoned by his earlier duties as commissioner to the harsh necessity of occasionally dealing severely with natives. The *Alaskan* complained about the excess of Sitka's "mangy dogs." Governor Brady repeatedly requested that the Indians control their filthy and forever-multiplying animals. His warnings unheeded, John walked through the Ranche, twelve-gauge shotgun in hand. There was a brief fusillade and Sitka's canine pestilence abruptly diminished. Afterward an angry Tlingit, Yaska by name, confronted him and demanded reimbursement for his dead dog: compensation or else. John frowned, shook his head, and then ducked as Yaska swung at him. His son Hugh never forgot how nimble his father's footwork was, nor how ridiculous Yaska looked sprawled on the ground. Equally disagreeable were those incidents when a stroll from Satchahnee to town brought a collision between

Alaska's governor and intoxicated Indians. John, Jr., remembered his father's quiet patience; in a few instances Brady firmly escorted an inebriated native either to a friend's or to the Sitka jail.[45]

The Ranche's diversions were a source of ceaseless wonderment to their nonaboriginal neighbors. One time the Indians decided to stage their own authentic crucifixion. Apparently an illustrated article in a current picture magazine featuring the Oberammergau passion play had overheated their religious fervor. As an apt figure to hang from a cross, they picked an Indian dying of tuberculosis. Another was cast for the Roman soldier who plunged his spear into Jesus' side, only in this case the Tlingit planned to hasten the execution with a bullet from his hunting rifle. Brady heard about the gruesome theatrical when a customer at the local boat shop just happened to inquire who had ordered the large cross-shaped object. Accompanied by two marines and Commissioner De Groff, the governor hurried to the crucifixion site. The natives were indeed eagerly preparing to crucify their comrade. The tubercular Christ did not seem particularly grateful that his life had been spared.[46]

Quite as astonishing, but infinitely more inexplicable, was the intra-Ranche squabble that erupted over which Indian families were entitled to display the frog totem. During February of 1899 a good portion of the Ranche populace gathered to rejoice at the construction of a new native home. It was not a pre-1867 Tlingit massive-beamed, multifamily dwelling, of course. Like most native houses erected during the past few decades, it was a lumber-framed, shiplap-enclosed, one-family structure, not unlike those built by the cottage Indians at the east end of town. Predictably, the housewarming turned into a roaring good party, lasting for well over a week. Quite as predictable, the boisterous libertines nettled Sitka's whites; doubly worrisome, cottage Indians were seen crossing town and joining the festivities.[47]

Daniel Benson, aglow with largeheartedness, promised to carve a unique wooden frog to adorn the new domicile. And indeed, the frog totem eventually gazed down at passersby. Late one night Brady was awakened by a native policeman and informed that approximately a dozen men equipped with ladder and cutting tools had disfigured Humpback Daniel's frog. The police officer had the culprits' names; John thanked him and promised action. The following morning the vandals quietly surrendered, explaining that the frog emblem was theirs and not that of the new home's occupants. After some hours of talking, listening, sitting quietly, talking, listening, gazing at Sitka's scenic splendors, talking, and listening, John evidently convinced the victims that a salmon would be a more appropriate clan symbol than a frog. The aggrieved Tlingits took no chances. Their totem obtained the protection of white law: Judge Johnson actually issued a temporary injunction restraining those who would steal a totem. Apparently the matter was amicably resolved—or so it seemed. A few years later one of those who had defaced the frog got drunk and hacked up Humpback Daniel's salmon![48]

William Kelly, training school principal and humorless Calvinist, was disgusted by the natives' heel-dragging Americanization. Kelly's letter to John remains a classic of cultural naivete:

> It is high time some law was enacted to abolish such of their old customs as tend to stir up strife and engender bad blood. Could you not have a law enacted to forever prohibit witchcraft, shamanism, and the erection of totems, the tearing up [of] blankets and distribution of goods at public feasts and such other ancient rites and ceremonies as tend to keep the native people in a state of semi-barbarism? If you could have such a law enacted at once you will advance the state of the natives a hundred percent at one bound and make it possible to civilize and educate them with a degree of rapidity unparalleled in this history.

Kelly was confident: "The leading natives would be glad of it, and I am sure the missionaries and better class of citizens would rejoice."[49]

How convenient it would be if passing a law could terminate attitudes and customs that stretched back to antiquity. Age had taught Alaska's governor the folly of such shallow solutions. Laws were imperative, but persuasion and addressing the people directly were much better. M. D. McClelland, a fellow white who watched him mingling with the Chilkats at Haines in 1900, recalled Brady's speech "to an assemblage of natives." The governor "spoke logically, vigorously and strongly against the continuation of these native customs using perhaps every argument that could be urged in favor of their abandonment." McClelland wrote Jackson:

> Not only a financial loss and embarrassment is caused by these feasts and potlatches, but the assembly of such a large concourse of natives many of whom are dissipated and dissolute characters, always results in serious moral injury to our native Christians, and the relapsing of many into grave sin can be traced humanly speaking, to the temptations which beset them at these assemblages. . . . they are also the perpetuation of prejudices, superstition, rivalries and customs which formed the old life of sin and darkness among their ancestors.[50]

A half century later the governor's sons vividly recalled their father's distaste for "ruinously wasteful potlatches." "By all means," Governor Brady wrote a missionary teacher in 1901, "encourage the natives to invest their money in some enterprise and not spend it all in potlatches." One suspects that Brady had a hand the following year in circulating

249

a Panhandle petition denouncing the potlatch. What is especially intriguing about that entreaty are its 144 signers. Those who urged "a
law enacted against 'potlatches' or public feast, which carry with them
the old-time customs of distribution of gifts for service performed in
honor of the dead," appear to be entirely Tlingits or "mixed bloods."
John included the document in his annual report.[51]

Jackson urged a crackdown. "There are great barriers in the way of
breaking up the old customs," John replied. "I think I am as much
opposed to potlatches and feasts as any one-else but I have my way in
trying to combat them." No doubt he was pleased when some eighty
of Sitka's Christianized Indians—they called themselves the New Covenant League—proposed "to abandon all their old laws and customs
and accept those which the white man is enforcing." "Like all true
reformers," John averred, "they have been zealous and oftentimes I
fear without patience or knowledge." The league demanded that he
"command all natives to change and that if they did not they should
be punished." Not wishing to become a Savonarola, John reproved the
New Covenant League and counseled a meeting in the Ranche where
a cross-section of grievances could be aired.

Convened in Annahootz's home, the gathering reinforced what John
had heard on his archipelago trips aboard the *Rush*. Later Governor
Brady spelled out his concerns to his Washington chief:

> They have been thinking seriously about [the old customs]. They knew
> that things are not right but they seem helpless and unable to extricate
> themselves. They are living more and more under a dual system as we
> make them subject to our laws. Their laws of property have reference to
> the clan and as much property is to be kept in the clan as possible. The
> children belong to the mother and her clan. When the husband dies his
> brothers and sisters take everything. This just now causes much trouble
> for the widows and children. . . . Their customs allow plural wives and
> many have two wives. This has been the source of much trouble.[52]

His misgivings bespoke a magistrate as much as a clergyman. In a
lengthy paragraph he detailed a fatal family row. The murdered wife's
relatives insisted on the Tlingit's customary property retribution. Brady
had patiently explained the complexities of Anglo-American law to the
Indians—that since both parties were intoxicated it was seen as man-
slaughter. "It was not much consolation" for the widower, Brady added,
"for he knew that the other parties would not respect his rights under
our law even when explained to them. When he returned, he and his
clan made a settlement with the clan of the woman."[53]

"These are hardworking self supporting people," he reminded Hitchcock, "but some of their customs keep them on a low plane." And of

all these undesirable practices, Brady ranked the potlatch among the worst. John described the ceremony as one in which "a head man goes through in giving away all his property save his house, canoe and gun. Bales of blankets are torn into strips, bolts of calico and brown sheeting into fathoms and handed out as each name is called, hundreds of cases of pilot bread, barrels of sugar, rice, apples, etc. There were $17,000 spent at one potlatch last year at Chilcat when several head men joined. They invited guests from all the settlements who are at some future time expected to return the compliment. Their savings are thus largely dissipated and they are kept from advancing as they should."[54] For all its conspicuous costs, the widely condemned potlatch also served to sublimate intense combative competition. Furthermore, the profligate giving assured reciprocity at a later date—a primitive form of social security.

At a 1901 Chilkat celebration, a number of elderly Tlingit leaders seem to have conceded "that the time had come for [the Indians] to abandon their old ways." Conscious that they could accomplish nothing without "a concert of action," Brady advised Secretary Hitchcock to secure funds so that a large and representative body of Panhandle Indians might attend "a general conference to be held in Sitka." John visualized about a hundred participants. Cost for their transportation and entertainment while at the capital he estimated at three thousand dollars. "These people are in a transition state and such an act on the part of the government is in accord with common sense and justice."[55]

During December 1904 an elaborate native gathering convened at the territory's capital. The *Alaskan* heralded it as the "grand potlatch, the last of its kind given by the Sitka Indians to tribes of Killisnoo, Hoonah, Juneau, Chilkat and other villages." Although it is unclear whether the federal government allotted the Far North governor money to underwrite this colorful affair, it is obvious that the military services were alerted. Tlingit leaders were hosted at the military installations ashore and afloat, and a section of Japonski Island was turned over to the visitors for their festivities.[56] It was quite a pageant. Stretched out in a single column, the large wooden canoes representing the various native communities of southeastern Alaska slowly approached the Sitka waterfront. Ancient chants echoed across the water, while over the vessels fluttered an incongruous mix of native banners and the Stars and Stripes. Within each craft were Tlingits whose attire was no less an olio: white man's pants and coats and wide-brimmed Indian straw hats. Following formal greetings by the Sitkans, singing and feasting began. Those whites lucky enough to be invited relished fish, shellfish, berry and seaweed dishes never dreamed of—and that was only the

Killisnoo Tlingit don their tribal regalia for the last potlatch, in 1904. (Reproduced by permission of the Beinecke Rare Book and Manuscript Library, Yale University.)

beginning. Off came the machine-made clothes. Suddenly it was 1804 instead of 1904: elaborate headdresses, Chilkat robes, handcrafted garments and jewelry—all profusely decorated with dazzling bird and animal designs. Fortunately photographers captured the face-painted celebrants. In a sense it was the Tlingits' last hurrah. Nor did the Indians have any desire to abbreviate the affair—it was months before Sitkans, red and white, bid farewell to the last exhausted merrymaker.[57]

Governor Brady missed much of the grand potlatch for he was enmeshed in one of his own: Alaska's extensive participation in the 1904 Louisiana Purchase Exposition at Saint Louis. However, he did confer with the major clan leaders and heard them renounce both their law of retribution and the potlatch. Before the native hierarchy had dispersed to their insular villages, the governor staged a formal ceremony to dramatize what he hoped would be the final potlatch. Katlean, Annahootz, Kitchcock, Kolnish, and a few other Tlingit leaders came forward and presented him with the historic raven hat, a headpiece said to predate Baranov's arrival. They solemnly renounced their old customs. Hands were shaken. Then, accompanied by the aged Tlingits, John walked to the Sheldon Jackson Museum. There, after further ceremony, John deposited the raven hat. "An emblem," he told them, "always to be saved, in memory of what they had done."[58]

More truly abhorrent as a lingering legacy from a barbaric past were the Indian practices of witchcraft and enslavement. Both customs persisted throughout the Alexander Archipelago despite actions by the military and civil authorities to root them out.[59] Slavery and its frequent corollary, witchcraft, proved especially difficult to eradicate wherever an influential shaman perpetuated them. Officials did all they could to humiliate publicly these physician-exorcists. A few shamans received lengthy prison terms. By the time Brady became governor, the Indians in Hoonah and Yakutat seem to have been the worst offenders when it came to tolerating or being exploited by these infuriatingly clever clairvoyants.

In 1902 Tlingit Samuel McKinley, one of Hoonah's leading men, hurried to Sitka to explain his village's disavowal of the recent murder of a witch. After calming the anxious McKinley, John penned warnings to his old Sitka acquaintances Moses Jamestown and Jim Nelson, now Hoonah residents: "I hope that the people of your village will try to behave themselves, keep sober and having nothing to do with witchcraft so that they will not have to be punished."[60] But the febrile act of destroying a witch could not be so quickly cured. Two years later Brady heard, probably from a native policeman, that the Hoonah Tlingits had captured another witch, in this instance a young man. Prompt execution

awaited him. The governor decided that it was imperative that he in-
tervene; the revenue cutter was soon on its way. Hardly had John landed
on Hoonah's beach before he saw the witch staked out on the wet sand.
The tide had ebbed; a few more hours and the incoming ocean would
have drowned the lad. Peter, as the Bradys called him, lived at Satchahnee for almost a year. After study at the training school, he joined
the Revenue Marine and developed into a fine seaman.[61]

Even the well-policed Alaska capital was not entirely safe from shamans and dangerous superstition. Brady attested that no resident *icht*
(Tlingit for shaman) threatened the Ranche. He admitted, however,
that local Indians "have been consulting Ka-shu-da-klock, an old sor-
cerer who lives at Angoon, seventy miles from Sitka." Little wonder,
since Ka-shu-da-klock promised to cure the Ranche's tubercular invalids. After some of the latter adamantly maintained that this or that
neighbor had bewitched them, John determined to demonstrate the
foolishness of such notions. A group of the malcontents were invited
to his office, where he had arranged some impressive physiological
charts: "I displayed the vital organs of the body, telling them the causes
of consumption, from which the white people suffer as well as they. I
talked all forenoon, and in the afternoon we had another session. They
had listened all day, but as I ended my talk an Indian chief cried aloud,
'Well, that is what the white men say. We are Indians, and we know
that there are witches.'"[62]

Yakutat, some two hundred fifty miles north of Sitka, was bedeviled
by an especially unsavory shaman. An English traveler described the
icht as "a filthy old scoundrel, with hair about six feet long; he had
been half blind for years." His loss of sight and grotesque face had
resulted from an assault on a trader. The merchant "had checked the
onslaught with a well-aimed dose of sulphuric acid."[63] Very likely this
was the shaman who became such a bane to Yakutat's Chief George.
Exacerbating community discord was the tension between those natives
who had been influenced by the local Swedish Evangelical Mission and
a gang of unruly red-white hedonists who cared little about family uplift
and nothing about their souls. In 1897 Chief George requested that the
governor send north a gunboat "to look into matters here." The gunboat
Wheeling was made available. John and navy commander W. F. Burwell
found that the Indians had recently been brawling and that polygamy
remained popular. Yakutat, however, was quieter than they had anticipated.[64] The troublesome shaman had vanished.

Three years later, and again in response to appeals from Yakutat's
stable element, John returned. This time his police vessel was the cutter

254

Rush, skippered by William F. Kilgore, "an active Christian man," Brady wrote Hitchcock; "he and I understand each other well and our minds are in accord with the things which should be done." Unlike the rather leisurely pace pursued by navy commander Burwell, Kilgore moved with dispatch. Not long before the *Rush* dropped anchor at Yakutat, the mail steamer *Newport* had "dealt out a large quantity of whiskey, the natives became furiously drunk and turned to fighting." After the villagers sobered up from their three-day binge, those accused of lawbreaking were brought to trial. For two days and a long evening, De Groff held open court. When the *Rush* returned to Sitka, eight convicted prisoners were locked in its brig. Robert A. Friedrich, the U.S. attorney, Sitka district, and John's neighbor, promised that he would prosecute "most vigorously" the liquor dealers at the next term of court.

Behind them at Yakutat the governmental authorities left "five white men who had been living with Indian women [who], when they saw the Government vessel come to anchor, hastened to the missionary and were married." One hundred sixty-nine Yakutatans had also been inoculated against smallpox. Doubtless an equal number heard their district governor declaim on the virtues of sobriety and thrift.[65] As to the wily shaman, he once again eluded capture. One has the feeling that Yakutat's Tlingits prized their *icht*, for all his ugly appearance and notorious reputation.

Excessive domestic discord among native Alaskans was an unpleasant reality. The disintegration of ancient native mores both magnified their discontent and eroded traditional village control. Doubly serious, these sociopolitical vacuums inevitably seemed to attract nonnative parasites, men whose predatory principles not only unraveled what remained of the indigenous social fabric but offered nothing constructive in its place. At Yakutat, for example, it appears that the white men who had so hurriedly taken native wives gained considerable status by introducing quantities of liquor. In 1905 a missionary, E. A. Rasmuson, bemoaned what he viewed as a worsening situation. After the *Portland* unloaded its whiskey kegs and barrels of beer, he informed Brady, the people began "fighting, breaking the windows and disturbing the peace."[66]

From the Panhandle to the Bering Sea, different versions of the same story never stopped moving across Governor Brady's desk. At Killisnoo drunken youths "assaulted an elderly man who was crippled and accused him of being a witch." Captain W. N. Lazier of Tee Harbor found the natives so demoralized by liquor that "his business is menaced." From Kenai, Father Sebastian Dabrovich denounced the importation of whiskey, which left the people "stupified from Saturday till Monday." The citizens and natives of Seldovia petitioned John "to prohibit a certain Captain Fillmore [who] make distill and to sell whiskey, spirits and liquors, in our neighborhood, especially to the natives." Creoles of Kodiak protested "turbulent" drunks and petitioned for the appointment of a native policeman.[67] In 1901 Frank A. Golder, the public school teacher at Unga, complained of "degraded white men" and two saloons inimical to local natives. Four years later Charles Valentine asked, "Can't we have any justice to protect our families and small children growing up? . . . the judge . . . is owned body and soul by the saloon men." Moravian missionaries from Carmel on Nushagak Bay deplored Chinese cannery workers bringing whiskey into the country. "It is considered amusing to drink until they lie round like dogs."[68] And wherever prospectors settled for any duration, a liquor dealer soon set up shop, even though in some instances "a majority of the miners . . . don't want them."

Commander Jefferson Moser of the U.S. Fish Commission steamer *Albatross* communicated another familiar litany to Alaska's governor: "The missionary element is some what exercised here over a small schooner that has been in these waters for some time and reported as selling spirits to whites and Indians. The name of the vessel is the DAUNTLESS hailing from Everett. . . . The schooner men are fine looking fellows that rather impress one with their honesty; nevertheless it is my belief that the schooner is a whiskey shop and is peddling whiskey. It is also said that . . . the Indians obtain liquor from the steamers stopping here."[69] By 1902 John's repeated requests that the district's executive arm be strengthened by an enlarged maritime police force had been realized. He believed that these Revenue Marine cutters were "the most effective way to enforce the law in all the out-lying settlements."[70] Equally patent, all the king's horses and all the king's men could not separate Alaskans from alcohol. In 1915 missionary-author Hudson Stuck, who knew the totality of the Great Land about as well as any man, lamented: "The country is a very large one, very sparsely populated; the distances are enormous, the means of transportation entirely primitive, and the police and legal machinery insufficient to the end of suppressing this illicit traffic, especially in view of the fact that a considerable part of the whole population does not look with favor upon any rigorous attempt to suppress it."[71]

"My own sympathy is with the Indians," John admitted. "But history will no doubt repeat itself here, as in other portions of our country,

A group of Indian and Creole Alaskans with Governor Brady in 1897, probably at Sitka. (Reproduced by permission of the Beinecke Rare Book and Manuscript Library, Yale University.)

where the aboriginals have come in contact with the civilizing influence of the white man, where rum, disease, and mercenary dealings have slowly but surely exterminated them." When John wrote that the natives "acknowledge the white men's superiority; all they want is suitable encouragement to imitate him," he again revealed his ethnocentric bias.[72] Nevertheless, the decades ultimately confirmed the painful truth that not until the native possessed the socioeconomic tools and finally the political skills of the invader could he assure himself of justice.

Governor Brady's maturing opinions of the territory's natives further confirmed his belief that the Eskimos were a people apart. Although he continued to fear the havoc that feverish gold seekers might wreak upon them, he comforted himself that the Eskimos' "mental capacity is greater than any others" and that their children at Carlisle "stand at the head of their classes."[73] Among the indigenes of southeastern Alaska, the vices and virtues of the invader's culture had been far more pervasive. Juneau dockworkers might still beat up Indians who undercut their wages, just as cannery operators continued to prefer "Chinese automatons" to Tlingit employees too easily lured away by salmon runs. And the number of Indians who had mastered even two of the venerated four Rs remained discouragingly small. On the bright side, the native who did master white men's skills wielded real leverage for prying open a place within Alaskan society. When John applauded their "upward tendency" he did not mean that they had accepted Jesus as their Savior; rather, they had embraced what the *Douglas Island News* labeled a "christian mode of life."[74] Vital concomitants were church membership, schooling for themselves and their children, and a monogamous marriage in a single-family dwelling. Equally crucial were the manifestations of their economic acculturation.

A few years after he had stepped down as governor, John informed a New York audience that Alaska's Northwest Coast peoples "were willing to work for just wages. They are fishermen by choice, and are not often surpassed in this industry. . . . With axe and saw in the logging camps they hold their own with the whites." Furthermore, they had "given entire satisfaction at the Treadwell Mine in whatever capacity employed. . . . They are natural mechanics."[75] As measured against Athapascans of the Yukon River Valley, the aboriginals of the Alexander Archipelago were far better off. How did they compare with contemporary Sioux, Apache, or even California's mission Indians? Were they better prepared to stand up to "the whites crowding into the country," as John described the situation, "and make complaint" and "know what their rights are"? For all the hazards inherent in such a comparison, a qualified yes does seem justified.[76]

1. Wilcomb E. Washburn, *The Indian in America* (New York, 1975), chap. 11; and Harold M. Hyman, ed., *The Assault on Indian Tribalism: The General Allotment Law (Dawes Act) of 1887* (Philadelphia, 1975), review this historic enactment. Richardson, *Messages and Papers*, 15:6674.

2. Elaine Goodale Eastman, in her examination of the soldier-educator (*Pratt: The Red Man's Moses* [Norman, Okla., 1935], p. 149), notes the distinction between the Plains Indians and the Northwest Coast natives so steadily promoted by the Presbyterians; see John G. Brady, *Annual Report of the Governor of Alaska, 1903* (Washington, D.C., 1903), p. 10. It is a curious fact that the uniqueness that the churchmen accorded the Panhandle inhabitants was later substantiated by America's eminent anthropologist A. L. Kroeber ("American Culture and the Northwest Coast," *American Anthropologist* 25 [January–March 1923]:7). A valuable study of Pratt's achievements is Everett Arthur Gilcreast, "Richard Henry Pratt and American Indian Policy, 1877–1906: A Study of the Assimilation Movement" (Ph.D dissertation, Yale University, 1967).

3. S. Lyman Tyler, *A History of Indian Policy* (Washington, D.C., 1973), chap. 5. William Hagan, *The American Indian* (Chicago, 1959), pp. 123–50. Francis Paul Prucha, ed., *Americanizing the American Indians: Writings by the "Friends of the Indian," 1880–1900* (Cambridge, Mass., 1973), offers the reader a useful, if one-sided, view of the reformers' ethnocentric patronizing.

4. AGP, box 13, Duncan to Harris, 15 February 1901. William Gilbert Beattie, *Marsden of Alaska: A Modern Indian* (New York, 1955), pp. 60–108. Marsden's cocky self-centeredness had not made it any easier for the increasingly misanthropic Duncan to welcome his return. See Marsden's blunt letter, ibid., pp. 62–66. Thomas H. Carter, comp., *Annual Report of the Commissioner of the General Land Office, 1891* (Washington, D.C., 1891), pp. 183–84.

5. AGP, box 10, Brady to Merrill E. Gates, 18 March 1901.

6. TAP, mf. 8, Brady to Hitchcock, 6 August 1901; JGB, mf. 3, Duncan to Brady, 17 May 1899. Ibid., mf. 1, Brady to his wife, 2 November 1903.

7. Brady, *Annual Report, 1901*, pp. 34–36; JGB, mf. 2, Brady to his wife, 26 March 1905. By 1902 Alaskan enrollees at Carlisle numbered fifty and included Eskimos, Aleuts, and Indians. Jackson, *Annual Report, 1902*, p. 1240.

8. JGB, unfiled, invitation card, "Twenty-first Anniversary and Twelfth Graduating Exercises," 13, 14, and 15 March 1900; JCorr, 19:175, Pratt to Jackson, 23 February 1900. JGB, unfiled, Brady to W. L. Bunard, 25 May 1903. Thomas G. Tousey, *Military History of Carlisle and Carlisle Barracks* (Richmond, 1939), pp. 334–35.

9. Brady, *Annual Report, 1905*, pp. 34–36.

10. JGB, mf. 4, Brady to Jackson, 8 October 1903.

11. Robert M. Utley, ed., *Richard Henry Pratt, Battlefield and Classroom: Four Decades with the American Indian, 1867–1904*, (New Haven, 1964), p. 323. R. N. DeArmond, "Authors' Roundup," *Alaska Journal* 1 (Summer 1971): 65; see also William L. Paul, Sr.'s article in that same issue, "The Real Story of the Lincoln Totem," pp. 2–16.

12. Harris, *Annual Report, 1904*, chap. 10 (pp. 715–66), contains the entire grammar and vocabulary.

13. William T. Harris, *Annual Report of the Commissioner of Education, 1902*, 2 vols. (Washington, D.C., 1902), 2:1232. AGP, box 12, Brady to Patrick Mason, 12 September 1905.

14. Brady, *Annual Report, 1901*, p. 31.

15. *Alaskan*, 1 November 1902. Brady, *Annual Report, 1905*, p. 101.

16. John G. Brady, *Annual Report of the Governor of Alaska, 1904* (Washington, D.C., 1904), p. 5.

17. White Alaskans objected that having to support native education from district tax revenues was "a discrimination against the people of Alaska" (McLain, *Alaska and the*

Klondike, p. 261). And because publicly funded aboriginal education throughout the U.S. territories had historically been drawn from federal funds, there was a measure of truth in their protest.

18. AGP, box 10, Harris to Brady, 23 May 1901. By 1902 the following Alaskan incorporated towns had their own school boards: Juneau, Skagway, Ketchikan, Treadwell, and Nome. Schools in the rest of the district were ostensibly "managed by the Alaska Division of the Bureau of Education, Washington, D.C." (ibid., box 11, Brady to George W. Attenberg, 18 January 1901). Jackson, *Annual Report, 1902*, p. 1239. AGP, box 13, Board of Education to Brady, 14 September 1901.

19. Jackson, *Annual Report, 1902*, p. 1239.

20. JGB, mf. 4, Brady to J. W. Heskett, 20 January 1903.

21. TAP, mf. 8, Brady to Hitchcock, 24 October 1900.

22. Quite early in his governorship John urged expanded congressional spending for white as well as red youngsters. Brady, *Annual Report, 1898*, p. 220; Harris, *Annual Report, 1904*, 1:1xi. Darrell Hevenor Smith, *The Bureau of Education: Its History, Activities, and Organization* (Baltimore, 1923), p. 137.

23. TAP, mf. 13, table 9.

24. Ibid. and mf. 14 are filled with Brady's correspondence detailing his 1905–6 educational concerns. AGP, box 10, Hunter to Roosevelt, 14 August 1905; ibid., Hitchcock to Brady, 10 October 1905.

25. *Alaskan*, 16 December 1905.

26. On 20 March 1905 Alaska's governor inquired about how the schools under his charge were to be paid and the teachers' salaries met. Hitchcock replied that the sum would be "one fourth of the amount collected for licenses outside of incorporated towns" during the period 27 January to 30 June. Jackson thought the twenty-five percent "ample for the first two or three years." Surely the general agent's sanguine prediction was an attempt to boost morale. AGP, box 10, Hitchcock to Brady, 22 March 1905; ibid., Jackson to Brady, 1 April 1905; ibid., 2 May 1905.

27. Brady, *Annual Report, 1903*, p. 57.

28. TAP, mf. 12, Brady to Hitchcock, 24 January 1906; ibid., claim of Dr. S. E. Stone and Miss Lulu Bert, 7 April 1906. JGB, unfiled, Brady to (probably) Knute Nelson, 1 January 1906.

29. AGP, box 10, John Hay to Brady, 5 July 1902 and 21 May 1903. Brady, *Annual Report, 1900*, p. 38.

30. AGP, box 10, Harris to Brady, 18 April 1901; TAP, mf. 8, Harris to Hitchcock, 30 August and 28 September 1901.

31. TAP, mf. 13, Brady to Leslie M Shaw, secretary of the treasury, 25 August 1905; ibid., R. J. Tracewell to Shaw, 21 July 1905; ibid., Brady to Hitchcock, 3 July 1905; ibid., memorandum on establishment of school districts in Alaska, 21 July 1905.

32. AGP, box 10, Jackson to Brady, 1 April 1905.

33. Ibid., 2 May 1905. JGB, mf. 2, news bulletin, 5 July 1900.

34. JGB, mf. 4, Brady to Mary Kline, 18 June 1902. Ibid., Brady to Vespasian Warner, 27 June 1902.

35. AGP, box 12, contains the exchange of letters of 26–29 January 1906.

36. Ibid., box 10, petition to Governor Brady from James Jackson, and others, n.d.; JGB, unfiled, Elizabeth Brady to commissioner of education, 12 October 1925. *Thlinget*, December 1908; *Alaskan*, 30 November 1889; ibid., 30 October 1897.

37. Brady, *Annual Report, 1900*, pp. 33–34.

38. *Alaskan*, 30 October 1897.

39. Ibid., 21 January 1899; *Thlinget*, October 1909.

40. TAP, mf. 8, Brady to Hitchcock, 11 April and 12 December 1901. AGP, box 11, Brady to Hitchcock, 1 April 1901, and ibid., box 13, Curtis P. Coe to Brady, 25 July 1901. Interview with Hugh Brady, 6 1963, San Jose, Calif.; JGB, unfiled, Brady to M. A. Sellon, 28 May 1901, and ibid., Brady to Hitchcock, 6 August 1901. AGP, box 13, L. Leonhardt to Brady, 6 May 1901, and ibid., box 10, O. L. Spaulding to Hitchcock, 21 February 1902.

41. TAP, mf. 13, Brady to Hitchcock, 31 October 1905; U.S., Congress, Senate, *Supplies Furnished Indians in the Vicinity of Fort Yukon*, 59th Cong., 1st sess., Doc. No. 67, 12 December 1905. Helpful on evaluating Bishop Peter Trimble Rowe is Thomas Jenkin's biography, *The Man of Alaska* (New York, 1943); and Hudson Stuck, *The Alaskan Missions of the Episcopal Church* (New York, 1920).

42. Brady, *Annual Report, 1902*, p. 51, and idem, *Annual Report, 1903*, p. 56.

43. TAP, mf. 6, W. R. Abercrombie recommendations; ibid., Abercrombie to Welsh, 3 July 1899; ibid., Elihu Root (secretary of war) to Hitchcock, 15 August 1899. *New York Times*, 5 November 1900. TAP, mf. 9, G. S. Clevenger to Brady, 11 August 1903; ibid., Brady to Clevenger, 4 September 1903. AGP, box 10, Thomas Ryan (acting secretary of the interior) to Brady, 22 September 1903. TAP, mf. 12, Clevenger to Brady, 23 May 1905.

44. TAP, mf. 6, Harris to Hitchcock, 8 May 1899; JGB, unfiled, Brady to Hitchcock, 3 March 1900; *Alaskan*, 15 July 1899. AGP, box 10, Ryan to Brady, 7 January 1903, and ibid., Wilson to Hitchcock, 30 December 1902.

45. *Alaskan*, 27 August 1898. Hugh Brady to author, 16 August 1960; interviews with Hugh Brady, 9 April 1967, San Francisco, and John Brady, Jr., 14 August 1968, Seattle.

46. Interview with John and Hugh Brady, 23 June 1962.

47. JCorr, 19:26, Olga Hilton to Jackson, 4 February 1899.

48. JGB, mf. 2, Elizabeth Brady to her husband, 18 December 1900. Interview with Bradys, 23 June 1962. AGP, box 13, Robert A. Friedrich to Brady, 28 February 1901. For the native view of this embroilment, see Frederica de Laguna, *Under Mount Saint Elias: The History and Culture of the Yakutat Tlingit* (Washington, D.C., 1972), pp. 288–91, 1132–33.

49. JCorr, 19:24, Kelly to Brady, 1 February 1899.

50. Ibid., p. 251, McClelland to Jackson, 15 October 1900.

51. Dictated tape to author's questions by Hugh Brady, 15 April 1975, Seattle. AGP, box 11, Brady to D. Waggoner, 20 November 1901. Brady, *Annual Report, 1902*, pp. 24–25.

52. JCorr, 20:96, Brady to Jackson, 20 February 1902. TAP, mf. 9, Brady to Hitchcock, 6 January 1902.

53. TAP, mf. 9, Brady to Hitchcock, 6 January 1902.

54. Ibid.

55. Ibid.

56. *Alaskan*, 29 October 1904.

57. Dictated tape, Hugh Brady, 15 April 1975. The literature on the potlatch is extensive. A splendid summary is Laguna, *Under Mount Saint Elias*, pp. 606–52. For other fresh insights see Abraham Rosman and Paula G. Rubel, "The Potlatch: A Structural Analysis," *American Anthropologist* 74 (June 1972): 658:71, and Robin Fisher, *Contact and Conflict: Indian European Relations in British Columbia, 1774–1890* (Vancouver, B.C., 1977), pp. 206–7.

58. Rosman and Rubel, "Potlatch," 658–71.

59. *Alaska Searchlight*, 25 April 1896; *New York Times*, 19 December 1903; TAP, mf. 13, correspondence on white slavery at Unalaska, 25 August 1905; also, AGP, box 10, William A. Davis testimony, 4 August 1905.

60. *Alaskan*, 8 and 15 November 1902. JGB, mf. 4, Brady's letter of introduction for Samuel McKinley, 29 November 1902.

61. Interview with John and Hugh Brady, 23 June 1962. AGP, box 12, Brady to Peter, Moses Jamestown, and Jim Nelson, 6 November 1902.

62. John G. Brady, "Witchcraft in Alaska," *Independent*, December 1898, p. 1912; and ibid., December 1904, p. 1499.

63. For a contemporary glimpse of Yakutat see National Archives, Microfilm Record Group 720, Alaska File of the Secretary of the Treasury, 1868–1903, mf. 19, W. L. Beasley to J. K. Luttrell, 25 August 1893 (hereafter cited as NAST). *Alaskan*, 2 November 1895. The definitive study of Yakutat's natives is Laguna, *Under Mount Saint Elias*.

64. JCorr, 18:182, Brady to Jackson, 5 December 1897; TAP, mf. 5, Brady to Hitchcock, 22 November 1899; ibid., Chief George to Brady, n.d.; ibid., Burwell to John D. Long (secretary of the navy), 1 February 1898.

65. AGP, box 13, Robert A. Friedrich to Brady, 30 August 1901. TAP, mf. 8, Brady to Hitchcock, 19 August 1901.

66. TAP, mf. 14, Rasmuson to Brady, 17 November 1905.

67. Ibid., mf. 5, Brady to Hitchcock, 12 February 1898; ibid., mf. 14, L. F. Jones to Brady, 16 November 1905; ibid., mf. 9, Sabastian Dabovich to Brady, 29 July and 6 August 1902; JGB, mf. 4, Brady to Dabovich, 17 January 1903; TAP, mf. 9, twenty-four natives of Seldovia to Brady, 8 August 1902; JGB, mf. 1, citizens of Kodiak to Brady, 8 September 1897; TAP, mf. 9, F. A. Golder to Brady, 19 October 1901. Ibid., mf. 12, Charles Valentine to Brady, 1 May 1905.

68. James W. VanStone, *Eskimos of the Nushagak River: An Ethnographic History* (Seattle, 1967), pp. 76–77.

69. AGP, box 13, H. H. Hildreth to Brady, 15 May 1901, and ibid., Moser to Brady, 6 July 1901.

70. Brady, *Annual Report, 1898*, pp. 223–24; TAP, mf. 5, Brady to Hitchcock, 5 May 1899; Brady, *Annual Report, 1901*, p. 37; JCorr, 20:96, Brady to Jackson, 20 February 1902. To expedite prompt law enforcement Brady went so far as to recommend that the *Rush*'s commander be appointed an Alaskan commissioner (AGP, box 10, L. M. Shaw to Hitchcock, 10 January 1906).

71. Stuck, *Ten Thousand Miles*, p. 363.

72. Brady, *Annual Report, 1899*, p. 7.

73. Brady, *Annual Report, 1902*, p. 26.

74. TAP, mf. 5, Brady to Hitchcock, 3 February 1898. Brady, *Annual Report, 1900*, p. 33. E. A. Hitchcock, *Annual Report of the Secretary of the Interior, 1905*, (Washington, D.C., 1905), pp. 100–101. Quoted in the *Alaskan*, 5 May 1900.

75. Brady, "The Present Status of the Alaskan Natives," p. 79.

76. Brady, *Annual Report, 1900*, pp. 33–34.

CHAPTER FOURTEEN

Safeguarding and Settling Alaska

Since 1867 the U.S. Navy and Revenue Marine had "shown the flag" along Alaska's coast. Although none of the navy's powerful new fighting ships ever replaced the diminutive U.S.S. *Pinta* on permanent Alaska station, some of them periodically visited Sitka and Juneau. Governor Brady and his fellow townsfolk greeted each vessel warmly. On the world scene the warships epitomized American strength. Along Alaska's littoral the flag-bedecked weapons stimulated patriotic ardor and provided relief from Panhandle ennui. Understandably, the arrival of free-spending bluejackets warmed the hearts of native and white traders.[1]

One of Governor Brady's first formal acts was to call upon the local marine commandant. He and Elizabeth had every reason to perpetuate the generally pleasant social relationship with military representatives living at Sitka. In the case of the navy officer R. E. Coontz, twice assigned Alaskan duty and ultimately an admiral, the Bradys built a friendship that extended beyond John's governorship. As for law enforcement, Alaska's governors depended not only on revenue cutters but also on naval vessels.[2] Significantly, when the *Pinta* was withdrawn from Sitka, the capital's Marine Corps unit remained.

During 1902, despite his previous healthy relations with these marines, John tried to relieve their commanding officer, Captain Joseph H. Pendleton. Like Coontz, Pendleton had returned to Alaska's capital after an earlier tour of duty there. For some reason the marine officer chose to deal arbitrarily with the local natives. He began by restricting native access to Sitka's wharf. Then he impeded their movements on the capital commons, even prohibiting baseball games. Finally he threatened to destroy native boats drawn up on the beach of Japonski Island.[3]

One explanation for these proscriptions was Pendleton's fear that smallpox-infected Sitkans would spread the disease among the whites. Inexplicably, his policy was enforced only against Indians, whose protests he ignored. Even before they sought redress from the governor, John had argued vainly with the marine commandant over his discriminatory actions. John did succeed in getting the district's quarantine officer to remove the marines guarding the commons. But the captain could not so easily be dissuaded from his zealous protection of Japonski Island. The marines set adrift some of the native vessels. Preparations to destroy a native sloop were begun on a day that John happened to be away from the capital: "The natives ran to tell my wife and she went and pleaded with the Captain not to burn the sloop." An Indian policeman ominously warned "that the Captain was in great danger if he presumed too far." Luckily, the sailing vessel was saved from the torch.[4]

By April of 1903 John felt obliged to write a long letter to the commandant of the U.S. Marines, General Charles Heywood. Brady carefully reviewed Pendleton's actions, declaring that the officer "for some unaccountable reasons . . . seems to have cherished a hostility toward the natives and they knew it." Furthermore, Pendleton appeared "vexed with the town." First, he had tightened up access to the inexpensive medical service heretofore supplied by the resident navy physician; he then sparked a silly friction over the boundary of the Presbyterian church as it adjoined the commons. Regrettably, John overstated his case to General Heywood. He closed: "I believe that we have never had a Marine officer from Ellsworth to Pendleton who has gained such illwill of the people by his domineering ways. . . . Why not build [the new marine] quarters upon Japonski that will be suitable and commensurate with the demands of the service." His suggestion that the marines be isolated from Sitka by a mere channel of water was not so objectionable, and he was entirely correct in saying that "the difficulty with the Marine barracks . . . is that it is in the heart of the town and confined to a small plot of ground." Nevertheless Pendleton stayed on, and the marines were not transferred to Japonski Island.[5]

During May of 1903 General Heywood sailed north and made a brief inspection of Captain Pendleton's command. Somehow he failed to pay his respects to Alaska's governor. No toady to military brass, and still indignant that Heywood had not removed Pendleton, John wrote another tactless letter, this one to the secretary of the navy. "Since I have been in office every officer of the Navy department who has come to Sitka has made it his duty to call upon the Governor," he remonstrated.

"This I suppose is a duty required when they visit any government however small. Now Mr. Secretary . . . I believe that the General's conduct was intended to be an insult to this office and the person who fills it." Both navy secretary William H. Moody and secretary of the interior E. A. Hitchcock reminded him that the marine commandant "is not required by Navy regulations, when visiting the capital of Alaska, to call upon the Governor. . . . the matter therefore becomes one of . . . social rather than official in character."[6]

Some citizens questioned whether Alaska even required marines now that the gold rushes had crested. Others pointed to tiny Japan's astonishing defeat of the Russian leviathan in 1904–5. By 1905 energetic Japanese fishing—the Alaskans called it poaching—posed an annual problem.[7] They were disregarding laws regulating the harvesting of marine life. After Japanese representatives approached Brady requesting permission to fish in Alaskan waters, John alerted interior secretary Hitchcock and the Navy Department to the problem.[8] It was the job of the Treasury Department's revenue cutters to check their activities. The governor also urged diplomatic accords with Japan to prevent the extermination of the Pribilof seals. To Hitchcock he speculated: "I believe it would be a wise thing for the State Department to sound out the Japanese minister and see if his Government would have a friendly understanding for us to seize several of their vessels and let them protest and thus open the whole question again to be submitted to the Board of Arbitration, which has been provided by the Hague. I do not see how else we can treat Japan, as she practically was snubbed when she desired to come into the original conference on the subject."[9]

John was aware of Japan's rising ambitions. Earlier he had told a reporter from the *New Orleans Picayune*, "The Japanese and other eastern nations are showing so much activity at present that the people of Alaska are keeping an eye on them . . . they may make some encroachment on the territory."[10] Where Japanese fishing schooners went, Asian warships might someday follow. John advised that two naval vessels be maintained in "continual service" in Alaskan waters. After leaving office, he continued to urge the necessity of constructing a fortified base in the Aleutians.[11]

Governor Knapp had made every effort to organize and arm a territorial militia; his successor, Sheakley, gladly dropped the entire idea. Governor Brady's opinion on the value of an Alaska national guard fell somewhere between these attitudes. For all of his concern over domestic lawbreaking and his anxiety about Alaska's vulnerability to Pacific attack, John never really took a fancy to civilians playing soldier. But many male Alaskans did not share their governor's misgivings about militia arsenals scattered around the territory. Not long in office, John received requests to organize town militia companies.[12]

A number of Alaska's recently arrived gold seekers, or opportunity seekers, had previously participated in western state or territorial militia bodies. Some had actually performed military service of one type or another. It is a safe assumption that most of those who pushed for local militia units did so because of the anticipated fellowship that these groups had traditionally assured. "In the [militia] apportionment of the four hundred thousand dollars among the states and territories," Governor Brady reminded one inquirer, "Alaska's place is blank." John did promise to confer with the War Department and inform his petitioner of Washington's answer. He channeled his letter to Secretary Hitchcock, briefly summarizing his own pros and cons on the activating of semi-military bodies in 1897 Alaska. That December Hitchcock authorized "the organization of a National Guard in Alaska."[13]

By 1899 irrepressible cheechakos, no doubt propelled by the recent Spanish-American War, had organized militia companies at Juneau, Douglas Island, and Skagway. The White Pass and Yukon Railroad at Skagway and the Alaska-Treadwell Company at Douglas Island assisted in the formation of the community-based militia. "This movement to organize a National Guard has had the sympathy of our best citizens and corporations," John informed Hitchcock. "The recent [acts of labor violence] in Idaho have taught the capitalists here the value of having well organized militia on the ground for their protection." John commissioned F. D. Kelsey of Juneau adjutant general with rank of colonel and W. H. McNair of Sitka assistant adjutant general with rank of major. The governor was, of course, ex officio commanding general. He assured his staff that before long uniforms would be on the way; guns would follow.[14]

Months passed and no military paraphernalia of any kind arrived. The aspiring civilian soldiers pressured their governor, and he in turn leaned on his superior. "Colonel Kelsey, the Adjutant General of the District, informs me," John notified Hitchcock, "that the different companies that has [sic] organized are becoming a little impatient for the reason of not getting their uniforms. These companies are organized a good deal for local and social ambition and a sort of rivalry between the different towns." Rivalry with more lethal implications forced Washington to review prospects for a Far North militia.

On 22 April 1899 the *Alaskan* crowed that the governor "has now succeeded and the Alaska National Guard has been organized." That same day Hitchcock dispatched a letter of caution to John. After conferring with secretaries Root and Hay, Hitchcock now concluded: "In view of the existing state of affairs in the Territory as regards the boundary line in Alaska, I do not deem it wise to equip the militia at this time. . . . The furnishing of arms for an organized militia . . . might possibly be misconstrued, and indirectly tend to bring about open hostilities between the persons along the disputed line."[15] John then wrote the War Department asking that at least the federal money apportioned for Alaska's militia be assigned to the district's credit. For this he got a prompt reproof: "As soon as, in the judgment of the Secretary of State, conditions will permit of the organization of militia in Alaska, you will be promptly advised." "In the meantime," snapped Hitchcock, "you will not communicate with any other branch of the Government service on this subject except through the Secretary of the Interior."[16]

Secretary Hay's caution was well advised. During the Spanish-American War an entire company of "able fighting men" had organized at Skagway, eager to join the fray. Two years later, when Governor Brady visited Nome, over a hundred of its citizens sought to volunteer for China duty, in this instance to protect "the lives and property of Americans" besieged by the frantic Boxers at Peking. Hay knew his countrymen's avidity for guns. Jingoism remained a staple in the Western press. Until the possibility of friction along the Alaska-Canada boundary had vanished, a Far North militia could wait, particularly with the creation of a regular U.S. Military Department of Alaska. The army's return to Alaska certainly had undercut any imperative need for a Far North militia.

An October 1901 letter from Jasper H. Rice of Ketchikan again spurred Governor Brady to see what could be done. Rice was confident that "there are quite a number of young men here regularly employed who are anxious to have a company organized." A few weeks later John received word from Washington that the Interior Department had "no further objections to interpose to the issue of quartermasters and ordnance stores to the militia of Alaska."[17] Months slipped by and no military stores arrived.

Next it was Joseph MacDonald, superintendent of the Alaska Treadwell Gold Mining Company Douglas Island who prodded Brady. "I must have 300 guns with bayonets here as soon as possible," he informed Alaska's governor. "If the Government cannot or will not furnish these, I shall be compelled to buy them myself, because I must have them." MacDonald feared labor violence and was confident that there were "at least 300 men here who stand ready and willing to join the Militia." Since his hard-driving management in Idaho's blood-soaked Coeur d'Alene mines, MacDonald always went armed. The preceding year he had whipped out his pistol and killed a "religious crank" on the Tread-well grounds. Some called it murder. He insisted that it was self-defense. Although John promised to "hurry matters as fast as I can," he cautioned the rash MacDonald: "If the [arms] are issued out of the usual method you may have to give bonds to the government that [they] will be returned upon demand of the proper officer. They usually hold the governor responsible for every strap and buckle."[18]

To Hitchcock John expressed his reservations: "I have not much desire for [a territorial militia], but it is a duty that is expected and should be performed, and I earnestly solicit the sympathy and cooperation of the War Department in making a right start." In 1903 Congress passed the historic Dick Act "to promote the efficiency of the militia," a part of which directed regular army officers to instruct state and territorial national guards. Brady requested that "the Secretary of War detail a proper officer for one year to come here to Sitka and help me to properly organize and put in operation the militia of this District."[19]

By 1905 Rice, not having received so much as a scabbard, again queried Governor Brady "regarding the organization of a military company at this place." As before, the paper trail led nowhere. However, one sentence in Rice's letter is revealing. "We now have a population of some 1000 people and can get a good company of either white or native men who will be here nearly if not all the time."[20]

Rice's stress on the permanence of Ketchikan's citizenry was wise; however, his suggested union of native with white men in a militia body was notable. Obviously he intended to secure the support of the "Indian-loving Governor." It also bespoke a reality. Alaska already possessed a handsomely uniformed "militia company"—and they were Indians and mixed bloods!

Since its beginnings the Sitka Training School had required a degree of military housekeeping and personal hygiene from its student body. Eventually the smartly uniformed and popular boys' band gave rise to a cadet drill corps. In 1901 the school's physician, Dr. Wilbur, and a teacher, George J. Beck, assembled their native cadet corps (the *Alaskan* labeled them a militia company) for a most impressive photograph. The student's sense of pride breathes forth—the parallel with Pratt's Carlisle cadets is striking. To be sure, their rifles were for drill parades, not for killing.[21] And except for special government material scrounged by Dr. Jackson, the unit was not a part of any territorial or federal military component.

Governor Brady no doubt had the Sitka cadet corps in mind when during December of 1902 he wrote Hitchcock: "We are holding [the natives] amenable to our laws, trying them for crimes, admitting their testimony as witnesses where white men are accused, requiring them to pay licenses for doing business as the whites are required to do. They can sue and be sued in civil matters, and the District Court is hearing complaints and granting divorces. I do not see therefore any real objection to their organization [of a militia]."[22] Sensitive that some white Americans might blanch at the thought of a red man militia, John ended his letter: "With the younger men it would be a measure of separating them from their old customs. Under proper white officers I think they would quickly respond and learn all necessary tactics." A little over a year later, secretary of war Elihu Root, after deliberation with the judge advocate general, worded a legalistic denial. Root cited three documents to buttress his negative. First, the Dick Act did not entitle the district's natives to "eligibility for membership in the militia." Second, an 1886 Alaska district court decision held that, "No treaty having ever been made with the Alaska Indians, or tribal independence recognized," they did not fall under the precedent begun with the Ordinance of 1787 wherein Indian tribes of the Northwest Territory had been treated as free and independent. Finally, Root quoted from the Supreme Court case *Elk* v. *Wilkins*: "An Indian cannot make himself a citizen of the United States without the consent and cooperation of the government; the fact that he has abandoned his tribal relations does not affect his status."[23]

William Duncan, Sheldon Jackson, and John Brady firmly believed that, before Alaska's natives gained authentic legal equality, these people must themselves use western civilization's governmental tools. Jackson and Brady, more so than Duncan, sought judicial protection not just *for* the native but *by* the native. Alaskan aborigines had to learn how to make the law as well as how to enforce the law if they were to gain racial justice and upward mobility.

One of the most visible instruments of sociojudicial control utilized by the Northwest Coast indigenes was Metlakatla's corps of native volunteer constables established in 1862 by William Duncan. S. Hall Young recalled how Indian policemen kept order at Wrangell during the late seventies. During the next decade Indian agent John P. Clum and Captain Pratt publicized how some Indian warriors not only acquiesced to the constraints of a white society but also actually applied some of the civil instruments of that world.[24]

During his first year in Alaska, Brady solicited decisions from white Sitkans to support a local native constabulary. Evidently an Indian had implored him "to appoint Indian policemen to arrest those who steal, get drunk and fight." Later this makeshift arrangement obtained the backing of the resident navy commander. By the time Swineford became governor, five Ranche inhabitants policed their village. Carried on the navy payroll, they received a common seaman's pay; their uniforms, when they chose to wear them, were a patchwork of military discards. By the nineties Governor Knapp headed a native police force with members in Killisnoo, Juneau, Wrangell, Klawock, Howkan, Douglas, and Chilkat, as well as at Sitka and Metlakatla. Although Alaska's white population mushroomed in 1897–99, the number of policemen authorized by the Bureau of Indian Affairs dipped slightly from twenty-two to twenty.[25] But, then, their primary purpose was law enforcement among indigenes.

Once governor, John did his best to keep the assigned quota filled. For all practical purposes Brady, like his predecessors, was chief of Alaska's Indian police. Neither title nor badge was his, but the administrative headaches were. He was designated "Special Dispersing Agent and required to file an official bond" in funneling money to the widely dispersed policemen. Personnel records, hiring, firing, equipment, and periodic inspections were also his responsibilities.[26] By 1905, however, the Bureau of Indian Affairs had discontinued all Indian police in Alaska's incorporated towns. When Brady's governorship ended their number was smaller than when he began his term, though Eskimo and Athapascan lawmen had joined Panhandle Indians in policing their fellows at Circle, Tanana, Iliamna, and Bethel.[27]

As may be imagined, the position of the Indian policemen was frequently controversial. Some simply overlooked the illicit liquor traffic. Others practiced forms of nepotism or shakedown. Absenteeism was common. Governor Brady fired officer George Kla-hautch of the Chilkats for "drinking and gambling and setting a bad example to your people." Sometimes an Indian policeman would report a violation of the law months after the event.[28] When whites urged him to appoint native police in embryo mining towns, John had to remind them that his allotted quota was small. Furthermore, to appoint an Indian policeman where no white magistrate existed courted trouble. Jackson once chided his old friend for playing politics with the Sitka clans. John snapped back: "I did not appoint the present policemen because they were Kok-won-tons, but only because they are the best men to perform the service, and when I become convinced that they are not I shall dismiss them."[29]

In truth, Brady could have usefully tripled the number of Indian police. Gold rush Alaska created numerous new tensions between red and white people and among the aborigines as well. Competition between the natives for trail packing jobs and dock work too often ended

270

in physical violence. Angry spats over disputed property were endemic. Compulsory school attendance was a joke. These challenges and many more demanded the attention of the native police. Clearly the capital's Americanized Indians, such as W. S. Hammond, Augustus Bean, and James Jackson, were favored by Brady for the few available police billets.[30]

With over twenty years of dealings with the Northwest Coast Indians, Alaska's governor knew hundreds of them by name and reputation. Nevertheless, a number of his appointees failed to measure up to what was expected of them. John was not insensitive to the social risks confronting a red man duty bound to arrest his fellow indigenes who broke the "white man's law." Six years before John became governor, old Katlayan concluded that wearing an Indian policeman's uniform had stigmatized him among his people: "It makes no odds now where when or how I die; like Christ my friends have all foresaken [*sic*] me and persecute me for standing for the right." Katlayan then formed a noose out of fishline and hanged himself.[31]

Governor Brady urged policeman Yalth-hock: "Do all in your power to help your people. One of the best ways to do this is to [set] . . . a good example by your daily life. Encourage your people to save their money so that they can in time own sawmills, small steam vessels and stores." To Charles Gunnok, a recent appointee at Kake, Brady counseled: "It is now time for the people to abandon their old ways and customs and be ruled by the white man's laws." Furthermore, John cautioned: "If policemen get drunk, gamble and attend dances and potlatches it will be sufficient reason for their dismissal from the service." Little wonder, then, that products of Dr. Jackson's schools increasingly filled the ranks of native policemen.[32]

Although the Indian police generally refrained from arresting white lawbreakers, they provided an excellent intelligence source for the U.S. marshal and his deputies. One place where they served primarily as informants was in the profitable salmon canning industry.[33] As Alaska's mining ebbed, General A. W. Greely reminded his countrymen that salmon canning was "second only to gold in value . . . the catch reaching the astounding value of $10,185,783 in 1908." Brady correctly predicted that this bounty would before long equal mining as a prime money-maker.[34] But without better policing even this renewable resource might be ruined. In 1889 he had recommended a "sort of congress of all the principal persons engaged in the industry to formulate a new system of protection." Afterward John may have realized how impractical his suggestion was. Just about all that could result from having native chiefs mingle with corporate executives from San Fran-

271

cisco, Portland, and Seattle were frustration and further humiliation.[35] In January of that year Alaska's governor testified before the Senate Committee on Territories. "I do not want to see the [salmon] business all broken up," he insisted, but "I tell you in behalf of the cannery men themselves, that there needs to be some interference [by the federal government]." John then recalled how formidable was the might of Joseph Hume of Oregon; in the Pacific Northwest his relative R. D. Hume was known as the "Salmon King." Hume "sat with a Winchester on his knees, and to use his own language, said that 'he would shoot the guts out of the first man'" who attempted to interfere with his salmon operations.

The Committee on Territories then heard how another packing company had mounted a steam winch ashore and rigged "a net three quarters of a mile long, and they go into the open sea, into the roadstead there." When a competitor's craft sought to interfere, John explained, "the other fellows went right around and set their steam winch on shore going and hauled the whole thing in, steamboat and all." Senator Carter remarked, "That was a big catch."[36] For all John's exaggeration, his tale highlighted the problem.

As Alaska's gubernatorial lobbyist Brady fully appreciated the achievements of the mighty Alaska Packers Association and the Hume group. "It must not be lost sight of," John cautioned, "that these canneries have given to the world a vast amount of wholesome and nutritious food at a very moderate cost, which otherwise would have been completely wasted." Yet in 1899 these seasonal plants paid not a penny in property tax. John urged a four-cent tax per case. To replenish streams depleted of salmon, he recommended an expansion of the incipient hatcheries and more rigorous enforcement of the law against blocking the streams with wire nets. He voiced no objections to the gill nets, which allowed smaller fish to slip through and thereby maintained a balanced supply of salmon.[37]

To legalize native ownership of Alaska's waterways, specifically their fishing sites, appeared reasonable enough. But Brady believed that such a law, though fully justified, would be ineffectual. He cited Commander Jefferson F. Moser of the U.S. Fish Commission, who "would gladly recommend, if the way were clear, the establishment of [Indian] ownership in streams; but it is impracticable, and I can only ask for him [the native] a consideration of his claim." John advised the senators to consult Moser for more precise information on possible solutions. But the commander was a Jeremiah. "Alaskan Salmon inspection is considered by all who have any correct knowledge of the subject as a howling farce," Moser snorted. "The truth is any attempt to regulate the use of this method of taking salmon is bound to be embarrassing and difficult of rigid enforcement. There is just one remedy for the nuisance—total prohibition." Governor Brady recognized the futility of that kind of "remedy." No, Alaskans must settle for half a loaf, and be heartened that the recommended four-cent tax per case won Congress's approval and that public indignation over the appalling waste was rising.[38]

Whether American conservation consciousness was in fact rising many doubted. Greedy prospectors who had failed at gold mining were actually mining the streams with dynamite. "The rivalry is great among the canneries," Brady reported, "so great that at times one cannery will catch and destroy tens of thousands of fish which they are unable to can rather than to allow the rival cannery's fishermen to catch them."

By the end of his governorship, little had changed. Ruthless harvesting of the salmon continued; their rate of decline was exceeded only by the rapid disappearance of the old native culture once so dependent on the salmon, now increasingly dependent on the white world. One can only speculate whether John Brady ever sensed the contradictory aspects of his attempts to shield the native from acculturation's sharpest edge. He relished extolling the Americanization of Alexander Archipelago Indians: "The younger people are generally well dressed. They buy cook and heating stoves, bedsteads, carpets, chairs, and sewing machines. Many sit down to their meals at tables covered with linen and eat from dishes with knives and forks and spoons. They are sending their children to school and these children are making good progress in learning the English language."[39] John could also paint a pleasant picture of the natives' prewhite fishing lodges "near the mouth of a stream . . . where they would dry their fish and venison and pick berries and enjoy life during the summer and fall."[40] Yet John's cultural myopia could not deny what his eyes saw. Those who owned sewing machines and had children in school were a distinct minority. Those natives living near spores of white civilization whose advanced age or unadaptability denied them socioeconomic assimilation faced a bleak future.

Painfully typical was the 1905 letter from Tlingit George Shar-wan of Hoonah, which reached John via another Indian. "One cannery from Chilkat put up a trap [by] my place. They have been [operating there] for 3 summers all the salmon which go up the river the salmon trap got all." Twice in the crudely worded note the old man pleaded with the recipient to "show this letter to Gov. Brady." John forwarded a stiff letter of protest, closing it thus: "This whole business is in an unsatisfactory condition and I have repeatedly called attention to it in my annual reports."[41] The pro forma ring of that final sentence reveals the resignation of a weary public servant.

Ernest Gruening has rated George T. Emmons's 1905 *Report on the Condition and Needs of the Natives of Alaska* a "classic." Emmons, a navy lieutenant, was first assigned to Alaska in 1882. Over the next two decades this scholar in uniform became an acknowledged authority on Alaska's native peoples and a friend and neighbor of the Bradys. There is a remarkable similarity between Emmon's 1905 report and Governor Brady's annual reports over the years. Emmons not only agreed in virtually every detail with Alaska's governor, but his report's narrative flow and sanguine conclusions on eventual native assimilation are also pure Brady. This is not to impugn a tightly written summary. That he drew so heavily on Governor Brady's conclusions flatters his fellow humanitarian; conversely, John richly benefited from Emmons's ethnographic knowledge.[42]

Emmons believed that the worst was about over as far as the acculturation of the Northwest Coast peoples was concerned. Although expressing qualms about what the unregulated exploitation of the salmon had effected among the Panhandle indigenes, Emmons felt that "the benefit of the cannery has been undoubted to the majority of the coast people." Like Brady, he saw that it was to the west where the packers' excesses must be braked. Here Emmons advised "prohibiting the establishment of salmon canneries, or the fishing for the same in the waters of Bering Sea and the Arctic Ocean" north of the Kuskokwim River.[43] There had been repeated complaints of cannery iniquities along Alaska's gulf and Bering coasts. In 1899 mixed bloods at Afognak informed Brady that cannery fishermen stretched their seines "directly at the mouth of the stream. We tried to remonstrate with them and they threatened to smash our skulls." A few years later natives in the region of Kobuk went "on the warpath," as the *Alaskan* editorialized the tension, seeking "to stop the destruction of the salmon and bring back a plentiful supply of food once more."

Just as Governor Brady had persistently advocated tightened law enforcement across the western reaches of Alaska, so did he push for Aleut, Athapascan, and Eskimo employment as fishermen and cannery workers. And as Emmons, Dr. Jackson, and others correctly surmised, the shift to a money economy assured a replay of what had earlier occurred in southeastern Alaska.[44] White man's wage payments could not, though, guarantee a comfortable acculturation for nonwhites. "The condition of native labor is the same here, among the Eskimo, as it is in other sections of Alaska," asserted Commander Moser. "Money

The interior of Satchahnee, showing a mixture of aboriginal items and turn-of-the-century Victorian clutter. (Reproduced by permission of the Beinecke Rare Book and Manuscript Library, Yale University.)

seems to have no value to the native except to satisfy his immediate wants, and the traders cater to their taste for geegaws by supplying them with the things for which they have no use." As an ex-trader Brady well appreciated native fascination with cuckoo clocks, cheap jewelry, and silk dresses. As governor he wished that savings deposits, books, and tools might more quickly supplant such useless fripperies. Fortunately, John's daily contacts with cottage Indians and a variety of educated natives sustained his faith in Alaska's indigenes. "They are dressed like white people," he wrote in a 1900 *Assembly Herald* article; "they render labor for wages, build frame houses . . . and in fact, have as many wants as their white neighbors and live very much like them."[45] To safeguard these natives' improved socioeconomic parity, their legal equality now had to be achieved.

When Brady boasted about native use of Sears, Roebuck mail catalogs, he did so not merely to laud the materialistic dimension of their Americanization but also to provide further proof that natives were quite prepared "for Congress to declare them citizens." In his 1898 annual report he was unequivocal. They should "be admitted to the enjoyment of all the rights, advantages, and immunities as citizens of the United States, and shall be maintained and protected in the free enjoyment of their life, liberty and property."[46] Predictably, his outspoken concern for native rights won him few admirers from the district's recent immigrants.

The *Alaskan* defended Brady's advocacy of native enfranchisement: "Is he so condemned simply because he is Gov. Brady or have our learned brethren some better scheme for their final disposal? Why should not an aborigne [*sic*] of Alaska who can comply with the educational and intellectual qualifications demanded of any franchised citizen be allowed a voice in our politics as well as the immigrants from foreign countries who are incapable of self government and are controlled by the political bosses?" For John W. Troy, editor of the Skagway *Daily Alaskan*, the answer was simple: "The advent of the whites [into Alaska] has forced the natives into the same condition of servitude as witnessed the westward march of immigration into the Western States." Brady could declare that "one law in Alaska for everybody and everybody amenable to that law should be the motto." But to Swineford such a statement was absurd: "The average native Alaskan takes to lying as naturally as a duck to water." Worse, John offended not only the pervasive sense of racial superiority held by most whites but seemed to them also to be wasting his energies on a matter irrelevant to booming Alaska. "As a shouter in an Indian meeting," Troy characterized him, "the gentleman is a success but as chief executive of this great district he is not the right man."[47] Those who agreed with Troy and Swineford preferred to ignore the emerging and articulate Americanized Indian leadership. "The native Alaskans do not object to miners and commercial men coming to their country," commented Tsimshian Edward Marsden. However, "If they are grossly wronged [they] will be coerced to take extreme remedial measures." In 1901 another Tsimshian, E. K. Mather, "acquitted himself well" as a juror in a Ketchikan criminal case. Native village councils were passing laws, actions that had won approval from district governors. As to whether Alaska's natives had earned the privilege of citizenship, Emmons's recommendation in 1905 echoed what John had been saying for years: "Of course it would be but a limited number that would seek this privilege to-day. . . . The older people from their want of education, would necessarily be excluded from full franchise . . . but the old life must pass away, and every advantage should be accorded to those growing up under the changed conditions, so that they may become active and useful members of society."[48]

For a brief moment in 1901 Governor Brady apparently feared that the Supreme Court's precedent-breaking "insular cases" might jeopardize nonwhite Alaskans' prospects for full citizenship. Writing to the secretary of the Board of Indian Commissioners, John insisted that the "natives should have the same standing in the courts, and the same rights in the community as are enjoyed by the other races." When district judge M. C. Brown seemed hesitant to grant citizenship to Panhandle Indians, John invited the magistrate to join him on the *Rush*, tour the native villages, and decide for himself if these people fitted Brown's stereotype. In his final annual report Brady capsuled the matter: "The natives in southeastern Alaska are, to all intents and purposes, ready for citizenship. They are hardy, hard-working, industrious people, and have always been self-supporting." It had become a Brady chant. And not without effect. None other than President Roosevelt urged Congress to extend "the privilege of citizenship" to those Alaskans "as may be able to meet certain definite requirements."[49]

Great Land natives would not gain "full political and civil rights" until well after John Brady's governorship, albeit three legal steps taken during his administration moved directly toward that noble goal. In May of 1904 Judge Wickersham held that John Minook (also named Ivan Pavlof), born of a Russian father and an Eskimo mother, could not become a naturalized American for the simple reason that he was a natural-born one. A copy of the decision was promptly sent to Governor Brady. "You have heretofore expressed great concern in this matter," Wickersham wrote, "and it is some satisfaction to know that the law recognizes that these people [mixed bloods] have rights of citizenship which are to be protected by the courts." John was elated. He appended the entire ten-page opinion to his annual report.[50]

Another Supreme Court decision the following year clarified Alaska's unique status among American noncontiguous territories. It appeared that the second-rate citizenship precedent born of the insular cases did not apply in Alaska. Finally, and not without a degree of symbolism, Congress passed the Native Allotment Act during John's last year in office. The law "provided for conveyance of 160 acres of public domain to adult natives." Like most reforms for the benefit of natives, this opportunity to homestead attracted little attention. Alaska was an enormous place; "most natives did not even know that such allotments could be obtained." Too many indigenes, "owing to their timidity," as Secretary Hitchcock euphemistically explained it, failed "to endorse their rights to the exclusive possession of lands occupied by them."[51]

No such timidity affected Alaska's whites, least of all the district's governor. Whereas aboriginals gave only passing note to what constituted legal individual land ownership, white Alaskans insisted upon "the right of fee simple land ownership." Governor Brady had hoped that Congress's 1898 homestead legislation, coupled the following year with an extension to Alaska of the public land survey, promised a long-overdue breakthrough for settlers. No swarm of pioneer farmers materialized. John blamed it on a lack of surveys and an ignorance of the Great Land. Thereafter his annual reports reiterated the pressing need for land title clarification and, above all, government surveys: "Let there be an appropriation of $200,000 for surveys. . . . This work should begin at many points within the territory." Nonetheless, a number of lawmakers continued to defend a discretionary policy in the northland. As Senator Stewart reminded his peers, California was not suddenly thrown open to homesteaders; "there were a dozen extensions made before those laws were finally extended over the entire country with appropriate limitations."[52]

John believed that potential Alaska farmers were being lost to Canada. He reminded congressmen that in 1901 twenty thousand Yankees crossed America's northern border. Canada practiced "systematic colonization of persons possessing a small amount of capital, for guiding them to the best locations, and for protecting them against the depredations of land sharks." "There are thousands of Finlanders," he insisted, "who would be glad to settle here if they could be assured that they can own their farms. Everyone of these would be worth more than a thousand dollars in his trained capacity to produce."[53] Appearing before the Senate Agricultural Committee, he evidenced a touch of desperation: "I still advocate the idea of giving [the Alaska settler] 160 acres or more, but we are willing to take one acre of land, because it is now impossible to get a title to 5 acres of ground." John G. Callbreath, whose Panhandle trading had predated Brady's, commiserated with Alaska's governor: "Is it not hard that an old frontiersman who for more than half a century has been in the vanguard of civilization must yield up the few hard earned dollars for a little piece of land that his toil and privations have helped make worth the having to speculate at many times its value. . . . I for one appreciate your noble efforts in our behalf. All the same if I get a few acres of barren Alaskan soil I must pay many times its value."[54]

Where Callbreath was resigned, John urged resistance. "All Alaskans," he entreated, should "bend every effort to have 160 acres granted as a homestead and to have the surveys begun at once." What about a small mineral claim? Here the law reflected the prospectors' historic practicality. The ephemeral nature of miners' claims, balanced by threat of swift "miners' justice," initially facilitated this type of transient land holding.[55] But once a prospector decided to become a permanent home-owner or establish a place of business, the vagueness of his land own-ership might soon haunt him. "Must I Sir, surrender all this or take a Shot Gun to defend my only home on earth," inquired an irate pioneer. H. E. Nicholai, a Dyea settler, wrote directly to President Roosevelt: "We have a country here that is unsurpassed by any of the other U.S. Territories. . . . the best citizens, the flower of the country and most of them would like to make Alaska their permanent home." Nicholai was confident that "Gov. Brady will present the matter more fully to you and Congress."[56]

When Brady urged Alaskans to stake out a homestead and then press for officially authorized surveys, he bespoke the hoary American tra-dition of squatter's rights. More concretely, he desired to breathe life into the feeble 1898 land law. During the period from 1900 to 1902, John once again surveyed his Sitka homestead, determined to nail down an uncontestable title to his beloved Satchahnee. Proceeding carefully, he obtained the approval of the district's surveyor general, then an endorsement from W. A. Richards, acting commissioner of the U.S. General Land Office. In December of 1902, leaving nothing to chance, he added President Roosevelt's signature to his patent. The Brady home-stead stretched to Swan Lake; supplementing this ground was an abut-ting forty-acre claim by his father-in-law, Hugh Patton. This final triumph meant that John Brady "and his heirs and assigns forever" had title to slightly over sixty-four acres, with an estimated value of less than a thousand dollars. Although Brady was primarily desirous of securing a home for his family, he deeply believed that his model farm would generate a life-style commendable to his fellow Alaskans.[57]

When the journalist J. S. McLain toured Satchahnee in 1903, he found the governor's "splendid garden around his residence in Sitka and its value as an object lesson in what are the agricultural possibilities of Alaska." Among the products of his two-acre garden, of which "Brady takes great pride," McLain noted several varieties of potatoes, raspberries, red currants, strawberries, cabbage, cauliflower, lettuce, radishes, turnips, peas, beans, celery, and "practically all the vegetables that thrive in our Minnesota gardens and some that do not." "I don't see any reason why we should not raise all the vegetables and cattle that we need here," Brady often repeated. Or, as a blunt editorial in the *Alaskan* stated, Far North farming enabled settlers to "prove our independence of the graft of steamship companies." Speaking at the nation's capital, John extolled: "The resources of agriculture are enormous. . . . the interior is made up of vast areas of farmland from which whole states can be carved out and where people can find good farms." Even his newspaper bête noire, Skagway's *Daily Alaskan,* conceded that Alaska's governor was "an obstructionist and pessimist upon everything but agriculture and totem poles."[58]

In 1897 Congress appropriated five thousand dollars to investigate Alaska's agricultural potential. The following year Danish-born Charles Christian Georgeson arrived at Sitka to commence the first U.S. agricultural station in Alaska. Among the sites selected for his experiments was the Brady farm. Professor Georgeson and Governor Brady quickly became agrarian allies. Within a few years Alaska boasted three additional stations: one at Kenai (on Cook Inlet), examining native and imported grasses and dairying opportunities, and one station each at Copper Center and at Rampart, on the Yukon River, for testing grains. Georgeson's first official report appeared in 1901. Thereafter, and for the next three decades, Georgeson acclaimed home garden patch potentialities "even beyond the Arctic Circle." It must have been doubly gratifying to John when scientists George Davidson and Luther Burbank recognized his own botanical accomplishments.[59]

Town boosters from Nome to Ketchikan paid slight heed to these latter-day Jeffersonians with their visions of Alaskan nesters. Like Juneauites two decades earlier, they preferred to believe that the Great Land's sheer immensity, not a large, productive resident population, accorded her a primacy among America's territories. Then, when their overblown demands proved unacceptable, they could lay the blame on

Betty Brady picking flowers in her father's tourist-attraction garden, about 1900. (Reproduced by permission of the Beinecke Rare Book and Manuscript Library, Yale University.)

predatory big businesses, congressional indifference, or Alaska's obstructionist governor. Quite different were the dictates of economic reality. Tiny, newly acquired Puerto Rico quickly became a larger market for American goods than Alaska. As for the relative value of the products shipped into the contiguous United States from her overseas territories, during 1903–4 the worth of Hawaii's exports overshadowed that of Alaska's by more than two to one. Lobbying sojourns at the nation's capital doubtless acquainted John with these disconcerting facts.

Sitka's *Alaskan* bragged that Governor Brady had been "bitterly fought by the commercial interests."[60] Again the facts revealed a quite different picture. When operating the *Leo*, John had indeed been hounded by the large San Francisco–based shippers. But as governor John could ill afford to estrange himself from any allies in the U.S. Senate, particularly men like Senator George C. Perkins who were important Pacific Slope businessmen. Although their cooperation was indispensable for the district, Alaska's trade was not indispensable to West Coast businessmen. David Starr Jordan viewed it from another angle: "The interest of these corporations is in general that of the government, because they cannot wish to destroy the basis of their own prosperity." This interaction tended to reinforce Alaska's law-and-order factions; unquestionably it facilitated the labors of lobbyist Brady.[61]

Anti-Brady newspapers like Swineford's *Ketchikan Mining Journal* and Troy's *Daily Alaskan* never seriously weighed the efficacy of those protracted East Coast sojourns by the man denounced as "Alaska's tory lobbyist." At one moment they bemoaned the district's failure to have a delegate seated in Congress with other U.S. territories. Then, soon afterward, they attacked Governor Brady for not representing "Alaska's people" at the capital. President McKinley had invited him to a cabinet meeting. Following McKinley's assassination Theodore Roosevelt kept John Brady at Alaska's helm. Important private and public groups listened to his speeches and read his annual reports. And now, in the spring of 1903, "the patron saint of the tories" had at long last won Congress's concurrence "that all the provisions of the homestead laws of the United States . . . are hereby extended to the District of Alaska."

"I am very glad that we now have a liberal land law," wrote the forever optimistic Brady. "This will induce homesteaders to come here in great numbers." In his annual report for that year, John could hardly restrain himself: "The people are reading and thinking, and have the hunger for more land, as has been painfully witnessed in the mad rush to Oklahoma and the Kiowa Reservation. The days of the ox teams and prairie schooners are past, but the desire and necessity for new homes abide. . . . Although the whole country is unsurveyed, the homesteader may select his claim of 320 acres, and by complying with plain and just provisions . . . be assured that he will receive a patent for same. This law will prove to be the foundation of Alaska's real prosperity."[62] John was not alone in his optimism. Judge James Wickersham, already viewed by some residents of continental Alaska as a "second governor," believed that sections of Alaska would match the Dakotas. "There are some very good areas of agricultural land in this country," he informed a group of visiting senators in 1904.

Time would demonstrate that Georgeson, Wickersham, and Brady were excessively sanguine in their predictions about Great Land agricultural potential. None of them lived to see anything that could even remotely be categorized as a farmers' frontier. In this instance editor Troy proved to be a better seer: "Gov. Brady would people the country with farmers to sell their products in the states at prices that obtain down there, by representing to prospective immigrants that foodstuffs can be raised as cheaply here as there. It is contended by those who are in touch with the actual development of the district that such doctrine is preposterous. The fact that Gov. Brady's homestead law has proved to be a dead letter is sufficient evidence on the point."[63]

Settlement of Alaska would balloon, but not for four more decades. Then, however, the catalytic elements were war, not peace, Washington's dollars, not Alaska's resources. As for the "farm families from the Middle West" on which John pinned such hope—"the most desireable [sic] element in the world for building up our institutions in this district"—they never formed more than well-publicized drops in the resident bucket. Alaska's mid twentieth century home seekers, like most Americans, would choose urbanity over rusticity.[64]

1. Brady, *Annual Report, 1905*, p. 43.

2. JGB, ledgerbook 1897, 26 July entry; ibid., pocket notebook, Coontz 1907 address; and interview with Hugh Brady, 26 June 1970, San Francisco. *Alaskan*, 1 September 1900.

3. TAP, mf. 9, Brady to General Charles Heywood, 7 April 1902.

4. Ibid., Brady to Pendleton, 25 September 1901; ibid., Brady to Heywood, 7 April 1902.

5. Ibid.; and ibid., Heywood to Brady, 25 June 1902. JGB, mf. 4, Brady to Hitchcock, 20 September 1902. Brady, *Annual Report, 1900*, p. 39.

6. TAP, mf. 9, Brady to Moody, 1 June 1903; ibid., Moody to Hitchcock, 23 June and 10 July 1903.

7. Ibid., mf. 13, Brady to Hitchcock, 29 September 1905. *Alaskan*, 27 May 1905.

8. AGP, box 10, S. Hayashis, Japanese Consul at Seattle, to Brady, 20 September 1901; ibid., Thomas Ryan to Brady, 26 September 1902. TAP, mf. 9, Leslie M. Shaw to Hitchcock, 15 September 1902.

9. Brady, *Annual Report, 1905*, p. 38. TAP, mf. 9, Brady to Hitchcock, 30 August 1902.

10. *Alaskan*, 3 April 1897.

11. TAP, mf. 11, Brady to Hitchcock, 19 January 1905; AGP, box 10, Paul Morton to Brady, 25 January 1905. Interview with Hugh Brady, 23 June 1962.

12. AGP, box 6, Brady to Burnette G. Haskell, 12 October 1897.

13. Ibid. TAP, mf. 4, Brady to Hitchcock, 16 October 1897. Ibid., mf. 6, Brady to Hitchcock, 6 April 1898.

14. TAP, mf. 6, Brady to Hitchcock, 24 July 1899. *Alaskan*, 22 April 1899.

15. AGP, box 10, Hitchcock to Brady, 22 April 1899.

16. TAP, mf. 8, Brady to Adjutant General, 13 February 1901; AGP, box 10, Hitchcock to Brady, 21 March 1901.

17. Brady, *Annual Report, 1900*, p. 38. AGP, box 13, Rice to Brady, 18 October 1902; ibid., box 10, Hitchcock to Brady, 25 October 1902.

18. AGP, box 10, MacDonald to Brady, 9 May 1903; ibid., 18 May 1903. *Valdez News*, 24 May 1902, and *Alaskan*, 24 May 1902. JGB, mf. 4, Brady to MacDonald, 26 May 1903. Brady, *Annual Report, 1903*, p. 26.

19. TAP, mf. 9, Brady to Hitchcock, 27 May 1903. Arthur A. Ekirch, *The Civilian and the Military* (New York, 1956), pp. 142–43; and Walter Millis, *Arms and Men: A Study in American Military History* (New York, 1956), pp. 179–80.

20. AGP, box 13, Rice to Brady, 5 April 1905. Brady, *Annual Report, 1905*, pp. 42–43.

21. *Alaskan*, 1 December 1900. John appointed Dr. Wilbur "Surgeon General with rank of Colonel on the staff of the Governor" (*Alaskan*, 22 July 1899).

22. TAP, mf. 6, Brady to Hitchcock, 19 December 1902.

23. Ibid., Root to Hitchcock, 9 February 1903.

24. Jean Usher, "William Duncan of Metlakatla: A Victorian Missionary in British Columbia" (Ph.D. dissertation, University of British Columbia, 1969), p. 208. Young, *Hall Young*, p. 220. William Hagan, *Indian Police and Judges: Experiments in Acculturation and Control* (New Haven, 1966), p. 27.

25. JGB, unfiled, Brady to (probably) Jackson, 18 March 1878; ibid., Brady to the people of Sitka, 12 November 1878. Ibid., mf. 2, Swineford statement, 24 May 1888; ibid., unfiled, Indian police pay vouchers, signed by Governor Knapp, 1891. TAP, mf. 5, Brady to Hitchcock, 14 September 1898.

26. AGP, box 10, Hitchcock to Brady, 17 January 1905. JGB, mf. 4, Brady to W. T. Bunard, 6 November 1902. AGP, box 8, Duncan to Brady, 26 December 1900; ibid., 27 December 1905; ibid., 6 November 1903; ibid., W. A. Jones, commissioner of Indian affairs, to Brady, 24 June 1904; ibid., box 12, Brady to Jones, 28 November 1903.

27. AGP, box 12, Cassia Patton to Daniel Benson, 30 September 1904; ibid., Brady to William Dickinson, 10 April 1905. Brady, *Annual Report, 1905*, p. 52.

28. AGP, box 12, Brady to Joseph Zuboff, 27 December 1905. *Alaska Journal*, 24 June 1893, and *Juneau City Mining Record*, 27 January 1894. JCorr, 25:43, Brady to Jackson, 14 April 1905. AGP, box 12, Brady to Kla-hautch, 29 December 1902. TAP, mf. 11, W. F. Burwell to secretary of the navy, 1 February 1898.

29. AGP, box 12, Brady to Royal Gunnison, 20 November 1905; JCorr, 20:96, Brady to Jackson, 20 February 1902.

30. TAP, mf. 5, R. T. Yeatman to adjutant general, Department of the Columbia, 4 July 1898; ibid., John M. Smith to Bliss, 13 December 1897; JGB, mf. 4, Brady to

Jackson, 15 December 1902. "Journal of Criminal Cases, May 1901–December 1901," cases of 2 September and 17 November 1901; and "Commissioners Docket Book, November 1901–September 1901," cases of 14 December 1901 and 10 February and 13 March 1902. Both record books located at State Superior Court House, Sitka, Alaska.

31. AGP, box 11, Brady to H. Folsom, 1 May 1901. *Alaskan*, 11 April 1891.

32. JGB, mf. 4, Brady to Yalth-hock, 29 December 1902; ibid., Brady to Gunnok, 21 March 1903.

33. TAP, mf. 5, W. A. Jenner to Hitchcock, 14 September 1898. NAST, mf. 20, Robert A. Friedrich to P. C. Knox (attorney general), 22 April 1901.

34. A. W. Greely, "The Economic Evolution of Alaska," *National Geographic Magazine* 20 (July 1909): 589. Hitchcock, *Annual Report, 1905*, p. 97.

35. Kutchin, *Report on the Salmon*, p. 29.

36. Senate, *Criminal Code*, 55th Cong., 3d sess., Exec. Doc. 122, 15 February 1899, pp. 1–4.

37. Ibid., pp. 2–4. Brady, *Annual Report, 1899*, p. 9. TAP, mf. 8, Brady to Hitchcock, 6 August 1901.

38. NAST, mf. 20, Moser's testimony, ca. 1900; Senate, *Criminal Code*, p. 3. *Congressional Record*, House, 56th Cong., 1st sess., 24 May 1900, p. 5967.

39. NAST, mf. 20, report of A. D. Harlan, 26 June 1901. Brady, *Annual Report, 1899*, p. 10. Brady, *Annual Report, 1900*, p. 33.

40. Brady, *Annual Report, 1900*, pp. 33–34.

41. TAP, mf. 12, George Shar-wan to Mr. Katlayan, 3 May 1905; ibid., Brady to Hitchcock, 6 July 1905.

42. Gruening, *State of Alaska*, p. 359. G. T. Emmons, *A Report on the Condition and Needs of the Natives of Alaska* (Washington, D.C., 1905). David E. Conrad, "Emmons of Alaska," *Pacific Northwest Quarterly* 69 (April 1978): 49–60; Jean Low, "George Thornton Emmons," *Alaska Journal* 7 (Winter 1977): 2–11.

43. Emmons, *Report on the Condition*, pp. 2, 10, 19–20.

44. Brady, *Annual Report, 1899*, p. 8. *Alaskan*, 16 May 1903. Brady, *Annual Report, 1898*, p. 212; and idem, *Annual Report, 1905*, p. 32. JGB, mf. 4, Brady to W. T. Bunard, 6 November 1902.

45. VanStone, *Eskimos of the Nushagak River*, pp. 77, 76. Brooks, *Blazing*, p. 439. Brady, "Peculiar Problems," p. 617.

46. Brady, *Annual Report, 1898*, p. 221.

47. *Alaskan*, 27 October 1900. Brady, *Annual Report, 1900*, p. 34. *Ketchikan Mining Journal*, 5 October 1901. *Daily Alaskan*, 11 August 1904.

48. EMC, vol. 3, MS "The Native Alaskans and the Klondike Miners." TAP, mf. 8, Brady to Hitchcock, 6 August 1901. Brady, *Annual Report, 1902*, pp. 22–26; idem, *Annual Report, 1901*, pp. 34, 86–88; Emmons, *Report on the Condition*, p. 16.

49. Nichols, *Alaska*, pp. 249 ff. AGP, box 10, Brady to Merrill E. Gates, 18 March 1901. *Alaskan*, 1 December 1900. JGB, unfiled, Brady to Brown, 14 March 1902. Brady, *Annual Report, 1905*, p. 31. Richardson, *Messages and Papers*, 15:6921. Section 6 of the Dawes Act included a clause that provided that citizenship could be obtained by Indians who had "adopted the habits of civilized life." Had Alaska's natives then been armed with the legal assistance Amerindians possessed by the 1970s, a significant number would no doubt have taken advantage of that clause. Most Great Land aboriginals did not become citizens until 1924 when citizenship was granted to all American Indians (Robert D. Arnold, *Alaska Native Land Claims* [Anchorage, 1976], p. 83).

50. JGB, mf. 2, James Wickersham to Brady, 4 June 1904. Brady, *Annual Report, 1904*, pp. 106–17.

51. Gruening, *State of Alaska*, pp. 144–45. Hitchcock, *Annual Report, 1905*, p. 100.

52. Wolcott, *Compiled Laws*, p. 167. *Alaskan*, 3 January 1903. Brady, *Annual Report, 1901*, pp. 5–12, traces Alaska's land disposition question in historical perspective; idem, *Annual Report, 1902*, pp. 8–12. *Congressional Record*, 55th Cong., 2d sess., 28 February 1898, p. 2277.

53. Brady, *Annual Report, 1902*, p. 15; idem, *Annual Report, 1903*, p. 17; idem, *Annual Report, 1901*, p. 12.

54. CLASJC, unfiled offprint, Brady's statement before the Senate Committee on Agriculture, 7 February 1900, p. 8. JGB, mf. 3, Callbreath to Brady, 28 November 1900.

55. *Portland Oregonian*, 23 May 1900. JGB, mf. 4, Brady to George M. Esterly, 18 November 1901. *Alaskan*, 12 March 1898.

56. AGP, box 13, M. V. Ley to William L. Distin, 21 April 1901. TAP, mf. 8, Nicolai to Roosevelt, 23 November 1901.

57. JGB, mf. 1, Brady to his wife, 16 December 1900. The patents and supplementary documentation concerning Satchahnee are unfiled in JGB. N. E. Keeler, *A Trip to Alaska and the Klondike in the Summer of 1905* (Cincinnati, 1906), p. 25.

58. McLain, *Alaska and the Klondike*, p. 262. AGP, box 11, Brady to [?], 25 February 1898. *Alaskan*, 30 January 1906. John G. Brady, "The Resources of Alaska," *New Voice*, 25 February 1899, p. 1. *Daily Alaskan*, 1 August 1904.

59. Witten, *Agricultural Prospects*, pp. 8–9. *Alaskan*, 15 and 22 April 1899. Brady, *Annual Report, 1902*, p. 21. C. C. Georgeson, "Agricultural Experiments in Alaska," *Department of Agriculture Yearbook, 1898* (Washington, D.C., 1898), pp. 515–24. JGB, mf. 4, Brady to James Wilson (secretary of agriculture), 3 October 1902. C. C. Georgeson, "Agricultural Capacity of Alaska: What Population Can the Territory Support?", *National Geographic Magazine* 20 (July 1909): 677. Of the thriving beauty spots that Georgeson developed around Sitka, virtually all of them have returned to "a wilderness of brush and muskeg" (*Sitka Troika*, April–May 1974, p. 4).

60. The standard Alaskan rebuttal to figures that demonstrated their inferior commercial status was to insist that America's Far North investment had been a profitable one. Few would dispute that $7,200,000 was an astonishing bargain, but of course this line of reasoning completely dodged the relative economic argument. See, for example, Wickersham's testimony, *Congressional Record*, 58th Cong., 2d sess., 6 April 1904, p. 4394. O. P. Austin, ed., *The Foreign Commerce and Navigation of the United States, 1904*, 2 vols. (Washington, D.C., 1904), 1:1073. *Alaskan*, 18 August 1900.

61. Brady, *Annual Report, 1899*, p. 42; idem, *Annual Report, 1901*, pp. 20–21. AGP, box 10, Perkins to Brady, 1 June 1890. *Congressional Record*, 55th Cong., 3d sess., 2 March 1899, p. 2702. JGB, mf. 2, Brady to his wife, 18 December 1904. Jordan, *Imperial Democracy*, p. 194. David J. Rothman, *Politics and Power: The United States Senate, 1869–1901* (New York, 1969), pp. 263–67. George H. Mayer, *The Republican Party, 1854–1964* (London, 1967), chaps. 6, 7, and 8.

62. *Daily Alaskan*, 2 and 15 April, 6 May, and 2 August 1904. Wolcott, *Compiled Laws*, pp. 124–25. JGB, unfiled, Brady to Henry Baldwin, 9 April 1903. Brady, *Annual Report, 1903*, pp. 8, 14.

63. U.S., Congress, Senate, *Conditions in Alaska*, 58th Cong., 2d sess., Rept. No. 282, 12 January 1904, pp. 105–20. *Daily Alaskan*, 5 November 1904.

64. An overall study of agricultural development in Alaska is Orlando Miller, *The Frontier in Alaska and the Matanuska Colony* (New Haven, 1975). Two indispensable articles by James R. Shortridge in the *Pacific Northwest Quarterly* are "The Alaskan Agricultural Empire: An American Agrarian Vision, 1898–1929" (69 [October 1978]: 145–58) and "The Evaluation of the Agricultural Potential of Alaska, 1867–1897" (68 [April 1977]: 88–98). For an appreciation of Alaska's accelerated growth since 1941 see Claus-M. Naske and Herman E. Slotnick, *Alaska: A History of the Forty-ninth State* (Grand Rapids, 1979), chaps. 6–9.

CHAPTER FIFTEEN

Administrator and Politician

In April of 1904 Walter E. Clark, Washington, D.C., correspondent for the *Seattle Post-Intelligencer*, commented on the probable reappointment of John Brady as Alaska's governor: "It has been represented to the president . . . that the governor has given an honest administration, and that honesty, when it can be found, goes a long way in Alaska." Clark described him as "an intelligent and progressive advocate of the best things for the territory."[1] Had he appended a photograph of Brady, it would have revealed a silver-bearded, slightly portly, fifty-five-year-old Alaskan. Traces of diabetes now compelled John to watch his diet; otherwise he appeared reasonably healthy.

That same month, despite all Brady's politicking, the office of the U.S. customs collector was formally moved from Sitka to Juneau. Clearly, keeping the capital at Sitka would require far more than Brady's persuasiveness. So, too, would winning reappointment for an unprecedented third term. Leaving nothing to chance, Sheldon Jackson circulated a letter that recalled that "the friends of good order and the substantial property holders of Alaska are in favor of Governor Brady's reappointment." Alaska's remarkably durable general agent for education then asked, "If you are willing to help us in Alaska to good government, will you not write President Roosevelt and ask that Mr. Brady may be continued governor?"[2]

Equally determined to terminate Brady's "monarchical rule," John Troy collected no-confidence petitions from Skagway's local chamber of commerce and Republican Club. Swineford did what he could to counter support for John at Ketchikan and Juneau. Earlier Troy had promised his readers, "John G. Brady will never hold a commission bearing the signature of President Roosevelt. Long before his term expires his whole traitorous and disgraceful career will be laid bare before the president and that will suffice with Roosevelt."

To satisfy himself of Governor Brady's competence, President Roosevelt dispatched judge W. A. Day, assistant attorney general of the United States, to investigate Far North affairs. By mid-October Day had returned and reported to the president. He branded the accusations of maladministration against Brady a "mare's nest" and "greatly exaggerated." However, Day's opinion of judge Melville C. Brown of Juneau resulted in the latter's replacement. Judge Brown had become too cozy with a Ketchikan utilities company. Muckraking and reform filled the air. Both the Big Stick President and his cabinet secretaries wanted the executive branch kept not merely free of corruption but also free of any charge of impropriety. Clearly Brady and his fellow public servants had been warned.

The Bradys cheered Theodore Roosevelt's overwhelming personal victory in 1904. Both Alaska and its governor appeared to have a friend in the White House; Roosevelt urged that "the land laws of the United States be extended in their fullness to Alaska." When the president recommended her husband for a third four-year term, Elizabeth was overjoyed. John, however, was less than happy with the formal relationship between himself and the dynamic president: "When I think of the unflagging energy that I have put forth, and am putting forth, in behalf of the territory, I wonder what Alaska would be if she only had a Governor up to the proper standard of strenuosity."[3]

Troy greeted "His incompetency's" third-term confirmation with an angry growl: "The people of Alaska have been turned down and Gov. Brady with eastern pull has triumphed! . . . Against him have been 90 per cent of the people of the district, including those of all classes and all sections."[4] Gross exaggeration, but then Troy spoke the idiom of a frontier journalist. If a pioneer newspaper was to succeed—and that often meant political office for its editor as well as black ink in the company's ledger—chimeras must be fought.

By 1901 Governor Brady had doubtless resigned himself to the editorial lances of Troy and Swineford, the price of public office, the glory of a free press. Year after year the pages of the *Daily Alaskan* and the *Ketchikan Mining Journal* hurled rocks and cast shafts at his management of Far North affairs. Troy's magnified accusations, like Swineford's, too frequently misrepresented the truth. For example, the Skagwayan claimed: "There is no disguising the fact that the feeling in the governor's home town is one of disappointment among the larger part of the citizens. Gov. Brady's affiliations with the Presbyterian missions have created a great prejudice against him and have caused

288

a wide spread feeling that he is opposed to the advancement of Sitka commercially because such advancement would hamper the missionary work now being pushed among the natives here."[5] Brady's protracted struggle to keep the capital at Sitka, to promote business there, made Troy's imputation preposterous. But then, Troy and Swineford had set out to destroy him politically, and that goal left little room for fairness.

Well-educated and cosmopolitan in outlook, John understood the opinions and the ambitions that motivated his journalist adversaries. They were as much a part of America's political process as were John's own increasingly overblown pro-Alaska assertions. Of course their attacks hurt. And of course, when Alaska's governor and his lady visited Skagway in 1905, the *Daily Alaskan* accorded them respect, though continuing to fire away at the "impractical Tory governor." Brady had long since inured himself to Alaska's political free-for-all. Nothing constructive could be accomplished by reacting to these nettlesome editors. John did his best to ignore their unending sallies. Immediately after his reappointment had been confirmed by the Senate on 14 January 1905, John wrote Elizabeth: "How can I be grateful enough to my friends. I am not cherishing any vindictive feelings. I want to render the best service possible so that my friends shall not regret their support."[6]

Troy's and Swineford's claim that Alaska's governor was kept in office merely by "eastern friends," although overstated, was in part correct. In addition to leading churchmen and key congressmen, an impressive body of business leaders had endorsed John's reappointment. Among these prominent easterners were Robert C. Ogden, Samuel Sloan, D. O. Mills, J. Whitelaw Reid, Chauncey Depew, and Frederick W. Seward, son of the man who had "purchased Alaska." Throughout the Northeast, Republican clubs and Yale alumni groups had loyally supported the Republican son of Old Eli. Brady and Jackson stimulated numerous pro-Brady letters even before Roosevelt was himself re-elected. John facetiously commented to Elizabeth, "If such letters keep pouring in at the White House Roosevelt will have to send me off as a foreign ambassador."[7] The repeated charge by Swineford and Troy that Brady was unpopular in the northland wronged him. Sitka had forwarded a petition on his behalf, and across the territory numerous newspapermen and businessmen approved his record. Dr. Jackson must have been stunned at the endorsement that flamboyant James Carroll desired to have forwarded to President Roosevelt. Legendary as a liquor smuggler and famous as an Inside Passage steamer captain, Carroll had been antagonistic to the missionaries since the eighties. Yet in 1904 he wrote Jackson: "Governor Brady has done more for Alaska and its

ALASKAN JOHN G. BRADY

people than any other governor ever appointed there. He works hard for the interests of the people and the territory. A great many have found fault because he takes such an interest in the natives; but if most of these people who do the talking in this direction would make as good citizens as the natives are, Alaska would have some very good citizens." As for the national politicians who echoed the opinions of Swineford and Troy: "I was permitted to go to Washington and face these people before the Senate Committee upon Territories," John recalled later, "and when the hour arrived for them to make their charges and sustain them they had not one word to say before myself and friends in the committee room."[8]

Alaska's fifth governor refused to play the typical backslapping frontier politician. Although few in or out of the north country would have disagreed with the American who stamped John Brady "a man of high honor and honesty," no one ever referred to him as a hail-fellow-well-met. "I am aloof from them all and have kept from any entangling alliances," he wrote Jackson. "If it takes Alaska politics to keep me in office, I am bound to go under. . . . I have simply my record and the influence of my friends in the East." Callused by the dutiful deprivations of his Calvinist upbringing, he eschewed fraternization that subtracted from his gubernatorial chores, his business, and his family. One searches in vain for evidence of any active participation by Governor Brady in such men's groups as the popular Arctic Brotherhood and the Alaska Bar Association, although he was an honorary member of both organizations. Yet whenever official obligations required, Brady could be the very embodiment of the warmhearted, gregarious Celt. And because the latchstring was always out at Satchahnee, he and Elizabeth escaped being stigmatized as snobs.[9]

To a degree Governor Brady's decision not to bend elbows with his constituents also reflected his disdain for Far North politics. In 1903 he snapped, "politics in Alaska is a farce and all upright men here believe it." Alaska's chaotic—indeed, kaleidoscopic—party organization reflected the traditional political pandemonium within America's rapidly changing western territories. Given the hugeness of the Great Land and the astonishing fluidity of its population, responsible and representative political parties were a virtual impossibility. Typical were the Republican territorial convention and the nonpartisan convention, each of which was held at Juneau during late 1903. Both Governor Brady and ex-governor Swineford attended the ill-named nonpartisan gathering; each left disgusted. Swineford ridiculed the GOP assemblage as "an affair rather of the monkey and parrot kind" and complained that the nonpartisan meeting (which he had hoped to control) was

Governor John Brady not long after assuming office in 1897. (Reproduced by permission of the Alaska State Historical Library.)

"completely under the domination of Joseph MacDonald" of Juneau. The Republican convention had split into two distinct groups. Each faction "proceeded to do business in the same hall at the same time."[10] Brady called the meetings farcical and henceforth avoided them. Swineford, hungering to regain Far North public office, resigned himself to future attendance at these noisy powwows.

Certainly the turbulent, faction-ridden behavior of the Juneau conventions contributed to John's antipathy for frontier politicking. Yet for all their bombastic harangues, these political carnivals did not disperse before formulating specific proposals. Naturally, the Republicans endorsed Theodore Roosevelt. They also urged an Alaska delegate, or delegates, to Congress. The nonpartisan conventioneers, or what was left of them, resolved that

. . . a Territorial form of Government for Alaska, is not at this time expedient or desirable.
. . . Congress provide for a means of securing patent to coal lands in Alaska, by providing for private surveys
. . . each of the three Judicial Divisions of the District be given a delegate to Congress . . .
. . . $50,000 [appropriation] be made by Congress to make a creditable exhibit at the Louisiana Purchase Exposition at St. Louis.
. . . it is imperatively necessary for the future welfare of the whole District that Congress immediately provide for the construction of a permanent road from Valdez [on the Gulf of Alaska] to the great Yukon Valley. . . . [11]

Governor Brady bristled at the resolution specifying that Congress not "extend the franchise to the original natives of the District." Yet except for this racist insertion and the multiple delegate proposal—John now advocated a single appointed delegate—these resolutions had his backing. For all his love of Alaska and deep identity with her people, John also subconsciously coupled himself with well-educated, less obstreperous easterners. This bias beclouded his ability to discriminate between the shadow and substance of vociferous frontier politicking.

Unfortunately, the very nature of Brady's official position did little to strengthen his relationship with Alaska's office seekers, often the next generation of district leaders. Since the eighteenth century America's territorial governors had been appointed. They therefore lacked a direct obligation to an electorate. Although these governors exercised "a stewardship of sorts, supervising the conduct of affairs in the territory," they usually did so with a minimum of guidance from the national government.[12] Finally, because territorial political parties were unrepresentative and irresponsible, the governors had difficulty gauging the acceptability of their policies.

In 1905 the newsman and congressional amanuensis J. S. McLain wrote, "There have been no scandals in the governor's office, and there will be none while he is its occupant." Brady doubtless concurred with McLain's other perception, although it was less agreeable: "There are those in Alaska . . . who are out of sympathy with the governor on moral and religious grounds, who feel a more aggressive and progressive policy than he has pursued would have been of advantage to the district." Acutely conscious of his office's ambiguities, Brady, like his predecessors, mixed ingenuousness with realism in answering these critics: "The truth is, that the people of Alaska are as well governed, for what it is costing them, as any people on earth. Everything is not perfect by any means, nor has every necessity been fully provided for; but when our condition is contrasted with the conditions existing in any of the other Territories it can be easily shown that there is no cause for complaint."[13]

Late-twentieth-century Alaska governors might well envy the administrative limbo in which Governor Brady operated: no legislature to wrestle and woo, no local party bigwigs hounding him for favors, no Washington superiors tying him down with endless red tape. And when it came to the exhaustive task of managing Alaska's executive office, John had only two employees to worry about, his part-time secretary, sister-in-law Cassia Patton, and the experienced ex officio secretary of Alaska, William L. Distin.[14]

Of course, there was an obverse to this gratifying autonomy: Congress made Alaska's laws, and appropriate cabinet secretaries thousands of miles from Alaska were supposed to interpret them and see to their execution. David Starr Jordan exaggerated when he designated the secretary of the treasury "the virtual ruler of Alaska," for as Jordan admitted, "no single person or bureau is responsible for Alaska." Still, his statement had a certain validity. Washington held Alaska's purse, policy, and patronage strings. To one questioner John wrote, "I am not in a position to help you to an office because there are not any appointments which I control." With no spoils to dispense, John's feeble political power was further weakened. In interviews around the United States, he often grumbled about the excess of officials who were not resident Alaskans. Although he did not create the "carpetbagger chant," which had begun decades earlier, John harmonized with it beautifully: "These men are foreigners to our land. They have no interests in Alaska except to grab whatever they can and get away. . . . They are like a lot of hungry codfish."[15]

Since 1897, when Brady inaugurated his governorship, the primacy of the older archipelago towns of Sitka, Wrangell, and Juneau had been challenged by an increasing number of vigorous young communities.

Among the more pushy were Ketchikan, at the district's southeastern tip; Skagway, at the top of the Panhandle; Valdez, adjacent to the Gulf of Alaska; Fairbanks and Eagle, in central Alaska; and of course remote Nome, facing on the Bering Sea. Not unlike embryo Juneau in 1880, some had difficulty determining what they wished to be named and whether in fact civic life had even germinated. Local politicians emerged to resolve these and other questions. Until "settled social and political order" took firm root, there could be little sophisticated party activism. In these isolated communities, political questions usually turned upon the "real and vital concerns of only a relatively few individuals." Congress had encouraged the growth of Alaska's settlements first by permitting them local elections and then by releasing to the incorporated towns the entire license tax collected within their boundaries. In his annual report for 1903, Governor Brady rejoiced that the town councils' "right of self-government is well provided for, and by a few further amendments will be almost complete."[16]

Here again John reacted optimistically where his detractors bemoaned congressional apathy. Actually—and this can hardly be emphasized strongly enough—Brady, Swineford, Jackson, or whoever, among the pioneer generation, spoke optimistically or morosely about Uncle Sam's concern for Alaska, as circumstances dictated. Addressing a Seattle audience in 1902, James Wickersham adjudged the Carter Code of 1900: "Together with the penal code, it gave to Alaska the very latest and best code of laws, fully in line with the spirit of the West. . . . These two codes furnish a complete system for the prevention and punishment of crime, and the enforcement of civil rights and the redress of civil injuries. No state in the Union has a better penal and civil code system than Alaska and no amendments are necessary to either."[17] Wickersham would regret such hyperbole.

The historic American pattern of evolving legislation piecemeal to meet territorial needs had supplied Alaska with laws. Again, similar to that of its sister commonwealths, Alaska's governmental machinery could never stay abreast of domestic demands. After a 1903 tour of the territory, senator Knute Nelson declared, "Alaska has been sadly neglected by Congress." "The government there is of the scantiest kind"; the incorporated towns "have a limited municipal government." Yet some of Alaska's hermitlike trapper-traders and sourdoughs would have been unhappy with Senator Nelson's desire to introduce more meddlers. "The people outside of the incorporated towns," he fumed, "are practically without any government." The Minnesotan reminded his Capitol Hill colleagues: "The only government they have is administered through and in the hands of the district judges. . . . The [three] district judges and court commissioners—something like forty in all—constitute [Alaska's] administrative force."[18]

As it transpired, the three district judges had indeed become virtual executive officers for their vast regions. Too often they handled matters for which they were ill-suited. Brady repeatedly tried to remedy this condition. Once he complained by letter directly to attorney general Philander Knox. John was reminded that it had been congressional parsimony that burdened district judges with the job of being internal revenue officers. In 1903, after many a prod from Jackson and Brady, members of senator Albert Beveridge's Committee on Territories determined to go north and see for themselves what "legislative relief" was called for.

After a six-week inspection of the Great Land—commencing at Skagway, traveling northward to Dawson, and then down the Yukon River into Alaska's great interior to Eagle and on to Nome, followed by an ocean voyage to the Pribilofs and Kodiak—the subcommittee finally collected at the district capital on 22 August 1903. Assisted by their fellow Sitkans, the Bradys extended the legislators a hospitable welcome. Among the guests were senators W. P. Dillingham, chairman of the subcommittee; Henry E. Burnham of New Hampshire; Knute Nelson; and Thomas M. Patterson of Colorado. Senator Albert Beveridge was not among them; the Indianan was enmeshed in New Mexico's statehood battle.[19]

By January the subcommittee had submitted its report. Those in and out of Alaska vitally concerned with the territory's future quickly familiarized themselves with *Conditions in Alaska*. To no one's surprise, it lauded the region's land and sea resources. And because this was the railroad age, few readers probably questioned the report's emphasis on improving transportation, a theme to which Brady had already begun to devote increased attention. He also succeeded in convincing a member of the committee of Alaska's farming prospects. Afterward Senator Nelson informed his Senate colleagues that Alaska was not "wanting in agricultural possibilities. The valleys of the Copper, the Tanana, and Fortymile rivers are broad and fertile. . . . by degrees farms will be opened here that will to a considerable extent supply the mining camps."[20]

Personally aware of the region's vastness, the senators concentrated their attention on strengthening Alaska's judiciary. Here again they espoused a Brady solution: carve out an additional, fourth judicial district. Three other subcommittee recommendations of which he approved were: abandon the "abominable fee system" (by which commissioners were remunerated, thereby inviting litigation); remove each district judge's power to appoint commissioners (which John believed stopped appeals from a commissioner's court because judges too often felt bound to sustain their protégés); and curb the excessive use of powers of attorney. This latter judicial instrument had been employed to stake out astonishingly "large numbers of claims in the names of persons from whom they are professed to hold powers of attorney." In fact, by 1904 prospector engrossment was widespread "in every section of Alaska." Abraham Springs, a Fairbanks attorney and ex-miner, shamefacedly admitted to the senators that it was "the greed of the first comers." Springs further confessed that the sporting, self-governing tradition of pre-Klondike days (one claim per camp, or district, per man) had vanished.

Finally, the senators' report lukewarmly supported an elected delegate from Alaska. However, for the present they saw no need to expand territorial government. In the eyes of John Troy, *Conditions in Alaska* merely rubber-stamped John Brady's proposals. It practically did so. At year's end President Roosevelt's annual message included the above suggested reforms, as well as a number of others for Alaska. Troy now included Roosevelt with those he satirized in his *Daily Alaskan.*[21]

Too often throughout his years as Alaska's chief administrator, John found himself district police chief. It was ludicrous, of course, but who else would wear the hat? As previously noted, he frequently called upon the military services, especially the Revenue Marine. After 1901 John increasingly depended upon the district judges and their respective staffs. To Secretary Hitchcock Alaska's governor confided that he felt "perfectly helpless" in enforcing the law. In 1904, seriously worried over the crush of litigation weighing on Judge Wickersham in his huge judicial district and beside himself at the impunity of certain criminals to the west, Brady championed a get-tough policy. In his annual report, after recounting some especially violent crimes about Bristol Bay, particularly at Nushagak and Karluk, he cried out for an end to this "horrible state of affairs": "The remedy is, to create the fourth judicial district and furnish it with a proper seagoing steamer, to be under the custody of the marshal and at the command of the court. It should be equipped with the best small arms and a Gatling gun and ammunition. All the communities which are along the thousands of miles of shore line of Kenai Peninsula, Cooks Inlet, Kodiak, Alaska Peninsula, Shumagin, Aleutian chain, and Bristol Bay can be visited in season, and as a consequence there will be a wholesome respect for law and order."[22]

Exactly why Judge Wickersham took such intense umbrage at the above section of John's annual report and attempted to inflate it into a sensational cause célèbre can only be surmised. Up to 1904 their professional relationship appears to have been quite cordial. Word of Brady's reappointment motivated Wickersham to write him: "Your administration has certainly been satisfactory to every good citizen in Alaska, although you have not escaped criticism which comes to all of us however earnestly we may try to do our duty." Unlike the Swineford-Troy territorial government advocates, Wickersham envisioned an evolving Alaska, the emergence of possibly four territories within the Great Land. Like Brady, he had publicly expressed his opposition to a territorial assembly, "for a time at least." John had repeatedly praised Wickersham's energetic qualities and quoted his opinions. "Personally I like him," John wrote in 1903. Ironically, the Gatling gun–armed vessel that so aroused the judge's ire was a law enforcement weapon that Brady had planned to have "constantly at the service of Judge Wickersham and his court so that every community may be visited at least once a year."[23]

On 29 May 1905 Wickersham addressed a twelve-page letter to Governor Brady. The judge saw that copies went to Secretary Hitchcock and the *Seattle Post-Intelligencer.* John later called it "as strange a letter as ever a man sent out." In it Wickersham directed some seventy-two questions at Brady; a number were condemnatory insinuations. The document's blistering, interrogatory tone reminds one of a hard-hitting prosecutor working over a hapless witness.

Surely Wickersham did not seriously envision a Gatling gun ripping into coastal settlements. For over twenty years Revenue Marine cutters had been patrolling the Bering coast. Their topside armament, as with the Coast Guard today, was relatively equivalent to or heavier than what John suggested, and these deck guns had not been used for "shooting up the people," as Wickersham put it. Brady may have written too loosely, but his intent to show a silent cannon's muzzle as a preventative measure seems obvious. Brady's annual report specified needed administrative reforms. Although none of these suggestions impugned Wickersham's judgeship, his diary indicates that he so interpreted them. Possibly Wickersham suffered misgivings about a likely reduction in the size of his gigantic judicial district or blamed Brady for the delay in his reappointment. His letter implied as much.[24] Brady knew how popular the "mushing magistrate" was in the north country. Although it does not appear that Brady ever criticized his fellow Alaskan in Washington, he might have.

If Wickersham hoped that his highly charged letter would produce an impassioned reply from Alaska's governor, he was disappointed. John's laconic riposte appeared in his next annual report. To assure the press as well as the public that he remained convinced of the need for a fourth judicial district, one reinforced by an armed vessel, John repeated word for word his Gatling gun request of the previous year. "This suggested remedy," John reminded his readers, "has been attacked in certain quarters with a light flippancy begotten of ignorance, and in disregard of the plain duty which the Government owes to every citizen to give him ready and efficient protection for himself and his property."[25] Not for some years did Brady or Wickersham choose to initiate amends.

A major impetus in the renewed pressure to improve district government north of the Alaska Range was the Great Land's last famous gold stampede: the 1903 rush to the Tanana Valley and its adjacent waterways. Fairbanks, a boom town on the Chena Slough, emerged as its nucleus. Gold production along this newest mineral belt fell only slightly below that at Klondike and Nome. No governor in American history had his administration rocked by three so diverse and lucrative gold rushes. By 1905 mining in the Fairbanks region provided over a third of Alaska's total annual output of $14,925,000. The *Seattle Post-Intelligencer* bragged: "Alaska is now crowding California, the golden state, for second place among all the states and territories in the production of gold." A year later only the state of Colorado continued to exceed the Great Land's extraction of the precious mineral.[26]

The central Alaska gold fields rather quickly became "rich men's placers." The richest gold-bearing strata lay deep under blankets of muck and gravel. Usually only complex, expensive equipment guaranteed a reasonable return on one's time and sweat. Alfred H. Brooks estimated that the cost of mining "probably consumed from one-third to one-half the output." The Fairbanks area mining camps circumvented the worst excesses of Alaska's earlier mining towns, possibly because the repeated river floods dampened the livelier spirits, but more likely because of tightened law enforcement. Certainly there was no lack of "ardent spirits" at Fairbanks. In 1905 the clerk of the district court notified Governor Brady that of the $173,219 license tax collection, well over half came from liquor licenses. That year John commented philosophically: "The rich alluvial deposits of gold in distant parts have attracted thousands of men who hope to secure fortunes quickly. In a few days a town of tents and light-frame buildings will arise, and all the accessories of a mining-camp life will be in full swing. If a report of [a] rich strike in another quarter is believed, there is a stampede, and the ambitious 'city' melts like snow before the summer sun. Nobody particularly regrets this for the result is sure. . . . some of these places will become centers of thriving industries."[27]

Though the veteran territorial governor now resigned himself to

Alaska's sojourners, he remained distressed at what happened to their mineral profits. "The successful placer miners," Brady reported, "who, in the aggregate, take out millions of gold, do not hunt up enterprises in the Territory for investment. Nearly every dollar of it finds its way south in the fall and seeks investment in other places."

Despite his lingering aversion to the gold hunters' unsettled way of life, John did what he could to comfort those broken in body and character. In temperatures of sixty below zero, locked within an ice prison, too many half-starved for food and family, a number of these marooned adventurers suffered tragic breakdowns; some committed suicide. After the mining rushes at the century's end, the number of Alaska's mentally ill increased to an alarming degree. Their plight compelled alleviation. The only certain way a demented individual might gain public assistance was to become a lawbreaker; then the court authorities could call on the Justice Department. "If an insane person can be turned into a criminal," decried Brady, "he can be taken care of, otherwise not." Even in their own capital, Alaskans knew nothing else to do but thrust a mentally ill person into Sitka's makeshift prison. "For several months a man here has been kept . . . in irons because he is insane. He has not received proper medical treatment," John protested to Hitchcock.[28]

The Carter Code promised some relief. It enabled Alaska's governor to advertise and receive bids for the "care and custody of persons legally adjudged insane." John contacted nine institutions. Taking no chances, he inserted an appeal in his 1900 annual report: "There are a number of persons who have been declared legally insane, and should be immediately removed from the jails and prisons to a place especially fitted for their care, comfort, and treatment." The following January, after additional correspondence and haggling, John toured the Oregon State Insane Asylum at Salem and signed a contract for the disposition of Alaska's mentally ill. Five years later John negotiated an improved agreement with the Sanitarium Company of Mount Tabor, Oregon. At that date sixty-five Alaskans were being cared for. A broken man no longer had to end his days as an object of derision in a Far North mining camp.

Just as John busied himself with institutions to house mental patients, so was he expected to concern himself with prisons for Alaska's criminals. Lawbreakers convicted of a felony and sentenced to a term longer than one year were sent to McNeil Island in the state of Washington; those sentenced for shorter periods usually were confined in the specific district where sentenced. By 1901 it seemed obvious to Brady that an increase of felons meant that "the time has arrived when a penitentiary should be built here. If an island was selected in Sitka Harbor for a penitentiary, nearly all the labor in its construction might be performed by prisoners who are now held in idleness in the Sitka jail."[29] Fortunately, capital residents would never have their lovely seaward view marred by a Far North Alcatraz; Alaska's criminals continued to be exiled to McNeil Island for some decades.

Governor Brady did demonstrate a degree of compassion toward lawbreakers suffering incarceration. After investigating the case of marine private Felix Hauk, confined to Sitka's jail for selling liquor to an elderly Indian, John freed the young man. Hauk had made no profit on the sale of liquor, had endured sufficient penalty, and was deeply humiliated by his imprisonment. Furthermore, Private Hauk had an honorable record in his marine company.

In the case of Mark Clinot, a Chilkat whom John had known since the Indian's boyhood, the matter was not so simple; indeed, it became a double death. Clinot, along with some others, had murdered a man and his wife. Now Clinot was rapidly dying from tuberculosis. The Indian pleaded to come home—"to die among his friends and family." John wrote directly to the president. Five months later it became John's sad duty to write the doomed man's brother: "I am sorry that he could not have been pardoned and sent home to die. I asked the President to do so and he turned the matter over to the Department of Justice. They were too slow. Will [Mark's] friends want his body brought back?"[30]

Another time President Roosevelt heard from his Alaska deputy about a boyish miner jailed for stealing a "suit of clothes and some gold nuggets." Possibly John sensed a frame-up. He urged Roosevelt to pardon him: "He is a young man and a fine looking fellow. It is a pity he had made such a start in the world." On a runaway wife in trouble at Nome whose Utah husband agreed to take her back, John was similarly forgiving: "The chances are that the caper she cut will keep her humble the balance of her days."[31]

In the case of the twice-convicted killer Homer Bird, Brady was anything but nonchalant. Bird, whose diabolical plans had luckily miscarried, symbolized precisely what Alaska did not want. John refused to forgive him, notwithstanding appeals from Bird's family and a petition from New Orleans citizens pleading that Alaska's governor pardon the convicted murderer. "In the face of his awful crimes and of the example it will furnish, I cannot constrain myself to ask the President to change the sentence of the Court," John wrote. Accordingly, Sitka authorities carried out one of their few executions.[32]

Among his Indian constituents, retribution remained quite as unyielding. A group of them from the Petersburg area left his office fuming because the murderer of their relatives was not being energetically pursued. "I would like very much to see this man run down and brought to justice," Brady notified the deputy marshal. "You know that three innocent lives may pay the penalty of this man's crime. The law of retaliation is not extinct among these people."[33]

Governor Brady's activities with another American minority, black citizens, was minimal. Little wonder: the 1900 census listed only 141 Negro adults residing in the entire territory. Requested to appoint "one colored man in Alaska on the Board of National Commissioners to the Frederick Douglass Memorial," John replied, "I am obliged to inform you that I do not know of a single colored man who is a resident of this District; so I am afraid Alaska can not be represented." Six months later a Georgia minister, and very likely a Negro, inquired about conditions in the Far North for black Americans. John's answer is revealing: "I am unable to give the name of a single colored person who resides and owns property in Alaska. A few have been here as servants and years ago Cato used to mine on the Stickine River and work as a blacksmith at Ft. Wrangell. I have tried to interest some of the porters on the cars to get up a party of young people to investigate the opportunities for colored people in Alaska and report to their society in St. Paul but nothing has been done. There is no hostile feeling here and the climate and chances for getting on well are favorable."[34]

By far the largest volume of unofficial incoming mail was poignant letters from wives, mothers, and sweethearts yearning for word of a beloved Jason, fearful he had perished in his quest for the golden fleece. The following response by Alaska's governor was typical: "Last summer when I went down the Yukon, I met many who had spent the winter of '98 and '99 on Kotzebue Sound and Kowak river. They told me that most of the men had a very hard time. . . . It is possible that your husband may be among them and that ere this you have heard from him. I am going to Nome soon and if I can obtain any information that will be of service to you, I shall send it to you." A year later John ruefully noted to a New York minister: "These letters concerning friends are sad and I receive some almost every mail."[35]

Less easy to escape was the rising number of inquiries and directives from various cabinet secretaries. The Department of Commerce and Labor, formed in 1903, had hardly organized its new Bureau of Corporations before John received a letter from its head, Commissioner James R. Garfield, who listed a series of questions on Alaska business, some virtually impossible to answer. Impossible to dismiss and sometimes impossible to expedite were Washington's ceaseless action memorandums: remove the Russian flags from Aleutian schools, but without incurring resentment among the Russian Orthodox priests; tighten up inspection of Yukon River steamboats to prevent them from exploding; find out if Alaska desires to participate in the 1904 Olympic Games; prepare to serve as special dispursing agent for the Treasury Department. Predictably, some Alaskans viewed their governor's collecting of statistical data as prying. He justified questions on the "cost of living, including rents, water rates, lights and a list of prices of groceries, coal oil, wood, candles" as imperative for his annual report and to the "benefit of intending residents."[36]

The formulation of his yearly summaries compelled Brady not only to review the district's present socioeconomic prospects but also to weigh its political maturity. In 1899, midst the feverish activity of the Klondike and Nome stampedes, the *New York Times* had quoted him as pleading for statehood. In fact, he pondered an evolutionary approach: "Alaska is large enough for many states. It might be admitted with definite provisions that as the population advanced with certain areas new States could be created. A people can attain under our form of government to their greatest degree of political happiness under a State and not as a Territory."[37]

Brady was not unique in his opinion that Alaska might later be politically divided. In 1884 the district's first governor had wondered if Alaska would forever remain "governed as a whole." President Benjamin Harrison had expressed similar speculations. At century's end California senator Perkins envisioned "two or three states the size of Texas and California" being formed from the Great Land. The *Alaska-Yukon Mining Journal* conjectured in 1901 "whether or not the district should be made into two or more territories, or whether it should remain intact." "There are differences of opinion among the permanent and temporary residents as to how the country should be governed," Brady reflected. "Some call for a full Territorial form of government . . . others ask for division into several Territories, and still others are content to remain as we are, under the direct control of Congress, until the political infant can grow stronger."[38]

As in America's Old Northwest, and later in the Pacific Northwest, most settlers seem to have preferred to let future settlement determine whether there would be one Alaska or an ultimate half-dozen Alaskas. Regional promoters, particularly those in Southeastern Alaska, refused to wait for what they shrewdly labeled "home rule." To some of them this meant full territorial status for the Panhandle with its own legislature and delegate. Others were understandably vague and inconsistent as to whether they wished for one Alaska Territory or four, as Judge Wickersham had suggested.

For editor Troy, change could not come without the defeat of the "pernicious Brady influence at Washington" and the demise of "the little knocker" whose "missionary cabal . . . keeps Alaskans gagged." Anger at John's leadership in blocking home rule was not confined to Alaskans such as Troy and Swineford. Seattle promoters whose businesses had benefited from the northern gold rushes resented a public leader reluctant to jump on the ballyhoo bandwagon. Indeed, as prematurely as 1891 its Chamber of Commerce had commended Congress "for the establishment of a territorial form of government over the territory of Alaska." In 1902 Donald Fletcher of Seattle, speaking before the Trans-Mississippi Congress, labeled Alaska's governor "an active agent of the great coal companies" who would delay territorial government until these powerful elements "gobbled up the best of the magnificent country."[39]

To an ally who approved his more moderate policy, John wrote, "I think many of the ones who are crying loudest for this kind of government, know that if we have it, it will be a political carcass upon which they can feast." "Carcass" was too harsh. What the establishment of a territorial legislature promised was fresh political offices. Brady's misgivings at the creation of a territorial government were primarily economic. He insisted that "Alaska as it is now governed entails the least possible expense upon the people residing here. The majority of the people here understand this quite well, and are not madly clamoring for a change at present. . . . Alaska is not ready for it. It would mean a more complex organization than we have, such as counties and townships and all their concomitants of buildings, officers, courts, etc. as we see in Territories to-day. This will entail an enormous expense upon a small population. It will discourage capital from investing [here]."[40] A major distinction between behaving merely as a politician and responding as a statesman is acting out of conviction and not swinging like a weathervane before the fickle winds of vox populi. For John, to have condemned big businesses "throttling Alaska development" would have been good Progressive rhetoric. He insisted, however, that "the cannery people and mill owners are complaining now that the license tax is too high compared with taxes elsewhere." For "the majority of the permanent residents who have property . . . a Territory would be too great a burden just yet." Journalist McLain summed up the situation rather well: "Those having large interests in Alaska are, as a rule, opposed to home government, claiming that it is the politicians and those owning nothing upon which taxes could be levied, who are agitating the subject. These claim that the few who have ventured heavily to develop Alaska could be compelled to bear the entire burden of heavy taxation. . . . On the other hand, those favoring territorial government claim that it is opposed only by the large corporations which 'have been bleeding Alaska for years.' "[41]

If Alaska's economic history has proved anything, it has conclusively demonstrated that large capital aggregates, public or private or a mix of both, are indispensable to Americanization. Although no corporate catspaw, Brady appreciated this hard truth. That it laid Alaska's governors open to being branded "a tool of those plundering Alaska" was also a painful truth. Lacking canneries, mining, and transportation companies, the Nome, Juneau, and Skagway mushrooms could never have sprouted and his detractors knew it. However, among Far North editors and politicians, "carpetbag corporations" (or the "Alaska Lobby") was simply too potent a stigma to discard. Certainly John never hesitated to utter the reproach whenever it served his argument.

Governor Brady warned his constituency to familiarize themselves with the penalties that New Mexico and Arizona had endured for their "fifty years in tutelage" as territories. A cautionary address to the House of Representatives on 20 May 1902 by Marcus A. Smith, Arizona Territory's delegate, "influenced my mind very profoundly," Brady admitted. To the Arizonian he wrote, "The idea I advocate is that we remain [a district] and devote ourselves in telling the truth about Alaska . . . , and in a few years there will be such a population of settlers here that we will be warranted in going to Congress and asking for statehood without undergoing the experiences you have had in Arizona."[42]

Year after year in speeches, interviews, and reports, Governor Brady insisted that the fundamental error of those who advocated territorial government was their miscalculation of Alaska's permanent population. The Troy-Swineford element blithely ignored his qualms, expressed in his 1903 annual report, that the white inhabitants of the Yukon Valley and Seward Peninsula were "migratory, almost simultaneously with the wild geese, which fly north and then fly south again." Three years later he reported that the migrants "do what they please and nobody is hurt or to blame, only this flotsam and jetsam multitude should not be recognized as part of a basis upon which a form of government is erected which will incur great expense to maintain."[43] In his 1905 annual report John estimated the district's total white population at 26,550. He knew the figure would infuriate what he called the "highflyers," and he challenged them to "make an estimate for comparison." Both Swineford and Troy had already done so. Swineford's *Ketchikan Mining Journal* reminded its readers that "Dakota, now two states of the union [was] organized in 1861, with a total population of 4,837." Alaska's second governor further buttressed his case by citing the creation of territorial governments in Colorado, Idaho, and Arizona in the 1860s, each with less than 35,000 citizens. Swineford failed to note, however, that during the 1860s the United States was in mortal danger of collapse, and President Lincoln had hurriedly reinforced the Union with Far West territorial political props. Swineford explained away Alaska's oceanic isolation by recalling that in Dakota and Idaho the railroad arrived after territorial status, thereby making "the impracticality of territorial government" in those instances greater "than can now be argued in the case of Alaska." In 1904, undaunted by the embarrassing loss of residents suffered by both Nome and Skagway, Troy chastised Brady "for slandering Alaska" with his total population estimate of "26,550 whites and 29,536 natives." A year later he crowed, "All the statistics that are available indicate that there has been a wonderful increase in the population of Alaska since 1900."[44] For these high-flyers' ballooning expectations, a territorial government assured a rising number of settlers. To soberly question one was to be guilty of weakening the likelihood of the other.

Time would confirm the wisdom of John's conviction that improved economic conditions were primary if Alaska was to hold its residents. Not that John was opposed to any Far North governmental reorganization. During 1904 he assisted Nebraska senator Charles Henry Dietrich in drawing up a plan for an "Alaska Government Board." In part a by-product of the recent senatorial tour, Dietrich's bill would have created a governing board of "seven members, three to be elected by the people of Alaska, three appointed by the President, and the governor of Alaska . . . to be ex-officio member thereof." Although a board was an untraditional means for managing a United States territory, Senator Dietrich explained that Alaska's "small populations, immense area and insufficiency of taxable property" dictated such a solution. Dietrich had resided in Deadwood, Dakota, in 1875 and knew all about mining camp lawlessness. Besides, America's New Empire, born of the Spanish-American War, was spawning a variety of governmental arrangements. The Nebraskan further recommended "that the powers of a delegate to Congress be conferred upon the Governor of Alaska, and that he should thus act as the agent of the government board and through it represent the people." The bill's backers cited the recent representative roles of "Governors [William H.] Taft and [Luke E.] Wright on the Philippine Commission." Finally, the measure advocated a supreme court and "a constabulary, to be patterned largely after the Canadian mounted police of the Northwest."[45]

"Governor Brady's pet measure," as Troy headlined it, never had a chance. To lump together Filipinos and Alaskans was bad enough, but to suggest that "law-abiding Yanks" needed an unbending police force like that which had so efficiently smothered serious crime at Dawson was intolerable. Equally objectionable, the Dietrich-Brady proposal, instead of dispersing political participation from Nome to Ketchikan, appeared to concentrate political power. Brady correctly judged that muscle for reacting to immediate problems now existed within Alaska's towns, centers that he asserted possessed "a great deal of latitude in self-government." Yet to the home rule men, Dietrich's bill was anathema. "You have given Porto [sic] Rico a legislature, Hawaii a Territorial form of government and are talking about self-government for the Philippines," snorted Swineford. "I can't conceive how Congress can hesitate to make a similar provision for us." For Swineford and his allies, nothing but the historic territorial form of government would do. Predictably, Dietrich's bill died in early 1905.[46]

Their persistent passion notwithstanding, the home rule enthusiasts simply did not hold sufficient political cards. Authority to affect administrative change in the northland lay in the hands of the Senate Committee on Territories. In their controversial 1904 report on conditions in Alaska, the solons had not dodged the question of a territorial assembly: "The strongest advocates of immediate action were residents of Ketchikan . . . and Skagway, . . . whose population in 1900 was 3,117 but which is now estimated at about 1200. They would undoubtedly be supported by a majority of the residents of Southeastern Alaska, provided that action could be set off into a territory by itself, but many of the last named class would oppose a legislative assembly of the whole district."[47]

Not until 1912 would Alaska win territorial status and her own legislative body. The delay was fortunate. By then Far North settlement had stabilized. In 1904 the governing board concept was all that Brady or any other governor probably could have secured from Congress. When in that same year the Democratic National Party Platform inserted a plank favoring "territorial government for Alaska and Porto Rico," few Americans viewed this as anything more than a pat on the back. In his fifth annual message, on 5 December 1905, President Theodore Roosevelt voiced the realities of pressure politics: "Nothing has taken up more time in the Congress during the past four years than the question as to statehood to be granted to the four Territories": Indian Territory, Oklahoma, Arizona, and New Mexico. Alaska, in other words, was not yet center stage America.[48]

The implacable opposition to home rule voiced by GOP senatorial leader Orville H. Platt astounded Brady. "I do not believe we can afford to let in states from outside our older territory," Platt stated. John characterized the legislator as visualizing "Alaska [as] a political inferno that all who enter are to leave hope behind." Cannot "American citizens in Alaska, who fulfill all possible qualifications as to numbers, intelligence, sobriety, patriotism, and morality," John pleaded, "come to Congress by their chosen representative and demand as a right that the republican form of government which they have created and ordained here, be admitted as a State of the Union?"[49] Fearful that Alaska might find itself lumped with the new "colonial dependencies," John urged that within Congress there be created "permanent committees on Alaska." The 1904 Supreme Court decision *Rasmussen v. United States* (197 U.S., 516) afforded Alaskans a degree of relief from the worrisome precedent of the insular cases. Henceforth Alaska, although still "an unorganized territory," had "precedence over all other noncontiguous areas as an unquestionably incorporated territory."[58]

One is entitled to ask whether the fifty-year-old Brady harbored any public ambitions beyond the governorship. John served at a time when, as he readily conceded, neither territorial government nor statehood was imminent. Yet there was a position atop Alaska's slowly maturing political plum tree whose attractiveness he surely pondered: the possible appointment as Alaska's first official delegate to Congress.

Congressmen had been considering the value of such an office, with or without territorial government, for decades. The gold rushes that coincided with Brady's gubernatorial appointment reinvigorated the impetus for a delegate. Beleaguered as he was with both internal and external problems during these first years, John gave limited attention to the matter. By 1900 the *Portland Oregonian* felt compelled to come to his defense: "He has been one of the hardest fighters for Alaskan rights, and the imputation against him for not insisting upon a representative for the newly-organized territory being elected immediately is a rather sharp thrust." In his annual report for that year, John reminded Alaska's congressional friends that, though they had recently accomplished much for the northland, they had failed to create the delegate post. The likelihood of Congress's granting Alaska an elected delegate in 1900 had run afoul an imponderable: how to manage an election across the enormous region among such an ephemeral population?[51]

After reviewing the role of the Far West territorial delegates, Earl Pomeroy and Clark Spence have concluded that "the delegate's influence was more a matter of his personal ability to charm, wheedle or inveigle, than of legal rights or privileges. Without a vote he was at a distinct disadvantage." Would becoming Alaska's official delegate rather than her unofficial one have made any practical difference for lobbyist Brady? In 1902 Brady described a delegate's limitations: "We know that he will have no vote and will therefore seldom be invited to a log-rolling; that he will sit at the foot of the committee table and will not often be allowed to open his mouth on the floor. Nevertheless people want their accredited representative there. He can persist in bringing measures for Alaska's welfare before the committees, look after the interests of her citizens before the Departments, and occasionally enlighten the House when it has Alaskan matters before it."[52] The Great Land surely had not lacked self-appointed and semiofficial delegates: William Gouverneur Morris, Henry Wood Elliott, Sheldon Jackson, Thomas Nowell, Captain James Carroll, John G. Price, and the recently self-appointed representative from Cold Foot, Alaska, whom congressmen tabbed "Icicle Ike."

If Brady itched to become Alaska's first bona fide delegate, there is no evidence of it. Indeed, in February of 1903 James Wickersham recorded in his diary that the governor "voluntarily said to me, plainly and positively that if the Alaska delegate bill passed he would support me for the place . . . though he kindly protested that I was of such value as judge that he regretted to lose me on the bench." A few months later in testimony to the 1903 senatorial investigators, Wickersham cut back his previous recommendation of four delegates. "Nature has divided [Alaska] at Mount St. Elias by impassable glaciers. The Eskimo tribes go no farther south than those glaciers and the Tlingit no farther north. That ought to be the division between the future commonwealths. I think that southeastern Alaska ought to be given a Delegate, and the district north of Mount St. Elias ought to have another or possibly two."[53]

Urged by Governor Brady, Senator Knute Nelson introduced yet another delegate proposal. Thanks to Senator Platt's veto, the bill quickly joined its predecessors in the legislative graveyard. As so often in the gestation of America's public institutions, it was a steady swelling of public pressure that ultimately caused Congress to grant Alaskans a voteless delegate. During 1903 Valdezians angrily added their resentment to the mounting "no representation" frustration. Valdez lawyer Volney T. Hoggatt, formerly of Nome, traveled to Sitka and dared John to elbow aside America's dilatory Congress. Northlanders, Hoggatt insisted, should publish a proclamation arbitrarily setting a day on the calendar for the election of a delegate and then let events run their course. Despite ridicule from Nome and Ketchikan newspapers, Hoggatt insisted that the Supreme Court case *Steamer Coquitlam v. United*

States (163 U.S., 346), among other decisions, legitimized such a pre-
cipitous step. John advised Hoggatt: "You are too reasonable and sensible a man . . . to issue a proclamation . . . irrespective of what the
President may say or think." Taking no chances, John apprised Secretary Hitchcock of the ferment.[54]

Hitchcock and Brady realized that, though President Roosevelt desired an Alaska delegate to Congress, he believed the northland un-
prepared for territorial status. It is entirely possible that the wily Roosevelt tacitly welcomed Hoggatt's impetuosity; Congress had dawdled
long enough on the delegate matter. On 4 March 1905 Valdez citizens
released a publicity declaration reminiscent of Captain Carroll's earlier
attention-getting offer to buy Alaska. Their flamboyant telegram to
President Roosevelt coincided with his inauguration day: "On behalf
of 60,000 American citizens in Alaska who are denied the right of
representation in any form, we demand, in mass meeting assembled,
that Alaska be annexed to Canada."[55] Later that year, with the persistence that only a dedicated lobbyist can sustain, Governor Brady once
again reminded Congress that a "majority of the resident population
want a delegate and would prefer to elect him." "It may be that the
law making power will have to act," John joked, "to get rid of the
annoyance of the large number of self and semi-appointed delegates
who bob up in the halls and the committee rooms in the Capitol." From
1900 until his last year in office, Governor Brady annually requested
that Congress provide Alaska with an elected delegate.[56]

By mid-1905 it appeared that the tide of both public and congressional interest in Alaska was cresting. Prodded by Alfred Swineford,
Americans who had cast their future with Alaska, as well as Puget
Sound businessmen with Far North investments, assembled at a nonpartisan convention in Seattle. Neither Brady nor Wickersham attended
the November 1905 gathering. However, John G. Price did, much to
the horror of the *Valdez News*:

> The convention was Alaskan only in name. It was controlled by Seat-
> tleites, as it was sure to be if held in Seattle. Take John G. Price for
> example. He was once in Alaska, it is true, but five years ago he moved
> bag and baggage to Seattle. . . . Many of the other delegates were no
> more entitled to represent Alaska than was John G. Price. . . . Most of
> the political ills from which Alaska has suffered during the past five
> years can be traced directly to one or more of these grafting outsiders
> who, in the name of Alaska, have imposed upon members of congress in
> the interest of their own private schemes and political jobs.[57]

The *Valdez News* was rather severe on Price. Furthermore, the Seattle
gathering was neither as un-Alaskan nor as futile as the newspaper
claimed.

Swineford was the most prominent participant, "the grand old man of Alaska," one magazine called him. Representatives from remote Nome and Fairbanks warmed up with an intensity astonishing to their southern brethren. The acrimonious regional clashes were made even hotter by bitter wrangling among individual delegates. In part this may explain why anti-Brady elements failed to roast Alaska's governor. Troy was shocked to hear that the convention had not demanded Brady's removal: "Gov. Brady has misrepresented the people of Alaska on every possible occasion. He has traduced them, slandered them, lied about them," and so on.[58]

After eight days of squabbling, the nonpartisan delegates patched together a memorial "to the people, the Congress, and the President of the United States." If their document is a reliable slice of Far North opinion, Brady's paramount emphasis on economic reform, rather than the political reform enunciated by Troy and Swineford, was what Alaska's upcoming leadership also desired. The Seattle memorial lists twelve measures, eight of them economic in nature (e.g., homesteads, transportation, postal facilities). Only three dealt with improving district administration, and these were aimed at judicial efficiency. On the matter of likely territorial zones, or a blueprint for a legislature, there was nothing at all. Troy had constantly chastised Brady for his "missionary instinct," for being a man for whom "the Indian has always had the preference." Yet here were these contentious "second-generation" pioneers memorializing Congress to put Alaska's aboriginals under the care of her governor.

Swineford, honored as permanent convention chairman, was one of three men selected to carry their memorial to Congress. Although touched by a five-minute ovation cheering his Great Land leadership, Swineford suffered a degree of embarrassment. Alaska's one-time governor, mining promoter, and editor had to ask his friends to pass the hat. A trip to Washington exceeded his financial resources.[59]

Jeannette P. Nichols has summed up the eight-day Seattle gathering as an "Alaska convulsion" whose "meetings were mutilated by personal, sectional, and political rivalries, with catastrophic results." In fact, the convention's lack of harmony was typically western, and the results were hardly catastrophic. The following month, as its three delegates traveled east to present their memorial to Congress, President Roosevelt addressed the men on Capitol Hill: "I earnestly ask that Alaska be given an elective delegate." Death having stilled Alaska nemesis Orville Platt, Congress finally granted the Great Land a delegate. In justifying the legislation, and probably without even realizing it, the House Committee on Territories both parroted and praised Brady: "There is a large and ever increasing body of the best kind of American citizens in Alaska, who have developed the country and made Alaska commercially great. . . . most of the relations with the Territory . . . fall in great measure upon the Governor who has been compelled to neglect his duties at home in the performance of more pressing and purely voluntary ones at Washington." As if to tease America's Far North province, the 1906 legislation declared "that the people of the *Territory of Alaska* shall be represented by a Delegate in the House of Representatives" who "shall be an inhabitant and qualified voter of the *district of Alaska*." As for the prospect of an actual territorial government, home rule remained an elusive dream. Swineford walked from the House weeping.[60]

Alaskans quickly picked two delegates, one for the short remaining term of the 59th Congress, the second for the regular term of the 60th. Neither bore the name Swineford, Brady, or Wickersham. The 1906 voting, Alaska's first territory-wide election, produced two other surprises. First, despite Brady's apprehensions at the efficacy of an election, Yankee common sense prevailed. Americans cast their ballots with relative smoothness, Alaska's dissected geography notwithstanding. Quite as unexpected, the two nominees who won did not represent Panhandle towns but came from continental Alaska, far to the north and west. Logrolling between shrewd miners clustered about Nome and those in the Fairbanks area had outpoliticked the cocky Skagway-Ketchikan aspirants. The Seward Peninsula men chose Frank H. Waskey, a youthful prospector. An older miner, Thomas Cale, originally from Wisconsin, was the Tanana area winner. Cale gained the long term.[61] Panhandle highflyers were dismayed, but none so totally as Swineford. His nomination and subsequent defeat proved a crushing blow. The previous year Swineford had been forced to sell the *Ketchikan Mining Journal*; two years later he was dead.

The year 1906 had signaled the start of formal territorial politics and had registered the all-time high in Alaska's gold production.[62] It also marked another climax: the collapse of the "Presbyterian hierarchy."

1. Quoted in *Daily Alaskan*, 15 April 1904.

2. JGB, undated entry in pocket memo book, 1902. Barker, *Compilation*, p. 110. Nichols, *Alaska*, p. 245.

3. President Theodore Roosevelt papers, Roosevelt to Brady (reappointment), 22 November 1904. JGB, mf. 2, Brady to Jackson, 6 July 1904.

4. Nichols, *Alaska*, p. 237. *Daily Alaskan*, 23 November and 2 December 1904. *Ketchikan Mining Journal*, 30 April 1904. *Daily Alaskan*, 15 May 1901; and 5 June, 19 July, 5 October and 23 November 1904.

5. JCorr, 19:253, Brady to Jackson, 16 October 1900. *Daily Alaskan*, 14 December 1904. In the second issue (12 January 1901) of his *Ketchikan Mining Journal*, Swineford explained his opposition to Governor Brady. Thereafter, as with Troy, his columns increasingly take on a sneering tone. The two men formed what inchoate opposition could be mounted against Brady (ibid., 19 January and 16 February 1901). Swineford's antipathy toward John was nothing in comparison to his contempt for Jackson, whom he denounced as "that distinguished and erudite publicist, bottle washer and cleaner of cuspidors" (ibid., 9 March 1901).

6. *Daily Alaskan*, 8,24, and 25 February 1905. JGB, mf. 2, Brady to Emmons, 20 April 1905; ibid., Brady to his wife, 16 January 1905. AGP, box 10, Hitchcock to Brady, 18 January 1905.

7. PTS, SJ letters, 15:161, Jackson to Roosevelt, 13 July 1904; ibid., 14:100, Jackson to Brady, 3 March 1904. JCorr, 21:61, Brady to Jackson, 11 June 1904. AGP, box 13, R. W. Kelly to Brady, 4 June 1901. JGB, mf. 2, Brady to Jackson, 16 July 1904; and ibid., Brady to his wife, 14 May and 10 June 1904.

8. *Ketchikan Mining Journal*, 25 May 1901. JCorr, 21:154, Elizabeth Brady to Jackson, 2 January 1905. PTS, SJ letters, 15:112, Jackson to Roosevelt, 19 October 1904, and ibid., 14:484, Carroll to Jackson, 23 August 1904. JGB, unfiled, Brady to Stuart Dodge, 18 April 1905.

9. Keeler, *Trip to Alaska*, p. 26. JCorr, 20:336, Brady to Jackson, 15 December 1903.

10. Delaney, *Alaska Bar Association*, pp. 33–46. *Alaskan*, 24 and 31 October 1903. Nichols, *Alaska*, pp. 216–19. *Ketchikan Mining Journal*, 7 and 14 November 1903.

11. *Alaskan*, 7 October 1903.

12. Hynding, *Life of Eugene Semple*, p. 75.

13. McLain, *Alaska and the Klondike*, p. 258. Brady, *Annual Report, 1905*, p. 6.

14. The "Correspondence of the Secretary of Alaska, 1900–1913" has now been microfilmed (National Archives, T 1201) and confirms that William L. Distin, who was also Alaska's surveyor general, did a capable job managing the routine bookkeeping and legal matters that funneled into Alaska's executive office at Sitka. Distin's two clerks, the receiver and the registrar, had their offices in Juneau (Brady, *Annual Report, 1902*, p. 70). On Distin see Atwood and DeArmond, *Who's Who in Alaskan Politics*, p. 24.

15. JGB, mf. 2, John Hay to Brady, 28 December 1901. Jordon, *Imperial Democracy*, pp. 192–93. AGP, box 12, Brady to Edwin Hofstead, 5 May 1905. *New Voice* (New York), 25 February 1899.

16. Owens, "Pattern and Structure," p. 164. PTS, SJ letters, 12:381, Jackson to Brady, 21 March 1903. Brady, *Annual Report, 1903*, p. 15.

17. James Wickersham, *Alaska: Its Resources, Present Condition and Needed Legislation* (Tacoma, 1902), pp. 12–13.

18. *Congressional Record*, 58th Cong., 2d sess., 18 April 1904, p. 4997.

19. McLain, *Alaska and the Klondike*, p. 260. Brady, *Annual Report, 1904*, p. 24. AGP, box 10, Philander Knox to Brady, 12 November 1902. *Alaskan*, 22 August 1903. Victor Westphall, *Thomas Benton Catron and His Era* (Tucson, 1973), pp. 327–29. Senator Beveridge's concern for the boreal territory had been but temporarily pushed aside (Claude G. Bowers, *Beveridge and the Progressive Era* [Cambridge, Mass., 1932], pp. 379–80; and John Braeman, *Albert J. Beveridge, American Nationalist* [Chicago, 1971], pp. 173 ff).

20. *Alaskan*, 30 January 1904. Senate, *Conditions in Alaska*, 58th Cong., 2d sess., Report No. 282, 12 January 1904. *Congressional Record*, 58th Cong., 2d sess., 18 April 1904, p. 4997.

21. Congressional Record, 58th Cong., 2d sess., 18 April 1904, pp. 26-ff, 94–98, 19; ibid., pp. 29–32. Ella Higginson, *Alaska: The Great Country* (New York, 1908), pp.

349–50. TAP, mf. 9, Brady to Hitchcock, 18 May 1903. Brady, *Annual Report, 1903*, pp. 48–49. Richardson, *Messages and Papers*, 15:6918–20. *Daily Alaskan*, 5 May and 20 July 1904.

22. AGP, box 11, Brady to Hitchcock, 21 April 1899. TAP, mf. 6, Brady to Hitchcock, 29 October 1899; ibid., mf. 9, Brady to Hitchcock, 18 May 1903. Brady, *Annual Report, 1904*, p. 13.

23. TAP, mf. 9, Brady to Wickersham, 8 September 1902; JGB, mf. 2, Wickersham to Brady, 4 June 1904. Wickersham, *Alaska* p. 2. Brady, *Annual Report, 1904*, pp. 5, 106–17. JGB, mf. 3, Brady to Roosevelt, ca. spring 1901. Ibid., mf. 4, Brady to Alice R. Crane, 10 April 1903; ibid., Brady to H. H. Hildreth, 4 September 1903.

24. TAP mf. 12, Wickersham to Hitchcock, 26 May 1905; ibid., Wickersham to Brady, 29 May 1905. JGB, mf. 3, Brady to Stanton J. Peelle, 27 January 1906. JWD, 30 May 1905. The full Wickersham letter first appeared in the *Seattle Post-Intelligencer*, 4 August 1905.

25. Despite his fine record, Judge Wickersham failed to obtain senatorial confirmation of his reappointment when his term ran out in June 1904. For three years he had to accept one-year presidential recess appointments. The Senate's failure to appreciate his accomplishments quite understandably disturbed him (Hunt, *North of 53°*, p. 283). Wickersham, *Old Yukon*, chap. 29. Senate, *Conditions in Alaska*, p. 105; *Alaskan*, 5 April 1902. Brady, *Annual Report, 1905*, p. 11. In 1892 Governor Knapp had suggested "Gatling gun from the deck of a transportation steamer" for the identical purpose (Lyman Knapp, *Annual Report of the Governor of Alaska, 1892* [Washington, D.C., 1892], p. 501).

26. Good accounts of this climax rush may be found in Andrews, *Story of Alaska*, chap. 33; Hunt *North of 53°*, pp. 136–76; Wharton, *Alaska Gold Rush*, chap. 12. *Seattle Post-Intelligencer*, 8 January 1905. Gruening, *State of Alaska*, p. 125.

27. *Alaskan*, 18 February 1905. AGP, box 13, Edward J. Stier to Brady, 6 November 1905. Brady, *Annual Report, 1905*, p. 5.

28. Brady, *Annual Report, 1904*, p. 36. Idem, *Annual Report, 1897*, p. 206. JGB, pocket memo book, entry for 28 July 1900. Thomas G. Smith, "The Treatment of the Mentally Ill in Alaska, 1884–1912," *Pacific Northwest Quarterly* 65 (January 1974): 22.

29. Barker, *Compilation*, p. 65. AGP, box 6, Brady to C. L. Vawter, 4 September 1900. Brady, *Annual Report, 1900*, pp. 42–44; and idem, *Annual Report, 1901*, p. 53. AGP, box 15, Ryan to Brady, 10 January 1903; ibid., box 10, Hitchcock to Brady, 19 November 1903; ibid., 25 February 1905. Brady, *Annual Report, 1905*, p. 12; and Hitchcock, *Annual Report, 1905*, p. 98. AGP, box 12, Brady to F. D. Whipp, 6 November 1905; Brady, *Annual Report, 1901*, pp. 48–49.

30. AGP, box 10, marine commander to U.S. district attorney, Sitka, 15 September 1899; ibid., J. K. Richards to Brady, 24 November 1899. Ibid., box 12, Clinot to Brady, 14 September 1903; ibid., Brady to Roosevelt, 13 October 1903; ibid., Brady to Dave Clinot, 24 March 1894.

31. AGP, box 13, Robert A. Lindsmith to Brady, 5 February 1901; ibid., box 11, Brady to Roosevelt, 6 August 1901. JGB, unfiled, Brady to Roosevelt, 18 April 1902.

32. AGP, box 11, Robert Friedrich to Brady, 30 August 1901; ibid., box 10, Brady to Philander Knox, 8 February 1900. *Alaskan*, 22 November 1902.

33. State Superior Court House, Sitka, Criminal Journal, vol. 4, 20 August 1903. JGB, mf. 4, Brady to W. D. Grant, 3 October 1902; ibid., mf. 2, John G. Heid to Brady, 26 January 1900.

34. Austin, *Commercial Alaska*, p. 4029. AGP, box 12, Brady to John G. Jones, 6 July 1905; ibid., Brady to A. Wilson, 22 December 1905.

35. AGP, box 11, Brady to Mrs. J. P. Crowley, 19 July 1900. Ibid., Brady to E. P. Marvin, 20 November 1901. TAP, mfs. 6–12, contains numerous samples of these sad missives.

36. AGP, box 10, James R. Garfield to Brady, 13 July 1903. TAP, mf. 12, Brady to Hitchcock, 18 May 1905; ibid., J. B. Loomis (acting secretary of state) to Hitchcock, 6 September 1905; AGP, box 12, Brady to Leslie M. Shaw, 28 January 1903; TAP, mf. 9, Brady to Hitchcock, 8 September 1902; AGP, box 10, Lyman J. Gage to Brady, 21 August 1900. Ibid., Brady to various towns, 22 September 1905.

37. *New York Times*, 24 November 1899. Brady, *Annual Report, 1899*, p. 47.

38. Kinkead, *Annual Report, 1884*, p. 641; Richardson, *Messages and Papers*, 12:5485. *Alaska-Yukon Mining Journal*, February 1901, p. 23. Brady, *Annual Report, 1905*, p. 4.

39. *Daily Alaskan*, 15 May 1902 and 23 June 1904. Brady, *Annual Report, 1901*, p. 8; and idem, *Annual Report, 1903*, pp. 8, 9. U.S., Congress, Senate, *Memorial by the Seattle Chamber of Commerce, Praying for the Establishment of a Territorial Form of Government over the Territory of Alaska*, 3 March 1891, 51st Cong., 2d sess., Misc. Doc. No. 93. JGB, mf. 1, *Seattle Daily Times*, 27 August 1902.

40. JGB, mf. 4, Brady to Joseph T. Gilbert, 13 October 1903. Brady, *Annual Report, 1902*, p. 18.

41. Brady, *Annual Report, 1900*, p. 44. McLain, *Alaska and the Klondike*, p. 350.

42. McLain, *Alaska and the Klondike*, pp. 17–18. JGB, mf. 4, Brady to Smith, 10 July 1903.

43. *Alaskan*, 11 December 1897; Brady, *Annual Report, 1905*, p. 5. Idem, *Annual Report, 1903*, pp. 8–9. JGB, unfiled, Brady to Charles S. Wiley, 15 January 1906. G. M. Irwin estimated these seasonal "birds of passage" to run between twenty and seventy thousand ("The Political Aspect of Alaska," *Alaskan Monthly*, May 1906, p. 2).

44. Brady, *Annual Report, 1905*, p. 8. Quoted in *Daily Alaskan*, 10 January 1903; 19 and 24 December 1904; and 25 February 1905.

45. JGB, mf. 2, Brady to his wife, 11 January 1905. U.S., Congress, Senate, *Alaska Government Board*, 58th Cong., 3d sess., Doc. No. 110, 21 January 1905.

46. *Daily Alaskan*, 27 February 1905; Brady, *Annual Report, 1903*, p. 9. Senate, *Conditions in Alaska*, p. 21. *Seattle Post-Intelligencer*, 5 July 1905.

47. Senate, *Conditions in Alaska*, p. 30.

48. *Daily Alaskan*, 13 July 1904. Richardson, *Messages and Papers*, 15:7020. Those who grieve over Alaska's neglectful delay in getting territorial status should consider the concurrent case of Arizona (Howard Roberts Lamar, *The Far Southwest, 1877–1900: A Territorial History* [New York, 1970], chap. 19).

49. Louise A. Coolidge, *An Old-Fashioned Senator: Orville H. Platt of Connecticut* (New York, 1910), p. 310. Brady, *Annual Report, 1904*, pp. 3–4.

50. Hitchcock, *Annual Report, 1905*, p. 102. Gruening, *State of Alaska*, pp. 144–45.

51. U.S., Congress, House, *Civil Government for Alaska*, 47th Cong., 1st sess., Report No. 1106, 11 May 1882; *Alaskan*, 6 September 1890. *Juneau Mining Record*, 17 June 1896. *Portland Oregonian*, 23 May 1900. Brady, *Annual Report, 1900*, p. 45. *Congressional Record*, 56th Cong., 1st sess., 24 May 1900, p. 5973; ibid., 58th Cong., 2d sess., 6 April 1904, p. 4395.

52. Pomeroy, *Territories and the United States*, chap. 8, and Clark C. Spence, "Beggars to Washington: Montana's Territorial Delegates," *Montana Magazine of Western History* 24 (January 1974): 4. Brady, *Annual Report, 1902*, p. 16.

53. Brooks, *Blazing*, p. 515. *Congressional Record*, 58th Cong., 2d sess., 6 April 1904, p. 4401. JWD, 28 February 1903. Senate, *Conditions in Alaska*, p. 125.

54. TAP, mf. 9, Brady to Hitchcock, 9 April 1903. *Ketchikan Mining Journal*, 6 December 1902. JGB, mf. 4, Brady to Hoggatt, 26 May 1903. The court had declared that "Alaska is one of the Territories of the United States." Constitutional expert Max Farrand warned, however, that "this assertion was made solely with reference to the

similarity of the judicial courts of Alaska to other territorial courts" and in no way invalidated the existing distinction made between a district and a territory ("Territory and District," *American Historical Review* 5 [July 1900]: 680). TAP, mf. 9, Brady to Hitchcock, 11 April 1903.

55. Nichols, *Alaska*, p. 246.

56. Brady, *Annual Report, 1905*, p. 7. *Portland Oregonian*, 23 May 1900; Brady, *Annual Report, 1901*, p. 13; and idem, *Annual Report, 1903*, pp. 10, 69; Hitchcock, *Annual Report, 1905*, p. 102.

57. Quoted in *Daily Alaskan*, 14 December 1905.

58. Joseph K. Smith, "Our Delegates to Congress," *Alaska's Magazine*, January 1906, p. 71. Both the *Seattle Daily Times* and the *Post-Intelligencer*, as well as the *Daily Alaskan*, followed the convention quite closely (*Daily Alaskan*, 17 November 1905).

59. *Daily Alaskan*, 2 May and 21 December 1904; ibid., 1 and 6 December 1905. The entire memorial appears in *Congressional Record*, 59th Cong., 1st sess., 22 January 1906, p. 1343.

60. Nichols, *Alaska*, p. 257. *Daily Alaskan*, 11 November and 6 December 1905. Richardson, *Messages and Papers*, 15:7019. *Seattle Post-Intelligencer*, 23 February 1906. Spicer, *Constitutional Status*, pp. 70–71, 25. *Daily Alaskan*, 3 March 1906.

61. Pat McCollom, "Alaska's First Delegates: Waskey and Cale," *Alaska Journal* 3 (Winter 1973): 50–55.

62. *Seattle Post-Intelligencer*, 11 and 12 January and 6 May 1906. *Ketchikan Mining Journal*, 31 March 1905. Alfred H. Brooks, *Mineral Resources of Alaska: Report on Progress of Investigations in 1911* (Washington, D.C., 1911), p. 21. *Marquette Daily Mining Journal*, 27 October 1909.

CHAPTER SIXTEEN

The Go-Getter Virus

The era from the end of the Civil War through the opening decades of the twentieth century witnessed an unparalleled expansion of American business. Economic historian Thomas C. Cochran believes nineteenth-century American culture "to have been one of the most favorable in world history for entrepreneurial activity"; social historian Daniel J. Boorstin styles the age as "the halcyon days of the Go-Getters."[1] John Brady's life amply demonstrates how pervasive, how unequivocal was this "go-ahead spirit."

From his Hoosier boyhood through the completion of his ministerial training, John Brady had been repeatedly counseled on the paradoxical power of wealth. To worship money was among the worst of idolatries. Yet a lack of money bespoke slothful, improvident living. Like millions of his countrymen, John had been infected by the go-getter virus for over half a century. Once he had cut his filial bonds with judge John Green and entered Yale, it multiplied dramatically. When the missionary turned merchant, the virus that had transformed a continent possessed him. Fortunately another boyhood homily, "Tell the truth," counteracted the bacteria's most noxious strain. This latter explains in part John's antipathy for the rhetorical excesses of certain Panhandle boomers. Nevertheless, the plunger's disease came close to ruining him.

How much simpler it had been for the bachelor clergyman to pursue a mendicant life-style in 1878 than it was for Alaska's governor, supporting a wife and family, to do so a quarter century later. Elizabeth, his five children, and his own expanded desires—indeed, the astonishing dynamism of his contemporaries—all generated Brady's acquisitive instincts. He was determined that his daughters as well as his sons acquire an eastern college education and that he and Elizabeth maintain a

316

respectable living and eventually a comfortable retirement. Grandfather Patton remained Satchahnee's foreman, minding its fruitful gardens and tending its stock, yet the old man's days were running out. John envisioned that in the not too distant future one of his own children might assume the direction of his Sitka properties.[2]

The distinction between a public-spirited citizen and a reckless promoter may not be quickly discernible, for just as an industrious, civic-minded person bespeaks a spirit of community confidence, so does a mercurial boomer. Furthermore, both citizens may germinate from the same seed, for in serving others, pride and greed insidiously magnify the self. Doubtless John and Elizabeth, as churchgoing, daily Bible-reading Christians, understood this timeless threat. If they did, it only furthered their practical devotion to their fellow Alaskans.

Within his hometown John promoted one worthwhile cause after another: a refurbished Lincoln Street sidewalk, a new chemical fire engine, a public subscription for cemetery improvement, a flagpole for Public School No. 1, and so on. Often these activities required that he speak publicly and sometimes forcefully before his friends and neighbors. First as Judge Brady and later as Governor Brady, he frequently addressed Sitka's summer visitors.[3] But now, instead of describing just Sitka's needs, he broadened his horizon to encompass all of Alaska's. At the annual national holiday celebrations his elocution took on effusive colorations; occasionally the governor's Calvinist predilections peeked out, as in the following, drawn from what was probably an Independence Day oration: "If the noted men who are at the head of the corporate enterprises and who for the most part congregate and or are represented in Wall Street, the pulsating financial heart of this continent, will only realize that all men are created equal, and that they are endowed by their Creator with certain unalienable rights; that among these are life, liberty, and the pursuit of happiness and conduct themselves and their great affairs accordingly all will be well, but if they do not and sneer at these broad principles of common equality a day of fearful reckoning will surely come." But John's faith in the republic was solid enough. It could hardly be otherwise for one who epitomized the "rags to riches," legend: "I for one do not believe that Andrew Carnegie, J. P. Morgan, J. J. Hill, E. H. Harriman and many others like them who are leaders and Captains in our great industries . . . are out of sympathy with these fundamental ideas. . . . Nay the large majority of these men have like our Presidents arisen from the humblest class of our citizens. They themselves are shining examples of the goodness of the system of laws under which they have been born and bred.[4]"

View from Sitka Commons (opposite view on p. 177). Sitkans celebrate the first Fourth of July in the new century. (Reproduced by permission of the Beinecke Rare Book and Manuscript Library, Yale University.)

John was fascinated by his adopted land's dazzling natural spectacles, its history, and its incalculable future prospects. All three stimulated his curiosity and thus exercised his habit of self-education. Like his mentor, Sheldon Jackson, he tried to peruse everything available on Alaska. Also like Jackson, John desired that all Alaskans appreciate their commonwealth's greatness. He encouraged this attitude by his energetic support of Sitka's Alaskan Society of Natural History and Ethnology, and especially by his commitment to the creation of a district library.[5]

Brady's official papers are laced with correspondence detailing aspects of the embryo district library. Unquestionably it was a labor of love. The 1900 Alaska civil code had instituted a library fund for a "district Historical Library and Museum." John made the most of this provision. In addition to the better known territorial newspapers, the library subscribed to such recently sprouted publications as the *Council City News, Valdez News, Seward Gateway, Alaska Sentinel, Alaska Transcript, Rampart Miner*, and the *Nome Weekly News*. Books were obtained from dozens of sources, among which were Seattle's Shorey Book Store, the Arthur Clark Company, state historical societies, and, most important of all, the Government Printing Office.[6] In 1901 he informed Jackson that "over four thousand volumes came from the Superintendent of Public Documents." John Wesley Powell, director of the Smithsonian's Bureau of American Ethnology, did what he could to supply back numbers of his bureau's annual reports. One afternoon, at the conclusion of a visit to the secretary of the navy, Secretary Long introduced Brady to Andrew Carnegie: "The Secretary jokingly remarked that the Governor would be wanting a library out in Alaska and I said yes—for this morning I have been buying a lot of books at an auction sale to take back to Alaska." Carnegie smiled and replied, "I will pay for them."[7]

John was relieved to let the Sheldon Jackson Museum handle the bulk of the memorabilia and artifacts. Indeed, for a few years this octagonal building stored the influx of printed matter, the expediency of which the governor's critics quickly condemned. A momentary setback occurred when the Treasury Department rejected John's request for the land where the historic Russian "Clubhouse" had previously stood. He and Elizabeth had hoped to construct a small town "library and reading room," a successor to the improvised Free Reading Room established some years before by the Patton sisters. After much correspondence and three years' delay, the government granted him a vault and some rooms on the second floor of the Custom House. It was not a moment too soon. John had recently acquired a number of rare books and assigned the venerable Sitkan Leo Nabokoff to translating valuable Russian documents. Charles Demmert, a native carpenter, probably constructed the district library shelves, and it may have been Elizabeth who hung the portraits of Peter the Great and Governor John Kinkead.[8]

Just as Governor Brady followed Jackson's lead in educating himself and his neighbors on their North Pacific homeland, so did he emulate Jackson's wide-ranging public relations campaign. From Washington to Chicago to California, John's magazine articles, his printed interviews with newsmen, and his spoken words reached tens of thousands of his countrymen. Detractors might refer to his annual reports as "senseless twaddle" and "incompetent vaporings," but an examination of them reveals quite the opposite. They are a storehouse of information on Alaska's commerce, inhabitants, natural resources, and much else. However, his critics were correct in their imputations that these documents were not solely factual compilations. Alaska's governor exhorted his general readers, admonished Congress, and ceaselessly praised his homeland's munificent prospects. As he presciently stated in the final paragraph of his last annual report: "The great returns from mines and fisheries go beyond our reach."[9]

John's respect for the truth checked him from excess bunkum. Nevertheless, his vibrant enthusiasm for the Great Land, a region so suddenly inflated by not one but a series of mining rushes, made exaggeration inevitable. And although he did not embrace Mark Twain's advice that truth should never be permitted to ruin a good story, John's Alaska opinions, especially those that fell from his mouth before a rapt eastern audience, revealed traces of Irish blarney. On one occasion Brady's son John, was among the deck passengers of the *Cottage City* being regaled by his father. As they passed a particular native village, Brady pointed out a well-wooded extension of the shoreline, recalling how the Tlingits of that region had succeeded in tying the tail of a sick whale to one of the trees. Then, unable to kill the leviathan, they drove a stake down the creature's blowhole. This done, Brady concluded, "the whale promptly drowned." This proved too much for the governor's eldest, who piped up, "And that's one I *never* heard before."

One might think that the only thing more dangerous than one boomer is two, puffing up each other's pipe dreams. But to set loose one boomer in Alaska may be even more dangerous. "Speaking of liars," a contemporary Valdez-to-Fairbanks traveler recalled, Alaska "held the per capita world record for liars. I do not know what the White population was. . . . whatever it was, that was the exact number of white liars running at large within the confines of the Territory." Far removed from the post-Klondike frenzies to the northwest, Sitka's populace was less ex-

320

posed to such hyperbolic contagion. "We feel," declared Brady, "that each [visitor to Alaska] when he or she returns home will be a sort of advertising agency to tell people something of the wonders of Alaska." And to ensure that this traffic did not wane, Jackson and Brady co-ordinated group tours to the Great Land. In 1899 they arranged to have the passenger steamer *City of Seattle* transport a synodical meeting through the Inside Passage. Brady chuckled with satisfaction after "the businessmen of Seattle, catching the spirit of the times, chartered the same steamship and sent her here with a large part of her leading merchants and prominent citizens."[10]

Some out-of-context Bradyisms, written to grab attention, will reveal how felicitous his role as Alaska's advocate was. Before New York's Chamber of Commerce he stated, "I have lived there twenty-two years, and I would rather live in Alaska than in New York State. I can live more healthfully and can obtain more good food for the amount of effort I put forth to obtain it than anywhere else." In a Chamber of Commerce pamphlet entitled *Facts of Alaska* Brady wrote, "The great river valleys like the Yukon, Tanana and Copper rivers embrace cultivatable areas large enough for four good sized states." From a Brady article in the *Chautauquan* one learns: "The placers of the Yukon and its tributaries and upon the headwaters of Cook's Inlet promise richer rewards than the fleece of which Jason dreamed." A prospectus for the Alaska Central Railway quotes him: "The climate of Southern and Central Alaska, as far north as the Yukon River, is better than the climate of Iowa." And in his final annual report he prophesied, "In twenty-five years Alaska will have a population of more than 1,00,000 developing mines, catching fish, and cutting timber."[11]

It is a heady experience to have senators and corporate magnates come to one's domicile in a distant land and return to the mother country echoing one's words. On the Senate floor Knute Nelson sometimes sounded exactly like John Brady: "In legislating for Alaska we are not legislating for a foreign race as in the case of the Philippine Islands, Hawaii, or Porto Rico. We are legislating for our own race and our own people, who have gone up there to build that country." The Minnesotan anticipated the time "when my children will see the day—when Alaska will have over a million thrifty, industrious and prosperous people. There is no end of gold all over that country. All that is needed to secure it is transportation." Congressman Dudley G. Wooten of Texas agreed: "The country has been neglected and misunderstood, its conditions have been misrepresented and disparaged. . . . An American railroad should be at once built on American territory opening up the great lower Yukon from Eagle City to St. Michael's." Appearing in

Seattle in 1903, President Theodore Roosevelt hyperbolized, "The men of my age who are in this great audience will not be old men before they see one of the greatest and most populous States of the entire Union in Alaska."[12]

Wherever Alaska's stocky, bewhiskered governor went, he was synonymous with the Great Land. Quite as understandable and just as flattering was the respect accorded his opinions. Senator Nelson arranged for him to address a group of University of Minnesota students; afterward John confidently predicted, "I shall be surprised if quite a number of that audience do not make their home in this country." The National Geographic Society and the American Academy of Political and Social Science were pleased to solicit his membership. Gratified at an honorary vice-presidency in the National Good Roads Association, John reminded its president: "Nothing will help Alaska so much as good wagon roads and railroads." Among the Yale alumni and their influential associations, he was "Mr. Alaska," no less than Sheldon Jackson had long since become "Mr. Alaska" among Presbyterians. This identification served their purposes and directly benefited Alaska.[13]

It was unavoidable that Governor Brady would be approached repeatedly by other businessmen weighing the merits of a Far North investment. The May 1900 banquet at the Waldorf Astoria, for example, served as more than a setting for presenting him with a bust of William Seward. Nor was there anything sinister or even wrong about the advances of these enterpreneurs: politicians are supposed to lure capital to their specific region. The same year as the Waldorf feast, Yale men honored him at New York's Union League Club. Of course, discussion of northland financial opportunities was interspersed among recollections of Yale days and talk of the current eleven's gridiron performance. In a personal letter written a couple of months later, John commented, "I know well what is here [in Alaska] and what can be done, but I have been hampered for capital. I once wrote a classmate of mine . . . asking him to make some investments here but he wrote back that he felt like the Indian . . . named 'Young Man Afraid of his Horses.'" Others were not so afraid of John's horses and Alaska's allure. One classmate, Nathan Edward Beckwith, first town engineer and local developer of Los Gatos, California, came north to investigate Alaska prospects. After several stints of working as a surveyor around Alexander Archipelago towns, Beckwith, like most such youths, returned to the states.[14]

At the outset Brady's gubernatorial duties had not seriously interfered with the profitable hum of his Sitka Sawmill Company's fifty-horse-power Corliss engine. The Skagway-Dyea construction boom provided a vigorous market. After 1900 Juneau's continued growth, as well as steady cannery sales took up the slack from Skagway's sagging economy. A 1903 visitor at the Sitka Sawmill Company heard that "the larger part of the lumber produced is now going into the manufacture of salmon boxes in southern Alaska." On occasion, John found himself middleman supplier for Panhandle customers, distributing products such as Puget Sound shingles and diverse building materials. Nevertheless, the pressing demands of Alaska's governorship meant that his commercial affairs received less and less attention. He worried that his "always small potatoes company" might fold.[15]

The Bradys were no doubt reminded just how insignificant their Sitka enterprise was by a summer 1899 visitor. That June one of the colossuses of American business, Edward H. Harriman, was their momentary guest. Hailed as a "scientific expedition," Harriman's cruise, on the steamer *George W. Elder*, included not only his family but possibly a larger number of distinguished savants than a single vessel had ever delivered to Sitka before or since. John Muir, William H. Dall, John Burroughs, Henry Gannett, B. E. Fernow, and George Bird Grinnell were among those entertained at the reception hosted by Governor Brady and his lady. Indian musicians from Sitka's Boys Band—those not absent at summer cannery jobs—mixed their Souza-cadenced greeting with native chants.[16] The photographer Edward S. Curtis came along to record the Harriman expedition on film. "Thlingit, Hydah and Tsimshean dancing songs and also a speech in each of these tongues" were captured by a large gramophone. "Mr. Harriman has the whole movement well in hand," John assured his Interior Department chief. "There is no friction and each fellow is working industriously." Apparently Harriman decided that for the present, steamships, not steam locomotives, were what Alaska required. But the transportation titan had sensed the Far North's crucial oil and coal potential. A few years later Governor Brady briefly assisted John B. Treadwell of California, who, as Harriman's agent, had briefly journeyed north "to examine the oil and coal fields of Alaska."

After four days the *Elder*, with Harriman's expedition, weighed anchor and continued northward. Reflecting later on the experience, the naturalist John Burroughs wrote, "People actually live in Sitka from choice, and seem to find life sweet. There are homes of culture and refinement there. Governor Brady is a Yale graduate, and his accomplished wife would shine in any society."[17] Sitka's press confirmed that the Bradys needed but the slightest excuse to host a party for their friends and neighbors. No wines or liquors were ever served. But this never lessened John's and Elizabeth's enthusiasm for squeezing townfolk into Satchahnee (or as often into the "Governor's Mansion" facing Sitka's Common) for their innumerable receptions honoring visiting dignitaries. This was no perfunctory duty. Nor need one be a touring dignitary for the Bradys to unroll their welcome mat. Seeking to borrow the derelect *Leo*'s anchor, some inconspicuous travelers called at the governor's residence. They "found His Excellency dressed in a blue suit of overalls and shoveling snow from a pile of lumber. This rather surprised me, for I had not thought of that as a dignified dress or seemly exercise for the Governor of so great a Territory." Surprise turned to gratitude when the overall-clad public servant "not only consented to loan us an anchor, but actually went along himself and helped us remove it to the ship which was no small undertaking."[18]

Governor Brady had persistently sought improved mail and cable links with America's West Coast. His efforts were hardly necessary. Commercial demands from Alaska's avaricious boom towns, the elementary requirements of maintaining public order and national defense, and, above all, outcries from the northland as well as from the conterminous United States seeking prompter postal deliveries—all combined to assure that the Great Land would quickly benefit from the latest in communication technology. As late as 1896 carrier pigeons had been advocated to overcome Alaska's awesome distances. In less than a decade a submarine cable united her Panhandle cities with Seattle, while Alaska's far-flung population centers were being knit together by telegraph wire. In his annual reports John lauded the "heroic accomplishments" of the Army Signal Corps under Major General A. W. Greely. The "Marconi system," which had seemed a fantasy only a few years earlier, became a reality. By 1905 General Greely boasted that on Alaska's Bering coast "the signal corps is today operating the longest successful wireless system in the world."[19]

Journalists noted that across Alaska "the telegraph has far out-distanced the iron horse." Half-century-old Americans could recall that during their youth electricity had also bested steam in connecting the East with the West Coast. Whereas it was inexpensive to lay and maintain a copper wire it was terribly costly to install and operate hundreds of miles of steel rails and rolling stock. But the colorful post–Civil War transcontinental railroads *had* repeatedly hurdled the frontier line. Understandably, then, Americans "knew in their bones" that, despite Alaska's slow population growth and cruel climatic handicaps, the railroad must ultimately come north—as railroaders like Charles Francis Adams and Leland Stanford had predicted well before the Klondike madness. At least until the 1893 depression, talk of a "Chicago to Paris through run" was common.[20]

The rush to Dawson City had given birth to the White Pass and Yukon Railroad. To be sure, the district's first genuine rail line was not Yankee owned and operated, but it was "a paying proposition." Furthermore, the railroad from Skagway to White Horse seemed to prove that snow, ice, and towering mountain barriers need not deter other like-minded men from "opening up Alaska." The WPYR was "a great undertaking in railroad construction," Brady exulted. Promoters agreed with him. By March of 1899 eleven companies had filed for railroad rights-of-way, terminals, and the nearby timber and stone needed for tracklaying.[21] After 1900 an increasing amount of John's official correspondence came from the owners of Alaska's budding lines. The Council City & Solomon River Railroad's general manager, J. Warren Dickson of Seattle, sent Brady a map of "the first standard gauge railroad to be built and operated in Alaska." Its owners modestly claimed that the railroad to be located in the Nome area, would open up "the richest mining section in the world." Congressman Wooten extolled the Yukon Valley's placer and quartz mines and "vast cattle ranges and agricultural lands," and urged that "the interior of Alaska [be] afforded a cheap, speedy and honest line of travel." He was confident that "all of this can be accomplished at comparatively small cost."[22]

Fortunately a number of Wooten's House colleagues knew better. In fact, Congress's original 14 May 1898 legislation authorizing Alaska railroad construction had placed rigorous restrictions on any Far North investors. At the outset of his governorship, John had envisioned wagon roads as the immediate solution to Alaska's lack of land transportation. By 1901 his mind had switched track: "Transportation companies are beginning to realize that what Alaska needs is a large population. . . . Railway capitalists would like to see what the drift of population will be before they make heavy ventures. Congress can aid such enterprises best by making it easy for the great multitudes of plain ordinary people who are ready and anxious to emigrate. If this is done it will not be many years before Alaska in its great valleys will be served with railways."[23] Alaska did get its homestead legislation, but all the inducements—both verbal and eatable—supplied by Brady, Georgeson, and numerous other publicists notwithstanding, the "multitudes of plain ordinary people" did not emigrate northward. Brady, probably without ever realizing it, then turned his argument upside down. His 1903 annual report began:

> Our railroads have accomplished wonders for us. Congress can do no better thing for Alaska just now than to encourage the construction of railroads across it. . . . We know enough now of the Yukon Valley and the whole region which lies between it and the sea, to assure the unbe-

lieving and doubtful that it is rich in precious metals, oil, coal, fish and is blessed with a salubrious climate. . . . The days of the ox teams and prairie schooners are past, but the desire and necessity for new homes abide. The people will follow up the lines which will give them access to the great valleys.[24]

The booming developments around the Fairbanks region can only have stimulated John's vision of a railroad, or railroads, prying open Alaska's heartland. He no doubt wondered where on the Gulf of Alaska the Great Land's future San Francisco or Seattle would be located, that bustling coastal emporium serving her continental frontier. Having successfully completed his governorship, might he not hope to achieve financial security as a corporate leader helping write this new, dynamic chapter in Alaskan history? For the present, however, his public duties had to come first.

By 1900 Governor Brady's extended sojourns in the nation's capital forced a slowdown at the Sitka mill. Hard pressed for funds, he twice attempted to lease out his equipment on a profit-sharing basis. For whatever reasons, he was unsuccessful. The following year John's output of wood products ranked at the bottom among the archipelago mills. Although his governor's salary, later raised to $416 a month, enabled the thrift-conscious Bradys to live comfortably, John never forgot that this income was sustained by unpredictable political winds.[25] Moreover, his children would not long remain at home to feed Satchahnee's chickens, pull its weeds, and milk the cows. Instead of producers, they would become costly college consumers. Fortunately, Elizabeth's stopgap management kept the Sitka mill from shutting down. Her sons later credited her with being "the business agent of the family." Clearly she could be tightfisted if the occasion demanded it. Once a small-scale mining company down the coast at Rodman Bay failed to return the Bradys' seventy-by-thirty-foot scow, or even to pay for the lumber the vessel had delivered. Finally, after some months, an incensed Elizabeth compelled a reluctant Judge De Groff to do his duty. The miners paid up. When they pleaded an inability to return the scow for lack of a tug to pull it, Elizabeth had no compunctions about calling on the Revenue Marine cutter *Perry* to tow it to Sitka.[26]

Far more vexatious to the Bradys was their dispute with two Sitka lumbermen and merchants, W. R. and W. P. Mills. Both Brady and his competitors possessed healthy markets. Periodically the Sitka Sawmill Company and the Mills firm had cooperated in supplying their respective customers. Nevertheless, in 1901 a nasty dispute erupted between them. What made the matter particularly awkward for Alaska's governor was that the quarrel once again involved the Ranche's senior citizens. From its inception the Brady mill had been dependent on native labor. After 1897 John more than ever had to rely on mission-trained millhands. In return for their dependability, John furnished them special building material rates in order that they might erect their own houses— what a few Tlingits still referred to as "Boston man houses." But if these mission Indians comfortably accepted absorption into a white man's society, a number of the Ranche inhabitants did not. Some still resented Brady's digging up their sacred ground.

Actually, since 1894 the Ranche inhabitants had enjoyed a degree of revenge. Only after protracted labor had John been able to widen the footpath connecting his Satchahnee enterprises into a road capable of handling a lumber wagon. By 1894 he had extended this wagon road from his mill to the boundary of the Indian village; his goal was Sitka's main wharf downtown. At this juncture the Ranche inhabitants refused to cooperate, and for almost five years Brady had to resort to rafting his wares to town at low tide along the inner harbor. What sardonic satisfaction this spectacle must have afforded the village elders. Imagine Alaska's governor forced to play out his winch line, heave it in, play it out and heave it in, laboriously kedging his cumbersome lumber along their village shorefront.[27]

The Brady family was convinced that W. P. and W. R. Mills had put the Indians up to this. Unquestionably the Mills firm had sold the Ranche Indians the lumber with which the Tlingits constructed their side-lock gate that further delayed the Satchahnee-to-Sitka wagon road. By 1900 the governor had gained land access to town, thanks to the aid of local penal labor supervised by Colonel Kostrometinoff. The Mills men, again allying themselves with certain Ranche elders, then tried to cripple Brady's business by legal action. The plaintiffs insisted that John's mill flume, which drew water from Swan Lake, plus his farm's demands were crippling their own power source. In January of 1902 the case got on the Juneau docket. Disputant W. R. Mills and John Brady boarded the *Cottage City* together, and once ashore at Juneau, both checked into the Occidental Hotel. Before the court even convened, they had resolved their dispute.

Brady was determined somehow to improve his low 1901 lumber output. However, Jackson questioned why Alaska's governor could not expend additional weeks lobbying in the nation's capital. "If my services are needed and I am ordered," John replied, "I shall gladly go and do what I can but it will not be a hardship to remain quietly at home in Sitka and look a little after my own affairs which have been too much neglected." Predictably, when John found himself on the Atlantic coast, he received letters from Elizabeth chiding him about how sorely the

327

family needed him. "It would be nice," she mused, "for us to have enough so we could do about going and coming as we like if the Lord is willing." Visits to Juneau left John with mixed feelings. Not only did the vast, roaring Treadwell complex shout forth "greatest in the world," but his 1880s store clerk had long since outpaced him. From virtually a penniless pioneer, B. M. Behrends had risen to become Alaska's most prominent banker and merchant, a businessman who boasted connections from Skagway to San Francisco to New York. Now it was banker Behrends who could patronize John's small business.[29]

Hardly a week passed that an investor's agent or engineer did not come north to scout out Alaska's coal, copper, and oil offerings. The actual extent of these minerals could only be estimated. Word that Standard Oil Company representatives were nosing along the Gulf coast induced speculation from Alaska's press. Although not oblivious to the threat of Standard Oil bullying, John wrote the governor of Texas: "We feel here that capital must be encouraged by allowing it to combine under suitable laws for it requires such to undertake the development of our resources." "The Secret of American Success" was how the *Alaska-Yukon Mining Journal* headlined a story on Standard's petroleum preeminence.[30]

Proof that Great Land prospects had won the attention of East as well as West Coast capitalists was ubiquitous. Of the twelve directors heading the North-American Mining and Development Company, only two were Alaskans; the others hailed from New York and Boston. During stopovers en route to Washington, Governor Brady often caught an avaricious glint in the eyes of businessmen as he warmed to his favorite topic. By 1903 he could rejoice that "many Seattle people have . . . large interests in different parts of Alaska." Ogling tourists, impressed by the Douglas Island din, heard that not Americans but Englishmen— the Rothschilds of London—now owned the Treadwell colossus. Indeed, the possibility loomed that English oilmen, not Texans, might pump out Alaska's oil revenues.[31]

John found more and more of his evening reading devoted to mineral matters. Here was where the fortunes were being made and even larger sums awaited to be won. His 1902 correspondence reveals a renewed interest in challenging once again Vulcan's tightfistedness. Writing of the nearby Silver Bay diggings, John commented knowledgeably:

I believe you are pursuing the right course namely developing your mine. It is well to develop thoroughly before spending money for patent, mills, or anything else that can be avoided. Just keep sinking holes to open up ore bodies which can be measured and calculated with mathematical certainty what you should do in the way of putting up a reduction works.

... In developing it is a question whether it is safer to sink on the ore
body and hoist and run drifts at certain levels or risk a long tunnel in
country rock to cut the ledge at great depth. Sinking and hoisting is no
doubt a safe way but most expensive.[32]

In 1901 Alfred H. Brooks of the U.S. Geological Survey inquired about
John's previous and unsuccessful coal-mining venture. "My partner and
I sank a shaft on Sullivan Point [southern part of Admiralty Island],
128 feet," Brady replied. "We obtained a very good grade of coal. I
brought 13 sacks of it to Sitka and found that it cooked well. . . . But
the vein was not large enough and we abandoned it for the time being."
Pleased at Brooks's 1903 appointment as Alaska chief for the USGS,
Brady asked Secretary Hitchcock for a resident mining commissioner.

John's initial interest in Alaskan mining seems to have resulted from
a marketing search for his sawmill's output. It is not difficult to grasp
John's preference for cutting sweet-smelling wood to grubbing in a
sunless, foul-smelling mine shaft. Certainly the lumbering industry was
considerably freer from the stink of commercial odium. Across the
West, mining scandals were endemic. The very first issue of the *Alaska-
Yukon Mining Journal* in 1901 featured an article entitled "How Mines
Are Salted." The vascillating value of Juneau's Silver Bow Basin and
of the nearby Bear's Nest Mine was standard barroom conversation.[33]
For every tippler who jubilantly toasted his lucrative "pay streak,"
probably another dozen disappointed gold seekers cursed the folly that
had driven them north. Yet, winner or loser, no Alaskan was totally
immune to the dizziness induced by the overly publicized riches won
on the Klondike, at Nome, and now "all over Alaska."

During the fall of 1902, as he completely overhauled his lumber mill,
John announced that shortly he would be able to process "10,000 feet
per day." By spring he had "found a place within 15 miles of Sitka
where I estimate one million feet of logs can be obtained." To attack
this stand of timber, John armed his men with one of Alaska's newest
steam loggers, the entire unit having cost him twenty-five hundred
dollars. Forthwith this Munday seven-by-twelve-inch double-drum engine began to pay for itself. Equipped with one thousand feet of steel
cable, Brady's "donkey" engine dragged stubborn, freshly toppled trees
to the water's edge and soon collected a raft within a fraction of the
time previously required by his hand loggers. Later at the mill these
shorn trunks were sawed into planking; some were smoothed by John's
California No. 1-1/2 planer. His donkey proved its versatility when
piles of the finished lumber had to be hauled and loaded. Peter Simpson,
a native lumberman, came up from Tongass to acquaint himself with
John's mechanical marvel and before long had the obedient creature

tearing out stumps from Grandfather Patton's vegetable garden. To really impress his aboriginal audience, Simpson reduced an oversized stump to manageable proportions with a half stick of dynamite.[34] No doubt this performance entertained the governor's children and not a few Sitkans, but unless the Sitka Sawmill Company very substantially increased its volume, the donkey, like the *Leo* rotting in the harbor, would become merely an expensive, rusting toy. Writing about the Alexander Archipelago timber operations in 1903, J. E. Defebaugh, editor of the *American Lumberman*, reported: "The saw mills in Alaska are of the most primitive kind. There is not a modern mill in the territory; in fact there are only three or four mills that make any pretension whatsoever of manufacturing lumber." John frankly admitted, "The bulk of the timber and lumber used has been shipped up from the sound." And then almost apologetically, "My mill is a small affair compared with those on the sound."[35] He had to face the disagreeable fact that the expansion of his firm seemed stalled for lack of capital. Was there no way out of this impasse? There was, and it took the form of an eastern go-getter.

H. D. (Harry) Reynolds embodied the turn-of-the-century boomer, the new man, born of the big city and dedicated to what it represented. Although Reynolds could be flamboyant in his speech, it was the man's charm and well-informed address that impressed people. Boston breeding had given him family status, education, money, and, above all, self-confidence. In H. D. Reynolds the older, genteel tradition had been hardened by a Yankee's sunup-to-sundown restless work day, a drive to attain affluence and dominate the environment.

Governor Brady first met his nemesis during the summer of 1902. Tall, of athletic bearing, Reynolds possessed handsomely cut features topped by unmanageable wavy blond hair. His ingenuousness was utterly disarming. In his mid-thirties when he arrived in Alaska, Reynolds must have appeared to John the perfect balance between yeasty youthfulness and seasoned experience. The easterner's blazing smile, his suave speech, and his enthusiasm for all kinds of work delighted Alaska's governor. This allure John soon transmuted to trust. Only years afterward could Brady admit how powerfully and how naively he had tied his fate and that of his family to Reynold's charm.

When the Bostonian arrived in Alaska, he joined dozens of other investors "hunting for a financial killing." He probably had only vague notions of where and what shape his corporate creation would ultimately assume. This much is known: Reynolds was part owner of some low-value Alaskan mining properties, and his faith in himself was unbounded. A risk-taker gambling for high stakes, the easterner appreciated that he, too, chanced total ruin.[36] Reynolds well understood the profitable possibilities inherent in combining mining, town growth, and railroad construction. Only later was his master design clear. By then he had traced a pattern very familiar to American entrepreneurs. At the outset, financial exigencies required showy, short-range achievements. Perforce, he had to concentrate his energies on immediate construction—a mine derrick, a wharf, storage sheds—it did not really matter what, as long as it demonstrated that human activity confirmed some Alaskan site's "superb investment possibilities." After his commercial undertakings had germinated, large capital aggregates could be secured and sustained growth would ensue. Should any one of his Potemkin ventures genuinely mushroom, such as those in the Juneau-Douglas region following Treadwell's magic touch, or more recently around Nome, the dividends could be immense. If none actually appreciated, Reynolds doubtless figured that he could pump up his shares and unload them at a handsome profit elsewhere. However, if he were astute and lucky, he might enjoy both inflated holdings and rich returns.

Reynolds came north in 1902 on behalf of eastern investors. As a fellow shareholder he hoped to arrange some means of resuscitating their Aurora Gold Mining Company on Kenai Peninsula. Situated approximately six miles from the village of Homer, Aurora—its tramways, power house, and even a partially constructed stamp mill—sat idle. It was here that John first met Harry Reynolds: "My impressions were favorable and after he told me what he had done he stood higher in my estimation. He found when he got around to examining matters at Aurora that things were not as bad as had been represented. . . . he brought matters to a halt would not allow the erection of the mill which has been shipped because there was not enough [ore?] in sight to justify such expense."[37] Before Reynolds returned to report to his eastern associates, he stopped awhile at Valdez and acquired some property in that neighborhood; the inconspicuous port of Valdez just might become Alaska's future San Francisco.

Nature was parsimonious when she shaped ice-free harbors adjacent to Alaska's sprawling interior. Although the Gulf of Alaska's coastline is sufficiently indented, a hinterland of enormous mountain ranges reinforced by rivers of ice—glaciers—blocks access from the North Pacific. A glance at a map shows that Cook Inlet and Prince William Sound to its east offer approaches to the interior. But precisely where man could obtain from nature an ice-free port and construct an entrepôt not cordoned off from continental Alaska by the massive Chugach and Saint Elias ranges was not clear. To pass these giant barriers required a valley entranceway. Ice-free Valdez on Prince William Sound, with the Copper River Valley to its east, seemed to be one answer. Another jack-in-the-box mining town, Valdez had earlier sprung up as a debarkation point for Klondike-bound gold seekers. Through its portal, advertised its promoters, miners could travel an "all-American route to the Yukon gold fields." Valdez sat on the distributary delta for the nearby Valdez Glacier, not the healthiest of geological locations, as circumstances later confirmed. By 1903 its citizens acclaimed it as the logical place for a major ship-rail terminal and boasted of its military roadway and "regular mail service [to] . . . Yukon River Points." Adding to its appeal were the ore bodies scattered about Prince William Sound waiting to be mined. However, Valdez had a competitor. Seward, a village to the west at the head of Resurrection Bay on the Kenai Peninsula, also aspired to become Alaska's great terminal city. Boomers were so excited at the inflated projections on the rate and volume of interior settlement that they foresaw rapidly emerging commercial hubs at both Seward and Valdez. Accordingly, starry-eyed entrepreneurs commenced laying track from these communities. Among their railroads' goals was Alaska's "future St. Paul and Minneapolis," the Fairbanks-Chena district. Not a single one of these corporate undertakings ever reached that objective. Only years afterward, having devoured breathtaking quantities of capital, amounts that none but the federal government could marshal, would a railroad connect Alaska's continental frontier to the gulf. But of course to men valiantly struggling in 1903 to overcome geography, that hindsight was not available.[38]

Spring of that year found the Sitka Sawmill Company throbbing with newfound vigor. It may well have resulted from a financial shot in the arm applied by H. D. Reynolds—at least, money to modernize Brady's business came from somewhere during 1902–3. We know that Reynolds returned to Alaska that year and that he was at the mill. Furthermore, he appears to have been a zestful worker. He may very well have shipped a load of lumber to his Aurora mine site. In any case, Reynolds's disarming manner and ingratiating actions erased any lingering suspicion from John's mind that the Easterner was all words and no work. In truth, John was an easy mark for any convert to his Alaska faith. Illustrative is a 1901 letter to the treasurer of the Alaska-Kodiak Mining Company: "I am in receipt of yours of May 8th, informing me that I am put down as a director of your company and that you have sent me a certificate of stock for 500 shares. This is all news to me as I have received no such certificate nor did I know that I was made a director of your company. The names which appear on your letter head please me very much but I should like to do something in compensation for stock which may be granted to me; after I have been informed upon what basis the company has been organized and how it proposes to act."[39]

During August of 1903 the Reynolds-Alaska Development Company was incorporated in the state of Washington, the "objects for which the said corporation is formed" being "to acquire, own, sell and operate gold, silver, copper, iron, coal and other mines; to carry and operate all reduction works and smelters . . . to operate there under concessions obtained in connection with the business; to engage in colonizing lands, agriculture, lumbering . . . acquire, hold, and dispose of real estate; to do a general contracting business; to act as agents for other parties . . . own, sell, and deal in bonds, stocks . . . to do a general manufacturing, trading and merchandising business . . . " The capital stock of the Reynolds-Alaska Development Company, according to its certificate of incorporation, was three million dollars. Fifty years was the specified life of the corporation. To manage the business five trustees were listed: Harry D. Reynolds, H. R. Reynolds (Harry's younger brother), Frank R. Fuller (these three men listed as residents of New York City), Eben Smith of Seattle (their attorney), and John Brady of Sitka.[40] Four months earlier Alaska's governor had written to a physician in Chicago: "I believe that Reynolds is honest, and capable and energetic. He sees that Alaska is full of great resources in minerals, fish timber and lands for stock raising and agriculture." His plan to gain profits was to "take up enterprises in these fields, put them in proper shape and dispose of them [to those] who are anxious to invest in some definite object."[41] This last line may well have been Reynolds's clincher, an argument that Brady found irrefutable: think what you as governor can do for your fellow Alaskans and American countrymen.

Promotional literature for the new enterprise soon began to circulate. Exactly when and where cannot be determined (it has no date) but a safe guess is that its distribution was primarily east of the Mississippi River during mid-1904. The complete first paragraph of their prospectus stated: "The Reynolds-Alaska Development Company was organized, under the Resident Directorship of the Governor of Alaska, to combine under one management valuable properties on the Southern Alaska coast, principally gold and copper mines, oil and coal and timber lands." The third paragraph, underlined in the original text, read in full: "No one is in [a] better position to judge values in Alaska than its Governor and his leadership has assured the best." Together these two paragraphs convey the impression that the company was a quasi-public corporation. Just as false is the misleading "organized, under the Resident Directorship . . . " John appears to have had virtually nothing to do with its organization. If only he had insisted on some factual answers to penetrating questions, his part in the impending disaster might have been averted. "The valuable properties" that the prospectus alluded to were the Boulder Bay Copper Mine, the Aurora Gold Mine, and the La Touche Island Copper Mine, all on, or adjacent to, Prince William Sound.[42]

Another Reynolds-Alaska Development Company promotional piece, an envelope brochure, included the reassurance: "The Hon. John G. Brady, Governor of Alaska and Resident Director of the Reynolds Alaska Development Company, is one of the founders and incorporators. Governor Brady is a Yale graduate; a man of great force of character and sterling integrity. His ripe knowledge of locations and conditions, gained by twenty-six years' residence in the Territory, has been an invaluable factor in determining the breadth and strength of the organization." It went on: "Nearly three hundred of the stockholders are now friends of the President, Mr. Reynolds"; among them "are the presidents and cashiers of three national banks, two private bankers, and a number of college professors, prominent physicians, lawyers and business men."[43] None of this early literature boosted an Alaska town or railroads.

Reynolds certainly protected himself. Englishman Blamey Stevens, the corporation's engineer and general manager, "a competent geologist, mineralogist, assayer, and engineer, careful conservative and with an infinite capacity for hard work," was his brother-in-law. His other sister and his brother H. R. managed affairs to the south, primarily among East Coast investors.

At first Elizabeth was charmed by the quick-witted and fast-paced Easterner. Before long, however, John's fixation on Reynolds's cloud castles began to alarm her. Finally the reality dawned on Elizabeth: her husband was mesmerized. The more she cautioned prudence, the more inexorable his faith. She must have been stunned the day she discovered that John had withdrawn their savings, earnings so slowly accumulated for the education of their children. Elizabeth implored him to get back the money: "You have given them your good name, isn't that enough?" His laconic answer, "That cost me nothing. I want to put my money where my mouth is—to show I have faith in the company."[44]

On 30 June 1904 Alaska's very naive governor once again endorsed the Reynolds-Alaska Development Company. "Governor Brady's Advisement" is surely a classic example of a man who trusted too much:

TO INVESTORS:

I believe that the Reynolds-Alaska Development Company is founded upon the true idea. The resources of Alaska are coming to light year after year and enough is now in sight to engage the attention of thoughtful men who are seeking places and opportunities where they can invest their money with assurance of a reasonable return.

In no part of our public domain is there such hopefulness in the way of development. Mining is the most marked industry at the present time. The wonderful management and rich returns from the Treadwell Mines on Douglas Island, Alaska, are a proof to the world of what can be done with a low-grade ore. Those who know Alaska well are sure that there are many such profitable opportunities, in mining and in other lines of industry.

The success of the Treadwell plant is due strictly to efficiency and honesty. The Reynolds-Alaska Development Company will be efficiently and honestly conducted. I do not wish to see a stock of any kind except what represents a real dollar and it is my earnest wish that those who put a dollar in shall get more than a dollar out within a reasonable time, and, to secure such a result, I willingly lend my personal supervision and aid to seize the best things and to manage them in a most economical and profitable way.

This is an age of concentration and combination, and Alaska is peculiarly adapted for such enterprises. A company of this kind, when so conducted, can, I believe, serve the purposes of men who are ready to make investments where they believe that they will be fairly dealt with. For such means and purposes I would advise my friends to take an interest in the enterprise.

John G. Brady
(Governor of Alaska)[45]

Late that year, conscious of Elizabeth's apprehensions and uncertain if he would again be reappointed now that President Roosevelt had won his own election, Governor Brady reassured his lady that he was still in the gubernatorial competition. "Reynolds will be in Washington tomorrow morning. I told him about matters, he wanted me to win out of course but would prefer to have me to go right in with him and give my whole time to the Development Company."[46] Despite his blundering endorsements over the past fifteen months, John obtained his reappointment.

Though he could not know it, Governor Brady had reached the apogee of his life, a state of affairs not entirely accounted for by his unprecedented third term and intoxicating dreams of financial security. The 1904 Saint Louis World's Fair permitted him to extol Alaska in a grandiose fashion. Indeed, there exists a dim possibility that, without the almost daily applause at the Louisiana Purchase Exposition, "Alaska's Grand Old Man" might have heard, and heeded, his wife's warnings.

Alaskan participation in U.S. expositions had grown in quantity and diversity since the 1876 Centennial Fair at Philadelphia. The spectacular success of Chicago's Columbian Exposition, and later Buffalo's, challenged Brady to do his best for the Great Land at the Saint Louis extravaganza scheduled for 1904.[47] As for the territory's outstanding human accomplishment, he believed that the handcrafted wood artistry of the Northwest Coast Indians surely matched Alaska's machine-wrought gold. And like native enthusiasts Emmons and Jackson, Brady grieved at the accelerating disappearance of this priceless heritage. What museum collectors, tourists, and thieves had not already removed from the archipelago the elements were rapidly destroying. Luckily, there still existed a few Indian house posts, wooden screens, and especially examples of the natives' world-famous totem poles. With the assistance of the Revenue Marine, John proposed to gather up those artifacts that could be moved—dry rot doomed many still standing—and see that they were preserved and painted at his Sitka yard. They could publicize Alaska in Saint Louis; then, when the exposition ended, they would be returned to Sitka, where they could be beautifully sequestered and appreciated at historic Indian River Park.

Four years prior to the Louisiana Purchase Exposition, Governor Brady initiated discussions with southeastern Alaska's native leaders. "I went with Captain Kilgore on the 'Perry' to different places," John wrote the general agent, busy trying to get federal support money. "At Ketchikan, I met a few of the Tongass people but could make no arrangements about getting any totem poles. The same was true at Kasaan village on Prince of Wales Island. If I succeed in getting any of these poles it must be by a lengthy negotiation and diplomacy."[48] John prudently visited Shakan, Klawock, Howkan, and Klinkwan. Without the cooperation of Kasaan's head man, Son-i-hat, his triumphant salvage of these treasures probably could not have been achieved. John later recounted the removal of the mightiest pole of all:

After obtaining [Son-i-hat's] consent the Captain anchored off the village and we went ashore with a working crew, tools and tackle and began work. The pole was nearly sixty feet high and you can imagine what a job it was when you know the base was four feet through and eleven feet in the ground. . . . Not being able to handle it on deck it was triced up alongside. . . . After cleaning [it] off we found that many parts of figures were badly decayed so I hired natives who were clever wood carvers to get to work upon it using some of the red cedar pieces we brought along for repair material. When all five [poles] were cleaned and repaired they were painted according to native ideas in such matters by a native artist.[49]

Collecting totem poles for exhibition at the Saint Louis Exposition. Governor Brady is directly to the right of the pole, and with a cane is Chief Son-i-hat of Kasaan, who contributed the largest totem. Standing beside Mary Brady is Captain W. F. Kilgore of the U.S.R.M., without whose cooperation the historic preservation could not have been accomplished. (Reproduced by permission of the Beinecke Rare Book and Manuscript Library, Yale University.)

Son-i-hat also agreed that Alaska's capital community might display an example of his people's maritime mastery. John had their gift, a large canoe, "repaired and painted in what the natives call Whalekiller style." He did what he could to allay native misgivings that their precious heirlooms would be treated irreverently: "The poles should be marked with the history giving the folk lore story, and the name of the donor, all to be put on a sheet of metal so that visitors can read the story." Whenever he was able to gather together the claimants of a specific pole, John drew up actual contracts with them. Descriptive marble tombstones were to be placed where the great crumbling shafts once stood.[50]

By 1902 the Brady clan had decided that two years hence all of them would attend the Saint Louis Exposition. John's annual report bubbled with his own anticipation: "There is to be a big show at St. Louis to display to the world the wonderful things that have been done since the Louisiana purchase by President Jefferson. . . . every fellow who can raise the car fare intends to go."[51]

For sheer size and heterogeneity of exhibits, the 1904 Louisiana Purchase Exposition surpassed many of the more highly touted world's fairs that would succeed it. Saint Louis's Forest Park did not glimmer with the sheen of modern technological triumphs so ubiquitous in later expositions, but its emphasis on people was unmistakable. Authentic living exhibits of African Zulus, Baluba, and Badingo, and Asian representatives ranging from Japanese to Ceylonese to Persians, all attired in native costumes and dwelling in structures and settings proximating their homelands—it was a babel.

Located among the various U.S. pavilions was the Alaska Building, a white stuccoed, two-story structure of fifty by one hundred feet. The totem poles that Brady had gathered flanked the building. Joining them on the east side stood a Haida cedar plank house, and within the Alaska Building lay an extensive array of native creations collected from all over the territory.[52] Gratifying to those anxious to accelerate aboriginal assimilation were neat, handwritten compositions and a fourteen-foot boat produced by students of Sitka's industrial school.

Vying successfully with the "native curios" was a pyramid of shimmering slabs of gold—gilded wood, in fact—set up by the Treadwell organization. Each bar was marked with a year and the annual gold output from the Douglas Island works. The top of the pyramid, representing the early 1880s, was small, but the base was huge. Ironically, that 1904 base would expand but a few more years and then begin its inevitable shrinking. Also located on the first floor of the Alaska Building were generous samples of Alaskan grain crops. Brady was determined to dispel popular notions that his homeland was one of "almost perpetual snow." Similarly, an abundance of lead, zinc, copper, asbestos, marble, iron, coal, and petroleum samples might dissuade Americans who believed that Alaskan earth held nothing but gold.[53] To make certain that every visitor "got the facts," Governor Brady insisted that each staff member be an Alaskan.

An attractive booklet, probably compiled by him for the occasion, is revealing. In it is reproduced Congress's "three hundred and twenty acres" clause from the 1903 homestead law. The booklet declares that "the greatest need of Alaska is railroads." And despite Valdez's low alphabetical listing and average historical rank, the port appears at the top of the list of "Cities and Towns" that is included: "It has a harbor which General Greely says will accommodate the navies of the world. It is open at all seasons of the year, and as a railroad terminal Valdez will some day undoubtedly become a town of the greatest importance."[54]

Secretary Hitchcock and his daughter inspected what the Alaskans had prepared. Laconic as always, he appeared content. Judging from Hitchcock's annual report, John's ability to stay within his budget, and even to return an unused portion, may have pleased him as much as anything. By and large, Alaskans seemed satisfied. *Alaska's Magazine* congratulated their executive commissioner for "his judicious selection of an exhibit representative of the varied resources of Alaska." John rejoiced that "thousands of people visit the halls, and very many express surprise and satisfaction at what they see. I think that we shall feel repaid by seeing emigration started our way." Certainly the cordial audience responses to his frequent stereopticon shows lifted his ego.[55]

For his children the Saint Louis exposition was an unforgettable fantasy world. Too young to be on their own, the girls saw the sights with their mother. But the boys tasted an unbelievable freedom. Before their father granted them the run of Forest Park, he reminded his sons that they "were not royalty," and the Pike was off limits until after lunch. Each morning they were to soak up the educational exhibits. Each evening John chuckled vicariously as his lads recalled their day's adventures: zooming into the sky aboard the Ferris wheel, watching the naval battles between miniature warships, and chattering with inhabitants from exotic lands. Quite rightly, the Brady boys considered themselves Alaskans. Nevertheless, they were as fascinated by the mock Eskimo village as any middle border hayseed. Large blocks of make-believe ice served as a backdrop for heavy sleds drawn by reindeer and dogs, and authentic Eskimo hunters demonstrated their deadly skill with harpoon lances. From the Moro, Visayan, Bagobo, Bontoc, and Igorot enclaves wafted strange smells; America's New Empire was quite a mystery. Apparently the children missed seeing Geronimo. But then they probably would not have recognized him: the Apache's fiery visage had long since softened. Spectators at the "Boer War" pageant, the boys almost yelled themselves hoarse. Here were actual English and Boer veterans from the just-ended African conflict firing away at each other on a battlefield replete with cannon and Red Cross ambulances. Only bullets and blood were missing.[56] None of the children seem to have been sobered by what all this implied.

October eighteenth was Alaska Day and therefore *the* day at the Alaska pavilion. The entire staff, the Bradys, and apparently every Alaskan on the exposition grounds posed for the cameraman. John and Elizabeth received an enthusiastic greeting. Fair officials complimented the Bradys on their handsome family and John for his dedicated and distinguished public service. Dazzled by the commotion, the euphora of the occasion, John Brady would have been a peculiar human being had he also heard hubris' eternal warning: "When a man thinks that he standeth, let him take heed lest he fall."

Two months later, his family having departed for home, John directed the packing of those precious native artifacts. To Jackson he expressed his thanks: "I have received many congratulations"; certainly the youngsters had "a splendid time." The object "I had in bringing the children here has been secured. . . . They return with a contented spirit, and I think they will better appreciate their own home and surrounds." Secretary Hitchcock also heard from John: "I had the attendants at different times to visit the Exhibition Palaces for the purpose of collecting the literature in connection with each. . . . Some of the works are valuable, as the large volumes from Portugal and three on the Antiquities of Mexico. We have a number of the State Books . . . altogether, it is a very desirable library of the World's Fair, and probably is as complete a collection as has been made. Now the question is, how to get it to Alaska?"[57]

Portland, Oregon, was preparing a fair of its own to honor the Lewis and Clark Centennial and requested that some of the totem poles temporarily adorn their grounds en route back to Indian River Park. The attention accorded these celebrated objects at both Saint Louis and Portland unquestionably helped stimulate America's archeological preservation program.

Paralleling the outcry over the "vanishing American" had been an expanding movement advocating the preservation of Indian antiquities. Sheldon Jackson and Benjamin Harrison had joined with men and women at the Smithsonian Institution, the Archeological Institute of America, and various other bodies condemning the destruction. In 1889 Pres-

Governor and Mrs. Brady and their family celebrate Alaska Day at the world-famous Saint Louis Exposition, 1904. (Reproduced by permission of the Beinecke Rare Book and Manuscript Library, Yale University.)

ident Harrison reserved Casa Grande in Arizona from dismemberment. By Theodore Roosevelt's presidency a number of sites were getting varying degrees of official protection. In 1905 John wrote to acting secretary of the interior Thomas Ryan strongly endorsing preservation of the "village of Kasaan entire." Joining John in this worthy effort was the retiring president of the American Library Association, Princeton librarian C. E. Richardson. Governor Brady, wrote Richardson, was "doing all in his power" to spark federal action. Mindful of how the "cash value" motivated Americans, the librarian closed on a pecuniary note: "It would be hard too to overestimate the practical importance of this matter with a regard to what Germans and Italians call the 'tourist industry.'"[58]

Throughout the early months of 1905, Brady traveled about the archipelago collecting fresh exhibits for the Portland exposition. "I am anxious to make a better display of our resources than we did at St. Louis," although a budget one-half of what had been appropriated for the Missouri exhibition made that improbable.

Both in correspondence with Secretary Hitchcock and in public documents, Brady had mentioned H. D. Reynolds.[59] Alaska's governor, however, had not informed his superior of his own business connection with the Reynolds company. If he gave the matter any thought, Brady probably presumed that after the 1904 circulation of the Reynolds-Alaska Development Company prospectus, Hitchcock would soon learn of his involvement. But given the secretary's diverse duties and exhaustive tug-of-war with Westerners hungering after land, water, forest, and game, one can comprehend his belated awareness. Not until a private citizen specifically informed the interior secretary of Brady's ill-advised endorsement did Hitchcock act. His rebuke was prompt. After pointing out how fulsome was the company's literature, "describing the richness of its mineral property in extravagant terms," he reminded Brady, that they had used his "official character to inspire public confidence in the concern and promote the sale of its stock." Hitchcock closed with a stern admonishment: "To permit your office to serve such a purpose ill comports with its dignity and character, is of questionable propriety, calculated to bring upon yourself and the administration unpleasant criticism, and I respectfully submit that you should take appropriate action in the matter without unnecessary delay." A month later, having received no answer from Brady, Hitchcock wired a telegram: "Wire immediately what action you have taken. . . ."[60]

No reply had been sent because John was busy aboard the USRM cutter *Rush* with preparations for the Portland exposition. A few days after returning to Sitka and finding Hitchcock's reprimand, John wrote Hitchcock (evidently the same day that Hitchcock had telegraphed him) reviewing his relationship with Reynolds. John frankly conceded:

> . . . you are right in calling my attention to the circular. This has been published since I saw Mr. Reynolds when I was east last. I think that the "Governor of Alaska" has been exploited much too freely in this circular and I shall have Mr. Reynolds discontinue them in their present form. . . . It did not occur to me that anything in [the prospectus] could be objectionable. . . . I have many times been quoted by those who were exploiting mining ventures. It is true that I have stood aloof from all companies and corporations until I took an interest in this present company and I cannot believe that I have done anything wrong. . . . I am writing to Mr. Reynolds to discontinue [the "letter of Advisement" circular] also.

Brady blithely admitted that "I have written to a number of my personal friends about these properties and advised them to take an interest." "I am not upon a salary in said company nor shall I receive any profits out of it until all preferred shareholders receive their dues." John expressed "entire confidence in Mr. Reynolds as an upright business man . . . and I have almost unbounded confidence in the character of the mining proposition which they have taken in hand."[61]

John also informed his chief that H. D. Reynolds and Stevens, the engineer, would "soon call upon you so that they may give an explanation of matters. . . ." Possibly Reynolds heard how austere the secretary of the interior was. Confrontation with a man who had made his wealth in the hazardous China trade, a cabinet officer whom the newspapers described as "scrupulously honest," "humorless and iron-willed," could prove embarrassing. After a perfunctory telephone call to the secretary's office, Reynolds retreated to the insulation of a letter. It contained few if any surprises for Hitchcock. "Mr. Brady was convinced he was working for the best interests of the country." In closing Reynolds sought to soothe the secretary: "You need have no apprehension of any acts of the Company bringing discredit upon Mr. Brady or through him the Administration."[62]

Hitchcock was apprehensive, but decades of managing men and money had taught him to skirt rash responses. Brady had demonstrated an amazing naivete; however, no laws had been broken. Discreet inquiries confirmed the secretary's instinctive suspicion: Reynolds was a sophisticated swindler. Fortunately, Alaska's governor was no fool. For all of his monomania concerning the Great Land, Brady would shortly sever his regrettable ties with the Reynolds crowd. "No man has a right to occupy a position of executive authority and mix his personality with a money-making scheme which his own acts at some time must affect," the Boston *Journal* editorialized; "Governors are human, and officials of mining companies more human still; the two occupations do not belong together." But the *Journal* was not worried: "Governor Brady has undoubtedly seen the point before this."[63] But had he?

1. Thomas C. Cochran, *The Inner Revolution: Essays on the Social Sciences in History* (New York, 1964), p. 91. Daniel J. Boorstin, *The Americans: The Democratic Experience* (New York, 1973), p. 3.

2. Readers who are curious about Brady's relationships with his family are urged to read Ted C. Hinckley, "A Victorian Family in Alaska," *American West* 16 (January–February 1979): 32–37, 60–63.

3. For a few samples see *Alaskan*, 21 January and 6 June 1891 and 23 July 1892; ibid., 6 June 1886, 4 June and 15 October 1892, and 3 June 1893. TAP, mf. 7, Thanksgiving proclamation, 29 November 1900; JGB, mf. 2, Memorial Day program; and *Alaskan*, 7 November 1903.

4. JGB, unfiled, fragment of speech by Brady.

5. Interview with John and Hugh Brady, 23 June 1962; JCorr, 16:383, Cassia Patton to Jackson, 22 December 1893; *Alaskan*, 9 December 1893, 15 June and 7 December 1895, 1 October 1898, 14 October 1899, and 28 January 1905.

6. Brady, *Annual Report, 1900*, p. 47, and idem, *Annual Report, 1905*, pp. 12–14. TAP, mf. 8–13, many vouchers signed by Governor Brady.

7. JCorr, 19:309–10, Brady to Jackson, 16 February 1901. AGP, box 12, Brady to S. F. Shorey, 26 December 1902; and TAP, mf. 9, bill from Arthur H. Clark Co., 20 November 1901. AGP, box 11, Brady to Louise P. Kellogg, 14 March 1902; and ibid., box 13, Powell to librarian, Alaska Library and Museum, 28 February 1901. JGB, mf. 1, Brady to his wife, 23 December 1900.

8. TAP, mf. 7, Brady to Hitchcock, 30 October 1900; and AGP, box 10, F. E. Vanderlip to Brady, 3 January 1901, JGB, mf. 4, Elizabeth Brady to D. H. Harvis, 15 December 1903. *Alaskan*, 3 September 1898. TAP, mf. 10, Brady to Hitchcock, 4 July 1904; ibid., H. A. Taylor (acting secretary of the treasury) to Hitchcock, 11 July 1904. AGP, box 12, Brady to V. L. Holt, 27 May 1905; ibid., Brady to William Distin, 15 December 1904. TAP, mf. 8, voucher for Charles Demmert, 29 June 1901; ibid., mf. 13, voucher for Leo Nabokoff, 20 September 1905; ibid., voucher for portrait bill, 6 May 1905. John G. Brady, "Notes on Pacific Libraries, Alaska District Historical Library and Museum" *Library Journal* 30 (September 1905): 141–43. Useful for an overview is Jeannette Stewart, "Library Service in Alaska: A Historical Study" (Master's thesis, American University, 1956).

9. *Daily Alaskan*, 29 May 1902, and *Ketchikan Mining Journal*, quoted in ibid.; Brady, *Annual Report, 1905*, p. 51.

10. Interview with John and Hugh Brady, 23 June 1962. Herbert L. Heller, ed., *Sourdough Sagas: The Journals, Memoirs, Tales, and Recollections of the Earliest Alaskan Gold Miners, 1883–1923* (Cleveland, 1967), p. 209. Hinckley, "Inside Passage," pp. 67–74. Brady, *Annual Report, 1903*, p. 54; idem, *Annual Report, 1899*, p. 42.

11. *Alaskan*, 24 February 1900. Brady, "Alaska," pp. 734–35. Idem, *Annual Report, 1905*, p. 102.

12. *Congressional Record*, 58th Cong., 2d sess., 18 April 1904, p. 4998. *Facts on Alaska* (Huntington Library pamphlet, n.a., n.p., ca. 1902). Andrew J. Stone, *Saw-Tooth Power: Its Value, Its Importance, Its Possibilities* (San Francisco, 1914), p. 28.

13. JGB, unfiled, Brady to Nelson, 20 April 1905; ibid., mf. 2, National Geographic

Society membership note; ibid., mf. 4, Brady to L. S. Rowe, 16 December 1902. Ibid., Brady to W. H. Moore, 19 October 1903. Ibid., unfiled, Ansley McCore to Roosevelt, 8 July 1904. AGP, box 13, F. S. Witherbee to Elihu Root, 27 January 1900.

14. JGB, unfiled, Brady to George W. McBride, 8 June 1900. *San Jose News*, 28 March 1975.

15. J. E. Defebaugh, "The Resources of Alaska," *American Lumberman*, 5 September 1903, p. 18.

16. *Alaskan*, 10 and 17 June 1899. Evidence that the expedition was not farcical and did accomplish something of scientific value may be found in Wickersham, *Bibliography*, pp. 211–12.

17. TAP, mf. 6, Brady to Hitchcock, 6 July 1899. JGB, mf. 4, Brady to G. T. Emmons, 2 September 1903, and ibid., Brady to Thomas Ryan, 10 September 1903. John Burroughs, *Far and Near* (Boston, 1904), p. 54.

18. For examples of the Bradys' levees, see *Alaskan*, 6 January 1894; 1 and 8 January, 5 and 26 February, and 23 July 1898; 18 February, 17 June, 22 July, and 28 October 1899; and 31 March 1906. AGP, box 6, Brady to auditor for State Department, 10 July 1899. Bruce Cotten, *An Adventure in Alaska during the Gold Excitement of 1897–1898* (Baltimore, 1922), pp. 43–44. A few white Sitkans did not approve of the Bradys' egalitarianism (James C. and Freda Campbell Klotter, "Mary Desha, Alaskan Schoolteacher of 1888," *Pacific Northwest Quarterly* 71 [April 1980]: 85).

19. AGP, box 10, G. F. Stone (acting second assistant postmaster general) to Brady, 7 February 1900; ibid., 9 May 1901. TAP, mf. 7, Brady to Hitchcock, 31 January 1900. *Alaska Searchlight*, 15 August 1896. Brady, *Annual Report, 1902*, pp. 48–49; idem, *Annual Report, 1903*, pp. 28–29; idem, *Annual Report, 1905*, pp. 25–26. *Ketchikan Mining Journal*, 29 March 1902; *Alaskan*, 11 November 1905.

20. William R. Stewart, "The Rich Empire in the North," *World's Work*, October 1903, p. 3978. John F. Stover, *American Railroads* (Chicago, 1961), p. 65. *Alaskan*, 4 July 1891, 18 May 1889; ibid., 13 December 1890 and 11 April and 3 October 1891. *Juneau City Mining Record*, 2 March 1893. Although it is true that all Alaska-bound tourists came by steam vessel, thousands first reached the West Coast ports by rail (Earl Pomeroy, *In Search of the Golden West: The Tourist in Western America* [New York, 1957], p. 57).

21. Stewart, "Rich Empire," p. 3976. Brady, *Annual Report, 1899*, p. 47. During July of 1898 Brady, accompanied by the Minneapolis investor George A. Brackett, inspected Skagway's Brackett wagon road. His informative comments are in TAP, mf. 5, Brady to Hitchcock 7 July 1898. Edwin M. Fitch, *The Alaska Railroad* (New York, 1967), p. 38.

22. TAP, mf. 7, Alfred Day to Brady, 12 August 1900; ibid., mf. 9, Dickson to Brady, 16 September 1903; AGP, box 12, Brady to Ray Morris, 29 December 1902. Wooten, *Facts on Alaska*, n.p.

23. Brady, *Annual Report, 1901*, p. 36.

24. Brady, *Annual Report, 1903*, p. 7. Governor Brady's vision was sound, but his enthusiasm failed to square with economic realities. Before his death he enjoyed the satisfaction of seeing the U.S. government initiate a railroad into Alaska's interior (William H. Wilson, *Railroad in the Clouds: The Alaska Railroad in the Age of Steam, 1914–1945* [Boulder, Colo, 1977]).

25. Defebaugh, "Resources of Alaska," p. 18. JGB, mf. 4, Brady to F. W. Baker, 12 July 1901; ibid., unfiled, Brady to A. E. Hall, 17 May 1899. AGP, box 13, A. E. Ainsworth to Brady, 25 January 1901. TAP, mf. 9, South-Eastern Alaskan Saw Mills, 1900–1901–1902. AGP, box 8, W. W. Lott to Brady, 20 October 1905.

26. Interview with John Brady, Jr., 14 August 1968.

27. JGB, mf. 1, Brady to his wife, 23 July 1898. *Alaskan*, 22 January 1897 and 12 February 1898. *Alaska-Yukon Director and Gazetteer, 1902* (Sitka, 1902), p. 695. *Alaskan*, 3 February 1894. Taped responses to author's questions by Hugh P. Brady, 15 April 1975, Seattle.

28. Tape of Hugh Brady, 15 April 1975. *Alaskan*, 26 October 1899. JGB, mf. 3, suit against Brady by W. P. and W. R. Mills, 28 May 1901; and ibid., pocket memo book, 6 January 1902 entry.

29. JCorr, 20:89, Brady to Jackson, 12 January 1902. JGB, mf. 2, Elizabeth Brady to her husband, 18 December 1900. Ibid., mf. 1, Brady to his wife, 3 July 1903. *Alaska Mining Record* (special mining edition), January 1898.

30. *Seattle Post-Intelligencer*, 30 July 1905. *Alaskan*, 10 June 1899. *Alaska Daily Guide* (Skagway), 2 July 1902; *Alaskan*, 11 July 1903; and Stewart, "Rich Empire," p. 3979. JGB, unfiled, Brady to Joseph D. Sayers, 31 July 1899. *Juneau City Mining Record, Alaska Mining Record* (special). *Alaska-Yukon Mining Journal*, 4 November 1901, p. 4.

31. *Alaska-Yukon Mining Journal*, 4 November 1901, p. 4. *Alaskan*, 19 August 1899. *Portland Oregonian*, 2 and 10 December 1905, and *Seattle Post-Intelligencer*, 28 August 1905. AGP, box 12, Brady to Howard H. Startzman, 2 September 1903. Elmo Richardson, *The Politics of Conservation: Crusades and Controversies, 1897–1913* (Berkeley, 1962), pp. 48–49. *Alaska-Yukon Mining Journal*, July 1901, p. 14. *Alaskan*, 14 May 1898 and 11 July 1903.

32. JGB, mf. 4, Brady to B. Loewenthal, 17 November 1902.

33. AGP, box 11, Brady to Brooks, 21 February 1901. Brady, *Annual Report, 1905*, pp. 95–96. *Alaska-Yukon Mining Journal*, 1 February 1901, p. 5. Morgan Sherwood, "Alfred Hulse Brooks, 1871–1924," in T. W. Freeman, M. Oughton, and P. Pinchemel, eds., *Geographers: Biobibliographical Studies* (London, 1977), 1:19–23. Scidmore, "Alaska's Mining Regions," p. 467.

34. *Alaskan*, 27 September 1902. JGB, unfiled, Brady to Henry Baldwin, 9 April 1903; and ibid., Brady to his wife, April 1903. AGP, box 12, Brady to H. D. Bartlett, 8 April 1903.

35. Defebaugh, "Resources of Alaska," p. 18. JGB, unfiled, Brady to George W. McBride, 8 June 1900.

36. It is manifest from the Brady correspondence that Reynolds rarely informed his business associates what he was doing until it was a fait accompli. To obtain a clear picture of what he did, much less what he intended, is now impossible. On Reynolds the man, the author has depended primarily on oral testimony from Governor Brady's sons and the periodical literature of that period.

37. *Alaskan*, 9 September 1905; 1 November 1902. JGB, unfiled, Brady to Wallace K. Harrison, 7 April 1903.

38. Donald J. Orth, *Dictionary of Alaska Place Names* (Washington, D.C., 1967), p. 1016. Senator Knute Nelson Papers, Minnesota Historical Society, Saint Paul, Minnesota, correspondence on Alaskan trip, Valdez Chamber of Commerce to Nelson, 8 June 1903. Alaskans were not of one mind on these Gulf boom towns. See, for example, *Ketchikan Mining Journal*, 17 August and 7 September 1901; and Senate, *Petition*, 57th Cong., 1st sess., Doc. No. 238, 6 March 1902.

39. JGB, mf. 2, Elizabeth Brady to her husband, 19 August 1903. Interview with Hugh Brady, 9 May 1968, Seattle. JGB, mf. 4, Brady to T. E. Sloan, 31 May 1901.

40. TAP, mf. 11, H. D. Reynolds to Brady, 14 September 1903; ibid., "Certificate of Incorporation of Reynolds-Alaska Development Company." It would seem that John Brady kept himself entirely removed from the company's legal and financial technicalities (ibid., William L. Distin to Frank C. Churchill, 25 September 1905).

41. JGB, unfiled, Brady to Wallace K. Harrison, 7 April 1903.

42. TAP, mf. 11, "Reynolds-Alaska Development Company: A Concrete Statement of Facts by the President of the Company."

43. Ibid., "Statement by the Reynolds-Alaska Development Company."

44. Interview with Hugh Brady, 9 May 1968, and letters from him to author of 5 October and 15 December 1969.

45. TAP, mf. 11, "Governor Brady's Advisement," 30 June 1904.

46. JGB, mf. 2, Brady to his wife, 18 December 1904.

47. *Alaskan*, 2 and 6 December 1890 and 21 October 1893. AGP, box 13, Arthur C. Jackson to Brady, 9 June 1901.

48. JCorr, 19:253, Brady to Jackson, 16 October 1900.

49. TAP, mf. 7, Brady to Thomas Ryan, 6 September 1905. *Alaskan*, 2 November and 8 March 1902.

50. *Alaskan*, 2 November and 8 March 1902. JGB, unfiled, "Memorandum of Agreement" with Kate Swanson, Tongass Indian, 24 July 1901; ibid., Brady to L. A. Babcock, 14 March 1902. There is an old canard floating around Alaska that Governor Brady "hoodwinked the Indians when he got those poles." Brady may well have promised more than the government could later deliver. However, the author does not believe that the evidence supports the accusation. Skeptics may wish to contact Professor Lawrence Rakestraw, Michigan Technological University, Houghton, Michigan, or examine for themselves TAP, mf. 7–12, and the Brady Collection at Yale University. It is worth noting that contemporary critics of Governor Brady's Indian art restoration efforts were not Tlingits, Haida, or Tsimshian but editors Troy and Swineford.

51. Brady, *Annual Report, 1902*, p. 57.

52. Mark Bennitt, comp., *History of the Louisiana Purchase Exposition* (St. Louis, 1905), pp. 443–45. "Gold Fields: World's Fair Souvenir" (handout for fair visitors), June 1904. JCorr, 21:27, Brady to Jackson, 18 March 1904.

53. Walter Williams, "Round the World at the World's Fair," *Century*, September 1904, p. 803.

54. [John Brady?], *District of Alaska Exhibits at the Louisiana Purchase Exposition, St. Louis, 1904* (St. Louis, 1904), pp. 10, 12, 15.

55. Hitchcock, *Annual Report, 1905*, pp. 217–18. JGB, mf. 2, Brady to his wife, 31 May 1904. EAH, unfiled, Brady to Hitchcock, 3 November 1904. Joseph K. Smith, "Alaska at St. Louis," *Alaska's Magazine*, April 1905, p. 16. TAP, mf. 10, Brady to Hitchcock, 4 July 1904.

56. Interview with Hugh Brady, 9 April 1967. JGB, pocket memo book, 1904, "Visit to St. Louis Fair by Brady Family." Ted C. Hinckly, "When the Boer War Came to St. Louis," *Missouri Historical Review* 61 (April 1967): 285–301.

57. JCorr, 21:121, Brady to Jackson, 3 December 1904. TAP, mf. 10, Brady to Hitchcock, 10 December 1904.

58. Helpful on the Portland fair are Robertus Love, "The Lewis and Clark Fair," *World's Work*, August 1905, pp. 6446 ff; and Agnes C. Laut, "What the Portland Exposition Really Celebrates," *American Monthly Review of Reviews*, April 1905, pp. 428–29. Hitchcock, *Annual Report, 1905*, pp. 218–19; Brady, *Annual Report, 1905*, pp. 100–125. Correspondence with Prof. Lawrence Rakestraw by author, 1970–74. TAP, mf. 7, Harry P. Corser to Brady, 5 June 1900; ibid., mf. 13, Brady to Ryan, 6 September 1905; ibid., Richardson to Ryan, 28 October 1905.

59. AGP, box 12, Brady to Charles A. Elwood, 2 May 1905. JGB, unfiled, Brady to Stuart Dodge, 18 April 1905; ibid., Brady to George Jamme, 20 April 1905. TAP, mf. 11, Brady to Ryan, 3 May 1905, ibid., mf. 10, Brady to Hitchcock, 4 July 1904. Brady, *Annual Report, 1904*, p. 34.

60. TAP, mf. 11, Edward Gore to Hitchcock, 25 February 1905, and ibid., Hitchcock to Brady, 6 March 1905.

61. TAP, mf. 11, Brady to Hitchcock, 7 April 1905; ibid., telegram, Brady to Hitchcock, 7 and 8 April 1905. Ibid., telegram, Brady to Reynolds, 8 April 1905.

62. Johnson and Malone, *DAB*, 5:74–75. TAP, mf. 11, Reynolds to Hitchcock, 20 April 1905.

63. Among the sources of information that Hitchcock tapped, probably indirectly, were Stephen Birch and Walter E. Clark (TAP, mf. 11, Birch to Clark, 11 April 1905). *Boston Journal*, 5 April 1905.

CHAPTER SEVENTEEN

Resignation

On 13 May 1905 the Reynolds-Alaska Development Company formally dropped Governor Brady from its board of directors. He remained a stockholder, his faith in the organization unshaken. Eastern friends continued to receive his praise of the company, and during an inspection trip to Alaskan mining properties, a group of prospective shareholders had the pleasure of the governor's company.

Seeking to jar him to his senses, Hitchcock abruptly denied John the role at Portland's fair that he had played so well in Saint Louis. Making the best of it, John called himself "temporary executive commissioner" and appointed William Kelly the "permanent executive commissioner."[1] To Joseph B. Marvin, whom Hitchcock sent west to fill the Portland hiatus until Kelly's arrival, John wrote, "The mining proposition is a good one." "Mr. Reynolds is in my opinion an upright man and there is no intention to run a fake concern and cheat the people out of their money, on the contrary his anxiety and mine was to see that those who put their money in should get it back with interest." And in a letter to his old friend Emmons: "I sincerely regret that in a circular without my knowledge or consent, the President of the Company expatiated the 'Governor of Alaska' too much, but otherwise my conscience does not probe me with the feeling that I have done wrong."

The newspapers quickly caught the scent of Brady's blunder. News of John's endorsement, his superior's rebuke, and his official separation from Reynolds-Alaska's board spilled out across the country. He was chided, even denounced. However, there was no widespread call for his dismissal. As a whole, Alaska's press did not rush for his throat, although Skagway's *Daily Alaskan* and the *Ketchikan Mining Journal* did.[2] Juneau's *Dispatch* was in fact sympathetic: "How the executive of any state, territory or district could be induced to get out such a fool letter of endorsement is beyond comprehension. . . . We hope that the Governor will come out with a statement and clear himself." Unfortunately, Brady's reluctance to transfer the capital to Juneau had inured him to press hostility from that quarter, for the *Alaska Record-Miner* could have warned him that the Alfred M. Lamar Company of New York "went broke as a result" of a Reynolds "escapade."[3]

Copy unsympathetic to Governor Brady made the front page of the *Seattle Post-Intelligencer*. Alaska's governor could ill afford to disregard these dispatches by Walter E. Clark. A *Post-Intelligencer* reporter assigned to the nation's capital since 1900, Clark had friends in the Interior Department. Furthermore, like many another Pacific Slope newsman, he was swept along by America's Progressive wave dedicated to washing out "corrupt office-holders." Within a month after Hitchcock's March rebuke, Clark reported that "Secretary Hitchcock will call for the resignation of Gov. Brady, of Alaska, as the result of the governor's letter explaining his connection with the Reynolds-Alaska Development Company." Although wrong, Clarks' column was broadcast to other organs. Clark quite correctly perceived that "the governor seems totally unable to understand the secretary's point of view." John exposed his obdurate stance to Senator Nelson: "My enemies have stirred up quite a fuss about my being interested in mining and a director in the Reynolds-Alaska Development Company. The newspapers try to make out that it is a fake to cheat street car conductors and servant girls. It is a legitimate enterprise and I have advised personal friends to become shareholders."[4] And the more John's friends acted on his advice, the more committed he was to sticking by Reynolds, who now controlled their savings.

As early as the letter of 7 April in which Brady first asked Reynolds henceforth to refer to him only by name and to "leave out all references to me as 'Governor of Alaska,'" John denied himself what might have been the politically expedient thing to do: "I cannot resign at this juncture for it would look as if I were trying to escape an investigation or hush up a wrong. . . . it would be a great injustice to a great number of my friends who fought for my reappointment." By the end of May John reassured Reynolds: "I went into the company with my eyes open and I cannot play the baby act in any way. I believe in you."[5]

Throughout 1904–5 Brady entangled himself in a web from which there really was no escape. Intoxicated by the elixir of go-getting, bewitched by the Bostonian, he rushed blindly on. John had begun to quote the famous Colorado governor William Gilpin, a man who today ranks as the quintessential Western boomer. John's enthusiasm for

349

Alaskan investment had approached the point where he would state for the record: "If *three* lines of railroad were built from the ports on the southern border across to the Yukon River, an industrious, wide-awake American population will follow them as they build, and by dint of hard work will produce results equal to any that we have seen on the western frontier."[6]

In mid-May president Theodore Roosevelt received a letter from H. D. Reynolds. It reemphasized the company's soundness and Brady's "creditable" role. Reynolds's last sentence included the promise that "to relieve the Administration of possible embarrassment, all literature mentioning Brady has been withdrawn from circulation." That same day Reynolds issued from his New York office a "President's *Confidential* Report to the Stockholders." It included three paragraphs once again flattering Brady as an "invaluable guide in the organization of the Company and all subsequent plans." The report then proceeded to make a mockery of time, common sense, and the term *public servant*: "In order to circumvent all political machinations, it was deemed advisable that Mr. Brady withdraw from the Directorate, temporarily, during the remainder of his term as Governor of Alaska. Thereafter, he will give his entire time and attention to the interests of our company."[7] When Hitchcock read that astonishing sentence he may well have anticipated that it would break Brady's hypnosis. If he did so, the secretary waited in vain.

For Reynolds to declare in one breath that by the resignation of his "Directorate" Governor Brady could "circumvent all political machinations" and in the next state that his absence would be "temporary" when Brady still had over three years remaining in his governorship was patently ridiculous. As Juneau's *Dispatch* snapped, "If Mr. Brady . . . will persist in using his official position as an advertisement of stock in a mining company . . . he should receive immediate opportunity to devote all of his time and attention to the interests of the mining company to which he is so unswervingly loyal."[8] Reynolds's careless copy may not have resulted from ignorance. Since 1904 Reynolds had been badgering John to give more, if not all, of his time to the company. Possibly he sought to manipulate John into an untenable position, one where there was no alternative but to resign and devote all his energies to the Reynolds-Alaska Development Company. The steadfast fidelity of Alaska's defiant old man could not help but win over some fence-sitting investors, Easterners possibly dubious of Reynolds's claims. That July a Seattle reporter snared Reynolds en route to Alaska. "The charges against Brady were without foundation," he angrily insisted. "The charges were brought by politicians who have always opposed Gov. Brady."[9]

Throughout 1905 one event after another kept afloat the buoyant aspirations of Brady and Reynolds. Alaska's commerce showed a fourteen percent increase over the preceding year. Two railroad companies promised to thrust railheads from Valdez, hurdle the Chugach Mountains, and enter the interior to the north. Deep in the interior, on 17 July, a golden spike linked Fairbanks and Chena. It did not matter that this narrow-gauge track ran only thirty-two miles—Alaska was rolling![10] Alfred Brooks had joined the railroad chorus, and Senator Nelson's peers heard that the all-American route "passes through the best portion—the very heart of Alaska; through the great Copper River Valley, rich in gold and copper; through the upper Tanana River Valley—the garden spot of Alaska. . . ." Congress seemed impressed. Money was appropriated for the construction and maintenance of a wagon road to the interior. Before the year ended America's go-getter in the White House, who had just demonstrated his ability for action by initiating construction of the Panama Canal, recommended that "Congress should aid in the construction of a railroad from the Gulf of Alaska to the Yukon River, in American territory."[11]

Unlike paradoxical President Roosevelt, a boomer and a conservationist almost in the same breath, Hitchcock acquired the reputation of being a bulldog guarding the national domain. Even Gifford Pinchot complained to President Roosevelt of Hitchcock's punctiliousness about forest utilization. In 1905 Hitchcock had the grim satisfaction of convicting a U.S. Senator, Oregon's John H. Mitchell, of land fraud. And this notorious judicial battle was not an exception. Cases of plundering the national domain arose in Utah, Nebraska, and Wyoming. Understandably, Hitchcock's general opinion of Far West politicians was low. With John Brady, Hitchcock had never fostered anything but a formal relationship. It had always nettled him to have Alaska's governor lobbying in the capital. In 1902 Brady had wondered whether the secretary of the interior "has a personal animus toward me or an ill will toward Alaska and the west in general."

Governor Brady did not fear an "investigation for I have nothing to tell but the truth." He had broken no law; his sense of rectitude was pure. As he wrote Reynolds, "I have not felt conscious of doing a wrong act." It is true that John Troy had once accused the lumberman of "sawmill graft," but it appears that Brady did his best to avoid confusing his private ledger with his public trust. John was "waiting for the Sec'y to pronounce me guilty or not guilty," never doubting the verdict.[12]

Surrounded by controversy, whipsawed by departmental disputes, Hitchcock was not going to judge a territorial official with Brady's public reputation guilty or not guilty, at least not until he had proof. For the moment he continued to fill up the governor's dossier with data pertaining to his Alaskan management. One such letter came from General Greely. Across continental Alaska, "without a single exception it was agreed" that John Brady's endorsement of the Reynolds-Alaska Development Company had been "most impolitic and inadvisable." Greely added, "with scarcely an exception the honesty and integrity of Governor Brady were admitted with the qualification that he had been overreached and exploited by mining speculators."[13]

For years Dr. Jackson's educational and reindeer programs had become almost routinely controversial. Hitchcock had gladly let his commissioner of education, William Torrey Harris, resolve these frictions. However, in mid-1905 Secretary Hitchcock assigned a special agent to uncover what he could about Far North affairs, specifically the administrative competence of Alaska's general agent for education and her territorial governor. Brady had been investigated before, and when special agent Frank C. Churchill arrived at Sitka, the governor welcomed him warmly enough. Churchill, an experienced Land Office employee, carefully wrote down everything that Brady told him. After their interviews he permitted John to check his notes. "I was much taken to him as a man and stranger," Brady wrote Jackson; "I surely have no complaint of Mr. Churchill for his treatment of me while he remained here."[14]

In his confidential report of 28 October 1905, Churchill detailed his findings on Governor Brady's relationship with Reynolds. He later submitted separate, strongly critical summaries of Dr. Jackson's work. Much of the testimony in the document John had already supplied in letters to Hitchcock.[15] Pertinent fresh information on Brady's ties to Reynolds included that Brady could give the names of only three stockholders besides the directors; he had given Reynolds the names of "class mates and acquaintances in different parts of the United States [he] thought would be likely to interest themselves in the Company"; and at the Saint Louis fair Brady had instructed the attendants "to draw the attention of visitors" to information blanks promoting the company. Rather quickly Churchill discerned that the Reynolds-Alaska Development Company was a fraud. It "has no [working] mines in Alaska and never had," he reported. "There is no town of Aurora and the only thing I know of it has to sell there is water power, unless it be hot air." Churchill was equally astute in his estimate of Reynolds: "As a promoter his skill approaches brilliancy."

Churchill detailed Governor Brady's relationship with Reynolds:

> He stated to me in so many words that he admired the young man. He even used the word "hypnotism," but perhaps only in a half serious way. In view of all the facts and the Governor's loyalty to Reynolds, I must conclude that the Governor has been grossly deluded and that he persists in upholding his deceiver to a degree bordering on obstinacy. To my mind it is a clear case of what is sometimes termed a confidence game. . . . The crafty Reynolds appears to have seen an opportunity to enlist his influence in a developing and stock selling enterprise by giving nothing in return but a block of stock which at the time had, in my opinion, absolutely no value. . . . To the credit of Governor Brady . . . he actually knows nothing of consequence about the company's management.

Later Churchill interviewed H. D. Reynolds in Boston:

> He claims they are employing from 12 to 16 men, which I doubt very much. . . . He states that the amount of cash that was actually paid in to the new company and repaid by the common stock, amounts to $130,000. Mr. Reynolds claims that he sells the greater part of the stock himself and that he draws a small salary for his service. . . . It may yet develop that the mining claims will prove to be of great value, but at the present time I cannot regard their business as anything but a speculation, in which the Governor has been used as a tool by a very clever promotor.[16]

The special agent judged John Brady to be "an honest man . . . but that he should be separated from the public service in Alaska is my unqualified conclusion."

By the end of 1905, with leakage from the "confidential" report beginning to spot American newspapers, Governor Brady was ready to withdraw. The reasons were trivial and overriding, of long duration and spur-of-the-moment, positive and negative. More tired than usual and finding himself "becoming somewhat fidgety" about his food, he finally surrendered to Elizabeth's insistence to see a doctor. They were shaken to hear the diagnosis: diabetes. The reality of death sobered him. Old friends John Eaton, Charles Johnson, and Arthur K. Delaney had recently died. Resignation would not be so dreadful. Dr. Jackson must soon abandon the field. And as prominent an educator-humanitarian as Superintendent Pratt had been pushed aside.[17] Public service was a thankless burden; even popular Judge Wickersham appeared unable to win reappointment.

Brady had accustomed himself to virulent attacks from such as John Troy, but the racial prejudice that swelled up in Sitka during January 1906 disgusted him. For over three years he and Elizabeth had been distressed about the deterioration of the local public school. The sudden preoccupation of some Sitkans with "the dangers of mixing the races" was the last straw. Bigots on the local school board strenuously opposed the admission of a few Ranche children, mixed bloods, some of whom were as white as their own. John arranged to have Cassia Patton escort the youngsters to the school. Here they encountered board members W. P. Mills and Mrs. George Stowell, who denied them admission. The third board member, William Kelly, had just resigned in disgust. Mrs. Stowell was a member of John's church; worse, the pastor sided with her and Mills. John sought "a writ of mandamus to compel the acceptance of these children." For the moment Juneau's superior court judge agreed that Sitka's school board had the authority to reject the mixed-blood children not "leading a civilized life." Doubly mortifying to the Bradys, a majority of the townsmen seemed tacitly to concur with the board's decision. "The one thing wanting in it all is Christian charity," groaned John to his mentor. "We are more truly heathen than the natives." "Can you blame us for wanting to get out of it?"[18]

On 27 January 1906 John wrote Stanton J. Peelle, chief justice of the U.S. Court of Claims in Washington. Peelle was an old friend, and in his letter John "opened up my soul": "I believe that the time has arrived for me to retire. My children need school advantages which they cannot get in Sitka or elsewhere in Alaska. The oldest boy is now in the Portland Academy. I desire that they shall have the best school training in the East. In a financial way while the salary of the office has been rather liberal I have not derived any real benefit from it because I have had to neglect my own business affairs. . . . By resigning now I can accept a position which will pay me as well and be continuous." But John could not step down without fulminating. E. A. Hitchcock received some of his anger, but most of it fell on "the Vardman-Swineford type. . . . They accuse me of being unprogressive— behind the times—a drag—unpopular—an Indian shouter and usually end the climax by classifying me as a damn missionary." John felt "honored by the latter title" and only wished he were "not more worthy to deserve it."[19] In closing, Alaska's governor admitted, "I do not want to leave office as though forced out with the impression that I am under a cloud. I feel jealous of my good name." Enclosed was John's one-sentence letter of resignation addressed to the president: "My request to you as my friend is that you go to President Roosevelt and have a talk with him and if you deem proper read him this letter. I then want you to place my resignation in his hands."[20]

As on previous occasions, reporter Walter Clark confused the facts. Fortunately, he tried to distinguish between John's honest character and his poor judgment. By mid-February it was known everywhere that as soon as President Roosevelt could pick a successor, Brady's tenure would end. On 2 March 1906 Juneau businessman Wilford B. Hoggatt

354

The "changing of the guard" at Sitka in 1906; incoming governor Wilford B. Hoggatt poses with "old man Brady." (Reproduced by permission of the Beinecke Rare Book and Manuscript Library, Yale University.)

became Alaska's sixth governor. In the years ahead both Clark and Troy would have their turns as Great Land governors, but not until Ernest Gruening did an Alaska chief executive exceed the longevity of Governor John G. Brady.[21]

Brady's resignation is recalled as "the end of the Presbyterian hierarchy." Reduced in responsibility but not in title or pay, Sheldon Jackson retained his job until 1908. Unquestionably Jackson and Brady, working with a collection of missionaries and teachers and supported by lay Christians in the district and throughout the United States, had influenced Alaskan history. Their actual Far North power had invariably been restricted by distance, time, and tradition. In just ten years the relationships between these three elements had largely changed. Indeed, John's inability fully to appreciate this change helps explain his political demise. It was ironic that Governor Brady, so long a voice of moderation amidst a multitude of intemperate boomers, had fallen victim to his unbounded enthusiasm for Alaska.

Churchill believed that "the little settlement of Sitka" with its "isolation" had caused John "to be out of touch with the people of the District." "Whether true or false," cautioned the special agent, "Alaska people believe that Governor Brady and a small coterie of his friends constitute a sort of closed corporation in the management of public affairs." In mid-July 1906, symbolizing the advent of a new political era, Alaska's capital moved from quaint, historic Sitka to bustling Juneau.[22]

In a relative sense, Alaska's population had not grown much—Sitka still had fewer than five hundred white citizens—but many other human factors had been modified, some radically. John discerned the commercial implications of all this and heralded them. But his humanistic revulsion at the exploitation of people inhibited him, made him, as he put it, "a drag" and "unprogressive." He was surely a devoted Alaskan, but he lacked that hard, practical touch so indispensable to the durable politician.

One other factor may well have hastened John's decision to depart Alaska's political arena. In September 1905 the militant Western Federation of Miners arrived in the northland. Alaska had tasted industrial bitterness earlier at the Treadwell Mines, but Nome's waterfront strike that autumn had worried him. Here again was a pervasive, disturbing, dimly understood change. John was the official primarily entrusted with safeguarding public order. Although he was not personally afraid of violence, the bloody December murder of Idaho's ex-governor Frank Steunenberg chilled him. That year had also witnessed the birth of the Industrial Workers of the World. To judge from their rhetoric, these allies of the Western Federation of Miners would indeed "raise a lot of hell."[23]

As the Bradys busied themselves for their move east, Alaska's departing governor turned his attention to those matters he valued most. "With a full heart I wish you a happy new year," he wrote Reynolds on January first. "The *Cottage City* will be here in two days and will probably have all the totems . . . returned to me. I have had to plead earnestly to get these sent back for Alaska." By 8 March John rejoiced that "thirteen totem poles, presented by native Alaskans, have been returned . . . and placed in Indian River Park, a government reservation. Mr. E. W. Merrill has been in charge of the painting, repairing and erecting of the same, the work being done by natives, Hydahs and Tlingits." And then in mid-May came a real sense of triumph—vindication for John and Elizabeth, in fact, every member of the "missionary crowd": Congress finally permitted Alaska's natives to acquire 160-acre homesteads.[24]

Elizabeth and John could not leave without parties for old friends among Sitka's polyglot citizenry. Pro forma, an "elaborate dinner" honored the new governor. John wished Hoggatt "a strong hand and a courageous heart" and could not resist reviewing Alaska's needs: "the treatment of the natives" ranked number one. His sister-in-law, still boiling over the school board's bigotry, decided that with the removal of the Bradys, she must sell the *Alaskan*. Miss Patton, reported Juneau's *Daily Alaska Dispatch*, "has pluckily kept the paper on its feet, regretting to see the oldest paper in the territory . . . consigned to the journalistic graveyard." Cassia had the last say; indeed, her editorial was a valedictory statement from the Bradys: "So today, wholly through the [natives'] own exertions and industry, without any material assistance from the general government, they have established themselves as an independent, self-supporting population, fully capable of rendering such labor as the conditions of the country demand. . . . the natives are not by any means to be despised or belittled. Their status is a vital point to be considered. . . . The idea of segregating the children of mixed blood living in the Indian village from those living amongst the whites is absurd."[25] That September, her last month as editor, Cassia testily replied to an editor who belittled her brother-in-law: "While he has gone to Boston . . . he leaves every cent he has made in Alaska, invested in her mines. Governor Brady during the last five years has started more capital toward Alaska than any other two men, and is busily engaged in developing one of the biggest copper propositions in Alaska."

By August Elizabeth and the children were on their way to Brookline,

Massachusetts, temporarily leasing a house from the Reynolds family. To his new employer John wrote, "Anxious to get on my business harness and work." Unable to arrange a satisfactory lease for his mill, he began to cannibalize it. Apparently some of his machinery and a good portion of his lumber ended up at the Reynolds properties across the gulf. Wasting no time, Reynolds quickly assigned John promotional duties as a "company representative." John soon bore the impressive title "Treasurer" and was advertising Reynolds-Alaska all the way from Seattle to New England. Concurrently, Blamey Stevens pushed construction of "an aerial tramway" to exploit the rich copper deposits near the southern end of Latouche Island. Before long, enthusiastic Brady, accompanied by prospective investors, inspected this activity and other development sites about the Sound. After visiting Valdez John was less concerned about the damage left from recent glacial floods than about the two competing railroads, which might "get to quarreling and neither road be built." He assumed that "these matters will be thrashed out in Washington."[26]

American legislators were indeed thrashing. As one of them said when discussing aid for Alaska railroad construction, "I think it will be a long time before the American people will be willing to go into Federal Government–aided railroad building again, after all the rottenness and corruption of the Crédit Mobilier and the De Golyer–Oakes Ames affairs." Undismayed by Congress's hesitancy, Reynolds pushed ahead; in the East he instituted a Boston-Alaska Society. John became editor of its monthly publication. And then, with speculative ardor, Reynolds bought, leased, or in some fashion united the following "Affiliated Companies" with the Reynolds-Alaska Development Company:

> Alaska-Coast Copper Co., Arthur H. Elliott, Pres., Capital $1,000,000
> Alaska Coast Co., Robt. N. Cummings, Pres., Capital $1,000,000
> Reynolds Smelter Co., Blamey Stevens, M.Sc., Pres., Capital $1,000,000
> Alaska Realty Co., Adam Swan, Pres., Capital $1,000,000
> Inter-Island Co., James Bettles, Pres., Capital $100,000
> Alaska Dock Co., Frank E. Youngs, Pres., Capital $100,000
> Alaska Utilities Co., Charles Kramer, Pres., Capital $1,000,000
> Alaska Construction Co., J. D. Sheldon, Press., Capital $100,000
> Copper River Drayage Co., Edward Wood, Pres., Capital $100,000
> Alaska Prospector Co., Wm. H. Crary, Pres., Capital $50,000
> Alaska Hotel Co., Simeon Poot, Pres., Capital $100,000
> Alaska Roadhouse Co., C. C. Roberts, Pres., Capital $100,000
> Copper River Lumber Co., William Finnical, Pres., Capital $50,000.[27]

Reynolds apparently put all of these companies together in about eighteen months. John exuberantly forwarded a 1907 prospectus to Sheldon Jackson urging him to buy in before the value of the financial edifice became prohibitive. Jackson replied, "My confidence in your Company is in the men connected with it and a prospectus without a knowledge of the men behind it is of no value whatever to me. It usually goes into the waste basket without being read." Later, Jackson warned Elizabeth, he had his "doubts about the conservatism and safety of Mr. Reynolds. It looks very much as if he was 'biting off more than he can chew.'"[28] By August of 1907 Brady compared Reynolds to "a whirlwind [who] drives with astonishing speed."

The tenth of that month found John Brady presiding at a mass meeting of Valdez townsmen determined to drive their stalled railroad northward. Standing beside him was handsome, winning Harry Reynolds, whom John laughingly introduced as the "piston rod." A special correspondent for the *Alaska-Yukon Magazine* was in the audience. His prose is a classic of its type:

> On August 10th of this year the horoscope of the city of Valdez must have shown that the town had emerged from under the evil influence of all the baleful planets . . . . This meeting was called by the former Governor of Alaska John G. Brady and Henry D. Reynolds. Both of these gentlemen were personally known to most of the residents of Valdez. . . . Mr. Reynolds, who had planned the work that was to be done, delivered a spirited address. Coatless, dressed in a flannel shirt, trousers tucked in miner's boots, his youthful face animated with enthusiasm over his subject, he presented a unique figure. His enthusiasm was infectious. His plan was to organize the Home Railway Company, capitalize it at $10,000 the mile and begin work immediately. He reviewed the history of previous attempts at railroad building from Valdez; pointed out the mistakes made and the way to avoid similar mistakes in the future. He told of how railroads have been built in western states and showed how simple the problem is when properly handled. He directed attention to the steady encroachment of the eastern trusts. He said that they had gradually bought nearly every Alaska steamship line save the one now owned by himself and his associates.

And then, after more on the "inevitable fight to a finish between Alaskans and the trusts," Reynolds delivered his peroration: "Mere money and avarice will not prevail against earnest and determined men. Alaskans are men of more than ordinary ability. We have the richest resources in the world to draw from, and we have here tonight the survival of ten years of pioneering. Gentlemen, the hour has come to show the grasping corporations that we can meet combination with combination, money with money, brain with brain, and we can hold our own against them."[29] Best of all, Mr. Reynolds had a plan. Slapping down his own $10,000 check on the speaker's table, he challenged his audience to build a railroad to the summit of the coast range, thirty-four miles away, in ninety days.

A hubbub ensued. Only after $106,000 of the $340,000 necessary to construct the road had been subscribed did the tumult subside. Blamey Stevens promised to take "charge of the engineering without salary and contributed $5,000 besides." As for Reynolds, "he will take no salary or promotion shares, and insist upon no high salaries or promotion stock to anyone. . . . but his copper mines are reputedly fabulously rich, and he is evidently inspired by the principle that his wealth is in trust for Alaska and should be utilized for its advancement." On 13 August Brady turned the first shovelful of earth for the Alaska Home Railway's line; a few days later hundreds of men were at work grading. By the end of the month the Alaska Home Railway had been incorporated for $10,000,000. During September Brady and Reynolds "addressed the various civic organizations of Seattle. . . . $9,000 was subscribed the first day. . . . The people are keyed to a pitch of enthusiasm that makes failure impossible."[30]

To accompany his ten-million-dollar railroad, Reynolds would have his town too. "At the Reynolds Alaska Mine on Prince William Sound is the town of Reynolds, one of the cleanest and best-equipped towns on the coast, where every building is painted white and the dirt and soot usually found in mining camps are not allowed to accumulate." The *Alaska-Yukon Magazine* reporter who wrote this must have been hallucinating. "The town has a bank, store, hotel, barber shop, laundry, hospital, a hall, and other accessories of an up-to-date mining camp. . . . There never has been a strike among the workmen of Reynolds-Alaska Mine." No wonder—the community described here never existed! There were some sheds, the start of a smelter, and, most symbolic of all, an aerial tramway, but little else.[31]

Sensing the impending disaster and appalled at the inescapable labyrinth into which her husband had wandered, Elizabeth became seriously ill. Her letters to John took on an embittered edge. She would as soon "take the shares in a railroad to the moon" as the Alaska Home Railway. She was frightened, for "you the Treasurer will be held responsible." "It will all go crash . . ."[32]

During September forebodings beset John. He tried to calm his wife's fears with letters to both Cassia and Elizabeth. By October he willingly confessed to Cassia: "We have undertaken to do too much, but we are in for it and must fight it through. Understand we and R.A.D. Co. do not own the Alaska Home Ry. but we are backing it and have gone to the extent of our resources." As if to confirm this, rifle shots echoed off the walls of Keystone Canyon north of Valdez. Alaska Home Railway laborers and the Alaska Syndicate's construction workers had spilled blood. John believed that the violent encounter "put the Guggenheims in a bad light" and "will doubtless call for a Congressional investigation." "I know not what Providence has in store for us," he sighed, "but I am praying and working as best I can."[33]

What Providence had in store was the grim Bankers' Panic of 1907. By the end of October the paper pyramid of H. D. Reynolds and John G. Brady had all gone crash, as Elizabeth predicted. "Reynolds has simply been crazy in the scope of his transactions," John groaned. "The man went wild and beyond the reach of everybody." And then, ashamed and cursing his folly, John confessed, "I am overwhelmed in disgrace and must take it all. I am dazed over it all and can hardly realize where I stand." He was, in truth, financially ruined. Possibly that made it a little easier when he tried to apologize to his friends for their losses. John was thankful that no criminal charges were brought against him. As for H. D. Reynolds, a complete nervous breakdown enabled him to substitute an asylum for a prison.[34]

With his personal estate in rubble, John's first reaction was to return to Satchahnee. Second thoughts reminded him that his mill no longer functioned. Above all, he wanted his children to continue to benefit from a superior education. Generous invitations from Yale classmates probably decided the matter. John joined his family in Brookline.

The story of the Brady family over the next few years is a study in stoic frugality. Elizabeth and John cut costs to the bone. To provide an occasional little nicety for his family, or simply to pay a utility bill, John periodically parted with yet another of his precious native artifacts. These choice items had taken him decades to collect. In the space of a few years they were sold. As quickly as possible his sons commenced to pay their own educational expenses, not to their father's regret: "it tempered them." And at Phillips Academy they were getting the finest college preparatory training America could offer.

Old Yale friends Arthur Dodge, Robert Kelly, F. S. Witherbee, and especially the Reverend Samuel Bushnell, a member of the "Black and Tans" class, rallied to assist John in finding employment. Most important, their words and actions enabled him to maintain his self-respect.[35] Financial panics were a hazard common to their epoch, associates reassured him. Alaska's grand old man would bounce back. Certainly the convivial, invariably optimistic westerner tried. Among the business ventures in which Brady involved himself over the next ten years were a proposed elevated monorail for Long Island, silent movie films set in the Great Land, the manufacture of mahogany furniture, and, in 1913, a business trip to China.

For a few years the General Manifold and Printing Company of New York City seems to have been Brady's major employer. The corporation plant was so large, so impersonal, that even the sanguine Brady must occasionally have felt uncomfortable. In his mid-sixties, he found keeping up with the younger men virtually impossible. Employment with General Manifold had required the Bradys to move to Manhattan. It was an environment they disliked, but Elizabeth loyally supported the surrender. Gotham did have its simple, inexpensive pleasures. Accompanied by Elizabeth, John visited his childhood haunts. Once they checked the church records and discovered that he was a year older than he had believed.

An oasis to which John found himself increasingly attracted was the Public Documents Room of New York's Public Library. Here he could escape the frenzy of factory and boulevard and return to his beloved homeland. He began writing an autobiography. When he reached Union Theological Seminary days, his pen faltered and stopped. Although incapable of disciplined self-analysis, he ground out some copy on Alaska for popular commercial journals. These successes spurred him to author a book on Alaska. He copied hundreds and hundreds of pages of Great Land information from government documents, the *Overland Monthly*, and rare books. But publishers rejected his drafts. Alaska was not newsworthy. Her gold production was in decline and her population had peaked. The Author's Service Bureau urged him to hunt up fellow New Yorker Rex Beach, "Write articles on Alaska happenings, try and get a little love fiction if you can." But fiction was not John's bent. Furthermore, he may have felt uncomfortable about looking up Beach, for though the novelist's opinions paralleled many of his own, they were astringent and probably aggravated his Reynolds scars. Random letters full of questions from an up-and-coming Alaska historian, Clarence L. Andrews, reminded John how much history he had lived and seen and helped make.[36]

Inevitably John's desire to communicate his knowledge of Alaska was capitalized on by numerous program chairmen. Businessmen's groups, women's clubs, church bodies, and schools enjoyed having the good-natured ex-governor talk about his Great Land. "We have never had a lecture that was more eagerly and earnestly listened to," one listener commented. "The speaker was profoundly interested in his topic." In 1912 John informed Yale's alumni, "Much of my time is now given to lecturing with globe, charts, maps, and slides, trying to tell and instruct the people what Alaska really is and how much it has in store for our young people who will be brave and resolute enough to go there and appropriate their share." Whose share and how much were questions that Brady was increasingly asked to address.[37]

In 1902 and then again in 1907 and 1908, President Theodore Roosevelt had withdrawn from private development vast Alaska timber lands in the national domain. Governor Brady had doubted the wisdom of simply a "you can't" policy, as he called it. "Would it not be more for the public good to invite people rather to cut off and utilize this grown timber and clean off the mountain sides of it, and let the young growth have a chance to mature?" He noted the remarkable fresh cover of trees that quickly sprang up from abandoned native villages and across storm-shattered stands. "The earth is the Lord's and the fullness thereof," he insisted, "and it should be our motto to ask the people living upon the earth to enjoy it in all ways without committing waste or wanton destruction." Alaskans were especially antagonized by President Roosevelt's 1906 executive order withdrawing Alaskan coal lands within the public domain.[38]

Five years later, still sensitive to unhappy memories of his resignation-Reynolds denouement, John had shifted to a testy anti-Roosevelt, anti-conservationist position. Conservation had penetrated the public mind through such widely headlined feuds as the Ballinger-Pinchot controversy and heated disputes over exactly how much conservation should be practiced. To the north, Alaskans had worked themselves into a lather over the restrictive federal coal policy. In 1911, incensed at being prevented from selling "their coal," Cordova citizens dumped a cargo of Canadian coal into the nearby bay. Their burlesque of Boston's Tea Party attracted the desired publicity to Cordova's "Coal Party." In a series of hotly written articles penned for *Commerce and Industries*, John expressed opinions no doubt voiced in his lectures. "President Roosevelt, as the all powerful champion of Pinchot's ideas, struck the knockout blow to the coal business in Alaska." "Is there no balm in Gilead for Alaska's hurt?" he asked rhetorically. And then, in a reply tinged with sarcasm, "Yea, verily! It is the leasing system." The present laws governing Alaska were bad, and Roosevelt and Pinchot had made them worse. "The Morgan-Guggenheim Syndicate and other malefactors of great wealth, who have avaricious eye [*sic*] upon all the people's wealth in Alaska, can be properly restrained by a [coal and timber] leasing system. The United States Government must assume the functions of a landlord and still further its bureaucratic power at Washington." John Brady's conclusion had a John Troy ring to it: "Mr. Roosevelt and his inspirers have said in their haste and leisure that all Alaskans are liars." Rex Beach also condemned the federal government for permitting America's conservationist pressure to descend with special severity on "the last frontier." When Washington insisted that Alaskans could neither sell nor receive money for their coal lands, the law, snorted Beach, "made perjurers out of nine-tenths of the miners."[39]

That same year John addressed the Twenty-ninth Annual Meeting of the Lake Mohonk Conference. Joining this band of humanitarians and detailing the advances of Alaska's native peoples proved a heart-warming experience. In his speech, entitled "The Present Status of the Alaskan Natives," John reviewed the pathos of culture shock among the Northwest Coast Indians, showing how important the subsequent role of the missionary-educator was in alleviating their distress. He praised the Indians as "progressive, self-supporting" people. And with an eye to his times, John added, "The woman is quite the equal of the husband." It vexed him that the law still regarded the Indians as "uncivilized tribes," yet "he was confident that the country could find no more willing and braver defenders if their services were asked." Clarification of their legal status was overdue; protection of their "ancient fishing grounds" was imperative. John liked nothing better than to contrast the conditions a half-century before with those of 1911:

> They are not manufacturing rum; they are not torturing and putting witches to the stake; they are not holding and dealing [in] slaves. The old communal structure and the *icht*, or Shaman, have disappeared. In their stead one beholds the single family dwelling and the visits of the physician at the call of the sick. The canoe and paddles are giving way to the more serviceable boat ribbed with oak and sheathed with spruce or red cedar, and propelled by oars or gasolene. Young men are carpenters, machinists, smiths, shoemakers, coopers, boat builders, miners, engineers on land and water; young women eagerly pursue the domestic arts, as one can see when he enters a home and beholds the children and the surroundings. That they have changed is well established by a visit to the store which supplies their wants . . . sugar, tea, coffee, cured meats, fresh fruits, canned goods of all kinds even to salmon, tables, chairs, stoves, pictures, musical instruments, ready-made suits, fine coffins . . . [40]

Two years later he was again asked to address the Lake Mohonk Conference. Again he concentrated his comments on Alaska's native population, only this time he traced Jackson's work among the Eskimos.

News that "God had called" Dr. Jackson saddened the Bradys. It was he who had induced John to become an Alaskan and thereafter had played such an intimate part of their personal and professional lives. Months earlier they had regretted their inability "to personally tender you our heartfelt congratulations" on "the 50th anniversary of your wedding and of your noble missionary life." Elizabeth bespoke her deep respect for the Presbyterian leader with a booklet extolling *Rev. Sheldon Jackson, D.D.: A Progressive Missionary*. News in the fall of 1910 that the "Sitka Training School has closed its doors forever!" and that the "Sheldon Jackson School will stand ready to carry on the work" formalized a long-overdue name change.[41]

To some degree these aroused Presbyterians had moderated America's red-white tragedy in Alaska. It simply is not true that they cared little about the education of the pioneers' youngsters. John took as much pride in the appointment of the first Alaskan to a U.S. military academy (Daniel D. Pullen to West Point in 1906), though he happened to be white, as he would have if he had been a nonwhite. In fact, Cassia listed his efforts to obtain a cadet appointment for Alaskans among his important accomplishments. One of those few occasions when ex-governor Brady poked his nose into governmental matters was a 1911 letter to James Wickersham, then Alaska's territorial delegate to Congress. As one might guess, the communication dealt with native rights and suggestions for improving Far North schools.[42]

A later generation can only envy Brady's contemporaries their immense confidence in the transforming power of formal education. When John was a student at Yale, William Graham Sumner's prodigious industry and voracious appetite for all kinds of knowledge had stimulated his search for truth. John was likewise inspired as he read Sumner's widely discussed *Folkways* in 1907. Education and experience had provided John that supreme gift of a catholic mind; thus he probably found little difficulty in accepting Sumner's evolutionary views. Both men were ordained ministers, had "preached the gospel," yet each had found his ministry outside the church. Although John can hardly have been comfortable with Sumner's emphasis on the aleatory element as a basis for religion, he must have been impressed by the brilliant sociopsychological hypotheses expressed in *Folkways*. Although neither man lived to witness the runaway consumerism that would engulf their nation a half-century hence, they had moved toward a materialistic ethic.[43] Fortunately circumstances enabled John to keep his particular Christian priorities straight. He might have put too high a value on things, but his fellow man, his family, and above all his relationship with a Christian God remained paramount.

Through good times and bad, Elizabeth had been a rudder. By 1914 she realized that she must soon be the engine and, sooner than she might like, the family compass. Her father had passed on, both of her sisters were married, and John was fading faster than anyone cared to admit. His constant reflections on Sitka and Satchahnee and their mutual antipathy for clamorous New York City dictated a return to Alaska. With typical hardheadedness Elizabeth had prepared herself. Three years of summer study at nearby Columbia University had equipped her with the latest teacher training "industrial arts for elementary school." Helpful in reformulating her own educational philosophy was the pamphlet she wrote for the Woman's Board of Home

Missions, *The First Presbyterian Missionary in Alaska, Mrs. Amanda McFarland.*

In 1914, weighed down by the educational expenses of their five children, Elizabeth returned to teaching. Doubly painful to John, circumstances dictated that her employment separate them. For two years her part-time employer was Hampton Institute in Virginia. Working in an environment similar to famed Tuskegee, Elizabeth justified their sacrifice as but a necessary prelude to an eventual return to Sitka and her reemployment there.[44] John, Jr., busy as yard salesman at the Mills lumber company, urged them to "hurry on home."

In late August of 1916 John and Elizabeth, accompanied by their eldest daughter, Mary, steamed northward. Elizabeth had a teaching position and Mary would assist in Sitka's other school. After a wonderfully relaxing voyage midst the insular beauty of the Alexander Archipelago forests, the Bradys rejoiced when their passage through these vistas finally revealed Sitka. John was jubilant. Tomorrow he would begin rebuilding his mill and training a new generation of natives. He was extremely proud of his own youngsters. Hugh was a Yale graduate and Sheldon soon to be one; Mary graduated from Vassar, and Betty was obtaining a Simmons education. He and Elizabeth had accomplished what they had gone east for, and now he could begin again.

The *Prince of Wales* slowed and its engine shifted from idle to reverse as it came to rest at Sitka's wharf. No boys' band greeted them; the town seemed even more languid than at their departure almost ten years before. Midway down the gangplank Alaska's ex-governor stopped, staggered, and fell against his son John. Disabled by a stroke, he was carried by his family to their temporary quarters, the teacher's rooms atop Sitka's public school. John G. Brady had come home, broken in mind and body but not in spirit.[45]

1. TAP, mf. 11, President's Confidential Report to the Stockholders of the Reynolds-Alaska Development Company Presented at the Annual Stockholders' Meeting in New York, 13 May 1905. JGB, unfiled, Brady to John C. Martin, 19 April 1905. Hitchcock, *Annual Report, 1905,* p. 98; TAP, mf. 11, Brady to Hitchcock, 8 July 1905. *Seattle Post-Intelligencer,* 30 August 1905.

2. JGB, unfiled, Brady to Marvin, 18 April 1905; ibid., Brady to Emmons, 20 April 1905. *Ketchikan Mining Journal,* 11 February 1905, and *Daily Alaskan,* 4 April 1905. Swineford's denunciations of Brady were almost cool when compared with the blazing headlines and hot copy that Troy's tireless bellows produced.

3. Samples of press reaction may be found in EAH, box 45, "Newspaper Clippings Oct. 11, 1900 to Jan. 6, 1907." *New York Evening Post,* 4 April 1905; *Washington Post,* 5 April 1905; *Boston Journal,* 5 April 1905. *New York Times,* 5 April 1905. *Dispatch,* 16 March 1905, and *Alaska Record-Miner,* 16 March 1905.

4. *Seattle Post-Intelligencer*, 21 April 1905. *Courant* (Hartford, Conn.), 27 April 1904. JGB, unfiled, Brady to Nelson, 20 April 1905.

5. JGB, unfiled, Brady to Reynolds, 7 April 1905, and ibid., 29 May 1905.

6. Brady, *Annual Report, 1904*, pp. 10–11, 36 (italics added). Hitchcock, *Annual Report, 1905*, p. 93, parroted John's opinion on the imperative need for "better transportation facilities."

7. TAP, mf. 1, Reynolds to Roosevelt, 13 May 1905; ibid., president's confidential report, 13 May 1905.

8. *Dispatch*, 6 July 1905.

9. *Seattle Post-Intelligencer*, 8 July 1905.

10. Ibid., 28 August 1905. Brady, *Annual Report, 1905*, p. 24. Wickersham, *Old Yukon*, p. 475.

11. *Seattle Post-Intelligencer*, 6 July 1905. *Congressional Record*, 58th Cong., 2d sess., 18 April 1904, p. 4997. Hitchcock, *Annual Report, 1905*, p. 94. Richardson, *Messages and Papers*, 15:7019.

12. JGB, unfiled, Brady to Reynolds, 29 May 1905. *Daily Alaskan*, 15 May 1902. JCorr, 20:266, Brady to Jackson, 8 April 1903; TAP, mf. 9, Brady to Hitchcock, 5 May 1903.

13. TAP, mf. 13, Greely to Hitchcock, 10 October 1905.

14. JCorr, 22:284–85, Brady to Jackson, 27 October 1905.

15. TAP, mf. 11, report of Frank C. Churchill, special agent, concerning Hon. John G. Brady, governor of the district of Alaska and his connection with the Reynolds-Alaska Development Company, 28 October 1905. The printed Churchill findings, U.S., Congress, Senate, *Reports of Conditions of Education and School Service and Management of Reindeer Service in Alaska*, Doc. No. 483, 59th Cong., 1st sess., 12 June 1906, were especially hard on Sheldon Jackson and his reindeer program. Strongly worded defenses came from the general agent's superiors in and out of government.

16. TAP, mf. 11, report of Frank C. Churchill.

17. JGB, mf. 2, Brady to his wife, 22 December 1904; ibid., 11 January 1905; ibid., 26 March 1905. Interview with Hugh Brady, 6 June 1962. *Daily Alaskan*, 11 October 1905. Ibid., 3 March 1906 and 24 January 1905. Johnson and Malone, *DAB*, 8:176. Thomas G. Tousey, *Military History of Carlisle and Carlisle Barracks* (Richmond, Va., 1939), pp. 336–37. *Daily Alaskan*, 6 January 1906. Utley, *Richard Henry Pratt*, p. 337.

18. Utley, *Richard Henry Pratt*, p. 337.

19. JGB, mf. 3, Brady to Peelle, 27 January 1906. JCorr, 22:381, Brady to Jackson, 7 January 1907; JGB, unfiled, Brady to Nelson, 17 February 1906; ibid., Brady to Peelle, 13 April 1906.

20. The accompanying letter to the president was postdated 29 January and read: "I herewith tender my resignation as Governor of the District of Alaska to take effect at your earliest convenience." Thus the statements by Henry W. Clark, *Alaska: The Last Frontier* (New York, 1930), p. 130, that President Roosevelt "ousted" Governor Brady, and Merle Colby, *A Guide to Alaska: Last American Frontier* (New York, 1941), p. 168, that he was "removed" are incorrect.

21. *Seattle Post-Intelligencer*, 21 January and 15 February 1906. James T. White & Co., *National Cyclopedia of American Biography*, 47 vols. (New York, 1940), 28:463. An Annapolis graduate familiar with Alaska since the 1880s and successful in both public and private careers, Hoggatt was a responsible choice. After three and a half years, he gladly stepped down as governor.

22. TAP, mf. 11, report of Frank C. Churchill. *Alaskan*, 24 February and 28 July 1906. TAP, mf. 15, W. H. Moody (attorney general) to various government officials authorizing movement of the capital from Sitka to Juneau, 17 and 23 July 1906.

23. James C. Foster, "The Western Federation Comes to Alaska," *Pacific Northwest Quarterly* 66 (October 1975): 161–76. *Military Telegraph Bulletin* (Eagle), 24 and 27 October 1905, and other reports indicate that as the "easy pickings" played out, violence increased. Continental Alaska was following the pattern set earlier in the Panhandle and across the Far West: corporate mining succeeded the individual prospector.

24. JGB, unfiled, Brady to Reynolds, 1 January 1906; ibid., 28 February 1906; and AGP, box 12, Brady to Distin, 8 March 1906. *Seattle Post-Intelligencer,* 12 April 1906. Robert D. Arnold, *Alaska Native Land Claims* (Anchorage, 1976), pp. 80–81.

25. *Alaskan,* 28 April and 5 May 1906. *Daily Alaska Dispatch,* 13 September 1906. Cassia was quoting George T. Emmons. *Alaskan,* 7 April 1906.

26. *Alaskan,* 1 September 1906. JGB, unfiled, Brady to Reynolds, 7 April 1906; ibid., 28 February 1906. *Alaskan,* 18 August and 15 September 1906 and 23 February 1907. Interview with Hugh Brady, 12 July 1973. *Seattle Post-Intelligencer,* 22 and 24 July 1905; and TAP, mf. 14, Brady to Hitchcock, 23 December 1905.

27. *Congressional Record,* 59th Cong., 1st sess., 21 May 1906, p. 7202. R. L. Polk & Co., *Alaska-Yukon Gazetteer and Business Directory, 1907–1908* (Seattle, 1907), p. 94A. Some insight on how Reynolds accomplished this can be gleaned from JGB, mf. 3, especially "To the Stockholders of the Reynolds Alaska Development Company," ca. December 1907.

28. PTS, SJ letters, 19:343, Jackson to H. D. Reynolds Company, 11 January 1907; ibid., 20:194, Jackson to Elizabeth Brady, 19 October 1907.

29. JGB, mf. 2, Brady to Cassia Patton, 10 August 1907. Unidentified "special Valdez correspondent," "Renascent Valdez," *Alaska-Yukon Magazine,* October 1907, pp. 162–70.

30. "Renascent Valdez," pp. 162–70.

31. Ibid. Although Orth, *Alaska Place Names,* p. 803, makes no mention of the town of Reynolds, the highflyer is appropriately immortalized on Latouche Island by Reynolds Peak.

32. JGB, mf. 3, Brady to Cassia Patton, 24 September 1907; ibid., Elizabeth Brady to her husband, 17 September 1907.

33. Hunt, *North of 53°,* chap. 26. Andrews, *Story of Alaska,* p. 213. JGB, mf. 2, Brady to Cassia Patton, 8 October 1907.

34. Reynolds was not crazy, just too eager. For an example of successful promotion in the same region by a more prudent go-getter, see Roberta A. Stearns's assessment of Stephen Birch, "Alaska's Kennecott Copper and the Kennecott Copper Corporation," *Alaska Journal* 5 (Summer 1975): 130–39. Interview with Hugh Brady, 9 April 1967. JGB, mf. 2, Brady to Cassia Patton, 17 October 1907. *Seattle Post-Intelligencer,* 20 October 1907. So embarrassed was the *Alaska-Yukon Magazine* editor, E. S. Harrison, over the October "Renascent Valdez" article that his post-crash November issue included a rather pathetic apology to his readers (*Alaska-Yukon Magazine,* November 1907, pp. 267–69). The Reynolds-Alaska Development Company did not formally expire until 1933, when its charter lapsed (Hugh P. Brady, personal business records).

35. *Kansas City Star,* 20 November 1906. Interview with Hugh Brady, 9 May 1968; Yale University Alumni Association to author, 31 July 1975.

36. John G. Brady, "Alaska and the Yukon," *Independent,* 24 July 1909, pp. 1379–85; also his "Alaska's New Found Resources," *Assembly Herald,* June 1910, pp. 255–57. Series of four articles by Brady in *Commerce and Industries Magazine*: "Mal-Administration in Alaska," September 1911, pp. 103–17; "Alaska's Grievances," October 1911, pp. 217–18; "A Condition of Mind," October 1911, pp. 181–86; "Conservation in Alaska," October 1911, pp. 187–95. JGB, unfiled, report on Brady manuscript, n.d. Rex Beach, "What Is the Matter with Alaska?", *Saturday Evening Post,* 25 February 1911, pp. 3 ff. CLASJC, unfiled, Andrews to Brady, 20 April 1915, and ibid., Brady to Andrews, 17 July 1914 and 2 February and 9 November 1915.

37. JGB, unfiled, W. B. Gunnison to whom it may concern, 27 October 1914. Yale College, *Biographical Record of the Class of 1874 of Yale College: Part Fourth, 1874–1909* (New Haven, 1912), p. 30.

38. Originally referred to as the Alexander Archipelago Forest Reserve, 20 August 1902, this reserve, along with other large parcels, ultimately became America's largest national forest, the Tongass National Forest (Brady, *Annual Report, 1903*, p. 22). Governor Brady favored the protection of wildlife and decried wasteful killings by natives as well as whites (Brady, *Annual Report, 1901*, pp. 18–19, and idem, *Annual Report, 1902*, p. 50). David E. Conrad, "Creating the Nation's Largest Forest Reserve: Roosevelt, Emmons, and the Tongass National Forest," *Pacific Historical Review* 46 (February 1977): 65–83.

39. As is now rather generally known, Ballinger deserved his exoneration by the congressional investigating committee, but Pinchot won in the court of public opinion. For a balanced view of this highly charged episode, see James Penick, Jr., *Progressive Politics and Conservation: The Ballinger-Pinchot Affair* (Chicago, 1968). A fine overview of the conservation question at that time is Samuel P. Hays, *Conservation and the Gospel of Efficiency: The Progressive Conservation Movement, 1890–1920* (Cambridge, Mass., 1959). Brady, *Commerce and Industries*, pp. 181–83, 117. Beach, "What Is the Matter with Alaska?", p. 40.

40. Brady, "Alaskan Natives," pp. 75–82.

41. John G. Brady, "Conditions in Alaska," *Report of the Thirty-First Annual Lake Mohonk Conference* (Washington, D.C., 1913), pp. 185–89. JCorr, 22:501, Brady to Dr. and Mrs. Jackson, 14 May 1908. Elizabeth P. Brady, *Rev. Sheldon Jackson, D.D.: A Progressive Missionary* (New York, 1911). *Thlinget*, August 1910.

42. *Congressional Record*, 58th Cong., 3d sess., 12 December 1904, p. 124. *Seattle Post-Intelligencer*, 15 February 1906. *Alaskan*, 5 May 1906. JGB, mf. 3, Brady to Wickersham, 26 December 1911.

43. Sydney E. Ahlstrom, *The American Protestant Encounter with World Religions* (Beloit, Wisc., 1962), p. 33. Robert Green McCloskey, *American Conservatism in the Age of Enterprise, 1865–1910: A Study of William Graham Sumner, Stephen J. Field, and Andrew Carnegie* (New York, 1951), pp. 68–71, seems as applicable to Brady as to Sumner.

44. Interview with John, Hugh, Mary, and Elizabeth Brady, 24 November 1967, Seattle. Registrar, Teacher's College, Columbia University, to author, 10 April 1973. Elizabeth Brady, *The First Missionary in Alaska: A Sketch* (New York, 1912). Eleanor A. Gilman, Hampton Institute, to author, 20 June 1973. CLASJC, Elizabeth Brady to Andrews, 3 October 1936.

45. JGB, mf. 3, Elizabeth Brady to Anson P. Stokes, 10 February 1926. Yale University, *Obituary Record of Graduates of Yale University, 1918–1919* (New Haven, 1920), p. 922. Interview with John and Hugh Brady, 23 June 1962.

CHAPTER EIGHTEEN

Home Again

Cursing his invalid status and eager to begin digging in his garden, John was glad when Satchahnee's repairs were finished and he could at last go home. His son John had done much to improve its water system and generally "bring the house up to grade."

Alaska's ex-governor had never envisioned himself as Sitka's Dr. Pangloss. His voice was not yet squeeky, nor was his frame a frail reed. It nettled him when his ladies enjoined him "not to work so hard." Once while dragging some kelp up from the beach to his garden for fertilizer, he did indeed make an old fool out of himself. His oldest son had rebuked him for demanding too much from his body, and when he spotted his father sweating with the seaweed, John ran down the beach, angrily admonishing him to cease such labor. The old man bristled, threw down the kelp, and raised his fists. "Put up your dukes," he challenged his astonished son. The inroads of diabetes, the aftershocks of his stroke, increasing dropsy—his strength could no longer match his will.

Reduced to puttering about, and always a saver, John took to dismantling the launch *Gertrude*, rotting on chocks near his mill. Then came a second cerebral blow. Fallen off his ladder and sprawled on the beach, his arm broken, he probably would have drowned from the incoming tide had not a native boy rescued him.[1] Chained by his infirmities to a bed, capable of reading for but brief periods, the worn-out old man had plenty of time for reflecting on his full life.

Now, a half-century later, it is easier to evaluate John G. Brady as a person. Was he a great man? He galvanized no political movement, built no industrial empire, left no important discovery or body of writings. Did he bequeath any enduring monument to his heirs, to society?

At his death his personal estate represented only three thousand dollars. Elizabeth even failed in her later attempts to give away Satchahnee to Sitka's public school system. Yet John thought that his life said something. Bedridden and aware that he was dying, he again tried to construct an autobiography and, for a second time, got no further than Yale.[2]

As an Alaskan pioneer, he compiled a creditable list of epithets: lawmaker, educator, businessman, publicist, and humanitarian. But no single law, judicial controversy, economic development, or sociocultural achievement bears Brady's name; hence Alaskan histories usually give him little if any attention. James Wickersham left a valuable *Bibliography of Alaskan Literature*. By contrast, few northlanders today are aware of Brady's Alaskan informational efforts or of his struggle not only to preserve the region's past but also to uplift its peoples and perpetuate their advances by appropriate legislation.

Brady's historical significance should not be judged merely in an Alaskan context. In a number of illuminating ways he embodied his age, an epoch in American history that, as one historian has recently suggested, witnessed more fundamental social and economic changes than any "other period of equal length in the history of the United States."[3]

Satchahnee, "home on a hill"—was its name happenstance or did Brady have in mind Matthew 5:14: "Ye are the light of the world. A city that is set on a hill cannot be hid"? He no doubt visualized the Brady farm and his handsome family as the best kind of appeal for potential pioneers. Verse sixteen of that same chapter is an injunction that he repeated many times to his children: "Let your light so shine before men, that they may see your good works, and glorify your Father which is in heaven." From his youth John had felt the compulsion to do good and to serve God. And like millions of his fellow nineteenth-century Christians, he was confident that educated men could attain great heights. In steady retreat was the Calvinist's suspicion of man's prideful absorption in his own works instead of glorifying those of God. For Brady and his age, Saint Augustine's spiritual City of God stood little chance against the mushrooming marvel, science's modern metropolis.

But John, like a growing number of twentieth-century Americans, had ambivalent feelings about the City of Man. Visiting the agrarian democracy that later shaped John's youth, Alexis de Tocqueville had worried lest the aggressive individualism of a richly endowed America might separate man from his contemporaries and his past. At the end of the century, John faced a similar dilemma. Initially uneasy about those Alaska sojourners so thoughtless of the Great Land's future, John eventually ceased to worry once he succumbed to the go-getter disease. If he represented an America of brave ideals, alarmed at an industrial society spinning faster and faster, he was also mesmerized, perhaps, by the prospects that the Merlins of manufacturing and money held before them. On the one hand, by giving his children the best eastern education available, he made certain that they were well equipped to keep step with the quickening pace of life. On the other, he dreamed that they might all become Far North homemakers and enjoy a quality of life that Boston and New York were rapidly discarding. It was probably just as well that the tired old man's vision could not penetrate beyond 1918; not one of his sons or daughters would settle in Alaska.

Like every other Alaska governor, John had to master his frustration with far-off federal officials who so conveniently forgot the Great Land, its size notwithstanding. In time, America's resource demands and modern technology would change that. Curiously, a malicious comment by John Troy about Governor Brady ended up in President Roosevelt's fourth annual message. In 1904 Troy had written: "The governor of Alaska comes in contact with the people but little. He is an executive in name only. His powers are largely confined to the appointment of notaries public, the writing of absurd Thanksgiving proclamations and the preparation of an abominable report once a year." Later that year Theodore Roosevelt declared that the Far North governor "has nothing specific to do except to make annual reports, issue Thanksgiving Day proclamations, and appoint Indian policemen and notaries public."[4] John knew how hard he worked, how year after year he sacrificed months at the capital lobbying for Alaska at his own expense. The president's ignorance of his labors must surely have hurt. Then again, such eastern slights may only have reinforced John's conviction—and that of just about every other Alaskan—that unless they exaggerated their handicaps, and did so with stentorian lungs, their needs would be overlooked by a government whose New Empire stretched south to Panama and west to the Philippines.

Later generations would agree that the rather sudden disillusionment by Americans in the glories of an overseas empire was a healthy and fortuitous phenomenon. Quite unhealthy was the ethnocentric basis for this shift in mood. As speaker Thomas Reed growled, "I suppose we had niggers enough in this country without buying any more of 'em." John and his fellow Christians helped counter this blatant racism. That these humanitarians were clothed in restrictive ethnocentric garb is unquestioned. What is of vital importance, they fostered leadership within Alaska's indigenous societies. It was no coincidence that the

Alaskan Native Brotherhood was born in Sitka in 1912 and that over half of its original Tlingit founders were men who in their youth had been associated with John Brady. Scientific-minded citizens, such as William H. Dall, Alice Fletcher, and George T. Emmons, concurred with Alfred Brooks's balanced evaluation of the work of "the missionary and his teachers" in protecting the natives.[5] John and Elizabeth Brady *had* made a crucial difference in improving red-white relations in the northland.

John Brady's abiding faith in the abilities of Alaska's natives may have shielded him from the diminution of the Victorian faith in progress. Certainly he glimpsed the onrush of the dynamo that so alarmed Henry Adams. But John also appreciated that there were millions of "uncivilized" people who hungered for the benefits that the dynamo seemed to promise. Raised on a Protestant's diet of dutiful vitality, John never lost confidence in himself as an instrument of God. He was, as Mark Twain had put it, a man "who had the confidence of a Christian holding four aces." Of course the world was a moral battleground, but God knew which was the right side.

What made it all so confusing to John was that the battlegrounds kept changing. The Puritan had started with God and self. Brady's generation increasingly viewed the conflict through social gospel lenses with less emphasis on saving one's soul and far greater attention to saving pagans. Evangelism took on the characteristics of advertising. Superficial faith supplanted study, quantity was more critical than quality, and uplift centered on raising money. As in the business world where "capital was frequently squandered in ways that made it hard to draw the line between optimism and outright dishonesty," religious beliefs became vague and sloppy.[6] Each year the complexities of America's technocratic society made the nuances of moral responsibility, personal conscience, and corporate conscience more difficult to discern. As John so painfully learned, even the go-getter's "sure thing" proved illusory.

Life promised only one sure thing, and by December of 1918 death approached seventy-year-old John Green Brady. John guessed it would not be long. There is never a right time to die, and he knew how lucky he had been. For all life's rigors, a merciful God had made the game worthwhile. He wished that his son John could be at his bedside, but the army had called him. A month earlier, in November 1918, his prayers had been answered: an armistice had been won and the world war was over at last.

Peaceful tools were what he and Elizabeth had bequeathed their progeny. Had John Brady lived a few more years, he would have seen all his family launched upon lives in which, directly or indirectly, they did indeed manifest Christ's injunction: "Go thou and do likewise." Even as his father was passing away, his namesake urged three of his mixed-blood playmates, Ralph Young, Frank Price, and Don Cameron, now grown men, to vote. To their dejected "But they won't let us," John spoke as would his father: "Go ahead and vote. If you are challenged, swear in your vote. If you are challenged and they want to carry it any further it will only take one case. And if they do that, the rest of you can chip in and help defend him." Some seventy natives voted and continued to do so thereafter.[7]

December 17—Christmas would soon be upon them. How gentle was the Sitka winter. Light, feathery snow brushed Satchahnee's windows, and the mountain giants guarding the little harbor town donned their ermine robes. Elizabeth, Mary, and Betty waited quietly. Death had waited long enough.

The news of Governor Brady's death spread rapidly across the community. Word was telegraphed to Juneau, and Governor Thomas Riggs ordered that flags be lowered to half-mast for thirty days. Afterward the Brady women marveled at the spontaneity of it all. Native men, young and old, appeared at Satchahnee, their arms filled with evergreen boughs, their voices as soft as the snowfall. Quickly the house came alive with festooned hemlock, spruce, and other verdant decorations. Everyone felt calmed by the pungent smells. Through her tears, Elizabeth noted that among her comforters were Ranche as well as mission people. They wished to conduct the Christian burial. In spite of her protestations that the family could at least pay for the coffin, the Alaska Native Brotherhood insisted that they would do it. Furthermore, the church service would be in the Tlingit Presbyterian Church, the sanctuary Governor Brady had helped them build.

In respect for their deceased and honored townsman, Sitka's schools closed and shop doors shut. A Ford truck covered with evergreens carried the heavy coffin from Satchahnee to the burial at the other end of town. Up the slope to the National Cemetery moved the column of mourners, the funeral's solemn sadness partially alleviated by the boys' brass band. Sounds from its trumpets, tubas, and trombones were clearly discernible on the campus of nearby Sheldon Jackson School. "Lead Kindly Light," "Rock of Ages," "Jesus Lover of My Soul"—the band intermixed dignity and celebration in its renditions of the hymns that Elizabeth and John had so often sung together. Hardly a mile from the water's edge, the gravesite was a beautiful resting place. Prayers, eulogies, more hymns, lots of love—then it was all over.

The funeral procession trailed back down the ridge. Midway the native band raised their instruments to their lips. "There'll Be a Hot

Time in the Old Town Tonight" reverberated across Alaska's most historic community.[8]

1. Interview with John and Hugh Brady, 23 June 1962. Hugh Brady to author, 5 June 1975.

2. JGB, mf. 3, Elizabeth Brady to Anson Phelps Stokes, 10 February 1926. JGB, unfiled, Elizabeth Brady to U.S. commissioner of education, 12 October 1925. Interview with Hugh Brady, 9 May 1968. JGB, unfiled, order and decree of distribution for Brady, 3 May 1920, Sitka.

3. Walter T. K. Nugent, *From Centennial to World War: American Society, 1876–1917* (Indianapolis, 1977), p. xiv.

4. *Daily Alaskan*, 16 April 1904. Richardson, *Messages and Papers*, 15:6919. Even more intriguing is how Troy's slur finally ended up as fact in Gruening, *The State of Alaska*, p. 122, and Nichols, *Alaska*, p. 242.

5. Mayer, *The Republican Party*, p. 268. Philip Drucker, *The Native Brotherhoods: Modern Intertribal Organizations on the Northwest Coast* (Washington, D.C., 1958), pp. 16–17; Arnold, *Alaska Native Land Claims*, pp. 82–83. Brooks, *Blazing*, pp. 495–500.

6. Thomas C. Cochran, *The Inner Revolution: Essays on the Social Sciences in History* (New York, 1964), p. 96.

7. Interview with John and Hugh Brady, 23 June 1962.

8. JGB, unfiled, Brady's death certificate, 17 December 1918, burial on 18 December signed by U.S. commissioner R. W. DeArmond. *Alaska Daily Empire*, 18 December 1918; *Seattle Post-Intelligencer*, 19 December 1918. Interview with John, Hugh, Mary, and Elizabeth Brady, 24 November 1967. MsEB.

Bibliographic Sources

The most productive body of historical evidence used in writing this biography of an Alaskan pioneer is located in two Atlantic Coast depositories. Of paramount importance has been the John G. Brady Collection housed in Yale University's Beinecke Library; here are his personal papers as well as a considerable portion of his official correspondence. Sadly, Elizabeth Brady destroyed virtually all of her deceased husband's business records. Nevertheless, Beinecke's Brady Collection forms by far the largest single extant manuscript assemblage of any nineteenth-century Alaska governor. Letterpress volumes, unclassified personal and professional correspondence, diaries, and a wide assortment of miscellany extend from Brady's days as a New York City foundling to his postgovernorship years. All of these papers were utilized in this study.

Another preeminent source for writing Far North history is the Sheldon Jackson Collection housed at the Presbyterian Historical Society, Philadelphia. For the period from approximately 1877 to 1906, Jackson's scrapbooks (sixty-five volumes), coupled with his correspondence (some twenty-six volumes of typed transcripts), offer an unparalleled Alaska cache. These scrapbooks comprise an unpredictable accumulation of printed material, everything from steamer tickets to pending Alaska legislation. Fortunately Jackson accurately dated the newspaper clippings, which reflect editorial opinion from all over the United States. There are frequent references to his coworker Brady. This mass of Alaska memorabilia does not always speak favorably of their mutual labors, however. Because Jackson served as both mentor and father-confessor for the one-time New York street arab, his vast correspondence enables one to trace Brady's career from that of tyro missionary through his Alaska governorship.

After the collapse of the Reynolds Development Company and the move of the Brady family to New York City, John Brady vainly attempted an autobiography. He apparently had a number of his important letters to Jackson copied to assist him while writing his "Zigzags of a New York Street Boy" (manuscript in the Beinecke Collection). Today, therefore, these informative communications exist in both New Haven and Philadelphia. Researchers should be warned that these letters drawn from the huge Jackson Collection are but pieces of a mosaic. Furthermore, serious investigators will first wish to exhaust Jackson's correspondence, if for no other reason than that the Presbyterian

377

Historical Society staff has superbly indexed—by sender, the location from which sent, and the date the document originated—the entire mass of letters showered upon him from all over Alaska and the United States. Supplementing this mine of documentary raw material are Jackson's books, magazines, government reports, photographs, and much else acquired by the insatiable collector.

Two vital manuscript sources that the author used and that have now been made available on microfilm are the records of the Office of the Governor of Alaska, 1884–1958, housed in the Seattle branch of the National Archives and Records Service, and the extensive Alaska Customs Records, initially deposited in the Alaska State Historical Library, Juneau. The former neatly supplements Brady's other official papers located at Yale. Furthermore, the various governors' letterpress volumes and boxes of correspondence provide the major source for analyzing the administrations of the district leaders who preceded him to the governorship. The Customs Records help one understand southeastern Alaska's commercial, essentially maritime, activities. Happily, the National Archives records, Microcopy No. 430, "Interior Department Territorial Papers Alaska, 1869–1911," were finished in time to assist this biography. Although carelessly organized, these microfilm rolls contain extensive information on every aspect of Alaskan development during Brady's crucial years.

Numerous other depositories possess manuscript collections that yielded critical bits and pieces. For example, the Clarence L. Andrews Collection, located at Sheldon Jackson College in Sitka, contains some vital postgovernorship letters, and the Speer Library at Princeton Theological Seminary holds Jackson's letterpress volumes covering much of his church and school responsibilities related to Brady's specific duties. Both the Michael Healey papers at the Huntington Library, San Marino, California, and the Court Proceedings volumes filed at the Alaska State Superior Court, Sitka, are invaluable for obtaining information on Far North law enforcement. The author has made repeated use of Alaska's own two major manuscript depositories, the library at the University of Alaska, Fairbanks, which contains the Alaska Commercial Company Papers and much James Wickersham material, and the especially rewarding Alaska State Historical Library at Juneau. Here has been amassed the finest Alaska newspaper collection in existence. Robert N. DeArmond has provided a wonderful key with his *Subject Index to the Alaskan, 1885–1907: A Sitka Newspaper* (Juneau, 1974). The Alaska State Historical Library also possesses one of the best periodical and book collections on the forty-ninth state.

Two microfilmed non-Alaskan newspapers which include considerable copy on the region are the *New York Times* and *Seattle Post-Intelligencer*. The *Times* is doubly useful because of its remarkable index.

Although unindexed and varying greatly in quality, the annual reports penned by each of the district governors are valuable for concrete opinions on virtually every aspect of Far North development. Governors Brady and Swineford took considerable pride in their yearly compendiums. Quite as informative are the U.S. House and Senate reports examining specific district problems. Fortunately the *Congressional Record* not only contains debate on Alaska questions but also possesses time-saving indexes. The same should be noted for James D. Richardson's multivolume *Compilation of the Messages and the Papers of the Presidents* (New York, 1917), which offers so prompt a means for identifying the Alaska consciousness of America's presidents. To locate precise data on

Great Land public servants see the compilation of Evangeline Atwood and Robert N. DeArmond, *Who's Who in Alaskan Politics: A Biographical Dictionary of Alaskan Political Personalities, 1884–1974* (Portland, Ore., 1977).

There are a number of bibliographies detailing how to get at Alaska's past. As a guide for the printed source materials, James Wickersham's *Bibliography of Alaskan Literature, 1724–1924* (Cordova, Alaska, 1927) remains the preeminent tool for prying open the years between 1867 and 1912. Although incomplete even for its time—for example, a number of Brady items are unlisted—the scope, accuracy, and sound organization of Wickersham's bibliography continue to make it indispensable. To avail oneself of the recent scholarly periodical literature on Alaska, Dwight L. Smith's *The American and Canadian West: A Bibliography* (Santa Barbara, Calif., 1979) is recommended. Beginners seeking a brief bibliographic guide may profit from the author's "Researching Alaska's Pioneer Years, 1867–1912," *Journal of the West* 16 (October 1977): 52–62.

Because this biography's footnotes review the range of specific books related to Alaska history, 1877–1912, it would be redundant to do so again here. Suffice it to note that despite the abundance of Alaska primary source material, there remains a discouraging lack of secondary studies on Great Land history. Yet seen from the perspective of the eager and capable scholar, this deficiency means magnified opportunities for writing fresh history.

Index

Abercrombie, W. R., 247

Adams, Charles Francis, 324

Adams, Henry and Brooks, 196

Admiralty Island, 37

Afognak, Alaska, 68, 154, 274

Agricultural Committee, U.S. Senate, 279, 295

Agricultural experimental farms, 242, 280–83

Agriculture in Alaska. *See* Brady, John G., and agricultural potential of Alaska

Alaska. *See under subject matter* (Crime in Alaska; Laws applicable to Alaska; Politics in Alaska; *and so forth*)

Alaska Appeal, 45, 81

Alaska Bar Association, 138, 290

Alaska-Canada boundary controversy, 179–80, 189, 226–30

Alaska Central Railroad (Railway), 189, 321

Alaska Chamber of Commerce, 219

Alaska Commercial Company, 29, 51, 101, 111, 164, 181

Alaska district government: and "Alaska Government Board," 305–6; by Army, U.S. (1867–77), 34, 182; cabinet officers and, 47, 95, 160–61, 171, 265, 293; and "carpetbag corporations" ("Alaska lobby"), 303–4 (*see also* Shipping; Politics in Alaska); and Carter Code ("Carter Bill"), 203, 210, 213, 218–19; and Code of Criminal Procedure, 203; commis-sioners' duties in, 90–91; and Congress and management of "New Empire," 194–95, 282, 295–96, 305–7; deficiencies and problems of, 40, 51, 80, 88, 92, 161, 210, 216, 256, 290, 293–95 (*see also* Brady, John G.; Politics in Alaska); and federal government, 29, 35, 40, 47, 49, 87, 161, 205, 218, 351; first territorial election of (1906), 311; and geography, 115, 134–37, 158, 161, 216, 218, 311, 356; governors of (*see names of individual governors*; Politics in Alaska); interpreter for, 33, 79, 98; judicial administration of (*see* Law enforcement); by Navy, U.S., 50–52, 61–63; officials of (1878–85), 40, 50, 60, 78, 89–96; officials' salaries of, 213, 232 n. 17; and Organic Act of 17 May 1884, 60, 88–89; and taxation, 92, 116, 175, 203–6; and Territorial Committee, U.S. Congress, 103, 136, 161, 202, 272, 290, 295, 306, 310–11; by Treasury Department, U.S., 34, 40. *See also* Brady, John G.; Law enforcement; Politics in Alaska

Alaska Gold Mining Company, 221–22. *See also* "Spoilers"

Alaska Herald, 50, 61

Alaska Home Railway Company, 359–60

Alaska Journal, 155

Alaska-Kodiak Mining Company, 332

"Alaska lobby," 111, 215

Alaska Mill and Mining Company, 145

Alaskan (Sitka), 70, 78, 79–81, 138, 155; birth and early years of, 81–82, 99, 112;

Alaskan (continued)
on liquor licenses, 204; on salmon destruction, 274; Bradys' valedictory statement in, 357
Alaska Native Brotherhood, 372–74
Alaska Nowell Gold Mining Company, 101
Alaska Packers Association, 272
Alaska Range, 156, 188
Alaska Record-Miner (Juneau), 349
Alaska Searchlight (Juneau), 158–59, 163, 191
Alaska Sentinel, 319
Alaska Syndicate. *See* Guggenheims
Alaska Transcript, 319
Alaska Yukon Magazine, 359
Alaska-Yukon Mining Journal, 302, 328–29
Albatross, U.S.F.C.S., 256
Aleutian Islands, 30, 68, 265; and defense, 231; and justice, 92; schools of, 302
Aleuts, 30
Alexander Archipelago, 28, 30, 330
Alfred M. Lamar Company, 349
Alger, R. A., 178
American Academy of Political and Social Science, 322
Americanization of Alaska, 111, 142, 146
American Library Association, 342
American Lumberman, 330
American Russian Company, 51
Ancient Society (Morgan), 36
Andreasfky, Alaska, 181
Andrews, Clarence L., 193, 362
Annahootz, Chief, 98, 104, 250, 253
Annapolis, U.S. Naval Academy at, 243
Annette Island, 237–38
Anti-Saloon League, 198, 201
Anvik, Alaska, 181
Anvil City. *See* Nome
Anvil Creek, Alaska, 192
Archeological Institute of America, 340
Arctic Brotherhood, 188–89, 290
Arctic coast, 155
Arctic Slope, 30
"Aristocrats," 162
Arizona, 28, 135, 161, 212–14, 218, 304–6
Armstrong, Samuel Chapman, 45

Army, U.S., 31, 34, 47; communications work of, 189, 324; in Nome, 194; response of, to Klondike gold rush, 172, 178, 180–83
Arthur, Chester A., 89, 93
Athapascans, 30, 190–91, 258, 270
Atkins, Barton, 99
Atwater, Lyman, 20
Aurora, Alaska, 331–32, 353
Aurora Gold Mining Company, 331, 334
Austin, Alonzo E., 49–51, 57–58, 60, 81, 119
Austin, Olinda and Ettie, 50
Author's Service Bureau, 362

Ball, Mottrom D., 50, 82, 88–89, 99
Ballinger-Pinchot controversy, 363, 369 n. 39
Bankers' Panic of 1907, 361
Bank of California, 156
Baptist Church, 68
Baranov's (Governor's) Castle, 56, 79, 83
Bartlett, George, 123
Bauer, Herman A., 66, 124
Beach, Rex, 221, 362–63
Bean, Augustus, 271
Bean, Edmund, 97
Bear, U.S.R.M.C., 172, 247
Beardslee, Lester A., 50–52, 54, 57, 61–63, 88, 133
Bear's Nest Mine, 329
Beck, George J., 268
Beckwith, Nathan E., 322
Beecher, Henry Ward, 25
Behrends, Bernard M., 64, 66, 162, 328
Bennett, Lake, 160
Benson, Billy, 239
Benson, Daniel S., 245, 248–49
Bering Sea Coast, 30, 155, 195
Berners Bay Mining and Milling Company, 101
Berry, M. P., 51
Bethel, Alaska, 270
Beveridge, Albert Jeremiah, 195, 295
Bird, H. Homer, 190, 300
Black and Tans, 19, 361
Blackford, Eugene G., 152

Blacks (Negroes) in Alaska, 81, 301

Blaine, James G., 137

Blair, Henry W., 200

Bliss, C. N., 164–65, 169, 178, 196, 201, 210

Blount, Joseph, 11

Board of Home Missions. *See* Presbyterians, and Board of Home Missions; Presbyterians, and Woman's Board of Home Missions

Board of Indian Commissioners, 277

Boer War, 277, 340

Bolles, T. Dix, 95

Bolshanin, W., 79, 106

Bonanza Creek, Alaska, 159

Boorstin, Daniel J., 316

Booster speculators, 111, 214, 331. *See also* Reynolds, Harry

Boston-Alaska Society, 358

Bouchet, Edward Alexander, 19

Boulder Bay Copper Mine, 334

Boyce, John J., 244–45

"Boyd" hanging, 91

Brace, Charles Loring, 5–6, 20, 25–26, 264

Brady, Elizabeth Patton, 75; adoption of witch Peter by, 253–54; booklet by, on Sheldon Jackson, 364; and Brady's post-governorship, 365–66; and business, 126, 326; children of, 129; correspondence of, with husband, 164, 238–39, 327; and Cottage Missionary Society, 246; courted by John G. Brady, 75–78; defense of native sloop by, 264; marriage of, to John G. Brady, 78; and Maternity Society, 83; promotion of capital library by, 319–20, 340; and racism, 245, 264; reaction of, to Reynolds-Alaska Development Company, 334, 360; and Sitka, 370, 373–75; and Society of Alaskan Natural History and Ethnology, 82–83; as student at Normal Park School, Chicago, 75

Brady, Elizabeth Patton (daughter), 129, 366

Brady, Hugh P., 129, 246, 366

Brady, John G.: and agricultural potential of Alaska, 51, 64, 67, 134, 183, 189, 225, 278–83, 338–39; Alaska career of, beginning of, 29; and *Alaskan*, 82; and Aleutians, fortifications of, 231; annual reports of, as governor, 170–71, 175, 195, 199, 205, 276, 278, 294, 299, 302, 304, 320, 325–26; as author, 158, 199, 212, 321, 362–63; autobiography of, 362, 371; birth of, 3; and Black and Tans (class of 1874 of Yale College), 19; business activities of (in 1880s), 54–70, 75–78, 117, 123 (*see also* Brady, John G., and lumber business); and Canadian boundary controversy, 179–80, 189, 226–30, 267; career change of, from clergyman to businessman, 38–52; children of, 129, 316–17, 326, 354, 357–58, 361, 366, 372–74 (*see also* Brady, Elizabeth Patton; Brady, Hugh P.; Brady, John, Jr.; Brady, Mary Beattie; Brady, Sheldon Jackson); and Christianity, 14; colporteur's commission of, 15; as commissioner at Sitka, 89–106; conservationist actions and opinions of, 147, 195, 230, 247, 265, 272, 362–63; correspondence of, official, 301–2; courtship of Elizabeth Patton by, 75–78; and criminal code, 203; cultural interests of, 20–21, 36, 98; death and funeral of, 374–75; and delegate issue (*see* Politics in Alaska); denouncements of governorship by, 213, 215, 217, 276–77, 280, 282, 288–89, 294, 303, 305–6, 310, 348–49; and district government, 87–88, 96, 171, 183; education of (in Indiana, 6–16; in New York City, 3–6, 224; at Union [Theological] Seminary, 19–21; at Yale College, 16–19); and Eskimos, 191, 195, 258; evaluation of, 370–74; as ex officio U.S. Superintendent of Public Instruction, 242–45, 260 n. 18; and *Facts of Alaska*, 321; Far East commercial struggle predicted by, 231; and father's death, 21; and first civil government appointees, 94–96; fishing site defended by, 153–54; governorship of (ambition toward, 119–21; campaign for, 162–66; beginning of, 169; and Klondike rush, 169–76, 184; third term of, 287–88, 335; resignation from, 353–57); and grand potlatch, 251–53; and Judge John Green, 6–16; and high license struggle, 197–203; and Ethan Allen Hitchcock, 223, 267, 339, 342–44, 348, 351; as Hoosier farm boy, 9–13; hospitality of, 78, 83, 116, 163, 176, 323–24, 357; Indian police management by, 269–71; Ireland trip of, 21; and Sheldon Jackson, 26–28, 56–58, 66–68, 89, 162–65, 171, 239, 287, 356, 364; and Klondike rush, 169–76, 184; and Lyman E. Knapp, 135; and land titles, stalling of, 40, 116, 126–30, 133–42, 183, 197, 278–82; and La Touche Island Cop-

Brady, John G. *(continued)*
per Mine, 334; law enforcement duties
of, 196–301; law reforms advocated by,
174, 178; lobbying activities of, 170–72,
178, 188, 200–203, 210, 239, 272–73,
282, 309, 327, 372 (*see also individual
issues*); and lumber business, 18, 116,
123–30, 142–46, 150, 158, 322–23,
326–30; and Marine Corps, 263–65;
mental patients, disposition of, by, 299;
and W. P. Mills, quarrel with, 326–27;
mining ventures of, 96–97, 155, 160,
328–29; missionary labors in Alaska by,
33–40, 87–88; and National Guard issue,
178, 265–69; native education promoted
by, 68, 83, 205–6, 236–45; native militia
proposed by, 269; New York City childhood of, 3–6, 22 n. 1, 224; parents of, 3;
patronage power of, 293; and penal facility need, 299–300; philosophy of life
of, 48–49, 81, 224, 316–17, 365; political
attitudes and opinions of, 96, 116, 195,
217, 289–90, 293; postgovernorship of (in
eastern U.S., 361–66; in Sitka, 370–75);
and Presbyterian Board of Home Missions, 30–31; and Ranche Indians, quarrels with, 117–18, 139–42, 326–27; and
Reynolds-Alaska Development Company (*see* Reynolds, Harry); and Theodore
Roosevelt, 224–25, 282, 287–88, 300,
335, 354, 363, 372; and salary question,
213, 326; and Satchahnee, 116–18, 129,
184, 279–80, 326, 370–71; as schoolmaster at Mud Creek, Ind., 13–14; and
settlers for Alaska, 178, 183, 189, 212,
278–83, 325; and Sitka Sawmill Company, 124–30, 150, 323, 326–30, 332; and
Sitka Training School, 57–60; as spokesman for Alaska, 46–47, 52, 189, 210–11,
280, 294, 317, 320–22, 325–26, 362–64;
and statehood for Alaska (*see* Politics in
Alaska); and Alfred P. Swineford, 82,
103–4, 112, 114–17, 119; and territorial
proposed government (*see* Politics in
Alaska); Texas manual arts school aspiration of, 26–28, 44; and totem poles,
336–40, 347 n. 50; tours, official, of, 169,
180–81, 188–90, 204, 213, 295, 301; and
trial of "fur seal pirates," 101–3; and
James Wickersham, 222, 296–98, 365;
witch's life saved by, 253–54; and Yale
College alumni, 19, 26, 46, 160, 288, 322,
361–62
Brady, John, Jr., 129, 366, 370, 378
Brady, Mary Beattie, 129, 366, 374

Brady, Sheldon Jackson, 129, 366
Brainerd, Erastus, 160
Breweries, 79, 92
Brewster, B. H., 92, 95
British Columbia, 28, 34, 82, 88, 146, 172, 237
Brooks, Alfred H., 329, 351, 373
Brown, Melville C., 277, 288
Bugbee, John S., 139, 162
Burbank, Luther, 280
Bureau of American Ethnology, 319
Bureau of Education, U.S., 31, 68
Bureau of Indian Affairs, U.S., 31, 270
Burke, Andrew, 6, 237
Burnham, Henry E., 295
Burroughs, John, 323
Burwell, W. F., 254
Bushnell, Samuel, 361

Cale, Thomas, 311
California, S.S., 29, 35, 51
Callbreath, John C., 279
Callsen, Peter, 83
Cameron, Don, 374
Canada: fur seal controversy and, 101–3;
systematic colonization of, 278. *See also*
British Columbia; Diplomatic issues re-
lated to Alaska; Klondike
Canneries. *See* Salmon canning
Cape Nome. *See* Nome
Capital move controversy, 217–19, 356. *See
also* Juneau, in competition with Sitka
Caplin, Lazar, 61–62
Carlisle Indian School, 6, 59, 236–40, 258, 268
Carmack, George Washington, 155, 159
Carmel, Alaska, 256
Carnegie, Andrew, 317, 319
Carpetbaggers, 96, 157, 161, 293
Carroll, James C., 65, 136, 289–90
Carter, Thomas H., 203, 214
Carter Code, 203, 210, 213, 218, 294, 299
Catella, Alaska, 243
Catholics. *See* Roman Catholic Church
Centennial Fair, Philadelphia, 336
Chautauquan, 158, 199, 321
"Cheechako," definition of, 158

Chee-tee-teek, 104

Chichagof Island, Alaska, 37

Chignik, Alaska, 242

Children's Aid Society, 5–8, 12–13, 18, 25–26

Chilkat Canning Company, 153

Chilkat Indians, 38, 59, 88, 95, 103, 153, 156, 172, 229, 251, 270

Chilkoot Pass, 156, 179

Chinese: expulsion of, from Juneau, 99–100; as laborers, 80, 205, 256; prejudice against, 81, 99

Chinook jargon, 98

Christian Church (Disciples of Christ), 9

Chugach Mountains, 331, 351

Churches. See names of individual denominations

Churchill, Frank C., 352–53, 356

Circle City, Alaska, 158–59, 181–82, 270

City of Seattle (passenger steamer), 321

"Civilization Fund," 31

Civil War, 11–12, 111

Clark, Walter E., 287, 349, 354, 356

Cleveland, Grover, 93, 96, 99, 118, 134, 137, 157

Clinot, Mark, 300

Clum, John P., 269

Coal lands, 292, 323, 329, 363

Cochran, Thomas C., 316

Coeur d'Alene mines, 266–67

Cohen, Abraham, 79, 88; daughters of, 79

Cohen, Marcus, 79–80

Cohen, Pauline, 49, 79

Cole, G. H., 159

Colonial status of Alaska, 139, 225

Columbian Exposition, Chicago, 336

Commerce. See Merchants; Shipping

Commerce and Industries, 363

Commerce, U.S. Department of, 301

Communication, 174, 189, 220, 324. See also Mail Service; Railroads in Alaska; Shipping; Transportation

Comstock, Anthony, 200–201

Concord, U.S.S., 159

Conditions in Alaska (U.S. Senate), 295

Congregational Church, 68

Conservation, 195, 206; fur seal, 101–2, 146, 230, 265; salmon, 152–54, 272–74; sea

lion, 247; timber, 146, 230, 351, 362–63

Cook Inlet, Alaska, 51, 158, 181, 188, 242, 280, 331

Coontz, Robert E., 79, 81, 83, 137, 154, 263

Copper Center, Alaska, 280

Copper River, 173

Cordova "Coal Party," 363

Corwin, U.S.R.M.C., 101

Cottage City, S.S., 178, 320, 327, 357

Cottage Missionary Society, 246

Council City and Solomon River Railroad, 325

Council City News, 319

Cowles, Byron, 99

Crafts, Wilbur F., 200–202

Crédit Mobilier affair, 358

Creoles, 29–30, 79, 133, 192; appearances of, in commissioner's court, 98–99, 104–6; friction of, with Presbyterians, 93–96; of Kodiak, 256

Crime in Alaska. See Brady, John G., as commissioner at Sitka; Laboring class, and violence; Liquor problem; McNeil Island penitentiary; Native Alaskans, as Indian police; Slavery; Witchcraft

Crittenden, R. B., 64, 91

Curtis, Edward S., 323

Customs, U.S., Collector of, 34, 40, 51, 58, 66, 88, 287, 296

Cutting and Company, 51

Czolgosz, Leon, 224

Dabrovich, Sebastian, 256

Daily Alaska Dispatch (Juneau), 357

Daily Alaskan (Skagway), 276, 280, 288–89

Daily Times (Seattle), 165

Dakota, S.S., 63

Dall, William Healey, 88, 133, 191, 323, 373

Danskoy, V. P., 83

Dauntless (schooner), 256

Davidson, George, 280

Davis, A. J., 94–95

Davis, Jefferson C., 64

Dawes, Henry L., 135

Dawes Severalty Act (General Allotment Act), 135, 236

Dawson City, Alaska, 137, 159, 179; Mounties at, 176, 179–81. *See also* Klondike

Day, W. A., 288

Dead Horse Trail, 188

Defebaugh, J. E., 330

Defense of Alaska. *See names of individual branches of the military*; National Guard in Alaska; Pacific Basin

De Golyer–Oakes Ames affair, 358

De Groff, Edward, 76, 248, 255, 326

Delaney, Arthur K., 117, 200, 353

Delegate issue, 87, 89, 112, 161–62, 175, 215, 219, 292, 296, 307–11. *See also* Politics in Alaska

Demmert, Charles, 320

Demmert, George, 239

Democratic National Convention: of 1888, 137; of 1904, 306

Democratic Party. *See* Politics in Alaska

Dennis, I. C., 87

Depew, Chauncey, 210, 289

Depression: of 1870s, 25–27, 49; of 1890s, 150, 161, 170, 324

Desert Land Act, 134

Dewey, George, 178

Dick Act, 268–69

Dickenson, Sara, 34

Dickson, Cyrus, 37, 49

Dickson, J. Warren, 325

Dietrich, Charles Henry, 305

Dillingham, W. P., 295

Dingley, Nelson, 201

Diplomatic issues related to Alaska: Canadian boundary dispute, 179–80, 189, 226–30; fur seal controversy, 101–3

Disease, 191, 246

Dispatch (Juneau), 348–50

Distin, William L., 174, 293, 312 n. 14

District courts. *See* Law enforcement, district courts and

Dodge, Arthur, 20, 26–27, 361

Dodge, William E., 20, 26, 45

Doran, Thomas C., 124

Dougherty, Will, 9

Douglas Island, Alaska, 57, 74, 97, 154–55, 243, 265–68

Douglas Island News, 215, 258

Douglass, Frederick, Memorial, 301

Duncan, William, 35, 45, 57, 126; autocratic policy of, 237–39; and native constables, 269

Dunn, James B., 202

Dwight, Timothy, III, 16–18

Dyea, Alaska, 156, 159–60, 172–76, 182, 229, 279

Eagle, Alaska, 189, 210, 243

Eastern Alaska Mill and Mining Company, 145

Eaton, John, 31, 67, 162–64, 216, 353

Education (public schools), 67, 236, 238–45; at Afognak, 242; and attendance problem, 241–42, 271; at Catella, 243; at Chignik, 242; at Cook Inlet, 242; at Douglas, 243; at Eagle, 243; at Ellamar, 242–43; financing of, 260 n. 26; at Haines, 242; at Hope, 242; at Juneau, 241, 243–44; at Kenai, 242; at Ketchikan, 241–43; at Kodiak, 242–44; at Kyak, 243; at Nome, 241, 243; and racism, 243–45; and Russian flags, 242; at Seldova, 242; at Seward, 242–43; at Sitka, 242–45; at Skagway, 243; at Teller, 242; town school boards and, 260 n. 18; at Treadwell, 243; at Unalaska, 242, 244; at Unga, 242; at Valdez, 243; at Wood Island, 242; at Wrangell, 242–43; at Yakutat, 243. *See also* Jackson, Sheldon; Missionaries; Presbyterians; Sitka Training School

Eggleston, Edward, 10

Ellamar, Alaska, 242

Elliott, Charles P., 152

Elliott, Henry Wood, 197

Ellis, M. D., 202

Emmons, George T., 83, 274, 277, 348, 373

Episcopal Church, 9, 68

Erikson, Erik H., 49

Eskimos, 30, 68, 83, 247, 270; and reindeer, 162–63, 364

Evarts, W. M., 46

Exploration of Alaska, 155

Fairbanks, Charles Warren, 189

Fairbanks, Alaska, 212, 296, 298, 326

Fairbanks-Chena mining district, 212, 298, 332

Fast, Edward S., 82

Favorite (steamer), 61

Fee system. *See* Law enforcement, fee system and

Fernow, B. E., 323

Field, George, 239

Fillmore, Captain, 256

Fischer, Frederick T., 66

Fish Commission, U.S., 152–54, 256, 272–73

Fishing industry. *See* Salmon canning

Fletcher, Alice, 373

Fletcher, Donald, 303

Folkways (Sumner), 365

Foreign affairs, U.S., related to Alaska. *See* Diplomatic issues related to Alaska; Pacific Basin

Forest Grove Indian School, 59

Forest Reserve Act of 1891. *See* Land: Land Act of 1891

Forests. *See* Lumbering

Fort Davis, Alaska, 194

Fort Egbert, Alaska, 189

Fort Saint Michael, Alaska, 193

Fort Wrangell. *See* Wrangell

Fortymile, Alaska, 158–59

Fort Yukon, Alaska, 181, 246

Free Press (Juneau), 120

Friedgen, H., 13

Friedrich, Robert A., 214–15, 255

Frye, William P., 228

Fuller, Frank, 101

Fuller, Frank R., 333

Funston, Frederick, 155

Fur seal hunting, 101–3

Fur Seal Islands. *See* Pribilof Islands

Gaines, John W., 213

Gannett, Henry, 323

Garfield, James R., 301

Gastineau Channel, 57, 97

Gee, Charles, 144

Gem (lumber vessel), 144–46

General Allotment Act. *See* Dawes Severalty Act

General Manifold and Printing Company, 361–62

Geological Survey, U.S., 157, 329

George, Chief, 254

Georgeson, Charles Christian, 280, 283

George W. Elder, S.S., 323

Gertrude (launch), 370

Gibson, Esther, 246

Gilded Age, 16; business environment of, 316; and Congress, 29; natural resources and, 214; philanthropy in, 18, 20, 26–27, 31; progress and, 20, 44–45, 48, 371–73; Protestantism in, 20, 48–49

Gilpin, William, 349

Gladden, Washington, 20, 48

Glass, Henry, 57

Glave, E. J., 155

Gold Creek. *See* Juneau

Golder, Frank A., 256

Gold mining. *See* Mining; *names of individual companies*

Golovin, Alaska, 192

Goodall, Perkins and Company, 65

Governor's Castle. *See* Baranov's Castle

Grammar and Vocabulary of the Thlingit Language of Southeastern Alaska (Willard and Kelly), 240

Grand Old Party. *See* Politics; *names of individual Republican politicians*

Grant, U. S., 31

Gravina Island, Alaska, 126

Great Eastern Mine, 97

"Great rapprochement," 179, 227–28

Great (Railroad) Strike of 1877, 25, 27

Greely, A. W., 182–83, 271, 324

Green, John, 6; family of, 9

Green, Milton, 9–10

Greyling, Alaska, 191

Grinnell, George Bird, 323

Gruening, Ernest, 274, 356

Guggenheims, 360–61, 363

Gulf of Alaska, 326, 331

Gunnok, Charles, 271

Haida Indians, 28

Haley, Nicholas, 97

Hallock, Charles, 65

Haltern, Theo, 122–23, 145

Hamilton, Mark, 126

Hamilton, Simpson and Company, 126

Hammond, W. S., 271

Hampton Institute, 45, 366
Hanna, Mark, 164
Harriman, E. H., 210–11, 317, 323
Harris, William T., 215, 237, 352
Harrisburg. See Juneau
Harrison, Benjamin, 60–61, 118–21, 135, 162, 302
Harrison, E. S., 368 n. 34
Haskett, E. W., 90–96
Hassler, U.S.C.S.S., 79
Hauk, Felix, 300
Hawaii, 44, 78, 165, 194, 196, 214, 231, 306
Hay, John, 227–29
Hayden. Henry E., 115–16, 138
Hayes, Rutherford B., 46–47
Healy, John J., 153, 157
Henderson, Robert, 159
Hendricks, Thomas A., 116
Heywood, Charles, 264
High license struggle, 92–93, 163, 197–203. See also Law enforcement; Liquor problem
Hill, J. J., 317
Hillyer, Munson C., 90–96
Hilton, Olga, 246
Historic preservation, 79, 83, 323, 336–42, 357. See also Jackson, Sheldon, and museums honoring natives
Hitchcock, Ethan Allen, 171, 176, 196–97, 227–29; and Brady, 342–44; as conservationist, 351; at Louisiana Purchase Exposition, 339; and National Guard, 265–68, 278
Hoggatt, Volney T., 308–9
Hoggatt, Wilford B., 354–57, 367 n. 21
Homer, Alaska, 331
Home rule. See Politics in Alaska; Territorial government
Homestead Act, 134. See also Land
Homesteading. See Land: homesteading
Hoonahs, 37, 59, 123, 246, 251, 273; and witchcraft, 253–54
Hope, Alaska, 242
Howkan, Alaska, 59, 270
Hume, Joseph, 272
Hume, R. D., 272
Hummerrikhouse, Catherine, 14
Hunt, Richard Morris, 16

Hunter, William J., 242

"Icicle Ike," 308
Idaho, 161, 212, 266–67, 305
Idaho, S.S., 103
Iliamna, Alaska, 270
Immigrants, 3, 133. See also Chinese
Independent (New York), 20
Indiana, 6–16
Indian police, 87–88, 98, 241, 253, 264; Brady's management of, 269–71. See also Law enforcement; Native Alaskans
Indian Rights Association, 247
Indian River Park (Sitka), 336, 340
Indians, 31, 35–36. See also Native Alaskans; Northwest Coast Indians; names of individual Indian tribes
Indian Wars, 31
Industrial Workers of the World, 356
Inside Passage, 63
Insular cases, 277–78, 305–7
Interior, U.S. Department of the, 31, 145–46
Irish Americans, 3–4
Irvin, William, 61
Isham, Charles, 161
Italians, 80, 205

Jackson, James, 245, 271
Jackson, Sheldon: and Alaskan, 82; Brady's candidacy promoted by, 1888, 118–21; and Churchill report, 352, 367 n. 15; as Colorado's synodical secretary ("Rocky Mountain Superintendent"), 26–29; death of, 364; early Alaska labors by, 27–29, 36, 38; election of, as Presbyterian Moderator, 165; and first civil government appointees of, 89–96; as General Agent for Education in Alaska, 60, 67, 89, 236–43; and Benjamin Harrison, 118–21, 340–42; and Lyman B. Knapp, 135; and Aaron L. Lindsley, 28, 35, 60; and liquor control, 198–201; in Washington, D.C., 56; and museums honoring natives, 57, 82, 253, 318–19; and organic act, 60, 88–89; and Presbytery of Alaska, 60–61; public schools and, 83; reindeer scheme of, 162–63, 191; retirement of, 356; and Sitka Training School, 57–60; and Alfred P. Swineford, 112–15, 118–21, 215–16; tours of, 89

Jamestown, Moses, 253

Jamestown, U.S.S., 50–52

Japan, 103, 178; utilization of Alaskan resources by, 147, 265

Japonski Island, Alaska, 246, 251, 263–64

Jefferson, Thomas, 137

Jews, 79–80. *See also* Cohen, Abraham

Jim Crow. *See* Native Alaskans; Racism

Johnson, Charles S., 141, 145, 162, 172, 176, 194, 205, 213, 218, 249, 353

Joint High Commission, 189, 227

Jordan, David Starr, 115, 175, 201, 282, 293

Juneau, Alaska, 59, 63, 66, 90, 156; birth of, 57; brewery at, 79, 92; Chinese expelled from, 99–100; in competition with Sitka, 74, 79–80, 112, 126, 160, 215, 219, 287, 356; conventions at (*see* Politics in Alaska); Indian police at, 270; militia in, 265–68; mining at, 329; public school of, 84; violence at, 88, 172. *See also* Douglas Island; Mining

Juneau City Mining Record, 120, 153, 155

Juneau Placer Mining Company, 101

Kah-du-shan, 206

Kahkeitch, 105

Kake, Alaska, 240, 271

Karluk River, Alaska, 152, 296

Kasaan, Alaska, 336–38, 342

Kashevarovs, 79

Ka-shu-da-klock, 254

Katlayan, 271

Katlean, 253

Katz-Kay-ish, 105

Keatley, John, 161, 197

Kellogg, Fannie, 36–38, 49, 79

Kelly, Robert, 361

Kelly, William, 154, 215, 240, 249, 348, 354

Kelsey, F. D., 266

Kenai, Alaska, 242, 280

Kendall, Henry, 38, 47, 57

Ketchikan, Alaska, 163, 216, 219, 288

Ketchikan Mining Journal, 216, 288, 305, 311

Keystone Canyon, Alaska, 360

Kilgore, William F., 255, 336

Killisnoo, Alaska, 104, 114–15, 270

Kinkead, John H., 90–96, 135

Kipling, Rudyard, 195

Kirk, James W., and Mrs., 189

Kitchcock, 253

Kla-hautch, George, 270

Klanat, Chief, 103

Kla-sha, 105

Klawock, Alaska, 153–54, 205, 270

"Klondicitis," 169

Klondike, 84, 128, 134, 155–60, 169, 205; Brady's governship of, 169–76, 184. *See also* Dawson City

Klukwan, Alaska, 229

Knapp, George E., 83

Knapp, Gertrude (née Patton): marriage of, to George Knapp, 84; remarriage of, 86 n. 40; as secretary to Governor Brady, 176–78

Knapp, Lyman E., 83, 128, 135, 139, 153, 155, 198, 265, 270, 313 n. 25

Knox, Philander, 295

Kobuk, Alaska, 274

Kodiak, Alaska, 242–44

Kodiak Island, Alaska, 51, 66, 256

Kok-won-ton Indians, 270

Kolnish, 253

Kootsnoo Indians, 37

Kootznahoo Inlet, 155

Kostrometinoff, George J., 33, 79, 88, 98, 140, 154, 327

Kudlik, Alaska, 181

Kuskokwim Valley, 191

Kutchin, Howard M., 152, 203

Kyak, Alaska, 243

Laboring class: in Alaska, 80, 205; in eastern U.S., 3–4, 20, 25; Nome strike by, 356; penal, 105, 327; seasonal, 80, 128, 216, 298–99, 304, 314 n. 43; and violence, 80, 99–100, 265–68; and Western Federation of Miners, 356–57

Lacey, John F., 213

Lake Mohonk Conferences, 364

Lake Mountain Mining Company, 145

Lamar, L. Q. C., 67, 100, 117–18

Land: Homestead Act of 1898, 183, 197;

Land *(continued)*
  homesteading, 40, 134; Land Act of 1891, 137–39, 145; Land Office, U.S., 134, 140–44, 197, 243, 279; ownership problem, 93, 116, 126–30, 133–42, 163, 279–80; Native Allotment Act of 1906, 278, 357; Section 14, Land Act of 1891, fish culture stations, 154; surveys, 278. *See also* Brady, John G., and agricultural potential of Alaska; Politics in Alaska; Mining; "Spoilers,"

Latouche Island, Alaska, 358

Laurier, Wilfrid, 226

Law enforcement, 34; apathy of officials toward, 119; commissioners' courts and, 90–91, 94–95, 98–106, 194, 294–95; and commissionership, 172; district courts and, 90–92, 198, 210, 213, 215–16, 294–95; fee system and, 195–96, 222, 225; impeding of, 92; by Indian police, 87–88, 98, 241, 253, 264, 269–71; and juries, 99; and Klondike rush, 172–76, 180–83; and martial law, 181; and miners' justice, 91, 99–100, 172, 175, 194–96; in Nome, 222; and penal facilities, 299–300; Sitka town council and, 50–51; and Sitka Training School, 93–96. *See also* Alaska district government; Conservation; National Guard in Alaska; Royal Canadian Mounted Police; Timber, trespass and; *names of individual branches of the military, law cases, legal issues*

Laws applicable to Alaska, 51, 90–92

Lazier, W. N., 255–56

Lear, W. K. ("King"), 61

Lee, Robert E., 12

Leo (schooner), 65–70, 75, 123

Lewis, A. T., 90, 95–97

Lewis and Clark Centennial Fair, 340–42

Library, district, 319–20, 340

Lincoln, Abraham, 11, 305

Lindemann, Lake, 156

Lindsley, Aaron L., 28–29, 33, 35–36, 38, 48, 60, 75

Liquor problem, 33, 35, 37, 50–51, 54, 61–63, 92–93, 104–6, 197–204. *See also* High license struggle; Law enforcement; Native Alaskans

Lomen, Carl, 193

Louisiana Purchase Exposition of 1904, 253, 292; Brady's participation in, 335–40; Alaska exhibits at, 338–40

"Lucky Swedes," 192, 221

Lumbering: in Alaska, from mid-eighties on, 123–29, 142–46, 174, 322–23, 326, 329–30; in twentieth century, on Pacific Coast and in Alaska, 65, 121–23, 132 n. 53, 158

Lutheran Church, 28

Lynch law, 88, 91, 104

Lynn Canal, 153, 156, 160, 188, 228–29

Lynn Canal Military District, 182

McAllister, Ward, Jr., 90–96

McClures Magazine, 195

MacDonald, Joseph, 267–68

McFarland, Amanda, 28–29, 34, 38, 44–45, 59; Elizabeth Brady on, 366

McKenzie, Alexander, 221–23

McKinley, Samuel, 253

McKinley, William, 160–65, 174, 196, 201, 210, 222, 240, 282; death of, 223–24; and "full dinner pail prosperity," 212; and Joint High Commission, 189

McLain, J. S., 280, 293, 303

McNair, W. H., 266

McNeil Island penitentiary, 299–300

Mail and Express, 210

Mail service, 56, 80, 255, 324

Manning, Daniel, 66

Manook (Minook Creek). *See* Rampart City

Marines, U.S., 83, 100, 105, 240, 263–65

Marquette Mining Journal, 82

Marsden, Edward, 164, 237–38, 277

Martial law, 181. *See also* Law enforcement

Martin, E. K., 164

Marvin, Florence, 160

Marvin, Joseph B., 348

Maternity Society, 83

Mather, E. K., 277

Mental illness, 299

Merchants, 54–57, 112, 126, 157, 181, 275–76, 328. *See also* Sitka Trading Company; Shipping

Merrill, E. W., 357

Methodist Church, 11, 68

Metlakatla (Old), 35, 45, 57, 269

Metlakatla (New), 237–39, 270

Military Affairs Committee, U.S. Congress, 182
Military Department of Alaska, U.S., 267
Militia. *See* National Guard in Alaska
Mills, D. O., 289
Mills, W. P., 123, 326–27, 354
Mills, W. R., 326–27
Miner (Douglas), 81
Mineral hot springs. *See* Sitka, Hot Springs
Miners, 50, 63, 80, 157–58, 195–96, 279, 298–301
Mining: in British Columbia, 28, 34; and claims issue, 97–98, 101, 194, 219–23, 279, 296; coal, 292, 323, 329, 363; and dream of Forty-niner super bonanza, 155; exhibits of, at Louisiana Purchase Exposition, 338–39; in Fairbanks-Chena Mining District, 212, 298, 332; gold, production peaks in, 311; in Juneau, 329; and Klondike rush, 159–60, 169–76, 183; and loss of profits, 298–99; and Nome gold rush, 192–94; and petroleum claims, 97–98; placer, 193; quartz, 97; silver, 207 n. 21; in Silver Bay and Sitka District, 96–97, 328–29; and "Spoilers," 219–23; at Treadwell complex, 57, 97, 99–100, 154–56; in Yukon Valley, 134, 155–60, 184, 188–90, 298. *See also names of individual mines, mining corporations, miners*
Minook, John (Ivan Pavlof), 277–78
Minook Creek. *See* Rampart City
Missionaries, 20, 25, 28–29, 44–45, 50, 52, 56–61, 67, 75, 165, 181, 198, 321, 354. *See also* Brady, John G.; Jackson, Sheldon; Presbyterians; Sitka Training School; Young, S. Hall; *names of individual denominations*
Mitchell, John H., 351
Mohican, U.S.S., 79
Montfort, Isaac, 14
Montojo, Admiral, 178
Moody, Dwight L., 25
Moody, William H., 201
Moravian Church, 68, 256
Morgan, J. P., 317
Morgan, Lewis Henry, 36
Morgan-Guggenheim Syndicate. *See* Guggenheims
Morris, William G., 49, 197
Morrow, William W., 223

Moser, Jefferson, 256, 272–73
Mounties. *See* Royal Canadian Mounted Police
Muir, John, 323
Muldrow, Henry L., 103
Myers, Frank, 99, 120

Nabokoff, Leo, 320
National Geographic Society, 322
National Good Roads Association, 322
National Guard (militia) in Alaska, 161, 178, 265–69
Native Alaskans: acculturation of, 28, 33–37, 44–45, 56–58, 67, 81, 124, 191, 236–38, 240, 245, 249, 258, 268, 273; and Alaska Native Brotherhood, 372–73; artifacts and crafts of, 30, 44, 54, 63, 66, 82; assimilation of, 103, 123–26, 237–40, 258, 277, 364; burial ground quarrel of, with Brady, 117–18, 139–42; cannery and mining employment of, 152–53, 240; and Christianity, 59–61, 124, 250, 258; citizenship of, 47, 236, 269, 276–77, 285 n. 49; commissioner's court appearances by, 98, 103–6; cottages of, 93–94, 123, 132 n. 45, 240, 327; crucifixion attempt by, 248; and disease, 28, 56, 80, 190–91, 246, 264; education of (public), 236–45 (*see also* Education; Missionaries; Sitka Training School); Eskimos, 68, 83, 162–63, 190–92; fishing sites of, 153–54; and frog totem quarrel, 248–49; funeral practices of, 105, 117–18, 374–75; homesteads of, 278, 357; as Indian police, 87–88, 98, 241, 253, 264, 269, 271; and Lyman E. Knapp, 135–36, 153; and law of retaliation, 300–301; and liquor control problem, 28, 33, 35, 50, 61–63, 98, 104–6, 153, 172, 197–200, 256; and lumbering, 123–26; medical facilities for, at Sitka, 83, 246; militia of, proposed, 269; Minook decision concerning, 277–78; and money economy, 275–76; as packers, 103, 124, 156, 172, 270–71; and patriotism, 103, 240, 364; compared with Plains Indians, 28, 33, 47, 67, 91, 238; population of, 30; and potlatch, 249–53; and property inheritance dilemma, 250; and prostitution, 28, 37, 67, 95; and racism, 70, 93–94, 99–100, 194, 243–45, 292, 353–54, 357; and raven hat presented by chiefs, 253; reaction of, to missionary Brady, 34–35; Roosevelt's opinions of, 225, 236, 277; and shamanism,

Native Alaskans *(continued)* 104, 253–55, 364; and Sitka Training School, 92–95; and slavery, 34, 94, 253; and Alfred P. Swineford, 103–4, 114–17, 142; and totem poles, 336–40, 357; villages of, destroyed by U.S. military actions, 91, 107 n. 19; voting rights of, 276, 374; and witchcraft, 37, 104, 118, 253–55. *See also individual Indian tribes* (Aleuts; Athapascans; *and so on*); Ranche Indians; *names of individuals dealing with natives*

Native Allotment Act, 278

Navy, U.S., 34, 46–47, 50–52, 57–59, 78–79, 92, 103, 153, 263. *See also names of individual officers, vessels*

Nelson, Jim, 253

Nelson, Knute, 294–95, 308, 321–22, 349, 351

New Covenant League, 250

Newell, W. A., 89

"New Empire," 194–95, 282, 305–7, 321, 372; and Louisiana Purchase Exposition, 339–40. *See also* Insular cases; Hawaii

New Mexico, 161, 214, 218, 295, 304, 306

New Orleans Picayune, 265

Newport (mail steamer), 255

New York Central Railroad, 16

New York City: Bowery, 4, 21; Brady in, 20, 25–26; Chatham Street Theater, 4–5; churches of, 20; East Side, 3–5; newsboys' lodging house, 26; public library, 362; socioeconomic conditions in, 3–4, 20; Union League Club, 211, 322; Waldorf-Astoria Hotel, 210–11; Young Men's Christian Association, 26

New York Herald, 45

New York Times, 88, 90, 302

Nicholai, H. E., 279

Noble, John W., 120

Nome, Alaska: courts of, 210; gold rush in, 134, 192–94, 212; public school and missionary work in, 194; reaction of, to Boxers, 267; and "Spoilers" scandal, 219–23

Nome Weekly News, 319

North-American Mining and Development Company, 328

North American Trading and Transportation Company, 157, 181

Northern Pacific Railroad, 63

Northrup, Cyrus, 18

North Star (Sitka Industrial School newspaper), 78, 82

Northwest Coast Indians, 28, 30, 57, 67, 82, 140, 258, 336, 364. *See also* Haida Indians; Native Alaskans; Tlingit Indians; Tsimshian Indians

Nowell, Thomas S., 101, 120

Noyes, Arthur H., 221–23

Nukeukahyet (Nuklukayet). *See* Tanana

Nulato, Alaska, 181

Nushagak, Alaska, 296

Ogden, Robert C., 289

Oil. *See* Petroleum

Oklahoma, 134, 161, 218

Ophir Gold Mining Company, 101

Oregon Steam Navigation Company, 61

Organic Act of 17 May 1884, 60, 88–89. *See also* Alaska district government; Jackson, Sheldon; Politics in Alaska

Osprey, H.M.S., 46

Ounalaska. *See* Unalaska

Overland Monthly, 362

Owens, Kenneth N., 137

Pacific Basin, 20, 78; "New Empire" markets in, 230–31; and Spanish-American War, 179

Pacific Coast Steamship Company, 65, 89, 156

Panama Canal, 227, 351, 372

Paris Lode, 97

Patterson, Thomas M., 295

Patton, Cassia, 75, 84, 97, 293, 319, 354, 357

Patton, Elizabeth. *See* Brady, Elizabeth Patton

Patton, Gertrude, 75, 84, 97, 319

Patton, Hugh, 75, 78, 84, 97

Paul, Tillie, 98

Paul, William L., 239–40

Pavolf, Ivan. *See* Minook, John

P. B. Weare (steamer), 157

Peckinpaugh, Nicholas R., 169

Pedro, Felix, 212

Peelle, Stanton J., 354

Pelagic seal hunting. *See* Fur seal hunting

Pendleton, Joseph H., 263–64

Perkins, George C., 164, 174, 218, 229, 301

Perry, U.S.R.M.C., 326, 336

Petroff, Ivan, 45–46, 80, 133, 197, 234 n. 64

Petroleum, 323, 328

Philippines, 194, 305–7, 372

Phillips, William, 10

Picken, John, 54

Pilz, George, 51

Pinchot, Gifford, 351, 363

Pinta, U.S.S., 76, 78–79, 92, 100, 153–54, 263

Placer mining. *See* Mining, placer

Platt, Orville H., 136, 307–8, 310

Platt, Rutherford Hayes, 46

Platt, Thomas C., 210

Point Barrow, Alaska, 68

Police, native. *See* Law enforcement, by Indian police; Native Alaskans, as police

Politics in Alaska: capital move controversy, 217–19, 356 (*see also* Juneau, in competition with Sitka); "carpetbaggers," 96, 157, 161, 293; "chaotic factionalism," 136–37, 216–18, 221, 294; convention of 1881, Juneau, 88–89; delegates to Congress (proposed, 87, 89, 111–12, 161–63, 215, 292, 296, 307–11; unofficial, 88–89, 217–18); Democratic and Republican conventions, Juneau, 1896, 161–62; Democratic National Convention (of 1888, 137; of 1904, 306); division of Alaska, 181, 218, 302–3, 306; floating electorate, 216–18, 221; "neglect" opinion, 134, 179, 294, 321; nonpartisan convention, Juneau (of 1890, 136; of 1899, 216–17, 229–30; of 1903, 290–92); nonpartisan convention, Seattle, 1905, 309–10; Republican convention, Juneau, 1900, 217; Republican Territorial Convention, Juneau, 1903, 190–92; Seattle Trans-Mississippi Congress, 1902, 303; statehood issue, 87, 161, 170, 218, 302, 322; territorial government ("home rule"), 89, 111–12, 163, 175, 212, 292, 302–7

Pomeroy, Earl, 307

Population of Alaska, 29–30, 128, 158, 192, 304–6, 356, 362

Porcupine Creek, Alaska, 228–29

Porter, Noah, 16–18

Portland, Ore., 28–29, 60–61, 96–97, 181

Portland Oregonian, 307

Postal service. *See* Mail service

Potlatch. *See* Native Alaskans, and potlatch

Powell, John Wesley, 36, 319

Powell, Margaret, 75–76

Pratt, Richard H., 59, 236–40, 269, 353

Preemption Act of 1841, 137

Presbyterians, 68; Alaska mission commenced by, 27–29; and Alaska Presbytery, 38, 48, 60, 119–20; Board of Publication of, 15; and Board of Home Missions, 27–29, 31, 45, 47, 49–50, 52, 56–61; and Brady's gubernatorial candidacy, 164; and Chinese schools, 31; and First Presbyterian Church, Portland, Ore., 28; General Assembly of (of 1884, Saratoga, N.Y., 60; of 1897, Winona, Minn., 165); Benjamin Harrison and, 60–61; Mexicans and Mormon outreach and, 31; and Muncie, Ind., presbytery, 14; and native Presbyterian church, 124; and Oregon Presbytery, 60; "Presbyterian hierarchy" of, 96, 311, 356; and *Presbyterian Quarterly and Princeton Review*, 20; and *Rocky Mountain Presbyterian*, 28; sawmill imported by, 123; and Sheldon Jackson College, 42 n. 40; and Sitka First Presbyterian Church, 60–61; and Sitka native (Tlingit) Presbyterian church, 245; and Sitka Training School, 57–60, 93–96, 116; and Synod of the Columbia, 44; synodical meeting of, aboard *City of Seattle*, 321; and Tipton, Ind., Presbyterian church, 9, 11; and Woman's Board of Home Missions, 365–66

Preservation. *See* Historic preservation

Press in Alaska, 81–82, 99, 112, 215–16, 288–89, 304

Pribilof Islands, 101–2

Price, Frank, 374

Price, John Garland, 217–18, 309

Prince of Wales (steamer), 366

Prince William Sound, 173, 181, 188–89, 331–32

Progressive period of U.S. history, 170, 349

Prohibitionists, 174, 197–202

Public schools. *See* Education

Pullen, Daniel D., 365

Pyramid Harbor, Alaska, 228–29

Pyramid Harbor Packing Company, 153, 159

Quarles, Joseph V., 196
Queen, S.S., 165

Racism, 81, 111, 353–54, 357, 371. See
also Native Alaskans, racism and;
Chinese

Railroads in Alaska, 137, 183, 321–26, 339,
358; Alaska Central Railroad (Railway),
189, 321; Alaska Home Railway Company, 359–60; Alaska Railroad, 345 n.
24; congressional railroad authorization,
325; Fairbanks and Chena linked by, 351;
Juneau to Chilkat, proposed, 156; in Yukon Valley, 350, 358–60

Rampart City (Minook Creek), Alaska,
181–82, 280

Rampart Miner, 319

Ranche Indians, 33, 35, 44, 50, 56–58, 88,
104–5; and Brady, 117–18, 139–42, 247,
326–27; crucifixion attempt by, 248; frog
totem quarrel among, 248–49; and Sheldon Jackson, 93–95; threatened by speculators, 133

Randall, George M., 182

Rankin, Elias, 105

Rasmuson, E. A., 255

Rauschenbusch, Walter, 48

Ray, P. H., 181–82, 189, 221

Reconstruction period of U.S. history, 19,
29, 45

Reed, Thomas B., 372

Reed, W. F., 121

Reform Bureau, 200

Reid, Frank H., 176

Reid, J. Whitelaw, 289

Reindeer, importation of, 162–63, 191, 352

Reliance, U.S.R.M.C. See Leo

Report on the Condition and Needs of the
Natives of Alaska (Emmons), 274

Republican Party. See Politics; names of
individual politicians

Revenue Marine, U.S., 34, 65, 89, 180, 246,
256, 296–97, 326; and totem poles,
336–38; policing shaman, 253–55. See
also names of individual vessels

Reynolds, Douglas, 123

Reynolds, Harry (H. D.): Brady's relations
with, 330–35, 342–44, 348–53; climax
and collapse of Alaska speculation of,
358–61, 368 n. 34. See also Reynolds-
Alaska Development Company

Reynolds, H. R., 333–34

Reynolds-Alaska Development Company:
"Affiliated Companies" with, 358; Brady's endorsement of, 335. See also Reynolds, Harry

Reynolds Peak, 368 n. 31

Rice, Jasper H., 267–68

Richards, W. A., 279

Richardson, C. E., 342

Richardson, W. P., 181, 220

Riggs, Thomas, 374

River transportation, 156–57, 181, 302

Roads. See Wagon roads

Roman Catholic Church, 68, 101

Roosevelt, Theodore, 222, 226, 296, 306,
310, 321, 350–51; and Brady, 224–25,
282, 287–88, 354, 372; and conservation,
362–63; and natives, 236

Roosevelt, Theodore, Sr., 5, 26

Root, Elihu, 267, 269

Rose (steam launch), 54, 61, 65–66

Rothschilds, 156, 328

Rowe, P. T., 246

Royal Canadian Mounted Police, 176,
179–81, 220, 228

Rumsey, Edgar, 14–15

Rush, U.S.R.M.C., 246, 254–55, 342

Russian Alaskans, 50, 79, 242, 302. See
also Creoles

Russian-American Company, 54

Russian Orthodox Church, 33, 242

Ryan, Thomas, 342

Saint Augustine, 371

Saint Elias Range, 332

Saint Lawrence Island, 191

Saint Louis Fair of 1904. See Louisiana
Purchase Exposition

St. Louis Globe Democrat, 67

Saint Michael, Alaska, 172, 181–82, 210

Saint Michael's Cathedral, 54, 79, 83

Salmon canning, 37, 50–51, 150–54, 271–74

San Francisco Bulletin, 81

San Francisco Chronicle, 67, 81, 89

San Francisco commerce, 51, 57, 65–66,
88, 92, 123, 128, 144

Sankey, Ira D., 25

Satchahnee. See Brady, John G., and Satchahnee

Schaeffer, Charles, 105

Schools, public. *See* Education

Schurtz, Carl, 47

Schwatka, Frederick, 155

Scidmore, Eliza R., 99, 137

Seals. *See* Fur seal hunting

Seattle, 66, 81, 100, 128, 160, 303, 309–10, 324

Seattle Post-Intelligencer, 178, 287, 297–98, 349

Seghers, Charles J., 101, 103

Senator, S.S., 246

Seton-Karr, H., 155

Seward, Frederick W., 289

Seward, William H., 211

Seward, Alaska, 242–43, 332

Seward Gateway, 319

Seward Peninsula, 192, 311

"Seward's Folly," 211

Sewell, William J., 202

Shakan, Alaska, 239

Shar-wan, George, 273

Sheakley, James, 157–58, 161, 163, 198, 265

Sheep Camp, Alaska, 175

Sheldon Jackson College, 42 n. 40

Sheldon Jackson School. *See* Sitka Training School

Sherman, John, 47, 161, 201

Shields, James H., 64

Shipping: coastal, 29, 35, 61, 65–70, 88, 103, 280; by great circle route, 230–31; liquor smuggling by, 197–98; lumber, 122–28, 144; mining related, 156–57, 172–73, 193, 220–21

Shmakoff, Alga, 106

Shumakoff, Anna, 98

Shutnovs, 79

Signal Corps, U.S. Army, 323

Silliman, Benjamin, 46

Silver Bay, Alaska, 96–97, 328–29

Silver Bow Basin, Alaska, 329

Simpson, Peter, 123, 126, 329–30

Sing, Lung, 81

Sitka, Alaska: agricultural station, U.S., at, 280; Lester A. Beardslee's leadership of, 50–52, 54, 57, 61–63, 88, 133; Brady's missionary work in, 33–37, 87, 88; brew-

ery at, 79, 92; John Burroughs's opinion of, 323; cadet corps of, 268; collector's office of, moved to Juneau, 287; commerce in, 29, 37, 50–52, 79, 97, 144–45; in competition with Juneau, 74, 79–80, 112, 126, 160, 215–19, 287, 356; Customs House, 176; diseases in, 246, 264; dogs, pests of, 247; fire brigade of, 83, 161; Governor's House, 176; historic preservation at, 83; Hot Springs (*see* Sitka, mineral springs of); Indian band of, 178, 240, 323, 374–75; Indian police of, 270–71; Indian River Park, 357; and Indian threat of 1879, 46, 50; Industrial School (*see* Sitka Training School); jail of, 70, 92, 98, 101, 104–5, 300; library of, 319–20, 340; local government of, 50–51; marines as police force in, 50, 263–64; medical facilities of, 83, 246; mineral (hot) springs of, 64–65, 76, 117; National Cemetery, U.S., in, 374; native cottages in, 93; native (Tlingit) Presbyterian church of, 52, 374; penal labor in, 105, 327; polyglot citizens of, 50, 353–54, 357; public schools of, 49–50, 83–84, 353–54, 357, 374; quarantine station at, 70; recreational activities of, 76, 81, 82–83, 119, 178, 252–53; Russian sawmill at, 122–23; socioeconomic conditions at (in 1879–86, 50–52, 54–70, 74–84; in 1886–97, 78–84); town councils of, 50–51

Sitka Sawmill Company, 124–30, 150, 323, 326–30, 332. *See also* Brady, John G., and lumber business

Sitka Times, 133

Sitka Trading Company, 54–70, 116–17, 123–24

Sitka Training (Industrial) School, 44, 45, 52, 57–60, 82–83; becomes Sheldon Jackson School, 364; cadet corps of, 268; compulsory boarding at, 93–96, 123, 245

Skagway, Alaska, 92, 159–60, 172–78, 180–82, 188, 204, 210, 219, 229, 265, 322–23; opposition to Brady in, 217, 282

Skookum Bob, 153

Slavery, 34, 94, 253

Sloan, Samuel, 289

Sloss, Louis, 164

Smith, Eben, 333

Smith, Jefferson Randolph ("Soapy"), 92, 175–76, 182

Smith, Marcus A., 304

Smithsonian Institution, 319, 340
Social gospel, 20, 48–49
Society of Alaskan Natural History and Ethnology, 82–83, 319
Son-i-hat, Chief, 336–38
"Sourdough," definition of, 158
Spanish-American War, 170, 178–79, 194, 266
Sparks, Andrew Jackson, 134, 144
Spaulding, Oliver, 193
Spence, Clark C., 307
"Spoilers," 219–23
Springs, Abraham, 296
"Squawmen," 162
Stanford, Leland, 324
Stanley, Henry M., 155
Statehood issue, 87, 161, 170, 218, 302. See also Politics in Alaska: division of Alaska
Steele, Samuel B., 180–81
Steunenberg, Frank, 212, 356
Stevens, Blamey, 334, 358, 360
Steward, William M., 195, 214, 278
Stikine River, 28
Stoneman, George, 155
Stowell, Mrs. George, 354
Stuck, Hudson, 191, 256
Sumner, William Graham, 18, 365
Sutro, Adolph, 157
Swedish Evangelical Mission, 254–55
Swineford, Alfred P.: and Alaskan, 82; and anti-Chinese crisis, 99–100; and Brady, 82, 103–4, 112, 114–17, 119, 163; as chairman at Juneau Territorial Convention, 1899, 216–17, 229–30; as chairman at Seattle nonpartisan convention, 1905, 310; death of, 311; as governor, 96, 111–21, 144, 198; and Sheldon Jackson, 82, 112–15, 118–21, 312 n. 5; and Ketchikan Mining Journal, 215–16; and natives, 103–4, 142, 276; and nonpartisan convention, 1903, 290–92; political constituency of, 111–14; and shaman, 114–15; and James Sheakley, comparison of, 157
Swineford, C. A., 119
Symonds, F. M., 57, 59

Taft, William Howard, 305

Talmage, Thomas De Witt, 25
Tanana(h) (Nuklukayet), Alaska, 181, 270
Tanana Valley, 298, 311
Tate, C. T., 82
Tawney, James, 126
Taxation, 92, 116, 175, 203–6, 272–73, 294, 304–5; without representation, 205, 215. See also Alaska district government; Law enforcement
Technology, impact of, 192, 196, 272–74, 324, 329–30, 371
Telegraph. See Communication
Teller, Henry M., 214
Teller, Alaska, 242
Territorial government (home rule), 87, 111–12, 163, 175, 212, 292, 302–7. See also Politics in Alaska
Thatcher, Thomas A., 18
Thompson, R. W., 47
Thonegal, William, 144
Thwing, Clarence, 83
Timber: conservation of, 146, 230, 351, 362–63; Timber Culture Act, 134; trespass and, 126–28, 133, 144–46. See also Lumbering
Tlantich, 118
Tlingit Indians, 28, 44–45, 70, 83, 123. See also Chilkat Indians; Northwest Coast Indians; Ranche Indians; names of other Indian groups
Tipton, Ind., 6–16, 27, 48
Tocqueville, Alexis de, 18, 371
Tongass, Alaska, 34, 47
Tongass National Forest, 369 n. 38
Tongue, Thomas H., 203
Tourism, 59, 63, 65, 74, 82, 321
Towns, incorporation and self-government of, 205–6, 219, 241, 270, 293–95, 306
Transisthmian canal. See Panama Canal
Trans-Mississippi Congress, 303
Transportation, 295, 322–25. See also Railroads in Alaska; River transportation; Shipping; Wagon roads
Travers, Michael, 98
Treadwell, John, 97, 99–100, 323
Treadwell Mines, 57, 79, 97, 156, 203, 267–68
Treasury Department, U.S., 34, 40, 47, 49, 293, 302

Troy, John W., 276–77, 282, 288–89, 303, 305–6, 310, 348, 351, 356, 372
Tsimshian Indians, 30, 34, 45, 126, 237–38
Twain, Mark, 196, 373

Unalaska, Alaska, 68, 90, 122, 242, 244
Unga, Alaska, 68, 242, 256
Union Pacific Company, 150
Union (Theological) Seminary, 19–21
United States Army. *See* Army, U.S.
United States Army Signal Corps. *See* Signal Corps, U.S. Army
United States Military Academy. *See* West Point, U.S. Military Academy at
United States Naval Academy. *See* Annapolis, U.S. Naval Academy at
United States Navy. *See* Navy, U.S.
United States Revenue Marine. *See* Revenue Marine, U.S.

Valdez, Alaska, 243, 308–9; Harry Reynolds's speculation in, 331, 332, 339, 351, 358–60
Valdez News, 309, 319
Valentine, Charles, 256
Vanderbilt, John M., 61
Van Dyke, Henry, 25
"Vanishing American" theme, 191, 236–37
Vedder, C. P., 211
Vest, George C., 184

Wadleigh, A. S., 154, 205
Wagon roads, 292, 322, 325
Wallace, Edwart T., 11
Wallace, Lew, 11
Wall Street Journal, 212
Walton, Rudolph, 244–45, 353–54, 357
War Department, U.S., 247
Warner, Vespasian, 214, 218
Washington, Booker T., 59, 200, 239
Washington Post, 195
Waskey, Frank H., 311
Watts, C. W., 172
Welsh, Herbert, 245
West Point, U.S. Military Academy at, 243, 365
Wood Island, Alaska, 242

Western America and Alaska: comparison of gold rushes in, 158–59, 173; historic comparisons of, 28–29, 74, 82–84, 137, 282–83; Indian acculturation in, 31, 59; jingoism in, 180; natural resources of, 80, 116, 121–22, 133–34, 137, 213; territorial government of, 87, 90, 111, 293–94, 302, 304–7; transportation effects on, 115, 324–26, 349–50, 358; violence in, 91, 100, 180, 184
Western Federation of Miners, 356–57
Western Fur and Trading Company, 51
Whalers, 190–91
Wheeling, U.S.S., 180, 254
Whitehorse Rapids, 189
"White Man's Burden" (Kipling), 195
White Pass and Yukon Railroad, 188, 266, 325
Whitford, Amos T., 36, 54, 61, 64–65, 68–70, 88, 124
Wickersham, James, 223, 277–78, 365; *Bibliography of Alaskan Literature*, 371; and Brady, 202, 296–98; opinions of, on Alaska, 283, 294, 303, 308; reappointment of, 313 n. 25, 353
Wilbur, B. K., 268
Wilkinson, M. C., 59
Willard, Carrie, 95
Willard, Eugene S., 95
Willard, Frances A., 240
Wilson, James, 247
Wilson, John L., 164
Windom, William, 64
Witchcraft, 37, 104, 118, 253–55
Woman's Board of Home Missions, 365–66
Women's Christian Temperance Union, 120, 202
Wooten, Dudley G., 321, 325
Wrangell, Alaska, 28–29, 34, 35, 38, 45, 47, 59, 61, 90, 91, 122, 269–70
Wrangell Girls' School, 59
Wright, Luke E., 305

Yakutat, Alaska, 243, 253–55
Yale College, 16–19, 46. *See also* Brady, John G., and Yale Alumni
Yalth-hock, 271
Yash-noosh, 206
Yaska, 247

Yas-touch, 105
Yeatman, R. T., 182
Young, Ralph, 374
Young, S. Hall, 38, 60, 89, 164, 194, 269
Young Man Luther (Erikson), 49
Yukon Field Force, 180

Yukon Indians, 30
Yukon River Valley, 101, 134, 156–60, 188–90, 210, 298; need for railroads in, 322–26, 350; starvation threat in, 174, 181. *See also* Klondike

"Zigzags" (Brady), 4, 362, 371